THE ROUTLEDGE COMPANION TO
MUSIC AND VISUAL CULTURE

THE ROUTLEDGE COMPANION TO MUSIC AND VISUAL CULTURE

Edited by
Tim Shephard and Anne Leonard

NEW YORK AND LONDON

First published 2019
by Routledge

52 Vanderbilt Avenue, New York, NY 10017
Simultaneously published in the UK
by Routledge
2 Park Square, Milton Park, Abingdon, Oxon OX14 4RN

Routledge is an imprint of the Taylor & Francis Group, an informa business

Library of Congress Cataloging-in-Publication Data
The Routledge companion to music and visual culture / edited by
Tim Shephard and Anne Leonard.
pages cm
Includes bibliographical references and index.
1. Art and music. 2. Music in art. 3. Art in music. 4. Visual communication.
5. Arts. I. Shephard, Tim, editor of compilation. II. Leonard, Anne (Anne Rachel),
editor of compilation.
ML3849.R82 2014
780'.07—dc23
2013001499

ISBN: 978-0-415-62925-6 (hbk)
ISBN: 978-0-367-14865-2 (pbk)
ISBN: 978-0-203-62998-7 (ebk)

Typeset in Goudy by Swales & Willis Ltd, Exeter, Devon

Senior Editor: Constance Ditzel
Editorial Assistant: Elysse Preposi
Production Editor: Emma Håkonsen
Marketing Manager: Joon Won Moon
Project Manager: Swales and Willis
Copy Editor: Judith Oppenheimer
Proofreader: Tamsin Ballard
Cover Design: Jayne Varney

CONTENTS

CONTENTS

CONTENTS

CONTENTS

LIST OF
ILLUSTRATIONS

Figures in plate section

Examples in text

PREFACE

This book was initially proposed to Routledge by Tim Shephard in a more modest form, for their "Routledge Music Bibliography Series." The intention was to fill the gap between existing treatments of the sub-discipline of "music iconography," rooted quite self-consciously in the methods of celebrated art historians of the earlier twentieth century, and the possibilities offered by the rather different perspectives that have emerged within musicology and art history more recently. It is a testament to the publisher's commendable investment in this area of scholarship that they immediately prompted expansion to the much more ambitious dimensions of a "Companion."

The process of substantially adapting and revising the proposal began with the enlisting of a co-editor, Anne Leonard, making a team comprising one musicologist and one art historian—something that we hope has decisively increased the cross-disciplinary credibility and scope of the book. In the following months, as we built our roster of contributors, we encountered approval of the project from many quarters, which not only was personally heartening, but also and more importantly confirmed our impression that the book was both needed and timely.

The explosion in scholarly approaches to music and visual culture over the past ten to fifteen years—characterized not just by a greater methodological diversity but also by considerably greater geographic and chronological breadth than in the past—calls for a current assessment of the field, which this *Companion* aims to provide. Newcomers to this field of research in particular may find its fast-changing parameters not immediately or intuitively navigable. The book's primary goal, then, is to offer a "one-stop-shop" for anyone coming to this field of research for the first time. Its secondary goal is to constitute a useful reference work for established researchers in the field.

Accordingly, we have divided the book into five parts. The first of them offers reflections on the relationship between music and the visual in general terms, from two different perspectives, and serves as a thought-provoking starting point for the volume. The chapters in Part II present and explain a range of relevant disciplinary methodologies both old and new. These include the approaches most obviously implicated in this field of research as it has traditionally been defined—namely musicology, music iconography, and art history—but also a range of disciplines which, by virtue of method or materials, are intrinsically concerned with musical and visual elements in combination. Cultural history, for example, insists on studying cultural activity in the round, rather than isolating individual arts; ethnomusicology, meanwhile, draws increasingly on visual evidence in addressing conceptions of music that, unlike that common in the West, do not always restrict it to sound alone; and film studies and performance studies both use highly developed methods and refined theory to address their inescapably hybrid objects of study. Our aim in this second section has been partly to support and promote the methodological variety evident in the remainder of the volume, but partly also to help improve cross-disciplinary comprehension, especially as regards approaches to dealing with musical and visual materials.

Part III tackles points of contact and patterns of intersection between music and visual culture. The topics covered, which are wide-ranging but by no means exhaustive, divide into two categories: the musical in visual culture, and the visual in musical culture. The fourth and fifth parts showcase the kinds of questions that interdisciplinary research in music and visual culture can address. The approach in each case has not been to provide comprehensive coverage of a given topic or area, but rather to offer sustained examples of the kind of work that can be undertaken within this field of study. Our hope is that these chapters, in giving clearer definition to a field that is still not well known, will spark new inspiration and a yet broader scope for research in coming years.

That broadening of scope is signaled by our use of the term "visual culture" in the title of the book—which should perhaps have been balanced by a corresponding appeal to "sonic" or "audio culture." Our aim in choosing that term was twofold. On the one hand, visual culture is meant to invoke the wider range of visual media and objects that many art historians now study. On the other, it allows us to include within the book's remit a recent wave of rewarding musicological work dealing with "the visual" generally, rather than visual art specifically, and drawing on geography, performance studies, and film studies as much as on traditional art history. The broad label provides space for less discipline- or canon-bound approaches to the topic, responding to the extremely multifarious nature of this area of study.

That said, it is incumbent upon us to acknowledge that the book has inevitably been shaped by the knowledge and interests of its editors. Our professional experience lies within musicology and art history, and our expertise covers European artistic culture in the Renaissance and the nineteenth century. While we have set out to make the book's geographical and chronological horizons as broad as possible—and have drawn liberally on the expertise of friends and colleagues to help us do so—the coverage remains somewhat uneven. The book has also been shaped to a certain degree by circumstance, and sometimes in ways that we would not have chosen: there are further topics and chapters that we had hoped to include, but that have been eliminated by factors beyond our control. While it seems appropriate to point out these shortcomings, however, it is also important to recall that a book such as this could never achieve complete coverage in any of the various dimensions of its theme.

To continue in the confessional vein, the reader may notice that, owing to practical constraints, this book incorporates fewer images than the topic might support. Contributors have responded to this in two very helpful ways: by discussing images that can easily be found online, and by providing references to publications replete with relevant images under "Further Reading." We suggest that readers follow these two strategies to supplement the images published here as they read.

Over the course of the project we have incurred several specific debts that it will be our pleasure to acknowledge here. Most obviously, our thanks are due to our commissioning editor, Constance Ditzel, and her assistant Elysse Preposi, for their confidence, support, and exemplary organization throughout the process of creating the book. They have made our task much simpler than it might have been. Special thanks are also due to a few friends and colleagues who offered helpful and constructive feedback on the project at an early stage: the members of the Royal Musical Association's Music and Visual Art study group, Charlotte de Mille, Diane Silverthorne, Flora Dennis, and Anne-Marie Hanlon; Marsha Morton; James H. Rubin; Therese Dolan; Karen Painter; Riccardo Marchi; the late Charles Rosen; and also Henry Stobart, who helped us to push the book beyond the limited horizons of our own Eurocentric expertise.

Most importantly, we owe a great debt of thanks to our thirty-nine contributors, all of whom have engaged with the project with enthusiasm, producing insightful and inspiring prose to fill the pages of this book. The quality of our roster of contributors is without doubt the single greatest asset of the book; and in more senses than just the obvious one, without them this project would not have been possible.

Tim Shephard and Anne Leonard
February 2013

NOTES ON
CONTRIBUTORS

Stephen A. Bergquist is a retired lawyer and banker in Boston, Massachusetts. He has contributed articles to *The Beethoven Journal, Print Quarterly* , and *Music in Art*, and is the author of *Musical Prints 1568–1949*, the catalogue of an exhibition held at the University of Connecticut in 2011.

Gurminder Kaur Bhogal is Associate Professor of Music at Wellesley College, USA. She has published widely on the music of Ravel, Debussy, and Léo Delibes. Her book, *Details of Consequence: Ornament, Music, and Art in Paris*, is forthcoming in the AMS Studies in Music Series from Oxford University Press.

Alexander Binns studied music at the University of Oxford, followed by research at the Sorbonne and in Hong Kong, and he is now Lecturer in Music at the University of Hull. His research interests include music in film and the music of Japan.

Jan Butler is Lecturer in Popular Music at Oxford Brookes University. In 2010 she completed her thesis exploring the ideology of authenticity in 1960s American rock, and she has published on the Beach Boys and cover versions. Her other research interests include popular music in film, music production, and institutional structures that affect the creation and reception of recorded music.

Antonio Cascelli is Lecturer in Performance Studies at the National University of Ireland Maynooth. He received his PhD from the University of Southampton, and has published on Chopin, Schenker (Schenker Studies series, forthcoming), and twentieth-century Italian composer Goffredo Petrassi. He is currently working on a project about the role of metaphors in sixteenth- and seventeenth-century Italian music treatises.

William L. Coleman is a PhD candidate in history of art at the University of California, Berkeley. He earned a bachelor's degree from Haverford College, a master's from the Courtauld Institute, both in history of art, and a master's in music from Oxford University.

Laura Cull is Senior Lecturer in Theatre Studies and Director of Postgraduate Research for the School of Arts at the University of Surrey, UK. She is author of the book *Theatres of Immanence: Deleuze and the Ethics of Performance* (Palgrave, 2012) and editor of *Deleuze and Performance* (Edinburgh University Press, 2009).

Alan Davison is Senior Lecturer and convener of music at the University of New England (Australia), and his research interests include music and visual culture, performance practice, and music aesthetics. His doctoral thesis was on the iconography of Franz Liszt, and he has published widely on portraiture of musicians.

Charlotte de Mille is Lecturer at Sussex University and Visiting Lecturer at the Courtauld Institute of Art. She curates music for exhibitions at the Courtauld Gallery and is Chair of the RMA Music and Visual Art Group. Her research studies the intersection of painting, music, and philosophy c. 1848–1950.

Therese Dolan is Professor of Art History at Tyler School of Art, Temple University. She is the author, most recently, of *Perspectives on Manet* (Ashgate, 2012) and the forthcoming *Manet, Wagner and the Musical Culture of Their Time* (Ashgate, 2013). She has also published numerous articles in scholarly journals and contributed an essay to *Women and Impressionism*.

Kelley Harness is an Associate Professor of Music at the University of Minnesota and Editor-in-Chief of the *Journal of Seventeenth-Century Music*. She is the author of *Echoes of Women's Voices: Music, Art, and Female Patronage in Early Modern Florence* (University of Chicago Press, 2006) and is currently at work on a book about equestrian entertainments in seventeenth-century Florence.

Sarah Hibberd is Associate Professor in Music at the University of Nottingham. Her research focuses on opera, ballet, and melodrama in nineteenth-century Paris, and their relationship with wider visual, literary, and political cultures. Her publications include *French Grand Opera and the Historical Imagination* (Cambridge University Press, 2009) and the edited volume *Melodramatic Voices: Understanding Music Drama* (Ashgate, 2011).

Jonathan Hicks is the Lord Crewe Junior Research Fellow in music at Lincoln College, Oxford. His interests include late-nineteenth- and early-twentieth-century French music, especially music in and about Paris. Having completed his doctoral thesis on "Music, Place, and Mobility in Erik Satie's Paris," he is now working on street music and the politics of public space in the same city c. 1880–1930.

Fabian Holt is Associate Professor at the University of Roskilde, where he teaches in the Department of Communication, Business, and Information Technologies. Holt specializes in the area of popular music and cultural events in the contexts of capitalism, media, and urbanization. His publications include *Genre in Popular Music* (University of Chicago Press, 2007) and the co-edited volume *Musical Performance and the Changing City* (Routledge, 2012).

Clare Hornsby's PhD was on the work of Giovanni Servandoni, the Italian artist and opera set designer. She has published widely on eighteenth-century cultural history, including Grand Tour studies and the art market. In 2010 and 2011 she was Honorary Research Fellow at the Royal Academy of Music, teaching a course on artistic and cultural contexts for music. Her current research is for a book on art and music patronage and aesthetics in the eighteenth century.

Jonathan B. Katz is a linguist and musicologist teaching at Brasenose and St Anne's Colleges, Oxford University. His interests combine Western and Indian music and literatures, and his publications include work on Indian musical theory and practice through Sanskrit and vernacular sources.

Robert L. Kendrick teaches music history and ethnomusicology at the University of Chicago, and has worked on music, ritual, devotion, and space in early modern Italy. His books include *Celestial Sirens* (Clarendon Press, 1996) and *The Sounds of Milan 1585–1650* (Oxford University Press, 2002).

Andrew Killick is a Senior Lecturer in Ethnomusicology at the University of Sheffield. His main research areas are the music and musical theater of Korea (including *In Search of Korean Traditional Opera: Discourses of Ch'anggŭk*, University of Hawai'i Press, 2010, and a forthcoming book on composer Hwang Byungki) and popular musical theater worldwide.

Liv Lande is an independent scholar, currently working as Cultural Affairs Adviser at the Embassy of Japan in Oslo, Norway. She earned her PhD in Ethnomusicology from the University of California, Los Angeles, and Masters degrees in musicology from Japan and Norway. She has specialized in Japanese music, and plays the koto and shamisen.

Laura Leante is a Lecturer in Ethnomusicology at Durham University. Her research interests include Indian classical and folk music, music of the South Asian diaspora, performance analysis, music and globalization, popular music, and music semiotics. Since October 2009, she has been directing the AHRC-funded project "The Reception of Performance in North Indian Classical Music."

Anne Leonard is a curator at the Smart Museum of Art and lecturer in the Department of Art History, University of Chicago. Her research on musical aspects of nineteenth-century art has appeared in articles, conference papers, and an exhibition catalogue, *Looking and Listening in Nineteenth-Century France* (University of Chicago Press, 2007). She holds a PhD from Harvard University.

Ayla Lepine has held an Andrew W. Mellon Postdoctoral Fellowship at the Courtauld Institute of Art and is a 2013 Fellow at Yale University's Institute of Sacred Music. She has taught and lectured widely in the US and Europe. She is co-editor of the books *Gothic Legacies* (Cambridge Scholars Press, 2012) and *Building the Kingdom: Architecture for Religious Communities* (Pickering and Chatto, 2013).

Richard Leppert, a musicologist, is Regents Professor in the Department of Cultural Studies and Comparative Literature at the University of Minnesota, Minneapolis. The most recent of his books are *Beyond the Soundtrack: Representing Music in Cinema*, co-edited with Daniel Goldmark and Lawrence Kramer (University of California Press, 2007); and an essay collection, *Sound Judgment* (Ashgate, 2007).

Dominic McHugh is Lecturer in Musicology at the University of Sheffield, where he teaches modules on the Broadway and Hollywood musical. His publications include *Loverly: The Life and Times of "My Fair Lady"* (Oxford University Press, 2012) and *The Lerner Letters* (forthcoming from Oxford University Press, 2014).

Sheila McTighe is Senior Lecturer at the Courtauld Institute of Art and held a Leverhulme Major Research Grant, 2005–08. She specializes in French and Italian seventeenth-century art and has published on Poussin, Caravaggio, and Annibale Carracci, among other early modern artists.

Anna Morcom teaches at Royal Holloway, University of London, and specializes in music and dance in India and Tibet. Her research focuses on phases of modernity ranging from nation building to globalization and neoliberalism, and spans issues of politics, ideology, and inequality as well as media and marketization.

Laura Moretti is the author of the book *Dagli Incurabili alla Pietà. Le chiese degli Ospedali Grandi veneziani tra architettura e musica (1522–1790)* (Olschki, 2008), and the joint author, with Deborah Howard, of *Sound and Space in Renaissance Venice* (Yale University Press, 2009). She is a Lecturer in Art History at the University of St Andrews.

Marsha Morton is a Professor of Art History at Pratt Institute and has published frequently on topics related to art, music, and science in nineteenth-century Germany and Austria. Her books include the forthcoming *Max Klinger and Wilhelmine Culture* (Ashgate), and her co-edited *The Arts Entwined: Music and Painting in the Nineteenth Century* (Garland, 2000).

Roger Moseley is an Assistant Professor in the Department of Music at Cornell University. His publications address topics including the music of Brahms, eighteenth-century keyboard improvisation, and music-themed digital games. His most recent research brings together his interests in play, musical performance, and digital media under the disciplinary banner of ludomusicology, and he is currently working on a book entitled *Digital Analogies: Music, Play, and Games*.

David Neumeyer is Marlene and Morton Meyerson Professor of Music at the University of Texas at Austin. With James Buhler and Rob Deemer, he is the author of *Hearing the Movies: Music and Sound in Film History* (Oxford University Press, 2010), and editor of the *Oxford Handbook of Film Music Studies* (forthcoming, 2013).

Holly Rogers is Senior Lecturer in Music at the University of Liverpool and a Fulbright Scholar at San Francisco's DocFilm Institute. She has published on a variety of audiovisual topics, including music and experimental cinema, visual music, and composer biopics, and is author of *Sounding the Gallery: Video and the Rise of Art-Music* (Oxford University Press, 2013).

Flaviana Xavier Antunes Sampaio is a Professor at the State University of Southwestern Bahia, Jequié, BA Brazil, where she teaches courses in dance and drama. She received her master's degree in dance from Bahia Federal University.

Peter L. Schmunk, educated in musicology and comparative arts, has taught art history since 1987 at Wofford College, where he is currently Garrison Professor of Humanities. His principal research interest lies in the influence of musical culture on painting in the nineteenth century.

Simon Shaw-Miller is Professor of the History of Art at the University of Bristol, having previously held the chair of History of Art and Music at Birkbeck College, University of London. He is an Honorary Research Fellow and Associate of the Royal Academy of Music, London. His many publications include *Visible Deeds of Music: Art and Music from Wagner to Cage* (Yale University Press, 2002), and the forthcoming *Eye hEar: The Visual in Music*.

Tim Shephard is a Lecturer in Musicology at the University of Sheffield, and also a Visiting Research Fellow at the Centre for Music, Gender and Identity, University of Huddersfield. His research concerns music, identity, and visual culture at the courts of Renaissance Italy, and has appeared in several journals.

Diane V. Silverthorne specializes in modernism in the German-speaking world, particularly Wagnerism and the convergence of music and art from the mid-nineteenth century onwards. Having earned her PhD on Alfred Roller and fin-de-siècle Vienna at the Royal College of Art, she has contributed to several anthologies, including *Music and Modernism* (Cambridge Scholars Press, 2011). She is Associate Lecturer at Birkbeck, University of London.

Marica S. Tacconi is Professor of Musicology at the Pennsylvania State University. She holds a PhD in Musicology from Yale University and is a specialist in the music, art, and culture of late medieval and Renaissance Italy. She has published extensively on the liturgical manuscripts of the cathedral of Florence.

Kate van Orden is Professor of Music at the University of California, Berkeley, where she specializes in cultural history. She has produced major studies of vernacular culture and the Renaissance chanson, and has just finished a book on the interrelationships between material culture and song. Her first book, *Music, Discipline, and Arms in Early Modern France* (University of Chicago Press, 2005), won the Lewis Lockwood Award from the American Musicological Society.

Philip Weller studied at the Universities of Cambridge, Heidelberg, Paris, and London. He was a Yates Fellow at the Warburg Institute, and more recently Visiting Research Fellow at the University of Tours. His interests include the field of research where language, image, and music converge (multimedia stage genres, Renaissance, Enlightenment). He has taught at the Universities of Liverpool and (currently) Nottingham.

Abigail Wood teaches ethnomusicology at the University of Haifa, Israel and SOAS, University of London. Her current research focuses on music and sound in public spaces in the Old City in Jerusalem; she has also worked extensively on contemporary diasporic Jewish musics.

Mingmei Yip received her PhD in Ethnomusicology from the University of Paris, Sorbonne. She was Lecturer at the Chinese University of Hong Kong (1981–86), and Senior Lecturer at Hong Kong Baptist University (1987–92). She has published twelve books, including two on the qin.

INTRODUCTION

Tim Shephard and Anne Leonard

It may seem surprising that a volume such as this is appearing only now, in 2013: art and music, as two major categories of creative production, have often been considered two aspects of a single phenomenon ("culture"), and it is very seldom that developments affecting one of them would have left the other untouched. Although the fields of musicology and art history have not been total strangers to each other in the academy, it is nevertheless only rather recently that they began to affirm shared interests, areas of study, and methodological approaches. It is quite recently, too, that their formerly sovereign territories—the musical and the visual—have found new students with new agendas right across the amorphous landscape of the modern humanities, making interdisciplinarity in scholarship on music and visual culture an inescapable reality.

The late arrival of this book probably owes a great deal to the mystique of specialized discourse. Art historians have over the years, quite reasonably, developed a range of specialized conceptual tools to help describe and explain visual art. In addition to the technical knowledge of materials and media necessary for visual analysis, the art historian may also take into consideration a variety of theoretical approaches pertaining to the status of the art object. The exclusivity of musical discourse, meanwhile, is greatly enhanced by the barrier presented to many by musical notation(s); and the language deployed within specialized music analysis is opaque even to many musicians. There has therefore been an understandable reluctance on each side to learn and participate in the specialized discourse of the other, and efforts to bridge the divide have sometimes suffered from problems of disciplinary translation.

The histories of the disciplines of art history and music have by no means run in parallel. Yet, even if the major inflection points and methodological shifts are asynchronous, both fields have been swept by broader theoretical currents in the humanities (notably those coming from literary studies); and these currents have, because of their wide scope, encouraged closer dialogue between the two fields. The same impetus has prompted some significant deregulation of materials and methodologies across the arts and humanities, with hugely positive implications for interdisciplinary research.

Certainly the desire to draw connections between music and visual art, between the "building blocks" or structures of their making, is very ancient, and has passed through quasi-mystical phases when such a correspondence has been thought, or wished, to be divinely ordained. Coming up to the much more recent past, one might argue that fundamental connections between the visual and the musical have been not so much philosophically as technologically enabled: the reality of combined media, or multimedia, has caught up to or indeed overtaken what had been imagined as the possible correspondences between visual and sonic forms. Alongside the rich and ancient vein of aesthetic discourse, and apart from the varied artistic possibilities of combined or hybrid media, music and the visual have always participated together (if not always in coordination) within the same lived experiences, and the same historical realities, at the most practical level; and a combined perspective is therefore of enormous value to "contextualist" scholarship.

Between the music of the spheres, lived historical realities, and the latest multimedia there is, to say the least, a lot of ground to cover. Hybrid arts, such as dance and opera, are after all nothing new. But, to be useful in providing for increased cross-disciplinary comprehension, a *Companion* such as this must take into account not just the different kinds of works that have attempted to engage the eyes and ears in something like equal measure, and the types of historical scenario that might be illuminated by combined study, but also the different kinds of scholarship that have more recently integrated the study of both arts into a new, synthesized understanding.

If the only, or primary, possibility for such integration was to study visual depictions of musical instruments, their players and listeners, there would be no need for the present volume. Musical iconography (the identification and description of musical subject matter in images, including its symbolic value)—and the related subdiscipline of organology (the study of musical instruments, often through visual sources)—was a mainstay of studies in music and the visual arts for much of the twentieth century, and had indeed been the dominant approach of most volumes published on the subject until quite recently. As the disciplinary landscape has changed in the last few decades, however, a kaleidoscope of alternative approaches has come into play, posing a much wider range of questions and addressing a correspondingly broader range of materials than had been traditional within musical iconography.

That growth and diversification is exemplified in the current spate of conferences and publications within this field of research. During the past four years alone, study days exclusively devoted to the topic have been held at the Courtauld Institute of Art, the University of Nottingham, the Royal Academy of Music, University College Cork, the Metropolitan Museum of Art/Columbia University, and Stony Brook University—to take only the US and UK instances of which we are aware. Monographs and essay collections have likewise begun to proliferate. While the field is still young enough not to have a fixed curricular presence at most universities, the exceptions to this are significant and can be expected to increase.[1]

This is, clearly, a moment of great energy and productivity in the youthful field of music and visual culture. Yet, in all the enthusiasm around "intermediality" and related topics (or buzzwords), certain problems can present themselves. To what extent do the different arts maintain distinct characteristics even as they converge or hybridize into new forms? How should such subjects be taught, within a disciplinary structure that may not yet be sufficiently flexible to accommodate inter-arts inquiry? And, on a practical level, how many art historians can claim equal mastery in musicology, or vice versa? How can we ensure the production of worthwhile, responsible scholarship that also remains intelligible, accessible, and (above all) useful to researchers in both fields and beyond?

While the challenges to effective cross-disciplinary research are substantial, current realities demand that there be a place for such scholarship, and means and tools for teaching it. There is reason to believe that as the field of music and visual culture comes to maturity, it will be seen neither as a middle term between two disciplines nor as an unusual species of scholarship in one or the other of them. Rather, studies in music and visual culture will be appreciated as integral to each domain, participating equally in each disciplinary discourse. Many of the chapters in this book chart a path to how this might come about. It will be interesting to see whether the vanguard moves to establish specialized degree programs, majors, and modules bearing this name (as mentioned earlier) will leave a lasting legacy, or whether indeed the scholarship being undertaken in the field thus defined will be progressively subsumed into each of its "parent" disciplines—such that one could not imagine teaching Poussin without reference to the musical modes, or teaching ragas without reference to the visual and gestural components of their performance.

In the meantime, we can simply acknowledge that the examples elaborated in this book are necessarily selective, reflecting the areas of research that have been found thus far to be most fruitful. If readers of this book thirty years from now find it incomplete, with many gaping holes, that, paradoxically, will be a sign of its success in fulfilling its brief. From those future readers' perspective, the book may appear well intentioned yet limited, just as limited as the musical iconography of mid-twentieth-century path-breakers such as Emanuel Winternitz and Albert Pomme de Mirimonde looks to us today. That will mean that the approaches explored here will by then have been thoroughly assimilated, and that they will have raised the possibility of many further research directions and links between the two fields that are as yet undreamed of.

For the moment, we hope to have resisted the idea that the connections between music and visual culture, or our understanding of them, are natural—that they are simply there for the taking. For in the vast majority of cases, they need to be teased out, pulled apart, and placed under the most careful scrutiny if they are going to yield anything of interest or lasting value. Therefore let this book be your "eyes and ears," a preliminary exercise in orientation as you go forth into this fascinating realm of inquiry.

Note

1 Some examples drawn from a casual investigation conducted online in 2012: the University of Brighton has a "Music and Visual Art" degree program; Anglia Ruskin a module called "Art, Music and Performance." Berklee College of Music in Boston offers a "Visual Culture and New Media" minor; Columbia College (Chicago) an MA in "Interdisciplinary Arts"; and Bard College gives students an "Integrated Arts" option, allowing them to study two or more arts-related disciplines in tandem.

Part I

STARTING POINTS

1

SEEING MUSIC

Richard Leppert

Precisely because musical sound is abstract, intangible, and ethereal—lost as soon as it is gained—the visual experience of its production is crucial to both musicians and audience alike for locating and communicating the place of music within society and culture. That is, the slippage between the physical activity to produce musical sound and the abstract nature of that which is produced creates a semiotic uncertainty that is ultimately "resolved" to a significant degree via the agency of human sight; in brief, music's visual-performative aspect is central to its meanings. All of this is obvious enough when witnessing live performance, and no matter the music: classical (orchestral, chamber, solo instrumental, lieder, opera), jazz ensemble, rock and pop bands, etc. It's equally obvious when the performance is shunted to the video screens at arena concerts or the product of a music video. The point is this: performers gesture; they do so, of course, simply in order to make musical sound. But musicians likewise gesture in order to make meaning, to visually inflect the sounds they produce. That is, musicians' gestures commonly exceed the physical movements necessary to produce the wanted sounds.

Take singing, and again no particular matter the sort: art-variety or popular. Singers gesture: facial expression, to be sure, but also more general body language involving hands, arms, legs, and torso. Performers act out music somatically, and they do so as a critical supplement to sonority. The visual aspect of music making is constitutive of the more general enactment of what we more commonly consider performance. The visual component of performance helps to render music expressive; as such, it is part and parcel of the multiple forms of knowledge that music offers its auditors. Music, in short, is not simply made, it is simultaneously *acted*. (Historical efforts to hide performers from sight are the exceptions that underscore the rule. And to be sure, the separation of sound from sight with the advent of the gramophone alters the equation—just as the "invention" of the music video, in fact long antedating MTV, constitutes a kind of pushback against the separation.)

The visual performance code functions through the human body in its efforts to produce and receive music. When people hear a musical performance they see it as an embodied activity. What they hear they also witness: how the performers look, of course, but also how they are costumed, how they interact with their instruments and with one another, how they regard the audience, etc. Listeners also see themselves in relation to other listeners as well as to the performers—and in this regard the musical event is realized as a rampantly socialized activity.

Musicology seeks to make sense of music in time and place, and it does so first and foremost by paying close heed to music itself, that is, to what *sounds*. Musicology also and necessarily takes near equal interest in the relationships between musical activity and the extra-musical contexts of which music is at once an agent and a product.

If we want to understand, say, Beethoven, first and appropriately foremost we have his notated musical survivals: sketches, manuscripts, published scores. We have biographical details, those that come from him and others. We have records of performances, the stuff that makes up reception history. And so on. And we have visual survivals in the form—prior to the invention of photography—of paintings, drawings, engravings, doodles, what have you. Some are formal and studied and self-reflexively flattering. Others might be off-hand; some are satirical. Some are aesthetically accomplished, others distinctly not. And so on. In the end, as regards Beethoven, we have a very great deal. In what sorts of ways does the visual record of Beethoven matter to the writing of Beethoven history? What can that record tell us about (his) music? What are the potentialities of visual-cultural survivals for the writing of history, and in relation to what sorts of caveats? Caveats first.

In the early decades of interest in iconography as a source for music history, a great deal of attention was commonly paid to two subjects, and often nearly to the exclusion of anything else. The first: what could the visual record tell us about organology, the design of musical instruments, especially those that have not survived or that survive only in very small numbers; and the second: what can the visual record tell us about past performance practice? While research of this sort can, and indeed has, paid considerable dividends, the simple or perhaps sad fact is that the record on both scores is at best mixed. The early researches of Emanuel Winternitz in particular make clear the sorts of problems endemic at once to visual source material and to how it is (mis)used:

> [There has been a tendency] often [to] take pictures at face value, without critical discrimination between real and imaginary objects; without sufficient regard for successive styles, technical peculiarities, and mannerisms of pictorial representations; without an awareness of the artist's lack of freedom, in certain periods, in choosing his topic and often even in delineating his objects; without sufficient familiarity with the theological or political doctrines which controlled allegorical representation and therefore detracted from faithful adherence to the actual appearance of the object. Furthermore [some scholars] frequently take a pitiful handful of depictions as adequate evidence, ignorant of the possibility that these may be atypical or that rarity or profusion of certain pictorial representations may not at all correspond to actual historical distribution of instruments and ensembles, or to actual performing practices.[1]

To summarize Winternitz's point: a picture is sometimes worth a good deal less than a thousand words, and especially when regarded as the unproblematic and objective record of the past available just for the looking. An image of Beethoven will indeed tell us something about Beethoven, and quite possibly something not available in any other kind of source. But like any other kind of evidence, it must be responsibly interpreted with regard to the conventions of the discursive practices through which it is realized.

The potentialities of visual culture to musicology, aside from what it can provide to organology and performance practice research, center especially on the relationship between music (and musicians) and society. In this regard, in 1968, Pierre Francastel articulated a critical point about the entwined histories of music and art:

> Music itself is never present [in art]: what the painters set down is the place that it occupies—not as music but as a regulated activity—in the social intercourse of men [*sic*] at a certain time in history and in a certain environment which views painting and music itself as an exterior manifestation less of a personal culture than of a fact of belonging to a certain group of initiates.[2]

Visual representation in effect summarizes by encapsulation musical *function*, not as a disinterested record of events but as a coherent and discursive, commonly dialectical vision of the varied relations within the context of which sound occurs and, hence, sound means. Visual evidence (whether aesthetically accomplished, second rate, technically clumsy, or worse) obviously cannot replicate sound, but it can provide an invaluable—and often pointedly hortatory—account of how and why a given people experienced music. Visual representations, except perhaps those that include decipherable musical inscriptions, tell us nothing specific about particular pieces of music; instead they suggest the range of semiotic possibilities for specific compositions performed under conditions similar to those represented.

The visual record of musical activity translates the three-dimensional and sonoric world into a two-dimensional and silent argument for and about the world—though this is not to deny the role that language plays in processing imagery. Reference to music occurs in visual art not because musical sound exists but because musical sound has meaning. As a topos in visual art, music itself is silenced, existing only as a remembrance of things past: all that remains of music in the image is its trace as a socialized activity. The question arising from visual representation is hence one of music's socio-cultural function. This in turn leads directly back from the abstract realm of ideas and their history to a grounding in social practice. As regards visual art, only certain kinds of musical activity typically get represented, and this is particularly the case with art of the more official sort. Portraiture, for example, typically restricts representation to those musical activities that constitute recognizable signs of socio-culturally sanctioned modes of behavior and thought (of greater significance than music itself), which it is a function of the image not only to attest but also to assert. Put differently, the point of visual representation, art-sort or other, was hardly to render a neutral record of a real or imagined event; representation is inevitably *interested*. It's hardly an accident, for example, that seventeenth- and eighteenth-century genre paintings of European peasantry represent them enjoying their peasant lives, drinking, dancing, making love, making music: happy one and all. It's precisely on account of the ubiquity of such images that the more rare sort representing the miseries of the poor can to this day engender shock (in Low Countries painting, for example, the work of Adrian Brouwer or David Vinckboons).

Music's effects and meanings, which in performance are produced both aurally and visually, in paintings or other forms of visual representation must be rendered visually only. The way of seeing hence incorporates the way of hearing: the artist must produce images in such a way that their meanings will be congruent with those produced by sight and sound together in the lived experience of the original and intended viewer, and commonly if hardly always reflecting the point of view of whomever has ordered up the image or will otherwise be a likely buyer. To render visually meaningful the acoustic phenomenon of music, the artist engages semiotic codes that operate as a sight when music is actually made. The artist doesn't invent a visual code entirely divorced from life-practice, for the simple reason that there is no point in doing so. If artists failed in their endeavor, if their envisioning confused viewers, it is inconceivable that musical subjects could have been produced in the West for many centuries with such abundance as survives. Again, this is not to suggest that artists were unproblematically bound to reproduce in paint what "is" in life; there exists a mutually mediating relation between life-practice and external pressures to flatter taste and ideological fixation. The rich array of caricatures relating to music, performance, and audience reception abundantly demonstrates this point, often with high degrees of trenchant social irony, commonly tinged with biting sarcasm.

Representation is necessarily highly selective. Whatever is visualized is intended not only as the mirror of that which *is*, but as the indicator of that which *is and is to be*. That is, visual representation is the product of an act whose conscious or unconscious purpose is to perpetuate (or critique) a particular way of life: by definition, the image re-presents the past (for time stops in art), but is *about* the future. And once again, when music plays its part in representation it does so precisely by providing a visual means of registering the correctness (or incorrectness) of the present-past and, hence, the correctness (or incorrectness) of the future toward which this present-past directs the viewer. Thus the image of music, re-presented as a social practice, is always already by definition political, to the extent that the future necessarily must be shaped, in effect caused and produced. As such, the future is a dimension of social contestation.

Music history's interest in visual art lies in equal measure with the adjective (visual) and the noun it modifies (art). What's essential about visual art is that it is first and foremost art (i.e., artifice). The importance of vision to visual art is not the physiological phenomenon of seeing (animals see; they do not make art) but perceiving, which of course is governed by the eyes in conjunction with the brain and, indeed, with the entire human organism in its relation to external reality. That is, musicological interest is invested in the ways that music functioned as a visualized activity, but not in the literal sense of how it looked. Instead, it is how it was *made to look* in art that draws attention. This naturally raises the question of original intent; yet recovering intention, were it ever possible, is not the goal. For what the artist (consciously) thought he or she was representing, even if that could be known, in no sense circumscribes what the image "contains" or means, either to its original (and ideal) audience or to the historian. A more useful effort than fussing about intention is self-reflexive engagement with conventions of representation.

Conventions, pictorial or otherwise, reflect the way people do things at a certain moment in time and place, though they are neither innocent nor accidental. They are inevitably the product of efforts to naturalize, hence render unproblematic, the hegemony of certain modes of action or behavior—even when, as in art or etiquette, such actions or behaviors may otherwise be quite arbitrary. In fact the more a behavior is arbitrary, the greater is the necessity to naturalize it. And the greater the extent to which conventions have been naturalized, the more they are explicit

10

responses to certain social demands and certain definitions of culture. Conventions are operative principles of order, just as order itself is the expression of power. In a social context, conventions are the rendered-unconscious expressions of ideology. Representational conventions are a visual condensation of social praxis, however veiled. And to be sure, however inaccessible, intention lies behind conventions as a driving force, even—perhaps especially—once intention itself is long forgotten, precisely what gives agency to, and extends the half-life of, a convention.

The visual representation of people making and listening to music, governed by conventions, encapsulates music's ideological use value, conscious or unconscious, for it is unreasonable to assume that music would be represented in such a way as to appear patently false or out of accord with perceived reality as defined by those who constituted the image's ideal audience. The audience, after all, comprised the very individuals whose dominant social position largely determined their signifi-cant-if-partial control over the construction of culture. Such is the ultimate truth behind the often false appearance of music in art. It is obvious that images commonly underscore, and in turn serve to justify, the ideological grounding of those commissioning the art work. Yet, beyond this quite narrowly interested function, images simultaneously imply an audience of the unconverted.

Art reveals; it also hides. It creates a self-enclosed world unique to itself. But it invites its viewer to recognize that world either as his or her own, or as what that world ought to look like. Visual art reveals in the precise degree to which it attempts to hide—art's conventions are the means by which something is both "said" and left unsaid. By naturalizing modes of representation, conventions stabilize certain behaviors, certain ways of seeing the world. Stated crassly, conventions, through their selectivity, are fundamentally ways of telling highly partial truths—and some-times truth lies, precisely, in the lie (consider the official portraits of history's butch-ers). Art works are never objective, but always *interested*. I don't mean by this that paintings never tell the truth. Indeed, paintings always tell both truth and untruth simultaneously. But what is usually the more important for the historian to deter-mine is not what truth the image seems to assert, but what it wants us to forget by making the assertion. In other words, visual art is about memory, or the construc-tion of memory. And the construction and control of memory takes on an obvious social dimension as the record of a past employed to help determine the present and future. (Considering the degree to which societies from time immemorial have attempted to control musical practices, it's no surprise the care with which visual art often takes to render music history culturally safe, whether in a flattering Eng-lish eighteenth-century conversation-piece group portrait of an elegant family at elegant music or, conversely and contemporaneously, to render an extreme distaste for common street music, as Hogarth satirized in *The Enraged Musician*.)

Consider portraiture. Whatever practices (such as music) any portrait incorpo-rates, it necessarily leaves out even more, by which I do not refer to the ordinary practical limitations about what can be included in a picture. My point is this: Whatever is incorporated must contribute to one all-determining goal. Portraits represent a sitter and the world she or he inhabits as metaphorically or literally in order. Portraits represent achievement. The world of the portrait is settled, no longer up for grabs. The portrait world seems to be an Eden, when in reality of course it is not and cannot be. But, like all half-truths (or even lies), the portrait contains truth by the very attempt to hide the unspoken truth and, by that means, to incorporate

11

a recognizable present absence. Portraits admit antagonism only to the extent that antagonism is overcome—conquered—leaving in its place a symbolic surface as smooth as the paint surface itself. Portraits were always more than monuments to personal vanity, their function considerably less passive than mere commemoration permits. Portraits served as primary tools for managing social position, in some measure because of their singularity. And though portraiture, the example chosen to make my point, is one representational subject among a nearly endless panoply of others, more or less the same points hold true for other sorts of representation.

Musicological research engaging visual culture faces an obvious challenge. It must acknowledge and respect the discursive specificity of representation, and this is especially the case with visual art as a highly developed, self-conscious, self-reflexive discourse operating through complex and historically unstable codes of practice, responsive to myriad cultural, social, and political pressures. In other words, visual representation, art especially, is not mere illustration standing ready, innocently, for the historian's dissection. To write about visual culture as a record of musical practice, one must know the specific histories that attach to the practice, one must understand, in other words, the various means—educational, technical, economic, aesthetic, etc.—by which it was made and its making was mediated. One must know the external histories within which it functioned and to which it explicitly responded, and which it in turn helped to shape. So doing brings dividends, making the effort well worthwhile.

Notes

1 Emanuel Winternitz, "The Visual Arts as a Source for the Historian of Music," in Winternitz, *Musical Instruments and Their Symbolism in Western Art* (London: Faber and Faber, 1967), 31.
2 Pierre Francastel, preface to François Lesure, *Music and Art in Society*, trans. Denis Stevens and Sheila Stevens (University Park: Pennsylvania State University Press, 1968), xx.

Further Reading

Leppert, Richard. *The Sight of Sound: Music, Representation, and the History of the Body*. Berkeley: University of California Press, 1993.
Lesure, François. *Music and Art in Society*. Translated by Denis Stevens and Sheila Stevens. College Park: Pennsylvania State University Press, 1968.
Shaw-Miller, Simon. *Visible Deeds of Music: Art and Music from Wagner to Cage*. New Haven: Yale University Press, 2002.
Winternitz, Emanuel. *Musical Instruments and Their Symbolism in Western Art*. London: Faber and Faber, 1967.

2

SYNAESTHESIA

Simon Shaw-Miller

Synaesthesia is manifest at two principal levels of signification: neurological and cultural. As one might expect from a transgressive phenomenon, there is inevitable crossover and mingling. While reference will be made in this essay to the former, my main area of focus is the latter.

At its most general, synaesthesia can be defined as the cross-stimulation of sensory modalities. Neurologically, synaesthesia occurs when the stimulation of one sensory modality automatically, and instantly, triggers a perception in a second modality, in the absence of any direct stimulation to this second modality. To give an example from the most common case (and the subject of this book), a piece of music might automatically and instantly trigger the perception of vivid colors. The interaction of sight and sound (music and the visual) constitutes about 90 percent of neurological synaesthetic cases.

At the cultural level, cross-sensory stimulation is sometimes referred to by scientists as "pseudo-synaesthesia." However, the position adopted here is that the distinction between so-called "real" (neurological) and "pseudo" (cultural) synaesthesia is often overstated. The existence of a physiological phenomenon and the rich experiences of those who have involuntary color hearing should not distract from the real and widespread existence of sensory experience outside the demarcation of clear-cut sensory and linguistic frames: experiences which can as appropriately be designated synaesthesia. The key concept which is frequently employed to discriminate cultural from neurological synaesthesia is metaphor, but metaphor is not simply a rhetorical device. As Lakoff and Johnson have argued, "metaphor is not just a matter of language, that is, of mere words.... On the contrary, human *thought processes* are largely metaphorical."[1] In other words, "Metaphors as linguistic expressions are possible precisely because there are metaphors in a person's conceptual system."[2] They call this "conceptual metaphor theory." Synaesthetic metaphors are extremely common, perhaps because they are simply special cases of the general rule of metaphor and understanding itself: "The essence of metaphor is understanding and experiencing one kind of thing in terms of another."[3] Our understanding of music is, in fundamental ways, grounded in the visual.

First I should like to address a few examples of individuals who have or have had synaesthestic experiences, and who may or may not be classifiable as neurological synaesthetes. The American composer Michael Torke (b. 1961) has musical key synaesthesia and, perhaps not incidentally, also has perfect pitch. He has, for as long as he can remember, always experienced the simultaneous coincidence of certain keys (B minor, E major etc.) with certain colors. His color–key associations have been fixed and consistent over forty years and, what is more, there are strict diatonic relationships: the colors of the major and minor keys are always related. For example, G minor is for him experienced as a subdued yellow ocher, G major bright yellow; D major is blue, D minor flint or blue-gray. The tonalities, in both musical and color terms, are closely related. It should be noted, however, that while the color terms employed are approximate, the color experiences and sensations are not. The musical and visual events are difficult to translate into words. Indeed, for him some keys have colors which hardly exist at all in the external world. This sensation of color and key for Torke is experienced against a sort of screen, but one that does not affect, in any way, his normal vision or color perception—he shares this with many other neurological synaesthetes. In addition, colors are never experienced in relation to isolated pitches or tonally ambiguous intervals. For example, a fifth will not invoke a color, whereas a third (major or minor) might. Torke's synaesthesia is deeply rooted in tonality; he explains that for him everything is related to the tonic. Brahms's 2nd symphony is blue (being in D major), and the movement that is in G minor will still be blue if heard as part of the whole work, but if that movement is read, or heard separately, it will appear ocher. This means that tonality is colorful not just as a consequence of the experienced sound, but as a consequence of the imagined sound, the sound heard in the mind's ear, just as the color is real in the mind's eye.

Another composer whom it is necessary to mention in relation to the concept of synaesthesia is Olivier Messiaen (1908–92). In conversation with Claude Samuel (published under the telling title *Music and Color*), Messiaen explains that for himself and, he believes, many other composers, color and music are always linked. Indeed, he goes so far as to say, "those who haven't taken it into consideration have committed a grave error."[4] However, beyond the metaphorical implications of this assertion (as regards timbre or texture), the fact remains that these correspondences are aspects of "an inward reality." This inward reality may be fixed for particular individuals and may also inspire a variegated range of sound combinations, suggested by Messiaen's "modes of limited transposition" (Example 2.1), for example. Unlike Torke, whose musical language is essentially tonal, Messiaen did not experience color–key associations in any straightforward way. Rather, as he put it himself, "colors are complex and are linked to equally complex chords and sonorities."[5] Messiaen's harmonic language is not simply tonal; his use of seven modes of limited transposition allowed him to create outside conventional diatonic structures.

The musicologist Jonathan Bernard has shown how only 4 of the 7 modes of limited transposition are color linked: 2, 3, 4 and 6. Bernard's research into Messiaen's mode–color associations further discovered that various transpositions within each mode can give rise to new colors, but that there is still usually a predominant color for the overall mode itself. For example, in the last of his eight piano Préludes (1959), entitled "Un Reflet Dans le Vent," Messiaen described the second theme as blue-orange in its first presentation and green-orange in its second presentation, the first being in a "kind of A," the second being in a "kind of D." While synaesthesia was not always the impetus for his compositional choices, Messiaen clearly uses it as an important part of his compositional toolbox.

Such color perception is subjective, but real. For clinical color–sound synaesthetes, color is not added to the musical experience, it is not extra-musical; it is a fundamental characteristic of the musical experience. However, this subjectivity

14

Example 2.1 Messiaen's modes of limited transposition.

also means that color–key associations, to take a common example, are rarely, if ever, shared between synaesthetes.

While never a clinically confirmed synaesthete, György Ligeti did report color–music associations:

> I am inclined to synaesthetic perception. I associate sounds with colors and shapes. Like Rimbaud, I feel that all letters have a color. Major chords are red or pink, minor chords are somewhere between green and brown. I do not have perfect pitch, so when I say that C minor has a rusty red-brown color and D minor is brown this does not come from the pitch but from

the letters C and D. I think it must go back to my childhood. I find, for instance, that numbers also have colors; 1 is steely grey, 2 is orange, 5 is green. At some point these associations must have got fixed, perhaps I saw the green number 5 on a stamp or on a shop sign. But there must be some collective associations too. For most people the sound of a trumpet is probably yellow although I find it red because of its shrillness ...[6]

So for Ligeti it is possible that the color associations (rather than experiences) may be culturally established, rather than innate. This may also have been the case with the American composer Amy Beach, who, according to at least one account, was encouraged by her mother to associate melodic patterns with colors, a skill (or predisposition) that developed into a life-long association: "Amy's mother encouraged her to relate melodies to the colors blue, pink, or purple, but before long Amy had a wider range of colors, which she associated with certain major keys. Thus C was white, F# black, E yellow, G red, A green, A♭ blue, D♭ violet or purple, and E♭ pink. Until the end of her life she associated these colors with those keys."[7] In contrast, the Russian composer Nikolai Rimsky-Korsakov's experience of colors in relation to musical keys was quite different from both Torke's and Beach's. For him, for example, the key of C major was white, B major was a gloomy dark blue with a steely shine, the key of A major was pink, Ab gray-violet, Eb was a dark gray-blue.

While Rimsky-Korsakov never attempted to develop this color–key association (above his wonderful ear for orchestral color), a fellow countryman of his did. A composer with a much more mythological bent, Alexander Scriabin, sought to create a synthesized aesthetic that incorporated not only sight and sounds, but also tastes and smells and the end of the universe. This synaesthetic and synthetic impulse came to dominate his thinking and to define his last major orchestral works. This is most dramatic in his unrealized (and perhaps unrealizable) Gesamtkunstwerk, a magnum opus known as the Mysterium. While this work was never completed, there was another work in which elements of this synthetic aspiration were realized: his fifth symphony, most commonly known as Prometheus—The Poem of Fire, opus 60, his last completed orchestral score, which he composed between 1908 and 1910. By no means as ambitious a work as the Mysterium, it nevertheless sought to synthesize two elements: color and sound. Scriabin took the mix of music and color further than Messiaen, by proposing the simultaneous projection of color with the performance of his music.

Prometheus is scored for large orchestra, including quadruple woodwind, eight horns, five trumpets, eight trombones and tuba, two harps, piano, a large percussion section (including celesta), organ, wordless chorus and, to add to this palette of timbre, a tastiera per luce (light keyboard: notated on the top line of the score in conventional music notation). There is no detail in the score as regards how the light is to be projected (on a screen or throughout the concert hall?), or by what precise means it is to be "played." The first version of this light device was devised by Scriabin in consultation with Alexander Moser, a photographer and professor of electromechanics at the Moscow School for Higher Technical Training. However, there is no evidence that the design of this "instrument" got off the drawing board.

Light seems to have been a central conceptual strand of the composition process. The notation for this tastiera per luce is written on a single stave in two parts (in three parts for four bars): one part forms the "background" which changes slowly, ten times in all, each change lasting about two minutes (Example 2.2). This part

Example 2.2 Bars 15–25 of Scriabin's *Prometheus* with the *tastiera per luce* part (top) and with the composer's color annotations transcribed from the Paris score.

moves in whole tones, from F# (blue) to the mid-point C (red). This divides the octave in half through a tritone, onto the "resolution" in F#, where the piece concludes on the only true triad of the piece (F#, A#, C#), signifying spirit or will (in opposition to C=red which signifies material will, human spirit). The move from F# to F#₁ represents a complete revolution of the cycle of fifths. However, the inclusion of very occasional "passing notes" (B, D♭, E#) skews the gradual move through the color circle by introducing colors from diverse parts of the color circle, for although moves between "pitches" may be only by a notated semi-tone, the corresponding color is more distant. This is because the division of color into twelve separate units is a matter of nomenclature rather than physical fact. The mapping of color onto pitch (the chromatic scale) is then neatly achieved, although totally arbitrary. In short, the slow-moving part played by the *tastiera per luce* appears to have been conceived to provide an indication of the overall conceptual framework of the piece, which has in practice occasional "wrong notes." Either this, or it appears to have no relation to the music at all.

In Messiaen, unlike Scriabin, color–sound relationships remain part of the conception if not reception of his works. I quote the *New York Times* of Sunday, March 25, 1915:

> At the last concert of the Russian Symphony Orchestra last evening in Carnegie Hall, Modest Altschuler, the conductor, produced what is apparently supposed to be the crowing triumph of Russian art, "The Poem of Fire," "Prometheus" by Alex. Scriabin ... M Altschuler is understood to claim [the] honor of giving the composition for the first time anywhere complete, that is with the accompaniment of "mobile lights" ... The piece was performed in darkness ... Behind the orchestra on the rear wall was a screen. On this the "clavier a luminers," operated by an invisible performer, threw changing, merging, colored lights. The composition ... was given twice in order that the listeners or spectators might have the opportunity to take in fully the revolutionary significance of it.

After a few disparaging remarks about the modern cacophony of the music—"The harmonic substance is ... practically unintelligible"—the reviewer concludes with comments on the lights: "They are continually shifting and melting, but without visible relations to the sounds ... to the first bewildered beneficiaries of the new art, it seemed still to be a sealed book."

The aspiration to realize instruments that might be able to play color in the way in which a musician plays notes has a surprisingly long history. One of the earliest experimentalists in this area was the sixteenth-century artist Giuseppe Arcimboldo (1527–1593). There is an account of his theories in *Il Figino, overo del Fine della Pittura* (Mantova, 1591). Most color–music associations up to the eighteenth century were based on Aristotle's theories of color (for example, Athanasius Kircher's *Ars magna lucis et umbrae* of 1646). But with the proposal for the construction by Louis Bertrand Castel (1688–1757) of a *clavecin oculaire*, or "harpsichord for the eyes," the model shifted to Isaac Newton. There appears to be no evidence that the instrument was ever effectively constructed, but whether or not he found a practical solution, Castel does seem to be the first person to have proposed the concept of an independent "color music." As he wrote in 1757 in *La Musique en Couleur*:

18

Can one imagine anything in the arts which would surpass the visible rendering of sound, which would enable the eyes to partake of all the pleasures which music gives to the ears? ... What could [w]e say of an art which did not only simply awaken the idea of speech, and of sound, by means of arbitrary and inanimate characters, such as the letters of the alphabet, or the notes of music; but painted it really; that is painted it with colors; in one word, rendered it felt and present to the eyes, as it is to the ears, in such a manner that a deaf person can enjoy and judge the beauty of music as well as he who can hear.[8]

This wish to "make music for the eyes" took on a greater emphasis in the nineteenth century as the development of technology provided more effective means of realizing it. In 1877 the American inventor Bainbridge Bishop got a patent for the first Color Organ. But perhaps the most well-known early pioneer in this area was the British painter and Professor of Fine Art at Queen's College, University of London, Alexander Wallace Rimington (1854–1918), whose electric-powered color organ was first demonstrated in London in 1895 (Figure 2.1).

This instrument made no sound, but was designed to accompany music through the projection of color onto a screen (its patent specification number is No. 24814/1893 Great Britain). In his book *Colour-Music: The Art of Mobile Colour*, Rimington wrote: "But though, in the case of sound, the great art of music has been created, no such art with colour for its main object has yet been built up. There is however, no reason why this should continue to be so, or why a great colour art analogous to the art of music should not be developed."[9]

He claimed his "new art" would mobilize color to create a new visual experience that would free art from the two-dimensional restrictions of the canvas. Although these experiments continued for many years with Vladmir Baranoff Rossiné in Russia, the Danish-born Thomas Wilfred, the American Mary Hallock-Greenewalt, Alexander Laszlo in Hungary, and Charles Blanc-Gatti in Switzerland, for example, it was with the development of another temporal medium that the idea of color music really found its technological fulfillment. That medium was, of course, film.

While by no means the only abstract color–music filmmaker, the Bauhaus artist Oskar Fischinger was a pioneer in this area and made fourteen animated studies between 1928 and 1932. In all of these films he closely coordinated the music with the images, his aim being to produce a new art form called "color rhythm," which for him fulfilled the true vocation of film: the manifestation of an abstract color music. In October 1933, at the third *Kongresse zur Farbe-Ton-Forschung* (Congress for Color-Tone Research) in Hamburg, his films were shown alongside Blanc-Gatti's color organ. Here Fischinger attended a meeting of anti-Nazis, where the president of the Congress, Georg Anschutz, called upon all present to maintain abstract filmmaking and color music in the face of Nazi threats to such abstract artistic experimentation, even if they had to use the term "ornamental." But by 1935 all non-representational art works had been labeled "degenerate," seen as snobbish and elitist and opposed to the true sensibilities of the *Volk*. In that same year Fischinger wrote: "I wish for 1935 the first, great, feature-length color-film work—an absolute color-work, born of music, comprehensible to all the people on earth—and bringing massive amounts of currency into the country! That is what I wish with all my heart!"[10] This wish had to wait until 1940 to find a kind of fruition—but not directly for Fischinger, and not in Germany, rather for Walt Disney and in America.

With the help of Paramount Pictures Corporation, Fischinger left Germany in early 1937 to settle in Hollywood. There he eventually found his way to Disney's studio, where one of his first tasks was to animate the sparkle of the blue fairy's wand in *Pinocchio*. Fischinger had, some years before working for Disney, talked to the conductor Leopold Stokowski about the possibility of adding animation to Bach's music. This idea found its way to Disney himself (via Stokowski), and, as Disney had seen color organs (in 1928), the idea was not foreign to him. In the preparatory planning stages of what was to become the animated film *Fantasia* (it had the working title *The Concert Feature*), Disney and Stokowski had tried a synaesthetic experiment: they had recorded their visual experiences while listening to Bach's music. Perhaps not surprisingly, while Disney saw orange in one passage, Stokowski insisted on purple. Fischinger's abstract animated color-music films were a significant inspiration for Disney's *Fantasia*, especially in the sequence animating Bach's toccata and fugue in D minor BWV 565 (Figure 2.2), but Disney judged that if the film remained too abstract it would alienate the audience (a not dissimilar judgment, ironically, from the National Socialists'). Instead he encouraged his animators to pursue narrative figurative realizations (e.g. Figure 2.3). Fischinger does not appear in the credits to *Fantasia* (at his own request). In a letter about his time at Disney he wrote:

> The film *Toccata and Fugue by Bach* is really not my work, though my work may be present at some points [e.g. it was his idea to have a visible, animated, soundtrack]; rather it is the most inartistic product of a factory. Many people worked on it, and whenever I put out an idea or suggestion for this film, it was immediately cut to pieces and killed.[11]

If the ambition to develop filmic synaesthetic color-music was to dry up, then the pursuit of instrumental solutions to the manifestation of synaesthetic perceptions was a relatively small, if diverting, tributary. Such ambitions may be generated either by an unavoidable neurological cross-sensory stimulation, or by the desire to extend and enlarge the creative process. As I mentioned earlier, some (scientists) insist on a clear-cut distinction between neurological syaesthesia and what John Harrison calls its "close-bosomed friend, metaphor."[12] My suggestion in the context of this collection of essays is that synaesthesia is frequently fundamental both to our thinking about the arts, and to an artist's or musician's own creative process.

We might perceive this metaphorical manifestation in the language we use to talk about music, although such relationships are rarely *only* functioning at the linguistic level. For example, non-diatonic music—that is, music that moves away from the centrality of key—is known as chromatic music. Similarly we refer to an elaborate and decorated melody, particularly in operatic singing in the eighteenth and nineteenth centuries, as coloratura. Most centrally, we refer to the *quality* of a note or sound as "timbre" or "tone-color," or in German *Klangfarbe*. Our ears tend to group harmonically related frequency components into a single sensation. Rather than perceiving the individual harmonics of a musical tone, we perceive them together as a "tone color" or *timbre*, and we hear the overall pitch as the fundamental of the harmonic series being experienced. Furthermore, if we hear a sound that is made up of just a few simultaneous tones, and if the intervals among those tones form part of a harmonic series, our brains tend to group this input into a sensation of the pitch of the fundamental of that series, even if the fundamental is not sounding. Most Western instruments produce harmonic sounds subject to these rules. But some produce inharmonic tones, and these, such as cymbals and other indefinite-pitched percussion instruments, are often used by composers to "add color or texture." But such speech does not just flow in one direction. In painting we talk of color in terms of "tonality," and of color and shape combinations as being "loud" or "quiet" (as in "that's a loud shirt"). Likewise we talk of tonal saturation in terms of highs and lows, like pitch.

The issue here is not really the appropriateness or otherwise of such language, nor more fundamentally the "accuracy" and measurability of one "synaesthetic" response over another in conventional scientific terms. Rather, the most important point is the very ubiquity of such synaesthetic responses, aspirations, expressions, and approaches.

The concepts of "cognitive metaphors," "conceptual blending,"[13] and "sensory mixing"[14] make the idea of clear boundaries between neurological and cultural synaesthesia much more difficult to be certain about. Lakoff and Johnson argue that the understanding of one idea or cultural domain in terms of another is fundamental not just to our communication, but also to the way we think and act. Conceptual blending is likewise proposed as a subconscious process that forms the very foundation of creative thinking. Even among some leading cognitive neurologists and psychologists interested in synaesthesia, a dominant view is that all human neonates have synaesthesia, but by about four months of age the senses have become modularized to the extent that we no longer experience it in the same way. Whether this is demonstrable or not, some have argued that even the idea of "modularization" in these terms is not so pure and demarcated as we might like to think. The Austrian-American psychoanalyst Paul Schilder wrote in 1935:

> But we should not forget that every sensation is generally synaesthetic. This means that there does not exist any primary isolation between the different senses. The isolation is secondary. We perceive and we may with some difficulty decide that one part of the perception is based upon optic impressions. The synaesthesia, therefore, is the normal situation. The isolated sensation is the product of an analysis. In the scheme of the body tactile-kinaesthetic and optic impulses can only be separated from each other by artificial methods. What we have studied is the change in the unity of the postural model of the body by change in the sensation of the tactile and optic sphere. The nervous system acts as a unit according to the total situation. The unit of perception is the object which presents itself through the senses and through all the senses. Perception is synaesthetic. There is no question that the object "body" presents itself to all senses.[15]

The work of the philosopher Michel Serres proposes that at the experiential level, foundational to that of metaphorical cognition as explored by Lakoff and Johnson, the body is essentially mingled. Art may then help to bypass this dominance of language and cognition: "We have lost hopelessly the memory of a world heard, seen, perceived, experienced joyfully by a body naked of language. This forgotten, unknown animal has become speaking man, and the word has petrified his flesh, not merely his collective flesh of exchange, perception, custom and power, but also and above all his corporeal flesh: thighs, feet, chest, and throat vibrate, dense with words."[16] The notion that there are five senses is principally a consequence of the physical (visual) existence of sense organs: eyes, ears, nose, tongue, and skin. But of course the ear does not hear, it merely receives vibration in air (usually) before passing it on to the cochlea and translating it into a liquid medium, then further translations take place into nerve impulses before the brain can finally interpret and hear. Sound happens throughout this process, not as a simple unitary phenomenon, but as a mingled one. Additionally, as any "deaf" musician will tell you, sound is never just experienced through the ear: the body hears. A case in point is the British percussionist Dame Evelyn Glennie, as reported in the *Globe and Mail* of March 1, 2011:

> Glennie may be one of the best listeners in the world, because she has had to develop the listening abilities of her entire body. Since the age of 12, she has been profoundly deaf, which means her ears deliver only a fraction of the sound vibrations that she picks up most vividly through her feet, hands, chest and whatever else in her frame responds to the vibrations from her various instruments. "The body's like a huge ear," she says. "It's as simple as that."

The important point is that she is not alone, we all hear like this. Serres again:

> [T]he whole body or organism raises a taut sculpture or statue of skin, vibrating to the voluminous sound, open-closed like a cylindrical drum, trapping what traps it. We hear through our skin and feet. We hear through our skull, abdomen and thorax. We hear through our muscles, nerves and tendons. Our body-box, strung tight, is covered head to toe with a tympanum. We live in noises and shouts, in sound waves just as much as in spaces … resonating within us: a column of air and water and solids … as though our bodies were the union of ear and orchestra, transmission and reception … We wear two question marks, one on each side of our heads like placards, two treble clefs, with neither repercussions nor answers.[17]

To return to the two central terms of this book, "music" and "visual culture," and their relationship to synaesthesia: sound and vision merge, music and visual culture converge. Synaesthsia is a mingling; sounds carry vision, and vision, or more specifically looking, is not a purely sense-limited activity. Looking may be biologically grounded in the same way as hearing, but as visuality, that is, as a screen of social constructs and discourses through which we have no choice but to look, it is also fundamentally grounded in culture. It is framed (and framing), affect laden and cognitive. This makes hearing and looking (and other sense-based activities) permeable, subject to infection from neighbors. What we see is not just sights, but textures, sounds. This is not only the case in multimedia or mixed media; it is more fundamental than that. Looking and hearing are inherently and unavoidably synaesthetic. Music is visual.

Notes

1 George Lakoff and Mark Johnson, *Metaphors We Live By*, rev. ed. (Chicago: University of Chicago Press, 2003), 6.
2 Ibid.
3 Ibid., 5.
4 Olivier Messiaen, *Music and Color: Conversations with Claude Samuel and Olivier Messiaen*, trans. E. Thomas Glasow (Portland, OR: Amadeus Press, 1994), 42.
5 Ibid.
6 *György Ligeti in Conversation with Péter Várnai, Josef Häusler, Claude Samuel, and Himself* (London: Eulenburg Books, 1983), 58.
7 Walter S. Jenkins, *The Remarkable Mrs. Beach, American Composer* (Warren, MI: Harmonie Park Press, 1994), 5–6.
8 Quoted in Adrian B. Klein, *Coloured Light: An Art Medium* (London: The Technical Press, 1937), 2.
9 Alexander W. Rimington, *Colour-Music: The Art of Mobile Colour* (London: Hutchinson, 1912), 2.
10 William Moritz, "Oskar Fischinger," in *Optische Poesie: Oskar Fischinger, Leben und Werk*, ed. Hilmar Hoffman and Walter Schobert, exh. cat. (Frankfurt am Main: Deutsches Filmmuseum, 1993), 40.
11 See Moritz, "Oskar Fischinger," 85.
12 John Harrison, *Synaesthesia: The Strangest Thing* (Oxford: Oxford University Press, 2001), 139.
13 Mark Turner and Gilles Fauconnier, *The Way We Think: Conceptual Blending and the Mind's Hidden Complexities* (New York: Basic Books, 2002).
14 Michel Serres, *The Five Senses: A Philosophy of Mingled Bodies*, trans. Margaret Sankey and Peter Cowley (London: Continuum, 2009).
15 Paul Schilder, *The Image and Appearance of the Human Body: Studies in the Constructive Energies of the Psyche* (London: Kegan Paul, 1935), 38–39.
16 Quoted after *Mapping Michel Serres*, ed. Niran Abbas (Ann Arbor: University of Michigan Press, 2005), 165.
17 Serres, *The Five Senses*, 141 and 144.

Further Reading

Bacci, Francesca, and David Melcher, eds. *Art and the Senses*. Oxford: Oxford University Press, 2011.
Baron-Cohen, Simon, and John E. Harrison, eds. *Synaesthesia: Classic and Contemporary Readings*. Oxford: Blackwell, 1997.
Campen, Cretien van. *The Hidden Sense: Synesthesia in Art and Science*. Cambridge, MA: MIT Press, 2007.
Cytowic, Richard. *Synesthesia: A Union of the Senses*. Cambridge, MA: MIT Press, 2002.
Di Bello, Patrizia, and Gabriel Koureas, eds. *Art, History and the Senses: 1830 to the Present*. Farnham: Ashgate, 2010.
Harrison, John. *Synaesthesia: The Strangest Thing*. Oxford: Oxford University Press, 2001.
Jewanski, Jörg. *Ist C=Rot?: Eine Kultur- und Wissenschaftsgeschichte zum Problem der wechselseitigen Beziehung zwischen Ton und Farbe: von Aristoteles bis Goethe*. Sinzig: Studio, 1999.
Serres, Michel. *The Five Senses: A Philosophy of Mingled Bodies*. Translated by Margaret Sankey and Peter Cowley. London: Continuum, 2009.
Shaw-Miller, Simon. *Eye hEar: The Visual in Music*. Farnham: Ashgate, 2013.
——. *Visible Deeds of Music: Art and Music from Wagner to Cage*. New Haven: Yale University Press, 2002.
Torke, Michael. *Color Music*. 1. Green, 2. Purple, 3. Ecstatic Orange, 4. Ash, 5. Bright Blue Music. (Recorded by the Baltimore Symphony Orchestra, conducted by David Zinman on the Argo label, 1991 (B000004CVR).)

Part II
METHODOLOGIES

3

ART HISTORY FOR MUSICOLOGISTS

Charlotte de Mille

The paragone of the arts has a distinctive and illustrious past, having engaged artists, writers, and composers from Leonardo, Alberti, and Michelangelo to Lessing, Goethe, Wagner, and Greenberg. Paragone texts that address music and the visual arts often draw support for what is perceived as the close correspondence between the two arts in terms of their structural innovations and expressive intentions. Exchange between the arts commonly serves as a way of mediating qualities that are hard to describe, and in the modernist period in particular, critics, artists, and publics faced with the unexpected frequently resorted to metaphorical comparison.

By the beginning of the nineteenth century, comparisons between music and painting were increasingly common. Ostensibly non-visual, music offered the painter an alternative trajectory through which to negotiate multi-sensual experience or to defeat mimetic representation. Through alertness to the emotive affect of instrumental music (and of Wagner's in particular), critics extolled a "higher Realism," shifting the intention of painting from mimetic illustration to the realization of psychological experience.

Concerns for the relation between the arts rely, understandably perhaps, on the discussion of formal qualities, the study of which lies at the foundation of academic art history as it developed at the end of the nineteenth century. To study the relation between music and painting is then a productive means through which to reflect upon the origins of art history as a discipline. Such work is perhaps less complementary to the socially conscious and politically engaged "new" art history developed in the 1970s particularly by Norman Bryson, T. J. Clark, Amelia Jones, Fred Orton, Griselda Pollock, and Raymond Williams, but may find renewed engagement in relation to the questioning of representation undertaken by the "October Group," principally Yve-Alain Bois, Hal Foster, and Rosalind Krauss. Not to detract from "new art history," it is, however, for these reasons that the following outline will focus largely on the fathers of art history rather than its later exponents.

When the British artist and critic Roger Fry claimed that the painting of Wassily Kandinsky was "pure visual music," he quite probably had in mind the observation of fellow artist-critic Walter Pater that "all art aspires to the condition of music." For Pater, music is the ideal "identification of matter and form," yet it is little remembered that he opened his chapter "The School of Giorgione" in *The Renaissance* (1893) by stating that it is a "mistake" to regard the arts as "translations into different languages of one and the same fixed quantity of imaginative thought."[1] Pater's essential text exploring disciplinary boundaries therefore constitutes a warning to anyone embarking on work in this field. But whereas Pater's text at heart concerns comparison, Fry's statement was more daring for dispensing with metaphor. The difference marks the modernist emphasis on the affect of art, from which its formal means could be deduced *a posteriori*.

Fry was the translator of artist Maurice Denis's essay on Cézanne, published in the *Burlington Magazine* in 1910, and author of one of the founding texts of formalist art criticism in the Anglophone world, "An Essay in Aesthetics" (1909). Here Fry laid out six "emotional elements of design": rhythm of line; mass; space; light and shade; color; and the inclination of the picture plane. For Fry, these formal qualities inscribed emotions that were communicated to the viewer through his or her body. Rhythm of line was the "*gesture* of the artist's feeling," and mass the feeling of the object's "power of resisting movement, or communicating its own movement to other bodies."[2] The idea that gesture and movement instigate a sensation of movement in the viewer that is comparable to the movement on the picture plane confounds our expectations of a static plane. On this basis, Fry claimed that a work of art has a "direct and immediate appeal" not to the intellect but to emotion, because the first response from the viewer is to an arrangement of form, not to a set of ideas.

On the Continent shortly before Fry's text was published, one of the founders of art history, Alois Riegl, was developing his now-notorious concept of *Kunstwollen*, or "will to art," which he described in *Late Roman Art Industry* (1901). Riegl believed that this will was premised on quintessentially formal values in art: "the appearance of things as form and color in the plane or in space."[3] According to Riegl, it is our apprehension or perception of form that accounts for our response to works of art, generated by the work itself rather than what we might bring to it. Riegl's younger colleague Heinrich Wölfflin agreed. In his conclusion to *The Principles of Art History* (1915), Wölfflin described two kinds of art history, one that moved according to outward historical and societal forces, and another that evolved from its own momentum, autonomously: a history of "*forms* of apprehension and representation ... of form working itself out inwardly."[4] Of course art history can better be described as a mixture of the two, and this is where Riegl and Fry concur.

Riegl alleged that the viewer meets a work of art in selfless attentiveness, "like a part of the all-embracing world soul."[5] Engaging with a work of art should be so engrossing that it becomes internalized by the viewer as part of his or her own experience. However, through its apprehension, the work of art should inform him or her of the way in which humanity relates to the world. Riegl thought that overarching styles such as late Roman art, the Renaissance, or modernism spoke of the desires and wills of the societies and cultures that made them. Just as we can derive a view of what societies of the past valued, and how different people from different countries or backgrounds related to one another by looking at their art, so too can we read this, he believed, in art of our own day. It is worth clarifying that Riegl's view of "Modern art" (he was writing in 1902) was far from complimentary: modern art ignores the viewer because "it knows nothing but the subject; for according to its view, the so-called-objects are completely reducible to the perception of the subject."[6] Modern art, Riegl thought, was dangerously founded on *sight*, just when scientific discoveries were providing evidence that sight could no longer be understood as the same for everyone. In place of this, Riegl championed another sense, *touch*, and argued that we should have to both see and touch an object in order to understand what it is. But by addressing the senses, this meant that art was not simply a representation to be read intellectually, but was integral to what it was representing. It was both representation *and* reality, proactive in the viewer's experience. Moreover, that experience was profoundly multi-sensual.

By extension, one could wonder at the limits of this multi-sensual understanding of art. If touch, then why not taste or sound? Riegl himself did not turn his attention to music; however, rhythm was of central importance to his discussion of form. Indeed, in Michael Gubser's words, for Riegl, "rhythmic form organized art and nature, man's perception and the historical world." It was rhythm that "provided the basis for artistic form and development."[7] By identifying with the work's rhythmic contours (or gestures, in Fry's language), the viewer apprehends essential qualities otherwise obscured by concern for its narrative or representative subjects, which are commonly pursued in cognitive and deductive looking. In contrast, a response attuned to the formal rhythms of a work opens up an intuitive and immanent looking akin to the emotive affects of rhythmic, harmonic, and melodic structures in music. The implication is that even in visual art, we do not necessarily *see* the subject depicted first of all, but rather *feel* the impression of the structural organization through which that subject is manifested.

Riegl's theory has significant implications for the way we might regard abstraction, although Riegl himself would doubtless have regarded abstraction as part of the modern art he most disliked. Because art is part of our experience, *is* an experience in its own right, it can show us complicated ideas without having to explain them narratively. We comprehend without having to articulate this understanding in words. And because it is the sensory experience that counts, a work of art doesn't need to be "of" anything at all, as the experience will remain—in paint, color, and form. Indeed, arguably, the experience will be more intense if there is nothing to distract us from these sensations. If we can see a figure, landscape, or other subject, then our intellect kicks in: we relate the work to things we know already, rather than comprehending it as itself.

When Riegl disparaged modernizing tendencies that reduced the art object solely to the perception of the viewing subject, he was to an extent rehearsing a Kantian interpretation of painting that was later to become central to formalist interpretations of modernism. Kant says that we experience only appearances, not things in themselves: "What may be the case with objects in themselves and abstracted from all this receptivity of our sensibility remains entirely unknown to us. We are acquainted with nothing except our way of perceiving them."[8] On this basis, modern critics have laid emphasis on the *appearance* of art rather than what it represents, and have used this tenet to justify "pure" and "abstract" works. For them, a modernist work of art is about itself as an art object, about paint, canvas, texture, and so on; and where these works are representational, the objects they include are not metaphorical or symbolic of anything outside the restricted confines of "art." Abstraction is both a *property* (i.e., it is non-figurative, and it functions on internal relations between forms, colors, and planes); and a *process* (i.e., it chooses to emphasize one idea over another and uses the means of its medium to that end). In this regard, it is easy to see why early critics of painterly abstraction turned to music as a comparable art form whose internal structure is integral to its expression.

Two of the first painters to explore metaphysical abstraction through a painterly address to several senses were the Russian Wassily Kandinsky and the Czech František Kupka. Kupka, however, did not have anything "comparative" in mind in his recipe of visual and aural. Instead he claimed to have made "something between sight and hearing"—a structural and material translation of music.[9] He signed some of his letters to the Austrian critic Arthur Roessler "color symphonist," and described his painting as "concepts, syntheses, chords."[10] So what did he mean? In *Amorpha, Fugue in Two Colors* (1912; National Gallery, Prague), Kupka expanded his investigations into the splitting of light, combining his knowledge of the color wheel and of fugal technique in music. In fugue, progression is made through the repetition of the theme in the same key, commonly (although not necessarily) beginning on a note either a third or fifth away from the starting one. Transposing this for painting, the colors red and blue on a color wheel are either three or five colors apart, depending on the direction one moves around the circle. Kupka called his painting a "symmorphy, which, like a symphony, will develop in space."[11] He said that by employing "forms of different dimensions, composed according to rhythmic concerns, I will achieve a formal and directional structure, typical of fugue, in which the development of a theme across time, or here, space, is undertaken with limited harmonies."[12] His sweeping curves, variously expanding and contracting, manifest this unfolding by recurrence. The meeting points of the two consecutive themes are seen in harlequinesque sections: for example, the tight loop in the upper part of the canvas. Kupka's painting is about space, the disposition of forms, and, as his title *a-morpha* indicates, about the transcendence of media through formlessness: literally, the title means without "morpha," without form. His subject was the continuum of every movement in the cosmos, but he despaired: "I was obliged to be even more morphic than I would be when interpreting forms recorded in nature," because "*morphé*, or form, is the fundamental condition for art of any description."[13] For Kupka, the means of art—of any media—were inadequate for his ends.

There is, however, a counter-argument to the abstraction of Kupka and Kandinsky. Clement Greenberg, in "Towards a Newer Laocoon" (1940), addressed medium specificity rather than correspondence between the different media. He saw it as characteristic of modern art to define itself according to the limits of its medium, and he argued this in order to justify abstraction. The title of his article referred to two earlier texts: Gotthold Ephraim Lessing's *Laocoon: An essay on the limits of poetry and painting* (1766), which not only discussed the arts as separate entities but imposed a hierarchy on them, with poetry at the top; and Irving Babbitt's *The New Laocoon: An essay on the confusion of the arts* (1910), which argued that any mixing of the arts should stop. Babbitt was particularly reactionary in his views, and it is worth noting that Greenberg, as harbinger of the avant-garde, turned to a conservative critic. Greenberg entered the fray saying that "purism" springs from anxiety about the identity of the art in question. Greenberg's generic "purism" is a "salutary reaction against the mistakes of painting and sculpture ... which are due to such a confusion" in the arts.[14]

It is also in this essay that Greenberg considers the medium-specific qualities of the other arts. Musicologists will doubtless not enjoy his observation that "[m]usic was saved from the fate of the pictorial arts," by which he refers to their subservience to and imitation of literature, "by its comparatively rudimentary technique and the relative shortness of its development as a formal art."[15] At the same time, he goes on to suggest that the avant-garde of the twentieth century, in an attempt to secure the integrity of painting, looked to the *method* of music: its "abstract" nature, constructed according to its own laws. Music's formal sovereignty was something for other arts to aspire to. Bringing the *Laocoon* texts up to date, Greenberg concluded his essay with the happy assertion that each art is "safe now" (in 1940), having "accepted" both its own limitations and the powers of its sister arts. For the visual arts, the key was the physical affect of the object, and Greenberg stressed the vital importance of the picture plane which broke with realistic space to assert its own presence.

In the course of several major texts, Greenberg espoused a dominant definition of modernism that traced a teleological advancement from the work of Édouard Manet to Jackson Pollock, Mark Rothko, and Barnett Newman. In this movement toward purity, and toward a self-reflexive interest in the medium, painting moved toward flatness. In his 1960 essay "Modernist Painting," Greenberg claimed that modernism "uses art to draw attention to art," as opposed to the Renaissance tendency to "use art to conceal art." The text continued: "Modernism lies, as I see it, in the use of characteristic methods of a discipline to criticize the discipline itself ... to entrench it in its area of competence."[16]

What Greenberg's narrative lacks is a sustained consideration of the socio-political and historical context of the works in question. His is a very selective history: he despised Duchamp, for example, and gave little attention to Dada, or to the social-realist works contemporaneous with the start of Abstract Expressionism in America. Socialist realism is, after all, still regarded as being outside most definitions of modernism. Greenberg's scholarship, however, evolved. He had addressed some of these issues in one of his earliest articles, "Avant-garde and Kitsch," published in the American Trotskyist journal *Partisan Review* in 1939. Here Greenberg addressed what he regarded as an increasingly divisive tendency in art production, the double-edged sword of art that engages critically with its environment while bending to the needs of that environment. The article distinguishes between the avant-garde, which "keep[s] culture *moving*," and easily digestible kitsch, an "ersatz culture" which welcomes "insensibility" and "uses for raw material the debased and academicized simulacra of genuine culture."[17] It is clear on which side Greenberg's favor lies; nevertheless, it is in this article that he most fully examined the "relationship between aesthetic experience as met by the specific ... social and historical contexts in which that experience takes place."[18]

It is this attention to context that provides an unlikely moment of correspondence between Greenberg and Raymond Williams, an exponent of "new" critical theory. For both critics, modernism is recognizable for its interest in itself, supporting a transnational community based on a like-minded approach to the medium in question. It is also recognizable for its technical innovation and sophistication; its liberation from conventions, largely facilitated by its urban environment; and its rejection of domesticity in the pursuit of the new. "Creativity is all in new making, new construction," Williams writes in "The Politics of the Avant-Garde," before launching into an analysis of the combative strategies of manifesto-led movements.[19] But, Williams also writes: "Although Modernism can be clearly identified as a distinctive movement, in its deliberate distance from and challenge to more traditional forms of art and thought, it is also strongly characterized by its internal diversity of methods and emphases: a restless and often directly competitive sequence of innovations and experiments, always more immediately recognized by what they are breaking from than by what, in any simple way, they are breaking towards."[20]

This openness, or uncertainty, is similarly embedded in the version of modernism given by T. J. Clark in his revised introduction to *The Painting of Modern Life*. Here Clark pinpoints the moment of modernism as commencing with Manet, identifying the change as "a kind of scepticism, or at least unsureness, as to the nature of representation in art." As a result,

> Painting would replace or displace the Real ... for reasons having to do with the nature of subjectivity, or the truths revealed by higher mathematics. ... Unbrokenness of surface could be seen—by Cézanne par excellence—as standing for the evenness of itself, the actual form of our knowledge of things. That very claim, in turn, was repeatedly felt to be some kind of aggression on the audience, on the ordinary bourgeois. Flatness was construed as a barrier put up against the viewer's normal wish to enter a picture and dream, to have it be a space apart from life in which the mind would be free to make its own connections.[21]

In this passage, modernism is elitist in its address to a mind able to follow its abstract vision of the world, while also constricting in its demands for attention: we have to see as it sees, we cannot "dream." Clark's *The Painting of Modern Life*, however, goes on to entrench a modernist emphasis on form within a changing social structure. He is adamant that the "form of the new art is inseparable from its content."[22] The economic change of industrialization that brought "tourism, recreation, fashion and display" created a population with new tastes in art; correspondingly, some art was made to satisfy the new taste, while other art sought to reflect the change in modern patronage and modern life, and to reflect it critically. Central works of Impressionism—Manet's *Bar at the Folies-Bergère* (1882; Courtauld Institute of Art, London), Renoir's *La Loge* (1874; also Courtauld), or Seurat's *A Sunday on La Grande Jatte—1884* (1884–86; Art Institute of Chicago)—ambiguously negotiated the two demands, both mirroring modern leisure, yet perhaps, through innovative technique, questioning some of its pretensions to a more "civilized" experience of life.

Clark's groundbreaking book on Impressionism pulled back the façade of chocolate-box contentment to reveal a critically engaged history beneath the surface. In a different vein, but no less unsparingly, Rosalind Krauss and the critics involved with the journal *October* have, over the last thirty years, forcefully staged a reassessment of the intentions and limits of the art-historical canon. Krauss's *The Optical Unconscious* wages war against the selective and visually driven histories of modernism that occlude instances of anti-form, inter-media collaboration, and the daily lives of those who make and look at art. Resisting the "withdrawal of each discipline into that sphere of sensory experience unique to it," Krauss abandoned the objective, empirical, and analytical voice of art history to engage with literary and fictional texts by André Breton and Georges Bataille, works of psychoanalysis by Sigmund Freud and Jacques Lacan, and philosophical texts by Gilles Deleuze and Jean-François Lyotard.[23] Looking for what was absent in existing histories of modernism, Krauss also sought what was absent from our cognition or perception: what was seen, but not expressed.

Formalist questions return us to core concerns for art history—the material object, cultural analysis, and aesthetic practice. Formalism has often been chastised for regarding art as an end in itself. However, by tracing the processes of making, the aspiration was in fact the reverse: to record an index of cultural movements, desires, and intentions. Many of the themes broached in this short outline—the transference between internal and external, the enigma of presence implied through absence, the multi-sensual, and the temporal—find correspondence in responses to music. These formalist endeavors in both the art-works themselves and the criticism about them share a desire to give voice to an ineffable quality in art that eludes analysis yet, it is argued, is responsible for conveying meaning beneath (or separate from) surface content. This is, after all, the gist of the immediate aftermath of the contest between satyr and god in the myth of Apollo and Marsyas: Apollo's brutality in the defense of an art of harmony was incongruous with the powers of music, Harmonia, Rhythmos, and Logos understood as the components that ordered the spheres, of which the human world is an incomplete reflection. According to Diodorus, on flouting the musical balance of the spheres, Apollo stopped playing the lyre for some time. So Marsyas silenced the god of music: his aspiration to music un-did music altogether. In other words, we regard form and skill as ends in themselves at our peril, but to ignore them would be to ignore the very qualities that the arts—and only the arts—can express.

Notes

1 Walter Pater, *The Renaissance* (Mineola, NY: Dover, 2005), 90, 92, 87.
2 Roger Fry, "An Essay in Aesthetics" (1909), in *Vision and Design* (London: Chatto and Windus, 1947), 36–38.
3 Cited in Margaret Olin, "Forms of Respect: Alois Riegl's Concept of Attentiveness," *The Art Bulletin* 71, no. 2 (June 1989): 286.
4 Quoted in Robert S. Nelson and Richard Shiff, eds., *Critical Terms for Art History* (Chicago: University of Chicago Press, 2003), 113.
5 Alois Riegl, *The Group Portraiture of Holland* (1902), in Olin, "Forms of Respect," 287.
6 Riegl, *The Group Portraiture of Holland*, in Olin, "Forms of Respect," 291.
7 Michael Gubser, *Time's Visible Surface* (Detroit: Wayne State University Press, 2006), 187, 190.
8 Immanuel Kant, *Critique of Pure Reason*, ed. Paul Guyer and Allen W. Wood (Cambridge: Cambridge University Press, 1998), 59–60.
9 Kupka interview of 1913, quoted in Peter Vergo, "How to Paint a Fugue," in *Music and Modernism c. 1849–1950*, ed. Charlotte de Mille (Newcastle: Cambridge Scholars Press, 2011), 8.
10 Letter dated 1895, cited in *František Kupka 1871–1957*, exh. cat. (New York: Solomon R. Guggenheim Foundation, 1975), 26; and letter to Arthur Roessler dated 1905, cited in Dorothy Kosinski, ed., *Painting the Universe: František Kupka, Pioneer in Abstraction*, exh. cat. (Ostfildern-Ruit: Hatje, 1997), 24.
11 Cited in Margit Rowell, "František Kupka: a metaphysics of abstraction," in *František Kupka 1871– 1957*, 64. This musical metaphor is furthered in a letter to Roessler of February 2, 1913: "what I am seeking now are symphonies," cited in Meda Mladek, "Central European Influences," in *František Kupka 1871–1957*, 37.
12 Ibid.
13 Kupka, *Form in Art*, 1923, cited in Jaroslav Andel, "A wanderer between chaos and order," in Kosinski, ed., *Painting the Universe*, 93.
14 Clement Greenberg, "Towards a Newer Laocoon," quoted in Charles Harrison and Paul Wood, eds., *Art in Theory 1900–2000* (Oxford: Blackwell, 2003), 562–63.

15 Ibid., 563.
16 Clement Greenberg, "Modernist Painting," quoted in Harrison and Wood, eds., *Art in Theory 1900–2000*, 774–75.
17 Clement Greenberg, "Avant-garde and Kitsch," quoted in Harrison and Wood, eds., *Art in Theory 1900–2000*, 543.
18 Ibid., 540.
19 Raymond Williams, "The Politics of the Avant-Garde," in *The Politics of Modernism*, ed. Tony Pinkney (London: Verso, 2007), 53.
20 Raymond Williams, "The Emergence of Modernism," in ibid., 43.
21 T. J. Clark, *The Painting of Modern Life* (Princeton: Princeton University Press, 1984, rev. ed. 1999), 10, 13.
22 Ibid., 5.
23 Rosalind Krauss, *The Optical Unconscious* (Cambridge, MA: MIT Press, 1993), 8.

Further Reading

Albright, Daniel. *Untwisting the Serpent: Modernism in Music, Literature and Other Arts*. Chicago: University of Chicago Press, 2000.
Harrison, Charles. "Abstraction, Figuration, Representation." In *Primitivism, Cubism, Abstraction: The Early Twentieth Century*, edited by Charles Harrison, Francis Frascina and Gill Perry, 185–206. London and New Haven: Yale University Press and the Open University Press, 1993.
Leppert, Richard. *The Sight of Sound: Music, Representation, and the History of the Body*. Berkeley: University of California Press, 1993.
Nelson, Robert S. and Richard Shiff, eds. *Critical Terms for Art History*. 2nd ed. Chicago: University of Chicago Press, 2003.
Preziosi, Donald. *The Art of Art History: A Critical Anthology*. Oxford: Oxford University Press, 2009.
Shaw-Miller, Simon. *Visible Deeds of Music: Art and Music from Wagner to Cage*. New Haven and London: Yale University Press, 2002.
Vergo, Peter. *That Divine Order: Music and the Visual Arts from Antiquity to the Eighteenth Century*. London and New York: Phaidon, 2005.
——. *The Music of Painting: Music, Modernism and the Visual Arts from the Romantics to John Cage*. London and New York: Phaidon, 2010.

4
MUSICOLOGY FOR ART HISTORIANS
Jonathan Hicks

If you consider yourself a musicologist, this chapter may not be for you. As the title implies, my aim is not to break new ground in the field so much as to introduce the lay of the land, as I currently find it, to those whose disciplines do not ordinarily address music as an object of study. Since many scholars of visual culture will already be familiar with aspects of the academic study of music, the following pages are not intended as a beginner's guide or "how to" manual. Instead, I propose a holistic, if necessarily selective and subjective, account of the history and priorities of (predominantly Anglo-American) musicology. What this brief survey lacks in detail, I hope it makes up for in usefulness. At any rate, my remarks and observations are not offered as conclusive statements on the discipline, but rather as a means of "joining the dots" and focusing further discussion. I begin by addressing musicology's problematic disciplinary identity before introducing some late-nineteenth- and twentieth-century figures whose work has formed the backdrop to a number of ongoing debates. I then consider what might be called the "privileged objects" of musical study, as well as the challenge to music's object status signaled by performance-oriented approaches. The chapter ends in an optimistic mood with some personal reflections on the present state of musicology and speculation regarding future areas of research. While all of the above is offered with art historians in mind, I do not attempt to flag up each shared interest or every occasion for dialogue, but prefer to leave it to readers to establish such connections for themselves.

Discipline and Publish

Musicology has a discipline problem—in fact, it has several. Despite the distinguished position of something called "music" in the long history of the liberal arts, and the even longer history of musical inquiry reaching back to Al-Kindi, Aristoxenus, Pythagorus, et al., there remains a sense that musicology needs to justify its place in the modern academy. No doubt some of our colleagues in the "hard" sciences will always detect a whiff of dilettantism in the study of any form of art—I have been laughed at more than once by engineers and chemists when explaining what I teach to undergraduate students—and every musicologist has been exasperated at one time or another by the fundamental misunderstanding behind the question "what instrument do you play?" Yet the ever-present need to communicate our research and account for our positions is felt especially strongly in the current neoliberal climate wherein higher education is increasingly instrumentalized as a means of providing intellectual labor for the administrative cadres of trans-national corporations. As the recent funding cuts made by the UK's Coalition government demonstrate all too clearly, arts and humanities teaching is now considered a poor relation to the teaching of STEM subjects (science, technology, engineering, and mathematics), on account of the latter being understood to add more value to the workforce of "UK Plc." In practical terms, this has already resulted in departmental closures and has forced all of us working under such hostile conditions to reassess the arguments we make on our subject's behalf.

Though such existential crises are hardly unique to musicology—or the UK, for that matter—they underscore the extent to which the history of any discipline is inextricable from its ideological and institutional contexts. Back in 1885, when Guido Adler (1855–1941) was preparing his now-famous essay on "The Scope, Aim, and Method of Musicology" for the first issue of the *Vierteljahresschrift für Musikwissenschaft* (Musicology Quarterly), his disciplinary circumstances were considerably different from those of the present day. As a salaried academic in fin-de-siècle Vienna, Adler was not especially concerned with establishing the social or economic impact of the new "music-science," but he was passionately committed to securing its independence from general historical studies and, just as importantly, its credibility vis-à-vis the better-established fields of art and literary criticism. In addition to exemplifying the sometimes anxious positioning of musicology in relation to other forms of academic inquiry—musicologists, it seems, are perennially worried about "lagging behind" their colleagues in other subjects—Adler's essay highlights another source of institutional tension when it proposes a division between *historische Musikwissenschaft* and *systematische Musikwissenschaft*. The precise differences between Adler's "historical" and "systematic" approaches are less important than the pattern they set for subsequent distinctions within the study of music.

These internal divisions are perhaps clearest in North America, where there are separate graduate programs and scholarly societies for musicology, ethnomusicology, and music theory. Traditionally, the first of this trio has been concerned with the history of European art music, while the second has attended to the musical cultures of the wider world, and the third has taken a more note-based or "analytical" approach to the study of musical structures. In some ways, the boundaries between the three major groupings are becoming ever more porous: one recent conference, for example, brought together the annual meetings of the American Musicological Society, the Society for Ethnomusicology, and the Society for Music Theory in a single all-encompassing event. Yet it would be misleading to suggest that there are no antagonisms or suspicions between the established sub-disciplines, just as it would be misleading to suggest that there are no other ways of differentiating the study of music. As you would expect, it is common for professional conversations and solidarities to form around significant chronological periods, geographical areas, and/or sub-divisions of style. There is also a sizeable body of research incorporating the study of music into the psychological, neurological, and biological sciences, as well as work on music and dance, music in film, music therapy, music technology, arts administration, and, of course, performance training and composition. Taken as a whole, then, musicology—or "music studies" if you prefer, since musicology is more or less synonymous in North America with historical musicology—is a remarkably broad church. This breadth and diversity, arguably one of the discipline's greatest strengths, might also be a strategic weakness when it comes to articulating a coherent account of the subject's values in the face of the aforementioned threats to university teaching and research.

Landmarks in the Field

Musicology, like any such scholarly profession, has a number of "landmark" figures whose work is so familiar to practitioners in the field that it becomes a means of orienting oneself in relation to ongoing debates. Given the centrality of Austro-German repertoire in the early years of musical research—not to mention Adler's status as a "founding father" of the discipline—it is unsurprising that some of the most influential scholars of the early- and mid-twentieth century had names with a decidedly Teutonic ring. Heinrich Schenker (1868–1935), for example, developed a system of analysis based on the age-old principles of voice-leading and "species counterpoint" (essentially a set of practical instructions for composing multi-part vocal music), which encouraged users to look beyond the surface details of a composition in order to reveal—or arguably construct—the harmonic *Ursatz* (fundamental structure) underpinning the work as a whole. Schenker's interest in the "organic" unity of musical structures was informed by a prominent strand of nineteenth-century German aesthetics, and one of the expressed purposes of his analyses was to establish the supremacy of certain Austro-German works within the broader European tonal tradition. It is surely no coincidence that Schenker was working at a time when this very tradition was perceived to be under threat by post-tonal composers such as Arnold Schoenberg (1874–1951), who was himself an influential music theorist. Indeed, it is well documented that Schenker was an arch-reactionary whose analytical tracts are notorious for their aggressive nationalism and overt anti-Semitism. Luckily for him, however, the offending passages were edited out of the earliest translations of his works, thus leaving his techniques free to gain a lasting foothold in the music departments of the post-World War II United States.

Another German-speaking scholar to have a considerable posthumous impact on Anglophone musicology was the Frankfurt School social theorist Theodor W. Adorno (1903–69). As an anti-totalitarian leftist, Adorno was fiercely critical of both the "culture industry," as he termed it, and any form of art deemed complicit in the suppression of autonomous subjectivity: notably Igor Stravinsky's (1882–1971) anti-expressive neo-classicism and Jean Sibelius's (1865–1957) symphonic "cult of nature." Adorno's polemics against the emotional manipulation of film music and the de-individualizing tendencies of what he mis-termed "jazz" have been pored over and parodied in equal measure. His championing of Viennese serialism—which has sometimes been used to bolster the claims of an infamously unpopular repertoire—also leaves him open to the charge of music-philosophical nepotism, since he was not only a personal acquaintance of Schoenberg's but also took composition lessons from one of his best-known students, Alban Berg (1885–1935). Partly because of these criticisms—and also because of broader objections to work-centered analysis, which I shall come to shortly—the vogue for Adornian musicology has waned in recent years. Nevertheless, it would be hard to overstate the significance of his essays (and paraphrases thereof) to the course of recent debate: by insisting that the study of musical change was always already the study of social change, Adorno's idiosyncratic approach to musical aesthetics encouraged a great many writers to take note of, and develop alternative approaches to, what Tia DeNora has termed the "music and society nexus."[1]

One such writer was Carl Dahlhaus (1928–89), whose wide-ranging studies were, in the best dialectical tradition, simultaneously informed by and critical of Adorno's sociology of music. The key term for Dahlhaus was "relative autonomy," a notion that signaled the limitations of both aesthetic hermeticism and social determinism.[2] Appropriately enough, this disciplinary stance appears to have been at least partially contingent on the political circumstances in which Dahlhaus worked. As Anne C. Shreffler has argued, Dahlhaus's position as a West German musicologist operating at the height of the Cold War casts new light on his robust objections to the Marxist models of musical production favored by his East German counterpart, Georg Knepler (1906–2003). While the vast majority of Knepler's work remains untranslated, Dahlhaus's writings were something of a hit in English and North American music departments throughout the 1980s. The questions he raised about the objects and methods of musical inquiry may well have been shaped by the intellectual climate of Cold War Berlin, but they also marked a turning point in the history of the discipline: whatever the shortcomings of his own approach, musicology after Dahlhaus was more ambitious, reflexive, and theoretically literate than it had ever been before.

Treasure and Pleasure

The surest sign of disciplinary upheaval in the 1980s and 1990s was the critique of the musical "masterpiece." Once upon a time it was self-evident that the purpose of musicology was to attend to the great works of genius bestowed upon the present by the great men of the past. Chief among these celebrated figures were the likes of J. S. Bach (1685–1750), Ludwig van Beethoven (1770–1827), and Richard Wagner (1813–83)—all of whom, we might note, were German-speaking. While there is no need to rehearse the discourse on canon formation here—still less to repeat the truism that universalist claims can be grounded in particular times and places—it is worth addressing how canonicity has played out in the performing, as opposed to plastic or literary, arts. You might think it was obvious that a performing art requires performers, yet the role of performance has not always enjoyed a prominent place in the academic study of music. Indeed, it was long assumed that the principal treasures of musicology were the objects made by composers (i.e., scores), and that the task of scholarship was first to establish the provenance and authenticity of such objects (usually by reference to principles of textual criticism imported from the discipline of philology), then to consider the composer's intentions by relating the features of the object to what was known of the man—or, very, very occasionally, the woman—in question.

If the methodology described above sounds distinctly old-fashioned, it is only because a number of writers successfully campaigned against the fetishizing of musical objects in favor of a broader understanding of musical history and experience. One such writer was Lydia Goehr, whose account of *The Imaginary Museum of Musical Works* located a tipping point—sometime around 1800—when music ceased to be considered an activity for doing and started to be seen as an object of contemplation. According to Goehr, the paradigm of the musical work—whereby performance is understood to be the realization of a composer's ideal aesthetic object—has functioned as a "regulative concept" ever since, with deleterious consequences for the vibrancy and creativity of musical culture.[3] Richard Taruskin has argued along similar lines that the proponents of the historically informed performance movement were not, as they had hoped, reproducing the music of the past, but in fact creating new music for the present. Both Taruskin's back-handed compliment and Goehr's interventionist history of ideas are typical of a broader shift in musicology from privileging the composer and his score to the performer and his—or, just as often, her—audience.

The implicit association of composerly authority with a masculine subject has been hugely important in the reconfiguring of the discipline. Most importantly, it suggested that composer-centered accounts inevitably perpetuate the erasure of women from music history because they relegate to the margins those roles—of singer, instrumentalist, patron, etc.—that women have most often been in positions to perform. Rather than attempting to rectify the inherited, and inherently misogynist, musical canon by adding a relatively small number of works by female composers, a new wave of gender-conscious musicologists in the 1990s sought to disrupt the conventional wisdom that a work was the product of a single authorial voice. As Carolyn Abbate demonstrated in Unsung Voices: Opera and Musical Narrative in the Nineteenth Century, music's metaphorical polyphony is one of the conditions of its fascination. The fact that a performance exceeds any monological interpretation is both a source of pleasure and, crucially, a source of power. For, once operatic agency is understood to be distributed between not only the composer and librettist, but also the singers, musicians, conductor, director, designer, and—last but not least—the audience, it is no longer convincing to organize discussion around the one name in large print on the front of the score. In part this is an argument in favor of reception studies, which has affected musicology no less deeply than it has the rest of the humanities, but it is also something more than that: by "decentering" the object of musical inquiry to the point that object status could no longer be taken for granted, exponents of the polyphonic mode of interpretation came to celebrate the very intangibility of music and musical meaning. Needless to say, such dedication to the pleasures of imprecision were incommensurate with traditional score-bound analysis. Little wonder, then, that Abbate was not the only musicologist to question the validity of close reading and the methodological reliance on textual traces.

Approach and Reproach

In 1980, Joseph Kerman published an essay in Critical Inquiry entitled "How We Got into Analysis, and How to Get Out." The fact that a musicologist chose to publish his work in an interdisciplinary journal is itself worthy of note; that Kerman went on to expand his arguments into a book-length survey of the field—described by one reviewer as "a Who's Who of musicology, and a What's What of theory, analysis, and musical philosophy"—made his work compulsory reading for all music scholars at the time.[4] The thrust of Kerman's argument was that musicology, in the decades since World War II, had become a dry and dusty field of study. On the one hand, he took exception to an analytical enterprise that appeared to equate aesthetic worth exclusively with structural unity, and therefore ignored many of the aspects of musical experience most valuable to audiences and performers. On the other hand, he argued that music historians had become weighed down by their archival work to the point that they were good at collecting dates and facts, but indifferent—or worse—when it came to the interpretation of musical meaning. Both symptoms, Kerman suggested, could be diagnosed by the term "positivism," which has echoed down the years as a stinging critique of any under-theorized or merely descriptive form of musical study. While the temperature of debate surrounding Kerman's wide-ranging critique inevitably cooled in the decades that followed, his call for a more humanistic and hermeneutic form of inquiry set the standard for a generation of scholars whose work came to be known as the "New Musicology."

Predictably enough, few writers have welcomed a label that was destined to grow old almost as soon as it entered circulation. Nevertheless, the notion of a New Musicology retains its currency to this day, and helps to identify a particular disciplinary "moment," the like of which has not been seen since. In line with Kerman's pronouncements, many of the practitioners who came to prominence in the 1980s and 1990s were concerned with building bridges between musicology and the broader humanities. Gary Tomlinson's widely cited essay on "The Web of Culture"—which, as it happens, was published in a special journal issue of "Essays for Joseph Kerman"—advocated a contextualist approach to the study of music informed by the cultural anthropology of Clifford Geertz. Later on, Tomlinson combined Paul Ricoeur's hermeneutics with Michel Foucault's archaeology of knowledge in his study *Music in Renaissance Magic* —a book that famously included not a single extract from a musical score. Lawrence Kramer's *Music as Cultural Practice*, first published in 1990, proposed a method of interpretation that aimed to render music's meanings no less legible than literature's. Kramer's next book, *Classical Music and Postmodern Knowledge*, added yet more theorists to musicological reading lists, while placing particular importance on questions of poststructuralism and epistemology. The early 1990s also witnessed Susan McClary's *Feminine Endings*, which brought musicology—sometimes kicking and screaming—into conversation with gender studies. No less important, however, was McClary's discussion in *Feminine Endings* of both popular musicians and high-art composers: though it may now seem unremarkable for an academic career to take in Madonna as well as Monteverdi, the initial breaching of sub-disciplinary barriers was yet another sign of the turbulent musicological times.

The New Musicology thus refers to both a new set of approaches to musical study and a broadening of disciplinary horizons in terms of repertoire, agency, and geography. One way of acknowledging this enlargement of interests is to consider the treatment of Gioacchino Rossini (1792–1868) by successive generations of musicologists. For Dahlhaus, writing in 1980, Rossini represented the lesser of the "twin styles" that typified the musical culture of the early nineteenth century: whereas Beethoven's instrumental music embodied the full breadth and depth of artistic genius, Rossini's operas belonged in the populist realm of spectacular entertainment. By the time of James H. Johnson's 1996 account of *Listening in Paris*, this sort of critical evaluation was less important than understanding why audiences for both Rossini's and Beethoven's music became increasingly attentive and subdued. More recently still, Benjamin Walton has researched the reception of Italian opera in South America, thus challenging the tacit Eurocentrism of traditional accounts of nineteenth-century music. Indeed, some historical musicologists now see their work as a branch of cultural history, just as ethnomusicology can be seen as a branch of cultural anthropology. Thanks to the opening out of disciplinary purview associated with the New Musicology, the academic study of music is far less isolated than it once was. Nevertheless, the subjects and objects of music studies retain a specificity that justifies a unique—if problematic—disciplinary identity.

Feeling Hopeful

Predicting the future is a fool's game, but forgetting the future is no less foolish. From the vantage point of the early twenty-first century, the New Musicology looks a lot like the New Orthodoxy. What emerged as a series of sometimes acrimonious disciplinary arguments about the aims, methods, and scope of music studies has now settled into a relatively familiar curriculum of performativity, anti-elitism, and identity politics. While I welcome these considerable intellectual advancements, the current generation cannot simply rest on inherited laurels. Our responsibility to the present is first to historicize past achievements, then to attend to what remains undone. In arguing for continued progress—and, yes, there is such a thing as progress—I wish to draw attention to more than the inevitable mellowing of critical voices when repositioned as the declarations of authority. In fact, some recent commentaries on the history of the discipline have suggested that the critical edge of the New Musicology was never all that sharp in the first place.

James R. Currie's 2009 essay "Music After All" investigated the cultural politics underlying the contextualist approach to musical study, arguing for a strategic return to widely debunked notions of "the music itself." Currie's claims rest on the possibility that music's relative autonomy, to borrow Dahlhaus's well-worn phrase, harbors a promise of freedom, which any progressive scholar ought not to waste by immediately reducing the aesthetic to the level of the social. Another leftist musicologist, J. P. E. Harper-Scott, has ventured a more strident critique of contemporary musicology by focusing on the work of its best-known exponent, Richard Taruskin. Specifically, Harper-Scott suggests that the latter two volumes of Taruskin's *Oxford History of Western Music* are deliberately biased toward Russian and American subjects so that the work as a whole can reach its climax in the post-Cold War triumph of North American liberal capitalism. This "end of history" narrative, Harper-Scott argues, does considerable ideological work in support of a free market approach to the making and receiving of musical "products." The fact that Taruskin has elsewhere criticized scholars for privileging art over entertainment leads Harper-Scott to describe Taruskin's work as "the longest suicide note in musicological history."[5]

It would be misleading to suggest that the two authors discussed above represent a large section of the musicological community, but that is beside the point: their work suggests that ideology critique—which has been linked too closely in musicology with the single figure of Adorno—has a significant role to play in the future of the discipline. This role need not be as resistant to contextualist or sociological approaches as Currie and Harper-Scott might suggest. The late Adam Krims's essays in *Music and Urban Geography*, for example, combine analyses of popular music and political economy in order to elaborate on the relations between modern cities and expressive culture. Krims's work also belongs to a broader category of studies that can be grouped under the banner of "music, space, and place." Significantly, this emerging body of research does not fit easily into any one of the three disciplinary sub-groupings listed earlier in this chapter. Michael Bull's *Sound Moves: iPod*

Culture and Urban Experience, Steven Feld's *Sound and Sentiment*, and Daniel M. Grimley's extensive writing on English and Scandinavian composers' associations with landscape, all draw on symbolic and material geographies to inform our understanding of particular practices of listening, singing, and composing. Above all, the concern that these writers share for "re-materializing" the study of music—in terms of both the tangible objects of musical culture and the ephemeral materialities of acoustic encounter—holds great promise for future inquiries and suggests a link, if not a merger, with the relatively new field of sound studies. This may seem an odd place to end a survey of musicology for art historians, since sound studies and visual culture are not the most obvious of colleagues, but it may be precisely in attending to the locations of expressive culture—whether noisy, spectacular, or a combination of these and more—that our disciplines might find most common ground.

Notes

1 Tia DeNora, "Formulating Questions—the 'Music and Society' Nexus," in DeNora, *Music in Everyday Life* (Cambridge: Cambridge University Press, 2000), 1–20.
2 See, for example, Carl Dahlhaus, "The 'Relative Autonomy' of Music History," in Dahlhaus, *Foundations of Music History*, trans. J. B. Robinson (Cambridge: Cambridge University Press, 1983), 108–128.
3 Lydia Goehr, *The Imaginary Museum of Musical Works: An Essay in the Philosophy of Music* (Oxford: Oxford University Press, 1994), 7–8.
4 The reviewer in question was Erich Leinsdorf, whose comments, written for the *New York Times* (26 May 1985), were proudly displayed on the front cover of Kerman's *Contemplating Music: Challenges to Musicology* (Cambridge, MA: Harvard University Press, 1985).
5 J. P. E. Harper-Scott, "Modernism as We Know It, Ideology, and the Quilting Point," in Harper-Scott, *The Quilting Points of Musical Modernism* (Cambridge: Cambridge University Press, 2012), 3.

Further Reading

Auslander, Philip. *Liveness: Performance in a Mediatized Culture*. New York: Routledge, 1999.
Bergeron, Katherine and Philip V. Bohlman, eds. *Disciplining Music: Musicology and Its Canons*. Chicago: University of Chicago Press, 1992.
Born, Georgina and David Hesmondalgh, eds. *Western Music and its Others: Difference, Representation, and Appropriation in Music*. Berkeley: University of California Press, 2000.
Clayton, Martin, Trevor Herbert, and Richard Middleton, eds. *The Cultural Study of Music: A Critical Introduction*. 2nd ed. New York: Routledge, 2012.
Leyshon, Andrew, David Matless, and George Revill, eds. *The Place of Music*. New York: The Guilford Press, 1998.
MacGregor, Emily. "Whoever Pays the Piper Calls the Tune: Pressures on Academic Freedom and the Discipline of Music in the UK." *Critical Quarterly* 54, no. 4 (2012): 54–73.
Shreffler, Anne C. "Berlin Walls: Dahlhaus, Knepler, and Ideologies of Music History." *The Journal of Musicology* 20, no. 4 (2003): 498–525.
Solie, Ruth A., ed. *Musicology and Difference: Gender and Sexuality in Musical Scholarship*. Berkeley: University of California Press, 1993.
Stobart, Henry, ed. *The New (Ethno)musicologies*. Lanham, MD: The Scarecrow Press, 2008.
Taruskin, Richard. *Text and Act: Essays on Music and Performance*. Oxford: Oxford University Press, 1995.

5
ICONOGRAPHY
Robert L. Kendrick

There are various ways to define musical iconography, ranging from the study of musical activity or objects (instruments) in images (traditionally defined as paintings) to the analysis of music's aesthetic and ideological function in visual media. For a number of reasons, the field has not enjoyed academic prestige, either from the side of music studies or from visual culture/art history, commensurate with the quite interesting and often painstaking work that has been done in it. This is all the more striking in light of the historical intersection between visual and sonic culture, not to mention the ways in which visuality, in a digital and video age, has become central to popular understanding (as anyone who has taught music to North American undergraduates over the past generation can testify). Here, I examine the issues around the academic study of iconography as they developed in one cultural matrix that was central to early scholarship: late medieval/early modern Europe (1450–1800). But we should also recognize the ways in which such issues are present in other cultural situations: the high literary level of ekphrasis around jazz photographs, the modes of narration and referentiality in film music, or the studies of pop and rock album covers.

In some ways, early iconography followed the models of collection and classification present in the first wave of late nineteenth-century musicology, the Austro-German school around Guido Adler (1855–1941) and, for ethnomusicology, Erich Moritz von Hornbostel (1874–1935). In its emphasis on forms and objects, we might consider this a parallel to Alois Riegl's "historical grammar" of art forms; it should be remembered that Adler, Hornbostel, and Riegl were all in Vienna at the same time. Musical iconography has shared, and preserved, some aspects of the first generation of music scholarship: its willingness to engage objects from world cultures, not just Western European societies, and an interest in archaeology, evolution, and even *Kulturkreis* theory. For obvious reasons, it began largely by studying musical instruments as objects of sonic culture. In classical studies this was aided by the fact that much evidence for music in Greek and Roman culture is precisely images (vase paintings). The diverse representations of practice, instruments, and notation were evident in the German series *Musikgeschichte in Bildern* (Leipzig, 1961–), which covered both historical and ethnological aspects of music cultures. As the practical discovery of pre-1750 music progressed through the twentieth century, the focus on instruments was linked to the nascent early music movement—quite different among its French, German, and British versions—and its emphasis on recreating or restoring early examples, not least with an ear to using them in performance. The focus on instruments, though, has co-existed uneasily with the reality that most surviving music up to 1700 is actually vocal, and a good deal of it does not use instruments at all.

The sub-discipline of iconography might also have seemed central, due to the roughly contemporary emergence of art history and musicology as disciplines between Vienna and Berlin around 1900. Certainly the emphasis on valorized cultural periods—such as the early Italian Renaissance, seen as inaugurated by Masaccio's frescoes in the Brancacci Chapel (S. Maria del Carmine, Florence; 1424–28) and by the music of Guillaume Du Fay's Italian years (essentially 1420–33)—was shared by the two disciplines. Further periodization was aided by the adoption across the humanities of Wölfflin's criteria for—and valorization of—"Renaissance" and "Baroque." Indeed, music historiography has often perceived 1600 as a kind of watershed equivalent to the pictorial revolution of the Carraccis and Caravaggio, even though this has been challenged in more recent scholarship in both fields.

In some ways, art history and musicology followed parallel if not entirely mutually intelligible paths up to the 1980s, with an emphasis on great figures, stylistic attributions of disputed works, and the establishment of artistic chronologies based on "progressive" features. Still, it was hard to link the Berensonian emphasis on connoisseurship and visual detail to musicology's concerns with source studies, pitch structures, and compositional process. In Renaissance studies, the implied (and sometimes explicit) parallels between "protagonists" in the two arts (e.g. Josquin des Prez as a kind of Michelangelo figure, or Edward Lowinsky's valorization of the "Renaissance avant-garde" in the madrigals of Cipriano de Rore as generated by the similar aesthetics of Venetian painting) ultimately found resonance in neither discipline. For all the seeming congruity between art history and music, their objects and methods were not really compatible.

Thus iconography came to be something of an outsider in both disciplines, despite some of the excellent work outlined below. For Renaissance art history, the images it studied were sometimes marginal, with the notable exception of Raphael's *Ecstasy of St. Cecilia* (Bologna, Pinacoteca Nazionale). The roles played by musical instruments in these images were difficult to discern beyond the Neoplatonic commonplaces of celestial harmony, especially for non-music scholars. For music, it became evident that the visual conventions of early modern Europe limited images' heuristic usefulness even for performance practice, let alone what was defined as the discipline's central concerns. Even the rise of patronage studies in the 1970s, affecting both fields in a short time, was largely unable to link specifically musical with specifically visual products coming from the taste or needs of a given noble patron (or, after the rise of women's history changed both disciplines, patroness).

Still, at least for iconography, the kind of historically aware scholarship coming largely from German refugees from Fascism who found a home at London's Warburg Institute would have immediate and also longer-term results. Certainly Erwin Panofsky's systems of iconography—less so his ideas on iconology (e.g. the codes implicit in the idea of "disguised symbolism")—have continued to influence the sub-discipline, especially around issues of meaning. In a different vein, Ernst Gombrich's concern with historically differentiated visual perception found a certain reception among music scholars, not least in those influenced by Gombrich's student Michael Baxandall's ideas of a "period eye" as transferred to be a "period ear."

In light of iconography's uneasy dwelling between two disciplines, it is perhaps no surprise that one of the figures who shaped it after 1945 had advanced training in neither. Emanuel Winternitz's degree was in law, although he systematically collected photographs and details about historical musical instruments even before he fled Austria after the Nazi takeover. Although he had frequented the neo-positivist Viennese intellectual circles around Moritz Schlick in the 1920s, it is not clear how much of that approach filtered into his remarkable activity and writings on iconography after he arrived in New York in 1941 and found a job as the instrument curator at the Metropolitan Museum of Art. From that position, and with only temporary academic jobs, he built up the museum's collection, along with an archive of images that would become systematized in the 1970s as the Research Center for Musical Iconography (see "Further Reading"). As part of his universalist background, he also supervised a major collection of what were defined as "non-European" instruments.

Winternitz's work in iconography was certainly a tribute to the powers of central European *Bildung*. Besides his organological interests, he published largely on the depictions of instruments, and in that sense his writings undergirded one stream in musical iconography. Winternitz's focus on instruments also led to important collaborations (e.g. with Paul Hindemith and Noah Greenberg) around the revival of early music in the United States during and after World War II. In his activity, writing, and collecting, he set the tone for a generation of musical iconography.

The closest approach to a theoretical focus is found in the opening essays to his *Musical Instruments and their Symbolism in Western Art* (1967/R1979), in which he explained the advantages of the "other" discipline for music historians and art historians, respectively, with most examples taken from the Italian Renaissance. It should be noted that, for all its immense erudition, the volume is essentially a collection of essays; the kind of chapter-driven, highly focused monograph on a single cultural moment or musical idea has been harder to achieve in iconography, at least of the pre-1800 period.

As both art history and musicology developed along largely positivist paths in the 1950s and 1960s, several music scholars who had made their mark elsewhere in the discipline also began to address iconography, again largely with a medieval/Renaissance focus, as the field of music history was defined at the time. These included comprehensive and detailed works by François Lesure, Reinhold Hammerschmidt, Howard M. Brown, Walter Salmen, and Albert Pomme de Mirimonde. But in the 1970s the sub-discipline of iconography, still largely traditionally defined, was broadened by works with wider ethnographic or art-historical sophistication. These included the medieval but also ethnomusicological studies of Tilman Seebass, and the deeper grounding in both musical sources and pictorial techniques that H. Colin Slim brought to the study of Renaissance painting and music. Seebass's work, grounded in the best Central European traditions of comparative music studies, reinforced the wider scope of iconography and reaffirmed its multicultural scope. Around the same time, a series of Slim's essays addressed musical issues in paintings by Giorgione, Titian, and Tintoretto, employing a deep knowledge of musical sources as well as critical awareness of the art-historical literature on those painters.

Two very different, more recent, monographs on Raphael's canonical St. Cecilia altarpiece displayed these streams. Thomas Connolly's "prehistory" of the image, rooted deeply in scriptural exegesis and patristic writing, gave a sense of the devotional attitudes that undergirded the contemporary gaze and intellectual perception of the painting, while Nico Staiti's more ethnographic and reception-oriented approach tracked its influence further into the early modern era, including the decipherable music depicted. Both, however, noted the issues of musical ecstasy or trance, an aspect that would become important in the seventeenth century.

Given the universalist heritage of iconography, it was no surprise that one comprehensive study treated an orally transmitted musical repertory culture contemporary with early modern Europe. Bonnie Wade's *Imaging Sound* (1998) used the manuscript painting of musical practice in Mughal culture during the era of Akbar the Great (r. 1556–1605) to recreate cultural synthesis at this north Indian court. Some aspects of the work (e.g. its focus on the forms of musical instruments) resonated with earlier iconographic approaches, but Wade's other concerns—princely self-representation, the visual depiction of an imagined past, and even women's agency (via dance, in what might have seemed to be a patriarchal system)—transcended traditional categories: indeed, her topics anticipated more recent concerns of Renaissance music historiography. Similarly, Susan E. Nelson's consideration of conventions in Chinese representations of listening focused on certain tropes that spanned Ming- and Qing-dynasty visual production, often treating the perception of *qin* (classical zither) repertories.

In a different vein, the intellectual revolution in the two fields—first art history, then musicology at a distance of about a decade—involving gender studies, postmodernism, or Frankfurt-School critical theory—has been differentially evident in the iconographic literature, especially in medieval/Renaissance studies. In Anglophone scholarship, at least, it was two remarkable books by Richard Leppert that brought the sub-discipline much closer to the critical and theoretical approaches evident in the rest of the humanities around 1990. Trained as an iconographer working on early modern Europe (with a dissertation on music in Flemish painting and another book on the pastoral trope in music and art at the French court), Leppert has produced work that speaks both to music's place in society and to the visual projection of class ideology via music. In *Music and Image* (1988), his focus on British upper-class culture in a "long" eighteenth century (1660–1820) gave a sense of how social standing as a whole was projected in musical images of both "high" and "low" register. The book benefited from its appearance at a moment of new studies, across literary and social history, of material culture and ideological expression in eighteenth-century Britain. Essentially this was a project in the (re)production of ideology via images that indexed music, and its theoretical scope is evident in its prescient realization that "gender studies" involved studying both genders. Hence the book is framed by paired chapters on male and female roles and activity in music-making. Just as theoretically central, Leppert's book was one of the first Anglophone monographs in early modern studies to engage the Frankfurt School systematically. It was evidently the first work that could be considered as "musical iconography" that used Adorno's "negative dialectics," or differentiation between concept and object, to discuss an eighteenth-century portrait.

The essays in Leppert's *The Sight of Sound* (1993) both extended Adorno's social aesthetics into nineteenth-century images and revisited music/image relationships, in light of the social and material basis of class and gender, in early modern Europe. Leppert employed both social history and contemporary views to shape his interpretations of the musical body at either end of his longer time frame, although several essays attempt to trace the projection of the body, musical gaze, and issues of gender over the entire chronological trajectory of the book. Certainly this heuristic sophistication allowed him to engage art historians on their own terms in the intellectual moment of the book's appearance.

The trajectories that different strains of iconography have outlined, even in early modern Europe, point up the diversity of problems inherent in finding its place in academic art history and musicology. Even in terms of the field's traditional focus on Renaissance and Baroque Europe, as much as has been done in the iconography of sixteenth- or eighteenth-century musical images, issues in the century in between still remain to be investigated. This is in line with the seventeenth century's relative neglect by both art historians (beyond six or seven major artists studied) and musicologists (about the same number of composers).

Yet the expansion of pictorial styles after 1600 also implied the depiction of a new range of musical activity. The turn in Rome around 1620 to images of music in public spaces, which were to some degree lower class, was matched by paintings of "refined" music, meant for highly select viewers, and by a diversity of such standard types as St. Cecilia. In Dutch and Flemish painting, the concept of representing family values by domestic music-making, and the silently sounding interiority most familiar from a half-dozen of Vermeer's paintings, also represented new possible meanings for "visual" music (some of these images were addressed in Leppert's work). That such iconographic novelty or complexity was not limited to Europe is evident from the famed anonymous series of paintings depicting Cuzco's Corpus Christi procession around 1675 (Cuzco, Archiepiscopal Museum), with its musical floats as markers of status, origin, and devotion in a complex New World society. Less well known but just a few years later, Cristóbal de Villalpando's *Sweetest Name of Mary* altarpiece from New Spain (Mexico City, Museum of the Basilica of Guadalupe) featured angel musicians singing and playing both contemporary (harp) and anachronistic (vielle) instruments, thus recasting a medieval visual topos in the service of a new (and somewhat abstract, in the tradition of contemporary mystical science) devotion that was also beginning to receive musical emphasis elsewhere in the New World.

The iconography of seventeenth-century visual culture also seems to gain from the patent connections of music and painting in the century, as music and art intertwined both theoretically and practically: the best-known cases are Nicolas Poussin's 1647 letter to Paul Fréart de Chantelou on the usefulness of the Greek musical modes for the "modalities" of painting, Domenichino's late-life fixation on chromatic and experimental music as practiced and theorized in Naples, or even Rubens's painting to the sounds of a viola da gamba consort in his studio. The collector, banker, patron, and aesthete Vincenzo Giustiniani (1564–1637) not only supported Caravaggio while amassing a fabled avant-garde art collection, but also wrote two foundational texts for new visual and musical aesthetics ("Discorso sopra la pittura" and "Discorso sopra la musica" of c. 1630). Even more centrally, the spectacular visual and musical ekphrasis of Giambattista Marino's epic poem on the story of Venus and Adonis, *L'Adone*, was matched by two parts of his carefully crafted exercises in devotional aesthetics (more precisely, aesthetic devotion): the *Dicerie sacre* (1614), with its discourses on "La pittura" and "La musica" as instantiations of the Shroud of Turin and the Seven Last Words of Christ, respectively. For all its upheavals of epistemological and aesthetic norms, the century's conceptual

47

universe was still indebted to antiquity as a discursive model and trope, the devotional concepts of late-medieval Christianity, and Renaissance visual procedures.

Still, the parallels need to be treated with some caution. Poussin, taking his categories from Gioseffo Zarlino's *Istitutioni harmoniche* of a century earlier, may not have understood the complexities of contemporary Italian theorizing of the Greek modes at the hands of G. B. Doni. Athanasius Kircher's universal "sonology," extending from animal song to the most recent and affective examples of passages in musical oratorios (for instance, those of Giacomo Carissimi), also was different from this kind of painterly discourse. Likewise, it is striking that Marino's approaches to painting and to music, produced in the environment of the avant-garde art collections and musical styles of the court of his Savoyard patrons in Turin around 1610, do not engage each other directly, but only through their common tie to poetry, thus returning to the familiar models of *ut pictura poesis* and "music as servant of the words," respectively.

One seventeenth-century iconographic topos that both has had a certain tradition of study and could be revisited based on newer work is that of musical ecstasy and its relationship to contemporary theories of mysticism. The plethora of seventeenth-century St. Cecilias—along with other, less-studied associations of music and trance, as in the depictions of St. Francis of Assisi or Mary Magdalene—might encourage viewing such images in light of early modern theories of true and false ecstasy (and ecstatics), and this state's relationship to playing or hearing music.

Certainly the century's mystical epistemology outlined by Michel de Certeau (*La fable mystique*, 1982) provided a context for descriptions and depictions of ecstasy, induced or not by music. In terms of social history, the efforts on the part of Catholic prelates and theologians to differentiate between "true" and "false" rapture among the sometimes socially humble are evident in the treatise of the art patron (and musically not unimportant) Cardinal Federigo Borromeo (1564–1631), whose treatise *De ecstaticis mulieribus et illusis* dealt with such issues in the cases of female mystics, like that of the Sienese courtesan-turned-nun Caterina Vannini, whose raptures were sometimes induced by playing the lute. First-person testimonials by nuns in Milan and Siena also underscore the connection. At the same time, ecstasy on the part of men seems to have been both rarer and less subject to ecclesiastical "certification."

Two *Saint Cecilias* from the still-understudied milieu of seventeenth-century Naples highlight this. In Carlo Sellitto's 1613 altarpiece for the musicians' chapel in S. Maria della Solitaria (Naples, Museo di Capodimonte), the saint gazes to heaven as if looking for inspiration or communication. Her surrounding music-making companions may well be representations, metaphorical or not, of the members of the musicians' guild that commissioned the work, led by the organist and composer Giovanni Maria Trabaci (1575–1647). On the other hand, Bernardino Cavallino's 1645 version (Florence, Palazzo Vecchio) shows her instrument (here a violin, in accordance with one branch of the iconographic tradition) far away from her, on the ground, as she is crowned by the angel while her unaware companions continue to play. The distance between the representations shows the visual possibilities for seventeenth-century musical ecstasy.

The study of ecstasy and music plays into a wider tradition of the musical ethnography of trance. In terms of early modern Europe, it might also suggest a field of rapprochement between visual and sonic studies around the ideas of historical

48

anthropology, especially those of ritual, cultic, or liturgical behavior that framed both images and musical practice/perception. Whatever the actual musical information of these images, the persistence of oral, memorized, and improvised music-making throughout the century suggests that they give us a wider, and perhaps socially more "authentic" view of musical praxis than do the musical sources alone. In the world of early modern culture, iconography, conceived broadly, still has much to reveal, sonically and visually.

Further Reading

Journals and Websites

Imago Musicae (now Lucca: LIM, 1984–).

Music and Art: International Journal for Music Iconography (New York: Research Group on Musical Iconography at the City University of New York, 1998–).

Répertoire Internationale d'Iconographie Musicale (now housed between London and Columbus, OH; www.ridim.org).

Research Group on Musical Iconography at the City University of New York (rcmi.gc.cuny.edu).

Study Group on Iconography of the Performing Arts of the International Council for Traditional Music (www.ictmusic.org/groups/iconography-performing-arts).

Books and Articles

Ausoni, Alberto. Music in Art. Los Angeles: Getty Museum, 2009.

Connolly, Thomas. Mourning into Joy: Music, Raphael and Saint Cecilia. New Haven: Yale University Press, 1994.

Leppert, Richard D. Music and Image: Domesticity, Ideology and Socio-cultural Formation in Eighteenth-Century England. Cambridge: Cambridge University Press, 1988.

———. The Sight of Sound: Music, Representation, and the History of the Body. Berkeley: University of California Press, 1992.

Lesure, François. Music and Art in Society. University Park, PA: Penn State University Press, 1968.

Nelson, Susan E. "Pictorial Listening: The Sight of Sound in Chinese Painting," Archives of Asian Art 51 (1998/99): 30–55.

Seebass, Tilman. "Iconography," in New Grove Dictionary of Music and Musicians, edited by Stanley Sadie, 12: 54–71. London: Macmillan, 2000.

Slim, H. Colin. Painting Music in the Sixteenth Century: Essays in Iconography. Aldershot: Ashgate, 2002.

Staiti, Nico. Le metamorfosi di santa Cecilia: l'immagine e la musica. Lucca: LIM, 2002.

Wade, Bonnie C. Imaging Sound: An Ethnomusicological Study of Music, Art, and Culture in Mughal India. Chicago: University of Chicago Press, 1998.

6

CULTURAL HISTORY

Marsha Morton

Cultural history originated and developed during the late eighteenth and nineteenth centuries as history's "other." Conceived in a spirit of opposition, it defended marginalized topics against the prevailing modes of historical writing centered on military events, politics, and leaders. By contrast, culture encompassed ways of life—social beliefs, habits, and practices—and within these, the arts both high and low. The French philosopher Voltaire, who called for a history of domestic family life, succinctly observed that "a lock on the canal … a painting by Poussin, [and] a fine tragedy are things a thousand times more precious than all the court annals and all the campaign reports put together."[1] Underpinning cultural history was the notion, theorized by the German philosopher Johann Gottfried Herder, that individual groups or nations were united by shared traditions of thought and behavior whose essence was encoded in their art and language. While cultural history would develop in many different directions, this sense of a comprehensive whole would continue to differentiate it from the disciplinary histories of art and music, whether singular or comparative. Cultural historians not only embed the arts in a broader social context that customarily includes politics, economics, and religion; they also seek to identify the underlying unifying "deeper general themes" that are foundational to "patterns of life, art and thought," as the Dutch historian Johan Huizinga wrote in the 1920s.[2] Committed to the belief that all culture is a product of human agency, cultural historians are concerned with uncovering unconscious mental structures, whether general worldviews or more specific psychological or linguistic frameworks, "that combine diverse expressions of human consciousness at a given time into patterns or networks of meaning."[3]

Within these parameters significant variations can be found, and it is the purpose of this essay to delineate approaches used by cultural historians when they discuss both music and the visual arts. What follows is a selective survey of representative trends. Not only is culture an elastic concept, but writers differ in the degrees to which they describe or analyze and balance detailed factual information with an all-inclusive thesis. Music and the arts are generally considered according to one of two basic models that correspond to the dual meanings of culture: as social practices or as studies of artists and their work. Overall, cultural history has moved from a classic phase pioneered by Jacob Burckhardt, Aby Warburg, and Huizinga, to the current period of new cultural history emerging in the late 1970s under the influence of anthropological and linguistic theorists. Correspondingly, conceptualizations of the relationship between the arts and society have shifted from ones of reflection to construction. Until recently, musical compositions have received less attention than works of visual art, due probably to their technical nature and the paucity of musicologists writing books on cultural history. Of the three pioneers cited above, only Burckhardt—an amateur composer and artist—included music.

Burckhardt is regarded as the founder of cultural history with his books *Civilization of the Renaissance in Italy* (1860) and *The Greeks and Greek Civilization* (published posthumously in 1898), the introduction to the latter being an essay that defined the new discipline. Aware of Hegel's "spirit of an age" concept, though not sympathetic to the philosopher's belief in teleological progress, Burckhardt marshaled myriad facts gleaned from written documents that revealed the period's characteristic worldview. He bequeathed to cultural historians a sustaining interpretive methodology that sought to discover latent, unintentional meanings in sources where "secrets" were betrayed unconsciously. In this pursuit, beliefs, "habits of thought," "mental attitudes," and "desires and assumptions" were as important as events and actions.[4] Burckhardt's treatment of the arts also established precedents, followed by several generations of historians, in which the two meanings of culture were fused: art, music, and literature were considered in relation to social life with an eye to affirming general themes.

In his study of the Renaissance, Burckhardt very rarely mentions specific works of art. Music and art are discussed in terms of reception, patronage, collecting, social status, education, and performance practices by professionals and amateurs. In conjunction with his governing thesis that the Italian Renaissance was defined by the growth of modern individualism, Burckhardt tracks the rise of celebrities; the formation of musical "virtuosi"; the dominance of solos in singing; and the creation of the new genre of portraiture. Two artists, Leon Battista Alberti and Leonardo da Vinci, receive more extensive coverage as exemplars of the new breed of "many-sided men" who emerged during the age of the individual. While Burckhardt's primary focus is on high art and educated society, he also introduces topics that would be increasingly central for later historians: the popular culture of festivals and comparative studies of gender equality.

Burckhardt's preoccupation with socio-political conditions, power, and the production of art is equally central to his exploration of Greek civilization from polis to democracy, from community to the individual, and from a largely political to a cultural force. While Burckhardt provides a fairly conventional survey of sculpture and music during the later centuries, his consideration of the arts in earlier periods is pegged to social developments. Music is highlighted for its key role, along with gymnastics, in developing the dominant spirit of the Greek "agonal" age of the polis (pre-fifth century BCE) through choral competitions at the Olympic festivals and Delphi games. Burckhardt cites the occasional painting agon, but his primary interest in art is as visual documentation: sculptural monuments representing victors, and prize vases depicting the activities of the games. By the fifth century BCE, music and dance primarily served as entertainment at symposia, the preferred social activity in an era that valued private life. Burckhardt also evaluates the status of artists, ranked in descending order from musicians to sculptors, according to prevailing Greek attitudes contemptuous of manual labor.

Variations of Burckhardt's basic methodology continued to dominate the writings of prominent cultural historians of the early twentieth century, such as Huizinga and Charles Beard. In collaboration with his wife, Mary, Beard wrote the three-volume bestseller *The Rise of American Civilization* (1927). According to the Beards' socio-economic theory of cultural change, the arts and music benefited from developments in industry, technology, business, and a democratic system of government. In an egalitarian spirit, the Beards' book was intended to be read by the general public (footnotes are excluded) and tracks the arts in conjunction with the ascendancy of democratic populism from the eighteenth to twentieth centuries. The book emphasizes patronage and the growth of musical and artistic institutions, the founding of orchestras and academies, the expansion of educational opportunities, and the formation of taste. It is no surprise to Beard that the American arts originally thrived in urban centers of the Northeast that were also home to industrial development and wealth, or that musicians arrived from Europe (especially Germany) in the wake of swifter and safer steamboat designs. Throughout, the book compares music and art transformed by economic and social forces. The Beards explore topics such as the impact of the automobile on art and science and the accessibility of culture in the nineteenth century (through improved printmaking techniques and the manufacture of more affordable pianos). Treatments of the two art forms differ, however, in that paintings and prints are discussed according to content and style, while musical compositions and composers go unmentioned. The Beards' book is also noteworthy for the attention given to the role of middle-class women, primarily as consumers of culture, but occasionally as artists.

Sociological and economic orientations, frequently Marxist, prevailed during the next three decades in the writings of cultural historians such as the Hungarian exiles Arnold Hauser, Francis Klingender, and Frederick Antal, and British historians Raymond Williams and E. P. Thompson. Although none of these authors addressed music, their concerns with socio-economic factors were appropriated in major studies appearing in the 1970s by Peter Burke and Theodore Zeldin. Those studies also took inspiration from the theoretical frameworks formulated by Williams, Thompson, and, especially, the French *Annales* historians (Marc Bloch, Lucien Febvre, and Fernand Braudel) from the 1920s. Burke and Zeldin jettisoned unifying *Zeitgeist* patterns in favor of assemblages of detailed information taken from primary sources. Zeldin referred to his methodology as "pointillism," in which the facts were disengaged "from what holds them together" and "the reader can make what links he thinks fit himself."[5] Publications by all three authors were highly innovative at the time as textbooks, both in their thematic rather than chronological organization and in their cultural-historical orientation that included states of mind and emotions. Each author sought to avoid generalizations applied to all of society (e.g. "the Renaissance mind") and instead looked at attitudes and practices specific to different classes and groups.

Among these historians, Burke contributed the only book in which the arts were the central focus. *The Italian Renaissance: Culture and Society in Italy* (1972), written in the late 1960s, revisited Burckhardt's territory according to recent approaches linking cultural values and attitudes with the socio-economic and political structures, while avoiding an economics-determined theory of change. His goal was to account for collective, rather than individual, artistic innovation using interpretations of texts and quantitative statistics based on a sample group of six hundred artists, musicians, and writers. Burke began his book with comparative characterizations of the arts, testing assumptions regarding increased innovation, autonomy, secularization, and fantasy. The heart of his book is a lengthy examination of the arts in their milieu—from the "microsocial" to the "macrosocial" context—in which practices and systems are compared to other institutions (religious, political, economic) in larger geographic areas (Italy, the Netherlands, and Japan). Featured topics include demographic profiles of artists, the development of guilds and universities, social status, traveling patterns, patronage, performance practices, the role of the marketplace, and taste in music and art as determined by an analysis of word usage in treatises and letters.

In one of the book's final sections, the narrative shifts to determining worldviews and whether they are embodied in the arts. This endeavor references, in addition to Burckhardt, Williams's "structures of feelings" and the *Annales* school's "collective mentalities," defined as patterned structural systems of thought which, according to Burke, convey unstated "assumptions and feelings as well as conscious thought."[6] Burke discovers, for example, new notions of measurable time and space in mechanical clocks and pictorial perspective, which co-exist with traditional views of the cosmos and astrological planets as evidenced by imagery in paintings and songs. Although this book confined itself to high art, Burke soon published his groundbreaking *Popular Culture in Early Modern Europe* (1978), which borrowed methodologies from social anthropologists and folklorists to recuperate the unrecorded non-elite culture of everyday life in Europe between 1500 and 1800. Filled with information about minstrels, actors, carnivals, festivals, and songs, the book limits its coverage of the visual arts to relatively brief discussions of broadsheets and popular prints. Several of these are reproduced for their documentary value as source material.

Zeldin's two-volume *France 1848–1945* (1977) broke new ground in the Oxford History of Modern Europe series with thematic categories of ambition, love, anxiety, and artistic taste. Oriented more toward the nineteenth century and the visual arts, Zeldin, like Burke, sets out to challenge clichés such as the opposition between academic and avant-garde art by marshaling an impressive array of statistics fleshed out through case studies and anecdotes. Proceeding empirically from individual attitudes, he is led to the eventual conclusion that there is no common core of values shared by all Frenchmen in a specific period. Topics are covered with an eye to different constituencies determined by class, gender, and urban or provincial location. These include marketing (galleries, dealers, exhibition histories), the motivations and practices of patronage (whether private or state-sponsored), museums, art and music education, Parisian popular concert venues, the formation of choral societies, and the production and use of musical instruments. Zeldin is at his most innovative, however, in the area of the psychology of taste, the role of critics, and the relationship of the artist to the larger community. By evaluating exhibition attendance records, opinion surveys, and types of art images illustrated in magazines or sold as reproductive prints or photographs, he constructs a profile of French taste (high art fares poorly) according to class and social background.

The arts also feature prominently in Peter Gay's five-volume *The Bourgeois Experience: Victoria to Freud* (1984–98), which, even more than Zeldin's work, is a cultural history of feelings, sensibilities, and tastes that synthesizes myriad sources to challenge stereotypes about a homogeneous and repressed bourgeoisie. With a nod to Bloch and the anthropologist Clifford Geertz, Gay seeks to portray the mindset of the European and American middle class: "its passions and prejudices, its self-scrutinies and its tastes embedded in its economic, political and social world."[7] While methodologically similar to Zeldin's utilization of primary sources and case studies, Gay's sociological treatment of the arts is informed by psychoanalysis, seeking latent content and recondite meanings with the interpretive tools of human drives and early childhood experiences unlocking the subtexts of bourgeois sexuality. This leads to perceptive observations about the eroticism of music (in advance of most feminist musicologists), the courtship role of pianos in middle-class homes, and the conflict between the nineteenth century's silent concert etiquette and bodily impulses. Freudian perspectives also provide insightful commentary on the motivations of collecting and the vagaries of aesthetic preferences rooted as much in "buried memories" and "submerged psychological content" as in material affluence.[8]

Art and music are considered separately in volumes one and two as evidence of physical and psychological desires fulfilled by the socially acceptable forms of high art, whether painted nudes, Wagnerian music, or ballet. Volume four explores art's role in reflecting and engendering the era's preoccupation with self-contemplation and emotional absorption. This collective "pilgrimage to the interior" is discovered in self-portraiture, landscape painting, confessional novels, and above all in attentive meditative attitudes for listening to music, whether in life (concert halls and private homes) or art (the experience visualized).[9] The final volume is devoted entirely to the "political economy of art" (John Ruskin's phrase) as Gay charts the rise of a democratized consumer culture via the increased availability and affordability of artistic pleasures. Chapters include art in the age of reproduction and modernizing media; the growth of institutions (museums, symphonies, galleries); collectors and consumers; and the role of what theorist Pierre Bourdieu has called cultural capital as a means of securing social status.

Gay's Freudian orientation, shared by many intellectuals trained in America in the 1950s, also characterizes Carl Schorske, whose book *Fin-de-Siècle Vienna: Politics and Culture* (1980) expanded on established traditions while also breaking new ground in cultural history. Schorske returns to the Burckhardt model of a comprehensive theme, albeit (as he insists) derived from empirical study, to encapsulate "shared concerns and shared ways of confronting existence."[10] His unifying context is the decline of Viennese liberalism and historicism amid "the acutely felt tremors of social and political disintegration."[11] Progressive rationalism and order are, according to Schorske, supplanted during cultural crisis and flux with a behavioral view of man governed by instincts. This conclusion, based on his examination of politics, music, painting, literature, architecture/urban planning, and Freud's writing (*The Interpretation of Dreams*), is framed in psychoanalytic terms as a "revolt of the young culture against the authority of the paternal culture."[12] Running throughout the chapters devoted to the individual arts is the continuous motif of how politics and culture interact. Schorske's innovation with regard to previous sociological approaches is his way of analyzing artistic texts to locate, in their style and content, parallels with the social-political tensions of the late Habsburg Empire. He is one of the first English-language cultural historians to illustrate musical scores as well as paintings.

Schorske's book abounds in interdisciplinary connections and artistic metaphors. The development of Klimt's career unfolds from high-society Ringstrasse muralist to radical Secessionist to painter-decorator disengaged from the avant-garde. This progression is shown to correspond to the role of the arts in bourgeois life, beginning as vehicles of assimilation into the aristocracy and ending as escape and refuge in defeat. The last two chapters are centered on the image of the garden as a symbol of social order and middle-class attitudes, with the final one ("Explosion in the Garden") tracking the birth of Expressionism in the work of Oskar Kokoschka and Arnold Schoenberg. Schorske's analysis of Schoenberg's atonality exemplifies the book's basis in interconnecting political-cultural references. Schoenberg's "expansion of dissonance" and chromatic "erosion of the fixed key" are presented as musical counterparts to the spirit of the nineteenth century, in which the forces of movement challenged those of order. Previous periods (and Habsburg Vienna) were dominated by musical consonance and established government control. "In fact," Schorske concludes, "tonality in music belonged to the same socio-cultural system as the science of perspective in art ... the Baroque status system in society ... legal absolutism in politics ... [and] the geometric garden."[13]

Fin-de-Siècle Vienna typifies two trends in cultural historical studies that incorporate art and music: an interest in cities, and a focus on Germany and Central Europe. While William Johnson's Vienna-based *The Austrian Mind* and Oliver Logan's *Culture and Society in Venice 1470–1790* (both published in 1972) include chapters on high art that merely list facts without interpretive social contexts, Schorske and Thomas Bender's edited anthology *Budapest and New York: Studies in Metropolitan Transformation 1870–1930* (1994) integrates the role of popular and high culture within a study of two urban centers with contrasting national ideologies and attitudes to ethnicity. The prevalence of culture in studies of German history may stem from the national origins of the discipline or from a tradition of cultural, rather than political, identity in the years before unification in 1871. Schorske's return to Burckhardt was preceded by the five-volume investigation of turn-of-the-century German arts, *Deutsche Kunst und Kultur von der Gründerzeit bis zum Expressionismus* (1965–75), by Richard Hamann and Jost Hermann, who link extensive stylistic and content-based analyses of art, music, and literary texts with socio-political themes. Hermann later extended this methodology to three books on twentieth-century German culture.

Many German historical periods are identified by their cultural components, so that books and exhibitions on the Biedermeier (1820s–1850s) and Weimar (1920s) eras invariably include high and popular art and music within a larger socio-political framework. German composers like Beethoven and Wagner have become interdisciplinary cultural movements in themselves, with Wagner stimulating many studies—from *Wagnerism in European Culture and Politics* (1984) by David Large and William Weber to *Modernism after Wagner* (2010) by Juliet Koss—that consider his music together with his views on spectatorship, politics, religion, and sexuality in national and international contexts.

Beginning in the 1970s, a theoretical turn in cultural history has significantly changed interpretations of the arts. In the wake of writings by anthropologist Clifford Geertz, political theorists Antonio Gramsci and Pierre Bourdieu, and poststructuralists Michel Foucault and Jacques Derrida, cultural expressions (signs, gestures, performances, artifacts, language) are now regarded as constructed, with symbolic meanings and values capable of being decoded (as per Geertz), and containing content with latent binary hegemonic relations. Among cultural historians, this has led to new investigations of social subgroups (especially those defined by gender and race) and to studies of how dominant social classes maintain their control through art (Bourdieu's "cultural reproduction"). The new concepts are rooted in Foucault's notions of discourse, in which the articulation of knowledge becomes an expression of power, and the *episteme*, or underlying "mental grid" through which information and experience are processed. Foucault's formulation of discourses and *epistemes* as collective and characteristic of a given historical period, however, reveals distant echoes of Burckhardt.

Scholars of gender (feminist literary and art historians) and colonialism were among the first to apply these theories to cultural studies, revisiting areas with long traditions in the discipline such as cultural encounters, reception, consumerism, and patronage. Orientalism became a prominent focus of interdisciplinary research following the publication of Edward Said's books *Orientalism* (1978) and *Culture and Imperialism* (1993). Said described Western representations of the East as a "style" created "for dominating, restructuring and having authority over the Orient" and proceeded to unmask high cultural products for their complicity with European (mainly British and French) political and economic agendas.[14] Said dealt primarily with literature, apart from his analysis of Verdi's opera *Aida* in *Culture and Imperialism*. These books, together with Linda Nochlin's Said-inspired article on painting, "The Imaginary Orient" (1983), engendered numerous publications by art historians and musicologists, but very few comparative ones.[15]

In the Orientalist vein, the book most centered on music and the visual arts as well as design, architecture, and theater is John MacKenzie's *Orientalism: History, Theory and the Arts* (1995), which, ironically, is a polemic against Said and his followers. MacKenzie, a historian of imperialism, attacks these scholars for demonizing Orientalism. He attempts to erase twentieth-century biases (and linguistic theories) and to return to a time when the term had fewer negative connotations. It is the book's contention that the East provided stylistic revitalization to Western arts, in that Orientalist paintings offered visions of a positive, albeit conservative, "other": a pre-modern and pre-industrial society. The chapter on music takes a very different approach, with ideological positions and thematic organization replaced by an introductory chronological survey tracing the influence of Eastern music as a source of destabilizing renewal for European composers from the seventeenth to the twentieth centuries. The discussion delves into formal elements (melodic, harmonic, and rhythmic conventions), exotic instruments, texts for program music, and biography, to the exclusion of patronage, reception, and popular culture.

An alternative paradigm integrating art and music emerges in Richard Leppert's essay "Music, Domestic Life and Cultural Chauvinism: Images of British Subjects at Home in India" (1987) and, following his example, Claire Mabilat's book *Orientalism and Representation of Music in the Nineteenth-Century British Popular Arts* (2008). In these, music and its relation to non-Western culture and colonialism are read through its visual and literary representations. Mabilat examines case studies in British musical stage productions, fiction, book illustrations, paintings, and photography in order to determine the part played by music—more specifically Eastern instruments and musicians—in Orientalist stereotypes, especially with regard to gender and sexuality. Leppert analyzes late-eighteenth-century portraits of British residents in India staged in musical settings to reveal the active role that painting and music played as signifiers and transmitters of cultural values in England's program of economic and social colonization. As a study of power relations, the essay evaluates standards of gendered domestic conduct and parallel theoretical structures of order and control formulated in musical, architectural, and political treatises.

Leppert's essay was published in 1987 in the anthology *Music and Society*, which he co-edited with Susan McClary. This book, containing important writings by Janet Wolff and Rose Rosengard Subotnik, functioned as a clarion call for change in musicology in opposition to the formalist autonomy that had dominated the field for a century. Some of the ground had been prepared, however, by Leo Treitler's interrogation of music history in his essay "What Kind of Story is History?" (*19th-Century Music*, April 3, 1984). Rejecting progressive "Whig" narratives and histories of style ("the autonomy of art"), Treitler proposed a new narrative methodology that grounded the history of forms and culture in the "internal constitution" of the work itself. Like Burckhardt, Treitler emphasized the constructed nature of historical fact determined by the sensibilities of the era in which it is written.

Stimulated by the same critical theories that had transformed art history during the previous decade, McClary and Leppert, together with other pioneers such as Lawrence Kramer, Jeffrey Kallberg, and Ralph Locke, interpreted musical texts to reveal discursive cultural meanings and social values. Recurring topics, shared with art historians and new cultural historians, have included gender, sexuality, race, ethnicity, the body, and emotion. McClary, inspired by Foucault, Theodor Adorno, and writers on ethnomusicology, uncovered the gendered associations of musical composition (major-minor chords, tonalities, cadences, sonata-allegro forms) from the nineteenth-century European canon of Chopin and Tchaikovsky forward to Madonna in her book *Feminine Endings* (1991). In it, she considers how music "contributes to the shaping of the self or enacts models of social interaction."[16] Kramer, in *Music as Cultural Practice 1800–1900* (1990), drew upon psychoanalysis, feminism, and deconstruction theory to embed texts "in a network of social, intellectual and material conditions."[17] These writings, however, apart from Kramer's occasional references to paintings, remain in the realm of musicology, though the developments in that field have facilitated new cultural-historical studies of both art forms.

Leppert's methodology, discussed above, offers one such option whose origins can be traced to François Lesure's *Music and Art in Society* (1968), which explored the social background of musical figures in portraits. In *Music and Image* (1988), Leppert looks at how music is shaped by and contributes to socio-cultural formation. The practice and idea of music are considered as determinants of the "ideologies of self, class and national identity" among the eighteenth-century British upper class.[18] Here, and throughout his other writings, Leppert's primary concern is with music as a visualized and embodied activity. Other recent studies of musical images have chosen to largely exclude or move beyond poststructural theory, as with the essays in *Art and Music in the Early Modern Period* (2003). In "Musical Indulgence and Pleasurable Sound in Seventeenth-Century Dutch Art," for example, Roy Sonnema rejects the monolithic binary options of agency or reflection to evaluate the content in portraits and genre paintings as evidence of a new musical subjectivity.

Future directions for the arts in cultural history, having shifted from a sociological orientation to one that also delves into textual analysis, would seem to necessitate a larger role for musicologists beyond their previously limited participation in the field. The turn to new cultural history in music may presage multidisciplinary publications by musicologists. Visual studies and music history have, for two decades, been following parallel tracks, whether dealing with identities and experiences related to the self or to the nation, and it is easy to imagine books that would assemble research from these collective endeavors. Daniel Grimley's *Grieg:*

Music, Landscape and Norwegian Identity (2006) or Bruce Holsinger's *Music, Body, and Desire in Medieval Culture* (2001) would, with the addition of more material from the visual arts, offer excellent examples. For the moment, formats involving multiple authors (such as anthologies and exhibition catalogues) have proven to be successful paradigms allowing for technical expertise in individual fields. Books with diverse contributors may additionally expand the field through deepened considerations of science, religious beliefs, and spiritualism alongside the arts as shapers of cultural mentalities and productions.

Notes

1 Voltaire, quoted by Peter Gay, "Introduction," in Jacob Burckhardt, *The Civilization of the Renaissance in Italy* (New York: The Modern Library, 2002), xvi.
2 Johan Huizinga, "The Task of Cultural History," in *Men and Ideas*, trans. James S. Holmes and Hans van Marle (New York: Meridian Books, 1959), 28.
3 Anna Green, *Cultural History* (London and New York: Palgrave Macmillan, 2008), 5.
4 Jacob Burckhardt, "Introduction," in *The Greeks and Greek Civilization* (New York: St. Martin's Press, 1998), 5.
5 Theodore Zeldin, *France 1848–1945* (Oxford: Oxford University Press, 1977), 1156–1157.
6 Peter Burke, *The Italian Renaissance: Culture and Society in Italy*, 2nd ed. (Cambridge: Polity Press, 1986), 181.
7 Peter Gay, *Pleasure Wars*, vol. 5 of *The Bourgeois Experience: Victoria to Freud* (New York: W. W. Norton & Co., 1998), 230.
8 Gay, *Pleasure Wars*, 107.
9 Gay, *The Naked Heart*, vol. 4 of *The Bourgeois Experience* (New York: W. W. Norton & Co., 1996), 5.
10 Carl E. Schorske, *Fin-de-siècle Vienna: Politics and Culture* (New York: Alfred A. Knopf, 1980), xxii.
11 Ibid., xviii.
12 Ibid., xxvi.
13 Ibid., 346.
14 Edward Said, *Orientalism* (New York: Vintage Books, 1979), 3.
15 Linda Nochlin, "The Imaginary Orient," in *Art in America* 71 (May 1983): 118–131, 187–191, reprinted in *The Politics of Vision* (New York: Harper and Row, 1989), 33–59. The seminal study in musical history is Ralph Locke, "Cutthroats and Casbah Dancers, Muezzins and Timeless Sands: Musical Images of the Middle East," in *Nineteenth-Century Music* 22 (1998–99): 20–53.
16 Susan McClary, *Feminine Endings: Music, Gender, and Sexuality* (Minneapolis: University of Minnesota Press, 1991; 2002 reprint), xiii.
17 Lawrence Kramer, *Music as Cultural Practice, 1800–1900* (Berkeley: University of California Press, 1990), xii.
18 Richard Leppert, *Music and Image: Domesticity, Ideology and Socio-Cultural Formation in Eighteenth-Century England* (Cambridge: Cambridge University Press, 1988), 1–2.

Further Reading

Burke, Peter. *Varieties of Cultural History*. Ithaca: Cornell University Press, 1997.
Burke, Peter. *What is Cultural History?* 2nd ed. Cambridge: Polity, 2008.
Gombrich, E. H. "In Search of Cultural History." In *Ideals and Idols* , 24–59. Oxford: Phaidon, 1974.
Gossmann, Lionel. *Basel in the Age of Burckhardt: A Study in Unseasonable Ideas*. Chicago: University of Chicago, 2000.
Norberg, Kathryn and Sara E. Melzer, eds. *From the Royal to the Republican Body: Incorporating the Political in Seventeenth- and Eighteenth-Century France*. Berkeley: University of California Press, 1998.
Pfister, Joel and Nancy Schnog, eds. *Inventing the Psychological: Toward a Cultural History of Emotional Life in America*. New Haven: Yale University Press, 1997.
Ward, Martha and Anne Leonard, eds. *Looking and Listening in Nineteenth-Century France*. Exhibition catalogue. Chicago: Smart Museum of Art, 2007.

7

PERFORMANCE STUDIES

Laura Cull

Having established itself in the United States in the 1980s and 1990s and expanded to become an established discipline in institutions across the world, performance studies has, unapologetically, borrowed and combined approaches to its subject from a vast range of other disciplines. In this essay, however, I want to focus on those methodologies that might be considered more specific to performance studies itself. For his part, in 1995, the leading performance studies researcher and ethnographer Dwight Conquergood argued that the "distinctive contribution" of performance studies is "the heuristic potential of performance as concept, practice, and epistemology."[1] In what follows, I will try to touch on each of these aspects. First, I will consider the idea of looking at something "as" performance, particularly in relation to what Richard Schechner—arguably the principal architect of performance studies as a discipline—conceived as the "broad spectrum" approach to performance. Here, we will see how concepts of performance constitute theoretical frameworks for the analysis of a wide range of activities and behaviors, not just those traditionally understood as the performing arts. But second, we will explore how performance (as the practice of producing and participating in performance activities) is not only an object to be studied using such conceptual frames, but also operates as *a valued research method in itself.*

As Performance (But What is Performance?)

It could be argued that the primary methodological contribution of performance studies lies in its multiple (re)conceptualizations of the notion of "performance" itself. Among various competing definitions, the most influential thus far has been Schechner's argument that "performance must be construed as a 'broad spectrum' or 'continuum' of human actions ranging from ritual, play, sports, popular entertainments, the performing arts (theater, dance, music), and everyday life performances to the enactment of social, professional, gender, race, and class roles, and on to healing (from shamanism to surgery), the media, and the internet." The broad spectrum approach asserts that "any action that is framed, presented, highlighted, or displayed is a performance" and that performance can be defined as "showing doing … pointing to, underlining, and displaying doing," such that performance studies can be defined as "explaining 'showing doing.'" Most simply expressed, Schechner conceives performance studies as a discipline that focuses on "what people do in the activity of their doing it" and on *what that doing does* to those involved in it and in relation to its context.[2]

Schechner proposes an is/as distinction, noting the difference between saying something *is* performance and studying it *as* performance. What is deemed to be performance varies over time and across cultures; it is determined by convention and tradition—as is the case with what the West calls the performing arts (to the exclusion of non-artistic activities). However, Schechner argues, there can be no fixed parameters assigned to performance studies, since any activity whatever may be studied *as* performance, whether or not convention will accept that it *is* performance. In turn, for Baz Kershaw, this is where the paradox of performance studies lies: on the one hand, it will admit no limit to what might be studied *as* (or from the perspective of) performance, but on the other, it remains focused on performance's absolute specificity.

As Schechner acknowledges, the broad spectrum definition of performance has a number of precedents from across the disciplines, not least in the historic *theatrum mundi* metaphor. Other examples include the work of the Canadian sociologist Erving Goffman, who used a theatrical metaphor to examine social interaction in works such as *The Presentation of Self in Everyday Life* (1959). It could also be seen as preceded by the philosopher of language J. L. Austin's work on performativity, which we will address shortly, and by work in anthropology, including Victor Turner's concept of "social drama" and Milton Singer's theory of "cultural performance," which proposes that "human behavior is largely governed by the acting out of predesigned roles, whether consciously or not."[3] However, music scholars will also appreciate how the broad spectrum approach is prefigured by John Cage's various calls to us to alter our perception of what counts as music, and by the artist (and Cage's student) Allan Kaprow's insistence on the fluidity between art and life.

In turn, Schechner argues that performance studies is not only defined by *what* it studies (which, as we've seen, he argues is unlimited), but also by *how* it studies it; indeed, he defends performance studies against accusations of a lack of disciplinary focus with reference to its methodological principles. Performance studies is "*fundamentally* relational, dynamic and processual," he argues.[4] Likewise, in 1991, Conquergood proposed that one of the key areas of performance studies investigation should be to explore the implications of conceiving culture as a verb rather than as a noun. To some extent, this emphasis on events over objects registers Schechner's critique of existing theater studies as he perceived it in the 1980s, and his call to theater studies scholars to de-emphasize the text-oriented approaches they had inherited from literary studies. Instead, he thought they should generate analyses specifically focused on the event of performance. As Marvin Carlson has discussed, drawing particularly from Gerald Hinkle's *Art as Event* (1979), performance analysis has suffered from the application of literature-based methods, with the result that, even when the traditional focus on the authorship of the scripted text was extended to include its realization in performance, the performance itself still tended to be treated as an autonomous aesthetic object rather than as a thoroughly situated event. In contrast, Carlson argues, a performance studies approach is often characterized by a concern with the physical, social, and cultural contexts of specific instances of performance and the contribution of all these factors, not just what is happening on stage, to our understanding of the nature and meanings of that event. In part, we could say that this shift in attention has also been prompted by the nature of aesthetic performances themselves, given that the interrogation of the conventional separation of the performance and the audience has been a core concern of avant-garde work since at least the late 1950s. As Schechner puts it: "Audience participation expands the field of what a performance is, because *audience participation takes place precisely at the point where the performance breaks down and becomes a social event*"—whether in intended or unintended ways, and to varying degrees of good or ill effect.[5]

But Schechner's objections to theater studies—as he perceived them at the time— run deeper than this problem of a text-centered approach. For instance, Schechner among others argued that the dominant concept of "theater" limited theater studies' research domain to specifically European models, excluding a huge amount of other performance activity encompassing both popular and non-European forms. In contrast, it was argued that the broad-spectrum concept of performance would allow scholars to take a more intercultural (or international) and democratic approach to the field. Performance studies was construed as a corrective to the conventional academic focus on theater (and indeed, dance or music) as an art form. This tended to lead to an emphasis on performance as conceived by the various movements of the aesthetic avant-garde, and a parallel neglect of public uses of performance and the roles it might play in society more widely. Schechner's concept of performance also constituted an explicit critique of the evolutionary model that had hitherto dominated theater history, suggesting that "the origin of theater (tragedy and comedy) was to be found in a common Primal Ritual."[6] It was argued that Cambridge theater scholars of the early twentieth century had problematically constituted (European models of) theater as the conclusion of a linear, historical progression such that theater and ritual were positioned in a vertical, hierarchical relationship.

In contrast, Schechner argued in favor of conceiving a wide range of different cultural activities as belonging to a horizontal continuum of performance with a view to moving beyond evaluations derived from text-based, Western norms. That said, many contemporary performance studies scholars, such as Paul Rae and Jon McKenzie, have recently noted the extent to which Anglo-American concepts of performance—albeit broad ones—continue to dominate the ways in which performance is thought and encountered. As such, the idea that the extended object of performance studies research can be co-constructed by multiple different cultural models of performance, and by relationships between these models in the context of globalization, arguably remains more of an aim than an achievement of the field.

Correlatively, from the outset, theater studies scholars raised concerns as to the value that this seemingly all-encompassing concept of performance could have as an analytic category. If everything is performance, or at least can be seen *as* performance, then what use is the concept of "performance" as a way of thinking about the qualitative complexity of the world? Likewise, more recently, Stephen Bottoms has questioned what we gain from seeing such a broad range of activities as performances. In contrast, though, one could also argue that any attempts to fix the necessary conditions for "performance" will have a limiting effect on the discipline—necessarily excluding what might, from another point of view, be the most radical developments within the field.

In turn, performance studies has labored to articulate the specificity not only of what performance is, but of what it *does* through a range of engagements with concepts deriving from other disciplines, perhaps most prominently "liminality" and "performativity." With respect to the first of these, the exchange of ideas between theater and anthropology (for instance, as manifested in Schechner's various collaborations with Victor Turner) contributed to a growth of interest in ritual, more precisely in the idea of rituals and rites of passage as particular types of performance characterized by liminality and a suspension of social norms. As Jon McKenzie explains, anthropology provided scholars with a "functional model" in which all kinds of performance events—including but not limited to theater—could be understood as liminal rituals. Through such ideas, Schechner and other scholars in the field came to study performance less in terms of entertainment and more in terms of efficacy or transformative potential, whether that efficacious quality was understood in terms of transgression or of resistance. Indeed, ironically, as McKenzie influentially proposed, the idea of performance as having the destructuring power to suspend social norms became the dominant structure through which to analyze performance (and indeed the operations of performance studies as a paradigm), such that the field has tended to overlook events with more normative effects.

Secondly, performance studies scholars have also done significant work to conceive what performance does as performativity—a concept that originates from the speech act theory of J. L. Austin, the British philosopher of language. In *How To Do Things With Words* (1962), Austin argued that language not only could have a descriptive or "constative" function, but could also be "performative"—by which he meant language can act on and in the world, not just represent it. Famously, Austin excluded theatrical language from his category of performative utterances, describing it as operating parasitically on real performatives—merely citing or quoting performatives in a context that renders them empty. Austin's ideas were subsequently construed as relevant to performance, particularly on account of Judith Butler's argument that identity per se, and gender identity in particular, could be construed as performative: not something we simply *have*, but something we *do* through "a stylized repetition of acts." Gender reality, Butler argues "is created through sustained social performances ... It is real only to the extent that it is performed."[7] This leads to us mistaking the effect of these performances (the production of a "male" or "female" subject) for a cause (as if our actions were the result of an essential "male" or "female" nature). More recently, performance studies scholars have taken up the concept of performativity to address how performances can be seen not only to enact but also to refute and rewrite the dominant scripts in relation to the production of gender, as well as race, class, and sexual identity.

And as is the case with liminality and performativity, many of the other key conceptualizations of performance produced by scholars in the field rest on such considerations of the nature of the relation between difference and repetition, presence and representation, the original and the copy. For his part, Schechner also develops the idea of performance as "restored" or "twice-behaved" behavior. Akin to concepts of citation and iteration with respect to language, this complex concept is an attempt to think through the kind of repetition involved in everyday routines, whether they take the form of extended rituals or of the briefest of gestures. At its simplest, Schechner suggests, restored behavior is a reproduction of a pre-existing behavior of which there is no "original" version. All behavior has this repetitive aspect, and yet, Schechner acknowledges—citing Heraclitus's adage about the impossibility of stepping in the same river twice—every performance is, at the same time, new on account of its concrete specificity. Likewise, Joseph Roach characterizes performance as "an executed copy of an original that does not exist, except as a retrospective understanding or prescient expectation." Performance studies involves "investigations of behavior that is repeated, reinstated, or rehearsed for the purpose of being shown," investigations of performance as "the return of an act, but not as itself."[8] In this way, for some scholars at least, it is precisely difference or (self-)differentiation that defines performance (as undefinable in any fixed sense).

Resisting an entirely open definition, Gay McAuley believes that certain basic factors are necessary criteria for performance: i.e., performers and witnesses, even if those roles may be unstable. Such claims make clear why the concepts of "liveness" and "presence" have also become central concerns of performance studies, as it works to explore what difference, if any, there might be between its own object of study—given the technologically mediated nature of much twentieth- and twenty-first-century performance experience—and that of media, film, and television studies. For Peggy Phelan, for instance, performance studies as a discipline relies on an understanding of performance as ephemeral. In her highly influential book, *Unmarked* (1993), she argues that performance's "only life is in the present. Performance cannot be saved, recorded, documented, or otherwise participate in the circulation of representations of representations: once it does so, it becomes something other than performance."[9] In turn, she suggests that performance studies' resistant and radical edge lies in its affirmation of the excluded knowledge of the ephemeral and transient in the context of a culture based on the (market) value of reproducibility and circulation. As such, Phelan construes performance studies as a historiographic project, the challenge of which is to find ways to preserve the fleeting but without eradicating the ephemeral qualities of its object, in a manner that would signal another kind of loss.

In contrast, Philip Auslander has argued against the idea that the live and the mediatized are somehow ontologically opposed; for instance, against the idea that repetition is somehow intrinsic to media such as film and video, suggesting instead that our experience of them, and of live performance, depends on how they are used. Auslander rejects the bias toward the live as more valuable than the mediatized, finding that this de-emphasizes technologically mediated events as legitimate objects of inquiry. Rather, Auslander argues, "In a cultural context dominated by reproduction and simulation, the value of live performance resides in its use as symbolic capital."[10] There is no ontological distinction between the experience offered by the live and the mediatized; rather, they differ in value because of the prestige afforded by the necessarily limited distribution of the live event relative to the majority of recordings. In more philosophical terms, Auslander's work was among the most influential in translating the implications of Derrida's deconstruction to performance and, in particular, to the value that performance studies has historically placed on the live as presence and immediacy. Echoing one of the core tenets of deconstruction, Auslander argues that the very idea of liveness relies upon and yet denies a notion of reproduction (the recorded, the mediatized) as its fundamental "other" in order to define itself. Reproduction and the recorded make the idea of (pure) liveness possible, Auslander suggests, but they also ensure that it is always already differed and deferred from itself.

Performance as Method

In 2002, Dwight Conquergood argued that performance studies had from the start resisted persistent mind–body binaries and questioned the traditional hierarchization of methodologies themselves. Indeed, we could argue that the body is at the center of both the theoretical and practical aspects of performance studies' methodologies, a model for the performative turn across the arts, humanities, and social sciences. In turn, the embodied practice of performance is used as a research method, not only in the sense of 'practice as research' that has become so central to UK performance studies, but also as explored through the performance of literary texts and performative ethnography. For instance, many of the founding performance studies scholars were also performance practitioners, whether they were part of the artistic avant-garde (as Schechner was) or working in other contexts such as community performance, particularly with disadvantaged communities (as Conquergood did with refugees in Thailand and street gangs in Chicago).

So, performance studies puts great store in the notion of experiential knowledge, in ways that might be contextualized with reference to the broader practice-turn in academia in the late twentieth century: a turn away from the distanced production of abstract theories and toward investigations derived from active engagement with or participation in the thing studied. Indeed, at times, Schechner himself seems to value practical methods to the extent that he appears to be denigrating the theoretical; for instance, in his claim that the discipline's methods of researching performance emphasize doing over any kind of text- or archive-based study (as if reading and working in the archive were not forms of activity). Overall though, at both institutions that primarily pioneered the development of performance studies—New York University (where performance studies emerged from theater studies) and Northwestern (where it emerged from oral interpretation)—the emphasis was on a methodological exploration of the nature of the *relationship between* theory and practice, the concrete and the abstract. And perhaps all questions of method inevitably return to this dyad: to what extent is our embodied experience of the concrete constituted by our abstract concepts, and conversely, to what extent can the abstract be constituted by experience?

Given that Schechner's broad spectrum approach includes rituals and social displays on its performance continuum, we can understand the interest in methods developed by cultural anthropology, such as ethnographic description and participant observation. In the case of ethnography, though, one might argue that performance studies did not simply adopt pre-existing methods but, rather, reinvented them according to its own concepts and values. For instance, scholars like Schechner and Conquergood explicitly sought to rethink ethnography itself *as* performance. In particular, they contributed to development of the notion of *performative*, as distinct from informative, ethnography in which researchers might, among other things, re-perform the personal narratives of those they were studying, whether back to those communities, to academics, or to other non-academic audiences. Conquergood argued in favor of the empathetic potential of this approach, but at the same time, he was profoundly aware of and wrote extensively about its ethical risks.

In the UK and elsewhere, the notion of performance as method has also been developed in what has come to be known as 'practice as research' (PaR). PaR contends that new knowledge can be produced in and as performance, among other practices. Debates specifically concerned with this idea of performance practice as research first became prominent around the late 1990s, but by the end of the 2000s, the approach was well established at universities in the UK, Australia, Canada, and elsewhere. PaR relies on British philosopher Gilbert Ryle's distinction between "know-that" and "know-how" as two types of knowledge. To give an example of this distinction: I know how to ride a bicycle, even though I may not know how the bicycle works in principle or which muscles are involved in the act of cycling.

As a method, PaR raises a number of complex questions: To what extent can the research dimension of practice "speak for itself" or need to be explicated through supporting text? How can the "tacit" know-how of performance practitioners be rendered explicit and shareable? Furthermore, the field has had to generate its own criteria for what counts as research outside a purely written context. While PaR argues that all practice can be research, it also acknowledges that not all practice *is* research (or at least, not to the same degree).

In this way, performance methodologies often present a challenge to the values of traditional forms of scholarship, particularly in relation to the concept of "methodology" itself. For instance, Baz Kershaw and Helen Nicholson suggest that many working within the field use their work to challenge "outmoded perceptions that the terms 'method' and 'methodology' imply an attempt to capture, codify and categorize knowledge."[11] Performance methods might equally focus on what eludes knowledge, embracing the idea that in the event of research we do not always know what we are doing while we are doing it. For instance, approaches to performance research include experimental improvisation, embodied intuition, and the affirmation of unknowing and uncertainty as key elements of the process of creating performance, as much as they might involve the enactment of carefully honed skills and the development of specialist performer training. Indeed, this inventive, hybrid approach to research is the very reason why it becomes impossible to summarize performance studies methods in a chapter of this kind. Performance studies researchers are constantly creating new ways to approach performance as object and method, often precisely to question and unsettle their own methodological principles and assumptions.

And perhaps, it is in order to continue to explore the idea of performance as method that the fields of music and performance studies might most fruitfully intersect in future. Historically, Auslander argues, performance studies has "been reluctant to engage with musical performance":

> While performance-oriented scholars spurn music, music-oriented scholars generally spurn performance. Traditional musicologists remain focused on the textual dimensions of musical compositions, whereas scholars who look at music from the perspective of cultural studies are generally more concerned with audience and reception than with the actual performance behavior of musicians.[12]

The editors' commission of a chapter on performance studies in this collection, though, suggests otherwise, and it has been my (difficult) remit here to attempt to summarize some of the field's most prominent methodologies, in the hope that they might also suggest approaches to the study of music and visual culture. To conclude, we might draw from Auslander to suggest that these could involve a renewed consideration of music *as* performance and musicians as performers, or the analysis of musical performances including the role of their audiences—from the hushed attention of audiences at a conventional classical music performance to the screaming of fans at a pop concert. Or, it might invoke alternative approaches to the relationship between the live and the recorded, such as the study of how recordings of music function as performance to their listeners. Likewise, no doubt, performance studies has much to learn from music-based methods in ways that will allow it to continue to evolve as the discipline-in-process that it claims to be.

Notes

1 Dwight Conquergood, "Of Caravans and Carnivals: Performance Studies in Motion," *TDR: The Drama Review* 39, no. 4 (Autumn 1995): 139.
2 Richard Schechner, *Performance Studies: An Introduction* (London; New York: Routledge, 2002), 1–2.
3 Gabrielle Cody and Evert Sprinchorn, *The Columbia Encyclopedia of Modern Drama* (New York: Columbia University Press, 2007), 1044.
4 Richard Schechner, "Foreword," in *Teaching Performance Studies*, ed. Nathan Stucky and Cynthia Vimmer (Carbondale: Southern Illinois University Press, 2002), x.
5 Richard Schechner, *Environmental Theater* (New York: Applause Books, 1994), 40. Emphasis in the original.
6 James Harding and Cindy Rosenthal, *The Rise of Performance Studies: Rethinking Richard Schechner's Broad Spectrum* (Basingstoke: Palgrave, 2011), 43.
7 Judith Butler, "Performative Acts and Gender Constitution: An Essay in Phenomenology and Feminist Theory," *Theatre Journal* 40, no. 4 (December 1988): 528.
8 Janelle Reinelt and Joseph Roach, eds., *Critical Theory and Performance* (Ann Arbor: University of Michigan Press, 2007), 457–458.
9 Peggy Phelan, *Unmarked: The Politics of Performance* (London; New York: Routledge, 1993), 146.
10 Philip Auslander, "Music as Performance: Living in the Immaterial World," *Theatre Survey* 47, no. 2 (November 2006): 265.
11 Baz Kershaw and Helen Nicholson, eds., *Research Methods in Theatre and Performance* (Edinburgh: Edinburgh University Press, 2011), 1.
12 Auslander, "Music as Performance," 261.

Further Reading

Allegue, Ludivine et al., eds. *Practice-as-Research: In Performance and Screen*. Basingstoke: Palgrave Macmillan, 2009.
Auslander, Philip. *Liveness: Performance in a Mediatized Culture*. London; New York: Routledge, 1999.
Bial, Henry, ed. *The Performance Studies Reader*. London; New York: Routledge, 2004.
Davis, Tracy, ed. *The Cambridge Companion to Performance Studies*. Cambridge: Cambridge University Press, 2008.
Harding, James and Cindy Rosenthal, eds. *The Rise of Performance Studies: Rethinking Richard Schechner's Broad Spectrum*. Basingstoke: Palgrave, 2011.
McKenzie, Jon. *Perform or Else: From Discipline to Performance*. London; New York: Routledge, 2001.
Phelan, Peggy. *Unmarked: The Politics of Performance*. London; New York: Routledge, 1993.
Schechner, Richard. *Performance Studies: An Introduction*. London; New York: Routledge, 2002.

8

STUDYING MUSIC AND SCREEN MEDIA

David Neumeyer

The history of the cinema may be mapped out broadly as consisting of two eras, with the dividing line around 1930: the so-called silent film (often called "early film" now) and the sound film. For the silent era, a further subdivision may be made at about 1915: very close ties to existing theatrical practices before that give way to an increasingly specific cinematic performance practice after, in great part because of a turn from one-reel films to multi-reel narrative feature films. Subdivisions of the sound era may be made by a number of different criteria, but the one perhaps most immediately relevant to analysis and criticism is the film's text-commodity status. Before the 1980s, films were essentially performances: one could buy fan magazines and memorabilia, sheet music, and sound track albums, but one went to the theater to watch the film—that is to say, audiences purchased the social experience of a film exhibition. If you watched a film on television, you "paid" for the performance by tolerating commercial interruptions and, in most cases, cuts and other distortions such as pan-and-scan. Only with the advent of the VCR and broad availability of VHS tapes did films themselves become text-commodities, physical entities one could buy, sell, and hold.

The field of film music studies is correspondingly young: only with VHS did it become possible to engage in close study of a film and its sound track or to make detailed comparisons of narrative and style traits efficiently across a group of films. From the early 1980s on, scholars interested in the musics of the cinema adopted and adapted to their object of study the varieties of scholarship and agendas already available. On the one hand, film music offered resistance to traditional methods of music studies, which are strongly biased in favor of historical concert musics and the "high-art" styles that dominate there. On the other hand, film studies were equally strongly biased toward the image and narrative, with the sound track only occasionally treated as a significant constructive or expressive element. Still, traditional modes of reading—of interpretation—in film studies (grounded in narratology and literary theory) have much to teach us about what happens to music when it becomes part of another text, and the historical and cultural knowledge reflected in music studies can teach us much about the emotional, expressive, referential, and symbolic effects of music in cinematic texts. Another field that has informed some basic aspects of the study of music in film—sound studies—has grown up alongside film music studies, and the relationship between the two remains quite fluid.

The commodification of the film text applies differently to the repertoires of the silent and sound eras. Film music before the transition period (1927–35) was a set of performance practices; sound film, by contrast, is a physical object, a "text" on which music was literally imprinted as part of a film's sound strip. Not only is it essential to the study of film music to recognize the differences between the silent and sound eras, but it is also important to keep in mind that we tend to treat film retrospectively—that is, as if its commodity form always existed, not that it came into being only thirty years ago. The social space of film exhibition is thus too easily forgotten, but so is the physical space, a fundamental consideration for the technological history of the sound track, including its musics.

The history of silent film is analogous to the chaotic history of nineteenth-century opera and operetta production, where—before Richard Wagner—the "score" was always understood to be secondary to the performance and productions could differ substantially. Sound film, by contrast, is more like a published score or literary text.

Wagner's notion of the *Gesamtkunstwerk*, a symbiosis of the arts that he attempted to realize in his later operas (especially the *Ring of the Nibelungen* cycle and *Parsifal*), was only the most ambitious of many combinations of music with painting, photography, and theatrical staging and action in the nineteenth century. On a much smaller scale, scenes in pantomime had long been accompanied by music, and thus it is hardly surprising that music later found steady employment for special-effects scenes (and also for scene transitions) in the popular action-filled melodramas that began proliferating in the early to mid-nineteenth century (and directly influenced opera as well). Later in the century, serious stage plays were routinely accompanied by music: overtures, entr'actes, and finales would fill the intervals and frame the performance. Composers would often repurpose such incidental music for concert use—Edvard Grieg's two *Peer Gynt Suites*, assembled from his music for the Ibsen play, are famous examples—while the transitions and similar musics would be used over and over, eventually finding their way into early (silent) film exhibition as "hurries," "agitatos," and "dramatic andantes."

Magic lantern shows, panoramas, and travelogues were among the many popular forms of image-based entertainment whose professional performers engaged musicians to provide accompaniments. Often this was a single pianist, who might be joined by a violinist; for more elaborate performances and larger venues the number could be as many as nine or ten, the standard orchestra of the vaudeville theater.

Thus their audience would certainly have expected that the Lumiére brothers would hire a pianist to play for their public presentations of projected film in Paris, December 1895, commonly (though incorrectly) regarded as the beginning of cinema history. A decade later, store-front theaters (essentially small vaudevilles) proliferated—the so-called nickelodeons that specialized in programs combining live performances with film exhibition—and musicians performed regularly there, either situated at the front of the theater as accompaniment to the performance or, more likely, near the back entrance as bally-hoo, to attract customers into the theater. At the same time, it was common practice for a singer and pianist to perform songs illustrated by color slides. By 1915 (and increasingly thereafter), the variety shows of the vaudeville theaters themselves would typically insert an occasional short film. About the same time, multi-reel narrative films came to dominate film exhibition, and musicians who previously had by and large simply played whatever music they knew or that the management required were now obliged to make closer connections of mood, pacing, and appropriate style—to "play to the film." By the 1920s, these practices had blossomed in the huge picture palaces, with their giant organs, percussion machines, and music directors conducting orchestras that approached or matched the size (and often the skill level) of symphony orchestras. *Don Juan* (1926) and *The Jazz Singer* (1927) memorialize these practices with recorded versions of the highest-quality picture-palace performance: both films use partly compiled, partly original scores assembled by New York-based music professionals, and the music is played by no less than the New York Philharmonic.

The Jazz Singer, of course, is famous not for its high-brow background music (in which Tchaikovsky's *Romeo and Juliet* figures prominently) but for Al Jolson's song performances and brief bits of speech. These were simply versions of shorts (one-reel films) that Warner Bros. had been distributing for a year or two already for use in the typical variety program. Many different musical styles were represented in these Vitaphone shorts, including opera, and marketing emphasized the idea that the high-quality performances of big-city venues were being brought to the hinterland. The Vitaphone sound recording and reproduction system, which used phonograph records whose player was ganged to the film projector, gave the highest-fidelity sound achievable at the time, but the clumsiness of the system was a major factor in its replacement, by the early 1930s, with optical sound systems, which imprinted a sound track directly onto the film strip and reproduced it electrically. By this time, also, the sound film had replaced the silent film in most countries, and music thus became part of the sound track, constructed and edited in the same way as the image track. Strong generic conventions had been established in multi-reel (that is, full length) feature films during the 1920s. The technique of continuity editing, or film editing for the most fluid sense of narrative, combined with the establishment of large-studio production structures, guaranteed that the image track would acquire a predictability in performance that sound could not. Strong generic conventions for sound did follow in the 1930s, so that by the end of the decade, a "classical" practice was in place that has continued to the present day.

The variety of musical styles represented in *The Jazz Singer* was typical of early film performance practices and was carried over as a characteristic of the sound film, as well, where, however, the distinction between symphonic background music and popular onscreen performance threatened to harden into a requirement. The distinction corresponded conveniently to the two basic levels of narration, the storyteller and the story, such that the background music held the authority of a narrator and performances were embedded in the story itself. The spaces associated with these two levels are nondiegetic (not part of the story world) and diegetic (within the story world). Early on, however, filmmakers, musicians, and sound editors realized that music did not function as directly along these lines as they expected but instead often inhabited an ambiguous middle space, and they lost no time in taking advantage of this "fantastical gap," as Robynn Stilwell has called it. We can see the range of options already at work in *Love on the Run*, an MGM A-level romantic comedy from 1937. Its composer was Franz Waxman, who had been hired a year earlier because of his combined experience in songwriting and arranging with UFA (the largest German studio of the time) and in symphonic underscore at Universal Pictures (where he wrote the music for *The Bride of Frankenstein*). An original song, "Gone," is given prominent placement in the orchestral main title cue of *Love on the*

Run and again later through a highlighted performance in a hotel nightclub setting. Immediately following, we hear a complete instrumental chorus played nondiegetically after a cut to Joan Crawford's hotel room. A similar transfer from diegetic to nondiegetic occurs later when Crawford and Clark Gable find a music box in an empty mansion, open it, and dance to the well-known Boccherini Menuet in A Major, then engage in more and more exaggerated antics as the music moves into the underscore.

Such flexibility in treatment rapidly became a hallmark of music, with respect both to style and to function. In the present day, every conceivable musical style, historical and contemporary, is potentially available as film music, but that wide availability has its roots in early practices. This stylistic variety, along with the functional range suggested by the "fantastical gap," serves to emphasize the broader point that film music is music in film, not simply music for film—or, those musics that appear in the sound track, not only original underscore.

It was silent-film practices in the 1920s that gave us the code of music in narrative film itself, that is, the convention that film exhibition could—and in most instances should—be accompanied by music, whether live or recorded. It is true that much experimentation was needed in the 1930s before the status of music in the sound film was settled, but a recognizably "modern" sound track was in place by the mid to late 1930s, and music necessarily evolved along with the sound track itself. The very idea, however, of a "music that narrates," and therefore music that acts as a strong mediating force, comes directly out of the early film practice of "playing to the film."

This constructed fiction, this myth of a music that narrates, is even more powerful than the impression of a music that directly expresses interiority, emotion, our internal sense of time passing, or some basic sense of obligation to the image. Consider, for example, a recent sound film, *Girl with a Pearl Earring* (2003). In one scene near the end (as the protagonist Griet [Scarlett Johansson], the subject of Vermeer's painting, is leaving the artist's house, having been driven out by his jealous wife), we see a seventeenth-century Dutch house on the screen and hear a seventeenth-century broom sweeping the floor but are asked to listen to modern instruments, whose acoustic sound has of course been affected by recording, performing music whose style cannot be taken as anything other than contemporary cinematic underscore. It is particularly striking that, as historical films attempt greater realism in the image—repeated views of the city canal emphasize how filthy it is, for instance—their attempts to match that authenticity in music remain sporadic, generally limited to source or diegetic music (as here when Catharina Vermeer plays the harpsichord). The sound track's constructed fiction, in other words, is heavily enculturated, and its century-old code for music still operates routinely.

This notion of a common practice has advantages and disadvantages for film music study. I can examine music in the Astaire–Rogers vehicle *Shall We Dance* (1937) in essentially the same way I might do for music in the ballroom competition film *Shall We Dance?* from 2004. And I can therefore compare their treatments on a common plane, which enables broadly applicable historical statements that provide a context for specific descriptions of film style and form. On the other hand, I could regard a limited set of options for the integrated sound track as a critical straitjacket and seek alternatives, the most influential of these historically being that proposed in the 1940s by Eisler and Adorno, who would have music challenge rather than accompany the image in order to awaken and foreground an ideological critique of the system that created the film. Like the French realist aesthetic that would ban all nondiegetic music, or its contrary, the 1970s–1980s documentaries with continuous nondiegetic background music, or even the more recent music video that inverts the terms of sound and image, Eisler and Adorno's contrary aesthetic has succeeded in informing both practice and criticism in important ways but has not thereby shaken or undermined the code of narrative music in sound film. The history of the cinema is now sufficiently deep that it is probably too late for music to acquire a fundamentally different role.

Music, then, is properly one of three components of the sound track – speech and effects (all sounds other than speech or music) being the other two. A sound film consists of two physical elements, image track and sound track (even in the digital era, these two components are separate). If one gives priority to the image track, one is generally giving priority to narrative; therefore, music is relevant as it serves narrative. This is the central thesis of Claudia Gorbman's 1987 book, *Unheard Melodies*, and the assumption behind most historical, archival, and analytic studies. Music's functions in narrative film are relatively limited, being tied mainly to one of three things: (1) referentiality, (2) the opposition sychronization/counterpoint (or playing with/playing against the picture), and (3) the opposition diegetic/nondiegetic (or source/background). These three functions are the familiar territory of close readings or analyses of film scores.

Music can refer, through motives or themes, style topics, or vocal and instrumental textures, to people, things, psychological states, and so forth. Music can also play with or against the image, and music can either be a sound of the narrative world of the film or address the spectator in the manner of voiceover narration. In the closing sequence from *Girl with a Pearl Earring*, covering the time period from the confrontation with Mrs. Vermeer through Griet's sitting in her parents' house and opening a handkerchief that contains the earring, the most notable function is referential, in this case the externalization of emotion. Music accompanies most of the scenes, and, because of the intense focus on Griet, it is readily heard as point-of-view (or "internal diegetic sound"), that is, as the aural expression and confirmation of her emotions. Symphonic underscore works well to depict, define, or enhance the emotions of the characters because it is often topically neutral, and therefore the sense of music as signifier of emotion (see Gorbman) can be all the more effectively foregrounded.

The situation in *Love on the Run* is more complicated. A performance, whether instrumental or vocal, by one of the leads is always tied to that character, whether topically (by the style of the music) or emotionally (by the mood and tempo) or through association (by linking the melody to the character, giving rise to the ability to refer to or "name" that character at some later point, even if not present). Recall, for example, that the first time we hear "As Time Goes By" in *Casablanca* (1943) is when Ingrid Bergman sings a fragment of it (albeit wordlessly). The audience for *Love on the Run* already had certain expectations for "Gone" because of its positioning in the main-title cue: it appears as a lyrical moment following the opening orchestral flourish, by convention where the film's "love theme"—the female lead's theme—was positioned. A famous instance of this device occurs in *Meet Me in St. Louis* (1944): we hear "The Boy Next Door" as the lyrical theme in the main title cue and then, early in the film, hear Judy Garland's performance, which cements

71

the connection to her and to the love relationship she seeks with her neighbor. In *Love on the Run*, thus, Joan Crawford's character, Sally Parker, would have been associated with this theme in any case; the onscreen performance by a singer in the nightclub confirms it (that is, the significance of the song); and the extra chorus played nondiegetically after the cut to her hotel room intensifies it.

The second of music's narrative functions refers to the degree of coordination between image and sound. Here, synchronization is the default: we expect that the sound track will be tied, both temporally and in meaning, to the image track. This means that speech and facial movements match, effects have visible or plausible sources, and music is topically and emotionally appropriate. Eisler and Adorno notwithstanding, music is the most difficult of the three sound track elements to set in opposition to the image because music is the least specific of the three. Speech is easily displaced (a person's words delayed by a second or more; a child's voice in the mouth of an old man), and effects almost as easily by the same methods (absent or delayed sound; sound not appropriate for available sources or for the ambient environment, as in seagull calls over Paris street traffic in Godard's *Prénom Carmen* [1983]), but music is often separated from a source, and a first evaluation of a strange bit of music will be at the level not of the diegesis, but of the narrator.

The third of the basic narrative functions—the opposition diegetic/nondiegetic—has already been discussed above. For additional examples, see the case studies in Chapter 42 of the present book. Here, then, we can summarize music's three narrative functions as relating to the basic narrative categories of agency (referentiality, "naming," character psychology); time (synchronization/counterpoint); and space (diegetic/nondiegetic).

Studying music's narrative functions necessarily tends to separate music out from the other sound track elements. Film is first of all a visual medium. It may not be quite the intensively visual medium that film studies often presumes, but it is obvious that none of the elements of the sound track—not dialogue, not sound effects, especially not music—can be adequately addressed in isolation, that is, outside the film altogether. This is not to say, however, that one cannot productively study individual sound track components. It may be difficult to focus on dialogue without collapsing it into narrative, but a study of acting can position dialogue differently. On the other hand, one can fairly readily study effects and, especially, music on their own. Indeed, it is quite common in the literature to carry out close readings of a film in terms of its music and never mention the sound track as a unit, as if speech were of a different species altogether and sound effects did not exist (except as they collude with or intrude on music). Music studies scholars are particularly prone to separating music out as a unique agent, but an analysis that singles out music and examines its functional relations to narrative independently will always be incomplete, rather like building an interpretation by pulling out a single verse from a poem. The notion of how film constitutes music, that is to say, how film participates in the social-cultural formations of music, or how a process of mediation works in reverse, is certainly interesting, but it also constantly pulls film music away to other questions, in fact is really concerned with other issues and other media altogether. Perhaps the most obvious representative of this in the scholarly literature over the past generation has been Lawrence Kramer, whose occasional readings of feature films focus intensely on the role of traditional (classical)

European music and emphasize what he sees as the enduring cultural and moral power of that repertoire.

Alternatively, one might focus on the sound track as a whole, in which case music is one element in sound design, or the "composing" of the sound track. In this case, the sound track is assigned a different ontological status, as if it were a separate "musical work" attached to the film. (To follow the analogy, the "composer" is the sound editor or sound designer, not the musical composer.) This is the method advocated by Michel Chion, who also argues that the image track is not complete and autonomous in itself—sound "adds value" to the image, but a sound track is also changed—transformed—by the image. Chion's audiovisual analysis is concerned particularly with the hierarchization and subsequent interaction of the sound track elements. As a simple example, we may describe the sequence mentioned above from *Girl with a Pearl Earring*: the stereotypical "live" modern sound track not only overlaps sound and effects at the beginning but makes the loud sweeping of the broom stand out over the music—all the more so because of the minor narrative mystery generated by the fact that the source of the sound is offscreen for the first moment or two and the nature of the source is unclear. Later, when the musical continuity is finally broken (with the cut from the lecherous patron's house to Griet in her parents' home), the sound track continuity is not broken—Griet herself may be silent, but the environment is substantially enlivened with bird noises in a very different register yet at a loudness level equivalent to that of the preceding music.

Finally, we should note that the methods and priorities of the study of music in the feature film have been mapped onto music in other screen media, while allowing for historical differences. Julie Brown, for example, notes that radio and vaudeville had a greater influence on early television than they did on the feature film. Music videos in the 1980s adapted and extended procedures long familiar from the montage (short scenes with rapid cuts, often used to show stages in the passage of time and almost always accompanied by music) and from onscreen musical performances. And contemporary internet venues such as YouTube present countless instances of amateurs tackling, with all possible levels of success or failure, some of the most basic issues in the combination of image and music, issues that would have been familiar to industry professionals in the late 1920s and early 1930s.

Further Reading

Brown, Julie. "Music in Film and Television." In *An Introduction to Music Studies*, edited by J. P. E. Harper-Scott and Jim Samson, 201–218. Cambridge: Cambridge University Press, 2009.

Buhler, James. "Analytical and Interpretive Approaches to Film Music (II): Analysing Interactions of Music and Film." In *Film Music: Critical Approaches*, edited by Kevin J. Donnelly, 39–61. Edinburgh: Edinburgh University Press, 2001.

Buhler, James and David Neumeyer. "Analytical and Interpretive Approaches to Film Music (I): Analysing the Music." In *Film Music: Critical Approaches*, edited by Donnelly, 16–38. 2001.

Buhler, James, David Neumeyer, and Rob Deemer. *Hearing the Movies: Music and Sound in Film History.* New York: Oxford University Press, 2010.

Gorbman, Claudia. *Unheard Melodies: Music in Narrative Film.* Bloomington: Indiana University Press, 1987.

Hubbert, Julie. *Celluloid Symphonies: Texts and Contexts in Film Music History.* Berkeley: University of California Press, 2011.

Laing, Heather. *The Gendered Score: Music in 1940s Melodrama and the Woman's Film.* Aldershot: Ashgate, 2007.

Stilwell, Robynn. "The Fantastical Gap between Diegetic and Nondiegetic." In *Beyond the Soundtrack*, edited by Daniel Goldmark, Lawrence Kramer, and Richard Leppert, 184–202. Berkeley: University of California Press, 2007.

Wierzbicki, James. *Film Music: A History*. New York: Routledge, 2008.

Wierzbicki, James, Nathan Platte, and Colin Roust. *The Routledge Film Music Sourcebook*. New York: Routledge, 2011.

9

VISUAL EVIDENCE IN ETHNOMUSICOLOGY

Andrew Killick

Definitions of ethnomusicology are many and varied, but one thing that they nearly all have in common is a focus on the relationships between musical sound and other aspects of human life. These "other aspects" often manifest themselves in visual forms—not only when music is performed in highly visual contexts such as theater, dance, or ritual, but also when the aural and visual products of a given society (say, the melodic ornamentation of Middle Eastern music and the "arabesques" of Islamic architecture) are interpreted as springing from the same underlying values, or when social groups are understood to express their identities and relationships through both aural and visual channels. Ethnomusicologists typically study music in performance rather than as "works," and regard the visual as well as the aural component of a musical performance as a source of insight into the aesthetic and ethical values of the people involved in it. From this perspective, the spatial arrangement and demeanor of the performers and audience (where such a distinction exists), the visual design of instruments, and the apparent age and gender of participants may convey as much information as the sounds that are produced. Where sound-structures do become a focus of analysis, a fixed, visual notation can be helpful, but, as many of the world's musics have no written form within their own tradition and are not readily accommodated by Western staff notation, the ethnomusicologist is often at pains to devise a visual representation that is intelligible to outsiders without distorting the actual sounds too much. In view of all this, it comes as no surprise that ethnomusicologists are constantly using visual evidence in their research, examining visual artifacts and behaviors as a part of musical life, documenting musical events with still and video photography as well as sound recording, and communicating their findings in visual as well as verbal ways.

What might be surprising, given the vital importance of visual evidence to their work, is that so few ethnomusicologists have tried to formulate any general principles for working with it. The standard texts on ethnomusicology might include sections on iconography, notation, transcription, and the use of photography and film as research techniques, but not on visual evidence in general as a methodological issue. An online search of ethnomusicology journals reveals only a handful of articles with the word "visual" in the title, despite the fact that, as Hilary Finchum-Sung has recently argued in one such article, "visuality can reveal much about the reconstitution of music performance's role within changing social circumstances"[1]—an important concern of ethnomusicologists in the twenty-first century. Nor does "visual" appear among the list of members' interests in the online directory of the Society for Ethnomusicology. While ethnomusicology has spawned a number of specialist sub-fields such as historical ethnomusicology, cognitive ethnomusicology, and applied ethnomusicology, no one appears to have proposed a "visual ethnomusicology" to correspond to the long-established equivalent in one of ethnomusicology's parent disciplines, "visual anthropology." Instead, the use of visual evidence has been taken for granted as an intrinsic part of what ethnomusicologists do, and has not been systematically theorized as a methodology in itself.

The present chapter cannot, therefore, be an overview of existing literature on its topic. Neither, within the current limitations of space and my own competence, can it attempt to provide the first full formulation of that topic. The most it can do is to survey some key examples of how the particular interests and methods that distinguish ethnomusicology from other approaches to the study of music have led ethnomusicologists to use visual evidence in particular ways, and to extrapolate from that a suggestion as to what ethnomusicology might have to contribute to the study of music and visual culture.

The initial problem is to define what ethnomusicology is. From the outside (by those who do not consider themselves ethnomusicologists), and in the organizational structure of academic institutions and conferences, the study of any music other than Western classical and popular tends to be regarded as ethnomusicology, whatever the methodology used. Thus, the textual study of old music manuscripts and theoretical treatises will be classed as historical musicology if the sources are European, and as ethnomusicology if they are Asian. Most scholars who identify themselves as ethnomusicologists, in contrast, prefer to define ethnomusicology as the study of *any* music (including Western classical and popular) using certain methodologies, typically centering on ethnographic fieldwork and theories about the connections between music and the broader life of its community. From the inside, that is, ethnomusicologists tend to define themselves less in terms of what they study than by how they study it.

Both kinds of definition have implications for the use of visual evidence in ethnomusicology. To take the "what" definition first: to the extent that ethnomusicologists study music outside the Western world, they study something that does not exactly correspond to what Westerners mean when they say "music." Different languages and cultures divide up the world differently, and few non-European languages have a term that covers quite the same range of phenomena as the English word "music." Instead, we find terms that are either narrower—referring for instance to singing, drumming, or secular music—or broader, embracing a song's text as well as its music, or encompassing other activities that take place while music is being performed. In India, the term *sangit* includes both music and dance, while in East Asia, the ideograph 楽 (pronounced *yue* in Mandarin Chinese, *ak* in Korean, and *gaku* in Japanese) can embrace virtually the whole realm of the performing arts, along with ritual, and only in modern times has it been combined with an ideograph meaning "sound" (音) to provide a direct translation for the European term "music" (*yinyue*, *ŭmak*, or *ongaku*). Thus, in many cultures, musical sound is conceptualized as part of a phenomenon that includes non-sonic elements, and, as Bruno Nettl has put it, "the widely held view of music as merely a kind of sound is a basis of operations too narrow for acceptance by ethnomusicologists."[2]

The non-sonic elements are, of course, often visual. Even where music is conceived as a form of sound, most kinds of music are more overtly visual in performance than is Western classical music, which for the last two centuries or so has adopted the unusual strategy of seeking to suppress the visual element in concerts through standardized monochrome dress codes, restrained stage etiquette, and functional instrument design, so as to focus the audience's attention on the musical work and its rendition as a sound-object. The separation of works from performances—first, ironically, through the visual medium of notations so detailed and complete that they are colloquially referred to as "the music," and later through sound recording—has further promoted within the Western classical tradition a concept of music as consisting of sound-structures independent of the visual elements associated with live performance. In the global context of human music-making, such a concept can only be regarded as anomalous. To study music outside the Western classical canon, therefore, is usually to study a phenomenon that is explicitly and unabashedly visual as well as aural, and the visual dimension has not been lost on ethnomusicologists, with their view of music as an activity rather than a repertoire of works. In that respect, "what" ethnomusicologists study influences their use of visual material by encouraging them to treat the performance event as a totality that is not only aural but also visual (and often tactile, gustatory, and olfactory as well, since the experience of dancing or playing an instrument highlights the sense of touch and movement, while many performance events involve the consumption of food and drink).

But of course, even Western classical music has not been able to escape the inherently visual quality of performance: many famous musicians have benefited from a commanding appearance and stage presence, and a conductor's role in performance is to communicate visually with the orchestra and/or choir rather than to produce sound—to say nothing of the more conspicuously visual appeal of opera, ballet, and the packaging of recent classical recordings. The classical tradition has also left a rich pictorial record that supports a burgeoning iconographic branch of the study of Western music history, as the work of several contributors to this volume attests. Thus, ethnomusicologists are not the only scholars to examine visual aspects of musical performance, and where their interests are primarily historical, their methods for doing so may not be particularly distinctive even if their focus on non-Western music classifies their work as ethnomusicology. Bonnie Wade's book on the musical culture of Mughal India, *Imaging Sound*, describes itself as an "ethnomusicological study" and was published in the Chicago Studies in Ethnomusicology series at a time when Wade was president-elect of the Society for Ethnomusicology, but its methodology is not strikingly different from that of Richard Leppert writing about Western musical culture in his similarly titled books *Music and Image* and *The Sight of Sound*.

Ethnomusicologists interested in the early history of non-Western musical cultures, for which written or pictorial sources may be unavailable or less informative than surviving artifacts such as instruments, have sometimes turned to the methods of archaeology, whose sources—physical objects—are also partly visual. In the introduction to a themed journal issue on "Music Archaeology: Mesoamerica," Dale Olsen proposed "music archaeology" (the study of music-related remains and of the sites where such remains are found) as one of four approaches to the study of ancient music cultures that could usefully be combined to form an interdisciplinary "archaeomusicology." The other three approaches are "music iconology" (the study of the "representation of music and music-related elements in the plastic arts"), "music historiography" (the study of contemporary written descriptions of musical artifacts or occasions), and "music ethnographic analogy" (the study of living music cultures for what they suggest about how things may have been in the past).[3] Of these, only "music ethnographic analogy" involves the characteristic ethnomusicological research technique of fieldwork, while it is the other three that rely on primarily or exclusively visual sources. Archaeomusicology does not, therefore, constitute a specifically ethnomusicological way of using visual evidence, and of course archaeological methods have been applied to the study of early European music too.

A similar case is found in organology, the study of musical instruments. A focus on non-Western musics has led many ethnomusicologists to examine the visual as well as the sound-producing qualities of instruments, for both are often culturally significant and to some extent independent. Yet the system of instrument classification that has been universally adopted in ethnomusicology for the past century is based only on properties that affect sound production. Alternative classifications based on visual criteria such as anthropomorphic, zoomorphic, and cosmological elements might also "reveal new genetic and cultural links" among the world's instruments (as the authors of the standard system claimed for their taxonomy),[4] but this possibility does not appear to have been thoroughly explored. Visual attributes unrelated to sound production have been studied for their significance within particular cultures, but this is also true of decorated instruments in earlier Western music culture, as studied for instance by Leppert. The visual study of musical instruments is no more a monopoly of ethnomusicologists than is organology itself; and the main journal of organology, the *Galpin Society Journal*, is independent of any disciplinary affiliation.

An interest in traditional and non-Western music, then, does not in itself result in a method of using visual evidence that is particular to ethnomusicology, at least where primary sources are concerned. Where it has led to such a method, ironically, is where a certain kind of visual primary source is absent, namely notation. In studying unwritten musics, ethnomusicologists have often found it expedient to create a notation of their own that allows them to "freeze" the music in time, analyze its structural features, and communicate something of it to others. The practice and skill of producing such notations, known as "transcription," was a hallmark of ethnomusicology's parent discipline, "comparative musicology," often characterized by what are now disparagingly termed "armchair scholars" staying home and transcribing music from recordings made by missionaries and colonial administrators on their travels, and using these transcriptions to construct global classificatory schemes based on cultural evolutionist assumptions. This kind of "visual evidence" was later rejected as a fabrication produced by forcing all the world's musics into the straitjacket of Western staff notation, in which only those features considered salient in Western music (chiefly discrete pitches and proportional rhythmic values) would be apparent, instead of considering each form of music in terms of its own salient features (which might include, for instance, timbre, microtonal intervals and pitch bends, or visual elements such as costuming and dance movements). Yet transcription and analysis has remained an important if increasingly optional technique in ethnomusicology even as ethnomusicologists have distanced themselves

from the ideology of the old comparative approach and agonized over the practical, epistemological, and ethical issues surrounding the representation of previously
unwritten musics in a visual form intelligible to Western readers. This long tradition of the practice and theory of musical transcription does constitute a distinctive
way of using visual evidence that has developed within the disciplinary lineage of
ethnomusicology, even if the "evidence" is created by the investigator.

A related technique is "transnotation," the transfer of written music from one
system of notation to another. Though less distinctive to ethnomusicology, having long been used by scholars of Western early music interpreting various systems
of neumes and instrumental tablature, transnotation has often been practiced by
ethnomusicologists studying non-Western musical scores, to create notations that
are both more intelligible to Western readers and more complete for analytical purposes. The indigenous notation of music for the Chinese zither *qin*, for instance, is
fantastically detailed in specifying fingering techniques for both hands, but gives no
explicit indication of rhythm. In performance, a given *qin* piece is played with fairly
consistent rhythms by different players, but this aspect of the music is transmitted
through oral tradition rather than notation. To create a notation reflecting actual
performance practice, the ethnomusicologist would consult recorded performances
as well as the written score—a combination of transnotation and transcription.

This is often necessary because notations used by practicing musicians around
the world are what is called "prescriptive": they tell the musician what to play or
sing. Because practicing musicians are already familiar in a general way with the stylistic conventions of the music they perform, the notation need not instruct them
on matters that are taken for granted or left to the performer's discretion. What
the ethnomusicologist wants for purposes of analysis, in contrast, is a "descriptive"
notation that closely reflects what is actually played, either in a typical performance or in one particular performance. The Western classical tradition presents an
unusual case in that the same notation is used for both prescriptive and descriptive
purposes: scores written by composers as instructions to performers are also used by
theorists analyzing the musical work. This is possible because the score is detailed
enough to enable a competent performer to learn the piece without having to rely
on oral tradition except for matters of general stylistic convention—a rare situation
among prescriptive notations worldwide—and thus contains all the information
required for an analysis of that particular piece by a theorist already familiar with
the style. Where the style is less familiar and the indigenous notation less complete
or lacking altogether, the analyst must create a descriptive notation that takes less
for granted.

Ethnomusicologists have become acutely aware that in producing these transcriptions and transnotations they are creating their own "visual evidence." A written
representation of musical sound can never be an objective record, for decisions must
be made as to which aspects of the sound are salient and how they can best be communicated. Moreover, an accurate transcription of a particular performance requires
a replayable recording, which is itself usually made by the ethnomusicologist and
is already far removed from the actual performance, being a product of decisions
about what to record and how, besides being detached from the social and sensory
experience of the performance event. Some ethnomusicologists have responded by
moving away from transcription and analysis and restricting their discussion to the
social uses and functions of music and the perceptions of insiders, but others have

felt that such a restriction excludes the special contribution that ethnomusicology has to make to the question of why people use the particular forms of music that they do in particular situations; and hence there has been a resurgence of analytical studies in world music, supported by visual transcriptions. To make these transcriptions more faithfully descriptive and avoid the ethnocentrism of comparative musicology, ethnomusicologists have developed a variety of strategies including modification of indigenous notations, invention of their own systems, and production of mechanical and computer-generated sound graphs. Recognizing that no single system will be suitable for all purposes, ethnomusicologists now choose whatever form of transcription best reveals the musical features that they wish to analyze, but, for the sake of communication among researchers of different musics, who mostly share a familiarity with Western staff notation, the prevalent approach remains the use of staff notation with adaptations to show features alien to Western music.

Other distinctly ethnomusicological ways of using visual evidence appear when we turn from the question of "what" ethnomusicologists study to "how" they study it. When the term "ethnomusicology" began to replace "comparative musicology" in the mid-twentieth century, it signaled a methodological shift away from analyzing and comparing transcribed examples of music as objects in isolation from their source, and toward seeking to understand any form of music in relation to the culture that produced it. This in itself is not enough to distinguish ethnomusicology from other ways of studying music, for historical musicologists are also often interested in music's relationship to its cultural context. What distinguishes ethnomusicology is the practice of studying that relationship through prolonged, intensive ethnographic fieldwork, as in another of ethnomusicology's parent disciplines, anthropology. So central has fieldwork become to the identity of ethnomusicology (and of ethnomusicologists) that any of the research methods described above as not specific to ethnomusicology might become so if informed by ethnographic techniques. Studying musical instruments as objects in a museum, for instance, is not a particularly ethnomusicological form of organology, but if the instruments are studied in the context where they are used and in relation to their users' ideas and practices concerning the functions, values, symbolism, social restrictions, and ritual sanctions associated with them, the study becomes an ethnomusicological one. It is the ethnographic method, more than anything else, that gives ethnomusicology a distinct methodological identity; even transcription and analysis is now mostly applied to music that the analyst has personally documented through fieldwork.

Thus, by the 1990s Jeff Todd Titon could write, "Today, it is not transcription but fieldwork that constitutes ethnomusicology. Fieldwork is no longer viewed principally as observing and collecting (although it surely involves that) but as experiencing and understanding music."[5] The problem here is that experience, like musical sound, is fleeting, and the kind of "evidence" needed for making an analysis and communicating it convincingly to others must be something that exists in a more permanent form. Hence, just as ethnomusicologists have made recordings and transcriptions to bring permanence to the musical sounds they study, they have sought to preserve other aspects of the fieldwork experience by creating a variety of permanent records. Among these records, besides written narratives that have become increasingly self-conscious and evocative—and often highly visual—are pieces of more directly visual evidence in the media of photography, film, and video. Here again, as with transcriptions and transnotations, ethnomusicologists create their own visual evidence; for as Steve Feld pointed out long ago, "just as pencils and typewriters don't write books, 'cameras don't take pictures' ... People take pictures";[6] and whether consciously or not, they do so in ways shaped by their values, assumptions, and agendas. Awareness of this has led ethnomusicologists to respond, not so much by trying to avoid the influence of such factors (which would be futile) as by making their ethnographies transparent as to how the visual and other evidence was created and how that process itself may have affected what was observed—for instance, by including photographs of themselves filming in a performance setting.

In the ethnographic study of music, still photography has been useful for examining inanimate objects such as performance venues, instruments, manuscripts, and art works of which the ethnographer's experience was "fleeting" in that they could not be taken away from the fieldwork site, but on the whole it has perhaps been used less for discovery than for communication. Lending itself to being reproduced in print, or projected from a transparency or PowerPoint slide without taking up any of the limited time allocated for a conference presentation, a photograph can be a powerful ally to an ethnomusicologist discussing a place and culture that may be quite unknown to the audience; it can convey an instant impression of what it was like to be there. Hence, many ethnomusicological books are lavishly and artistically illustrated with photographs that often serve to evoke a setting or put a face to the name of a musician rather than provide evidence for an analytical point. But, willy-nilly, the photographs that are not analyzed also communicate ideas and values, for a photograph can only show a subject from one point of view, and the frame always excludes more than it contains.

Film and video, with their ability to capture sound along with moving images, have been enthusiastically embraced by ethnomusicologists, some of whom have become accomplished documentary filmmakers. Films of musical performances preserve far more of the original performance event than do sound recordings and still photographs, enabling the ethnomusicologist to analyze the interaction of aural and visual elements in a multitude of ways. For instance, a major research project funded by Britain's Arts and Humanities Research Council in the late 2000s on "Experience and Meaning in Music Performance" included analysis of "the embodiment of sound as patterns of movement" in the physical gestures used by North Indian classical singers, for which audiovisual recordings of performances were indispensable.[7] But the physical movements of performers have also been studied in other fields, such as music psychology. Where ethnomusicology makes a distinctive use of performance films is for the information they contain about the interactions between people that take place during a musical performance—something of vital concern to ethnomusicologists with their understanding of music as social behavior. Some ethnomusicologists have deliberately included the audience within the camera's view in order to examine how musicians and audience may create a performance together, particularly where improvisation or spontaneous selection of material is involved. Regula Burckhardt Qureshi, studying the Islamic mystical song genre *qawwali*, used such footage to produce transcriptions showing the actions of audience members alongside the words and music sung, thus enabling her to "trace the interaction between the musician's ongoing performance decisions and the audience responses as he perceives them, along with the resulting song sequence."[8] This of course required the verbal input of the musician, commenting on his own recorded performance—and playback of video recordings to those involved in the performance has become an important strategy for eliciting insiders' knowledge and evaluations.

Examples of ethnomusicologists' uses of visual evidence could be multiplied indefinitely, but enough has perhaps been said to address the question of what ethnomusicology might have to contribute to the study of music and visual culture. One hint could be taken from pioneer ethnomusicologist Alan Merriam, who in the 1970s advocated a shift in thinking from the study of "music in its cultural context" or "music in culture" to "music *as* culture." By stressing "process rather than form," Merriam suggested, such an approach would "conceptualize music sound not as separate from, but as a part of the totality of society and culture."[9] Since then, ethnomusicologists, like anthropologists, have become uncomfortable at times with the concept of "culture," but they have never forgotten that music in performance is visual as well as aural. Rather than thinking of music as a separate, aural phenomenon that might have relationships of one kind or another with visual phenomena, an ethnomusicologist might re-define the topic and ask what can be learned by studying "music *as* visual culture."

Notes

1 Hilary V. Finchum-Sung, "Visual Excess: The Visuality of Traditional Music Performance in South Korea," *Ethnomusicology* 56, no. 3 (2012): 396–425.

2 Bruno Nettl, *The Study of Ethnomusicology: Thirty-one Issues and Concepts*, new ed. (Urbana: University of Illinois Press, 2005), at 23.

3 Dale A. Olsen, "The Complementarity and Interdisciplinarity of Archaeomusicology: An Introduction to the Field and this Volume," *The World of Music* 49, no. 2 (2007): 11–15.

4 Erich M. von Hornbostel and Curt Sachs, "Classification of Musical Instruments," trans. Anthony Baines and Klaus P. Wachsmann, *Galpin Society Journal* 14 (1961): 3–29, at 5. (First published in German in 1914.)

5 Jeff Todd Titon, "Knowing Fieldwork," in *Shadows in the Field: New Perspectives for Fieldwork in Ethnomusicology*, ed. Gregory F. Barz and Timothy J. Cooley (New York: Oxford University Press, 1997), 87–100, at 87.

6 Steve Feld, "Ethnomusicology and Visual Communication," *Ethnomusicology* 20, no. 2 (1976): 293–325, at 299. The embedded quotation is the title of an article by Paul Byers, *Columbia University Forum* 9, no. 1 (1966): 28–32.

7 Laura Leante, "The Lotus and the King: Imagery, Gesture and Meaning in a Hindustani *Rāg*," *Ethnomusicology Forum* 18, no. 2 (2009): 185–206, at 185.

8 Regula Burckhardt Qureshi, *Sufi Music of India and Pakistan: Sound, Context and Meaning in Qawwali* (Cambridge: Cambridge University Press, 1986), at 143.

9 Alan P. Merriam, "Definitions of 'Comparative Musicology' and 'Ethnomusicology': An Historical-Theoretical Perspective," *Ethnomusicology* 21, no. 2 (1977): 189–204, at 197.

Further Reading

Not all items in this list explicitly theorize the use of visual evidence; as mentioned above, studies of that kind are rather rare within ethnomusicology. The items by Rault and Reck, in particular, are intended to serve as examples of ethnomusicological books that rely heavily on visual material in the form of photographs and (in Reck's case) an innovative approach to transcription.

Marian-Bălaşa, Marin, ed. *Notation, Transcription, Visual Representation*. Themed issue of *The World of Music* 47, no. 2 (2005).

Mera, Miguel and Anna Morcom, eds. *Screened Music: Global Perspectives*. Themed issue of *Ethnomusicology Forum* 18, no. 1 (2009).

Olsen, Dale A. *Music of El Dorado: The Ethnomusicology of Ancient South American Cultures.* Gainesville: University Press of Florida, 2002.

Rault, Lucie. *Musical Instruments: A Worldwide Survey of Traditional Music-making.* London: Thames and Hudson, 2000.

Reck, David. *Music of the Whole Earth.* New York: Da Capo Press, 1977.

Tenzer, Michael, ed. *Analytical Studies in World Music.* New York: Oxford University Press, 2006.

Part III

RECIPROCATION

III.1 The Musical in Visual Culture

10
REPRESENTING MUSIC-MAKING

Alan Davison

That an image of musical performance can evoke within us a sense of the sonorous, even a sense of movement and the tactile, is a truism whose significance is both highlighted and obscured by the temptation to search for poetic metaphors. While rhetorical devices are significant in themselves as forms of expression, what is of particular interest for the purpose of this chapter is that they are deeply suggestive of the importance of images in our responses to, and engagement with, music. For the scholar, visual representations of music-making offer a vast repository for researching the role of music in society, the history of performance practices, and the interconnections between music and visual culture.

Representations of music-making date back well into ancient history, and their study has been a major concern of the relatively recent discipline of music iconography that emerged during the twentieth century. Most often, this concern was related to researching historical performance practices, and research by significant figures such as Emanuel Winternitz still stands today as a major contribution to the field. Winternitz's *Musical Instruments and Their Symbolism in Western Art* (1967) remains highly recommended reading for anyone seeking some erudite and cautionary case studies in how instruments were used in art. Richard Leppert's 1979 article published in *Early Music* is a landmark in scholarship into representations of music-making, and from around the early 1980s scholars such as Leppert argued for the role of musical images in understanding wider socio-cultural issues. Today, it is surely a reasonable expectation that any scholar attempting a study of musical imagery should display a sound understanding of broader social context as well as facility in visual analysis and depth of relevant musical knowledge.

Depending upon the specific cultural or historical context, an image of music-making may already be overtly and inextricably linked to performance traditions and even within a web of ritual, such that contemplating the image removed from these practices is nonsensical. Moreover, what even constitutes proper subject matter for a discussion on representations of music-making is worth pondering before we move on. Consider a cave painting, a rock engraving, or a religious totem imbued with ceremonial importance involving music and dance. To the uninitiated, such representations may fail to show any overt indication of music-making (i.e. musicians, instruments, or notation), and yet they are deeply embedded within—and evocative of—the activities that occur around them.

The scholarly value of any given image or genre of images can depend as much upon what questions are asked of it as it does upon the nature of the image itself. The challenge of developing some broad approaches is that one can easily ride roughshod over the specificities of time and place, or diminish the significance of distinct forms of musical and visual expression that periods, groups, or individuals exhibit. Theories that attempt to formulate pan-historical/cultural approaches run the risk of being little more than aprioristic templates that mold predetermined outcomes onto their object of investigation. In other words, images require what anthropologists would call "thick" description in order to generate valid findings to attach to them, and such descriptions would require at a minimum a consideration of genre, media, and context of viewing. Ultimately, however, if images are to have a value beyond being mere adjuncts to other source materials, then we must be able to derive something from their study as a *class* of objects. With this in mind, three points of reference are used to guide the discussion below:

1. visualizing performers
2. visualizing contexts and listeners
3. visualizing music as practice and idea.

While it is possibly the first point of interest, considering images for their performance practice value is more properly the last point arrived at in a thorough study of visual sources. Images can indeed provide a wealth of information relating to performing traditions and practices of the past or of societies different to that of the scholar's own. One obvious reason for this is the readily observed fact that images often record aspects of the world that do not get referenced in other forms, through neglect or the very commonplace nature of the activity. However, caution is needed when there is an underlying expectation that an image is an unproblematic "window" or "snapshot." A painting is not a photograph, nor indeed is a photograph simply a "photograph" in the sense of being an unmediated visual capturing of an event. Once other considerations have been taken into account, then we can make a case for what a picture can offer performance practice research, but it is a point to be arrived at, not taken a priori.

The power of images to elicit a response from an "inner" ear (what will be termed throughout this chapter as the "mind's ear") speaks of very real processes in brain function that recent scientific studies have begun to shed light on. While it is still in its infancy, research into brain function and into music and gesture has yielded some significant findings that bear direct relevance to the topic of this chapter. First, when viewing static images of objects in motion (such as an athlete jumping or a dancer pirouetting), those parts of the brain that are responsive to motion are activated and, to put it crudely, the mind attributes a sense of movement to the object in the picture. Second, when presented with silent movies of music-making, those parts of the brain that would normally be activated by sound are also stimulated; the mind's ear aligns the movements with the consequent sounds that the ear should be hearing.

The implications of such findings for research into images of music-making are considerable. Even as they are motionless, images that show clear music-making movements or gestures will have the potential to elicit a sense of both movement and sound in the viewer's mind. This goes some way to explaining the special fascination that images of music-making can have over us, for they are engaging our brains in a variety of tasks in order to "complete" what is missing from the image proper. In short, we strive to add movement and sound to images that show music-making. This striving, however, does not result in something that can be simplistically measured, as both visual and musical competency (knowledge of the object category) are crucial in influencing the level of response of an individual. In addition, neurological studies show that empathetic simulation is evoked within the observer when s/he is presented with images of expressive bodily gestures or depictions of highly tactile events. It stands to reason that images of musicians involved in music-making actions would likewise stimulate empathetic responses in the musically knowledgeable viewer, but that the degree of stimulation would depend upon familiarity with the instrument and the consequences of the actions being represented.

Consider Augustus John's painting of the great cellist Guilhermina Suggia, completed in 1923 (Tate, London). Suggia was an outstanding musician and a trailblazing figure for women seeking a professional career playing the cello. John's portrait is ablaze with movement, not least of which is implied by the drawn-out bowing arm. This implied movement is emphasized and also counterbalanced through the vibrant extension of Suggia's red dress into and beyond the bottom right frame of the painting. To say that this painting is full of movement is inadequate: it engages the mind of the viewer, and, through the overt sound-producing movement shown, it evokes a sonorous sense in the mind's ear. The degree to which individuals might respond to and engage with the picture will depend at least partly upon their knowledge of the instrument and its playing techniques (note the multiple stopping of the strongly placed left hand).

Not only do these emerging studies suggest a neurological basis for the attraction of gazing at pictures of musicians clearly in the act of making music, but they also hint at the appeal of viewing less straightforward images. D. G. Rossetti's various images of women stroking and pawing at unlikely string instruments have both captivated and perturbed critics for years; A Sea Spell (1877; Fogg Art Museum, Cambridge, MA) is a wonderful example. The fascination of such images may have as much to do with the cognitive dissonance of our subconscious, as it grapples to connect impractical music-making actions with imagined sounds, as it does with the visual appeal of color and flesh. (As an aside, this visual-sonic "work" of the viewer may also explain the bizarre appeal of air guitar playing for audiences: the brain strives to connect gestures that the conscious mind knows are irrelevant to the sound that the ear can hear, for it is apparently a human necessity to match movement and sound at some level.)

If the mind's ear is acknowledged as an essential partner to the viewer's eye, then we come to the intriguing issue of the alignment and interaction between these two senses. Admittedly, they are not of the same type, but the confluence or otherwise of the eye and the mind's ear when engaging with an image adds an additional level of interpretive potential to the points made above. An image typically situates the eye concretely in relation to what it is representing; perhaps as an audience member, "backstage," or in an idealized yet physically unobtainable position in relation to the performance. What are the implications for our mind's ear if an image positions us behind the performers? Would we not only have the sense of being "backstage" as a viewer but also strive to hear the music from there? In our mind's ear and imagination is it muffled, distorted, or as the players themselves hear it? Is, for example, a photograph by Herman Leonard showing a smoke-filled stage with iconic jazz performers at least partly appealing as a subconsciously evoked and privileged aural experience, just as much as it is a visual phenomenon alluding to intimacy and authenticity?

Another role that images can have in our engagement with music can be in providing cues to interpretation and meaning in performance that are in addition to the musical sounds themselves. Studies have shown that facial expression and bodily gestures aid audiences in attributing a sense of significance to musical performance, especially those audience members less highly trained in music. In other words, viewing actions adds to the sonic information obtained simply through listening, and some people will form judgments according to what is seen as well as heard.

Images may not offer the continuous flow of signals that we experience while witnessing a performer in action or a listener in response. All the same, images can supplement the listening experience and provide essential cues regarding musical meaning, interpretation, and appropriate behavior. Historically, images could well have functioned to help establish some broad parameters in "appropriate" aesthetic approaches: what cognitive researchers would categorize as "top-down" influences upon perception and responses. These indicators of appropriate listening might be explicit or implicit, intentional or unintentional, and generated from an image of the performer or of the listener. The extent to which such visual cues to meaning and response are presented in any given image is an important factor to tie back in to questions regarding socially expected modes of listening, and regarding variations among representations of different musical genres.

Just as images of musical performers can present visualizations of actual performance and ideas associated with performance, so images of audiences can provide historical and cultural insights into listening. A common trope in nineteenth-century paintings and prints is the "attentive listener." Typically shown with head somewhat bowed and chin perhaps resting on hand, this audience member epitomizes the deep and serious listening that was increasingly expected of music lovers as the nineteenth century progressed. The flourishing of images of music audiences in the nineteenth century is doubtless linked to the function of providing modeling exemplars of listening to culturally aspiring middle classes, and it fed highly politicized debates surrounding audience manners and class. As Nancy November has discussed, a print from 1846 in the *Illustrated London News*—"Quartet Party at the Musical Union"—exemplifies the representation and promotion of appropriate behavior through imagery. The image shows the four musicians seated in a semicircle, while off to the right, some Musical Union audience members read through program notes and/or scores. Attentive listening—aided through study—is not only represented in the image, but its evident merits are reinforced and encouraged. In short, the message of the image relates more to ways of listening and audience behavior than it does to the performers.

As Tilman Seebass notes, naturalistic depictions of music-making are, in fact, relatively rare in Western European formal portraits. The reasons for this may be many, relating to niceties of pictorial and social convention and—depending upon the historical context—to a tension between presenting music as a cerebral or a physical act. Nevertheless, many portraits show their musical sitter engaged in what might be called "nominal" music-making actions. These typically include gestures such as resting a hand on a piano keyboard or holding a bow against the strings of a violin. While not especially evocative of music-making, these types of images do emphasize the symbiotic link between performer and instrument, often presenting the latter as an extension of the body. For example, a photograph by Bernard Schwartz of the pianist Dame Moura Lympany (National Portrait Gallery, London) shows her posed with one hand in her lap and the other crossing her body in order to depress an Ab/G# with her index finger. The portrait is in a sense a double portrait: Lympany's gaze and attention are directed toward her instrument, as if to a lifelong partner.

A well-known oil painting of Liszt is a rich example with which to address the various facets discussed above. *Franz Liszt Fantasizing at the Piano* (1840; Staatliche Museen zu Berlin), painted by the Viennese artist Josef Danhauser, depicts the composer-pianist in a lush salon setting, surrounded by notables of the Romantic movement: from left to right these are Alexandre Dumas; Victor Hugo or Hector Berlioz (scholars disagree on the figure's identity); George Sand; Niccolò Paganini; Gioacchino Rossini; and Marie d'Agoult. Danhauser used pre-existing portraits for all of the assembled audience but appears not to have had a likeness of d'Agoult, whose face is unseen. The piano maker Conrad Graf commissioned the painting in 1839, and it is therefore hardly surprising that the instrument of his design receives particular care from the artist. Although the painting has attracted considerable scholarly attention, especially as it relates to Biedermeier sensibilities, salon culture, and the cult of Beethoven, the focus here will be on how the main points presented so far in this chapter can converge in a single image.

The scene is imaginary; no such gathering of Romantic worthies actually occurred, although Danhauser and Liszt knew each other quite well and the artist would certainly have seen the pianist play. He is shown with his head tilted back, eyes raised toward a prominent bust of Beethoven, while the sheet music on the piano is ignored. Liszt did indeed play without music, but in order for Danhauser to indicate the music being performed at or associated with the imagined concert, he has placed two scores on the piano stand; the slow funeral march movement of Beethoven's Piano Sonata op. 26 in Ab Major, and a Phantasie by Liszt himself. We are left in little doubt, however, that even if Liszt is not playing the great composer's somber *marcia funebre* specifically, his extemporization is at least in an appropriate mood for the late master. Liszt is shown here not just as a famous pianist, but as Beethoven's great champion and anointed interpreter. His famous "ivory profile" appears in sharp relief, and in clear parallel to the profile of the poet Byron, whose likeness is placed above Liszt on the wall. Liszt's distinctive hand and arm position, with raised wrists, helps to lead our eye from the keyboard to his highlighted head, and suggests that a chord has been struck.

The assembled audience is in various states of either contemplative listening or rapturous response. Sand, especially, is moved to close Dumas's book, while Hugo has already turned his volume over as the musical transcends the literary. All are clearly rapt with Liszt's channeling of Beethoven's spirit, and Danhauser has set his listeners in carefully contrived poses to show their individualized responses. While attention is most easily drawn to those in the greatest state of movement or response, it is an interesting exercise to align each with their reputation and significance at the time. Although at first easily overlooked, upon reflection Paganini stands out precisely because of his upright pose, fixed stare, and crossed arms; he was, after all, the greatest virtuoso of the day, and a major influence on Liszt's own artistic and technical development as a musician. The great Mephistophelian violinist is shown in the repose of utmost respect and reserve in the presence of his virtuoso successor.

While Danhauser's painting is rich in its depiction of differing listener responses and interactions, the solo musician himself is nonetheless shown as if in his own world and unaware of his audience (we know in fact that Liszt was highly aware of his influence upon his audience!). When an artist depicts a group of musicians, there is the added dimension of how communication between players can be represented or emphasized. Images of string quartets provide opportunities to see how an artist or photographer might seek to evoke a sense of the intimacy and unity of a group. György Gordon's oil painting of the Lindsay Quartet, completed in 2003 (National Portrait Gallery, London), shows the Quartet—minus music stands—huddled so closely around a mid-point in the visual space that their bodies merge impossibly into a central space in the canvas. The strong foreshortening not only places the viewer immediately in front of the quartet, it also creates a sense of being almost within the group itself because the viewer completes a circle around an imagined central point. Intimacy of musical thought and action emanating from the performers is visualized, but the viewer—and so the evoked listener—is part of the imagined experience. As a representation of music-making, Gordon's painting epitomizes the associations that we have of the depth and intimacy of the string quartet as a performative genre as well as a listened-to experience. More than a record of the Lindsay Quartet in rehearsal, this compelling group portrait visualizes the *idea* of the string quartet—and this quartet in particular—as an ensemble

Returning to Danhauser's *Franz Liszt Fantasizing*, the painting is still valuable as a performance practice source, even if it is not a representative of an actual concert. Danhauser's depiction of Liszt's high seating position, implied hand–arm gesture and gaze away from the keyboard are all aspects of Lisztian playing that are supported through written sources, although not seen consistently in visual material. It is actually caricatures and informal sketches—rather than formal oil portraits or even photographs—that provide the most compelling additional iconographical evidence that freedom of arm and wrist movement was a distinctive Lisztian "fingerprint."

Photographs as a medium might at first seem especially promising as the clearest possible record of actual performance and of fundamental aspects of Liszt's performing style, including such basics as the way he positioned himself in relation to the keyboard. Even here we need to pause to consider what leads up to and results in the captured image. As photographic technology becomes more portable and the "snapshot" more feasible, more apparently realistic images occur, including those in the photojournalistic tradition. Even with fundamental matters of technique, photographers make choices regarding exposure, lighting, and positioning (angle, distance)—and then there are factors like the relationship with the sitter.

With many photographs from the nineteenth century, long exposure times led to stiff poses. The setting was often the photographer's studio, where natural light was optimized. Studio props would be used, which might include a small upright piano and chair for the pianist. Do photographs of Liszt show him more "realistically" at the piano than do oil portraits or caricatures? Yes and no. As photographers used compositional conventions derived from painting, Liszt's pose at the piano is usually within a rather conservative tradition, feet neatly angled, with the right foot off the sustaining pedal and turned toward the viewer. The chair or stool he sat on might just as easily be lower or higher than what he used in concert, and the positioning of his hands might be a consequence of the requirements of sitting still rather than a natural shaping and gesture.

On the face of it, caricatures of musicians seem to be at the opposite end of the reliability spectrum from photographs. It is certainly true that the aesthetic of exaggeration and distortion leads to amusing excess, but many satirical illustrations capture what other genres avoid, and so they are of great interest on these grounds alone. Because they make fun of pictorial and social conventions, caricatures can often show distinctive features or gestures of a musician that are normally de-emphasized. As humorous images often use visual shorthand, they tend to rely on "signature" actions, poses, or physical features of their subject. For example, Liszt's well-known gesture of throwing his hands in the air is captured in caricatures, but not in serious portraiture.

By now it should be apparent that using images for performance practice research is a problematic task. Many artistic and social conventions regarding pose, gesture, expression, and overall composition must be considered alongside questions of performance practice value. In addition, the knowledge and skills of the artist, and his or her relationship with the performer(s), are crucial factors in what results in any given picture. Nonetheless, images of music-making do offer evidence of a particular kind that can be valuable, and indeed sometimes it is the only substantive evidence at all.

Although the focus of this chapter has been necessarily limited to selected examples, the goal was nonetheless to offer approaches that have validity for several different social and historical contexts. With this in mind, two essential ideas can be drawn out from the discussion and examples above: (1) whatever their precise manifestation, representations of music-making should be considered first and foremost as records of ideas associated with musical performance as much as they are records of music-making activities; and (2) these representations are not mere passive visual accounts of music-making, but active agents in how people have listened and even conceived of music through history.

The earlier point of referring to emerging scientific understanding of our engagement with images and music is not to push scholarship of musical images into a magnetic resonance imaging scanner but, rather, to show that the poets and painters were right: images of making music can evoke strong reactions of which most of us are only vaguely consciously aware, and to which metaphor and analogy seem entirely understandable responses. If we reverse the situation of the scientist and the music scholar, it is pictures of music-making over the centuries and across societies that provide scholars and researchers today with compelling yet challenging forms of evidence of the role of music and images in humanity's collective conscious and subconscious experiences.

Further Reading

Comini, Alessandra. *The Changing Face of Beethoven*. 2nd ed. Santa Fe: Sunstone, 2008.

Gritten, Anthony and Elaine King, eds. *New Perspectives on Music and Gesture*. Burlington: Ashgate, 2011.

ALAN DAVISON

Leppert, Richard. "Concert in a House: Musical Iconography and Musical Thought." *Early Music* 7 (1979): 3–17.
November, Nancy. "Theater Piece and Cabinetstück: Nineteenth-Century Visual Ideologies of the String Quartet." *Music in Art* 29, nos. 1–2 (2004): 134–150.
Pinson, Heather. *The Jazz Image: Seeing Music through Herman Leonard's Photography.* Jackson: University Press of Mississippi, 2010.
Seebass, Tilman. "Iconography." In *Grove Music Online. Oxford Music Online*, http://www.oxfordmusiconline.com/subscriber/article/grove/music/13698 (accessed September 19, 2012).
Winternitz, Emanuel. *Musical Instruments and Their Symbolism in Western Art: Studies in Musical Iconology.* New Haven: Yale University Press, 1979.

11
COMPOSER PORTRAIT PRINTS

Stephen A. Bergquist

Over the past five hundred years, composers have been depicted in all the major media—paintings, drawings, prints, and sculpture. Printmaking is an intimate medium, and while an etched or engraved portrait may lack the immediate impact of an imposing oil painting or a life-size sculpture, prints are an extraordinarily important source for the visual history of music. Even for composers whose images are familiar primarily from paintings, prints have made significant contributions to their iconographies, and for many composers, prints constitute the only visual record. They can thus be of great interest not only to the music lover, but to the musicologist and the music historian as well.

The first printed portraits of composers date from around the mid-sixteenth century, a few decades after etchings and engravings first began to appear in large numbers. At that time, composers were not yet writing for the general public. The public concert did not exist, and composers found their employment in the church or the court. Although the profession of printselling was already well established by the second half of the century, there would undoubtedly have been little or no demand by the public for portraits of composers, and it is thus not surprising that the earliest such portraits were not produced for sale as single sheets but, rather, for use as title-pages or frontispieces to books or printed music. The printing of music from engraved plates was becoming common by the 1540s, and this enabled composers to begin to address the general public as well as their own employers. Some publications of music began to appear with engraved frontispiece portraits, undoubtedly intended to enhance the attractiveness of these publications to potential purchasers. In 1553, a musical instruction manual by the Spanish composer Diego Ortiz was published in Rome; on the title-page is a portrait of Ortiz by an anonymous engraver. In 1565, an anonymous engraved portrait of the French composer Jean Maillard appeared as the frontispiece for the Paris publication of a collection of his motets, the *Modulorum Ioannis Maillardi*. Three years later, in 1568, Massimo Troiano, a composer, singer, and writer working at the Bavarian Hofkapelle in Munich under Orlando di Lasso, published a book describing the wedding festivities of Duke Wilhelm V and Renée of Lorraine; the second edition of this work, published in Venice the following year, contains a frontispiece portrait of Troiano by the Venetian engraver and printseller Niccolò Nelli, apparently the first engraved portrait of a composer by an identified artist.

Through the end of the sixteenth century, musical portrait prints remain uncommon, although there are a few portraits of composers among the many portraits engraved by members of the Sadeler and Kilian families of printmakers. Early in the seventeenth century, two notable composers' portraits were made by important artists: Claude Mellan's 1619 engraving of Girolamo Frescobaldi, and the 1624 portrait of Jan Pieterszoon Sweelinck by the Dutch Mannerist engraver Jan Muller. These portraits were produced as independent prints. It should be noted, however, that both composers would have been known in their day not primarily as composers, but as executants. Frescobaldi was famed as a keyboard player; in 1607 he became organist at S. Maria in Trastevere, and shortly afterwards he was appointed organist of the Cappella Giulia at St. Peter's. His fame spread throughout Europe, and the German keyboard player and composer Johann Jacob Froberger came to study with him for four years. Sweelinck likewise was known in his lifetime primarily as a keyboardist. For more than forty years he was organist at the Oude Kerk in Amsterdam, where his brilliant improvisations on the organ and the harpsichord earned him the nickname "The Orpheus of Amsterdam."

The second half of the seventeenth century saw a flourishing of portrait engraving in France, within which Gerard Edelinck's portraits of Jean-Baptiste Lully and the opera composer André Campra stand out. Again, however, these portraits would have been executed not simply because of their subjects' fame as composers, but because of their connection with the court or the church. Edelinck himself was court engraver to Louis XIV; Campra was for a few years *maître de musique* (composer and conductor) at Notre Dame in Paris and later a *sous-maître* at the royal chapel, and Lully was for the last twenty-five years of his life *maître de la musique de la famille royale* (music teacher to members of the royal family).

The institution of public concerts began in England in the 1660s, stimulated by a number of factors—the restoration of the monarchy in 1660, the enthusiasm of Londoners for foreign fashion, and the arrival of many musicians from the Continent, who saw London as a place of opportunity. The first public music-room in London opened in 1689, and public concerts were soon being advertised in newspapers. Musical evenings existed in Paris by 1678, and the *concert spirituel* was founded in 1725. The musical interests of the aristocracy and the emerging bourgeoisie began to have more and more in common over time, but the existence of public concerts did not yet result in any large demand for portraits of composers. Musical portrait prints were still not common in the first decades of the eighteenth century, and one of the most beautiful of all composer portraits—the engraving of Jean-Féry Rebel by Jean Moyreau, done in the 1720s (Figure 11.1)—owes its existence to an unusual circumstance. Jean de Jullienne, a wealthy art collector who owned many works by Jean-Antoine Watteau, commissioned a series of etchings and engravings after all of Watteau's paintings and drawings following the artist's death in 1721. These reproductive prints were published in a set of volumes known as the *Recueil Jullienne*. The beautiful print of Rebel thus has come down to us only because Watteau happened to draw a portrait of his friend the year before he, Watteau, died. Part of the attractiveness of this image is that it is not a formal portrait; rather, it depicts Rebel seated at a harpsichord, with pen in hand, writing, and turning his head to look out expectantly at the viewer, as if to answer a question that has just been posed.

By 1705, the Italian opera was becoming fashionable in London as a place to be seen by the *beau monde*. The Royal Academy of Music, which produced George

Frideric Handel's operas, was organized in 1719, and the rival Opera of the Nobility in 1733. Not only did London have a flourishing musical life by this time, but it was in the process of overtaking Paris as the center of the art world. Print publishing grew into a major business, and the ownership of prints was said to demonstrate "possession of taste and knowledge of fashion."[1] By the middle of the century, portraits of composers *as* composers were regularly appearing in the marketplace. The development of mezzotint, which was highly suited to the reproduction of paintings and was much used in England throughout the eighteenth century, resulted in many attractive portrait prints. Handel, Giovanni Bononcini, and Attilio Ariosti, three of the most important opera composers working in London, were all portrayed in mezzotint portraits, as were Nicola Cosimi and, later, Thomas Arne and Samuel Wesley.

The place of Handel in the history of musical portraiture is unique. After the decline of the Italian opera in London in the late 1730s, Handel turned to writing oratorios; indeed, he was the creator of the English oratorio. It was these works, and particularly the hugely successful *Messiah*, that secured for him a fame and popularity in England that last to this day. Although only five portrait prints of Handel (as well as several caricatures) were done during his lifetime, his popularity continued to grow after his death. In 1784 a Handel Commemoration was held in London, inaugurating a tradition of performances of *Messiah* with huge choruses, a tradition that lasted for a century and a half. This Commemoration spawned the publication of many new portraits of Handel. As Handel himself became an English institution, a small industry in portrait prints of the composer developed, which was to last until well into the nineteenth century. Needless to say, all of these posthumous portraits were based on prior models, and none of them offers anything new for the Handel iconography.

On the Continent, as well as in England, portraits of composers *as* composers began to appear with some frequency in the second quarter of the eighteenth century. Many of the later Baroque composers were portrayed in prints—Corelli, Vivaldi, Telemann, and Rameau, among others. Johann Sebastian Bach, the greatest of all Baroque composers, was never the subject of a portrait print during his lifetime, undoubtedly because he spent the last twenty-seven years of his life working as a church musician in Leipzig, and not in a major musical center such as London, Paris, Berlin, or even nearby Dresden. In the second half of the century a number of important French engravers produced portraits of composers: Jean Daullé (a portrait of Carlos Seixas), Simon Charles Miger (Gluck), Jean-Michel Moreau (Grétry), Louis-Jacques Cathelin (Antonio Sacchini and Niccolò Piccinni), and especially Augustin de Saint-Aubin (Gluck, Sacchini, Philidor, Mondonville, and Carl Friedrich Abel).

Early in 1764, Jean-Baptiste Delafosse made an engraving that can claim to be the most famous musical portrait print of all time: a portrait of the seven-year-old Mozart performing music with his father, Leopold, and his sister, Nannerl. In June of 1763 Leopold and his family set out from Salzburg on a three-year tour of Europe, with Paris and London as their major destinations. While they were in Paris, Louis Carrogis (known as "Carmontelle"), an artist in the employ of the Duke of Orléans, drew a watercolor portrait of Leopold and his children, and Delafosse immediately thereafter made his engraving from the watercolor. Leopold purchased from Delafosse a large number of impressions of the engraving, which he handed out as souvenirs on the family's subsequent travels. In 1765, when the family was in London, he presented an impression to the Trustees of the recently established British Museum, along with copies of Wolfgang's first two published compositions. This print has been reproduced endlessly in biographies of Mozart and in general histories of music, making the child prodigy almost a more familiar figure than the mature composer. (Only one portrait print of the adult Mozart appeared during his lifetime.)

The public concert came later to Vienna than to London and Paris. The first concert society in Vienna, the Tonkünstler-Societät, was formed in 1771; the popular concerts in the Augarten began in 1775; and the Gesellschaft der Musikfreunde was founded in 1808. Many members of the ruling Habsburg family were accomplished musicians, as were many of the aristocracy, both men and women, and Vienna at this time was an extraordinarily musical society. Haydn's fame, as a composer of symphonies and string quartets, had spread throughout Europe by the 1780s, and two of the most important portrait prints of him, by Francesco Bartolozzi and William Daniell, were made in London as a result of Haydn's visits there in 1791–92 and 1794–95, where he had a huge popular success. In Vienna itself a prosperous trade in musical portraits developed. The increase in public performances created an increased demand for portraits, and many of the music publishing houses, most notably Artaria & Co., began to commission artists to engrave portraits of important composers and performers, which they sold as a sideline to their main business of selling printed music. Many of the engravers engaged for these tasks were not major artists, and often their names are hardly known today, but they generally had an unexceptionable technical competence, and produced many highly attractive portraits. Among the most prolific makers of composer portraits at this time were Johann Joseph Neidl, Josef Lanzedelly, Friedrich Wilhelm Bollinger, Karl Riedel, and Josef Teltscher.

Beethoven's fame began to spread in the first decade of the nineteenth century, when he was in his thirties, and a number of portrait prints of him appeared during his lifetime, one of the most important being the 1814 stipple engraving by Blasius Höfel, after a drawing by Louis Letronne. Joseph Steinmüller's engraving, done for Artaria & Co. in 1827, the year of Beethoven's death, after an 1824 drawing by Stefan Decker, was considered by Carl Czerny to be the most faithful printed portrait of the composer.

Two series of composer portraits from the early nineteenth century deserve mention. In Paris, Edme Quenedey issued a series of portraits in etching and aquatint, from about 1808 to 1813, including Boieldieu, Dussek, Rodolphe Kreutzer, Méhul, Paër, Spontini, and Steibelt. These portraits were "physionotraces," done in profile by having the subject sit in a large box, a form of camera obscura, in which his image was projected onto a flat surface, from which a drawing was then made. In Munich Heinrich von Wintter published a series of eighty-eight portraits of composers, from 1815 to 1821, including many contemporaries, although some were posthumous portraits of musicians from the eighteenth century and earlier.

At the end of the eighteenth century an event occurred that was to have a profound effect not only on musical portraiture, but on print production in general, the publishing industry, and particularly music publishing: namely, the invention of lithography, around 1798, by the Bavarian Alois Senefelder. A lithograph is produced not from an incised or etched copper plate, but from a smoothed slab of limestone, on which an image has been drawn. From an artistic standpoint, drawing an image on the stone requires far less technical skill than engraving or etching a copper plate, and from a commercial standpoint, lithography offered a huge advantage over etching and engraving: not only is the process of obtaining each impression from the stone far less time consuming, but a very large number of impressions can be made. By contrast, etched or engraved copper plates start to wear out fairly quickly, sometimes after only a few impressions.

It was to be a couple of decades before Senefelder's invention came into general commercial use. In 1814, the Mühlhausen native Gottfried Engelmann went to Munich to learn the technique of lithography from Senefelder himself; later that year, he opened a lithographic publishing firm in his home-town, which was so successful that by June 1816 he had opened a branch in Paris. In the following year, Charles Motte started his own firm in Paris, and around the same time François-Séraphin Delpech followed suit. In the second quarter of the nineteenth century, the City of Light was indeed the glittering musical capital of the world, with Liszt, Chopin, Berlioz, Rossini, Meyerbeer, Auber, Adam, Hérold, and a host of other composers and performers competing for the favor of the public. This time and place saw the most considerable production of musical portrait prints ever, with the growth in the concert-going middle class, the concentration of musical talent, and the development of the lithographic process all combining to drive up demand and create the means of supply.

As the demand for portraits of favorite composers, instrumentalists, and singers (as well as actors, writers, and political figures) grew throughout the 1830s and 1840s, some lithographers turned out hundreds of portraits. In this age of *bel canto* and of virtuoso pianists and violinists, portraits of singers and instrumentalists abounded, but many composers achieved a level of fame equal to that of the great performers and were often depicted in prints—Rossini, Meyerbeer, Spontini, Berlioz, Boieldieu, Adam, and Auber being some of the most popular. Among the best portrait lithographers working in Paris at this time were Achille Devéria, Henri Grévedon, Pierre Roch Vigneron, and the Maurin brothers, Nicolas-Eustache and Antoine.

Franz Liszt, who was based in Paris from 1823 to 1847 (although often away on tour), is believed to have been portrayed more often in paintings, drawings, and prints than any other musician. An astounding virtuoso, and hardly averse to showmanship, he was lionized in Paris; he also concertized widely throughout Europe, from Portugal to Russia, to large and enthusiastic crowds. A child prodigy, he was performing in public by the age of ten, and the first portrait prints of him began to appear around that time. Although we tend to think of Liszt today as a composer, it was the virtuoso pianist whose portrait was in such demand during his lifetime.

The art of caricature flourished in Paris in the middle decades of the nineteenth century. In addition to Daumier, one of the great artists of his time, a number of other artists turned out large quantities of caricatures, among the most important of these artists being Gavarni (Hippolyte-Guillaume-Sulpice Chevalier), Gustave Doré, Cham (Amédée-Charles-Henry de Noé), Nadar (Gaspard-Félix Tournachon), and Étienne Carjat. Musicians who seemed to lend themselves to caricature, such as Rossini, Berlioz, Offenbach, and Wagner, were the subjects of many amusing sheets. Carjat did a number of large, full-page caricatures for various Parisian journals, including among his subjects Gounod, Berlioz, Meyerbeer, Offenbach, Rossini, and Félicien David.

Perhaps the most important, and certainly the most prolific, of all portrait lithographers was the Viennese artist Josef Kriehuber. Although he produced landscapes and other subjects in oils and watercolor, he is remembered today entirely for his portrait lithographs, of which he produced perhaps as many as three thousand. More than 130 of these are musical subjects. Kriehuber's career as a portraitist began to flourish around 1827, and his output peaked in the 1840s and 1850s. Much in demand, he often received as much as one hundred gulden for a portrait, a handsome sum in those days. He did portraits of local Viennese musicians as well as of musicians based in Paris and other cities. Some subjects he portrayed multiple times, including above all Liszt, meriting eight portraits from 1838 to 1856.

If the heyday of musical portraiture, and portrait prints in general, was ushered in by the invention of lithography, it was ushered out by another invention: photography. Several photographic processes had been invented by 1840, but, like lithography, photography took some time to become commercially feasible. By the middle of the century, however, photographs were being sold on the market, and in 1851 at an exhibition in Paris prizes were awarded in the category of portrait photography. This new invention eventually brought an end to reproductive printmaking, and its effect on portraiture was sudden and dramatic. Some artists adapted by taking up the new technique. The caricaturists Nadar and Carjat both became photographers; Nadar had a studio shortly after mid-century, and Carjat opened his studio in 1860. Perhaps their experience as caricaturists gave them a particular sensitivity to the portrayal of the human face, but whatever the reason, they became the two most important early French portrait photographers.

Although few interesting musical portrait prints were made in the last thirty or forty years of the nineteenth century, several attractive images are worth noting: for example, the French artist Paul Mathey's beautiful etched portraits of Lalo, Saint-Saëns, and Benjamin Godard from around 1889 or shortly after. Mathey produced most of his prints in editions of forty impressions and never sold any, so they are seldom encountered today. In England, Sir William Rothenstein did lithographic portraits of Charles Villiers Stanford and C. Hubert H. Parry, both in 1897.

In the first two decades of the twentieth century, portrait printmaking flowered in Vienna and Berlin. Both cities enjoyed vibrant musical cultures, with Gustav Mahler in charge of the court opera in Vienna and Arthur Nikisch the conductor of the Berlin Philharmonic. Emil Orlik—a native of Prague, who moved to Vienna in 1899 and exhibited with the Vienna Secession—did a number of musical portraits, the best known being his 1902 portrait of Mahler. He also portrayed Richard Strauss, Eugen d'Albert, Alexander Zemlinsky, and Wilhelm Furtwängler. Also active in Vienna at this time was Ferdinand Schmutzer, likewise a member of the Vienna Secession. Highly successful as a portraitist, he etched portraits of Joseph Joachim, Richard Strauss, Karl Goldmark, Hugo Wolf, and, among other non-musical personages, Freud, Einstein, Arthur Schnitzler, and the Emperor Franz Josef.

In Berlin, Hermann Struck, a member of the Berlin Secession, enjoyed great demand as a portraitist. He depicted many famous contemporaries, including Freud, Einstein, Ibsen, Nietzsche, and Oscar Wilde. His 1904 etching of Arthur Nikisch is a fine example of his ability as a portrait etcher. Finally, Ernst Oppler, born in Hanover, moved to Berlin in 1905, where he too became a member of the Secession. Like Schmutzer and Struck, he was in high demand as a portraitist, some of his musical subjects being Nikisch, Ermanno Wolf-Ferrari, and his friend Ferruccio Busoni. Not all of the portraits by these etchers went into the trade; many of them were done for the subjects themselves, presumably to be given out from time to time as gifts. Consequently, these portraits are sometimes fairly scarce, and when they do turn up, they are frequently signed by the subject.

Outside of Vienna and Berlin, not many musical portrait prints can be found from the early twentieth century. Despite many of the German Expressionists being prolific and innovative printmakers, their work includes extremely few interesting musical portraits. Conrad Felixmüller did a very fine portrait of Arnold Schoenberg in etching and drypoint in 1914 (just before Felixmüller's seventeenth birthday), and ten years later a large and impressive woodcut of Erwin Schulhoff. Max Beckmann made a lithographic portrait of Frederick Delius when that composer was visiting Frankfurt in the fall of 1922.

Elsewhere, the Scottish etcher William Strang, a prolific portraitist, depicted many of his famous contemporaries, including two musicians, Joseph Joachim and the conductor Hans Richter. The American etcher Arthur W. Heintzelman etched a number of plates of musical subjects, including four fantasies on Beethoven and three contemporary portraits (of the conductors Arturo Toscanini, Serge Koussevitsky, and Charles Munch). In France, the great caricaturist Jean Veber did an amusing lithographic portrait of the composer and pianist Gottfried Galston, looking rather fey as he performs for an audience of old ladies; this is ironic, for Galston, a protégé of Ferruccio Busoni, was a highly serious and intellectual musician, whose programs included the late Beethoven sonatas, Brahms's Handel Variations, and much Bach. The English artist John Copley produced an imposing etching in 1946 of a song recital that had taken place at Wigmore Hall the previous year, with Pierre Bernac singing, Francis Poulenc playing the piano, and Felix Aprahamian turning the pages for Poulenc. As a general matter, however, musical portrait prints in the twentieth century are only to be found here and there. This is undoubtedly due to a combination of circumstances—the waning of interest in classical music, the decline of print collecting, and artists' lack of interest in producing portrait prints. There remains, nevertheless, a rich legacy of portrait prints that allows us a glimpse at many of the composers of the past four-and-a-half centuries.

Note

1 Timothy Clayton, *The English Print 1688–1802* (New Haven and London: Yale University Press, 1997), xii.

Further Reading

There is almost no literature devoted specifically to musical portrait prints. There are catalogues raisonnés of the works of many printmakers, a list of which can be found on the website of the Print Council of America. Among the most fertile sources for illustrations of musical portrait prints are the iconographical studies devoted to particular musicians, of which four outstanding examples are listed below.

Bergquist, Stephen A. *Musical Prints 1568–1949*. Exhibition catalogue. Storrs: The William Benton Museum of Art, University of Connecticut, 2011.
Bory, Robert. *Ludwig van Beethoven: His Life and His Work in Pictures*. Zurich: Atlantis, 1960.
Burger, Ernst. *Franz Liszt: A Chronicle of His Life in Pictures and Documents*. Princeton: Princeton University Press, 1989.

Deutsch, Otto Erich. *Mozart und seine Welt in zeitgenössischen Bildern*. Kassel: Bärenreiter, 1961.

Kinsky, Georg. *A History of Music in Pictures*. London: Dent, 1930.

Kobbé, Gustav. "A Collection of Musicians' Portraits." *The Print-Collector's Quarterly* 5, no. 1 (February 1915): 84–108.

Somfai, László. *Joseph Haydn: His Life in Contemporary Pictures*. New York: Taplinger, 1969.

12

MUSIC, SYMBOLISM, AND ALLEGORY

Ayla Lepine

A symbol is an image or an object that represents something other than its own form, whether by convention, association, or resemblance. A triangular emblem may represent the Christian Trinity, or a particular flower may represent loyalty, mourning, or purity. Allegories are more complex. An allegory is an image or cluster of objects that may represent an abstract concept. A book may symbolize knowledge and a sword may be a symbol of strength. Taken together in a complex pictorial framework, which may also include references to literature and cultural context, symbols may support delicate allegories. In Raphael's painting *An Allegory* of 1504, which the National Gallery in London acquired in 1847 and which inspired numerous modern British painters, two women stand on either side of a sleeping knight who lies beneath a bay tree. In relation to a Roman first-century poem well known to Raphael and his contemporaries, these figures and their attributes arguably construct a cohesive allegory of a man's choice between Virtue and Pleasure.

Music, instruments, and the suggestion of melody and sound in visual culture have often been deployed to proclaim symbolic and allegorical meanings. This chapter will explore the capacity for aspects of music to be symbolic or to contribute meaning in an intricate pictorial allegory within nineteenth-century British visual culture. There are numerous trajectories, even within this single period and within the concentrated zone of relating music to symbol and allegory, that an assessment of Victorian approaches to music in visual culture could take. Working with material that interlinks the ideas and works of Victorian artists such as Julia Margaret Cameron, Edward Burne-Jones, George Frederic Watts, and the instrument maker Arnold Dolmetsch, this object-based strategy creates an assemblage of material that speaks to music's allegorical and symbolic potential for British artists.

One of the defining characteristics of the emergence of modern sensibilities in art, architecture, and design—and indeed in music—during the nineteenth century is the conscious notion of art's ability to transcend materiality, speak to the soul, align sensory and emotional experience in new ways, and aspire to the Romantic conception of symbolism. Symbolism, in this context, offered a unity between "form and content, word and world, art and life."[1] Symbolism as a trajectory in European modern art grew out of literature and soon lodged itself in art practices that privileged non-naturalistic representation and visionary moods as a method of declaring emotional content and an artist's personal expression. Its close connection with the British Aesthetic Movement's quest for beauty and its invest-ment in "art for art's sake" prompted new modes of image-making that prioritized sensuousness and intensity of feeling.

This quality in late-nineteenth-century art was an aesthetic shared by many, including the photographer Julia Margaret Cameron and the painters George Frederic Watts, Dante Gabriel Rossetti, and Edward Burne-Jones. The painters' intensely colored, mythologically and allegorically driven dreamscape canvases offered environments interlaced with music, literature, and historicism. Elizabeth Prettejohn has argued persuasively that Rossetti's allegorical work is informed by Dante's view that "interpretation may discover a literal, an allegorical, a moral and a spiritual significance in turn."[2] Rossetti's adoption and secularization of Dante's layers of interpretation uncoupled the power of allegory from the necessity of theol-ogy, however. A portrait of Jane Morris, William Morris's wife, could also stand as a Victorian artist's response to the legacy of Botticelli and the Italian Renaissance, as well as being an allegory of compassion, beauty, love, or art, and none of these powerful associations would necessarily supersede the other.

Music as Muse

In 1863, Julia Margaret Cameron acquired a camera. She had been experiment-ing with photography on the Isle of Wight for some time before she received this object as a Christmas present, but a camera of her own marked a key moment of transition toward her artistic vocation. By 1865, she had produced numerous series of images and had converted her domestic spaces, including a coal store and a small greenhouse, into sites for photographic production. She had become a member of the Photographic Societies of London and Scotland, made carbon prints of her more popular works, exhibited increasingly widely, and forged strong relationships with the British Museum and the museum at South Kensington. In the same year, the London dealers Colnaghi became her official agent. In this momentous year that saw Cameron's emergence as a prominent figure in photographic circles, she posed two young girls on either side of a bearded, sage-like figure in a garden on the Isle of Wight (Figure 12.1). The two girls are Elizabeth and Alice Keown. The bearded man with fingers thrust in and around the body of a violin is George Fred-eric Watts. The photograph's title is *The Whisper of the Muse*. The captivating stare of a Keown sister beckons to the viewer from the lower left corner of the image. Her gaze meets ours and draws us in, making the viewer witness to a moment that takes place in the private encounter between the musician (Watts) and the girl-muse (the other Keown sister). The leaves in the muse's hair, which flows out of the boundary of the top right corner of the photograph, create a border with the ivy clinging to the garden wall, framing her face and the musician's. The diagonal com-position of these three faces, one inviting, one listening, one whispering, is echoed in the placement of the violin at a gentle incline in the lower third of the image. Hands too—his two on the body and neck of the instrument, the muse's gently resting on his shoulder—assemble in a diagonal relation. The allegorical quality of photography itself and the importance of children in Cameron's art-making have been articulately explored by the art historian Carol Armstrong, who argues that Cameron repeatedly used children's bodies to allegorize photography as an exten-sion of maternal, feminine love. If Watts as painter becomes musician-artist for the purpose of allegorizing unplayed music as expectant inspiration in relation to the presence of children as muses, then Cameron's own relationship to the child-muse is figured in the photographic image she creates. In Armstrong's view, Cameron's photographs repeatedly oscillate "between outward bodily reference and inward self-reference: which is to say, between the indexically traced photographic referent, the fleshly body (of the child), and the allegorized evidence of the materiality of the photographic process."[3]

To audiences in 1865, the bearded figure with his violin in the appealingly blurred, light-streaked image would have been a very familiar face. Watts was ascending to the acme of his painting career in the 1860s. If the image, concentrating on the expectant hope for inspiration from an external, youthful, divine source, could be connected with any visible art in order to make its point, why would Cameron have chosen an unplayed violin, grasped with fingers interlacing the strings at their highest point above the instrument's hollow chamber? My contention is that with this provocative image that made the familiar strange, turning a celebrated painter into an anonymous musician and two family friends into divine bodies proffering inspiration, Cameron achieved an allegory of creativity itself, in all its potential and frustration, and inserted her photographic practice into a cross-media artistic interest in images of, about, or evocative of music. Age and youth, nature and culture, painting and music are all interlaced like the winding of Watts's fingers through the violin's taut strings.

Music as Longing

The poet and critic Algernon Charles Swinburne wrote *Laus Veneris* in 1866. Its stanzas praising Venus were conceived as an intensive and controversially visceral response to the medieval Tannhäuser epic, in which a knight is seduced by Venus and, repentant, then rides to Rome to purify his soul, leaving the lovesick love goddess in the Venusburg, surrounded by attendants who attempt to cheer her. The same story was a primary inspiration for Richard Wagner, whose opera was performed in London when Burne-Jones was painting his own representation of *Laus Veneris* in the 1870s. Swinburne and Burne-Jones knew one another well. Swinburne's emphasis on the merging of senses allows for permeable readings between sound, touch, smell, and sight:

> ... Her beds are full of perfume and sad sound,
> Her doors are made with music and barred round
> With singing and with laughter and with tears ...[4]

In Swinburne's writing, the structural elements of the Venusburg are musical, aligning the ineffable qualities of melody and rhythm with architecture. Following on Burne-Jones's attentiveness to Swinburne's alliance between music and space, Burne-Jones's representation of that space is suffused with music, and music is the primary material for its construction. Regarding construction and inspiration, it is notable that Burne-Jones's work from the 1870s onward has recently been described as "a coherent whole, harmonized around a color chord of silvery and golden shades."[5] Indeed, Burne-Jones himself wrote of his plans for a tapestry depicting the Adoration of the Kings (now at Exeter College Chapel, Oxford):

"It will be a blaze of color and look like a carol."[6] Burne-Jones's work is akin to a silvery-golden chord, a harmony of visuality, and this allows for a further link with a provocative argument for the interpretation of art as soundscape in nineteenth-century criticism. In Walter Pater's essay "The School of Giorgione," part of his influential collection of writings, *The Renaissance*, Pater claimed that "all art constantly aspires towards the condition of music."[7] The claim that music perpetually drives development, refinement, and improvement across the arts by setting itself as their hope and their goal is especially suggestive in relation to allegory, as music then becomes an allegory of artistic perfection in Pater's ideological system: that to which all else in creative output strives, not because it is compelled, but because it is impelled. In Pater's observation, music's abstract, inexpressible, ungraspable quality stands for the hope of art, the quest to represent the unrepresentable, and the ascent toward beauty.

Andrew Eastham's provocative research, which relates Walter Pater's writing on Giorgione to "acoustic space," posits that Pater's interpretation of Giorgione's *Fête Champêtre* "establishes a series of transitions between the motion of water, the progress of sound waves, the shape of the landscape, and the felt experience of air."[8] In Eastham's analysis, music is a vehicle by which the flat surface of the canvas opens out into a three-dimensional vision, not unlike the interrelation between Swinburne's and Burne-Jones's visions of Venus in their *Laus Veneris* projects, where music is the constructive material of architecture. Eastham writes that for Pater, "the presence of sound in air is able to overcome the limits of the plastic medium (the fixed body in space) and retrieve the plenitude of space for the flat surface of painting."[9]

Among Swinburne's contributions to British poetry was his invention of the roundel poetic form, based on French Renaissance poetic traditions. His first roundel, composed for the poet Christina Rossetti, references the role of music, sound, and vision in relation to cyclical ring (and ringing) lingual structures. Its inward-looking method of description produces a poem-as-symbol, wherein the musical and visual references bolster the symbolic conception of movement through a circular form:

> A roundel is wrought as a ring or a starbright sphere,
> With craft of delight and with cunning of sound unsought,
> That the heart of the hearer may smile if to pleasure his ear
> A roundel is wrought.
>
> Its jewel of music is carven of all or of aught –
> Love, laughter, or mourning – remembrance of rapture or fear
> That fancy may fashion to hang in the ear of thought.
>
> As a bird's quick song runs round, and the hearts in us hear
> Pause answer to pause, and again the same strain caught,
> So moves the device whence, round as a pearl or tear,
> A roundel is wrought.[10]

In Edward Burne-Jones's painting *Laus Veneris*, first exhibited in 1878, the alternate cascading swaths of reds and blues languidly direct the eye across a strongly horizontal surface. A densely ornamented interior confronts the viewer, and the figures are tightly anchored within rich decorative zones, from the intense hatching of the floor matting strewn with instruments and flowers, to the tapestries depicting Venus and Cupid triumphant that line the walls of this claustrophobic divine fantasy. The right side of the picture is dominated by Venus in bold, scaly orange folds of drapery, crown in lap, her entire body expressing a weary frustration. To the left, a group of women in sumptuous semi-classical garb prepare to play reed instruments and chime bells, following an illuminated hymnal or missal which Burne-Jones has populated with fragments of Latin, Old French, and square notation. Their text begins, "Laus Veneris ..." Through the window, in a world that seems simultaneously close and impossibly distant, knights can be seen arriving at the Venusburg, presumably to search for their comrade, who has abandoned Venus for penance. A mixture of legible and illegible text and square notation on the exposed pages of the illuminated manuscript is in play with the ambiguity and poetic references set in relation to one another in Burne-Jones's image. There are at least two literary models, the Tannhäuser story and Swinburne's poem, that underpin the image. And yet the image refuses an easy relationship with either of these textual sources. In order to elicit a legible meaning, we must turn to an allegorical framework, in which the poetry, set to unknown music and not yet played or sung, both praises and laments the condition of love. Within the image as a whole, symbols and emblems of music's presence together perform as an allegory for dissatisfaction and loss in the midst of sensuous reverie.

In his article "Visuality and Unmediation in Burne-Jones," art historian David Peters Corbett has lucidly argued that Burne-Jones's image is "all surface," in which time seems suspended and cloistered female space gives way to a meditation on inactivity paired with the expectation of movement and music.[11] Instruments and pages of red and black notation are present, but all remain unplayed. The absence of sound, heightened by the presence of instruments and the promise of music, positions music itself as a symbol of inhibited action and a barred path. There is no song here; the doors have been crafted with music, but the music of consolation and love is—in Burne-Jones's vision—unplayed.

Music as Love

In 1897, Arnold Dolmetsch designed and made a polygonal clavichord at his studio. This was clavichord "Number 10." He had made his first only three years before, and the appearance of this small revivalist instrument was, in George Bernard Shaw's view, nothing less than a revolution for how the new century might greet history and make something new. In *The World*, Shaw asserted, "He has actually turned out a little masterpiece ... I therefore estimate the birth of this little clavichord as, on a modern computation, about forty thousand times as important as the Handel Festival."[12] The 1897 No. 10 clavichord was commissioned by John William Mackail for his wife, Margaret. Edward Burne-Jones, Margaret Mackail's father, painted its surfaces, inside and out. Dolmetsch designed the instrument with an outer case, and crafted hinged panels so that the clavichord could be played either outside or within the case. Burne-Jones had introduced Dolmetsch to William Morris in 1894, and the three planned to work on a manuscript of 300 songs in the British Museum for the Kelmscott Press. Though this did not come to fruition, Dolmetsch and Morris became close allies, and Morris encouraged Dolmetsch to produce his first harpsichord for the Arts and Crafts Exhibition in 1896. As Morris died that same year, it is possible that Burne-Jones's close involvement in No. 10 a few months later had a memorial quality to it, even as it cemented his family ties with his daughter and son-in-law. The outer case, painted red, has two main decorative zones: a stylized roundel of leafy foliage, curled in on itself like a medieval carved boss, on which "CLAVIS : CORDIUM" is inscribed. The "L" nestles within the first "C" and the "O" within the second "C", the large C-forms themselves echoing the round nest of vegetation from which springs a series of tender shoots with leaves unfurling across the red-painted background of the instrument case. The other side of the case features an image of St. Margaret of Antioch leading a rather diminutive dragon on a loose silken cord, tied around its neck like a leash. Predator has become pet. Between these two decorative elements is a Latin inscription, the translation of which is:

> Into me, so that I might rejoice or mourn,
> the artificer put sound. Me the ancient flower
> of the muses, the muse arouses from Death.
> Once more therefore the disused voice sounds
> weeping, sounds joyfully, whenever Margaret opens
> the Clavichord.[13]

In Dolmetsch's 1915 publication, *The Interpretation of the Music of the Sixteenth and Seventeenth Centuries*, he explained that the clavichord "possesses a soul, or rather seems to have one, for under the fingers of some gifted player it reflects every shade of the player's feelings as a faithful mirror."[14] The instrument—due to its scale, the way in which it was built, and its lack of hammers, stops, pedals, or other "mechanical aid to variety of tone"—was perceived by Dolmetsch as an extension of the body and the sensibility of the player.[15] As a reflection, evocation, or even musical symbol for the self, the behavior of the clavichord in relation to a player's touch, and the symbolic resonances of its decoration, were particularly symbiotic. The decorative program for this clavichord makes its ownership and its status as a multi-authored project given from three men—friend–maker, father–decorator, husband–patron—to one woman, intimately connected with the identity of its recipient. Each of the decorative patterns, figures, and inscriptions indicates aspects of Margaret Mackail and her identity in relation to music, art, history, and symbolism.

Music as Regeneration

Starting in the 1870s, Burne-Jones developed a range of pictures with sound and music as core elements. The most monumental and articulate of these is his *Sleep of Arthur in Avalon*, which he began in 1881 and continued to work on until his death in 1898. In the summer of 1897, conversing with his studio assistant Thomas Rooke while he painted, Burne-Jones remarked: "It is a pity I was not born in the Middle Ages." Rooke responded, "Yes, it would have suited you exactly."[16] Edward Burne-Jones and William Morris had known each other since they were students in the 1850s, and, like many in their circle, they were captivated by medievalism. The vast

Sleep of Arthur in Avalon, measuring 6.5 by 3 meters, required Burne-Jones to rent the largest studio he could find, in Campden Hill in London. The picture's subject derives from Book 21 in Sir Thomas Malory's fifteenth-century *Morte d'Arthur*, in which "some men yet say that King Arthur is not dead, but hid away by the will of our Lord Jesus Christ into another place; and men say that he will come again."[17] Wounded in a battle with Mordred, Arthur is transported to Avalon, laid out on a catafalque, and surrounded (in Burne-Jones's image) by a solid Byzantine-inspired canopy featuring gilded panels that tell the legend of Arthur's activities and the narrative of the quest for the Holy Grail. (The latter subject also occupied Burne-Jones throughout the 1880s and 1890s.) Arthur's head rests in the lap of his half-sister Morgan le Fay as the queens of Northgalis and the Waste Lands look on. Surrounding this group is a further set of figures, who hold instruments. Watchers look into the distance with long horns at the ready, intending to sound a blast when Arthur wakes. Female figures in the middle ground hold instruments that, crucially, have no strings. The collection of symbols, from the flowers in the foreground to the grail imagery surrounding the sleeping king's body, collate together with the unplayable instruments to form an allegory of mourning and, more powerfully and suggestively, of expectation. This is an image that embodies a semi-death in relation to the faint but present hope of resurrection. The body of Arthur does not rise from sleep; the instruments held by the women will only gain strings in a world in which the king awakes.

Both *Laus Veneris* and *The Sleep of Arthur in Avalon* are meditations on the anxiety of teleology. They are suspended endings. Burne-Jones's exploration of music's meanings in his visual worlds led toward a pictorial embodiment of the fermata, if not of silence itself. A perpetual state, relieved perhaps in future but for now an aching constant, was made more still and yet more intensely anticipatory by the insistence on narrative moments and representational vigor, whether in the story of Arthur or the story of Tannhäuser. Music comes to perform a rich lack, in which the infusion of music within a pictorial composition symbolizes absence. The sleeping body and the languid body, resonant with death and regeneration, activate meanings that cannot be separated from the anxieties of absence and loss. Burne-Jones had focused on this theme as early as the 1860s, when he produced two wedding presents. One was a wardrobe painted for William and Jane Morris, with scenes from Chaucer's Prioress's Tale, in which a dead boy is revived by the Virgin Mary with a grain of corn. The other was a piano for his own wife, Georgiana, on which the panel beneath the keyboard was painted with a crowned figure of Death, standing outside a garden where several young women are sleeping. Toward the end of the artist's life, *The Sleep of Arthur in Avalon* become a symbol of Burne-Jones's own inevitable death. He wrote to his wife from his studio in 1898, "I am at Avalon, not yet in Avalon."[18]

Sight and touch are the boundaries of this exploration of music as allegory and symbol through a short, focused foray into late Victorian visual culture. The role of music in these images and objects, whether marshaled symbolically or allegorically, is to indicate the desire to hear and be heard, to listen for what cannot yet be heard, and to have that listening and hearing experience be one that transports the body and the mind beyond the material zone of the printed page, the painted canvas—or the smooth wooden surface of a new clavichord, whose wood was silent in life but sings in death.

Notes

1 Elizabeth Prettejohn, *Art for Art's Sake: Aestheticism in Victorian Painting* (London: Yale University Press, 2007), 230.
2 Ibid., 231.
3 Carol Armstrong, "Cupid's Pencil of Light: Julia Margaret Cameron and the Maternalization of Photography," *October* 76 (Spring 1996): 119.
4 Algernon Charles Swinburne, *Laus Veneris* (1866), http://www.victorianweb.org/authors/swinburne/laus.html [accessed 10 October 2012].
5 Stephen Calloway and Lynn Federle Orr, eds., *The Cult of Beauty: The Aesthetic Movement 1860–1900*, exh. cat. (London: V&A Publishing, 2011), 238.
6 Georgiana Burne-Jones, *The Memorials of Edward Burne-Jones* (London: Macmillan, 1904), 2: 176.
7 Walter Pater, *The Renaissance*, ed. Donald L. Hill (Berkeley: University of California Press, 1980), 106.
8 Andrew Eastham, "Walter Pater's Acoustic Space: The School of Giorgione, Dionysian *Andersstreben*, and the Politics of Soundscape," *Yearbook of English Studies* 40 (2010): 205.
9 Ibid.
10 Algernon Charles Swinburne, *A Century of Roundels* (London: Chatto and Windus, 1883), 52.
11 David Peters Corbett, "Visuality and Unmediation in Burne-Jones's *Laus Veneris*," *Art History* 24, no. 1 (February 2001): 83–102.
12 Quoted in Margaret Campbell, *Dolmetsch: The Man and His Work* (London: Hamish Hamilton, 1975), 83.
13 See Anne Stutchbury, "Instruments of Femininity: The Arnold Dolmetsch Clavichords of 1897, Nos. 8 and 10" (MA thesis, University of Sussex, 2011), 23.
14 Quoted in Mabel Dolmetsch, *Personal Recollections of Albert Dolmetsch* (London: Routledge and Kegan Paul, 1958), 11.
15 Ibid., 12.
16 Mary Lago, ed., *Burne-Jones Talking* (London: Murray, 1982), 90.
17 Quoted in Alison Smith, *The Sleep of Arthur in Avalon*, exh. cat. (London: Tate, 2008), 5.
18 Burne-Jones, *Memorials*, 2: 340.

Further Reading

Armstrong, Carol. "Cupid's Pencil of Light: Julia Margaret Cameron and the Maternalization of Photography," *October* 76 (Spring 1996): 114–141.

Brauchli, Bernard. *The Clavichord*. Cambridge: Cambridge University Press, 1998.

Campbell, Margaret. *Dolmetsch: The Man and His Work*. London: Hamish Hamilton, 1975.

Christian, John. *Symbolists and Decadents*. London: Thames and Hudson, 1977.

Fagence-Cooper, Suzanne. *St Cecilia's Halo: Music, Sex, and Death in Victorian Painting*. Crabapple Press, e-book, 2012.

Prettejohn, Elizabeth. *Art for Art's Sake: Aestheticism in Victorian Painting*. New Haven and London: Yale University Press, 2007.

Prettejohn, Elizabeth, ed. *The Cambridge Companion to the Pre-Raphaelites*. Cambridge: Cambridge University Press, 2012.

Wittkower, Rudolph. *Allegory and the Migration of Symbols*. London: Thames and Hudson, 1987.

13

MUSIC AS ATTRIBUTE
Idea, Image, Sound

Philip Weller

To whom, or what, can the distinctive qualities and characteristics of music be attributed? What type of idea (or person, or event) deserves the epithet "musical," and why? And conversely, how should we attempt by visual means to convey or connote the musical, whether as experience or as object? Through what visual cues or attributes, adroitly deployed by the artist, can musical ideas or experiences be evoked? These questions and others like them serve to make the important point that the "question of attribution" goes both ways. On the one hand we may ask: What types of visual device are able to connote music, and how do they work? What kinds of vocabulary and concepts best aid the viewer in his or her response to depictions of musical subjects? And on the other hand: To what kinds of phenomena, objects, individuals, or contexts do we attribute musical characteristics in the first place, and why?

Music—perhaps better, musicality—can be seen in the first place as a human gift or skill: an attribute of trained musicians, therefore, or of certain kinds of musically informed enthusiast. Yet tradition has always held that music possesses qualities which are in principle available to all, through contemplation and experience, so that the question of musical virtues and attributes needs to be addressed in regard to these larger horizons.

Conversely, music when understood (say) as harmonious proportion might be construed metaphorically as an attribute of the cosmos, or of certain kinds of architecture. Further, the idea of harmony might by extension be applied to human relations, and musical imagery then invoked to support that metaphor. Music has sometimes also been viewed more generally as a kind of complement to mathematics, to the varied permutations and applications of number, and even as an underlying ("latent") cognate of symbolist art and poetry—in the latter case backed up by the beautifully turned, if rather partial and perhaps ultimately misleading dictum of Walter Pater to the effect that all art "constantly aspires towards the condition of music" ("The School of Giorgione," 1877).

All these ways—and more—in which music functions in such a guise as to suggest mutual relationships between different media have the potential to enrich the perceptual and experiential world of music itself. Even if this may often happen in tangential or indirect fashion, music's extreme fitness as an attribute of some other reality or system offers myriad possibilities for associating visual and musical elements of various kinds in productive ways. Musical qualities are what they are, in and for themselves; but by this means they also find a wider applicability and frame of reference. Within this potentially vast field, this essay sets out to explore a few particular strands of connective thinking and artistic practice that will help to illuminate the range of possibilities, offering a range of thought-provoking historical materials and contexts as it does so, in more and less familiar places.

Music as Symbolic Order: A Classical-Medieval-Renaissance Model

To a classical or a medieval mind—one of a learned or poetically imaginative disposition, at least—it was relatively easy to see music as an attribute of the cosmos. To a modern sensibility, this might seem extravagant or simply incomprehensible, until we grasp the idea of the universe as having "beautiful" proportions and "lucid" structures, which, in motion, created the so-called harmony of the spheres. This theory had its critics even in antiquity, and in the Middle Ages it was a topic of discussion within élite clerical or humanistic culture, rather than common knowledge openly shared. But it was widely enough known in the Renaissance to allow a whole raft of English poets, including especially the public voice of Shakespearean theatre, to use it as a source of imagery evoking the beauty of the created order, the "well ordered state," or the "true and harmonious" human mind. In analogous fashion it offered a range of conceits and also deeper points of comparison that could inform a wide variety of lyric and longer poems by Milton, Dryden, and others.

And yet the idea of a linkage between cosmic order ("harmony") and planetary and human music (also "harmony") is a tradition that, while being a touchstone of the Renaissance reappropriation of classical learning in the fifteenth and sixteenth centuries, had also survived through late antiquity and the Middle Ages. The universal view of music which it articulates might be seen not so much as a decorative attribute of the cosmos, but rather as an ordering principle within it. Such a view permits us to interpret unusual images such as the frontispiece to the monumental anthology, kept in Florence since 1456, of French liturgical compositions famously styled the "Magnus Liber Organi" (Great Book of Polyphony; Paris, c. 1245–55; Biblioteca Medicea-Laurenziana, MS. Pluteus 29. 1). This is one of the greatest of all collections of medieval polyphony, and it is doubly striking that the whole magnificently produced volume should have been prefaced with a full-page illumination displaying not something musically anecdotal but a fully philosophical view of music.

The three-tiered framed image is laid out in two columns, with a personified figure of Musica in each of the left-hand niches. On each of the three levels she points with a stick (or wand) towards the right-hand column, where, from top to bottom, we can read the three "orders" of universal music as expounded by Boethius (c. 480–524/25 CE): *musica mundana*, the music of the heavens (shown by planets, stars, tides, the earth); *musica humana*, the music of the human mind and soul (shown by what appears to be a spiritual conversation); and *musica instrumentalis*, actual sounding music (shown by a practical musician playing a *vielle*, surrounded in his studio with a variety of instruments). This intellectual visualization of music, clarified by attributes which refer to the threefold Boethian doctrine, serves to show how important a familiarity with both sides of the representational system is.

A single counter-example will suffice to illustrate a different, but related, use of the system. It occurs, again as a frontispiece, in an English copy of Boethius's *De Musica* (early twelfth century, scriptorium of Christ Church, Canterbury; Cambridge University Library MS. li. 3. 12, fol. 61v). This tinted pen drawing (brown, red, green), laid out as a full-page framed miniature, is divided into four quarters, each quarter depicting a philosopher who was also a music theorist: Boethius himself (top left), facing Pythagoras; and Plato (bottom left), facing Nicomachus. Each figure has a particular stance and a characteristic attribute. Boethius has his monochord, Pythagoras his set of bells and hammers, while Plato and Nicomachus debate energetically with one another, each holding a text inscribed "MVSICA" and raising an index finger to reinforce a verbal point.

There would be hundreds of representations of cosmic harmony and music in the succeeding centuries. Many of them would have distinctive as well as typical features, showing the combination of familiarity and individuality that is a sign of a well-grounded—yet also resourceful, and therefore flexible—tradition.

"Musica" as Image and Idea

The classical system of representation in its Greek and Graeco-Roman form does not really employ a general allegorical figure of "Musica" of the kind that became common in the medieval, Renaissance, and Enlightenment periods. The nearest antiquity came to it was probably the depictions of a lyre-playing Muse that we find on a number of fifth-century BCE red-figure vases, and occasionally also in the form of marble relief sculpture. It shows a robed young woman holding (or playing) a lyre or cithara. This figure-type was later emulated, in Renaissance garb, by Paolo Veronese in his frescoes (c. 1560–61) at the Villa Barbaro, Maser; and it can be seen in a different context as part of a group of Muses around their leader, Apollo, in other depictions: e.g. Raphael, *Parnassus* (1511). In Mantegna's *Parnassus* (1497) the Muses are shown without attributes, performing a "dance of harmony" while Apollo himself plays the lyre.

This association of Muses with their divine leader was the origin of the ancient-classical conception of music, and showed how and why music had come into existence. As the Homeric *Hymn to the Muses and Apollo* announces: "I shall begin with the Muses and Apollo, and with Zeus: for it is through the Muses and far-shooting Apollo that there are singers and lyre-players upon the earth, and through Zeus there are kings. Happy is the man whom the Muses love, for sweet is the speech that flows from his lips."[1] A Greek circular mosaic from Elis (first century BCE) shows a whole series of attributes for the entire band—including no fewer than three lyres, one each for Apollo, Erato, and Terpsichore—as does the Roman "Muses Sarcophagus" (Louvre; second century CE), which shows only one Muse (probably Erato) with a lyre.

Other classical modes of depiction commonly showed the famous musical figures of mythology: Orpheus (sometimes also his fellow "Thracian bards" Thamyris and Musaeus), Amphion, Arion, Linus, and so on, and above all Apollo himself. The figure-type showing the god as a performing musician is known to scholarship as "Apollo citharoedus" (cithara player) and was a common sculptural subject, later appropriated into the Western tradition.

Female figures understood as abstract personifications with formalized attributes came into use from the time of Martianus Capella, writing in the fifth century CE.

Martianus's descriptions of the Seven Liberal Arts brought about a new way of depicting the different subjects within late-antique education; these then stood as the model and representational template for the entire Middle Ages. But the specific musical figures of mythology, not such abstract personifications, had typically conveyed the idea of music to the eye of the classical spectator.

The system of attributes, particularly the instruments carried (or played) by the Greek Muses and by Martianus's Latin female allegories, then gave rise to the conventional imagery that would become standardized in Cesare Ripa's famous book of emblems and images, *Iconologia* (Rome, 1593). A great many pictures and prints followed this scheme, broadly speaking, though many variations and independent versions are found. Music could be shown, Ripa said, as a "young woman who with both hands holds Apollo's lyre, and with diverse musical instruments at her feet."[2] What was pointedly lacking in the classical images was, of course, this assorted pile of instruments which was to become familiar in Western representations.

Also on red-figure vases we can observe figures of ecstatic male "citharoedi" (Gk. *kitharodes*) performing on the lyre, again from the years either side of 500 BCE: famous examples are in New York (attributed to the Berlin Painter: the Nolan Amphora) and in the Louvre (Andokides Painter, with two robed listeners). The latter image, probably misread as a picture of Orpheus ("the first Poet-Musician") by Franz Liszt when he saw it in Paris, may well have helped to inspire his symphonic poem *Orphée* (1853–54).

Many of these vase figures are keenly and beautifully observed, in their understated way, yet at the same time they have an idealizing clarity and definition. In observing and contemplating them we learn something of the detailed importance of music as a social and cultural reality (there are images, for example, showing a music lesson, a performance at a symposium-banquet, and even a young woman tuning a pair of lyres). But we also sense a representational urge to capture the idea of music, its essence almost—or at least to find a way of silently pinpointing its qualities and characteristic features.

Aspects of Musical Portraiture

The classical system of representation remained a semi-active presence in visual culture into the nineteenth century, such was the self-perpetuating force of received models and conventional imagery. Thus what seems the most accomplished and expressive of the portraits of Beethoven in all the vigor of his *Eroica* phase—that painted by Willibrord Joseph Mähler in 1804–5 (Wien Museum)—depicts a charismatic and forceful figure, decidedly unclassical, seated in front of a windswept Romantic treescape, but still holding a neoclassical lyre in his left hand, at the bottom of the picture. This anachronistic motif of the lyre corresponds, moreover, to the temple of Apollo located in the mid-background, to the left, opposite the windblown trees. Beethoven's fingers are strikingly delineated, full of expressive energy and vitality (they are the pianist's point of contact with his instrument), while his right hand seems to cleave the air in order to articulate time and tempo. Yet there is no sign anywhere of a fortepiano, an attribute one would surely have expected as obligatory for a musician whose reputation was grounded in his keyboard virtuosity and his sonatas, concertos, and chamber music for piano.

Two or three generations earlier, in 1738, Louis François Roubiliac had made (on commission) his seated marble statue of George Frideric Handel for display in London's Vauxhall Pleasure Gardens. Handel, too, is shown with a classical lyre, almost nonchalantly strumming it in an easy reclining position (Victoria and Albert Museum). He is dressed, with a certain informal elegance, as an Enlightenment "virtuoso" posed in the relaxed-yet-active context of free thought and artistic invention: at productive leisure. The closeness of Enlightenment intellectual self-awareness in its relationship to the tradition of scholarly and scientific classicizing Academies makes the lyre no doubt a shade less disconcerting here than in the case of Beethoven. The Handel statue certainly shows both wit and ease in managing to combine the attributes of Orpheus and those of a fashionable Georgian artist-about-town. And yet we may still legitimately feel that the presence of the lyre remains incongruous, especially since even the classical figure of Apollo was often depicted in the Renaissance with an instrument—the *lira da braccio*—that was in fact a modern, not a classical type (Raphael, Titian, and others all did this, seemingly as a matter of course). What is at stake here is the contemporaneity of the musical portrait and its imagery, as a culturally up-to-date statement of a musician's status and expertise.

One of the most widely recognizable musician portraits of the eighteenth century is undoubtedly that of J. S. Bach by Elias Gottlob Haussmann (1695–1774), of which two copies exist (1746, Leipzig, Altes Rathaus; and 1748, William H. Scheide Collection, Princeton, NJ). Bach in his early sixties is shown holding a small piece of manuscript paper with a real (if idiosyncratic) Bach piece—the concise, intricate Canon Triplex à 6 from the so-called "Goldberg" Canons BWV 1087—notated on it. Not Bach's virtuosity as organist or harpsichordist, nor his public status as "Director Musices" in Leipzig, nor even his authorship of the great religious works such as the Passions and the B Minor Mass, but, rather, his extreme compositional ingenuity is celebrated here. His powers of invention, specifically the intellectual and combinatorial genius of his musical temper, are what particularize the artist's visual statement and make the image so telling.

The portrait of Jean-Philippe Rameau in Dijon by Jacques André Joseph Aved (1728; Musée des Beaux-Arts) is visibly in the same representational tradition, yet subtly different from that of Bach. The conventional attributes within the picture— a small manuscript score and a violin bow—are there but hardly contribute very much to the pictorial message. Rameau, paying them no attention, instead faces the viewer slightly diffidently, holding a violin in plucked "guitar position." What could this possibly mean? Rameau was famous above all as a theoretician and composer, and as a moderately virtuosic harpsichordist and organist—not as a violinist or composer for the violin, as, say, Bach, Vivaldi, and his French contemporary Jean-Marie Leclair all were.

Perhaps the clue lies in Rameau's passion for theory, or better: his idea of uniting the theoretical and practical spheres of music, seeing them as two aspects or dimensions of the same larger reality. During the 1720s he published several volumes of harpsichord music, while he would not begin his operatic career until *Hippolyte et Aricie* in 1733. But he had published the large-scale *Traité de l'Harmonie* in 1722 and was already famous on this account. It seems that the violin in the 1728 portrait might be read as an allusion to his theoretical preoccupations, grounded in the phenomenon of the resonance of strings. It also, perhaps, prompts the viewer to "listen for" the instrument's imagined sounds: Rameau is in fact plucking a chord of G major voiced g-d'-b'-g" (in Helmholtz notation) using the bottom two open strings as the harmonic foundation. Music's main attribute is, in this instance, harmonic resonance as a natural (i.e. physical) phenomenon—made significant by the fact that resonance, embracing the overtone series, is in turn the fundamental principle of Rameau's tonal-harmonic system.

A further interesting variant on the composer portrait type is offered by the picture of Christoph Willibald Gluck by Joseph Duplessis (1725–1802) (1775; Vienna, Kunsthistorisches Museum). The composer is shown sitting at a large "domestic" spinet, but he has no score and no quill pen. Instead, he is shown looking upwards, with his brow illumined as if from above in a moment of inspiration. Here the artist has used a pictorial rhetoric to capture the idea of the creative act itself, in both its craftsmanlike and its inspirational dimension.

From Concert Pictures to Still Life: The Eighteenth Century

The eighteenth century saw the use of a wide variety of musical subjects and motifs within visual art, and, in the case of such figures as Watteau (1684–1721) and Gainsborough (1727–88), these reflected the artist's serious passion for music. Watteau excelled in such painterly genres as the so-called "fête galante" and the "bal" or "concert champêtre" (the famous Giorgione–Titian "pastoral concert" scene in the Louvre was probably given its title from this generic source). These types of scene have a strong musical element in their subject matter and atmosphere, and incorporate the fantasy and nuance of music as an imaginative medium into their pictorial world—though many of the individual musical motifs for such pictures were studied by Watteau from the life in astonishingly vivid and realistic colored chalk drawings. Parallel study of drawings, paintings, and prints is thus essential for a full understanding of Watteau's relationship to music.

Music was a supreme passion in Gainsborough's life, and his pictures of (mainly) London musicians, many of whom he knew well—including such luminary figures as J. C. Bach and Carl Friedrich Abel—represent one of the most brilliant musical galleries by one artist of the entire eighteenth century. Like Watteau, he was an obsessive draughtsman, and such keenly observed images as the red chalk study of a *Music Party* (c. 1765–70) in the British Museum brilliantly represent the spontaneous intensity of live music-making. Here the prime attribute of music is, precisely, its controlled liveliness and sense of productive energy: a quintessence of social and psychological interaction. Such qualities were a major part of the fascination that scenes of musical performance held for artists such as Watteau and Gainsborough. The argument can be made that the Enlightenment shared with the Italian and Flemish traditions of the sixteenth and seventeenth centuries a pictorial approach that was able to combine in equal measure a classical system of representation, with its resourceful visual conventions, and a vivid type of "empirical" depiction based on direct observation and an illusionistic style.

Over and above the making of images with a specific representational or emblematic aim in view, there is a striking decorative tradition based on musical motifs, of essentially Baroque–Rococo derivation, that existed through the later seventeenth and eighteenth centuries. Wall-mounted wood carvings of the greatest virtuosity and refinement by Grinling Gibbons (1648–1721) and painted musical "still lives" by Jean-Baptiste-Siméon Chardin (1699–1779) may stand as leading examples of this tendency, though the tradition is broader than this. Gibbons's most famous musical carvings are without doubt those on the elaborate panel (c. 1690) in the Carved Room at Petworth House, West Sussex. Here the viewer can observe a fabulous, virtuosic display of musical elements combined with other decorative motifs—the assemblage of which combines a sense of Baroque profusion with a supreme elegance of finish and outline.

In 1765 Chardin painted his *Attributes of Music* (Paris, Louvre), together with two companion pieces (*Attributes of the Sciences* and *Attributes of the Arts*), as overdoor panels for the Château de Choisy. They formed part of the new decorative scheme to revamp the interiors of this grand castle following Louis XV's purchase of the manor of Choisy in October 1759. Diderot saw all three pictures in Paris and reported on them in the *Salon de 1765* (see below). Fueled no doubt by the public success of this trio of canvases, Chardin went on in 1767 to paint, for the Château de Bellevue at Meudon, a further pair of musical overdoor panels: the *Attributes of Civil Music* and the *Attributes of Military Music*. These two showed mainly instruments (oboes and bassoons interestingly grouped among the equipment of the *musique militaire*).

For Diderot, Chardin is a demigod of visual depiction, rivaling on canvas the optical appearances of Nature herself: Chardin's painterly approach is more one of truth than one of rhetoric. In his comments on the 1765 Salon exhibition, Diderot makes a fanciful address directly to the artist:

> [Chardin,] great magician that you are, with your silent pictures—but which speak so eloquently to an artist! [...] If it is true what the philosophers say, that nothing is real except for our sensations ... then let them enlighten me, these philosophers, and teach me what difference there is, at a distance of four feet or so from one of your pictures, between you and the Creator![3]

He goes on to praise the selection of musical objects and their distribution on the table surface covered with a reddish carpet, but above all the color and aerial shading and the texture of truth that they communicate. This essentially art-critical discussion implies that Diderot viewed these pictures not as allegorical or emblematic, but as purely visual still lifes. They speak of types of music, clearly, but in a very concrete and physical form—presenting us, in a spiritualized form, with something of the "material culture" of music. This type of picture draws on, yet also stands against, the historical tradition of attributes, adapting it to new Chardinesque ends. It combines a coolly and delicately objective, quasi-scientific gaze (Enlightenment dispassion) with an exquisitely poetic sense of physical arrangement and observational truth.

In 1771 Diderot commented on a group of similar still lifes by a young, up-and-coming female artist known as Mademoiselle Vallayer (Anne Vallayer-Coster, 1744–1818) (Figure 13.1). Of her *Instruments de Musique Militaire*, he observed:

> Mlle Vallayer astonishes us, even as she delights us—here is Nature rendered with an inconceivable force of truth and, at the same time, a sense of color that is seductive. Everything is well observed and felt.[4]

Again, there is no hint here of any story or symbolism to tease out. This is a descriptive still life of the Chardin kind that presents an essentially visual set of attributes: form, color, texture, physical nature ("What truthfulness ... what vigour [there is] in this picture!" Diderot exclaims). It offers, no doubt, the artist's distilled visual experience of the instruments as observed objects; but if it also contains some residue of her impression of a military band playing (say) on a holiday parade, this memory is buried deep within or beyond the picture, and carries no representational charge. Her two still lifes of 1770, one of the arts and the other of music, submitted as reception pieces for the Academy, likewise aim at Enlightenment description rather than at baroque allegory (Figure 13.1).

Here we see the delight of a keen eighteenth-century mind reflecting not so much on the subject itself as on the world of illusion—a painterly illusion that configures the material world in visual form, and then plays on the viewer's optical sense. That the Enlightenment era was a culture of wit and understanding tends to support such a view of the still-life painter as potentially both *philosophe* and "poet of reality."

In between 1765 and 1771, however, the 1767 pictures by Chardin offer a kind of limited *rapprochement* with the classical system of attributes. In the two Bellevue paintings he depicts instruments that relate in general terms to two royal musical institutions, the Musique de la Chambre du Roi (Music of the King's Chamber) and the Musique de la Grande Écurie (Music of the Great Stable). So here the "pure" musical still life acquires a new—if somewhat remote—exemplary value. The instruments have come to symbolize, in an almost heraldic way, two musical ensembles, with their respective environments and identities. In the first picture (civil music, with a faintly pastoral accent) we see a Provençal drum (*tambourin*), a transverse flute, a treble *pardessus de viole* with its bow gently caught between the strings, a tambourine, a hurdy-gurdy (*vielle à roue*), an early boxwood clarinet, and a natural horn (the presence of the last two instruments in orchestras was relatively recent in France, suggesting that Chardin's information was up to date).

In the second (military) painting Chardin has shown kettledrums, cymbals, a fanfare trumpet, and also bassoon and oboe (which were still in use as part of a double-reed band for ceremonial and military music). Draped over the front edge of the table is a blue and red flag with the arms of the King of France and Navarre and the Cross of the Holy Spirit. This completes the quasi-heraldic message of this assemblage of musical instruments, and marks the point at which Chardin allows himself to make a gesture, at least, towards a system of traditional representation which he rarely embraced.

Conclusion

What has our process of observation and reflection offered us by way of reward? Are we in a position to begin to take stock of what the presence of music within visual culture makes possible, and what their mutual interactions can achieve? Music can be connoted within visual experience by a variety of means: through subject matter (direct representation of musical scenes or objects); through the use of signs and attributes, emblems, effects of ambience; and through specific musician portraits.

Moreover, through the evidence of visual materials—prints, drawings, paintings, sculptures, photographs—the viewer can contemplate a range of historical forms and cultural contexts, thereby finding points of imaginative contact with the musical practice of another age and with the ideas to which such visual images relate. Most importantly of all, perhaps, such contemplation prompts an active and highly responsive reading of any given musical image. It is precisely the *gaps* in the system of representation—the fact that visual cues can only suggest sound, rather than state it openly, and that ideas from a different culture or era will require our imaginative cooperation in order to reconstruct something of their continuity and immediacy—which force the viewer to respond actively. Paradoxically, then, these intellectual and experiential gaps act as part of the transmission of knowledge, and serve to keep alive something of the vivacity of the musical tradition in question.

Notes

1 Translation adapted from Apostolos N. Athanassakis, *The Homeric Hymns*, 2nd ed. (Baltimore: Johns Hopkins University Press, 2004), 57–58.
2 Cesare Ripa, *Iconologia* (Siena: Heredi di Matteo Florimi, 1613), 2: 75.
3 Denis Diderot, "Salon de 1765," in *Salons II*, ed. Else Marie Bukdahl and Annette Lorenceau (Paris: Hermann, 1984), 117.
4 Denis Diderot, "Salon de 1771," in *Héros et martyrs: Salons IV*, ed. Else Marie Bukdahl (Paris: Hermann, 1995), 196.

Further Reading

AA.VV. *Musiques au Louvre*. Paris: Éditions de la Réunion des musées nationaux, 1994.
Diderot, Denis. *Salons I–IV*. Edited by Jacques Chouillet et al. 4 vols. Paris: Hermann, I–II/1984, III–IV/1995.
Gétreau, Florence. "The Portraits of Rameau: A Methodological Approach," *Music in Art* 36, no. 1–2 (2011): 275–300.
—— "Watteau et la musique: réalités et interprétations." In *Antoine Watteau (1684–1721): Le peintre, son temps et sa légende*, edited by François Moureau and Margaret Morgan Grasselli, 235–246. Paris: Champion, 1987.
—— ed. *Voir la musique: les sujets musicaux dans les oeuvres d'art du 16e au 20e siècle*. Exhibition catalogue. Carcassonne: Musée des Beaux-Arts, 2010.
Mirimonde, Albert Pomme de. "Les sujets musicaux chez Watteau." *Gazette des Beaux-Arts* per. 6, 58 (November 1961):249–288.
Stainton, Lindsay. *Gainsborough and His Musical Friends*. Exhibition catalogue. London: Greater London Council, 1977.

14

LOOKING AND LISTENING

Music and Sound as Visual Trope in Ukiyo-e[1]

Alexander Binns

The word *ukiyo-e* comes from a combination of "Ukiyo" (浮世), which means "floating world," and "e" (絵), which means picture or image. So, *ukiyo-e* offer both a description of the world of Edo (present-day Tokyo)—in particular the pleasures, foods, daily life, and culture on offer there—and the heavy bustle of the city, at that stage the largest and most densely populated in the world (with over a million inhabitants by the eighteenth century). These prints present fantastical exaggerations of life and often insert historical and mythical characters into contemporary contexts. *Ukiyo* conjures up a sense of the cultural pursuits, pastimes, and pleasures that grew up to serve a growing merchant class. Furthermore, *ukiyo* contains within it the idea of a carefree existence; of living for the moment and relishing the aesthetic aspects of life. This attitude, prevalent in the urbane richness of Edo, is encapsulated in the dominant aesthetic known as "iki" (粋). It was hedonistic and largely indifferent to status or rank, though the city itself was governed elsewhere by strict hierarchy. The "floating world" was also a world of the theater and of music, but, crucially, this was a world accessible though money. This aesthetic, then, and the ways in which it was embedded within daily life and attitudes to nature, is central to the identity of the pictures that imagined *ukiyo*. Referring to a set of new fashions and voguish practices—urbane and cultured—*ukiyo-e* thus characterize the ways in which music, among many other themes, figured in Edo life.

The imagined space of *ukiyo* was a kind of conjured domain in which the distinctions between art and life and music were blurred or even concatenated, so that the pleasure one experienced was *through* music or required the presence of music. Thus, many *ukiyo-e* prints imagine scenes in which music justifies or completes other activities. A sense of this effect can be gained through the documents that survive—writings, maps, and of course the *ukiyo-e* themselves, describing events, individuals, scenes, and journeys.

Music in *ukiyo-e* figured in many ways: through the act of listening or playing, or through music's place in relation to a depicted character (perhaps an actor or a geisha), or to plays, or to nature; sometimes, however, the very idea of music gave embodiment to the image's narrative. In most of these instances, however, it is important to avoid considering music, and especially listening to music, as an isolated act. Music was always embedded within some other activity in Japan and only rarely appears for its own sake, even in the case of performances with shamisen. Therefore, the sight of music can tell us something interesting about its identity in Edo-period Japan.

Music's role as a widespread and culturally important activity in Japan is made clear by Hiroshige, in a print entitled "Matching the World and Music" (音曲世界合) (1849–50). Music here is not the central focus—this would defy the aesthetic of its place within nature. Instead, it seems to emerge organically from the scene; to be a natural activity in and among whatever else is taking place. This illustrates a kind of sensuous mixture of music making, in the so-called jōruri style (a style associated primarily with the shamisen, and with the chanted style of singing that accompanies it). Music is implicated in the notion of nature itself. Although, in broad terms, this idea is not confined to ukiyo-e—it can also be found in Western art contexts—ukiyo-e avoid associating nature with the sublime. In fact, the Japanese had not always made a distinction between natural sounds and musical sounds, and a merging of these types of listening occurs in literature as well as in visual culture. In a famous scene from The Tale of Genji (Genji Monogatari), there is a description of what the writer Kikkawa Eishi has referred to as "an ideal fusion or harmony between the sounds of nature and the sounds of music (or musical instruments),"[2] in a passage that outlines the ritual court dance:

> Under the tall autumn trees breath from a circle forty strong roused from the instruments an indescribable music that mingled with the wind's roaring and sighing as it swept, galelike, down the mountain, while through the flutter of bright falling leaves "Blue Sea Waves" shone forth with an awesome beauty.[3]

Clearly, then, it is the way in which sound is *experienced* that is central; it is regarded as natural or, at any rate, a fluid partner to nature, because it appears to emerge from nature, coalescing seamlessly with the experienced surroundings. Thus, to listen to music is to listen to nature. A sense of what is conveyed in Genji Monogatari in the form of written texts is also found in ukiyo-e, where, once again, listening to nature is presented as akin to listening to music. As a result, the distinction between musical instruments and the sounds of nature itself is not always made clear. Sounds, musical (from instruments) or not, are seen as emergent within the setting. What is clear, however, is the importance given to listening to nature. The construction and practice of listening to classical music in Western contexts often took the form of a composed seriousness, requiring earnest endeavor on the part of the listener as well as a type of structural connection to the artwork, also imbued with the context of the concert hall. It was implicitly understood that the artwork required such attention precisely because it was of human endeavor, in spite of what critics might have asserted. Nature did not demand or require this kind of culture-bound attention, for it was aesthetically separate. Participating in or merely observing the "performance" of nature is part of the aesthetic of Edo-period Japan.

This practice of listening to nature as though it were music, or even the idea that music collapses nature and humanity, is found in Japanese culture more widely. It can be witnessed in the frenzy and pleasure of *hanami*, the cherry blossom viewing, the period in March and April when people gather to enjoy the transient blossoms. The pleasure in *hanami*—one that is widely thematized in *ukiyo-e*—is that of both human contact *and* nature together, as can be seen in a print from 1765 by Suzuki Harunobu, *Girl Viewing Plum Blossoms at Night* (夜の梅).

The experience of listening seriously to nature also emerges from Hiroshige's famous "Listening to Insects on Dokan Hill" (道灌山虫聞之図), from the *Series of Illustrations of Famous Places in the Eastern Capital* (東都名所) (c. 1840). In this image, a couple of men and a woman sit on a mat toward the top right, in and among the trees on a slightly elevated outcrop. The scene is a stylized construction of listening. That they sit and listen intently together is made clear not only by the title of the print, but also by the figures' lack of interaction, in spite of the drinks and food they have. Instead, they concentrate on the sounds that nature is making, as though they were listening to a concert, but without a human/musical focus. Although this scene contrasts with the carnivalesque invocation of group pleasure during *hanami*, it nonetheless illustrates the same fundamental importance of nature, and the sound of nature, in art. The incorporation of nature and music appears also in Kitagawa Utamaro's "Brocade Prints of Beauties Performing as Jōrurihime" (c. 1800). Here the ideas of history and music are blended. We see a small garden with a gate, next to which a man is playing a flute. He is the twelfth-century figure Minamoto Yoshitsune. To his right is Reizei, the woman who (according to the legend) was instructed by Princess Jōruri to find the flautist. In the fantasy that emerges, history and music blend in a kind of aesthetic allegory.

This approach to understanding listening within Japanese visual culture has been commented on more widely in the context of pillow books—collections of notes or tales, often written in a scholarly classical style, that recounted certain periods in an individual's life—and even more generally as a way of suggesting that Japanese auditory sensibilities, extending beyond music, account for the visual and literary tropes of music so often encountered. However, the presentation of music in later *ukiyo-e* scenes from kabuki theater suggests that its field of influence expanded beyond capturing the aesthetics of nature.

Actors' Performances

Music plays a significant part in *ukiyo-e* actor portraits. Here, music—in particular through these individuals' stylized poses—is captured within a tradition of presenting famous actors of Edo in a deliberately exaggerated, almost caricatured way. The figuring of music in these images seems to trace its changing role in kabuki more widely. Such prints depicted a wide range of people, including kabuki actors, geisha, and so-called *bijin*—beauties, famed for their looks, who would also entertain with dance and usually music, mostly on the shamisen or koto. Indeed, in prints, music often authorized their beauty, completing their identity as *bijin* and marking them out as important.

Kabuki theater is not narrative in any continuous way. Instead, it focuses on captured moments, which take the form of sumptuous, ritualized performances—usually dances—often by star actors, who play out key episodes in the play. The actor's way of performing these scenes, or vignettes, captivates the audience, making them the most highly anticipated scenes. Part of this stylized action is the rhetorical pose (or *mie*) that actors adopt at various points and which usually lasts for a couple of seconds. At these moments, the actor freezes and squints with one eye. This produces the so-called "Mona Lisa Effect," in which each member of the audience assumes that the actor is looking specifically at him or her, and it is very often this pose (the most characteristic and individual) that is captured in *ukiyo-e* of kabuki actors. It is the dramatic high point of a scene, and the tension is further accentuated through the use of *tsuke*, wooden clap boards struck repeatedly together to mark the moment.

Reproducing this stylized pose in prints created a kind of "brand" for the actor in question, capturing what was considered to be his unique performance feature. *Ukiyo-e* of actors were generally sold as a way of enhancing their popularity, increasing their fame and income. It was thus important that the captured pose should remind kabuki audiences of the play and of the actor more specifically, with the print serving as a form of both memorabilia and promotion. These *ukiyo-e*, then, were not aimed at aesthetic contemplation in quite the same way as with the Hiroshige example above. Instead, they sought to recall scenes that the audience had experienced. In many prints, especially after the end of the eighteenth century, part of this recall of the actor was also the music, the singing, and the acting associated with that moment, or with a particular character's disposition. Mutō Junko has argued that these *ukiyo-e* could be enjoyed as much for the sound as for the image, and that they were designed to evoke (rather than invoke) the music that was part of a given character's identity.

The emphasis, therefore, was not so much on remembering the plot, as on remembering what the play felt like and sounded like. Each actor's performance is accompanied by onstage music, broadly divided as *nagauta* (lyrical) and *jōruri* (narrative) music. The songs performed by these onstage ensembles are known collectively as *degatari*, and the *ukiyo-e* that depict actors try to capture a sense of these musical aspects as an important part of how a scene is understood. In that sense, music is constructed as part of the actor's identity, and listening is presumed even within the highly stylized visual presentation.

It is also possible to trace these attitudes through the presentation or exaggeration, within certain *ukiyo-e*, of music that is normally hidden from the audience. Two such types of prints, in particular—so-called *degatari-zu* and *gekijō-ga*—deal with these subjects and offer interesting commentaries on the figuring of music. *Degatari-zu* refers to a type of *ukiyo-e* that depicts kabuki dance scenes featuring onstage musical ensembles.

Kabuki, richly dramatic, uses music as a central and consistent feature of its *mise-en-scène*. Broadly speaking, there are two types of music in kabuki: onstage and offstage. Their respective functions are very different, as is the instrumental make-up of each—though the shamisen is usually central to both types. The onstage music, called *jōruri*, tells a story: it is a sustained music that supplements the stage drama while the characters dance or perform. These onstage musicians, with shamisen as the centerpiece, accompany the dance scenes and play a type of music known as *shosa*. Offstage ensembles are known as *geza ongaku* (*geza* can be translated as "accompaniment"). These musicians are usually hidden from the audience behind a black screen, often made of bamboo (they are also known as *kuromisu-ongaku*, therefore). They provide musical fragments and sound effects that are not self-supporting outside the drama. The musical effects are richly symbolic rather than diegetic. The position on stage of these musicians also varies over time—it shifted from stage left to stage right when the so-called *hanamichi*, which is a walkway on the left-hand side for actors to enter the stage, started to assume greater importance.

Interestingly, very few prints depict music and musicians in this way before the end of the eighteenth century. Even though music was central to kabuki, it remained absent from *ukiyo-e* until Torii Kiyonaga began to include musicians in *degatari-zu*; his first print of this type was published in 1782. Many subgenres of *degatari-zu* appeared subsequently, but while music was an important feature in all of them, musicians were not represented until only a few years before these prints emerged. It is not clear what prompted the sudden foregrounding of musicians. A print from 1784 showing the kabuki actors Sawamura Sōjūrō and Iwai Hanshirō, again by Torii Kiyonaga, features a shamisen player to the right and two chanters sitting to the left, all of whom are identified because they are famous musicians. The shamisen player is Namisaki Tokuji, and the chanters are Tomimoto Buzendayū and Tomimoto Itsukidayū. This would suggest that the presentation of musicians in general, and even the identification of increasingly famous musicians, was becoming important in promoting kabuki. This makes sense, given that an important aspect of *ukiyo-e* depicting kabuki was to advertise the forthcoming plays and actors. Here, we know the name of the play (*Amijima*) and even the scene ("Nobe no kakioki") [field of letters left on the way to suicide], as well as the type of scene (*Michiyuki*, a dance interlude comprising two characters who usually commit suicide, as is the case here).

A further image by Kiyonaga frames a subgenre of the onstage musical ensembles known as *tokiwazu*, but it gives the impression that the musician and actor are placed almost together on stage. In fact, however, *tokiwazu* musicians are usually in the far stage right, with actors in the center. Given that the main purpose of these prints was the presentation of musicians (as the very name of the print type suggests), it is possible that the images reflect the increasing influence of musicians in kabuki plays and their ability to stand as emblems for kabuki's attractive dramatic character. One print by Toyokuni III even shows musicians more prominently than the actors, sug-gesting—perhaps—that kabuki is fundamentally a musical experience. Similarly, but with a different musical focus, the presence of offstage musicians or *geza* music in prints that depict the whole theater, including the audience (known as *gekijo-ga*), also suggests musicians' exaggerated importance in *ukiyo-e*. These musicians are never normally seen by the audience in kabuki, unlike onstage narrative ensembles, and yet from the 1790s onward, an increasing number of prints in this genre start to hint at the musicians' varied presence behind the bamboo curtain. As before, it is conceivable that the practice of depicting musical instruments and identifying particular musicians (there was quite often a large ensemble of *geza* musicians) was intended to underscore the lavish visual and musical features of kabuki, and in turn to reinforce its dramatic and spectacular identity—to which the range and variety of the *geza* contributed enormously.

Music and/as Beauty

Music in Japanese visual culture also functioned as an important accompaniment or endorsement of beauty. Mentioned above in connection with *ukiyo-e* of *bijin*, it can further be regarded as a type of companion to allegorical love, as a still-life *ukiyo-e* by Ryūryūkyo Shinai suggests. In this image, the Seven Gods of Fortune figure symbolically. The biwa (or lute) is associated with the goddess of love *and* music—Benten-sama. By virtue of the biwa's central position in the print, the symbolic presence of music fills the scene, and in other situations acts as the symbolic authority of love. We can see many examples of this. The *ukiyo-e* from 1886 "Ariko" (有子) by Tsukioka Yoshitoshi (Figure 14.1), from the series *One Hundred Aspects of the Moon* (月百姿), furthermore, is made more poignant by the inclusion of the biwa as a symbol of the power of love and, in this case, of its absence—evident in Ariko's weeping. At the upper right-hand side of the *ukiyo-e*, a poem reads:

はかなしや波の下にも
入ぬへし　つきの都の
人やみるとて　有子

(How hopeless it is, it would be better for me to sink beneath the waves; perhaps then I could see my man from the Moon Capital—Ariko)[4]

We see a young woman sitting in a small boat on a lake, weeping. Her right hand, wiping tears from her eyes, holds a plectrum with which she has been strumming the strings of her lute. She is dressed in a richly decorated kimono, and her hair is loose in the courtly Heian manner. Hopelessly in love, she is preparing to jump from the boat to drown herself, and music seems to frame this moment. In fact, it seems as though she is singing the poem before committing suicide. It is not uncommon for ritualistic suicide to be associated with music in these types of scenes. The use of the shamisen—most often associated with *geisha* in *ukiyo-e*—is part of what gives this *ukiyo-e* print its sense of beauty. Since *geiko* and *geisha* were regarded as the epitome of art and beauty, the presence of music seems to reinforce this way of understanding it. As such, beauty is not only visual, but also requires music to play out and complete the geisha's role. Witness Kitagawa Utamaro's famous image from 1800, "Flowers of Edo: young woman's narrative chanting to the shamisen" (江戸の花娘浄瑠璃), depicting a *geisha* and shamisen.

The musical allusions, however, did not always take the explicit form of instruments. Others were implied, by either the context or the individual. Another print by Utamaro, "Tomimoto Toyohina" (富本豊雛), depicts the famous musician of the same name, though she has no instrument. However, this *ukiyo-e* is a *surimono* (a more lavishly produced, often privately printed, version of the standard *ukiyo-e*), frequently used to announce musical performances. Thus the allusions to music would have been clear. In the image, she looks intently at the material she is holding with embossed green chrysanthemums, which appears to suggest the contemplation that music invites, just as it did in the Hiroshige example at the outset. Achieving this condition is regarded as beautiful, as an aesthetic achievement.

In 1766, Suzuki Harunobu, in a scene from "The Bridges of a Zither—Geese Alighting" (琴路の落雁) part of the parody series *Eight Parlor Views* (座敷八景), incorporates aspects of beauty, music, and nature more directly. Two women prepare to play the koto in a room whose door to the garden is open, thus allowing us to see the encroaching branch of a tree. It refers not only to music, by locating instruments and music-making within the space, but also to the preparation for music, to a state of listening required, and to music's visual place among nature and humans.

125

Both the koto and the plant seem to engender the kind of serenity and anticipation experienced by those listening to the insects in the Hiroshige print mentioned earlier. It is almost as though the plant and the instrument are connected: in so assuming, we are returned to the central premise of Japanese aesthetics in the Edo period: music is a branch of nature and thus inseparable from it.

Notes

1 I wish to record my gratitude to the Great Britain Sasakawa Foundation, which provided funding that enabled the completion of this article.
2 Kikkawa Eishi, "The Musical Sense of the Japanese," in *Contemporary Music Review* 1, no. 2 (1987): 86.
3 Murasaki Shikibu, *The Tale of Genji*, trans. Royall Tyler (New York: Penguin Books, 2003), 137.
4 John Stevenson, *Yoshitoshi's One Hundred Aspects of the Moon* (Redmond, WA: San Francisco Graphic Society, 1992), 146.

Further Reading

Clark, Timothy. *Hokusai's Great Wave*. London: British Museum Press, 2011.
Clark, Timothy and Osamu Ueda. *The Actor's Image: Print Makers of the Katsukawa School*. Chicago: The Art Institute of Chicago and Princeton University Press, 1994.
Hasegawa, Yumiko. "*Degatari-zu*: An Examination of the Transition in the Depiction of Onstage Kabuki Musical Ensembles in Color Woodblock Prints (1746–1866)." *RIdIM/RCMI Newsletter* 22, no. 2 (1997): 62–68.
Kikkawa, Eishi. "The Musical Sense of the Japanese." *Contemporary Music Review* 1, no. 2 (1987): 85–94.
Kiyoko, Motegi. 「枕草子」の記述に表された日本人の<音>への姿勢 ["The Japanese Attitude toward Sound, as Seen in Sei Shonagon's 'Pillow Book'."] *Bulletin of Joetsu University of Education. Sect. 2, Language, social studies, art and music* 6, no. 3 (1987): 213–231.
Kuki, Shūzō. 九鬼周造 (2008) 『(対訳)「いき」の構造』講談社 [*The Structure of Iki*. Translated by Hiroshi Nara. Tokyo: Kodansha, 2008].
Kyrova, Magda. *The Ear Catches the Eye: Music in Japanese Prints*. The Hague: Hotei Publishing, 2000.
Mutō, Junko. "Enjoying Actor Prints: Imagining the Voices of Actors and Music." In *Ukiyo-e*, edited by Gian Carlo Calza, 10–14. London: Phaidon Press, 2005.
Shikibu, Murasaki. *The Tale of Genji*. Translated by Royall Tyler. New York: Penguin Books, 2003.
Stevenson, John. *Yoshitoshi's One Hundred Aspects of the Moon*. Redmond, WA: San Francisco Graphic Society, 1992.

15

PAINTING AND MUSIC

Therese Dolan

Interior picturing rather than an ocular sensation, and internal perceptions rather than optical functions, began to partner closely with music when painting moved toward modernist abstraction over the course of the nineteenth century. The interrelationship of the arts became the *raison d'être* of the periodical *L'Artiste*, founded in Paris in 1831, as evidenced in the frontispiece wood engraving to the first issue that featured a writer, painter, sculptor, and musician practicing their crafts (Figure 15.1). Painting had been traditionally allied more closely with literature as a sister art because both were seen to imitate human action. This concept was encapsulated in the ancient phrase from Horace, *ut pictura poesis*. Its acoustic alternative—*ut pictura musica*—began to take precedence as Romantic artists sought to infuse their works with the ineffable world of feelings and emotions.

Music and painting shared a basic vocabulary, including terms such as color, tone, harmony, composition, improvisation, modulation, and scale. Hector Berlioz wrote that instrumentation in music was the exact equivalent of color in painting. The relation of the two arts had been a trope for centuries before Romanticism, as when Giorgio Vasari described the putto playing a lute in Fra Bartolommeo's *Saint Bartholomew* as being so lifelike that anyone who looks at him can almost hear his voice, due to his performative strumming of his instrument and opened mouth. Nicholas Poussin in 1647 made an analogy with the modes of ancient music to explain the kinds of emotion that certain subjects of art should elicit in the viewer. Joseph Haydn's 1798 oratorio, *The Creation*, became famous for its tone paintings of birds, fish, and whales, along with tonal evocations of the emergence of the oceans and mountains. However, a new notion of vision began to emerge as the arts gradually withdrew from imitating aspects of the natural world and moved to communicating internal states of mind. With the increasing economic capitalization of Europe, the decline of the authority of the Church and state after the French Revolution, and the rise of scientific positivism, many artists and writers looked to music's intangibility as a safeguard against the encroachment of materialism.

Music's indeterminacy had caused Immanuel Kant in his 1790 *Critique of Judgment* to rank it as the lowest of the fine arts because it advanced from sensation to indefinite ideas. As the Romantic movement began to emerge, music became valued for its nonreferentiality. In his influential 1810 review of Beethoven's Fifth Symphony, E. T. A. Hoffmann wrote: "Music reveals to man an unknown realm, a world quite separate from the outer sensual world surrounding him, a world in which he leaves behind all precise feelings in order to embrace an inexpressible longing."[1] One sees movement toward the interior in the portraits of virtuoso violinist Niccolò Paganini by the two dominant figures of early-nineteenth-century French art, Jean-Auguste-Dominique Ingres and Eugène Delacroix. In his 1819 pencil drawing of Paganini, Ingres carefully registered the virtuoso's facial features, staid appearance, and straightforward gaze. The artist, himself an accomplished violinist, carefully noted the right hand fingering the strings and the left hand professionally grasping the bow (Figure 15.2). Delacroix portrayed Paganini totally absorbed, eyes closed and body torqued as the music he is playing pulsates through his body (Figure 15.3). Ingres seems to faithfully record a musician's appearance, whereas Delacroix visualizes music's embodiment. Put otherwise, Ingres's rendition is a likeness of a musician; Delacroix gives us music personified.

Writing in his *Journal* in 1853, Delacroix explained how a work of art could transcend imitation to achieve a higher aesthetic goal: "[I]f, to a composition that is already interesting by the choice of subject, you add an arrangement of lines that augments the impression, a chiaroscuro that seizes the imagination, and color that fits the character of the work, you have solved a far more difficult problem and you are superior: you have harmony with all its combinations adapted to a single song. This is a musical tendency."[2] Delacroix further recorded in his *Journal* how the acoustic could transport him beyond external to internal vision. While attending a funeral, he saw a painting of Christ by Pierre-Paul Prud'hon, and claimed that listening to the solemn music of the requiem Mass liberated the emotional side of the painting for him. Further, when Delacroix worked on the Saint Sulpice murals in 1855, a morning service of musical chants put him in a state of exaltation favorable to painting.

Delacroix's art became a touchstone for those seeking a relation between music and painting. Théophile Gautier, a prolific novelist, poet, and critic, eagerly sought the transposition of the arts and found in Delacroix an ideal model. When he first saw Delacroix's *Death of the Bishop of Liège* in 1838, he described it as a tumultuous and sonorous painting that could be heard as plainly as it could be seen. Encountering it again in 1855 at the Universal Exhibition, Gautier exclaimed: "Who would have thought that one could paint uproar and tumult? Movement still occurs, but this small canvas howls, screams and blasphemes; it seems that one can hear flying above the table, in the bloody vapor of the wild fanatics, the hundred different idle remarks and the obscene songs in this drunken barracks."[3] Gautier's ideal work of art resonated with the characteristics of more than one art form. Rossini's music produced in him the same pleasure of pure art as the paintings of Paul Veronese; Donizetti's *Don Pasquale* evoked Tiepolo's ceiling paintings; Mozart's *Don Giovanni* made him think of Correggio; while Meyerbeer's *Les Huguenots* conjured up an immense fresco. Criticizing the lack of homogeneity in Charles Gounod's *Sappho* score, Gautier compared it to a beautiful woman with torso and face drawn by Ingres and legs and arms executed by Delacroix.

Faced with a work of art that moved him, Gautier quickly sought to connect it to senses other than the primary one to which the work was addressed. The vividness of Charles Louis Müller's painting of victims called to the guillotine during the Revolution led Gautier to describe the painting with chilling acoustical effects: "One can almost hear the blade whistle in its groove and become deadened on the bloody flesh with a dull thud."[4] In one of his very last statements on music, Gautier extolled its ability to transcend the real and lamented the incapacity of the verbal—his own art—to express the depths of thought and feeling. For him, the composer was the consummate artist, surpassing the writer, because of his ability to evoke vision: "The musical sound awakens mysterious echoes in the depths of the soul. It speaks to idea and sensation, stirring those obscure and profound thoughts that language is incapable of rendering. The composer stumps (*estompe*) the dry contour of the figures in the libretto by softened tones and smooth shadows; he bathes his characters in a mysterious chiaroscuro; he slips silvery highlights onto the highlighted side and sacrifices the background under bluish neutral tints. From the first notes one is transported to a higher and more distant realm."[5] Had Gautier lived long enough, he would have seen this idea come to fruition in Henri Fantin-Latour's pictorial evocations of Richard Wagner's operas in the 1880s.

Music and painting reached a crescendo in the writings of Charles Baudelaire at mid-century, with Delacroix's painting serving as his conduit. From the first mention of the artist in his writings, Baudelaire expressed his admiration for Delacroix in musical terms. Discussing Delacroix's *The Sultan of Morocco* in his *Salon of 1845*, Baudelaire asked rhetorically: "has anyone ever shown a greater musical seductiveness, at any time? ... Were melodies more fanciful ever set to sing upon a canvas?"[6] In the *Salon of 1846*, the *Universal Exposition of 1855*, and his 1857 poem "Les Phares," Baudelaire compared Delacroix's color to the plaintive melodies of Carl Maria von Weber. The poet expressed his frustration at the inadequacy of his own linguistic medium to express the notion of internal visualization suggested by Delacroix's art, asking the reader's pardon to express the subtle idea that Delacroix's color "*thinks for itself*, independently of the objects which it clothes."[7] Delacroix's color chords made Baudelaire dream of harmony and melody, prompting him to claim that the impression brought away from his paintings was musical. By the time Baudelaire wrote the *Salon of 1859*, his linkage of Delacroix's color with music had become a veritable *leitmotiv*, and Baudelaire called the painter an ardent and prolific composer. What Baudelaire saw in Delacroix was not so much literary subject matter as a taste for form provided by color and a resonating dramatic effect likewise stimulated by color rather than narrative.

According to Peter Vergo, it was in the 1840s that composers began to look to painting for inspiration. Franz Liszt, visiting the museum in Bologna, described himself dashing through rooms of Italian paintings in his eagerness to see Raphael's painting of Saint Cecilia. Vision quickly turned to internal musical vision as he stood before the work: "I do not know by what strange magic this picture presented itself suddenly with a *double appeal to my inner eye*: it is a fascinating expression of the human form and all that is noble and most ideal, a wonder of grace, purity and harmony; then at the same time, and without any effort of the imagination, I recognized in it an admirable and complete symbolism of the art to which we devote our lives [i.e., music]."[8] Liszt claimed that studying the works of Raphael and Michelangelo gave him insight into Mozart and Beethoven. But it was especially his experience of Wagner's music that illuminated for him the connection between music and painting, as it would do throughout the rest of the century. Wagner's rebellion against established tradition and contemporary authorities in his field impelled him to invent a new type of opera, which he preferred to differentiate by the term "music drama." Rather than set pieces such as duets, arias, recitatives, and choruses, music would continue without interruption throughout his operas and unify them. Innovative elements—increased chromaticism, unusual harmonic inventions, dissonant tones, and a melody that eluded any definite shape—broke radically with extant traditions and inaugurated a revolutionary musical language and form.

Liszt fully exploited the pictorial aspect of music in his 1849 article on Wagner's *Tannhäuser* for the *Journal des débats*. He allied Wagner's music with the growing trend in painting for realistic drawing, color, and perspective, concluding that music called out for more dramatic qualities and a more solidly constructed libretto. In October of that year, Liszt reported again to the *Journal des débats* on the premiere of Wagner's *Lohengrin* in Weimar. Wagner colored his language with antique tints, according to Liszt, and his opera portended a new system that would transform musical art. Liszt took what had been borrowed references to visual art in these articles and turned them into a sustained metaphor in his book on Wagner's *Lohengrin* and *Tannhäuser*, published in 1851. He described Wagner's works synaesthetically, invoking olfactory effects of incense and perfume, but more insistently giving visual renderings of the operas to the reader rather than describing their auditory effects or musical technicalities. Liszt confessed to being powerfully moved by Wagner's "visions." As in a mosaic, he claimed, nothing could be removed from the ensemble of Wagner's opera without ruining its effect. Liszt informed the reader that Wagner even wrote his score in differently colored inks in order to deepen the orchestra's understanding of the musical parts: black ink for strings, red ink for winds, and green for brass, seeking not a homogenous mass of sound but a spindle of variegated colors that produced interwoven designs like lace or a priceless tapestry. Not only did Wagner animate the feelings and passions that he put in play, but he strongly wanted their contours to be associated with colors assigned to the characters.

Baudelaire turned to Liszt's observations in his own essay on Wagner in 1861. For Liszt, Wagner's *Prelude to Lohengrin* had the power to make the listener see the castle of the Holy Grail, with its doors of gold and columns of opal. Liszt employed visual metaphors to explain the beauty of Wagner's music, and when Baudelaire cited him, he italicized Liszt's words to emphasize the visual aspects of the music: "At the beginning it is a *vast, slumbering lake* of melody, *a vaporous extending ether*, on which the holy picture may take form before our profane eyes ..." When the trumpets and trombones join the horns and bassoons, they create "*a dazzling burst of color*, as if at this unique moment the holy edifice *had blazed forth* before *our blinded eyes*, in *all its radiant and luminous magnificence*."[9] Liszt described the waxing and waning of celestial light in Wagner's opera and claimed that the *brasses* made the marvelous lines of the single motif of the prelude *shine forth*. In quoting these passages, Baudelaire specifically highlighted the words and phrases where Liszt united the acoustic with the visual. Baudelaire's italicization of the word brass—*cuivre*—conveniently reminds the reader that this word functions on two levels: as a color, and as a section of the orchestra.

After citing the program notes and Liszt's interpretation, Baudelaire went on to describe the "inevitable translation" that Wagner's music stimulated in his own imagination when he first heard it with his eyes closed, arguing that genuine music suggests analogous ideas in different minds. While Liszt employed material objects to suggest their acoustic analogues, Baudelaire experienced the music in terms of physical lightness, an immense horizon, diffused light, infinite immensity, warmth, and whiteness. His interpretation of Wagner's music entered the realm of pure abstraction by offering a sensation that was not related to any object but, rather, to his own corporeality. He had described this impression in similar terms in his February 1860 letter to Wagner, saying that he borrowed his language from painting: "I conjure in front of my eyes a vast spread of deep red. If this red represents passion, I see it make its way gradually, by all the transitions of red and rose, to the incandescence of a furnace. It would seem difficult, even impossible to arrive at something more fiery; but nevertheless a last flare traces a furrow more white than the white that serves as background."[10] One has the feeling that Baudelaire has just described a Barnett Newman zip painting a century before it was created.

In his essay on Wagner, Baudelaire justified his alliance of the acoustic and visual (communicated through the verbal), by observing that it would be more surprising if "sound *could not* suggest color, that colors *could not* evoke the idea of melody, and that sound and color were *unsuitable* for the translation of ideas."[11] Baudelaire's sustained interest in music and painting centered on the idea of an essential unity behind all sense impressions, and he pursued this tenaciously in the Wagner essay. If Delacroix exemplified Baudelaire's painter-musician, then Wagner became his musician-painter. It is as if Baudelaire then replaced the composer's pen with a paintbrush: "[Wagner] possesses the art of translating, by means of the subtlest shades, all that is excessive, immense and ambitious in spiritual and natural man. One seems sometimes, when listening to this fiery and peremptory music, to recapture the dizzy perceptions of an opium-dream, painted upon a backcloth of darkness."[12] For the privileged observer, listener, or reader of a work of art, the world becomes a unified system of interrelationships echoing and reinforcing one another. Sensory experiences overlap and interpenetrate in the true work of art: color is musical and poetic, music is poetic and painterly, poetry is painterly and musical.

Baudelaire's essay and Wagner's music became potent talismans during the 1880s and 1890s for the Symbolist painters and poets whose complex aesthetic relied strongly on evoking inner visions and dreams in search of an ideal that lies behind the world of appearances. Stéphane Mallarmé stated that his poetic goal was to paint in language not the thing, but the effect that it produces, thereby invoking not vision but its internal effects. The musicality of words became his vehicle to an introspective poetic world freed from conventional description. Paul Verlaine's motto—"De la Musique avant toute chose" ("Music before everything")—signaled the investment of creative resources into the production of works that expressed emotions in their purest form, and highlighted music's allusiveness and distance from quotidian expression. Odilon Redon grasped music's potential for his goal to place the logic of the visible at the service of the invisible when he stated that his drawings inspired rather than defined, and determined nothing. Like music, he insisted, they placed the viewer in the ambiguous world of the indeterminate. After attending a production of Wagner's *Tannhäuser* in 1895, Redon wrote enthusiastically to a friend that the music suggested a multitude of ideas and a new art also for the eyes. The increased mysticism of his subject matter in the 1890s leaves no doubt that he sought to convey abstract values rather than illustrations of Wagnerian subjects.

Georges Seurat also used Wagner as a touchstone for important aspects of his Neo-Impressionist art. Seurat knew from secondhand accounts that Wagner had darkened his theater at Bayreuth so as to focus the viewer's attention on the illuminated stage. This inspired him to paint dark frames around his pictures to draw the spectator's attention inexorably to the image. The musicality of Seurat's work was noted during his lifetime. In 1887 Paul Adam characterized Seurat's paintings as arrangements of symphonic patches. The alliance of painting and music is especially keen in Adam's description of Seurat's *Beach at Bas-Butin, Honfleur*: "the work will be perceived in accordance with the special charm that belongs to listening to a symphony: where, at the same time as the combination of sounds is felt, the value of each orchestral element is experienced as a unique and vibrant force ..."[13] Paul Smith, in his astute analysis of the Wagnerian aspects of Seurat's painting, observes that the artist's consistent use of gradation of hue in the later works might be considered Wagnerian, since it imitates the famous chromaticism of Wagner's music. Seurat combined his knowledge of Charles Henry's analysis of the musical qualities of certain groupings of lines and colors with his adherence to Teodor de Wyzewa's theories of "peinture wagnérienne." According to Wyzewa, the liberation of painting's non-mimetic and suggestive potential of line and color would allow the artist to attain the unallied emotional expressivity traditionally associated with music. Seurat's maintenance of an overall dominant harmony in his paintings, achieved through repeating color areas throughout all elements of the work, aligns him with Wagner: for he gives identity and expressive character to the details of his compositions by distinguishing them against, and simultaneously within, the continuous harmony of the whole work.

Vincent van Gogh claimed that he wanted to make his art as consoling as music. Wagner's revolutionary music impelled him as a young artist in Nuenen to pursue piano lessons. He recalled in a later letter to his brother Theo that he likened the notes to Prussian blue and dark greens and ocher. Wagner remained a sustaining model for the artist when he arrived in Arles from Paris in 1888 and embarked on a series of blossoming orchards: "But by intensifying *all* the colors one arrives once again at quietude and harmony. There occurs in nature something similar to what happens in Wagner's music, which, though played by a big orchestra, is nonetheless intimate."[14] Van Gogh wanted his painting to evoke some of the comfort he found in music. He titled his 1889 portrait of Madame Roulin *La Berceuse*, counting on its double meaning of a woman who rocks a cradle and the musical form of the lullaby. "Ah, my dear friend," he wrote to Gauguin, "to make painting into what the music of Berlioz and Wagner has already been before us: a consoling art for broken hearts!"[15] While convalescing at Saint-Rémy in 1889, he compared his copying of black-and-white reproductions after Millet and Delacroix to a musician executing a composition. The lack of colors in the reproductions led him to improvise, and he likened taking up his paintbrush to a violinist slipping the bow between his fingers as he sought what he called the vague consonance of colors which are at least right in feeling. Music inspired Van Gogh in the creation of a language of expressive forms through the catalyst of color. This led him to render an impression of a motif in nature as an expression of universal internal feelings.

Paul Gauguin's ambition to create an art of inner vision that mirrored the subjectivity of the creative imagination also found an impetus in music. Disillusioned with the opticality and instantaneity of Impressionism, Gauguin searched for a manner of painting that would take him beyond traditional figurative and narrative representation into what he called the mysterious centers of thought. Desiring a primitive simplicity in his life and art, Gauguin left Paris for Brittany in 1886 and noted in a letter how he sought to infuse the visual with the acoustic: "The flat sound of my wooden clogs on the cobblestones, deep, hollow, and powerful, is the note I seek in my painting."[16] Although he insisted that painting was the higher art, Gauguin resorted to musical analogies to justify the trajectory of his art away from facile decipherability and into the realm of disembodied ideas. In a letter explaining his 1892 Tahitian painting *Manao tupapau* Gauguin described the "musical part" of the painting as undulating horizontal lines with harmonies in orange and blue linked by yellows and violets. He concluded that the harmony was somber and frightening, sounding on the eye like a funeral knell.

In an important letter to the critic André Fontainas in March 1899, Gauguin defended the harsh coloration of his masterwork *Where Do We Come From? What Are We? Where Are We Going?* with words prophetic of twentieth-century art: "Think also of the musical role color will henceforth play in modern painting. Color, which is vibration just as music is, is able to attain what is most universal yet at the time most elusive in nature: its inner force."[17] Wassily Kandinsky was just a few years away from creating the first non-objective work of art, strongly impelled by both an exhibition of Claude Monet's *Grainstacks* and a performance of Wagner's *Lohengrin*. Works with titles such as *Lyrical* (1911), *Concert* (1911), and *Fugue* (1914)—as well as the *Composition* and *Improvisation* series (both 1911–13)—testify to the significant role music played in Kandinsky's creative process. According to Theodor Adorno, Wagner's unresolved chords marked "the historic spot where, for the first time, the multilayered, broken-up tone becomes emancipated and responsible for itself alone."[18] Music helped to free painting from a denotative account of reality and served as an acoustic impetus to artists as they challenged artistic conventions. This new art created an alternative way of seeing, freed from destructive worldly needs and focused on the idealistic emancipation of the spirit.

Notes

1 *E. T. A. Hoffmann's Musical Writings: Kreisleriana, The Poet and the Composer, Music Criticism*, ed. David Charlton, trans. Martyn Clarke (Cambridge: Cambridge University Press, 1989), 96.

2 Entry of May 20, 1853 from Eugène Delacroix, *Journal*, ed. Michèle Hannoosh (Paris: José Corti, 2009), 1: 661–62. Unless otherwise noted, translations are mine.

3 Théophile Gautier, *Les Beaux-Arts en Europe* (Paris: Michel Lévy Frères, 1855), 177.

4 Théophile Gautier, "Salon de 1850–1851," *La Presse* (February 6, 1851), 1.

5 Théophile Gautier, *Le Journal officiel* (January 17, 1870), 109.

6 Charles Baudelaire, "Salon of 1845," in *Art in Paris 1845–1862: Salons and Other Exhibitions*, trans. and ed. Jonathan Mayne (Ithaca: Cornell University Press, 1965), 6.

7 Charles Baudelaire, "The Exposition Universelle," in *Art in Paris*, 141. Emphasis in the original.

8 Franz Liszt, "La Sainte Cécile de Raphael," *Revue et gazette musicale* (April 14, 1839). Italics mine.

9 Charles Baudelaire, "Richard Wagner and Tannhäuser in Paris," in *The Painter of Modern Life and Other Essays*, trans. and ed. Jonathan Mayne (New York: Da Capo Press, 1964), 115.

10 Charles Baudelaire, *Correspondance*, ed. Claude Pichois with Jean Ziegler (Paris: Gallimard, 1973), 1: 673.

11 Baudelaire, "Richard Wagner," 116.

12 Ibid., 117.

13 Paul Adam as cited in Paul Smith, *Seurat and the Avant-Garde* (New Haven: Yale University Press, 1997), 147.

14 Van Gogh in *The Complete Letters of Vincent van Gogh* (Boston: Little, Brown and Company, 2000), 3: 431.

15 Van Gogh as cited in Debora Silverman, *Van Gogh and Gauguin: The Search for the Sacred in Art* (New York: Farrar, Straus and Giroux, 2000), 327.

16 Gauguin as cited in Naomi Maurer, *The Pursuit of Spiritual Wisdom: The Thought and Art of Vincent van Gogh and Paul Gauguin* (Madison, NJ: Fairleigh Dickinson University Press, 1998), 119.

17 Herschel Brown Chipp, *Theories of Modern Art: A Source Book by Artists* (Berkeley: University of California Press, 1968), 75.

18 Theodor Adorno as cited in Herbert Lindenberger, *Opera: The Extravagant Art* (Ithaca and London: Cornell University Press, 1984), 66.

Further Reading

Morton, Marsha L. and Peter L. Schmunk, eds. *The Arts Entwined: Music and Painting in the Nineteenth Century*. New York and London: Garland, 2000.

Shaw-Miller, Simon. *Visible Deeds of Music: Art and Music from Wagner to Cage*. New Haven: Yale University Press, 2002.

Smith, Paul. *Seurat and the Avant-Garde*. New Haven: Yale University Press, 1997.

Stevens, Maryanne. "The Transformation of the Symbolist Aesthetic." In Douglas W. Druick et al. *Odilon Redon: Prince of Dreams, 1840–1916*. Exhibition catalogue. Chicago: The Art Institute of Chicago, 1994.

Vergo, Peter. *The Music of Painting: Music, Modernism and the Visual Arts from the Romantics to John Cage*. London: Phaidon, 2010.

III.2 The Visual in Musical Culture

16
THE "REPRESENTATION" OF PAINTINGS IN MUSIC

William L. Coleman

The scholarship of Daniel Grimley, among others, has made it possible to describe with some precision the ways in which composers have rendered visual effects, most often landscape imagery, by means of music. For Grimley, "the organization of musical events in time suggests a structural parallel with the placement of landscape objects in visual space."[1] Examples come readily to mind: the suggestion of verdant countryside in Beethoven's *Pastoral* Symphony, sublime depths and crashing surf in Mendelssohn's *Fingal's Cave* overture, and the coming of the dawn in Sibelius's tone poem *Nightride and Sunrise*. Grimley's groundbreaking readings of Scandinavian music, in particular, have brought much-needed nuance to the discussion of the ways in which this music is visual and prompt another question for research: how have composers of Western art music used not just visual phenomena but specific paintings in their work?

This essay will endeavor to show some of the ways in which research might proceed on this particularly elusive category of musical–artistic exchange. While a number of composers have responded to paintings in their music, there has been little effort to move beyond generalizations to specificity about the paintings that composers have encountered and instances in which they have tried to incorporate known images into their work. What scholarship there is has often focused on musical and artistic abstraction because of the obvious kinship of these movements, to the detriment of other periods and styles. The lack of study of the "representation" of paintings in music can be explained not by a scarcity of instances in which this sort of response has occurred but by the precariousness of this field of research, always threatened by descent into unrigorous argument by comparison. The standards for documentary evidence and analysis before drawing connections between paintings and compositions must be very high to avoid traps, but the significant challenges should not discourage work on this important topic any longer, which stands to make a distinctive and important contribution to our understanding of the history of Western music.

Two case studies that require two very different sets of analytical tools will suggest some methods for research on the representation of paintings in music. The first example is the best-known case in which paintings have not just inspired music but been depicted through it: Modest Musorgsky's *Pictures at an Exhibition*. Using textual sources and surviving paintings from the exhibition mentioned in the work's title, it is possible to reconstruct the precise musical–artistic correlations at work in this piece and to draw conclusions from this analysis about the wider cultural sphere of Russia in the period. In the second example, the collaborative friendship of composer Jean Sibelius and painter Akseli Gallen-Kallela suggests new ways of studying the former's music, especially the creations of his early years when the visual arts were most prominent in his compositional thought. While documentary evidence is no less necessary in this example, we can suggest instances in which Sibelius's rare form of synaesthesia led him to render his tonal experience of certain of Gallen-Kallela's paintings in his music. While the particularities of these case studies make them especially ripe for the study of paintings as musical material, they are not isolated, and their implications for the study of other works and composers are manifold. A final section in this essay suggests some other directions and strategies for future research.

Case Study 1: Musorgsky's *Pictures at an Exhibition* (1874)

No volume on music and visual culture would be complete without some discussion of this famous instance of musical–artistic contact. *Kartinki s vystavki*, literally translated as "Pictures from an Exhibition" but more commonly known by the above title, was completed in 1874 but not published until Nikolai Rimsky-Korsakov's editorial intervention in 1886, five years after Musorgsky's death. The suite for solo piano does not seem to have been performed during the composer's lifetime, but it has become the work for which he is best known, largely on the basis of Maurice Ravel's now-canonical arrangement for orchestra of 1922. While *Pictures at an Exhibition* was itself inspired by painting, it has been at the center of a whirlwind of translations back into painting, including a series by Wassily Kandinsky and a watercolor by Frank Nelson Wilcox, and back into sound via a Klaus Peter Brehmer installation and composer Philip Corner's 1980 piece inspired by the latter: *Pictures of Pictures from Pictures of Pictures*. The unique challenges that the piece presents to scholars who would hope to attend to the work of Musorgsky instead of the rich tradition that has grown up around the piece can be largely overcome by focusing on the piano suite as published. With the use of surviving correspondence and other documentary evidence, it is possible to draw links between specific paintings and movements.

When Musorgsky's close friend Viktor Hartmann, an architect and painter, died suddenly in 1873 aged just 39, it came as a devastating blow to the composer. According to Vladimir Stasov—a major critic who had brought the two together—Musorgsky, who "loved Hartman passionately and was deeply moved by his death, planned to 'draw in music' the best pictures of his deceased friend."[2] The composer was afforded an opportunity by the memorial exhibition, arranged by Stasov, of four hundred of Hartmann's paintings and drawings that opened in St. Petersburg in February 1874. Stasov's description of the exhibition's contents in the *St. Petersburg Gazette* gives some idea of the wide array of subjects included:

> the lively elegant sketches of a genre painter, the majority being of scenes, types, figures from everyday life, caught from the environment that swirled

around him—on the streets and in the churches, in the Paris catacombs and Polish monasteries, in Roman side-streets and villages around Limoges, carnival types à la Gavarni, workers in smocks and Catholic priests on donkeys with umbrellas under their arms, old French women at prayer, Jews smiling from beneath their skull-caps, Parisian rag-pickers, ... country scenes with picturesque ruins, wonderful vistas including an urban panorama.[3]

By June, Musorgsky had completed his musical tribute. Although many of Hartmann's works have been lost or destroyed and he is remembered today almost exclusively on the basis of Pictures at an Exhibition rather than in his own right, six of the ten pieces Musorgsky responded to in music do survive. Not all of these were included in the memorial exhibition—the two pencil drawings that inspired the movement to which Stasov gave the derogatory title "Samuel Goldenberg and Schmuyle" had been gifts from Hartmann to the composer in 1868—but Musorgsky incorporated all into the exhibition context for coherence. The foremost scholar of Pictures at an Exhibition, Michael Russ, has argued that "[t]hese little pieces do not simply turn Hartmann's illustrations and designs into music, they bring them to life, creating little scenes out of them which, in turn, may carry messages about Russian culture and society."[4] Many musical vernaculars are called into service to describe the content of the paintings and the composer's emotional response to them, but this is no slavish imitation in a different medium. Musorgsky uses the paintings as points of departure for the exploration of new and exotic sound worlds.

Instead of discussing all of Pictures at an Exhibition and all the known paintings that were incorporated into the suite, it will be most productive in this context to focus on two parts of the piece that have proven challenging to scholars, the section titled "Catacombae: Sepulchrum Romanum," which I will refer to simply as "Catacombs," and the recurring "Promenade" theme. The challenge will be to describe precisely how Hartmann's art was useful to Musorgsky by studying the paintings in conjunction with the music. In the case of "Catacombs," we know the painting that the composer had in mind: Paris Catacombs of c. 1864–67, now in the Russian Museum in St. Petersburg.[5] The Promenade theme, on the other hand, does not refer to any painting in the show and presents its own challenges.

"Catacombs" is surely the strangest part of Pictures at an Exhibition. The sparse, jagged soundscape is strikingly different from the other movements. As a result, it has received a great deal of analytical attention, hoping to explain its structure. As one of these analysts notes, "It is unique among Musorgsky's non-vocal works in being athematic: a chant-like inner part (bars 4–11) ... seems to promise thematic development, but nothing comes of it, and the burgeoning melodic interest in bars 17–22 peters out at the cadence. ... The harmony is unpredictable, even non-functional (bars 23–4), its oddity emphasized by the sudden dynamic contrasts and unusual, Stravinsky-like spacings."[6] However, the painting to which this movement responds offers an alternative reading to that arrived at through structural analysis. The opening beats strike a listener like a haunting echo in a vast underground space. The dissonances that assail us in bars four and six might be understood as the brief thrill of fright experienced when torchlight passes over a wall of skulls. Unearthly sounds that seem so "Stravinsky-like" are only appropriate as a way of musically painting this otherworldly place. The mournful mood is the product not only of the setting but of the participants in it; this painting is the only self-portrait of Hartmann in *Pictures*, showing him visiting the catacombs of Paris alongside the architect Vasily Kenel and a guide. When the documentary evidence is considered in conjunction with the painting that was the source for "Catacombs," this movement becomes the emotional core of *Pictures at an Exhibition*, a searing expression of mourning for a friend and a frightening evocation of the inescapable presence of death in life.

Hartmann's own self-portrait encourages a re-interpretation of the Promenade theme that recurs throughout *Pictures at an Exhibition*. Although not based on a Hartmann painting, this theme can be productively understood as a direct response to Hartmann's art as well. Musorgsky emulates his friend's medium, rather than any single painting, by not merely depicting the process of moving around the exhibition but actually offering a changing series of self-portraits of his own. Musorgsky makes this clear in a letter to Stasov, in which he writes "My physiognomy is evident in the interludes."[7] A particularly interesting example of how the theme portrays the composer himself is the Promenade movement that follows "Catacombs," titled "Con Mortuis in Lingua Morta" ("With the dead in a dead language"). As Derrick Puffett has argued, "[Catacombs] depends on 'Con mortuis' to resolve the tonal and harmonic tensions that have been set up."[8] While the theme is still immediately audible, it has taken on the quavering, minor tones of the underworld. No longer the confident, brassy Promenade of the opening, now the tempo has slowed markedly from *allegro giusto* to *andante ma non troppo, con lamento*. Musorgsky's own marginal notes in the manuscript of "Con Mortuis in Lingua Morta" describe the movement thus: "The creative spirit of the departed Hartmann leads me towards the skulls and addresses them—a pale light radiates from the interior of the skulls."[9] We hear a portrayal of the composer in the act of being drawn into the world of Hartmann's painting of the catacombs of Paris, mourning as he moves. The artist is included alongside Musorgsky in this self-portrait by means of a citation from the end of Act II of *Boris Godunov*, Musorgsky's influential opera, which he had completed only at the urging of Hartmann. For this reason, the artist was intimately linked with this success. The inclusion of music from the opera can be understood as a way for Musorgsky to emulate the medium of painting to portray his lamented friend.

Case Study 2: Sibelius's Symphony No. 1 (1899)

Just as adequate textual evidence was a precondition for the search for paintings in the music of Musorgsky, so it must be for Sibelius. Ample documentation attests to the fact that Sibelius was passionate about painting and in sustained contact with it through his friendship with the pre-eminent Finnish painter of the fin-de-siècle, Akseli Gallen-Kallela, especially in the years from 1891 to 1902, when they were at their closest. Sibelius claimed, "The other arts fascinate me more than do [sic] other people's music," and said of himself, "really I am a tone painter and a poet."[10] In a reflection that is particularly important for the example that it provides of his desire to bridge disciplinary boundaries and respond to the visual arts in music, the composer wrote in the autumn of 1890, "When I was a boy I thought I would invent an altogether new art (it would be half-sculpture and half-music I thought). I began with sculpture and as you know that turned out disastrously."[11] Little is known of this brief foray into the visual arts, but the desire to incorporate them into his music would remain with him. His pupil Bengt de Törne wrote, "Unlike so many musicians, Sibelius is deeply interested in literature, fine art, history and other subjects.... Many of his happiest and most popular inspirations have originated in his reading and contact with other arts."[12] His long association with Gallen-Kallela was the most important instance of this contact; Sibelius called him "Finland's greatest painter" and composed *Surusoitto* ("Funeral Music") upon Gallen-Kallela's death in 1931.[13] Gallen-Kallela was equally invested in Sibelius's music: he painted the composer's portrait three times, including himself in the image on two of those occasions, and attempted to depict at least one of Sibelius's compositions in paint with the diptych *Sibelius as the Composer of 'En Saga'* of 1894. While these intriguing points of contact demonstrate the richness of their engagement with each other's work and are eminently deserving of further study, I will instead focus on Sibelius's efforts to represent specific paintings by Gallen-Kallela in his compositions.

Some bolder scholars have begun to suggest that there is more than a passing resemblance between certain of Gallen-Kallela's paintings and Sibelius's music, but none has been willing to make much of this, presumably because of the difficulty of proving such linkages. Eero Tarasti, for one, tantalizes his readers by hinting that "If we ... juxtapose Gallen-Kallela's painting [*Kullervo Departs for Battle*, 1901] with the earlier painting [*Kullervo Cursing*, 1899] and moreover the fourth and second movement in Sibelius's *Kullervo* Symphony [1892], we may discover interesting similitudes between them," and noted that "[t]he long pauses [in the 4th movement of *Kullervo*] may be interpreted there to symbolize the stillness and motionlessness of the surrounding nature analogically to Gallen-Kallela's painting [*Kullervo Cursing*]."[14] Tarasti is content to leave these pungent observations hanging in the air, without attempting to prove that Gallen-Kallela was responding to Sibelius's music as he had in his painting *Sibelius as the Composer of 'En Saga'*. However, Tarasti's recognition of a certain similarity between the work of Gallen-Kallela and Sibelius when they turned to subjects from the Finnish national epic, the *Kalevala*, of which the story of Kullervo was one, points the way to a new reading of Sibelius's next effort in the symphonic form.

While Sibelius's *Kullervo* preceded and cannot be a response to Gallen-Kallela's influential series of paintings of subjects from the *Kalevala*—works that caused one scholar to claim that the artist "gave the *Kalevala* its definitive 'look'"—Sibelius's Symphony No. 1 of 1899 is another matter.[15] Although not overtly programmatic like *Kullervo*, the symphony "evokes the Kullervo poem in the *Kalevala*," according to Ilmari Krohn, a musicologist and friend of Sibelius.[16] Because of his close association with Sibelius in the period and the fact that Krohn's own piece *Paimenessa* ("Shepherd's Song") was an important inspiration for Sibelius's turn to *Kalevala* subjects, Krohn's word on this is reliable. James Hepokoski has written of the First Symphony, "Here we encounter bold patches of color laid onto the sonic canvas with the broad strokes of the palette knife, not the fine brush," another indication that the sudden shifts of tone and mood may bear a structural resemblance to the characteristic bold, patchy colors of a Gallen-Kallela canvas.[17] Sibelius wrote in his sketchbook, "The wind blows cold, cold weather from the lake, motto for the first movement of the symphony."[18] This makes clear that the piece was not without visual content, despite the lack of an explicit program. Erik Tawaststjerna reports that Sibelius's description of the movement is taken from a "well-known Finnish folk song," encouraging us to consider Gallen-Kallela as a source because he was among the first to travel to the Karelia region to collect folk songs, giving rise to the move-ment known as "Karelianism," in which Sibelius was an enthusiastic participant.[19] Others have gone so far as to call this Sibelius's "Karelianist" symphony.[20] This wealth of textual evidence about the visual resonances of the first movement of the first symphony urges a search for Gallen-Kallela paintings that might enhance our understanding of it, but the difficulty remains of making such linkages more than self-serving aesthetic generalizations.

A route forward is offered by surviving documents that demonstrate that Sibelius had a rare form of synaesthesia that caused the sight of specific colors to produce an immediate, permanently linked tonal sensation in his mind, or tonal–seeing synaes-thesia, the inverse of a more common form known as *l'audition colorée*. In contrast to artists and composers who have affected "metaphoric pseudosynaesthesia" as a form of higher artistic consciousness—examples include Baudelaire, Scriabin, and Kandinsky—all evidence suggests that Sibelius had a neurological condition that he could not control.[21] The composer only rarely wrote of his experience with the condition himself, and as a result is usually omitted from lists of historical figures with synaesthesia. However, accounts of friends leave little doubt. Adolf Paul, a prominent writer and member of the same intellectual circle as Gallen-Kallela and Sibelius, offers a crucial account of the composer's childhood:

> For him there existed a strange mysterious connection between sound and colour, between the most secret perceptions of the eye and ear. Everything he saw produced a corresponding impression on his ear ... And this he thought natural, with as good reason as those who did not possess this fac-ulty, called him crazy or affectedly original. For this reason he only spoke of this in the strictest confidence and under a pledge of silence. 'For otherwise they will make fun of me!'[22]

Similarly, the composer and critic Karl Flodin wrote in a memoir of his first meeting with the student Sibelius in the 1880s, "Before we knew where we were, Sibelius was juggling with colours and sounds as if they were bright glass balls, made colours resound and sounds glow, so that A major became blue, C major red, F major green and D major yellow, and so on like that."[23] While it is unfortunate that this is all we know and no similar document indicates the colors Sibelius associated with minor tonalities, the surviving color–tone code permits a deeper understanding of the dis-tinctly painterly materials of the allegro of the First Symphony and encourages us to seek a painting that corresponds with the documentary evidence and would have been available to Sibelius while he was at work on the piece.

We know that Sibelius was in regular contact with Gallen-Kallela in Berlin in May of 1898 while he was writing the First Symphony. Because of these circum-stances, there can be little doubt that Sibelius saw *Kullervo Cursing* (Figure 16.1), which Gallen-Kallela was working on at the time, while writing the first movement. This painting, in which Eero Tarasti recognized something of Sibelius's musical vocabulary, is predominately a muted yellow, a color that we know was associated with the sound of D major. While the symphony is in E minor, there are two unmis-takable moments of D major in the strings at measures 203 and 241, the first a kind of appoggiatura and the second resolving a particularly eerie and directionless pas-sage that has come before it. These achingly sweet passages seem strikingly out of place in a movement that is all foreboding and bombast, so it is reasonable to look to the painting as a possible explanation for them. The fact that the figure of Kullervo stands next to a lake in the painting, as in Sibelius's own description of the movement, further reinforces this link. With this context in mind, a listener hears in the allegro of Sibelius's first symphony an evocation of Gallen-Kallela's painting, with its subject, the hot-headed slave boy of the title, pledging revenge on those who had wronged him. *Kullervo Cursing* lends the mood of the movement and there are distinct suggestions of its subject matter throughout.

The future directions for the study of the representation of paintings in music are many. For simplicity, this account has been limited to two instances in which composers have explicitly represented paintings. Still more examples could be mentioned if the terms are broadened to include other art-forms, such as sculpture and architecture, and other less literal categories of musical repurposing. Mendelssohn was mentioned earlier as an example of a composer who is known for the explicitly visual resonance of his music. However, his body of work is ripe for further study in the vein described here because of the depth of his engagement with the visual arts. Manuscript scores by Mendelssohn offer another way in which scholars might approach the use of the visual arts as musical material: by tracing correlations between drawings in the margins in Mendelssohn's own hand, his paintings, and his music. While Sibelius and Musorgsky were deeply invested in the visual arts, neither had Mendelssohn's talent as a painter, so there is every likelihood that his compositions contain sophisticated responses to the visual arts—his own creations and those of others—if we only search. The challenges of studying paintings in music are significant, but, with methodical research, it will be possible to offer new insights into the work of these and a great many more composers.

Notes

1 Daniel M. Grimley, "The Tone Poems: Genre, Landscape and Structural Perspective," in *The Cambridge Companion to Sibelius*, ed. Grimley (Cambridge: Cambridge University Press, 2004), 107.
2 Originally a footnote in Stasov's "Musorgsky: A Biographical Sketch," translated in Michael Russ, *Musorgsky: Pictures at an Exhibition* (Cambridge: Cambridge University Press, 1992), 16.
3 Translated in David Brown, *Musorgsky: His Life and Works* (Oxford: Oxford University Press, 2002), 230.
4 Russ, *Musorgsky*, x.
5 For a reproduction of this crucial image, see Russ, *Musorgsky*, plate 4 (between pages 49 and 50).
6 Derrick Puffett, "A Graphic Analysis of Musorgsky's 'Catacombs'," *Music Analysis* 9, no. 1 (1990): 67.
7 Translated in Brown, *Musorgsky*, 230.
8 Puffett, "A Graphic Analysis," 68.
9 Quoted in Alfred Frankenstein, "Victor Hartmann and Modeste Musorgsky," *The Musical Quarterly* 25, no. 3 (1939), 286.
10 Letter to Aino Sibelius of 28 July 1894, quoted in Erik Tawaststjerna, *Sibelius* (London: Faber and Faber, 1976), 1: 155; Letter to Aino Sibelius of 19 August 1894, quoted in Grimley, "The Tone Poems," 100.
11 Tawaststjerna, *Sibelius*, 1: 35.
12 Bengt de Törne, *Sibelius: A Close Up* (London: Faber and Faber, 1937), 92.
13 Editor's note, *Architectural Association Quarterly* 7, no. 3 (1975), 2.
14 Eero Tarasti, *Myth and Music: A Semiotic Approach to the Aesthetics of Myth in Music, especially that of Wagner, Sibelius and Stravinsky* (The Hague: Mouton, 1979), 264 and 266.

15 Patty Wageman, "Fired by Passion: The Life and Work of Akseli Gallen-Kallela," in *Akseli Gallen-Kallela: The Spirit of Finland*, ed. David Jackson and Patty Wageman, exh. cat. (Groningen: Groninger Museum, 2006), 11.

16 Tawaststjerna, *Sibelius*, 1: 217.

17 James Hepokoski, "Sibelius," in *The Nineteenth-Century Symphony*, ed. D. Holoman (New York: Schirmer Books, 1997), 422.

18 Tawaststjerna, *Sibelius*, 1: 201.

19 Ibid.

20 James Hepokoski and Fabian Dahlström, "Sibelius, Jean," *Grove Music Online, Oxford Music Online* (Oxford University Press).

21 Simon Baron-Cohen and John E. Harrison, "Synaesthesia: An Introduction," in *Synaesthesia: Classic and Contemporary Readings*, ed. Baron-Cohen and Harrison (Oxford: Blackwell, 1997), 8.

22 Quoted in Karl Ekman, *Jean Sibelius: His Life and Personality* (London: A. Wilmer Ltd., 1938), 38–9.

23 Ibid., 40.

Further Reading

Fink, Monika. *Musik nach Bildern: Programmbezognenes Komponieren im 19. und 20. Jahrhundert.* Innsbruck: Helbling, 1988.

Frankenstein, Alfred. "Victor Hartmann and Modeste Musorgsky." *The Musical Quarterly* 25, no. 3 (1939): 268–291.

Grimley, Daniel M., ed. *The Cambridge Companion to Sibelius.* Cambridge: Cambridge University Press, 2004.

Morton, Marsha L. and Peter L. Schmunk, ed. *The Arts Entwined: Music and Painting in the Nineteenth Century.* New York: Garland, 2000.

Russ, Michael. *Musorgsky: Pictures at an Exhibition.* Cambridge: Cambridge University Press, 1992.

Tawaststjerna, Erik. *Sibelius.* Edited and translated by Robert Layton. 3 vols. London: Faber and Faber, 1976–1997.

Vergo, Peter. *The Music of Painting: Music, Modernism and the Visual Arts from the Romantics to John Cage.* London: Phaidon, 2010.

Walton, Kendall. "Listening with Imagination: Is Music Representational?" *The Journal of Aesthetics and Art Criticism* 52, no. 1 (1994): 47–61.

17
GESTURE AND IMAGERY IN MUSIC PERFORMANCE
Perspectives from North Indian Classical Music

Laura Leante

The experience of music is a multi-faceted one, and entails complex visual and gestural engagement at different levels of sound production and reception. In the following pages I will discuss how a comprehensive understanding of this visual aspect necessarily involves consideration of bodily involvement in performance and how both are ultimately integral to the aural dimension of music.

Performers use their bodies to make music, whether through their voice or by playing instruments; they move—more or less ostensibly—to communicate with fellow musicians and audiences, and—more or less deliberately—to accompany the flow of the music, or to support meanings associated with it. Other participants and listeners also, depending on the context of performance, move their bodies to the music, for example to dance, clap, express appreciation, or communicate with each other and with musicians. All these behaviors are regulated by genre-specific cultural codes and are embedded in the role that each individual takes on in the music event. Most of all, these movements and gestures, together with the visual experience that accompanies them, are integral to processes of music-making and reception: participating in a performance as well as "just" listening to music implies sharing these movements—by seeing them, by making them, or by associating sounds and memories with them.

At the same time, musical sound is embodied through patterns of movement, and even listening (including remote listening to recordings, for example) involves experiencing this movement. Such embodiment of sound can be manifested through movement in performance, as well as in conversation, as people support the discussion of their experience of music through gesture and through imagery and metaphors; these images can be rich with extra-musical details, and can reveal information on the meanings and emotions that people associate with music. Rather than being *a posteriori* attachments, these visual elements are closely connected to musical sound: in fact, while retaining their cultural specificity, they are rooted in the same process that makes music a physical experience. Music experience is therefore a visual and bodily, as much as an auditory one: music is "seen," and is perceived as movement, as well as listened to.

In this chapter I challenge notions of a disembodied nature of music shared among certain cultures (including Western art music), where the invisibility of the sound object often leads to the assumption of the ineffability of an abstract musical experience. On the contrary, I will claim that music is experienced at a bodily level and—most importantly—that this experience can be expressed through images and gesture, which are integral and not incidental to processes of embodiment of music. Furthermore, the interconnectedness of these visual and gestural aspects is such that one cannot be fully understood without taking the other into account.

The cross-modal nature of musical experience and also the role of gesture in music performance are at the center of current scientific debate, and literature on this topic has increased in recent years, with contributions reflecting the interdisciplinary interest to which the subject lends itself. A lot of this work is grounded in research into embodied cognition, challenging the Cartesian dichotomy of body and mind, and in studies on the relationship of speech and gesture in verbal communication. Of particular relevance to the present discussion is David McNeill's acknowledgment that gesture and speech are co-expressive and non-redundant, and, most of all, that they both emerge from a common imagistic ground. Extending this to the analysis of performance, it can be argued that gesture, image, and sound stem from the same process of musical expression. Investigating these aspects necessarily involves not only analyzing each one of them but, more importantly, emphasizing their interrelationships, considering, for example, how connotations arising from a given music can convey kinetic qualities, how gesture can integrate aural information, or how certain visualizations accompany the production of musical sound.

The analysis of performance in both its musical and visual aspects needs to be supported by ethnographic research aimed at carrying out inquiries into how people describe their experience of music, the extra-musical associations, images, and emotions they attach to it, and, in particular, how they express them both verbally and through gesture. In the next section I will focus on Hindustani (North Indian) art—or "classical"—music, and in particular on ethnographic work on the vocal genre of khyal (nowadays the most commonly heard classical genre across the North of India), and on inquiries carried out between 2005 and 2010 with a number of khyal singers.[1] While I suggest that this tradition is far from being a unique case, the rich and often openly articulated body of extra-musical—including visual—associations attached to it makes North Indian classical music an ideal object of consideration for this discussion.

The Ethnography of Imagery and Gesture in Khyal

Khyal concerts take place in public halls and large auditoriums, as well as in private homes where artists and a few listeners sit together on the floor in close proximity. The latter, smaller venues reflect a more traditional way of listening to and appreciating this music, and even today members of the public sometimes spontaneously split into two groups, with men and women occupying different areas of the room.

The performance space can be unadorned, or decorated with flowers or a colored backdrop. The music is led by a singer (rarely a duo), who sits at the center of the stage. On his right and left side sit respectively a drum player on *tabla*, who provides the rhythmic accompaniment, and a harmonium (or *sarangi*) player, who shadows the melody performed by the singer. One or more musicians (often students of the singer) sit at the back, playing the drone on *tanpuras* and sometimes providing vocal support.

During the concert hand gestures, glances, and head nods are employed by the participants to fulfill a number of different functions. Musicians on stage exchange visual as well as aural musical cues to structure the unfolding of the music performance (by marking new sections or solos, for example), guide fellow performers, reward virtuosic passages, or to acknowledge the presence and seek the approval of the more knowledgeable listeners and senior artists who customarily sit in the front rows of the audience. Especially in smaller venues, these latter musicians are observed by other members of the public, who look at them, searching for signs of support for or disapproval of the performance. Moreover, audience members can tap along with the rhythmic cycle, and punctuate the event with nods, exclamations, and hand movements to show appreciation of the music. In any case, attending a concert involves ascertaining participants' roles and status, and visually following a complex web of relationships. The singer is at the center of these dynamics and the achievement of a successful performance relies on his capacity to manage them in an effective manner, as well as to focus on the delivery of his music. The accompanists' and audience's eyes are constantly on him, as his movements, therefore, both communicate with other participants and support and accompany the production of musical sound.

In contrast to other Indian performing arts (such as, for example, classical dance forms, or the more romantic vocal genre *thumri*), *khyal* singers are not expected to perform iconic or symbolic gestures fulfilling a depictive function to underline the text of a song or meanings associated with the music. Their movements are assumed to be more abstract, supporting the flow of the music in the improvised sections as well as in the performance of compositions with lyrics. I will now turn to these supporting movements, and I will discuss how gestures are integral to the singer's imagination in the production of musical sound, and how movement relates to the images and meanings that are associated with it.

Like other Hindustani classical genres, *khyal* is considered part of a complex tradition which can elicit profound emotions, often likened to and described in terms of religious feelings and deep, fulfilling aesthetic experiences. It is based on a system of modes (the *ragas*), which are defined in terms of musical features such as scale profiles, principal pitches, distinctive phrases, and melodic movements, and also in terms of extra-musical traits, including prescribed time of day and season of performance, moods, characters, or even contingent effects that some modes are believed to cause. At times, raga names can contribute to conjuring up certain associations and images, as in the case of toponyms like Multani (referring to the region of Multan), or direct references to seasons, like Basant (Spring), or characters, such as Durga, named after the Hindu goddess.

Moreover, song texts (often romantic and/or devotional) represent other sources of visual information attached to the music. There is no consensus among singers on the level of importance that the lyrics and their content should be given in

147

khyal, and different artists claim to be aware to different extents of the text's content when performing; however, these texts can still contribute to shaping the artist's imagination.

Each raga, therefore, is accompanied by a rich corpus of images and associations which combine to define its musical identity. The importance that this visual aspect has long had in North Indian classical music culture is corroborated by the *raga-mala* paintings, collections which flourished in India's princely states and depicted ragas as human or divine personifications, and which are discussed in more depth in Chapter 29 in this volume. Although nowadays musicians rarely make reference to these paintings when talking about music, they remain among the visual sources accessible to the imagination of performers and listeners alike.

Extensive enquiries among musicians have shown how each individual artist seems to create his or her own picture of a raga, by drawing on both personal experiences and shared imagery; recurrent examples of the latter are represented by images stemming from the time of performance, with evening ragas often associated with birds returning home, night ragas with dark or starry skies, and morning ragas with the sunrise. The analysis of this pool of visual resources shows how musicians often portray ragas by making recourse to common tropes, mythological references, local geographies, and cultural practices. A typical instance is the musician figuring himself in a contemplative mood by a river or by the ocean, or—in the case of more serious or devotional ragas—in the act of praying in front of a god. Other examples refer to specific ragas, like the description by Bengali singer Arun Bhaduri of the seriousness and the virility of Shree raga through the image of the god Shiva: for him, Shree is "king-like ... [It's a] very strong mood, [he's holding] a trident."[2] This mythological picture is very different from the one provided by Sudokshina Chatterjee when talking about her experience of another raga, Bihag. Although still tinged with devotional references, her depiction conveys a much more joyful mood, pointing at the myth of the young Krishna and his lover Radha in his birthplace, Vrindavan, the stories about his playful teasing of cowgirls, and the Spring festival of Holi, which people celebrate by throwing paint and colored powders at each other: "When I perform Bihag ... I try to imagine that I'm in Vrindavan and I can see that Lord Krishna and Radha [are] there ... throwing colors at each other ... and all beautiful girls also ... running here and there."[3]

The extent to which extra-musical associations are explicitly taught by a guru varies: the knowledge transmitted by the teacher generally includes—apart from the musical features—information about the time of performance, the mood, and a number of compositions set in a given raga. Some teachers make recourse to imagery to explain more effectively the feeling that a raga is supposed to convey, its melodic movement, or a technique of sound production.

Most importantly, musicians often use gesture to accompany and clarify these images or the performance of a specific melodic passage. An example is provided by Manjiri Asanare-Kelkar, who—during an interview—stated how hand movement had become essential to the explanation of musical content in her communication with her late guru Madhusudan S. Kanetkar, once his old age and fragile physical condition had started to affect his vocal strength: "Sometimes he just gives the action [and] I understand what he means."[4] Gestures depicting abstract designs were sufficient for Manjiri to understand, for instance, the melodic contour or emphasis of a musical phrase. To illustrate her point she performed a quick, contained circular movement of the hand and explained that she associated it with a short, smooth phrase, within a small interval range, emphasizing the first and, mostly, last pitches (Figure 17.1). Gesture, image and sound are all non-redundant parts of a single process: seeing the hand movement provides specific and unique information about how the musicians conceive their music and its performance.

While the explicit use of images associated with a raga's identity in didactic contexts is not practiced by all teachers, gesture—as in the case of Manjiri Asanare-Kelkar—plays a fundamental role in the transmission of North Indian musical knowledge, and its use is widespread. Picking up music is about both watching and listening, as well as reproducing sound: in fact, learning *khyal* involves the repetition by the student of a passage performed by the guru—a process which is usually accompanied by the imitation on the part of the disciple of the guru's gesture. Although this is not a topic often discussed explicitly by teachers during the lesson, and not all teachers openly encourage students to use hand movement to support their performance, it is easy to observe that the students' vocal improvements correspond to the development of smoother and more confident gestures. Sudokshina Chatterjee's experience confirms this co-expressiveness of gesture and sound in music production: "The hands give you psychological support ... when I started using my hand I was more expressive, the expression came more ... naturally."[5]

Literature on the transmission of gesture in Hindustani classical music is extremely scarce; however, it is plausible to hypothesize that a guru's movements would exert an influence on the development of his student's own gestures, as Ashwini Bhide Deshpande seems to suggest: "I think we have seen our senior artists also doing these gestures and it comes out unknowingly. When my mother was teaching me, probably she was doing these gestures; and it comes ... I [picked] up those qualities also along with [the music]."[6]

There is no agreement among musicians on the aesthetics of gesture in performance and therefore on the impact that more or less emphatic hand movement can have on the audience and on the effective delivery of a raga.

However, although there is ample margin for individual behavior (and in fact singers' movement on stage varies a lot), most claim to prefer a more restrained, rather than flamboyant comportment. In any case, as the musicians quoted above indicate, gesture is considered a natural part of music performance, as "[the] total body is singing, not [just the] voice."[7]

Singers describe their use of gesture as something which they do not deliberately control, something "unconscious,"[8] spontaneous, and at the same time idiosyncratic, as summarized by the seemingly contradictory words of Vijay Koparkar: "The movement of the hands is a natural thing, [it] is a habit."[9] Therefore, if on the one hand it is a key element for the acquisition of musical knowledge and it is learned through the observation of the guru, on the other hand bodily involvement is acknowledged by *khyal* singers as intrinsic in music production, since "gesture goes with the *swaras* [notes]."[10]

In performance, gesture often seems to stem from embodied metaphors of direction as, for example, conceptualizations of high and low musical pitch in melodic development can correspond to analogous trajectories in hand movement: some singers explain that in their mind they visualize, if not the single notes, at least these trajectories between phrases or pivotal pitches of the raga. Similarly, a number of pantomimic gestures can often be seen: for example, notes can be "held" or "sustained"—both with the hands and the voice, as the imaginary as well as the physical space around the performer is occupied by his arms. Some musicians—not coincidentally—liken performing a raga to making a design, drawing patterns, or painting on a canvas. Ashwini Bhide Deshpande, in particular, explained how she associates her singing with visualizing and organizing colors and architectures: the former are related to the identity and mood of the raga; the latter refer to the structure of the overall performance. She also specified that the way she manages them is not random, but can depend, for example, on the planned length given to a raga, as longer ragas (which usually last approximately forty-five to sixty minutes) are performed as the first item, and shorter ones as the second item in the standard format of a *khyal* concert:

> I sometimes do see colors, I sometimes do see pictures, some architectures; but, you know, I don't think that's very raga-specific ... Colors, maybe yes; architectures, no ... I think [the architecture] comes from the structure, the building of the raga. I'll give you an example: rag Ahir Bhairav ... has the potential of being expanded for over one hour ... in that case, I might build a bigger structure with that rag ... But now this same rag, if I am treating [it] now as a second rag of my performance ... I will not treat it the same way, I will not structure it the same way as I would if I am treating it like a first rag. In that case, I might just splash some colors, and not think about the structure at all, of the rag. It's that way.[11]

Ashwini Bhide's mention of color associations is not unique: other musicians too link ragas to shades and colors, which often stem from either the mood or the prescribed time of performance of a raga. However, as I pointed out earlier, the visual body that musicians draw on to shape their own idea of a raga is wider, and can include images (either shared or constructed by each individual), which can be quite detailed in their pictorial qualities. How do images connected with a given raga and with the singer's own experience of it relate to body movement?

An example of how intertwined gesture and imagery can be in both the production of music and the verbal discussion of the experience of its performance is provided by Arun Bhaduri's explanation of Kedar, a night raga, in which the fourth degree of the scale can be both natural and sharp, and which is characterized by oblique melodic phrases. During an interview, Arun Bhaduri described Kedar's characteristic melodic movement (*chalan*) with rolling, circular, and undulating movements of his hands (Figure 17.2 A and B). Then, when talking about the mood and the pictures that the raga arouses in him, he specified that Kedar reminds him of sea waves and of the feeling of standing by the seashore. While saying this, he repeated the same circular gestures he had made before (Figure 17.2 C): the common image of the musician standing by the sea is accompanied by the more precise, raga-specific detail of the movement of the water waves. Most of all, he immediately demonstrated the movement of the waves singing Kedar's *chalan*, and again, accompanying the music with circular and undulating gestures (Figure 17.2 D and E).

Kedar's *chalan* is therefore embodied as a pattern of movement which can be expressed by a circular, undulating, contained hand gesture, and by the image of sea waves; or, vice versa, it can be seen as the sonic rendition of an extra-musical, visual experience, i.e. the view of the waves. Most importantly, Arun Bhaduri adapts the shared common image of the musician standing by the seashore by adding and focusing on the detail of the waves' movement: these images are reflected in and at the same time stem from the process of embodiment of the music. His experience of raga Kedar is therefore a complex one, in which musical sound is inseparable from visual and gestural aspects.

Imagery and Gesture in Performance: Some Concluding Remarks

Arun Bhaduri's use of gesture in performance is, of course, more complex than the brief, clear hand movement displayed during our conversation. As discussed above, in fact, body movement during a concert fulfills a number of functions, including managing musical and social relationships with other participants, as well as structuring the development of the music and supporting the production of sound. The boundaries between these different kinds of movements are often blurred and it can be difficult to distinguish neatly between them.

However, analysis of video footage of a performance of raga Kedar that Arun Bhaduri gave the evening before the interview shows that he made circular hand gestures when singing Kedar's *chalan*, in particular during the first section of the raga, in which the mood and the character of Kedar are thoroughly explored and presented.[12] Whether in that moment the singer was visualizing the ocean waves is impossible to determine: what is important is that the kinetic qualities of the melodic movement he associated with the images of the water waves are reflected in the process of embodiment of musical sound and are expressed through gesture. Similarly, other participants, including listeners, will not have grasped Arun Bhaduri's specific image, but his hand movements will have contributed to conveying the character of the melody: this, in turn, will be integral to the shaping of their own experience of raga Kedar, as the shared body of images and extra-musical associations attached to a raga is complemented by one's own pictures and details.

Movement in performance will also reflect a singer's own idiosyncratic gestural behavior, which is developed through training and through the observation of the teacher, as part of the process of acquisition of musical knowledge. At the same time, it will be affected by the corpus of visual sources associated with different ragas, as well as by images employed to describe the performance of large-scale structures (such as architectures or colors), or specific phrases (as in the case of movements implying metaphors of trajectories).

The auditory, the visual, and the gestural are therefore integral parts of the experience and the performance of music. Acknowledging the importance of these aspects and their interconnectedness, and investigating them simultaneously rather than considering them as separate elements, is essential to an understanding of how people make and make sense of music.

Notes

1 The fieldwork in India was sponsored by the UK Arts and Humanities Research Council (grants MRG-AN6186 and AH/G012911/1), and the British Academy (grant SG38692). All interviews were carried out by the author together with Martin Clayton, unless otherwise stated. I would like to acknowledge the musicians who took part in the research, and in particular: Arun Bhaduri, Ashwini Bhide Deshpande, Chiranjib Chakraborti, Sudokshina Chatterjee, Babanrao Haldankar, Manjiri Asanare Kelkar, Vijay Koparkar, and Veena Sahasrabuddhe. Finally, I would like to thank

Martin Clayton for his comments on a first draft of this chapter, and Tarun Nayak for providing help with the translation of Arun Bhaduri's interview from Bengali.

2 Arun Bhaduri, 15 February 2007, interview first published in Laura Leante, "The Lotus and the King: Imagery, Gesture and Meaning in a Hindustani Rāg," *Ethnomusicology Forum* 18, no. 2 (2009): 185–206.

3 Sudokshina Chatterjee, 8 June 2006.

4 Manjiri Asanare Kelkar, 11 December 2006, interview first published in Gina Fatone, Martin Clayton, Laura Leante, and Matt Rahaim, "Imagery, Melody and Gesture in Cross-cultural Perspective," in *New Perspectives on Music and Gesture*, ed. Anthony Gritten, and Anthony and Elaine King (Farnham: Ashgate, 2011), 203–220.

5 Sudokshina Chatterjee, 8 June 2006.

6 Aswhini Bhide Deshpande, 5 February 2010. Interview carried out by the author together with Martin Clayton and Simone Tarsitani.

7 Chiranjib Chakraborti, 6 June 2009.

8 Babanrao Haldankar, 31 January 2010. Interview carried out by the author together with Martin Clayton and Simone Tarsitani.

9 Vijay Koparkar, 18 February 2010. Interview carried out by the author together with Martin Clayton, Tarun Nayak and Simone Tarsitani.

10 Veena Sahasrabuddhe, 5 May 2005.

11 Ashwini Bhide Deshpande, 5 February 2010. Interview carried out by the author together with Martin Clayton and Simone Tarsitani.

12 The concert took place in Raniganj, West Bengal, on 14 February 2007. The video recordings were made with Martin Clayton and Andrew McGuiness.

Further Reading

Clayton, Martin, Byron Dueck, and Laura Leante, eds. *Experience and Meaning in Music Performance*. New York: Oxford University Press, 2013.

Godøy, Rolf Inge and Marc Leman, eds. *Musical Gestures: Sound, Movement, and Meaning*. New York: Routledge, 2010.

Gritten, Anthony and Elaine King, eds. *New Perspectives on Music and Gesture*. Farnham: Ashgate, 2011.

Leante, Laura. "The Lotus and the King: Imagery, Gesture and Meaning in a Hindustani Rāg." *Ethnomusicology Forum* 18, no. 2 (2009): 185–206.

MacNeill, David. *Hand and Mind: What Gestures Reveal about Thought*. Chicago: University of Chicago Press, 1992.

——. *Gesture and Thought*. Chicago: University of Chicago Press, 2005.

Rahaim, Matt. *Musicking Bodies: Gesture and Voice in Hindustani Music*. Middletown, CT: Wesleyan University Press, 2012.

Tagg, Philip. "Gestural Interconversion and Connotative Precision." *Film International* 13, no. 1 (2005): 20–31.

18
NOTATIONS
Context and Structure in Japanese Traditional Music Notation

Liv Lande

Notation is a visual representation of musical sounds and/or of how these sounds should be reproduced. It is found in numerous music cultures all over the world, in their culture-specific forms. Notation performs diverse functions and roles, depending on its overall aim and the musical values predominant in its cultural context.

The music cultures of East Asia share a long history of notation. Coherent, well-established notation systems have been in use for hundreds of years, such as the Chinese *gongchepu* and the Korean *chŏngganbo*. Still, oral–aural transmission and rote learning have been the most central characteristics of these musical practices. In the East Asian context, notation has mainly functioned as an auxiliary means for musical memorization.

This chapter discusses the cultural context and structural qualities of notation in Japanese musical culture. Although there are distinct differences among the East Asian cultures in their musical values and practices, Japan shares with her neighbors the same two-fold relationship between oral–aural and written transmission.

The Cultural Context of Notation

In traditional Japanese music, notation has most often played a secondary role, subordinate to "face-to-face" oral transmission from teacher to student. Musical pieces were taught in a detailed, "strophe-by-strophe" manner, through practical kinesthetic imitation, visual observation, and listening. This method was the essential way of obtaining access to this type of music. In this context, notation was mainly applied as a tool for memorizing musical pieces.

Despite its subordinate position, written notation is found in all traditional music genres in Japan, and has a long history in many of them. Notations were introduced from China to Japan in the eighth century, at the latest. Moreover, one of the oldest extant printed music scores in the world is a Japanese *shōmyō* (Buddhist chant) notation associated with the Shingon Buddhist sect, dating back to 1472.

A central trait of notation in Japanese traditional music is the wide diversity of its systems. There is no common approach to notation used by all traditional genres and instruments. Rather, for each specific instrument or vocal style within each genre, there exists a particular notation system. For each instrument of a genre, there may be, again, slightly different notation systems in use, depending on school tradition and the branch of the school. In this way, the performer may not completely understand a type of notation unless he/she belongs to that school branch of a genre.

Various reasons can be offered for this complex diversity. Although music genres have influenced each other throughout history, most of the genres have still been formalized and carefully transmitted within their own small, isolated groups of devotees. Such groups have most often been families or specific groups of society, such as guilds of blind male musicians or female entertaining artists. In many of these isolated groups, their own music heritage was for a long time treated with secrecy in order to control and prevent dissemination. In this way, the artistic legacy was highly exclusive. These conditions were probably connected to the group's ability to secure income, and to preserve authentic transmission of their living masters' and ancestral masters' musical heritage. Such preservation practices can be associated with Confucian values, as I have argued in my own research. Further, in regard to the various notation systems, the information on how to play the music on specific instruments has been prioritized higher than indications of musical elements per se. Due to circumstances like these, the notation systems for each instrument in the respective genres have developed in their own unique ways.

In many genres, for instance in *koto* (thirteen-stringed, bridged, long zither) music, one may even find individual variations in the way music is transcribed. Each school branch and its masters often play specific pieces in a slightly different way to other schools or masters. Because of this, publicly published notations often cannot be used completely. It is therefore common for students to transcribe musical parts that are learned in the lesson. They do this either by writing everything out on their own, or by making individual corrections to a published version of the musical piece.

Today, audio and audiovisual recording technology provides ground-breaking possibilities for learning and transmitting music. Some teachers and schools of Japanese music have embraced these devices; others have not (yet).

Structural Characteristics in Japanese Notations

Despite the complex differences of musical notation in Japanese traditional music, as described above, there are still similarities between the notation systems, in terms of aims and information given. Below is an outline of two major categories of notation types in Japan. It is important to note, however, that although types of notation systems are listed separately within the two categories, some notation types may be combined or juxtaposed with each other in actual music scores today. This aspect can be observed in the concrete notation examples later in the chapter.

The first category of notations is tablature types mainly focusing on *how and where on the instrument to play*. These aspects represent fingering positions, fingerings, string names, playing techniques, and/or syllables referring to these above-mentioned elements. The second category mainly includes notations illustrating specific, selective *melodic and/or rhythmic patterns*. None of the notation systems has traditionally tended to prioritize accurate prescription of music-centered elements, such as pitch, rhythm, phrasing, meter, tempo, and timbre. Rather, an outline of the music is presented in the notations. Nevertheless, owing to massive Euro-American influence since the late nineteenth century, detailed denotations of musical aspects have become more common in vernacular notation forms.

Category 1: Notations focusing on *how and where on the instrument to play*

Shôga

Shôga syllables stand in a unique position in this notation context, since they function in both oral learning and transmission of music as well as in written notation. Shôga is a type of solmization, which consists of mnemonic, onomatopoeic-like syllables. David Hughes calls it an "acoustic-iconic mnemonic system."[1] As his term indicates, it consists of the acoustic sounds of syllables, and the syllables in written, "iconic" form. The specific syllables often imitate and refer to specific pitch (relative or absolute), rhythm, timbre, playing techniques, and/or melodic and rhythmic patterns on the actual instrument. All traditional instruments and genres have their own system of shôga, with their specific syllables, vowels, and consonants referring to their particular elements in the music. For instance, the shôga for the piece *Etenraku* used with the *hichiriki* (a short double-reed pipe used in the gagaku court music ensemble) starts like this: "to-ra-ro' o-ru-ro' ta-a-ro-ra' a-a." In written form, shôga functions as a type of notation. Today, in published music scores, shôga is often combined with other notation systems. In scores, shôga is written in Japanese syllabic, phonetic *katakana* letters. Katakana is now used exclusively for foreign-derived names and words, not for general texts where syllabic, phonetic *hiragana* letters and Chinese characters are applied. Therefore, the use of katakana for shôga may signal that the words do not convey conventional linguistic meanings. Although the iconic component of shôga helps in visually memorizing the syllables, it refers only to their pronunciations. The pitches and other indirect meanings of the syllables can only be acquired through practical training.

Shôga is often sung or recited independently from notation, for instance in the learning context. When a student begins to learn a musical instrument or a new piece of music, it is common to first learn to sing the piece by using shôga syllables. After a while, the student may hold the instrument and move her fingers on it as when playing, while still singing the shôga. Then, when these initial stages are completed, the student finally starts his training on the instrument itself. For koto, on the other hand, it is more customary to start playing the instrument from the beginning. The teacher then sings the shôga of the piece as the student plays it.

String instruments: fingering position or string name notation

For string instruments, two different methods of notation are employed. One is to describe musical performance mainly by illustrating where on the strings to use the left-hand fingers (finger positions). The second method is to show which strings to play. In order to illustrate the diversity of notation types that depend on genre and school traditions, and to exemplify the detailed structure of the notations, I will go into more depth for these string instrument notations than for the other types that follow. It must be stressed that a variety still exists in all genres and notation types.

155

Like several other string instruments, the *shamisen* (three-stringed, plucked, long-necked lute) employs a fingering position notation. It prescribes the left-hand finger positions on the respective strings of the instrument. The finger positions are indicated by Chinese characters, numerals, or symbols.

Depending on music genre and school tradition, the notation method and style for shamisen notation differ in a range of ways: in what symbols are used for strings, finger positions, and playing techniques; how to indicate musical elements such as time duration and rhythm; whether the notation is read horizontally or vertically; and so on. Below is a presentation of two common types of shamisen notation; yet more versions of shamisen notation exist.

The first type is called *kateishiki-fu* (chamber music style notation; see Example 18.1). This notation is a revised version of an earlier koto notation, formed at the beginning of the twentieth century. The notation is applied in *jiuta shamisen* music, a classical chamber music genre for shamisen, which includes singing. Written vertically, the notation should be read from top to bottom and right to left. Small, rectangular boxes (see 1, Example 18.1) lined up vertically in a group of four represent a bar (2). Each box refers to one quarter-tone (1). The bars are marked with horizontal double lines (3). Moreover, each "quarter-tone box" is partially subdivided horizontally into two parts, corresponding to eighth notes. The symbols for the finger positions are written inside the bar boxes, illustrating the duration of the tones. Time symbols and many other signs are influenced by Western five-line staff notation.

Using a large plectrum, which is held in the right hand, the performer plucks the three strings on the instrument box. The left hand moves up and down on the instrument neck while pressing the fingers at various positions on the strings. Finger positions on the first string are marked by Chinese numerals together with the Japanese letter イ (i.e., イ一, イ二, イ三). For the second and third strings, Chinese numerals (i.e., 一, 二, 三) and Arabic numerals are applied, respectively. For all strings, position one (イ一, 一, or 1) is the open string. The finger position two is a half tone above the open string. For each position upward, with a few exceptions, the pitch elevates a half tone. The symbol "•" beside the finger position numerals refers to one octave above, "• •" to two octaves above. Rests in various time durations have their specific signs, such as circles or triangles with a dot inside.

The notation also includes symbols for various playing techniques. These are written beside the finger position numerals. Some of the most common ones are *uchi* (ウ) (4), hitting the string with a left-hand finger; *suri* (c) (5), slipping the left fingers quickly upward or downward on the neck; and *sukui* (ス) (6), up-pluck with the plectrum on the indicated string and position. The left-hand index and middle and ring fingers are denoted as 人, 中 (7), and 工 (8), respectively.

On the top of the music score, the scale type used for the piece is specified (9). Although the tonal intervals in the respective scales are fixed, they can be tuned to various pitches. The shôga syllables, called *kuchi-jamisen* for shamisen (10), are likewise provided in the score. As the majority of jiuta shamisen music consists of vocal song with instrumental accompaniment, performed by the same person, the lyrics (12) are included in the music score together with the notation (11). The vocal notation is written in a small size with the same string name characters and additional symbols as for the shamisen part. All these elements (10–12) are written vertically in the notation, from top to bottom.

156

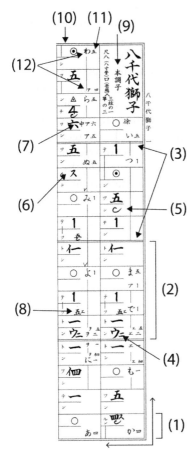

Example 18.1 Shamisen music scores of "Yachiyo-jishi," bars 1–8. Michio Miyagi, ed., Sangen-gakufu Yachiyo-jishi (Shamisen scores Yachiyo-jishi) (Tôkyô: Hôgakusha, 2011).

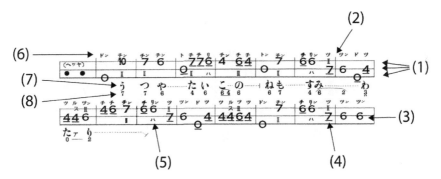

Example 18.2 Shamisen music scores of "Echigo-jishi," bars 16–31. 4th generation Yashichi Kine'ie, ed., *Shamisen bunka-fu Nagauta Echigo-jishi* (Civilized scores for shamisen, Nagauta piece Echigo-jishi) (Tôkyô: Hôgakusha, 2010).

The second example of shamisen notation is *shamisen bunka-fu* (civilized scores for shamisen), invented in 1922 (see Example 18.2). Contrary to the notation above, this one is written horizontally, from left to right and top to bottom. It uses three long horizontal lines to represent the three strings (see 1, Example 18.2), marked by vertical bar lines across the "string lines" (2). Finger positions are written on the respective string line, all with Arabic numerals. Short, horizontal lines under the finger position numerals denote the duration of the tone: "1" without an underline is a quarter note (3), "1" an eighth note (4), "1" a sixteenth note, and so on. Similarly, rests in various time durations have their specific signs. Playing techniques are indicated with their signs: some of them resemble the ones mentioned above, such as ハ for *hajiki* (5); some are different. Shôga syllables are written at the top of the music score (6), and the vocal text (7) and notation (8) at the bottom.

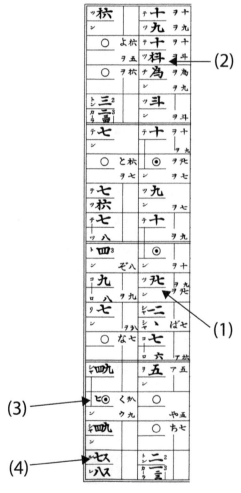

Example 18.3 Koto music scores of "Chidori no kyoku," bars 40–47. Michio Miyagi, ed., *Ikuta-ryu sokyoku: Chidori no kyoku* (Ikuta school koto music: Chidori no kyoku) (Tôkyô: Hôgakusha, 2012).

For the instrument koto (see Example 18.3), Chinese characters referring to the specific thirteen strings are used for its tablature. The notation, which is in "chamber music style," is read from top to bottom and right to left. Strings one to ten (designated by distance to the performer, ten being the closest) are illustrated with Chinese numerals (i.e., 一, 二, 三), while different characters are used for strings eleven to thirteen (i.e., 斗, 為, 巾). In addition, other characters represent specific playing techniques and/or timbres. For instance, common characters include the symbols for pressing a half tone (ヲ) (see 1, Example 18.3) or a whole tone up (オ) (2), the symbol for slightly slackening the strings (ヒ) (3), and *sukui* (ス) (4), the symbol for plucking the strings upward. These symbols are placed right beside the numeral for the actual string.

The scale type in use for the actual piece is written in the beginning of the music score. These can be tuned in various pitches, with the same interval relation between the tones. In newer contemporary art music for koto, by contrast, the exact pitch may often be given. As for the shamisen scores above, the shôga, the lyrics, and notation are included in the music score. Traditionally, vertically written koto notation is common, but horizontal scores are also in use today.

The above examples of notation demonstrate the visual variations within the notations. The combination of Chinese characters and numerals, Japanese phonetic letters, dedicated symbols, Arabic numerals, and Western-derived notation elements clearly illustrate Japan's cross-cultural encounters throughout history. The encounters have led to a process of the Japanization of foreign impulses. Retention of Chinese characters in the notation further suggests a continuing high status for the Chinese written language in Japanese culture. Similar acknowledgments of Chinese writing can be observed in Japanese Buddhist and literary traditions, and not least in the visual art tradition of calligraphy. Furthermore, written culture in general has been associated with the refined *literati*. The close connection with written culture has undoubtedly helped creative and spiritual traditions to maintain a high status.

Wind instrument notation

Wind varieties include a diversity of flutes and reed-type instruments, such as *shakuhachi* (five-holed vertical "notched" bamboo flute) and hichiriki, respectively. In general, notation for wind instruments focuses on fingering. Each instrument has its specific set of terms or syllables referring to their fingerings. The terms indirectly convey information on which holes to keep open or closed, and to what degree this should be done. The written notation with the fingering terms may consist of shôga syllables, such as for shakuhachi and hichiriki.

Category 2: Notation focusing on specific *rhythmic and/or melodic patterns*

Percussion signs notation: rhythmic patterns

Generally speaking, the various percussion instruments in Japanese traditional music typically perform a number of rhythmic patterns (*tegumi*) in a certain order of sequences. The rhythmic patterns are given instrument-specific terms, and their frame structures vary between instruments and genres. The broad range of percussion notations provide information on what rhythmic patterns to use, either by using characters which represent the terms, or by applying visual symbols such as dots which refer to these terms and their rhythmic patterns. For instance, in relation to the percussion instruments *kotsuzumi* and *ôtsuzumi* in nô theater, a dot notation system designates various rhythm patterns and playing techniques.

Vocal music notation: melodic patterns or movements

Vocal music notation can be divided into two groups. One is vocal notation incorporated into an accompanying instrument's notation. The other is independent, vocal-specific notation. The former is applied in vocal music with koto or shamisen accompaniment (Examples 18.1–3), when the same person performs both parts. In these cases, as mentioned above, the vocal lines are given in the same notation system as for the instrument.

Independent vocal notations are found in genres in which the vocalist plays an independent role separate from other instruments. Such types of notation exist, for instance, in shômyô (Buddhist chant), and in *jôruri* music, a type of narrative shamisen music. The common trait for independent vocal notations is that they mainly focus on prescribing melodic lines or musical patterns, whether in a detailed graphical or more simplified form.

In shômyô, the notation describes, up to a point at least, melodic contours and ornaments. There are many versions of such notation, depending on time period and school. The song text is usually placed in the center of the score, written in a large size. For some notation types, five Chinese characters (宮, 商, 角, 徵, 羽) are written beside the text and refer to the five basic tones in the music. These characters define the tonal starting points for the respective parts of the text. Next to this information, small or melismatic melodic movements may be indicated by lines and curves in various directions. Such melodic movements are, in their written form, often reminiscent of and associated with techniques in calligraphy. One may question whether the art of calligraphy has had an impact on musical notations. This suggested connection must nevertheless be further analyzed and confirmed by scholars of visual art.

For theatrical genres, such as *jôruri* music, the lyrics are likewise the center of the vocal notation. Beside the text, selective information is given for types of melodic patterns, pitch, breathing, or for tempo and dynamics. Both characters and symbols are employed to prescribe such elements. The information is given only sporadically, not in detail throughout the song.

The foregoing analysis of various notation forms aims to demonstrate the complex diversity of notation systems in Japanese traditional music. The notation systems are adapted to characteristic features and functions of the respective instruments. The instrument-specific constructions of these notation systems are interrelated with the oral–aural form of music learning, in which training with a master is necessary for learning and memorizing the music. Notation provides an overall idea of the music, but not details of the musical elements. The presentation has further illustrated the visual, cross-cultural variations within the notations, and the significant impact that East Asian written culture has had on musical notation.

The oral–aural pattern of learning and transmitting music has for centuries supported the Japanese idea of securing *the* "authentic tradition" of music. Through

160

imitation of "micro-kinesthetic" movements and their sounds, music heritage has been passed on in a presumably "static" way. Still, changes have naturally occurred throughout history.

Some Historical Developments in Modern Times

Since the latter half of the nineteenth century, Japan has experienced a massive state-initialized modernization, taking the form of Westernization. From this time, Euro-American music was introduced, establishing its central role in the country's musical life as well as in the national music curriculum. This development led in the first stage to an increased application of staff notation in Japanese traditional music. In 1888, the first collections of koto and shamisen music in staff notation were published. Soon, other similar publications followed for a variety of vernacular instruments and genres, such as for *biwa* (four- or five-stringed, pear-shaped plucked lute), shakuhachi, and shômyô. These were mainly publicized for research or preservation purposes, and did not become widespread for performance contexts. Rather, numerous instrument-specific, traditional notation forms were revised in the first half of the twentieth century, incorporating ideas and symbols influenced by staff notation. The shamisen and koto notations described above (Examples 18.1–3) emerged in this period, blending old notation practices with new ideas taken from European notation and instrument symbols.

Contemporary Japanese art music composers in the twentieth and twenty-first centuries have tended to compose in staff notation, even for works incorporating traditional Japanese instruments. Others, such as Tôru Takemitsu and Yoritsune Matsudaira, experimented with graphic forms or "open-form notation adapted from a free-form structure found in gagaku."[2] In all cases, traditional instrumentalists most often transcribe such compositions into their instrument-specific notation, in order to facilitate their playing. At the same time, some composers of traditional Japanese music, such as Shin Miyashita, have published new music combining staff notation and instrument-specific notation within the same score. This feature can be seen in the notation of Miyashita's work *Suikin-sho for Koto and Piano* (1994).

The national music curriculum, which was established in the late nineteenth century, was founded on Euro-American music and cultural perspectives. In this context, staff notation was applied exclusively in music education in schools during the twentieth century. As a result, the vast majority of the Japanese populace can read staff notation to some degree. On the other hand, only a small minority are literate in the wide range of vernacular notation forms. It must be added, however, that from 2002, the Japanese state has included traditional Japanese music in formal education. Since this traditional music constitutes just a marginal part of the curriculum, it is as yet unclear whether it will have an impact on notation literacy.

For most Japanese, therefore, the experienced connection between musical performance and the visual, notational aspect of music differs considerably from the situation described in this chapter. Furthermore, the vast majority of music performers in Japan today are educated in Western-style art music. The traditional form of musical practice, in which oral–aural transmission has been prioritized above the use of notation, has therefore become a "minority perspective" in Japan today.

The above Japanese case illustrates that different notation practices and their visual components influence people's experience of music. The most distinctive feature of the Japanese vernacular notation practice—compared to its Western counterpart—is first and foremost its intimate link to written culture and linguistic elements. Nevertheless, the notation symbols and characters do not always refer to something absolute or specific; rather, they offer vague suggestions of—or multiple alternative—meanings. In order to decode the information given in the notation, its reference system must be learned and experienced through oral–aural training together with a teacher. In Western staff notation, on the other hand, the symbolic reference system and its conveyed meanings appear more specific and consistent once learned. In this latter context, musical performance can be experienced as more independent and personal.

Despite the marginalized role of traditional, vernacular-style transmission, it undoubtedly colors today's Japanese music culture in distinct ways. This approach is, for instance, prevalent in the practice of Suzuki-style violin pedagogy, which emphasizes oral–aural aspects of learning. Moreover, performers belonging to the various traditional music genres are today, to a large extent, "bi-musical" or "multi-musical" in terms of notation literacy.[3] Most of them read both traditional Japanese notation(s) and staff notation. Such culturally compound, pluralized identities are highly distinctive features of the contemporary globalized world. This feature is present in Japanese notation literacy, as represented in a distinct, local form.

Notes

1 David W. Hughes, "No Nonsense: The Logic and Power of Acoustic-Iconic Mnemonic Systems," *British Journal of Ethnomusicology* 9, no. 2 (2000): 93–120.
2 Judith Ann Herd, "Western-influenced 'Classical' Music in Japan," in *The Ashgate Research Companion to Japanese Music*, ed. Alison McQueen Tokita and David W. Hughes (Aldershot: Ashgate, 2008), 363–381, at 374.
3 I borrow "bi-musical" from Mantle Hood, "The Challenge of Bi-Musicality," *Ethnomusicology* 4 (1960): 55–59.

Further Reading

Hughes, David W. "No Nonsense: the Logic and Power of Acoustic-Iconic Mnemonic Systems." *British Journal of Ethnomusicology* 9, no. 2 (2000): 93–120.
Kikkawa, Eishi, Satoaki Gamô, and Kenji Hirano. "Shamisen." In *Nihon Ongaku Daijiten* (The Big Encyclopedia of Japanese Music), edited by Hirano Kenji, Kamisangô Yûkô, and Gamô Satoaki, 299–312. Tôkyô: Heibonsha, 1989.
Komoda, Haruko, and Nogawa Mihoko. "Theory and Notation in Japan." In *The Garland Encyclopedia of World Music, Volume 7, East Asia: China, Japan, and Korea*, edited by Robert C. Provine, Yoshihiko Tokumaru, and J. Lawrence Witzleben, 565–584. New York: Routledge, 2002.
Tanaka, Yumiko, Nogawa Mihoko, and Haikawa Mika, eds. *Marugoto shamisen no hon* (A Book Completely about Shamisen). Tôkyô: Seikyûsha, 2009.
Tokita, Alison McQueen and David W. Hughes, eds. *The Ashgate Research Companion to Japanese Music*. Aldershot: Ashgate, 2008.
Tokumaru, Yosihiko and Osamu Yamaguti, eds. *The Oral and the Literate in Music*. Tôkyô: Academia Music, 1986.
Tukitani, Tuneko. *Nihon ongaku to no deai: nihon ongaku no rekishi to riron* (Encountering Japanese Music: The History and Theory of Japanese Music). Tôkyô: Tôkyôdô, 2010.

19
MANUSCRIPTS
Marica S. Tacconi

The boundaries between the musical and the visual can be remarkably murky in music manuscripts. Music books created in the Middle Ages and Renaissance were often so sumptuously decorated that, although fundamentally used for the purpose of musical performance, they became visual objects as much as they were musical objects. The two aspects are perfectly intertwined: the musical elements feed into the visual, and the visual elements feed into the musical.

Music notation itself could be a source of visual interest (see Chapter 18 in this volume). The manuscript's visual appeal could also extend to its binding, which sometimes went beyond the strictly functional and included decorated clasps and richly worked wood or metal plates. My focus here, however, is on the presence of extra-musical visual content in the form of decoration (drawings, illuminations, etc.) on one or more pages of the manuscript. Thousands of music manuscripts were decorated, with visual content ranging from decorations on the margins, to relatively simple decorated initials, to more elaborate historiated initials, to full-scale "paintings on the page" depicting complex scenes.

Why were manuscripts decorated in the first place? What prompted their creators to embellish them? These are broad questions that have many answers and, as such, this essay does not claim to cover the topic exhaustively. I will begin with some general considerations and then provide a few examples, drawn from a particular time and place, that will illustrate some of the broader points.

First and foremost, decorating a music manuscript served as a way to distinguish it from others. It made the book unique—an original object whose visual elements imprinted it with special features that signified its association with particular patrons or institutions, that underscored the relationship with its intended recipient or audience, or that served to clarify the subject, topic, or theological message contained within the music and its text. Along these lines, it is possible to identify three main types of decorated music manuscripts:

1 Manuscripts whose visual content illustrates the subject or text of the music with which it is associated. These manuscripts can be of a secular or religious nature. In the case of liturgical books, historiated initials or border illuminations can illustrate the religious feast with which they are associated. These visual elements can also serve as markers that aid the organization of the content. For example, decorated initials might mark the introits of each Mass contained in the book or, in the case of polyphonic music in choirbook format, they often indicate the beginning of each voice part.

2   Manuscripts whose visual content points to their function as objects of luxury and prestige. These manuscripts were lavishly decorated as a way to indicate status and bestow value upon a patron, institution, or civic center. They often included elements that could be associated with the patron, such as his/her coat of arms, portrait, or emblems. Similarly, when associated with a particular institution (e.g. a church, a monastery) or civic center, the visual elements could include civic emblems or depictions of that institution, or images related to the city's history or topography.

3   Manuscripts whose visual content points to their function as gifts or presentation objects. These manuscripts were crafted for specific recipients. They were often associated with events of significance to the recipient's life: an engagement, a wedding, the birth of a child, an election, a special honor, or military victory.

Examples in each of these categories abound. Some of the manuscripts produced for the liturgical needs of the cathedral of Florence in the late Middle Ages and Renaissance serve as interesting case studies and underscore the way in which visual elements fed into musical elements, making these books visual as much as musical objects.

First as Santa Reparata and then as Santa Maria del Fiore, the cathedral of Florence was well endowed throughout the centuries with manuscripts that served its liturgical needs. From the earliest extant books, these manuscripts were often embellished with elaborate decorations and illuminations. One of the earliest examples is the antiphonary from the Archivio Arcivescovile, produced around the middle of the twelfth century for the cathedral of Santa Reparata and embellished, originally, with as many as eighty-three illuminations.

After the founding of Santa Maria del Fiore in 1296, the cathedral acquired new manuscripts that were produced over the course of several well-defined and ambitious campaigns, spanning a period from the 1330s to 1526. As a whole, these books transcended their basic function as instruments of worship and became objects of marked civic pride. Made possible through a system of public funding (in essence, a "tax of Santa Maria del Fiore"[1]) and commissioned by the Opera del Duomo—the lay institution that was entrusted with the construction, maintenance, and overall administration of the cathedral—the service books were, to a large extent, "conceived as books *of* the people and *for* the people of Florence."[2] They are multifaceted objects of a richly composite nature: they are, at once, codicological, liturgical, musical, and artistic products. It is these manuscripts' visual apparatus, however, that points most directly to the nature of Renaissance Florentine culture, the values of Florentine society, and the ambitions of its proud citizens. The visual elements prevail not only on the viewer's eyes, but also in the minds of the commissioners—the head administrators of the Opera del Duomo, the *operai*—who ensured that the books would be decorated lavishly as a way to reflect the prestige of the church and of the city.

The cathedral service books produced in the fifteenth century are some of the most glorious ever made in the West. These manuscripts replaced those from the fourteenth century, not as a result of liturgical changes, but because the earlier books were now considered aesthetically inadequate. Two new psalters (Florence, Archivio dell'Opera di Santa Maria del Fiore, Cod. N.2 n. 3 and Cod. O n. 4) were the first service books to be produced as part of the fifteenth-century phase of manuscript production. They were specifically commissioned in January 1439 because in the cathedral there were no psalters deemed "appropriate," a fact that resulted "in the greatest shame and dishonor for the ... church and for the ... Operai." To remedy the situation, the new psalters had to be made "with the greatest possible value and beauty."[3] The *Trecento* psalters still owned by Santa Maria del Fiore were liturgically suitable (two existed; one is lost today, but the other is still identifiable as Florence, Biblioteca Medicea Laurenziana, Edili 131), but those early books must have been regarded as aesthetically inadequate for the figurative *domus* (home) of a people whose collective self-image and pride in their city had reached new heights in the early *Quattrocento*.

It took over ten years for the work on these two psalters to be carried out: nine artists and craftsmen were involved, including three illuminators, a silk merchant, and a goldsmith. One of these artists, Zanobi Strozzi, is regarded by some as "the most important Florentine illuminator of the early Renaissance."[4] Indeed, his employment must have been a significant coup for an institution that, at every level, was seeking to acquire objects worthy of its splendor and prestige. Strozzi was entrusted with the artistic highlights of the book—six illuminated figures—but it was to Filippo di Matteo Torelli that the commissioners turned first, entrusting him with the creation of forty-five foliate initials. In the hierarchical structure of manuscript illumination, Torelli's role was secondary to that of Strozzi. Torelli, however, was a great innovator, having established a new decorative style that departed significantly from the traditional ornamental white vine-stem motif known as *bianchi girari*. Instead, he employed light arabesques with leaves and fruit, populated by putti and animals. By hiring Torelli, the commissioners ensured that the manuscripts would be thoroughly embellished with some of the most innovative decorative elements.

Although the trend to decorate these music books with "the greatest possible value and beauty" expressly begins with the 1439 psalters, the highest example of this attitude is found in the production of four large choirbooks: one antiphonary (Florence, Biblioteca Medicea Laurenziana, Edili 148) and three graduals (Florence, Biblioteca Medicea Laurenziana, Edili 149–151), executed between 1445 and 1477/78. Collectively, "they represent one of the most glorious achievements in the history of Florentine manuscript production."[5] Never before in Florence had a liturgical book been as massive in size, as refined in script and musical notation, as spectacular in decoration, and as precious in binding. Many aspects of these sumptuous books point to the fact that they were commissioned and primarily regarded as objects of significant institutional and civic pride. Their visual apparatus trumps their liturgical and musical content, making them, above all, visual objects in which the viewer could feel great pride.

The antiphonary and three graduals are far from complete liturgically, as they omit many important and standard religious feasts. Moreover, the organization of the books' contents, especially in Edili 150 and 151, points to a desire to begin and end each volume with feasts of special significance for Florence and its cathedral. In covering the Proper of the Saints, Edili 150 begins with the vigil of St. John the Baptist (23 June), the patron saint of Florence, and concludes with the feast of the Purification of the Virgin (2 February), a Marian feast that was especially important in Florence and at Santa Maria del Fiore—thus spanning an eight-month

---

period. Similarly, Edili 151 begins with the feast of the Annunciation of the Virgin (25 March), which marked the start of the Florentine year and on which day the cathedral was consecrated in 1436, and concludes with the feast of St. Zenobius, the father of the Florentine church—thus covering only two months. Despite their lopsided arrangement, the manuscripts' organization guaranteed that stunning, full-page illuminations opened and closed the volumes as "visual bookends" of sorts.

It is clear from their organization and significant liturgical gaps that these books were never intended to be entirely practical in nature. Far from being exhaustive in their content, they would have been appropriate only for relatively few liturgical occasions, thus still requiring the use of earlier choirbooks from the fourteenth century. Instead, the primary motivation for their creation seems to have been aesthetic: these four lavish manuscripts met the new standards of opulence and magnificence of the cathedral, served as prized objects of luxury, and showed off the wealth of the Opera del Duomo, of the cathedral, and, by extension, of the city of Florence.

Through these manuscripts we see full well the extent to which these books were visual objects as much as musical objects. In fact, it can be argued that they transcended their musical and liturgical nature, and fundamentally served, instead, as objects of enormous institutional and civic pride. A glorious page from gradual Edili 151 illustrates this point.[6] A large, full-page illumination by Francesco d'Antonio del Chierico marks the introit of the Mass for the feast of the Dedication of the Church (f. 7r). It was on this day, celebrated in Florence on 25 March, that Santa Maria del Fiore was consecrated in 1436, an event of enormous religious, civic, and political significance. The scene shown in Edili 151 is set in front of the cathedral, depicted in considerable detail, presumably just before the grand entrance of Pope Eugene IV and Cardinal Giuliano degli Orsini, the officiators of the ceremony. The consecration Mass was of great musical significance because it included two works specifically composed for the occasion: the polyphonic motet *Nuper rosarum flores* and the monophonic sequence *Nuper almos rose flores*, both likely composed by the great Franco-Flemish master Guillaume Du Fay. The sequence is preserved in Edili 151 (ff. 10v–15v), the only known source for this unique chant. Despite the musical significance of the event, Edili 151, like the other choirbooks in the series, appears to have been produced with the main goal of awing the viewer, rather than of impressing the listener. This is supported by a curious detail: the introit chant "Terribilis est locus iste," marked by the full-page illumination, has a wrong note: the penultimate note on the page should be a C, not a B. The craftsmen and artists working on this page painted the scene inhabiting the large initial T in great detail, produced an elegant foliate border populated by birds, angels, and other imaginative creatures, painted the letters of the chant's textual incipit in a fanciful and colorful script, inscribed the names of the commissioning *operai* just above the chant, produced an exquisitely delicate lapis-lazuli blue filigree background for the music incipit, and laid out the music clef and notes in gold leaf. Yet, they copied the chant with a wrong note and the error was never corrected, despite the fact that this introit, like the rest of the Mass, was prescribed every year for the feast of the Dedication of the Church. This peculiar aspect reinforces the view that these four choirbooks may actually never have been used for singing. Edili 148–151 are, above all, lavish objects of immense luxury, books that most unabashedly exhibited the wealth of the

Opera del Duomo, of the cathedral, and of the city. As such, they are prestigious possessions, with distinctly civic overtones, intended to be viewed by a wide audience.

Most music manuscripts were functional: they were held or placed on a lectern when needed and then stowed away. But the service books of the cathedral of Florence, and especially the super-luxury items Edili 148–151, were different. Documentary evidence shows that these four choirbooks, together with an evangeliary, epistolary, and missal (identifiable as Florence, Biblioteca Medicea Laurenziana, Edili 115, Edili 112, and Edili 109, respectively), were lent to the cathedral's *cartolaio*, Domenico Parigi, from 20 to 22 June on at least two occasions (in 1491 and 1513) for display at the *mostra di San Giovanni* on 21 June. During this "exhibition," local merchants "ostentatiously show their things in the more frequented places of the city. For almost all the artisans and those with warehouses who do business in such places put whatever precious things they have outside if they have such things … for the greatest honor of the city, and perhaps for greater profit."[7] Although he provided the parchment leaves for at least one choirbook in 1517, there is no evidence that Parigi worked directly on the production of the books that he borrowed. Unlike other merchants who displayed their own handiwork at the *mostra*, Parigi exhibited objects belonging to the cathedral. This leads us to speculate that the Opera del Duomo may actually have initiated and actively promoted the public display of these books, seeking one of its craftsmen with a workshop along a well-traveled, highly public street, likely what is today the Via del Proconsolo, in the area of the Badia.

The layout of the cathedral choir in the fifteenth century also guaranteed full view of the choirbooks. When, in 1434, the Opera del Duomo turned its attention to the liturgical space of the cathedral, the placement of the lectern within the choir was a key consideration. Filippo Brunelleschi's winning design allowed room for the lectern and the singers in the center of the liturgical space. Indeed, the lectern was placed directly in front of the opening (the so-called *bocca*) that led to the nave. Keeping in mind that it was standard practice to leave the choirbooks on the lectern for the duration of their respective liturgical period, it is evident that the placement of the lectern in front of the *bocca* guaranteed a stunning, quasi-theatrical visual effect of the open choirbooks as one entered the church and proceeded down the nave.

Both in and out of the cathedral, most of the choirbooks would have been readily identifiable by the populace at large as books belonging to the cathedral, commissioned by the Opera del Duomo, and made possible through public funds. Nearly every full-page illumination exhibits the Agnus Dei, the emblem of the Opera del Duomo. Moreover, as commissioners of the books and as chief officers of the Opera del Duomo, the *operai* were honored through inscriptions found on as many as seventeen of the most lavish illuminated pages of the three graduals (Edili 149–151). These inscriptions provide the names of the two *operai* who were in office when the illumination was completed. The inclusion of the *operai*'s names among these pages may have served as a way to offset, at least in part, a period of institutional crisis, during which the Opera del Duomo and its officers were regarded unfavorably by the populace. The books offered their viewers a tangible and glorious example of what the *operai* did accomplish and of what the Opera del Duomo was able to produce by means of its public funds.

In 1508, the Opera del Duomo embarked on another ambitious campaign of manuscript production that, over the course of nineteen years, led to the creation of fourteen graduals and eighteen antiphonaries. Each set of graduals and antiphonaries constitutes a complete liturgical cycle, thus filling the liturgical gaps of the fifteenth-century choirbooks. Like Edili 148–151, these new manuscripts are in various ways both commemorative and celebratory in nature. But instead of being primarily concerned with the glorification of the Opera del Duomo and its *operai*, or with preserving the memory of significant events in the history of the cathedral (e.g. the consecration of Santa Maria del Fiore), the commemorative and celebratory elements now take on new forms, which are distinctly political and even more civic in nature.

Seven of the choirbooks produced in this period are overtly "Medicean" in their iconographic details. Their commission and production followed the 1512 return from exile of Giuliano de' Medici (1479–1516), son of Lorenzo "il Magnifico," and the subsequent restoration of the Medici re gime in the spheres of secular as well as religious power. Only six months after Giuliano's re-entry, his brother Giovanni (1475–1521) was elected to the throne of St. Peter as Pope Leo X. Despite the lack of any direct involvement in the commission or finance of these choirbooks, "the Medici were, in various ways, 'present' in as many as seven of these lavish instruments of worship. Whether through the portraits of Lorenzo 'il Magnifico' or of his son Giovanni (the newly elected Pope Leo X), or through the symbols of Medici power (their coat of arms and political devices), the Medici 'entered' the arena of the painted service book."[8]

The best example is found on a page that marks the first responsory of Matins for the feast of the Epiphany (Florence, Archivio dell'Opera di Santa Maria del Fiore, Cod. C n. 11, f. 4v). A rich border at the bottom of the page shows two lions, a lioness, a bear, and five golden balls (Figure 19.1). Moreover, two laurel branches, one cut, the other flowering, hold the shields of the City (left) and of the People of Florence (right). The laurel, or *lauro*, alludes onomatopoeically to Lorenzo, but is also one of the heraldic devices adopted by "il Magnifico." The flowering laurel branch, known as the *broncone*, was the symbol used by the contemporary ruler of Florence, Lorenzo II "il Giovane" (1492–1519), grandson of Lorenzo "il Magnifico" and nephew of Leo X. The bear, the *orso*, is likely an allusion to the Orsini, a prominent Roman family related to the Medici by marriage through Clarice Orsini (1450–88), wife of Lorenzo "il Magnifico" and mother of the pope, and Alfonsina Orsini (1472–1520), widow of Lorenzo's son Piero and Leo's sister-in-law. The lions carry a double reference. First, they are a prominent Florentine emblem, the *marzocchi*—a symbol of civic power and independence. At the same time, the *leoni* allude to *Leone* X. The balls, or *palle*, are the basic components of the Medici coat of arms. Their golden color points to the *pomo d'oro*, a device adopted by Cosimo "il Vecchio" (1389–1464) as the main vegetal symbol of Medici regeneration.

The historiated initial H frames the scene of the Baptism of Christ, which is commemorated on the Feast of the Epiphany. The illumination includes a portrait of Leo X, standing behind some angels as one of the witnesses to the holy event. The deeper message of the entire page is revealed only when one considers the text of the chant with which the initial is associated (ff. 4v–6r). The key phrase is "This is my beloved Son, with whom I am well pleased" ("Hic est filius meus dilectus in quo mihi bene complacui"). Derived from the biblical account of the Baptism of Christ, the text had special significance for Leo X. Together with an image of Leo's father, Lorenzo, the phrase was inscribed on one of the triumphal arches that marked the path of his Florentine entry on 30 November 1515. Contemporary eyewitnesses report that, upon viewing the arch with the image of his father and the inscription, Leo was moved to tears. By associating this key biblical text with such vivid Medici symbolism on the painted manuscript page, the liturgical message becomes a deeply personal one: it is Lorenzo who figuratively introduces his "beloved son" to his people, and his grand entry into Florence is thus juxtaposed to Christ's triumphal entry into Jerusalem.

The liturgical books produced for the cathedral of Florence over the course of four centuries provide, collectively, a superlative case study for the three main types of music manuscripts that traditionally received visual attention. Most fundamentally, as books that preserved the texts and chants for the celebration of the liturgy, their historiated initials and border illuminations illustrate the religious message or story of the day. However, these lavish books go beyond their most basic function as instruments of worship and take on a distinctly civic flavor. Everything about these cathedral manuscripts points to their function as objects of luxury and prestige. As books belonging to the cathedral of Florence, they reflected the wealth and distinct civic identity of Santa Maria del Fiore. Their pages often include civic emblems and they were widely recognized as books of the people and for the people of Florence. Finally, the visual content of some of these books points to their association with the Medici family in the wake of the 1512 Medici restoration. Although never belonging directly to the Medici family, some of the lavish "Medicean" pages clearly would have been viewed by Pope Leo X and his entourage during his 1515 Florentine visit.

The musical and the visual are inextricably connected in these and other books. Their association enables the listener and the viewer to consider the manuscript in ways that go beyond what each element alone would otherwise allow.

Notes

1 Lorenzo Fabbri, "La 'Gabella di Santa Maria del Fiore': Il finanziamento pubblico della Cattedrale di Firenze," in *Pouvoir et édilité: Les grands chantiers dans l'Italie communale et seigneuriale*, ed. Elisabeth Crouzet-Pavan, Collection de l'Ecole Française de Rome 302 (Rome: Ecole Française, 2003), 195–244.

2 Marica S. Tacconi, *Cathedral and Civic Ritual in Late Medieval and Renaissance Florence: The Service Books of Santa Maria del Fiore* (Cambridge: Cambridge University Press, 2005), 138.

3 Giovanni Poggi, *Il Duomo di Firenze. Documenti sulla decorazione della chiesa e del campanile tratti dall'archivio dell'Opera*. 2 vols. Vol. 2, ed. Margaret Haines (Florence: Edizioni Medicea, 1988), doc. 1615. Quoted in Tacconi, *Cathedral and Civic Ritual*, 27 and 143.

4 Mirella Levi D'Ancona, *Miniatura e miniatori a Firenze dal XIV al XVI secolo* (Florence: Olschki, 1962), 261.

5 Tacconi, *Cathedral and Civic Ritual*, 144.

6 For a color reproduction of this illuminated page, see Tacconi, *Cathedral and Civic Ritual*, 324.

7 From a 1475 letter written by the Florentine notary Piero Cennini to Pirrino Amerino; quoted in Tacconi, *Cathedral and Civic Ritual*, 40.

8 Tacconi, "Appropriating the Instruments of Worship: The 1512 Medici Restoration and the Florentine Cathedral Choirbooks," *Renaissance Quarterly* 56 (2003): 369.

Further Reading

Fabbri, Lorenzo and Marica Tacconi, eds. *I libri del Duomo di Firenze. Codici liturgici e Biblioteca di Santa Maria del Fiore (secoli XI–XVI)*. Exhibition catalogue. Florence: Centro Di, 1997.

Haines, Margaret. "Firenze e il finanziamento della Cattedrale e del Campanile." In *Alla riscoperta di Piazza del Duomo di Firenze*. Vol. 3, *Il Campanile di Giotto*, ed. Timothy Verdon, 71–83. Florence: Centro Di, 1994.

Levi D'Ancona, Mirella. *Miniatura e miniatori a Firenze dal XIV al XVI secolo*. Florence: Olschki, 1962.

Tacconi, Marica. "Appropriating the Instruments of Worship: The 1512 Medici Restoration and the Florentine Cathedral Choirbooks." *Renaissance Quarterly* 56 (2003): 333–376.

——. *Cathedral and Civic Ritual in Late Medieval and Renaissance Florence: The Service Books of Santa Maria del Fiore*. Cambridge: Cambridge University Press, 2005.

Wright, Craig. "A Sequence for the Dedication of the Cathedral of Florence: Dufay's (?) *Nuper almos rose flores*." In *Cantate Domino: Musica nei secoli per il Duomo di Firenze*. Edited by Carolyn Gianturco, Piero Gargiulo, and Gabriele Giacomelli. Florence: Edifir, 2001.

20
PRINTED MUSIC
Music Printing as Art

Kate van Orden

Music printing counts among the longest-standing interests of music historians, running right back to the eighteenth century, when the first grand histories of music appeared. In his *General History of Music from the Earliest Ages to the Present* (4 volumes, London, 1776–89), the English historian Charles Burney helped to launch this historiographic tradition by stressing the watershed effect of the new technology in a long chapter titled "Of the State of Music, from the Invention of Printing till the Middle of the XVIth Century," in which he discussed the work of Ottaviano Petrucci, the first printer to produce books of polyphonic music. Petrucci's work and his historical significance as a music printer were likewise well known to the first great Continental music historian, padre Giovanni Battista Martini of Bologna, who amassed a huge collection of sixteenth-century prints that fed his antiquarian passions and doubtless also served as source materials for his *Storia della musica* (3 of a projected 5 volumes, Bologna, 1757–81). Martini made a special effort to acquire Petrucci's work, and it may even have been during Burney's visit to Bologna that Martini called the Englishman's attention to Petrucci's prints, which—then as now—were a highlight of Martini's collection.

There is much to admire in Petrucci's craftsmanship, beginning with the sheer accomplishment of having devised a practical method for music printing. Polyphony proved highly resistant to print, and whereas Gutenberg's 42-line Bible came off the press in 1455, almost fifty years elapsed before Petrucci set up shop and turned out the first book of printed polyphony in 1501, the *Harmonice Musices Odhecaton A*, a collection of almost one hundred chansons for three and four voices. Other prints soon followed, fairly establishing Petrucci's claim to have been the first to print polyphony on any significant scale, but even so, his output was relatively limited, averaging only three titles a year across his twenty-year career as a music printer. Doubtless this modest pace owed not only to the limited market for his wares, but also to the technical difficulties that had hindered the establishment of commercial music printing altogether, for the techniques and inventions that Gutenberg combined to enable the printing of verbal texts were ill suited to the graphic requirements of music. Certainly the screw presses themselves and Gutenberg's recipe for oil-based ink enabled the printing of many genres of text and image, but the "Gutenberg Revolution" was, at heart, a typographical one, and herein lay a fundamental problem that would plague the printing of music for its first centuries. Printers did develop various typographic means of printing music, but the broader history of music printing ultimately coincides more closely with the history of the visual arts and the technologies used to produce fine art prints—woodcuts, copperplate engraving, etching, and lithography.

Unlike art-historical research into printmaking, however, histories of music printing are primarily content-driven repertorial studies that usually concentrate on individual music printing firms and culminate in detailed catalogues. Here musicology took its lead from bibliography, adopting the cataloguing techniques used to identify printed editions of verbal texts issued in books and pamphlets. Attention to "bookish" material elements such as format, foliation, and signatures is standard in studies of music printing, whereas other features such as paper, quality of impression, registration, "state," and corrections are less often brought into consideration. Essentially, music prints have been studied like books, not like "prints," by which is usually meant a picture or design printed from a block or plate or a photograph printed on paper. Yet the very strangeness of the fact that historians of music printing regularly refer to the objects that they study as "prints" rather than "books" shows up music's unusual position in an interstice between art and literature. The artistic quality of music notation, most particularly in manuscript, doubtless accounts for the significant attention that musical sources have always garnered as material objects meriting study qua objects, but much work remains to be done by musicologists who choose to break out of bibliography and investigate what the methods of art historians might bring to research into music printing.

The historiographic tensions I have just outlined originated in the sixteenth century, when the typographical revolution initiated by Gutenberg dominated printed production. Music was assimilated to the forms standardized for book production, despite the bad fit, particularly where type was concerned. Polyphonic notation consists of numerous discrete signs amenable to type—individual notes, rests, double bars, mensuration signs, sharps, flats, clefs, and so forth—for which punches could be cut and type could be founded on small rectangular bodies like those used for letters and punctuation in the printing of verbal texts. For these elements, Petrucci could employ Gutenberg's methods, using metal type for the notes and the words in his books of music. And, like other Venetian printers such as Aldus Manutius, he had a stock of large decorative initial letters cut into woodblocks that could be set into the formes at the beginning of lines of compiled type. The real trouble came with printing the staves, which demanded horizontal continuity across the entire page and in precisely the same zones for which type was being used to print the note heads. It is difficult to overstress the significance of this technical problem, and the enormity of it is probably best appreciated by considering the perpetually shifting solutions that music printers devised to overcome it, each one imperfect in its own way. The following section of this article retraces this history from the perspective of the visual arts and artists who played significant roles in its unfolding, and in closing I suggest avenues for future research that might recover alternative histories of music printing as a graphic art.

Petrucci was the first to devise a method that would allow polyphonic music to be printed using type, but it was not a simple solution. He printed the music staves separately from the notes and texts in his music books, using wooden blocks on which were mounted five metal bars for staff lines. But this meant that each sheet had to be run through the press twice, which severely undercut the speed and accuracy that made printing interesting in the first place. Certainly other printers did sometimes use double-impression methods (for instance, in rubricating liturgical and legal texts), but for Petrucci, it was absolutely necessary. He may even have used triple impressions for some sheets. Moreover, Petrucci's double-impression prints could support only the smallest margin of error in registration, since even slight misalignments would send the notes veering off the staff and botch the sheet being printed. In a world where the price of paper could represent as much as 75 percent of the overall cost of printing, these errors counted dearly, even more so than the extra hours of a pressman's labor required to print each sheet twice. Thus the quality of Petrucci's books came at a price. But they do impress with their beauty, their airy staves supporting elegant noteheads with finely cut heads and exceptionally long stems, and the ends of lines embellished with dashing custodes (Example 20.1).

Example 20.1 Specimen of the Double-Impression Typography of Ottaviano Petrucci, Venice, 1504. Note the stave that intersects the large initial "S" and the stems that run into the text—both signs of the double-impression method of printing.

Petrucci's first serious competitor, Andrea Antico, approached the conundrum of staff lines from a completely different vantage, one that played to his expertise as a cutter of woodblocks. Circumventing metal type altogether, he treated music entirely as a graphic image, engraving it in reverse in wood and printing each page as a visual artist would a picture. In quality of execution, Antico's work might be compared to the woodcuts of Lucas Cranach the Elder or Hans Holbein the Elder, a point worth insisting on if only to call attention to the middle ground that music occupied between text and image. Clearly, nothing in the two-dimensionality of musical notation demanded expertise in the representation of contour, light, and shade, but the graphic regularity of music brought its own challenges, for, as anyone who has tried to copy out a few bars of music at a page-turn well knows, drawing staff lines requires a precise and steady hand. Antico insisted that it took him three years to produce the woodcuts for his magnificent *Liber quindecim missarum* (Rome, 1516), a book consisting of 162 folios in large "royal" format fronted with a dedicatory engraving of Antico on bended knee presenting the book to Pope Leo X. Like Petrucci's music books, Antico's were works of art, painstaking, costly productions whose graphic beauty rivaled that of calligraphed manuscripts.

Throughout the sixteenth century, some music printers continued to work from woodcuts and with the double-impression method. Numerous monophonic psalters employed woodcuts, some of them strikingly delicate and in very small formats that required real precision work. Alternately, the occasional provincial press, like that of Francesco Moscheni in Milan, printed the staves and notes of part music in separate runs through the press, just as Petrucci had. But around 1528, Pierre Attaingnant, a printer working in Paris, began printing music books using a single-impression method that would come to dominate the trade and finally give music printing the boost that it needed to achieve commercial viability. In Attaingnant's sorts, each piece of type included both a notational symbol (note, rest, clef, etc.) and a small segment of staff lines, a typographic innovation that allowed the staves to be rendered in pieces that aligned, character by character, across the horizontal expanse of the page (Example 20.2). Music could now be typeset in its entirety, and the typographical "revolution" that had begun for verbal texts in the fifteenth century came to polyphony as well.

tez bien leur deuis Deſtoupez uoz eſcoutoz bien leur deuis deſtoupez uoz oreilles

Example 20.2 Specimen of the Single-Impression Typography of Pierre Attaingnant, Paris, 1544. Note the broken staves—emblematic of the single-impression method of printing.

Had single-impression printing for music been entirely satisfactory, fonts like Attaingnant's might well have been created much sooner, though one could also argue that this development occurred when and where it did in conjunction with a florescence in type design centered in Paris in the second third of the century. During these years Paris became the international capital of type founding, and a generation of highly artistic punchcutters, including Claude Garamont (c. 1510–61), Robert Granjon (1513–90), and Pierre Haultin (c. 1510–87) produced typefaces so perfect that they enjoyed centuries of subsequent use. Attaingnant adopted the upright roman typefaces and sweeping italics of their stylish fonts for his title-pages and text underlay, but, sadly, the musical notation never achieved the same balance and visual flow. The broken staff lines caused an inevitable choppiness, no matter how perfectly the type aligned, and any wear to the edge of each piece of type made the problem worse. The same flaws are evident in all single-impression typography for music, even in the lovely chansonniers printed by Robert Granjon in Lyons in the 1550s with a civility font for music that he cut himself. Some printers tried to mitigate the uneven effect in their books of tablature by compiling the type in a jigsaw of pieces that included longer metal bars to fill out portions of the staves with unbroken lines wherever possible, but even this remained a half-way solution, and one that was only possible for tablature, where the symbols on the "staff lines" were without stems.

Some of the largest music printing houses of the sixteenth century produced hundreds of editions. By rejecting xylography and multiple-impression printing in favor of his less elegant but more economical single-impression technology, Attaingnant managed to issue at least 170 editions between 1528 and 1551, almost quadrupling Petrucci's known rate of production, and this is to say nothing of the actual print runs, which may well have been higher for Attaingnant. In Venice, music printers quickly adopted Attaingnant's methods and music printing came into its own as an industry. The press of Girolamo Scotto issued hundreds of music titles between 1539 and 1613, of which exemplars from at least 724 editions survive; also in Venice, the Gardano press put out over a thousand music titles between 1538 and 1611, of which 1,425 survive in at least one partbook; and smaller presses in the Serenissima issued at least 74 music titles in the years up to 1572. If we use the conservative figure of 500 copies for print runs at that time and count only the surviving editions, Attaingnant's rather modest enterprise in Paris would have produced over 85,000 prints, and presses in La Serenissima well over one million.

But even this commercial success did not secure the future of music typography, which was challenged by the spread of copperplate music engraving throughout Europe in the early seventeenth century. Nothing, it seemed, could surpass the ability of the human hand to render music notation legibly and with continuity. In this light, it should come as no surprise that a calligrapher was responsible for producing some of the first path-breaking engravings of polyphony—Simone Verovio, a Dutchman working in Rome. Seemingly without effort, his extraordinary *Diletto spirituale canzonette a tre et a quattro voci … con l'intavolatura del cimbalo, et liuto* (Rome, 1586) combined three sorts of notation on each opening—vocal parts in mensural notation, keyboard tablature, and lute tablature—economically solving problems of layout that had long kept mensural notation separated from tablature in dedicated prints. Everything about Verovio's engravings seems designed to accentuate their crossing of typographical boundaries. Extravagant cursive italic lettering escapes the limits of the rectangular type-bodies that restrained the slope of italic type, reined in the horizontal flow of extenders, checked the reach of swash capitals, and reduced ligatures to a bare minimum. The same typographical rectitude and discretion that kept letters to themselves had long exerted a tyranny on individual notes in mensural music, preventing beaming in vocal lines and the rendering of chords in keyboard tablatures, and Verovio seems to have taken joy in bringing these elements to print. Beams, ties—nothing keeps his notes apart (Example 20.3). Even the noteheads are novel in the way they relax the straight-edged iron lozenges standard for music typography into teardrop-shaped noteheads reminiscent of those in hand-written manuscripts. Perhaps not incidentally they resemble the noteheads of the civility font cut by Robert Granjon, who had moved to Rome in 1578. Finally, the exuberance of the engraver's hand is palpable in the grand calligraphic flourishes that fill out the empty spaces and replace the blank broken staves that lined the bottoms of pages in contemporary prints with eye-catching penmanship. Visually, each opening projects motion, flair, and the utmost care in book design.

In the same years that Verovio issued the *Diletto spirituale* and other music editions such as the *Ghirlanda di fioretti musicali* of 1589, he was also busy printing handwriting manuals from copperplate engravings, copybooks such as *Il primo libro delli essempi* (Rome, 1587, with engravings by Martin van Buyten) and *Essemplare di lettere cancellaresche corsive* (Rome, 1593) that students could use to perfect their penmanship. The confluence of these two apparently very different sorts of publications—one for music-making, the other for handwriting—reflects significantly on both, illustrating their common roots in the graphic traditions of manuscript production. The centrality of the design element in these prints should encourage us to linger in our consideration of Verovio's background as a calligrapher, and, indeed,

Example 20.3 Specimen of the Engraved Music printed by Simone Verovio, Rome, c. 1590.

to push further in the broader analysis that I have pursued thus far, which aims to understand music printing as a series of technical issues that were resolved more or less successfully by artists. In such an analysis, the content of the prints—the music itself—is of secondary importance to understanding the world of book production into which they issued and the ways in which music notation was simply another sort of image to be cut into woodblocks, copperplates, or the steel punches from which type might be cast. Such an analysis would push behind the scenes at print shops to investigate the labor of the artists who incised notes and staves into wood and metal, to examine their aesthetic, design sense, and technical ability in their chosen medium, and to formulate a deeper appreciation of the effort required to transform their materials. The fine, flowing lines of Verovio's engravings convey lightness and ease, to be sure, but their production required strength, accuracy, and tendons of steel, not to mention working in reverse.

One place to begin is with the work of punchcutters, for sets of punches from the Renaissance survive in significant numbers. This is to say, the original "works of art"—steel punches, cut by the artist's own hand—can be inspected by us today, and even for typefaces for which the punches do not survive, the oeuvres of type designers such as Robert Granjon, Claude Garamont, and Pierre Haultin can be identified with precision from the catalogues and type specimens of early-modern type foundries. Thanks to recent research in palaeotypography, the corpus of these artists has already taken shape, and musicologists have increasingly sought to catalogue the types employed by the printers they study, making a significant amount of information available. Music types by Granjon, Haultin, and Guillaume I Le Bé are now well known. Less advanced is scholarship on individual copperplate engravers and woodcutters, at least those engaged in book production, but many did sign their work, so the way is clear to writing these untold histories and to tracking the activities of engravers who moved into music printing at some point in their pluralistic careers. Here we might take the lead suggested to me by Thomas Hill, a professional sculptor and musician with a studio in San Francisco, who writes, "copperplate is so expressive of the music itself: the allegros look allegro [in engravings of French Baroque music], the adagios look slow, the notes seem to have direction and move

176

across the page in a way that makes graphic sense. These engraved scores have the organic and expressive qualities of a visual work of art, you can see the Human Hand at work. Movable type and modern printing seem so static and unmusical by comparison. The scores of George Crumb, Karlheinz Stockhausen, and John Cage have some relation to this I think, works that have the intention to exist both as works of visual art and as sonic art."[1]

To date, connoisseurship of music printing as a visual art remains of but passing interest to music historians. Pressured foremost by the need to seize bibliographic control of a vast repertoire in print, the first objective of musicologists who study printed music has—as I have already remarked—inevitably been to produce catalogues, usually printer by printer. Intelligent analyses of type, colophons, decorative initials, and graphic features front many of these catalogues, and yet these investigations are generally motivated by bibliography—visual elements provide evidence in arguments concerning dating and attribution. Doubtless the assumption that printing standardized book production and made one edition much like another has also forestalled pointed graphic analysis of early printed music books, and in this respect, the "sociology of texts" proposed by D. F. McKenzie in his Panizzi Lectures at the British Library in 1985 has yet to be taken up consistently for music.[2] This corner can now be turned more easily than ever, thanks to numerous digitization projects that give direct access to high-quality digital images of primary source materials. For instance, the "Early Music Online" project at Royal Holloway, University of London, has made 300 sixteenth-century printed anthologies of music from the British Library freely available online, and approximately 1,800 polyphonic prints from the sixteenth and seventeenth centuries at the Bayerische Staatsbibliothek are rapidly coming online there. As never before, scholars can launch comparative studies of widely dispersed sources, and while nothing has yet replaced the detailed analysis of paper, watermarks, bindings, and quality of impression possible in person, sources can now be examined in a preliminary way with a facility impossible even just five years ago.

Perhaps the greatest obstacle to advances in our understanding of music printing as a visual art is the long-standing prejudice against printmaking that has always made it a poor cousin to painting and sculpture. Jacques Callot, William Hogarth, Giovanni Battista Piranesi, and Henri de Toulouse-Lautrec have always been considered lesser lights in the constellations formed by their contemporaries, whereas even those printmakers of universally acknowledged greatness, such as Albrecht Dürer and Hans Holbein the Younger, may still be better known for their few paintings. Keyed to an art market that prizes uniqueness and rarity, the value attributed to Dürer's painted self-portraits or Holbein's *Ambassadors*, all on permanent display and frequently anthologized in textbooks, completely eclipses that of whatever woodcuts or engravings of theirs might be visible in the cool darkness of the same museums' distant print rooms.

Certainly the art world took more interest in printmaking in the 1960s, when artists themselves forced the renegotiation of aesthetic boundaries between art and decoration, and scholarship opened up to new ranges of inquiry beyond the traditional fine art, museum-centric orientation of visual studies. Commercial illustration, silk screening, and lithography played significant roles in these aesthetic revolutions with the ascent of superstar Pop artists such as Andy Warhol and Roy Lichtenstein. Pop artists challenged the conventions of the art world by adopting the look, content, and techniques of mechanical reproduction, forcing collectors and dealers to confront printmaking as high art. Lichtenstein's famous comic-book paintings, with their Ben-Day dots, stock primary colors, and flat imagery magnified designs from the cheapest color prints on the market without seeking to transform them. Warhol, in turn, made some of his most iconic paintings with silk screens, initially employing hand-drawn images, but later using screens produced with stencils made from photographs, as in his Marilyn Monroe series. These works deliberately deny the body of the artist, avoiding the impasto and brush strokes so central to connoisseurship and—not incidentally—to the attribution and valuation of paintings, particularly those of Renaissance masters. In this way, Pop art pitted itself against a critical tradition that turned on direct appreciation of the artist's manipulation of materials, flouting a set of aesthetics that ruled a New York art scene then dominated by Abstract Expressionist paintings with highly worked surfaces, typified by Jackson Pollock's action paintings and Willem de Kooning's deep, frosting-like layers of pastel oils. By promoting the flat, blunt solids of offset printing and the immediately graspable forms of trademarks and mass marketing, Pop art effaced evidence of the artist's physical engagement with the canvas, using commercial designs and techniques to comment on the artist's fragile place in a culture of mass consumption that was accelerated by the advertising campaigns of big business. But, paradoxically, Pop artists nonetheless failed to contest the bad attitude toward printmaking in any fundamental way. For the works that they marketed through the trend-defining gallery of Leo Castelli employed oil on canvas as the medium of their message. Pop art may have tested the limits of what collectors would pay for paintings made under an aesthetic hostile to the painterly, but it did nothing to promote printmaking in and of itself. Paintings such as Andy Warhol's "Eight Elvises" (1963)—sold in 2008 for $100 million—garner prices rivaling those paid for paintings by Vincent van Gogh, Pablo Picasso, and the French Impressionists.

If art critics and collectors have traditionally accorded less value to art prints, printed music has fared dramatically worse, even by comparison with printed books. The look of sixteenth-century music prints eventually became outmoded as flowing engravings replaced the broken staves of single-impression typography. Formats shifted from oblong to upright quarto, parts were supplanted by scores, and the often intricate and dense counterpoint of the Renaissance was superseded by the soloistic textures of the Baroque. The lack of bar lines and antiquated mensuration signs in sixteenth-century part music rendered it illegible for many. As a result, even Petrucci's elegant double-impression prints ended up as scrap paper, something we know for a fact from Padre Martini, who sought for years to add Petrucci prints to his collection. In 1753, one of Martini's friends, ever on the lookout for books that Martini might desire, wrote to say that he had come across a huntsman using pages from a copy of Petrucci's *Odhecaton* as wadding for his musket, but the hunter refused to part with his book. Sadly, such stories were not unusual. Just the year before, one of Martini's agents rescued fifty madrigal partbooks from a *pizzicheria* in Rome, where they were being sold by the pound as second-hand sheets, and still others came to Martini from aging collectors who feared that otherwise their books would be used to wrap salami after their deaths. Thanks to Martini, the Biblioteca della Musica in Bologna preserves one of the world's largest collections of Verovio's gorgeously calligraphed engravings, otherwise exceedingly rare, despite their beauty. In the end, music prints, no matter how beautiful, have always been treated like the piles of sheet music one still finds loosely stacked in second-hand book stores and falling apart in piano benches, prints to be used and used up, not art per se.

Historical attitudes as deep as those toward printmaking are difficult to reverse, but the opportunity to develop new modes of connoisseurship awaits those scholars who wish to take a fresh look at music prints, thanks to the digital media that are facilitating research into the material cultures of the past. Ironically, the obstructive energy that still accrues to cults of genius may ultimately invigorate these new avenues of research as the lives and work of hitherto unknown artists are explored. Attaching names to objects inevitably increases their value, and just as it saved a good number of Petrucci's prints in the eighteenth century, working out a history of the artists responsible for printing music stands to further increase the cultural capital of printed music books in academic circles and at the auction block.

Notes

1 My thoughts on the relationship between music and printmaking techniques evolved partially in conversations with Thomas Hill, from which these lines were drawn and for which I am deeply grateful.
2 D. F. McKenzie, *Bibliography and the Sociology of Texts*, The Panizzi Lectures, 1985 (London: British Library, 1986).

Further Reading

Bernstein, Jane A. *Print Culture and Music in Sixteenth-Century Venice*. Oxford: Oxford University Press, 2001.

Bavarian State Library, with the Münchener Digitalisierungs Zentrum. "Notendrucke des 16. und 17. Jahrhunderts mit mehrstimmiger Musik in der BSB" ("Music Prints from the 16th- and 17th-centuries with Polyphonic Music in the Bavarian State Library"). http://daten.digitale-sammlungen. de/~db/ausgaben/uni_ausgabe.html?projekt=1328176523&ordnung=sig&recherche=ja (accessed 15 October 2012).

Boorman, Stanley. *Ottaviano Petrucci: Catalogue Raisonné*. New York: Oxford University Press, 2006.

Krummel, D. W. and Stanley Sadie, eds. *Music Printing and Publishing*. New York: W. W. Norton, 1990.

McKenzie, D. F. *Bibliography and the Sociology of Texts*. The Panizzi Lectures, 1985. London: British Library, 1986.

Royal Holloway, University of London. "Early Music Online." http://www.rhul.ac.uk/music/research/earlymusiconline/home.aspx (accessed 15 October 2012).

Saff, Donald, and Deli Sacilotto. *Printmaking: History and Process*. New York: Holt, Rinehart and Winston, 1978.

Vervliet, Hendrik D. L. *The Palaeotypography of the French Renaissance: Selected Papers on Sixteenth-Century Typefaces*. 2 vols. Leiden: Brill, 2008.

21

ALBUM ART AND POSTERS

The Psychedelic Interplay of Rock Art and Art Rock

Jan Butler

[The late sixties were] a time when, having purchased a new gatefold album, you would get it home and religiously study every image, comma and hieroglyph on the sleeve for any last nuance of possible meaning. It was vital to believe that the group were trying to contact you through the images, and were saying deep things through the juxtaposition of totally disparate things. I scrupulously read all the lyrics, all the credits, and spent hours thinking to myself: "Now what do they *mean*—Printed in Slough?"[1]

In his work on the role of records in people's lives, Evan Eisenberg goes so far as to suggest that the album cover, not the music contained on the record, becomes the coveted possession of a rock fan, as it is the only visual distinguishing feature among the records in his/her collection. Even in today's digital music environment, downloads of tracks are accompanied by digital images of album art which you can flick through on your iPhone, and fans upload their favorite tracks onto YouTube with self-made "videos" consisting of still images including that artwork, suggesting that the combination of music and image that started with the large, brightly colored LP sleeve in the 1950s is still important today. In the quote at the head of this chapter, Andy Partridge recalls that—at least in the 1960s, when album artworks first came into their own—the fan looked to the artwork not just as an item worth collecting but as in itself an expression of meaning from the band. Yet, despite the clear importance of album artwork to music fans, there has been little scholarship published on the topic; most writing about album art is contained within glossy collections of album covers which focus more on celebration than on analysis of their role in music culture.

Nonetheless, there are existing theoretical frameworks that will prove to be pertinent in such analysis. Sarah Thornton's exploration of the role of micro-media in subcultural formations in her study of 1990s club cultures, while not addressing album art specifically, could be a useful starting point for the use of art in extended musical subcultural formation, and is discussed briefly below. Perhaps more useful, however, is Jonathan Gray's work on how paratexts function in relation to film and television, which can also help us to understand the interrelationship between an album of music (which is usually considered to be the main "text" of study by popular musicologists) and its related texts, such as album covers and reviews. Gray borrows the idea of the paratext from literary theory and expands upon it to argue that the meaning of a cultural text cannot be fully understood without taking into account its related texts, such as advertisements, posters, trailers, and media coverage, all of which have the potential to affect the meaning and value of the text. Gray splits paratexts into two types: entryway paratexts that control and determine our entrance to new texts; and *in medias res* paratexts that inflect or redirect the text after our initial interaction. Working with film, Gray assumes that most paratexts will greet an audience before they ever see the filmic "text" itself. The album cover and music promotional materials are more complicated in their relation to the musical "text," as music can be heard without any visual framing devices of this sort (for example, on the radio), although it is unlikely to be bought or sought out without reference to them; so album covers could act as either entryway or *in medias res* paratexts. Despite this, the paratext concept is a useful one for considering the role and importance of album art and posters in the formation and maintenance of musical subcultures, and offers a means by which academic discussion of album art can be brought into popular music study. This chapter proposes that the album cover should be understood as a paratext, a text that is both distinct from and intrinsically linked to the main text, and that plays a crucial role in suggesting or confirming the meaning and value of the musical work contained on the record.

To explore this idea, I will focus on the sudden appearance of the psychedelic album cover in 1967. From the 1940s onward, it had been common to sell pop albums with a picture of the star on the cover (see, for example, Frank Sinatra, *Songs for Young Lovers* (1953), or Elvis Presley, *A Date with Elvis* (1959)). Even bands that were later associated with psychedelia were portrayed on their early album covers as groups of nice young men in matching outfits (for example, the Beatles, *Please Please Me* (1963), the Beach Boys, *Surfin' Safari* (1962), the Rolling Stones, *The Rolling Stones* (1964)). As their music developed, the cover images stayed much the same, although suits were exchanged for more casual dress and the length of hair crept closer to their collar-lines (the Beatles, *Rubber Soul*, the Beach Boys, *Beach Boys' Party!*, the Rolling Stones, *December's Children (and Everybody's)*, all 1965). The first hint of change in rock album design came in 1966, with the release of the Beatles' *Revolver*, which featured a collage of line drawings and photographs of the band designed by artist Klaus Voorman. This was followed by a flood of self-consciously artistic and psychedelic album covers in 1967, as psychedelic rock reached a mainstream audience. This chapter explores the reasons for and effects of this change, and argues that 1967 marked an important moment in which popular music and visual culture became closely aligned through the prism of psychedelia to help create a sense of rock as an artistic community.

The Rise of Psychedelic Art Rock

Psychedelia is a term used to describe a wide range of art forms dating from and influenced by the 1960s. It is generally considered to be very difficult to define and discuss in an academic manner, and as a result the literature on psychedelic art remains somewhat small. Although psychedelia was closely linked to elements of the counterculture (which is also notoriously difficult to define), and was often connected with the experience of taking LSD, it was not necessarily created or appreciated only by proponents of either. Probably the most wide-reaching form of psychedelic art, in terms of audience numbers and eventual global reach, was psychedelic rock, which emerged from the West Coast of America in the mid-1960s, coalesced into a movement combining visual art and music through 1966, and then became a global phenomenon in terms of record sales in 1967. The term "psychedelic rock" can be considered to be largely synonymous with art rock, progressive rock, and acid rock (terms more commonly used in the UK), and includes bands such as the Beatles, Pink Floyd, and Cream in the UK, and Jefferson Airplane, the Grateful Dead, and Quicksilver Messenger Service in the US. In relation to rock music, the term "psychedelic" tended to refer to writing, visuals, or music that either enhanced the sensory alterations that LSD caused or else imitated them, and was understood to help the listener to expand his/her consciousness and explore the possibilities of the self. LSD was also believed to enhance creativity, and both the Beatles and the Beach Boys have attributed their sudden changes in musical style around 1965—involving an expanded palette of sounds and greater range of harmonies—to taking LSD.

For the purposes of this chapter I use the term "psychedelic community" to refer to a segment of the counterculture that was concerned mainly with a personal revolution, not a political one. This psychedelic community was more concerned with the spreading of "positive vibes" and the opening of individuals' minds through artistic activity and the organization of live events and happenings than it was with direct political protest. It attempted to bypass politics and instead create a community of enlightened individuals. Psychedelic rock bands were considered to be key members of this community, as they were important providers—through live musical events—of a collective experience that also furnished the means whereby people could carry out "the search for the truth of the person and the attempt to set up an alternative lifestyle."[2]

In her work on progressive rock and the counterculture in the UK, Sheila Whiteley goes beyond the importance of live rock events as communal spaces to argue that psychedelic rock encoded the psychedelic experience in musical form through melodic shapes, timbral effects, and harmonic progressions, as well as in its lyrical subject matter. She also describes how psychedelic rock started to favor the LP album format over singles, which had previously accounted for the majority of the record sales in rock and pop. Whiteley argues that the greater musical freedom and space for extended displays of musicianship (such as guitar jams and solos) which the LP allowed led to its being linked to artistry in the second half of the 1960s. What Whiteley does not mention, however, is that the LP, unlike the single, was sold in a full-color sleeve, allowing for much greater artistry in the packaging of the music as well as in its content. As demonstrated below, it can be argued that, once a visual style associated with psychedelic rock music had started to develop, the artistic potential of the album cover as a paratext was taken advantage of, allowing not only a musical encoding of psychedelia on psychedelic rock records, but a visual one as well.

The Rise of Psychedelic Rock Art

Over the course of 1966, the psychedelic community developed synergies between rock music and other art forms, aligning rock and visual culture to help induce psychedelic effects in rock's audience. The year began with the Trips festival in late January in San Francisco. Organized by members of various local avant-garde groups in conjunction with the San Francisco Tape Music Center and local rock bands the Grateful Dead, Big Brother and the Holding Company, and Jefferson Airplane, the festival was an attempt to draw together various strands of San Francisco's artistic and psychedelic community. Described as a three-day "electronic happening," the Trips festival was promoted as "a non-drug re-creation of the psychedelic experience," designed to induce psychedelic effects in its audience through artistic means, and it marked the first occasion on which rock bands were accompanied by light-shows.[3] Lightshows were originally conceived in San Francisco in the late 1950s by painters interested in the possibility of literal movement in a work, and were developed through experimentation with film, projectors, and different light and paint effects. In the 1960s, they were regularly combined and synchronized with performances of avant-garde music by members of the San Francisco Tape Music Center. The combination of rock bands with lightshows at the festival was considered to be particularly effective, and the lightshow became a key part of rock "dances" at venues across San Francisco.

Perhaps taking their inspiration from this combination, five key artists working in San Francisco—Victor Stanley "Mouse" Miller and Alton Kelley of Mouse studios, Wes Wilson, Rick Griffin, and Victor Moscoso—developed a distinctive style of poster art to advertise these rock "dances" and events on local handbills and posters. These posters featured unusual lettering: uneven, "psychedelic" bubble styles, art nouveau references, old Western-style fonts, and almost unreadable lettering designed to fool the eye. They used clashing colors, recurring motifs such as "the Indian", the sun, mandalas, and yin–yang symbols, all of which became standard elements of psychedelic poster art. For example, Moscoso's 1967 Quicksilver Messenger Service poster combines clashing electric blue and red distorted lettering disguised as geometric shapes forming a yin and yang symbol which, if interpreted, tell you the line-up, venue, and date of the band's next gig. The difficulty of decoding the posters, which were working at one level as adverts for psychedelic events, was part of their appeal to the psychedelic community. The act of straining to decode the posters was in itself hoped to induce a psychedelic effect in viewers, providing them with a glimpse of the psychedelic event to come. Thus, these posters can be understood as entryway paratexts which "hold considerable power to direct our initial interpretations, telling us what to expect and establishing genre, gender, style, attitude and characterization."[4] They also had the social organization function of Thornton's micromedia, in that they relied on a large proportion of their audience possessing the subcultural capital needed to decode the poster accurately and find the details of the advertised event.

Links between rock music and multimedia shows were also being made elsewhere in 1966: in New York, Andy Warhol developed his Exploding Plastic Inevitable (EPI), a multimedia artwork experience featuring the band the Velvet Underground. Whether or not this could be considered psychedelic is debatable, as when Warhol toured the EPI to San Francisco in the summer of 1966 it was not well received. Yet it was advertised using the same psychedelic-style letter-ing as other gigs held at San Franciscan venues, suggesting that it was expected to be greeted with open arms by the psychedelic community. A more successful psychedelic development occurred across the Atlantic, starting in March 1966, when Pink Floyd started incorporating multicolored lights and extended musical numbers into their gigs. By October 1966, the band was performing regularly at the London Free School's Sound and Light workshop, where slides were projected over the band and their audience. In the same month, Pink Floyd permanently enlisted Joe Gannon, who synchronized his slides to underlying rhythms in the music to provide a direct link between visual and aural effect. By the end of 1966, then, links between psychedelic rock and visual artforms were firmly established in San Francisco and London, both places considered home to the psychedelic community.

The media coverage of rock also changed over the course of 1966, providing new paratexts for rock which moved toward constructing it as a new art form. The earliest examples can be found in *Crawdaddy!* magazine, founded in Febru-ary in the US, which described itself as providing "intelligent writing about pop music."[5] The jazz critic Ralph Gleason spent the year describing San Franciscan rock in artistic terms usually reserved for jazz in the *San Franciscan Chronicle*, and concurrently *Melody Maker* in the UK increasingly praised the musicianship and artistic value of rock bands. The early media recognition of rock as art arguably peaked with the broadcast of the first dedicated rock documentary in April 1967 on the American TV channel CBS, *Inside Pop: The Rock Revolution*. *Inside Pop* was produced at the latter end of 1966 by David Oppenheim, a well-respected maker of art-music documentaries, and included an introduction in which Leonard Bernstein compared the Beatles to Schumann in their ability to reflect emotional lines in their music, and discussed the inventiveness of many rock musicians. Although psychedelic rock was still not high in the charts at this point—with the exceptions of the Beatles and the Beach Boys' "Good Vibrations"—through the proliferating paratexts of record criticism, there was a growing awareness of the existence of the music associated with the psychedelic community, and growing discussion of it as a new art form.

The Psychedelic Explosion

It was in 1967—and in particular after the success of the Monterey Pop Festival in San Francisco and the release of the Beatles' *Sgt. Pepper's Lonely Hearts Club Band* in the same week—that psychedelic rock was brought to mainstream attention with widespread coverage in the press, and gained a large audience beyond the psych-edelic community. It was also largely from this point that rock album covers moved away from portraits of the band and toward covers inspired by psychedelic effects and imagery, and occasionally Pop art—see, for example, Andy Warhol's covers for the self-titled *The Velvet Underground and Nico* (1967) or the Rolling Stones' *Sticky Fingers* (1970). The most famous Pop art cover at the time was of course *Sgt. Pepper* itself, with its collage designed by Peter Blake, but this too was psychedelic in its visual busyness, bright, clashing colors, and the unusual dress of the Beatles. The remainder of the year's album releases from bands wishing to align themselves with the counterculture featured psychedelic artworks inspired by the artistic developments of the previous year: elements of the psychedelic posters originating in San Francisco (see the lettering and photo montage on Grateful Dead, *Grateful Dead* (1967) and the bright colors and lettering on the Beach Boys, *Smiley Smile* (1967)); impressions of lightshows (see Country Joe and the Fish, *Electric Music for the Mind and Body* (1967), or Iron Butterfly, *Inna Gadda Da Vida* (1968)); visual elements of psychedelic culture (see the combination of bright colors, hard-to-decipher writing, references to nature, yin–yang symbols, and the all-seeing eye on the cover of the Incredible String Band, *The 5000 Spirits* (1967), or the clashing colors and visual intensity of Cream, *Disraeli Gears* (1967)); or psychedelic visual effects (such as the "fish eye lens" on the American edition of the Jimi Hendrix Experience, *Are You Experienced* (1967), and on Captain Beefheart, *Safe as Milk* (1970)).

The Expanded Psychedelic Community

So what were the reasons for and meanings of this wholesale shift toward the psychedelic? As I have discussed elsewhere, the financial success of psychedelic rock after Monterey suggests that there was a developing awareness of how rock should be marketed, and key to this marketing strategy was the use of members of the psychedelic community as rock cultural intermediaries. One crucial role of the rock cultural intermediaries was the maintenance of the perceived authenticity of rock music, both for the wider audience and for the psychedelic community from which it emerged. Psychedelic album covers aided this process by acting as effective paratexts for both these audiences. For the psychedelic community, the album covers could act as reassuring confirmation that the authenticity of their psychedelic art had not been "corrupted" by its own commercial success and could still have a psychedelic effect, both through its use of their own symbols and through its difference from the pop marketing norm of straightforward portraits of the band. This use of art on albums to symbolize the artistic content within instead of portraying the musicians themselves had previously occurred in the 1950s, when jazz started to be taken seriously as an art. See, for example, the bright figures of the covers of *This is Benny Goodman and His Orchestra* (1956), the abstraction of *Jutta Hipp with Zoot Sims* (1956), and the line drawings of Andy Warhol's early forays into mass-produced art on the cover of Kenny Burrell's *Blue Lights* (1958). In the case of rock, it seems likely that, as cultural forces started to frame rock as art instead of as a commercial product, album covers moved toward more artistic statements, confirming and perpetuating rock's new-found art status.

After Monterey, the market for psychedelic rock far exceeded the geographical boundaries of the locations from which the psychedelic community emerged. For this much larger audience, now aware of the psychedelic community and its visual style, and perhaps also influenced by the larger cultural paratext of discussion of rock as an artform, psychedelic album covers could function as effective paratexts in a different way, either suggesting to the browser in a record shop that the music contained in the album was psychedelic, or confirming that it was psychedelic to someone who had first heard the music on the radio. However, I would argue that, for rock fans such as the one quoted at the head of this chapter, these paratexts could also function as more than this, being read as a direct message which could provide a simulacrum of the psychedelic experience for those unable or unwilling to be physically involved in the psychedelic community itself.

Records have long operated as symbols of belonging—as Eisenberg reports, a 1947 study of teenagers found that record collecting was largely used to announce membership of a particular social group—and theorists have discussed the function of records in the formation of a sense of community among disparate individuals in relation to the psychedelic community. Eisenberg argues that the gathering of fans to listen to psychedelic rock records on a friend's hi-fi system acted as a means of maintaining faith in the counterculture in between attendance at live events. Ellen Willis, a music critic, makes a similar but more detailed argument, describing albums in general as offering the basis through which disparate individuals can feel themselves to be part of a community while retaining a sense of their individual freedom. She calls this community the "mass-mediated crowd," a crowd in which it is possible to respond as an individual to records in the privacy of one's own home, but also, through the knowledge that others are listening to the same record, feel part of a community.

Sgt. Pepper is often identified as the album that first provided an extended sense of community in this way. This was an album that would never be performed live, that was a virtual performance in itself, and that was the first commercially successful work to be heralded by critics as a key element of psychedelia. The huge popularity of the Beatles meant that the album was played everywhere, and, according to Willis, there was a sense that "everyone was connected … through the Beatles—from twelve year old girls who were turned on by Paul McCartney to musicologists who were analyzing the chord structures."[6] Whiteley argues that the collective experience of this album provided the musical equivalent of the (psychedelic) community already established in San Francisco and London. As mentioned above, music's ability to reach an audience relatively free from paratexts makes it difficult to determine how important paratexts such as album artwork are in determining the value and meanings attributed to it. However, I would argue that—although the music was no doubt important—for the mainstream audience, their ability to feel part of the psychedelic community was largely due to rock's effective framing by psychedelic paratexts. The use of psychedelic artforms as reference points for visual paratexts such as album covers helped to confer a sense of meaning on this music, giving new importance to the visual in relation to popular music, binding it closely to the pre-existing psychedelic community and allowing a sense of a mass-mediated artistic rock community to emerge.

Notes

1 Andy Partridge in Storm Thorgerson, *Classic Album Covers of the 1960s* (London: Collins and Brown, 2005), 220.
2 Theodore Roszak, *The Making of a Counterculture: Reflections on the Technocratic Society and its Youthful Opposition* (Garden City, NY: Doubleday, 1969), quoted in Sheila Whiteley, *The Space Between the Notes: Rock and the Counter-culture* (London: Routledge, 1992), 1.
3 David W. Bernstein, *The San Francisco Tape Music Center: 1960s Counterculture and the Avant-garde* (Berkeley: University of California Press, 2008), 5.
4 Jonathan Gray, *Show Sold Separately: Promos, Spoilers, and Other Media Paratexts* (New York: New York University Press, 2010), 79.
5 Paul Williams, "Editorial," *Crawdaddy!* 1 (February 1966): 1.
6 Ellen Willis, "Crowds and Freedom," in *Stars Don't Stand Still in the Sky: Music and Myth*, ed. Karen Kelly and Evelyn McDonnell (London: Routledge, 1999), 155.

Further Reading

Butler, Jan. "Record Production and the Construction of an Ideology of Authenticity in the Beach Boys and Late-Sixties American Rock." PhD thesis, University of Nottingham, 2010.

Eisenberg, Evan. *The Recording Angel: Music, Records and Culture from Aristotle to Zappa.* London: Pan Books, 1988.

Gray, Jonathan. *Show Sold Separately: Promos, Spoilers, and Other Media Paratexts.* New York: New York University Press, 2010.

Grunenberg, Christoph and Jonathan Harris, ed. *Summer of Love: Psychedelic Art, Social Crisis and Counterculture in the 1960s.* Liverpool: Liverpool University Press and Tate Liverpool, 2005.

Thorgerson, Storm. *Classic Album Covers of the 1960s.* London: Collins and Brown, 2005.

Thornton, Sarah. *Club Cultures: Music, Media and Subcultural Capital.* Cambridge: Polity Press, 1995.

Whiteley, Sheila. *The Space Between the Notes: Rock and the Counter-culture.* London: Routledge, 1992.

Willis, Ellen. "Crowds and Freedom." In *Stars Don't Stand Still in the Sky: Music and Myth* , edited by Karen Kelly and Evelyn McDonnell, 153–159. London: Routledge, 1999.

Part IV

CONVERGENCE

IV.1 Convergence in Metaphor

22

VISUAL METAPHORS IN MUSIC ANALYSIS AND CRITICISM

Gurminder Kaur Bhogal

The "naturalness" with which art and music terminologies have co-existed in discussions on musical performance, analysis, and interpretation since the nineteenth century is intriguing and complicated. Pedagogues have been particularly skillful in creating analogies between music and the visual arts; those of us who have learned to play a musical instrument might recall how effectively a simile or metaphor could strike our imaginations, thereby changing our performance of a phrase or entire piece almost instantaneously. The aims of composers and music critics have been somewhat less strategic, but still oriented toward captivating their audiences. Although these figures routinely appropriated such terms as line, color, shape, and (somewhat later) texture from the art world, their subdued interest in acknowledging the source of their borrowed language, or considering the precise nuance and significance of visual correlates, seems to suggest that the visual origin of these terms was of little consequence. What seemed to matter more was how markers of visual practices could shed their original roles and meanings to accrue new ones upon entering the domain of music. For artists, musicians, and their critics, metaphors did more than establish broad parallels between disciplines; they also catalyzed the transformations of style and technique that propelled their respective media toward making contact.

From the standpoint of music, one might argue that it was an inherent meaninglessness that allowed it to benefit from association with pictorial art, a tradition whose capacity for representation lent an element of specificity to a medium which some nineteenth-century critics described (in positive and negative terms) as a complex arrangement of tones and rhythms. While offering new templates for the organization of musical ideas and articulation of formal structure, painting and literature served to endow music with narrative significance at the same time as they aspired "towards the condition of music," that is, the idealized purity of music's existence as captured in the famous words of Walter Pater. The abundance of metaphor in nineteenth- and twentieth-century cultural life—seen in the titles of works, critical reviews, and aesthetic writings—reflects the ease with which interdisciplinary associations were made, but conceals the work that these figures of speech actually did with regard to stimulating technical innovation and shaping the ways in which audiences made sense of what they saw and heard. This is why an analysis of the metaphors that permeate a work's creation and reception proves useful for understanding the social and cultural dynamics that link a creative work to its milieu.

How do metaphors function and what is it that they do? Cognitive theorists George Lakoff and Mark Johnson have argued that the formation of metaphors is deeply rooted in bodily experiences which the mind tries to interpret by conceptualizing one domain (unfamiliar) in terms of another (familiar). Before exploring how this process works, let us consider some metaphors that bring together the domains of music and art such as "instrumental color" and "melodic line." Hector Berlioz, in combining an unusual array of instruments with their distinct pitches and timbres, thought of his music as conveying colors. He spoke of "sharp contrasts of colour between the brass and wood," and enthused, "there is nothing so virginal or so pure as the shades of colour bestowed on certain melodies by the tone of the intermediate register of the clarinet in the hands of a skilful player."[1] The interpretation of timbre in terms of color was equally important for Claude Debussy, who described his composition *Printemps* (1887) as "a work in a special color." He also perceived the rhythmic fluidity of melody in terms of curve and line: the composer cherished "undulating music, swaying, full of curved lines."[2]

The extent to which these types of borrowings were reciprocated has been well documented. With regard to the application of color and development of line, art historians have examined the general use of such musical concepts as sonority, harmony, and melody in the critical writings of painters. More focused attention has been given to such figures as Paul Signac, who perceived melody in color and rhythm in line, and James Abbott McNeill Whistler, who alluded to specific musical genres in labeling certain works *Nocturnes* and *Symphonies*. In response to Whistler, Debussy later reversed the trend in arguing for a purely visual understanding of his *Trois Nocturnes* (1897–1899); he instructed his listeners, "the title 'Nocturnes' is to be interpreted here in a general and, more particularly, decorative sense. Therefore, it is not meant to designate the usual form of the Nocturne, but rather all the various impressions and the special effects of light that the word suggests."[3]

The reason why cross-disciplinary associations such as these make sense, or seem "natural," is because the connection established between domains to create a metaphor, and the cognitive process through which this conceptual product materializes, has considerable physiological resonance. For example, the metaphor of "melodic curve" is effective because the rising and falling pattern of neighboring pitches—to use a spatial metaphor—might encourage us to visualize a curve in our minds or evoke a corresponding gesture through the movement of our hands. In this case, the changing frequency of pitches is one that we understand as configuring our awareness of space and motion; listeners might actually *feel* a curve emerge with a completion of the melodic phrase. Another metaphor, "melodic line," is equally successful, given the facility with which the temporal succession of a group of pitches can map onto the continuity of a figure conceived in two-dimensional space. In this instance, the interaction between cognitive and perceptual efforts to register each pitch, and make sense of how they relate to one another, finds a correlate in the act of observation; the ear follows each note almost as the eye traces the linear extent of the figure.

Even though such conceptual mappings seem entirely feasible, some musicologists have been troubled by the lack of specificity inherent to these types of associations. A criticism voiced by Reinhold Brinkmann with regard to the notion of "musical Jugendstil" a few decades ago is still, to some degree, valid: "What, in the realm of music, are those sensitive, perfectly drawn asymmetric lines of apparently endless movement? What, in the technique of composition, corresponds to this visual phenomenon? Is it the melodies of irregular, ametrical structure, without *caesura*-stressing cadences? Is it the related contrapuntal parts?"[4] Rather than deter inter-art inquiry, however, criticisms such as these have impelled music scholars to move beyond establishing superficial affinities between the arts. In the spirit of Theodor Adorno's notion of "convergence," Walter Frisch has recently argued for the pursuit of a dialectical relationship between music and art, one that thrives on establishing points of contact, rather than parallels and signs of imitation.

Quite rightly, the fundamental concern of Brinkmann, Frisch, and others stems froman absense of critical reflection: just because composers, artists, and critics spoke about art and music with a considerable level of ease and fluidity, this doesn't mean that we should do the same, especially since scholars today don't have the same lack of terminology that musicians, composers, and critics had at the turn of the twentieth century. The evolution of music analysis as an activity and academic sub-discipline provides those who wish to analyze music with a vast vocabulary and ample terminology for describing and understanding complicated musical structures and processes. As a result, the question might be asked whether the use of metaphor has a place in the practice of music analysis.

Of course, such a query cannot be raised without first acknowledging the extent to which the language of Western music theory is firmly rooted in visual and spatial experience. A notion of space has come to inform conceptions of pitch as "high" and "low." That of perspective has allowed the perception of loud pitches to be equated with proximity and softer ones with distance. Motif, another visual concept, is commonly invoked to describe a succinct gesture whose precise arrangement of pitches or rhythm takes on a larger significance with regard to the organization of musical form, much as in the visual arts. Similarly, shape is used to address issues of organization, from the lowest level of the phrase to that of the entire movement or composition. Texture, too, has provided an effective way for analysts to grapple with the hierarchized delineation of musical material. The longevity of some of these terms in music criticism and analysis has meant that the original link to the visual realm has all but eroded. Still, an awareness of their roots can yield fruitful results for the purposes of analysis, especially in repertoires where visual stimuli served as an impetus for innovation. The case of Debussy demonstrates the importance of taking metaphors seriously.

Despite his disgust at being labeled a Symbolist or Impressionist composer— "useful terms of abuse," he called them—Debussy often turned to the visual arts to explain what was different and new about his music.[5] One term that featured copiously in his critical writings was "arabesque." In the visual realm, "arabesque" referred to a vegetal motif denoting vine, ivy, or acanthus leaves; it also alluded to the geometric and floral designs of Islamic art and architecture. Building on these associations, Debussy described this type of ornament as pure, adorable, beautiful, divine, capricious, supple, and fluid, all the while emphasizing its appearance in terms of line and curve. He made it virtually impossible for his audience to figure

GURMINDER KAUR BHOGAL

out what he truly meant by "arabesque." In addition to making such cryptic comments as, "in Bach's music it is not the character of the melody that moves us, it is its curve," Debussy professed his admiration for "the flowing curves of the melodic line," and praised "the parallel movement of several lines whose meeting, whether fortuitous or agreed-upon, stirs our emotions."[6] Based on his writings, we might well wonder whether the term "arabesque" referred to melody or harmony; the fact that he wrote a piano composition called *Deux Arabesques* in 1888–91 also draws into debate the significance of this term as generic designation. The broad scope of Debussy's remarks further raises the issue of whether the arabesque was—in keeping with Eduard Hanslick and the German Romantics—pure and devoid of meaning as observed by John Daverio; or if, in tandem with Debussy's colleagues in art, this ornament was valued equally for its capacity to evoke and narrate.

Debussy's music provides some answers to these questions, particularly the *Prélude à l'après-midi d'un faune* (1894), an orchestral piece inspired by Stéphane Mallarmé's poem, *L'Après-midi d'un faune* (1876). In a letter inviting Mallarmé to attend a performance of his piece, Debussy flattered the poet by claiming that the flute arabesques of Mallarmé's faun had dictated his composition. Even though the real and imagined music of Mallarmé's poetry seems to have anticipated Debussy's efforts to transform the arabesque from a visual to a musical gesture, the composer's solo flute melody shows the imaginative ways in which he chose to transcribe the visual figure of the arabesque into sound.

The shallow contour characteristic of arabesques is evident in this melody's tendency to gravitate around the opening C♯ (Example 22.1). In the first two measures, attempts to move beyond the opening pitch are heard in the form of short, rhythmic values whose slippery chromatic descent is balanced by a lugubrious whole-tone ascent in keeping with the balanced, undulating curves of arabesque lines; throughout this melody, ascending intervals are followed by descending intervals. Debussy evokes the intricacy of visual arabesque through a musical manifestation that is defined by variety in pitch and complexity of rhythm. He also points to the special status of the arabesque in his work by positioning it at the beginning, where a lack of harmonic support allows the listener's attention to be focused squarely on the horizontal dimension. Whispered by the soft dynamics of the flute, Debussy's arabesque, like many of its visual referents, is somewhat hazy, although structurally sufficient. This theme's inability to establish a tonal center reflects the composer's interest to privilege ambiguity as an expressive feature of musical arabesque. Furthermore, a

Example 22.1 Debussy, opening melody of *Prélude à l'après-midi d'un faune*.

194

meandering motion, accentuated here by the arabesque's failure to initiate a sense of meter, allows time to literally stand still as the listener is slowly drawn into the Faun's dream through the otherworldly allure of his captivating music.

The types of visual–musical correspondences that Debussy was keen to explore suggest how he might have taken his inspiration from such artists as Maurice Denis or Pierre Bonnard, even though his aims were markedly different. It is true that Debussy empowered the arabesque so that it came to assume a structural as well as expressive role, but while most painters conceived of the arabesque as generating motion, Debussy relied on this figure to convey the very opposite: that is, his arabesques tended toward suspending time through a non-teleological development and irregular transitions between long and short durations, as heard within a non-metered background. An example such as this serves to show that the simultaneous preoccupation with a single principle didn't necessarily lead composers and artists toward pursuing the same goals. This is especially true for inter-media relationships at the turn of the century, when interest to manipulate an audience's perception of art or music depended on the approximation of qualities that were antithetical to that medium. In the case of the arabesque, the evocation of motion in art, or stasis in music, demonstrated technical novelty, while touting a tendency for avant-garde subversion (as I have explored elsewhere).

The example of Debussy's Faun melody enacts a process of substitution as an undulating, intricate melodic phrase comes to stand in for an equivalent visual figure. Given the culture of reciprocity that held sway during the nineteenth century, it is perhaps no surprise that artists also sought varied ways for music to feature in their work. The topic of music entered the spatial arena through many ways, some of them concerned with the act of teaching (George Goodwin Kilburne, *The Music Lesson*), or the art of practicing an instrument (Paolo Bedini, *Girl Playing the Violin*); others showcased a formal performance (Edgar Degas, *L'orchestre de l'Opéra*, 1870), or a single listener deep in contemplation (Fernand Khnopff, *Listening to Schumann*, 1883). Examples such as these require us to re-create the music of these paintings in our minds. Others, such as Bonnard's colorful lithographs for a piano textbook, *Le Petit Solfège Illustré* (1893), were more literal in their presentation of music, as seen in his preoccupation with notation.

Commissioned by his brother-in-law, the composer Claude Terrasse, Bonnard's playful illustrations for this piano primer were designed to enliven a child's first encounter with music theory. Terrasse's somewhat dry explanation of the rudiments of music theory—how to read notation, understanding the formation of scales, learning rhythmic subdivision—is considerably offset by Bonnard's charming and entertaining visual commentary. While manipulating the signs of notation, Bonnard conveys the illusion of tone as wavy arabesques are transformed from abstract lines into anthropomorphized note-heads, note stems, the open mouths of singers, and outlines of musical instruments. Bonnard's equation of visual contour with sound evokes the topic of reverberation and suggests that "music [is] in the air," as described by Anne Leonard.[7] Significantly, the close interaction of figure with ground also has the remarkable ability to convey that music *is* line or contour as the accumulation of abstract lines forms images that compel us to imagine different facets of musical sound, while their unraveling falls back to reveal the constituent undulating contour. The ambiguity of lines and shapes in *Le Petit Solfège Illustré* points to the possibility for art to be conceived as music (or, rather, as an extension of music notation). In so doing, Bonnard also suggests the possibility for music notation to be conceived as art. We might thus ask ourselves whether, in composing the Faun's melody, Debussy imagined he was drawing an arabesque.

Although metaphor plays a crucial role in facilitating acts of transcription and transformation in the types of visual–musical exchanges outlined above, it is important not to dismiss the impulse that underlies its formation in the first place: an instinctive need for parallels. This essay has warned against the artificial observations and superficial alignments that sometimes hinder a critical evaluation of cross-domain interactions. However, when parallelisms are addressed through scrutiny of a common vocabulary, particularly the use of metaphor, then one might have an opportunity to glimpse the sources of inspiration that fueled technical innovation, especially in genres that thrived on collaboration between different media, such as opera and ballet. Certainly, for some creative figures of the early twentieth century, the opportunity to cultivate visual–musical relationships through this type of synchronic engagement lay at the heart of their creative enterprises. The ballet that cast Igor Stravinsky as the *enfant terrible* of Paris, *Le Sacre du Printemps* (1913), provides a useful case in point.

The language of first reviews has played a vital part in determining how Stravinsky's music has been analyzed ever since. To this end, some credit must also be given to Jean Cocteau's cuboid caricature of the composer; seated at the piano, Stravinsky is pursued by the flat profiles of the ballet's dancers as they trail off into the distance. Geometric, block-like, stratified, angular: these are just a few terms that have come to saturate Stravinsky scholarship as commentators strive to grapple with unusual shifts in the musical style of his so-called "Russian period." In early reception, for instance, a prominent music critic, Jean Marnold, saw Stravinsky's creation of repetitive motifs as presenting "one [idea] after another in changing blocks, in successive compartments."[8] A similar emphasis on processes of juxtaposition and repetition is evident in well-respected analyses of *Le Sacre* by Pierre Boulez and Pieter van den Toorn; even more recently, Gretchen Horlacher calls attention to Stravinsky's "penchant for layering repeating strata ... a form best described by words such as block and superimposition, terms associated more with assemblage."[9] Some of Stravinsky's stylistic novelties, such as an emphasis on repeating chords, and discontinuity in the transition from one musical idea to another, have been traced back to his experiments in an earlier ballet, *Petrushka* (1910–11). However, the unique designs of Nicholas Roerich's costumes, with which Stravinsky became familiar when sketching his ideas for *Le Sacre*, also proved pivotal in bringing his musical innovations to fruition. The juxtaposition of visual–musical elements is first witnessed in the opening dance of this ballet, "The Augurs of Spring," when the stage curtain is raised to reveal Roerich's costumes as dancers perform Vaslav Nijinsky's stylized choreography to the pulsating, repetitive chords of Stravinsky's music.

At this moment, several correspondences are established between visual and musical domains. Given a mutual emphasis on techniques of repetition, juxtaposition, and re-combination by designer and composer, we might experience how a geometric shape has a correlate in one of Stravinsky's succinct musical ideas. Roerich's use of repetition seems to be replicated in Stravinsky's treatment of ostinato, while the regular spacing of each shape conveys a visual rhythm that is mirrored in the periodic pulse of Stravinsky's metric patterns. The changing colors of

Roerich's repeated shapes correspond to the shifting timbres of repeated musical ideas, and the changing sizes of shapes relate to Stravinsky's techniques of rhythmic augmentation and diminution. Roerich's overall organization of motifs and patterns into horizontal reams is reflected in the linear trajectories of Stravinsky's musical material. These mappings strive to turn the mind's ear toward the complexities of Stravinsky's decorative organization at the same time as they place the mind's eye before the spectacle of Roerich's geometric designs (and Nijinsky's abstract dance formations). This example goes beyond placing visual and musical phenomena in proximate (but distinct) relationship to one another; it encourages us to imagine how sonic, visual, and choreographic intersections worked together in rendering the audible visible and the visible audible.

Despite the collaborative nature of Le Sacre, the inherent complexity of each medium spurred analysts toward investigating aspects of choreography, costumes, and music in isolation from one another. In fact, in hailing Stravinsky's composition as a masterpiece that surpassed the contribution of Roerich and Nijinsky in its vision and originality, some commentators have preferred to evaluate the composer's accomplishments in purely musical terms, going so far as to disavow (or disparage, in some cases) connections with the visual (Stravinsky, himself, advocated such interpretations later in his career). Undoubtedly, there is considerable value in undertaking a formalistic approach to visual, musical, and choreographic analysis, especially since each realm is intrinsically complete in and of itself. However, reading Stravinsky's music through Roerich's costumes, and Roerich's costumes through Stravinsky's music, makes it possible to re-create the multimedia framework in which this ballet was initially conceived. Thus, while Roerich's boldly colored costumes are characterized by repeating, oversized geometric shapes, his designs are brought to life only by musical techniques that emphasize qualities of stylization, intricacy, and linearity. Similarly, the unrelenting ostinati and abrupt juxtaposition of ideas that define Stravinsky's music are even more effective when they are visualized in the form of recurring, geometric patterns which similarly evolve to create complex structures in Roerich's fabrics. In comparison with Debussy, who sought to approximate visual techniques while applying them to vastly different expressive ends, Roerich and Stravinsky seemed more intent on nurturing convergences to create an inter-art aesthetic that is almost reminiscent of a Wagnerian Gesamtkunstwerk in tone and spirit.

The examples of Mallarmé and Debussy, Bonnard and Terrasse, and Roerich and Stravinsky, have served to show that metaphors do not arise because of a lack; the allusion to a visual domain while operating within the constraints of music, and vice versa, is not made with the purpose of compensating for an expressive meaning or mode of formal organization that music or art cannot achieve independently. Metaphors, along with similes, figures, and tropes, build on a framework of meaning that is already in existence; conceived of in ancient rhetoric as a component of elocutio, metaphors were understood to function as aspects of verbal decoration that rendered the argument more vivid through the remarkable imagery and feelings that they conjured. Certainly, their role as decoration is still implicit in the evocative titles and intriguing turns of phrase through which they pervaded the cultural spheres of the nineteenth and twentieth centuries. However, the status of metaphor became considerably elevated during this time, given a widespread interest in questioning the primacy of structure in creative theory and practice. Like all forms of ornament, metaphors function in subtle and powerful ways. In this regard, their hybrid identity—as conferred by the coming together of distinct domains—is especially significant, since it places them somewhat outside the primary realm of focus, in a peripheral space, from where they are able to stake out a considerable presence. By facilitating the synthesis of unrelated concepts, metaphors reveal their capacity for evoking ideas, sensations, and images that not only guide the imagination, but also shape one's engagement with creative work.

Despite the long relationship that music and visual art have enjoyed on the levels of creation, interpretation, and criticism, scholars are faced with several challenges when undertaking research of an interdisciplinary nature. It must be remembered that not every instance of linguistic crossover is of aesthetic or stylistic significance; just as musical concepts pertaining to duration have lost their specific meanings by becoming thoroughly assimilated into the language of art criticism (rhythm and harmony, to give two such examples), some visual concepts have also been transformed upon entering the language of music criticism (texture and line, to give two others). Although the mutual sharing of language is an important relationship to acknowledge between disciplines, equally significant is an awareness of the different ends to which specific terms are applied. Related to this issue is one that concerns the critical understanding of metaphors as they appear in historical sources, especially such documents as letters and reviews. In these instances, one must be willing to gauge the extent to which the use of metaphor is illuminating and informative, and, in the case of reviewers, the ideological ends to which such language is directed. With Debussy and Stravinsky, for instance, some critics established analogies with art so as to place negative emphasis on the specifically unmusical quality of their innovations, while others highlighted the same correlation in affirming these composers' musical experiments. When interpreting acts of substitution, transformation, parallelism, and convergence, it is up to the analyst to look beyond the obvious and, sometimes, tentative correlations, so as to extrapolate the larger issues that might be at stake.

Notes

1 Ernest Newman, ed. and trans., *Memoirs of Hector Berlioz from 1803–1865* (New York: Dover Publications, 1966), 84; and Hugh Macdonald, *Berlioz's Orchestration Treatise: A Translation and Commentary* (Cambridge: Cambridge University Press, 2004), 125.

2 See Claude Debussy, *Correspondance (1872–1918)*, ed. François Lesure, Denis Herlin, and Georges Liébert (Paris: Gallimard, 2005), 59; and François Lesure, "Une interview de Debussy," *Cahiers Debussy* 11 (1987): 5.

3 See Léon Vallas, *Claude Debussy: His Life and Works*, trans. Maire O'Brien and Grace O'Brien (New York: Dover Publications, 1973), 112.

4 See Reinhold Brinkmann, "On the Problem of Establishing 'Jugendstil' as a Category in the History of Music—with a Negative Plea," *Miscellanea Musicologica: Adelaide Studies in Musicology* 13 (1984): 24.

5 Claude Debussy, *Debussy on Music: The Critical Writings of the Great French Composer*, ed. Richard Langham Smith (Ithaca, NY: Cornell University Press, 1988), 48.

6 See Claude Debussy, "Musique: Vendredi Saint," *La Revue Blanche* (1 May 1901): 67–68; and "S.I.M. 15 March 1913" in *Debussy on Music*, 284.

7 Anne Leonard, "Picturing Listening in the Late Nineteenth Century," *Art Bulletin* 89, no. 2 (2007): 279.

8 Jean Marnold, "Musique," *Mercure de France* (1 October 1913): 628.

9 Gretchen Horlacher, *Building Blocks: Repetition and Continuity in the Music of Stravinsky* (Oxford: Oxford University Press, 2011), vii.

Further Reading

Bhogal, Gurminder Kaur. *Details of Consequence: Ornament, Music, and Art in Paris* (New York: Oxford University Press, forthcoming).

Daverio, John. "Schumann's 'Im Legendenton' and Friedrich Schlegel's *Arabeske*." *19th-Century Music* 11/12 (Autumn 1987): 150–163.

Frisch, Walter. *German Modernism: Music and the Arts*. Berkeley: University of California Press, 2005.

Leppert, Richard. *The Sight of Sound: Music, Representation, and the History of the Body*. Berkeley: University of California Press, 1993.

Pater, Walter. *Studies in the History of the Renaissance*. Oxford: Oxford University Press, 2010.

Tresize, Simon, ed. *The Cambridge Companion to Debussy*. Cambridge: Cambridge University Press, 2003.

Vallas, Léon. *Claude Debussy: His Life and Works*. Translated by Maire and Grace O'Brien. New York: Dover Publications Inc., 1973.

Zbikowski, Lawrence. *Conceptualizing Music: Cognitive Structure, Theory, and Analysis*. New York: Oxford University Press, 2002.

23

VISUAL METAPHORS IN MUSIC TREATISES

Metaphor as Experience in Vincenzo Galilei's *Dialogo della Musica Antica e della Moderna*

Antonio Cascelli

In his book *Metaphor and Musical Thought*, Michael Spitzer writes: "Calling discourse about music 'metaphorical' inevitably suggests that there is a more literal mode of engagement, one generally associated with technical music theory. And yet an argument that music theory brings us closer to music would cut little ice with the overwhelming majority of listeners, who actually find arcane categories such as 'tonics' and 'dominants,' 'voice leading,' 'retransition,' 'hemiola,' and so on, rather alienating, and for whom such metalanguage interferes with the cherished immediacy of the musical experience."[1] Indeed, descriptions of music in terms other than musical are abundant in the literature.

As Anne Leonard writes in another chapter in the present book, "[M]usic has been the object of seemingly limitless visual associations, as various as the listeners offering them for consideration."[2] Marcel Proust, for example, in his *In Search of Lost Time*, describes the melodies of Chopin, in the experience of Mme de Cambremer, as made of "sinuous and excessively long necks, so free, so flexible, so tactile, which begin by seeking out and exploring a place for themselves far outside and away from the direction in which they started, far beyond the point which one might have expected them to reach, and which frolic in this fantasy distance only to come back more deliberately—with a more premeditated return, with more precision, as though upon a crystal glass that resonates until you cry out—to strike you in the heart."[3]

The divide between such poetic descriptions and the allegedly more technical language of treatises on music theory is not as wide as one would think. However poor music theory might be "at describing how music is composed or heard," Spitzer argues, there is an imaginary dimension in music theory too: theorists "build models by drawing on domains of human experience—a knowledge of language and culture, but also the experience of what it is like to have a body, that is contained, that can move through a landscape, that can grasp and manipulate objects, and so on."[4]

The practice of discussing music with reference to other artistic disciplines, *in primis* painting, as Leslie Korrick states, was "already underway circa 1500 and gained momentum as the century progressed; during the last quarter of the cinquecento it had become almost commonplace."[5] But the question I would like to address here, with James Grant, is "what metaphor enables critics to achieve."[6] Grant proposes a theory of metaphor that he calls "minimal thesis," which does not make any claim concerning whether in a metaphor we understand the speaker's meaning or the actual content of the metaphor. For Grant, there are two types of property at work in a metaphor: likeness, i.e. the property of being like something else; and likeness-makers, i.e. the properties that give something that likeness. The elements in a metaphor are then twofold: the subject, i.e. what is being metaphorically discussed; and the metaphorical elements, i.e. the content other than the subject, "the expression(s) in the metaphor that are used metaphorically." The claim of the minimal thesis is thus about the relationship between the subject of the metaphor and the metaphorical elements:

> With certain exceptions … each property a metaphor's subject is characterized with the metaphorical elements as having is either (i) a likeness indicated by the metaphorical element or (ii) a likeness-maker for a likeness indicated by the metaphorical elements. The critic using metaphor attributes likeness indicated by the metaphorical element and/or likeness-makers for these likenesses. If a critic describes music metaphorically as 'chattering,' then she gives us to understand that (1) the music is like something chattering, and/or that (2) the music is F, G, H, etc. where Fness, Gness, Hness, etc. will be properties that would make the music like something chattering.[7]

Probably the most interesting aspect of Grant's theory, however, is the idea that metaphors provide "a certain experience, or elicit a certain response," forcing the recipient to look again at the subject of the metaphor in light of the response that the metaphor is eliciting. "So metaphors not only often prompt a reader to imagine or recall perceiving their subjects. Metaphors that are very specific characterizations prompt a reader to imagine or recall this experience very accurately."[8] As an example of this, Grant quotes a passage in which John Ruskin describes what he sees on his arrival in Venice by boat: "the long ranges of columned palaces,—each with its black boat moored at the portal,—each with its image cast down, beneath its feet, upon that green pavement which every breeze broke into new fantasies of rich tessellation, … the front of the Ducal palace, flushed with its sanguine veins, looks to the snowy dome of Our Lady of Salvation." In this very specific and "informative description of the way the waters of Venice look," its evocative and vivid metaphor "tends to cause the reader to imagine seeing the waters of Venice."[9]

Metaphors thus create an experience by forcing their recipient to recall an experience in order to comprehend the likeness proposed. They are not just rhetorical elements to embellish a discourse; they are actively and silently involved in the construction of meaning and experience. This point can be expanded, appropriately, through the elaboration of a simile linking music theory and architectural theory. Visual metaphors in music treatises create something similar to what Juhani Pallasmaa describes in relation to the work of architects: "When working, both the artist and craftsman are directly engaged with their bodies and their existential experiences rather than focused on an external and objectified problem. A wise architect works with his/her entire body and sense of self. While working on a building or an object, the architect is simultaneously engaged in a reverse perspective, his/her self-image—or more precisely existential experience. In creative work, a powerful identification and projection takes place; the entire bodily and mental constitution of the maker becomes the site of the work."[10]

In comparing music to other arts, either through a metaphor proper or through a simile or an analogy, the theorist brings together different senses, and as such she establishes a body and a subjectivity that experience the musical object not as an "external and objectified problem," but as a locus for a powerful identification and projection. And in the same way as the hand-drawn project and hand-made model "put the designer into a haptic contact with the object or space," the use of a metaphor puts the theorist and the reader/listener in wider contact with the musical object, so that in this respect exploiting a metaphor in music theory is akin to hand-drawing and model-making in architecture. "In our imagination," Pallasmaa writes, "the object is simultaneously held in the hand and inside the head, and the imagined and projected physical image is modeled by our bodies. We are inside and outside of the object at the same time. Creative work calls for a bodily and mental identification, empathy and compassion."[11] Likewise, the musical composition and all the creative metaphorical work that is involved in its production, but also in its theoretical presentation, or the creative work embedded in any music theory, when discussed through metaphorical mapping—as Michael Spitzer puts it—call for a bodily and mental identification, empathy, and compassion, because the musical experience is discussed through different senses: it is seen, it is heard as sound and as words, it is compared to images and objects that can be touched, and so on.

As a corollary, different metaphors, or different contexts for the same metaphors, different meanings ascribed to the same terms used in metaphors in different contexts, etc., present different existential experiences. For if we agree with Wittgenstein that "work on philosophy—like work in architecture in many respects—is really more a work on oneself," and if we are willing to stretch his sentence a little, then each metaphor presents a different work on oneself, a different interpretation of one's own, a different aspect of how one sees things.[12]

Leonardo da Vinci

Although this chapter is concerned mostly with visual metaphors in music treatises, I would like to start with the comparison between music and painting established by Leonardo da Vinci in his *Treatise on Painting*. I will follow on with Gioseffo Zarlino, and ultimately with Vincenzo Galilei, whose writings will be the main focus of the chapter. These three examples will exemplify how the use of metaphor and analogy represents the different ways in which the authors see things, and how something so apparently simple as a metaphor or analogy might reveal different cultural traits and visions. They will show how the interaction between music and the visual world reveals different world visions or world hearings, different ways to look at and listen to the world.

The manuscript of Leonardo's *Trattato della pittura*, first put together by Francesco Melzi around 1542, was first printed only in 1651, in both Italian and French. The main aim of the treatise was to demonstrate the scientific foundations of painting. Among the various discussions, in paragraph 25 Leonardo makes a comparison between painting and music, arguing that there is common ground between the two: "Music, must be called nothing other than the sister of painting, because she is subject to the ear, second sense to the eye, and she composes a harmony with the conjunction of its proportional parts made at the same time, forced to be born and die in one or more harmonic moments (*tempi armonici*), which surround the proportionality of the members which compose such harmony, not differently from the circumference [that surrounds] the members which generates human beauty."[13] It is clear that for Leonardo an ocularcentric view furnishes the criteria to judge even music. The famous image of the human body enclosed in a circumference represents for Leonardo a good model for music too. In his text, the subject of the metaphor/analogy is music (to say that music is the sister of painting is not dissimilar to saying it is like painting). The likeness-maker is proportionality. Proportionality here seems to be a declination of Alberti's idea of *istoria*, "that divine force which we are to think of as the moralizing content of what is being made legible by carefully worked out composition and the action of the figures."[14] "But," continues Leonardo, "painting excels and lords over music, because she does not die immediately after her creation, as does unfortunate music, on the contrary she stays alive, and shows alive what in fact is only one surface. Oh wonderful science, you keep alive the ephemeral mortal beauties. Which have more permanence than works of nature, which are continuously changed by time, which lead them to the dutiful old age; and this science, has such a proportion with the divine nature, like that her works have with the works of nature, and for this she is adored." For Leonardo, painting addressed to the eye is superior because it represents form and beauty as abstract and timeless concepts, whereas music dies immediately after its creation. In Leonardo's comparison thus, there is both a likeness-maker—the proportionality of painting akin to the proportionality of harmony—and a non-likeness-maker—the non-temporality of painting in contrast to the temporality of music. In this case the experience of the two arts concerned is different, and it seems that in Leonardo's comparison the non-likeness-maker is more important to the establishment of a hierarchy.

Gioseffo Zarlino

In his 1558 *Istitutioni Harmoniche* (Part II, Chapter 7), Zarlino's starting point in describing the effects and affects of music is a human being as a living web of feelings: "Nor should we be amazed if merely to see a painted story or fable, moves us sometimes to compassion, sometimes leads us to laughter, and sometimes to anger." So far, it seems there is an ocularcentric view, as in Leonardo's treatise, with a gaze open to compassion, laughter, and anger; but then the scenario changes, because "speaking can do this much better, because it can express things better than any painter can do with his brush." A few lines before, Zarlino had already noted that "speaking has greater strength when it is joined by harmony, for the similarity that this [i.e. harmony] has with us." (Zarlino refers here to the idea that music reflects both the macrocosmic harmony of the heavens and the microcosmic harmony of the human soul.)

Although there are obvious similarities between Zarlino's and Leonardo's positions, particularly in the connection between harmony and the human being, there is a reversed judgment. Again it is the non-likeness-maker which makes the crucial difference, swapping the positive and negative poles. What for Leonardo was a limitation—that is, music's temporal process—for Zarlino becomes music's special power:

> So that if we wanted to examine everything, we would find that four have been the things that have always concerted in such effects: of which if one was missing, it would have been possible to see nothing or just a little. The first was the Harmony, which is born from the sounds, or from voices; the second is Number determined and contained in the verse; which was called meter; the third was the narration of some thing, which would contain some moral, and this was the Oration, that is the speaking; the fourth and last then was a subject [i.e. a listener] well disposed, inclined to receive any passion.

In Zarlino we find the beginnings of opposition to the ocularcentric position of Leonardo and of Renaissance aesthetics more broadly. Indeed, Zarlino's and Leonardo's positions reflect epistemological changes in the sixteenth century: the exhaustion of the old cosmology in which music was understood to be part of the immutable structure of the cosmos, and the emergence of early-modern ideas in which music embodied the linguistic power of rhetoric, grammar, and dialectics. Narration and the presence of the listener are essential elements, with the temporality inherent to the experience, in the realization of effects and affect. Music thus becomes a better embodiment of the ideal of istoria as expressed in Alberti's humanistic view, and also of Leonardo's concept of beauty and proportion.

Vincenzo Galilei

In 1581 Galilei, a student of Zarlino, published his *Dialogo della Musica Antica e Moderna*, in which the characters Giovanni de' Bardi and Pietro Strozzi discuss the differences between ancient Greek music and contemporary practice. Particularly through Bardi's character, Galilei expresses his condemnation of polyphonic music and his preference for monodic music, in the context of texted music; indeed, he does not condemn polyphonic instrumental music. In the section where Bardi/Galilei discusses the superiority of monodic music in relation to the effects in both ancient and modern music, Galilei includes a very interesting image that warrants some investigation. It is worth citing the passage at length here:

> with all the height of excellence of the musical practice of the moderns, today one cannot hear or even see the smallest sign of that which ancient music did; nor can one read that those signs were visible fifty or hundred years ago when it was not so common and familiar to men, so that neither the novelty, nor the excellence of modern music has ever enabled our practitioners with the strength to operate any of those virtuous effects that the old music operated. ... I say that the nature of the low register sound is different from that of the high register, and the middle register

sound is different from both. So, likewise I say that the fast movement has one character, the slow another, and the moderate movement is far from both. Now since these two principles are very true, it is easy to deduce ... that singing in consonance in the manner that the modern practitioner does, is an impertinence, because consonance is nothing else than a mixture of low and high sounds, which mixture (as you have heard above) without offense, either with delight or most sweetly causes injury to the ear. If this contrasting affect is present between low and high sounds forming simple consonances [...] how much more of a different nature would be high and low sounds forming imperfect consonances, and even more than these the dissonances of which their songs are full? And if this happens between two voices, it happens even more strongly between four, or six or even more parts.[...] To these impediments that cause the diversity of sounds and the variety of voices, we need to add the effects that are born out of the different movements of the parts, impediments which are not less important than the first; that is, the many times when the Soprano hardly moves for the laziness of its notes, whereas the Bass with its [notes] flies [...] so that [...] one of the parts would pull the listener, the other, as its contrary, would push them; not differently from what would happen to a column: which, evenly placed on its base, if someone tried to make it fall by replacing the capital with two or more equal ropes pulling in opposite directions from equal distances with equal forces, this column would not move from its place, even with all this exertion, unless in some of its parts it is already defective; because each force would oppose the others. But if someone else with the same equipment, and with the same forces attacked the column pulling it from a single side, in my opinion it would not be a surprise, if all this effort together was sufficiently powerful to make it fall.

Bardi then goes on to explain that among the mentioned impediments in the making of fugues, modern musicians have "introduced the diversities of pauses or rests. Whatever we wish to call them, without worrying that at the same time one part is singing the beginning of the words, either in prose or in verse, another one sings not only the middle or the ending of the same, but the beginning or the middle, and sometimes the ending of a different phrase."

Although the presence of the visual image of the column might initially suggest an ocularcentric perspective as the correct one from which to access and evaluate musical experience, there are quite a few elements that might indicate that something different is happening here, diverging from both Leonardo's and Zarlino's views. The subject is not just music, it is music in a particular situation: contrapuntal writing in the context of a poem set to music. The metaphorical element is, likewise, another situation: the column pulled by various forces. The likeness-maker is thus the whole experience of watching the column well-balanced versus the column falling apart. Two very concrete experiences are put metaphorically in contact when Galilei states that music is like the column. The likeness-maker is the relationship between the forces applied to the column. In this case the likeness is important in itself as a feature that is attributed to the music, but it also recalls an experience: the listener becomes a viewer, looking at and experiencing the column either standing still or falling apart, but the viewer becomes a listener, because in the falling of the column she will experience the sound of the column breaking into pieces.

The inherently metaphorical visual language used to describe the movements of the various parts of the musical counterpoint becomes explicit in the visual image of the column. The "negatively judged" experience of listening to contrapuntal music is metaphorically understood through another experience, which is judged negatively because of its consequences—that is, the column falling apart. In this way, the image of the falling column seems to suggest that contrapuntal writing is not able to hold together a sense of unity; contrapuntal writing is a representation of fragmentation, the fragmentation of a human subject who cannot follow all the different parts at the same time, with the risk of the column falling apart. But this particular image brings with itself also a sound element, that of the column falling apart.

What do the two images of the column, stable and collapsing, indicate and what kind of experience do they represent? Both in fact partake of fundamental Renaissance aesthetic ideals and definitions of the human subject. The falling column is the image of a fragmented being that cannot be kept together, while the column standing still is the desire to overcome that fragmentation, a situation in which all forces are kept in proportional balance. The standing column thus represents "a graph of desire, for our own unattainable unity [represented by the falling column], and for the real existence of the world around us beyond our representation of it to ourselves," and interestingly enough, in this graph of desire, sound is completely internalized because the standing column does not produce any sound.[15] But indeed this is an unattainable desire in texted contrapuntal music, because, for Galilei, counterpoint results in the music falling apart and creating noise (as opposed to music), just as the column does when it falls apart.

Like Leonardo, Galilei participates in a characteristic Renaissance desire for unity; but for him this can no longer be realized through contrapuntal writing. Contrapuntal writing is to the falling column as melody/monody is to the column standing in balance. Leonardo argued, through a different comparison, that unity is achieved in the harmony made by the various parts that are composed together that correspond to the harmony of the human figure. For Galilei, however, the human subject cannot be defined through a comparison with contrapuntal writing because there is no harmony, no symmetry in contrapuntal writing. For him, the symmetry of perspectival view is no longer a valid reading, because in reality in music there is not a perspectival view at all; forces are not in balance, they pull the music in one direction only and will cause its collapse. In this sense, Galilei's visual but at the same time haptic metaphor catches the subject's "perpetual cycle of desire to overcome our own fragmentation, which manifests itself in the concept of the metaphysics."[16] For Hendrix, the Renaissance's "perspectival construction represents the dialectic of the inescapably fragmented and multiple nature of perception and the metaphysical unity towards which desire leads us."[17] In Galilei the dialectic between the fragmented nature of perception and the desire for unity can be resolved only by abandoning contrapuntal writing (in the context of song).

To summarize Galilei's trajectory, then: He starts from the experience of contrapuntal music, which of course is addressed principally to the ear. He then moves to the eye, but not just in its visual quality, also in connection with tactile and haptic qualities of human experience, because the column is something very physical, rather than an abstract concept or representation. At this stage the characteristic desire of the Renaissance eye for control and power seems to be at work; but the falling column becomes a critique of this desire of the eye, signaling a return to a distorted ear-experience, with the sounds of the falling column. The eye no longer solely provides the criteria with which to judge experience, at least in music, it no longer "embraces the beauty of the whole world," as Leonardo would put it, because in music the harmony that Leonardo indicated as the common ground between music and painting is, in Galilei's view, not harmonious beauty after all. A door is opened here, I suggest, to the possibility of a new-sounding gaze, one which effectively characterizes the Baroque sound and visual experience with its strongly tactile, haptic, and aural qualities, defined against the centered perspectival vision of the Renaissance. A metaphor that, in its experience, constitutes a window opened toward a new-sounding world vision.

Notes

1 Michael Spitzer, *Metaphor and Musical Thought* (Chicago: University of Chicago Press, 2004), 2.
2 See Chapter 24.
3 Marcel Proust, *The Way by Swann's*, trans. Lydia Davis (London: Penguin Books, 2002), 334.
4 Spitzer, *Metaphor*, 2.
5 Leslie Korrick, "Lomazzo's *trattato ... della pittura* and Galilei's *Fronimo*: Picturing Music and Sounding Images in 1584," in *Art and Music in the Early Modern Period: Essays in Honor of Franca Trinchieri Camiz*, ed. Katherine A. McIver (Aldershot: Ashgate, 2003), 194.
6 James Grant, "Metaphor and Criticism," *British Journal of Aesthetics* 51, no. 3 (2011): 237.
7 Ibid., 238–240.
8 Ibid., 256–257.
9 John Ruskin, *The Stones of Venice* (London: George Allen, 1900), 2: 3, as quoted in Grant, "Metaphor and Criticism," 251.
10 Juhani Pallasmaa, *The Eyes of the Skin: Architecture and the Senses* (Chichester: John Wiley & Sons, 2005), 12–13.
11 Ibid., 13.
12 Citation of Wittgenstein from MS 112 46: 14.10, 1932, cited in Pallasmaa, *The Eyes of the Skin*, 12.
13 Translations of this and other Italian texts have been prepared by the author of this chapter.
14 Charles H. Carman, "Meanings of Perspective in the Renaissance: Tensions and Resolution," in *Renaissance Theories of Vision*, ed. John Shannon Hendrix and Charles H. Carman (Aldershot: Ashgate, 2010), 34.
15 John S. Hendrix, "Perception as a Function of Desire in the Renaissance," in *Renaissance Theories of Vision*, ed. Hendrix and Carman, 99.
16 Ibid.
17 Ibid.

Further Reading

Carman, Charles H. "Meanings of Perspective in the Renaissance: Tensions and Resolution." In *Renaissance Theories of Vision*, edited by John Shannon Hendrix and Charles H. Carman, 31–44, Aldershot: Ashgate, 2010.
Grant, James. "Metaphor and Criticism." *British Journal of Aesthetics* 51, no. 3 (2011): 237–257.
Hendrix, John S. "Perception as a Function of Desire in the Renaissance." In *Renaissance Theories of Vision*, ed. Hendrix and Carman, 89–102.
Korrick, Leslie. "Lomazzo's *Trattato ... della pittura* and Galilei's *Fronimo*: Picturing Music and

Sounding Images in 1584." In *Art and Music in the Early Modern Period: Essays in Honor of Franca Trinchieri Camiz*, edited by Katherine A. McIver, 193–216. Aldershot: Ashgate, 2003.

Pallasmaa, Juhani. *The Eyes of the Skin: Architecture and the Senses*. Chichester: John Wiley & Sons, 2005.

Sanger, Alice E. and Siv Tove Kulbrandstad Walker. "Introduction: Making Sense of the Senses." In *Sense and the Senses in Early Modern Art and Cultural Practice*, edited by Alice E. Sanger and Siv Tove Kulbrandstad Walker, 1–18. Aldershot: Ashgate, 2012.

Spitzer, Michael. *Metaphor and Musical Thought*. Chicago: University of Chicago Press, 2004.

24

MUSICAL METAPHORS IN ART CRITICISM

Anne Leonard

That a painting can be infused with the qualities of music is a notion that flowered in the nineteenth century, though it appears well before that. In embryonic form, it underlies Leonardo da Vinci's engagement of musicians, as reported by Giorgio Vasari, to play during the painting of Mona Lisa: this was to ensure that the vivacity of the sitter would shine forth in the finished portrait. And indeed afterward, "it was considered a wondrous thing that [her smile] was as lively as the smile of the living original."[1] Four hundred and fifty years after Vasari's *Lives*, Maurice Denis returned to *Mona Lisa* as a benchmark of musicality—likening the "blue arabesques" in the background of Leonardo's painting to "the seduction of the violins in the overture to *Tannhäuser*."[2]

This is not to say that over a period of 450 years, critical assessments of visual art made steady reference to music—far from it. Musical metaphor could have no definable place in art criticism, nor could criticism itself develop as a category of literature, until music-listening and art-viewing had become established social practices in public places. This did not happen in Europe until well into the eighteenth century, with the rise of concert halls and museums. While affinities with music were no doubt noted and shared among art connoisseurs in private circles before that, public performances and exhibitions made available a common fund of experience to any who cared about such matters—an opportunity to compare works presented in the two different contexts, and in turn, a basis for building a critical lexicon that drew potentially upon both arts.

Quite apart from these social and cultural developments, it is worth asking why musical language would have been deemed appropriate for visual art in the first place. Nothing would inherently suggest this. It may seem to us a natural thing that musical metaphor be proffered as a form of praise for visual art—and the converse, too, that words such as noise, clangor, or din be applied to an unpleasing visual presentation. Yet the appeal of metaphor may be due, paradoxically, as much to the incommensurability of the two arts as to their recognized commonalities. Visual art, with its stubborn material presence, has had a long rhetorical romance with music, imagined by some writers and critics as its immaterial opposite. This distinction may be even more important than that of spatial vs. temporal, at least for purposes of metaphor. Metaphor turns out to be suitable for two arts that *can't* occupy the same field, leaving the comparison always purely hypothetical. In contrast, likening a work of art to a work of literature is a proposition that can be tested: image and text can be juxtaposed to see if one effectively illustrates the other. Although there have been willed attempts to introduce related music into art venues—notably Joséphin Péladan's Salons of the Rose + Croix (1892–97)—these experiments were more notable for their novelty than for any accumulated revelations concerning the affinities of one art for another.

The extent to which music might be considered equivalent to painting, and on what grounds, are questions that have been much worried over—not just in criticism, but also in celebrated passages of fiction such as E. M. Forster's *Howards End* (1910), where, after a Beethoven concert, the heroine, Margaret Schlegel, bursts out: "Helen's one aim is to translate tunes into the language of painting, and pictures into the language of music. It's very ingenious, and she says several pretty things in the process, but what's gained, I'd like to know? Oh, it's all rubbish, radically false. If Monet's really Debussy, and Debussy's really Monet, neither gentleman is worth his salt—that's my opinion."[3] A century after that passage was written, the Debussy–Monet comparison continues to inflect the reception of both figures' work (even if Debussy's music is now discussed more in terms of its Symbolist, rather than Impressionist, affinities). Questions of equivalence were prominent in the critical debate over Whistler's *Nocturnes*; and they became only knottier in the twentieth century with Kupka's *Amorpha: Fugue in Two Colors*, Kandinsky's *Compositions* and *Improvisations*, and Mondrian's *Broadway Boogie Woogie*, to name just a few examples.

Much of the appeal of ascribing musical qualities to art may stem from music's resistance to verbal description. Visual art, possessing a material form, is susceptible of physical description even when its meaning may be indecipherable; differently so for music, whose formal description relies on more specialist vocabulary. And whereas *ekphrasis* is a well-established concept with a distinguished classical pedigree, there is no comparable tradition of musical description. The fact that music in its sonic form possesses no visible or material aspect does not mean, however, that visual correlates have been in short supply. On the contrary, music has been the object of seemingly limitless visual associations, as various as the listeners offering them for consideration. In *Howards End*, earlier in the same scene cited before, Beethoven's Fifth conjures up for Helen Schlegel "[g]usts of splendor, gods and demi-gods contending with vast swords, color and fragrance broadcast on the field of battle, magnificent victory, magnificent death! Oh, it all burst before the girl, and she even stretched out her gloved hands as if it was tangible." In Helen's active imagination, taste is the only sense that comes up empty under the influence of Beethoven. But sight predominates; Forster is at pains to contrast Helen's dramatic visions with "the attenuated Cupids who encircle the ceiling of the Queen's Hall, inclining each to each with vapid gesture, and clad in sallow pantaloons."[4]

It was surely music's receptivity to visual imagery that made it such an irresistible tool in the hands of art critics. As a bonus, music's indeterminacy rendered any linkage immune to contradiction. Yet if musical references were simply strewn randomly over wide swaths of art criticism, they would be mere curiosities. What makes them of more compelling interest is the way that they build on each other to form a new language of criticism. Before 1800, such references are rare. But as musical analogies proliferate in the nineteenth century, it is productive to look at changing metaphors for music itself, and the ways that such metaphors respond to surrounding poetic and rhetorical climates. One finds that the impulse to link music and visual art could lead in many contradictory directions. Friedrich Wilhelm Joseph von Schelling's famous dictum (c. 1802) that "architecture is frozen music" was largely associated with Gothic cathedrals and the "sweet yearning melancholy" of religious services.[5] Like the landscape metaphors of vastness and distance that also prevailed at this period, Schelling's image participated in the discourse of the sublime, evoking ineffable grandeur. Formally, at least, it could not have less to do with the disordered, ephemeral images that music called up scarcely ten years later for another influential Romantic writer, E. T. A. Hoffmann. It was this latter strain emphasizing music's indeterminacy, not its architectonic solidity, that was to carry forward with such authority in the later nineteenth century. Most fin-de-siècle critics in France could see only the ethereal, diaphanous qualities of music.

The blossoming of musical metaphor in the nineteenth century followed on a consensus, datable to around 1800, that music is not a mimetic art and therefore should not seek to represent reality. At the same time, it was considered the best imitative art for purposes of expression, because mobile, variable, and lasting over a span of time. Music increasingly was seen as a language of sentiment. As Johann Gottfried von Herder put it, if music "quits her empire of feeling and emulates the painting eye, she is no longer music but a cacophony of sounds."[6] The role of instrumental music as an independent art, whose language signifies nothing, offered an intoxicating promise of freedom to visual artists hemmed in by the responsibility to a subject. According to Friedrich Schiller, the inability to define the subject of music creates a "bottomless depth" of meaning.[7] This became a model for other arts, emphasizing the role of the individual imagination in each of them—a proto-Mallarméan injunction to suggest and not describe.

Absence of meaning tended to alarm the critics, however, and is remarkably persistent as a trope of art criticism whether music is being invoked positively or negatively. John Constable noted that the French critics at the Salon of 1824 said his paintings were "like the rich preludes in musick, and the full harmonious warblings of the Aeolian lyre, which *mean* nothing."[8] Almost the same formula appears nearly fifty years later, though more tartly expressed, in response to James McNeill Whistler's *Nocturne: Blue and Silver—Chelsea*. When the painting was exhibited at London's Dudley Gallery in 1871, a critic likened it to "strains of the Aeolian harp, or to the sighing of the wind through a cracked casement. As best such pictorial melodies are as the pipes of Pan; [...] and so little subject have they that they are just as comprehensible when turned upside down."[9] The same meaninglessness that characterized music, and accounted for much of its prestige, could be taken as an insolent breach of decorum when painters set a value on it for their own art.

The accumulation of musical metaphors over the nineteenth century, particularly in France, produced a dramatic snowball effect and had reached surfeit by the late 1890s. Although early German Romanticism provided the intellectual origins for this development, its firm rooting on French soil at mid-century is largely due to the boundless critical energies of one man: the passionate, partisan, and poetic Charles Baudelaire. The originality of Baudelaire's remarks on the "music of painting" in Eugène Delacroix's art could hardly have failed to leave a trace; that this formula had lapsed into cliché by the end of the nineteenth century is only a measure of its enormous success.

In much the same way that Baudelaire's account of hearing Richard Wagner's music became paradigmatic for a generation and more of music criticism—it even gave rise, arguably, to a new aesthetics of listening—so Baudelaire's remarks on Delacroix's painting ushered in a new critical vocabulary. In the case of Wagner, Baudelaire's talent had been to give voice to the very sensations that others were too timid or obtuse to recognize in themselves, or to put into words. This awakened them, in effect, to a world of experience that would otherwise have remained uncharted. The sensuality of Baudelaire's impressions, unsettling at first, decisively shaped writing on Wagner over decades. Nor was its influence reserved for big-name writers; hacks and parodists adopted it, too.

Baudelaire's writing on art and music alike owes much of its enduring power to its convincing account of immediate, embodied sensation. This is not, however, to understate the importance of literary precursors like E. T. A. Hoffmann. A writer of fiction and music criticism as well as a composer and conductor, Hoffmann offered startling accounts of perceiving music through more than one sense. In his review of Beethoven's two piano trios op. 70, he wrote, "[T]here is a restless alternation of the most marvelous images, in which joy and pain, melancholy and ecstasy, appear beside and within each other. Strange shapes begin a merry dance, now converging into a single point of light, now flying apart like glittering sparks, now chasing each other in infinitely varied clusters."[10]

Hoffmann's synaesthetically based criticism, though vivid and highly imaged, was in the end too idiosyncratic to enter the language as a form of metaphor; its main legacy was to bring attention to the phenomenon of *audition colorée*, of which many other accounts followed. Baudelaire generalized the language of synaesthesia so that it could have much broader applicability and sweep. In this regard, it is important to remember that being receptive to the musical qualities of a painting does not depend on a capacity for synaesthesia. Analogies with music, by mental processes of transfer and substitution, are available to all. They are but one component in a whole network of associations that, taken together, intensify one's pleasure in a work of art. That is why even those who do not experience music or visual art through multiple senses can find themselves nodding their heads to Baudelaire's remark in "The Salon of 1846" that Delacroix's color "is as plaintive and deep-toned as a melody by Weber." Baudelaire elaborated on this notion in a poem that he included in "The Exposition Universelle" (1855) and explicated thus: "[Delacroix's] wonderful chords of color often give one ideas of melody and harmony, and the impression that one takes away from his pictures is often, as it were, a musical one."[11] These metaphors, less threatening because less sexually transgressive than the ones he used for Wagner's music, entered into widespread use.

The fact that Delacroix himself meditated on art's parallels with music in his *Journal,* and that these meditations were nourished by friendship with Chopin and regular attendance at concerts and operatic performances, can only have had a further legitimating effect on Baudelaire's pronouncements. Delacroix's journal entries offer proof against any suspicion that an overzealous critic might simply have been projecting his own ideas onto the art of the painter he most admired. In a claim that gains credibility from having been put forth by the artist, the "best head" in the *Bark of Dante*—that of the man trying to climb into the boat—is credited to a friend's melodious reading aloud of one of the cantos while Delacroix worked, inspiring him to paint "with tremendous speed and excitement." But the *Journal* addresses general principles as well as specific works. Delacroix's endorsement of Alphonse Karr's ideas on color is clear from a passage he copied: "Colors are the music of the eyes; they combine like notes; there are seven colors as there are seven notes, there are shades as there are semitones."[12] Noncontroversial statements like these, comparing the building blocks of the two arts rather than the caprices of individual aesthetic response, hastened acceptance of musical metaphors for art as a straightforward proposition.

Whistler echoed Delacroix in his "Ten O'Clock Lecture," stating that nature contains the elements of all pictures as the keyboard contains the notes of all music. The artist's task is to group elements of nature into beautiful pictures, just as the musician gathers notes into chords to bring forth harmony. Although the "Ten O'Clock Lecture" did not appear until 1885, this belies the fact that Whistler had been titling his paintings as Harmonies and Symphonies since the late 1860s. At his patron Frederick Leyland's suggestion, he adopted the title *Nocturne*, another term borrowed from music, for a half dozen or more of his night-time landscapes from the 1870s. By these titles, Whistler sought to direct the viewer's attention away from the painting's ostensible subject and toward more poetic aspects of perception, memory, and aesthetic experience.

Although many of Whistler's English critics derided his efforts at first, by the 1880s in France, the time was right. In 1881, Théodore Duret noted with approval the Wagnerian musical effect, quasi-abstract, that Whistler achieved in his *Nocturne* paintings. By then, the "music of painting" was not just in the air, but ready to serve heavy duty with the rise of Symbolist art. Musical metaphors were of only middling usefulness in Realism and Impressionism, art movements that focused on representing the visible world. But because the aim of Symbolism was itself metaphoric—to represent what could not be represented—musical metaphors could hardly have been more apt. As Théodule Ribot wrote in his *Essay on Creative Imagination*, Symbolist art "disdains clear, bright representation of the exterior world; it replaces it with a kind of music that aspires to express the mobile and fugitive intimacy of the human soul."[13] As Symbolist painting sought to emulate music's gift for expressing the inexpressible, musical metaphors in criticism would become the highest form of praise.

Many such metaphors continued to rest on matters of structure and form. They assumed that the building blocks of each art are analogous and that the practitioners of each proceed in comparable ways toward the completion of a discrete work. In 1884, for example, Octave Mirbeau likened the forms in Edgar Degas's paintings to those in Bach's fugues: "everything proceeds necessarily, mathematically, musically, if you will, from that first line and that first figure, as the fugues of Bach do from the first phrase or first sonority forming their base."[14] Mirbeau's conception is rather atypical for the period, not only for its focus on production instead of reception, but also for emphasizing line over color (which was usually the primary basis for comparison, following the example of Baudelaire and Delacroix).

Paul Gauguin's remarks on analogies to the musical art are often used as a reference: "Through arrangements of lines and colors, using an ordinary subject taken from life or nature as a pretext, I obtain symphonies, harmonies that do not represent anything wholly real in the vulgar sense of that word, not directly expressing any idea, but provoking thought, without the aid of ideas or images, simply through mysterious affinities between our brain and certain arrangements of colors and lines."[15] What Gauguin is pleading for above all is a liberation from subject matter as the major criterion for judging a painting. The same is the case for Édouard Vuillard, who wrote in a journal entry around the same time: "Who speaks of art speaks of poetry. There is no art without a poetic aim. There is a species of emotion particular to painting. There is an effect that results from a certain arrangement of colors, of lights, of shadows. It is this that one calls the music of painting."[16] Interestingly, these artists' statements on musical equivalence (unlike Whistler's) *follow* those of the critics. By 1894–95, when the Vuillard and Gauguin passages were written, the "music of painting" was anything but new, and it is difficult to disentangle what is coming from an already established strain of critical writing as opposed to personal discovery or engagement with the problem. Nonetheless, because of artists' particular credibility in explaining their craft, declarations like these helped to reinforce the critical tendency toward formal analogy.

What distinguishes Symbolist musical metaphor is the desire—hinted at in previous instances but never so well elaborated—to go beyond mere formal congruence and straight into the realm of feelings. Here, comparison depends on whether a painting can provoke an emotional state akin to what one experiences when listening to music. If so, it can be considered "musical painting" (or in Teodor de Wyzewa's term, "Wagnerian painting," for Wagner's music was credited with the most powerful emotional effects of all). De Wyzewa's contributions to Édouard Dujardin's *Revue wagnérienne* (1885–88) stoked much of the hype, as well as much of the confusion, around musicality in painting. Hardly a systematic thinker, de Wyzewa was nonetheless consistent on the point that a painting is musical to the extent that it succeeds in stirring the emotions. By this measure only, "colors and lines ... [can] become the notes of a new music."[17] From the mid-1880s, de Wyzewa expounded repeatedly on the features of Wagnerian painting, positing it as a fulfillment of the Symbolist goals of emotion and interiority.

Other critics were content to restrict their musical metaphors to formal aspects of art. Thadée Natanson used them to praise the harmony of composition in Pierre Bonnard's decorative painting ("tranquil melodies or vibrant rhythms"); André Fontainas resorted to musical terms to explain Henry de Groux's visionary aesthetic ("He knows from which wells to draw the divine flow of an always impassioned song"); and Léonce Bénédite ascribed sound qualities to Gustave Moreau's palette ("new tones, sonorous and vibrant, strident and high-pitched").[18] By the late 1890s, when all these reviews appeared, the Baudelairean vocabulary was ordinary, not to say shopworn—or, to put it another way, was so ensconced in the critical lexicon that it could be used automatically and unreflectively.

All musical metaphor, regardless of its specific premise, turned on age-old paragone debates over the relative stature of the different arts. Visual art, concrete and material, could never evade description. But what if it could be, nevertheless, beyond words? Music's elusive quality came to stand in for any kind of inexpressibility: this transcendence of words implied a purer, more ethereal realm. So clearly, the importance of paragone here concerns not just the contest between painting and music, but—equally if not more so—that between music and language. According to Romantic thinkers like E. T. A. Hoffmann, music had been the originary, universal language, before it "decomposed" into many mutually incomprehensible tongues. This made of the composer a seer, or perhaps hearer, who did not so much create something new as recognize these lost original melodies (beyond the threshold of ordinary perception) and recover them for the uninitiated. Likewise, from Novalis and others, we have the image of the artist as a decipherer of hiero-glyphic mysteries, a mediator between a spiritual realm and that of ordinary mortals. In Delacroix's version, the hieroglyphic mysteries became the dictionary of nature, from which the painter draws jumbled bits and recomposes them into self-sufficient works of art.

How critics would have liked to join this august company on such a noble mission! It is easy to see how they, as traffickers in ordinary "fallen" language, might reach for musical metaphor as the most powerful and prestigious language at their disposal. But, complicit in the belief that music expressed what was otherwise inex-pressible, they were only undermining their own cause. Seeking authority for criti-cism on these terms could feel more like abdication—as when Mirbeau, in the mid-1880s, declined to explain what he meant by the "musical sensation" elicited by a painting. Arthur Schopenhauer had defined a composer as one who "expresses the deepest wisdom in a language which his reason does not understand";[19] so how could the critic, coming after, claim to do better? Thus did art criticism come to a serious impasse, when the ultimate in praise was the speechless critic.

As a general rule, musical metaphors in art criticism tell us less about the specific relationship between individual works than about the relative values ascribed to art and music—and language—at a given moment and within a particular discourse. This is their primary usefulness to the historian. Metaphors can also help to sug-gest a cultural context or clarify a critic's frame of reference. Because Baudelaire's "chords of color" were inspired by the art of Delacroix, for example, they imme-diately evoke that painter's love of music and his relationship with Chopin and George Sand (memorialized in his infamously severed double portrait of them). Further, the phrase points up the growing interest in synaesthesia at that time, and most of all the pervasive Romantic belief in music as the art to which all others ought to aspire.

"All art constantly aspires toward the condition of music": the famous dictum is Walter Pater's in "The School of Giorgione," and he phrases it as an observation, not a directive.[20] For Pater, art has fulfilled its potential when, as in music, matter and form are indistinguishable. Music reigns as the supreme art, while the others scurry to bask in its prestige. There is no doubt that, from the beginning, musical metaphor was deployed in art criticism as a more or less furtive attempt to elevate the status of visual art. But to the extent that the attempt succeeded, it could do so only in rhetorical terms, not in evidentiary ones. Thus the claims to hear Rameau in looking at Vernet (as Diderot wrote), or to think of Bach when looking at Degas (as Mirbeau wrote), depended for their persuasiveness not on a reader's having the same experience, but on a general notion of plausibility, tied very much to the criti-cal and literary reputation of the writer. If the truth be told, the nineteenth-century use of musical metaphor for art has been tarnished by its association with a certain kind of purple prose. Some authors, it is felt, turned to musical comparisons as a way of grasping for effect or, worse, hiding the fact that they had really nothing to say. But the prevalence of such comparisons in art criticism only underscores the high regard in which music was held. More than that, it shows how the "journey toward the interior," a major tendency of the fin-de-siècle, required the resources of another art for its ultimate justification. In music, both visual art and the language of criticism found a purer, higher version of themselves, a beacon and a model.

Without question, musical metaphor is a flexible and adaptable concept in art criticism. Its nineteenth-century uses, my focus in this essay, were plentiful but hardly exhaustive. Eager as those period commentators were for tight analogies between art and music, they often chose to ignore one of music's most salient characteristics: its temporal dimension. Pater's "School of Giorgione" essay, as has been often pointed out, in fact speaks of music in very unmusical terms: static moments rescued from the flow of time. Later art movements—Orphism, Futurism, kinetic art, and so on—discovered metaphoric potential precisely in music's temporal flux, dynamic motion, and improvisatory freedom. Music was still a symbol for the aspirations of another art, but those aspirations had profoundly changed.

Notes

1 Giorgio Vasari, "Leonardo da Vinci," in *The Lives of the Artists*, trans. Julia Conaway Bondanella and Peter Bondanella (Oxford: Oxford University Press, 1991), 294.

2 In the conclusion to Denis's "Définition du néo-traditionnisme" (written in August 1890); quoted in Robert Goldwater and Marco Treves, eds., *Artists on Art: From the 14th to the 20th Century* (London: J. Murray, 1976), 380–381.

3 Chapter 5 of E. M. Forster, *Howards End* (New York: Alfred A. Knopf, 1946), 46.

4 Ibid., 40, 39.

5 See Hugh Honour, *Romanticism* (New York: Harper & Row, 1979), 148–150.

6 Quoted in John Neubauer, *The Emancipation of Music from Language* (New Haven: Yale University Press, 1986), 161.

7 Charles Rosen, *The Romantic Generation* (Cambridge, MA: Harvard University Press, 1995), 131.

8 Quoted in Rosen, *The Romantic Generation*, 75.

9 Anonymous critic for the *Saturday Review* (28 October 1871), quoted in Katharine Lochnan et al., *Turner Whistler Monet*, exh. cat. (London: Tate, 2004), 148.

10 E. T. A. Hoffmann, "Review of Beethoven's Piano Trios, Op. 70 Nos. 1 and 2," originally published in the *Allgemeine Musikalische Zeitung*, xv, 3 March 1813, unsigned; and reprinted in *E. T. A. Hoffmann's Musical Writings*, ed. David Charlton, trans. Martyn Clarke (Cambridge: Cambridge University Press, 1989), 303. The same passage appears in "Beethoven's Instrumental Music," section I-4 of *Kreisleriana* (102).

11 Charles Baudelaire, *Art in Paris 1845–1862*, trans. and ed. Jonathan Mayne (Oxford: Phaidon Press, 1965), 66, 141.

12 Quoted in Anne-Birgitte Fonsmark, *Delacroix: The Music of Painting*, exh. cat. (Copenhagen: Ordrupgaard, 2000), 13, 31.

13 Théodule Ribot, *Essai sur l'imagination créatrice*, 3rd ed. (Paris: Alcan, 1908), 169.

14 Octave Mirbeau, "Degas," *La France*, 15 November 1884, reprinted in *Combats esthétiques I: 1877–1892*, ed. Pierre Michel and J.-F. Nivet (Paris: Séguier, 1993), 78.

15 From an 1895 interview, quoted in Pierre-Louis Mathieu, *The Symbolist Generation 1870–1910*, trans. Michael Taylor (New York: Rizzoli, 1990), 19.

16 January 1894 journal entry, quoted in Katherine M. Kuenzli, *The Nabis and Intimate Modernism: Painting and the Decorative at the Fin-de-Siècle* (Farnham: Ashgate, 2010), 77.

17 Teodor de Wyzewa, "Une critique," *La revue indépendante*, n.s., 1 (November 1886): 63.

18 "mélodies tranquilles ou rythmes vibrants"; "Il sait à quelles sources d'harmonie puiser le flot divin d'un chant toujours passionné"; "tons nouveaux, sonores et vibrants, strients et aigus"; quoted in Jean-Paul Bouillon, *La promenade du critique influent: anthologie de la critique d'art en France, 1850–1900* (Paris: Hazan, 1990), 394, 406, and 411, respectively.

19 Arthur Schopenhauer, *The World as Will and Idea*, trans. R. B. Haldane and John Kemp (London: K. Paul, 1927), 1: 336.

20 Walter Pater, *The Renaissance: Studies in Art and Poetry* (London: Macmillan, 1910), 135.

Further Reading

Bouillon, Jean-Paul. *La promenade du critique influent: anthologie de la critique d'art en France, 1850–1900*. Paris: Hazan, 1990.

Fonsmark, Anne-Birgitte. *Delacroix: The Music of Painting*. Exhibition catalogue. Copenhagen: Ordrupgaard, 2000.

Johnson, Lee McKay. *The Metaphor of Painting: Essays on Baudelaire, Ruskin, Proust, and Pater*. Ann Arbor: UMI Research Press, 1980.

Lochnan, Katharine et al. *Turner Whistler Monet*. Exhibition catalogue. London: Tate, 2004.

Nectoux, Jean-Michel. *Harmonie en bleu et or: Debussy, la musique et les arts*. Paris: Fayard, 2005.

Neubauer, John. *The Emancipation of Music from Language: Departure from Mimesis in Eighteenth-Century Aesthetics*. New Haven: Yale University Press, 1986.

Rosen, Charles. *The Romantic Generation*. Cambridge, MA: Harvard University Press, 1995.

25

MUSICAL METAPHORS IN ART TREATISES

The Codification of Emotions in Eighteenth-Century Art Theory[1]

Clare Hornsby

In intellectual and academic terms, the eighteenth century was the era of explaining all human and natural phenomena in treatises. Art treatises are part of that culture, reflecting the breadth of the contemporary urge to taxonomy. While the *Encyclopédie* (1751–72) is perhaps the most famous of the attempts by eighteenth-century scholars and writers to classify and order a response to the world, others include Johnson's *Dictionary* (1755) and Linnaeus's *System of Nature* (1735–58). The common feature of the two art treatises that will be examined here—one concerning drawing, the other music performance practice—is the blend within them of the aesthetic with the moral, presented in a utilitarian manner that is educative and practical.

Both authors were artists who worked primarily as teachers in their respective fields. The painter Alexander Cozens was born in Russia in 1717, studied in Italy, and then came to England, where he earned a living by teaching drawing privately and also, notably, at Eton College. Francesco Geminiani, virtuoso violinist and composer, was of an older generation, Cozens's senior by thirty years. He was born in Lucca, Italy, in 1687, and in 1714 arrived in London from Rome, where he had been a pupil of Corelli. He spent much of his career as a teacher in London and Dublin, although he had broader artistic interests and was a successful dealer in paintings. As examples of the systematizing tendency in aesthetics of the period, texts such as Geminiani's *Rules for Playing in a True Taste* (c. 1748) and Cozens's *The Various Species of Landscape* (c. 1760) are valuable; they are texts designed with a didactic aim, created by professional teachers to form the artistic skills of their pupils—largely a male elite of wealthy, educated amateurs who in most cases studied both disciplines—in the composition and ornamentation of the work they practiced. But they also give insight into more subtle philosophical questions involving the identity of the art object and the nature of aesthetic experience.

Meditation on the meaning of the harmony of tones in music is a perennial presence in Western thought. The same mathematical structure that underlies musical intervals and their interrelationship has often been used in art, particularly architecture, to order forms within the visual plane. Art critics' application of the term "performance" to paintings in the eighteenth century is only one indicator that it helps to look at both media with the same critical eye. The extent to which various emotions could be made to be part of the "thisness" of a landscape composition, or directly expressed in musical performance, raises issues that can be elucidated when Geminiani's and Cozens's treatises are examined side by side.

In order to see them in their correct context, we must look back. Aristotle in his *Politics* (Book VIII, ch. V) contrasted the effect of music (and poetry) with that of the visual arts:

> But anger and mildness, courage and modesty, and their contraries, as well as all other dispositions of the mind, are most naturally imitated by music and poetry; which is plain by experience, for when we hear these our very soul is altered; and he who is affected either with joy or grief by the imitation of any objects, is in very nearly the same situation as if he was affected by the objects themselves; ... statues and paintings are not properly imitations of manners, but rather signs and marks which show the body is affected by some passion. But in poetry and music there are imitations of manners; and this is evident, for different harmonies differ from each other so much by nature, that those who hear them are differently affected, and are not in the same disposition of mind when one is performed as when another is.[2]

The distinction made here by Aristotle is between the creation of an affect within the person, as when hearing music or poetry, and the expression of the *idea* of a feeling, as seen in the visual arts, most notably in sculpture of the human form.

Joshua Reynolds, in his seventh *Discourse* to the Royal Academy in 1776, followed this distinction and extended it to include taste:

> All arts having the same general end, which is to please, and addressing themselves to the same faculties through the medium of the senses, it follows that their rules and principles must have as great affinity as the different materials and the different organs or vehicles by which they pass to the mind will permit them to retain. We may therefore conclude that the real substance, as it may be called, of what goes under the name of taste, is fixed and established in the nature of things; that there are certain and regular causes by which the imagination and passions of men are affected; and that the knowledge of these causes is acquired by a laborious and diligent investigation of nature ... however instantaneous its operations may appear when thus acquired.[3]

The historical legacy of the classical and patristic authors provided the terminologies for later writers, particularly those of the seventeenth century; for example, *passion* and *affect* derive from translations of the Greek *pathos* used by Aristotle, Augustine, and others. These models also drove the classification and placement of emotions—as volition, as appetite, and so on—in the modern period. The relationship between the emotions and the body, or emotions and motives for action, also received attention, as well as the possibility that a single, or similar, emotional source might produce conflicting tendencies.

The seventeenth century had a proto-scientific, organizing mission—seen in Charles Le Brun's lecture on expression, as followed later by Cozens—and a desire to present a rival position to that taken by the ancients and the scholastics. Descartes in his *Passions of the Soul* (1649) identified six passions: wonder, which he calls "the first of all the passions" (probably following Plato, who wrote in his *Theaetetus* that philosophy begins in wonder), love, hatred, desire, joy, and sadness; then more finely graded derivatives of these. Later, David Hume's *Dissertation on the Passions* of 1757 listed ten main passions, with numerous sub-types.

Cozens's famed and much-mocked blot system for creating landscape drawings is described in his first theoretical publication, the *Essay to Facilitate the Inventing of Landskips* (1759), the basis of his teaching at Eton in 1763–68. Some of his publications repeat the same material or re-present it differently, as we shall see also with Geminiani's treatises. Blot drawing was not the only teaching method Cozens used; he often combined it with the more traditional method of copying from manuals, which was less open to a creative response. Cozens's pupil Henry Angelo later described the blot system:

> Cozens dashed out upon several pieces of paper a series of accidental smudges and blots in black, brown, and grey, which being floated on, he impressed again upon other paper, and by the exercise of his fertile imagination, and a certain degree of ingenious coaxing, converted into romantic rocks, woods, towers, steeples, cottages, rivers, fields, and waterfalls. Blue and grey blots formed the mountains, clouds, and skies.[4]

In the 1780s, Cozens collected his thoughts or "systems" in the *New Method*;[5] while staying at Fonthill with William Beckford, a key figure in English literary and artistic Romanticism as well as art and music patronage, he was described as "very happy, very solitary and almost as full of systems as the universe."[6] Beckford's *The Vision*, begun in Switzerland, is dedicated to Cozens, his teacher and friend, and is deeply indebted to his system. The following quotation could serve as a textual illustration of blot drawing number two, *The tops of hills or mountains—the horizon below the bottom of the view*:

> Now I found my path finish its course and where think you did it lead to not to a summit from whence an extensive Landscape was to be surveyed nor to a forest of Pines the natural production of a Mountain, but to a gloomy dell skirted with huge Masses of Rock troubled by winds that howled Desolation and Torrents that flowed in narrow encumbered Channels sending forth a discordant hollow murmur.[7]

The results of Cozens's teaching method can be seen in a drawing that his Eton pupil Sir George Beaumont made in 1806, at his home in Coleorton in Leicestershire, which he annotated "From an accidental blot of Indian ink on a palette." Beaumont was working in this way in the 1780s and influenced John Constable;

he was also a friend of the poet William Wordsworth. Beaumont admired Reynolds greatly and was a major collector of Old Master art; later he became one of the founding donors of the National Gallery.

The frontispiece of the *New Method* clarifies the primacy of the creative imagination that informed Cozens's method with a pertinent quotation from *Antony and Cleopatra*—"Sometimes we see a cloud that's dragonish ..."—and another from Horace: "Not [so much] on the smoke from the flame does he dwell but on the light from the smoke, that marvellous wonders should it hence evoke."[8] At the end of the *New Method* appear *16 Descriptions of the Various Kinds of Compositions in Landscape*, with aquatints, which are the same or reversed versions of the landscape etchings included in the earlier unpublished treatise *Various Species of Landscape etc. in Nature*. It seems that Cozens had readapted his idea of a system for landscape for the teaching manual, although he had bigger plans; in letters to William Hoare he spoke about a "System of 35 pictures."

Various Species contains lists of factors that can be combined to create landscapes. While there are several versions, one contains two major categories, *Objects* and *Circumstances*. The *Objects* are those usually to be found in any landscape painting. The *Circumstances* are grouped according to times of day, seasons, and accidents of nature: fog, rain, wind, storm, and so on. The focus throughout is on either landscape, sky, or a mixture of both. The *Various Species* are those to be found in nature, not those that exist in pictures. "Why be original?" is the implication; after all, Reynolds was for nature, but "Improved." But Cozens was writing primarily as a practicing artist, not as a scholar, hence his frequent setting up and subsequent abandonment of systems. He certainly suffered from the still lowly classification of landscape among the genres accepted at the Royal Academy, which resembles the struggle of instrumental music to be ranked as highly as vocal music and opera by an educated audience over the preceding centuries.

The Rev. Charles Davy, an amateur musician and painter who was the tutor of the young George Beaumont, wrote a mnemonic for him and perhaps others to use that connects the *Various Species* compositions and gives a hint of the list of emotions that are paired with each; this list comes from Constable's notes on the system, made at Beaumont's house, probably in 1823. Constable painted *A Cenotaph to the Memory of Sir Joshua Reynolds* after a visit to Coleorton in October/November of that year. It depicts the memorial erected by Beaumont on the grounds of his home, inscribed with some lines of poetry composed by Wordsworth in 1811. Another influential Cozens treatise copied by Constable at that time was *Clouds*, not issued separately but as part of the *New Method*.

Charles Davy had written the only English eyewitness account of the cataclysmic 1755 Lisbon earthquake, the perfect circumstances in which to acquire a heightened sensitivity to nature and the sublime. Similarly, Burke's *Philosophical Enquiry into the Sublime and Beautiful*, written the year after the earthquake, was a distillation of responses to Shaftesbury's and Addison's writings after having seen the Alps, the key topos of what might be termed the landscape revolution.

The *Various Species* engravings demonstrate that the compositions could be formed from any object on the list. The relevant emotions are listed next to each. For example, the first is annotated "The edge of hill or mountain near the eye": "N. B. The spectator is supposed to be in a tranquil state of mind. Attention, caution, awe, expectation of an extensive country, admiration from contemplating great amount of sky, fear, terror." Number six describes "A single object, or a cluster of objects, at a distance" (here a house among trees) as evoking "Unity of idea, influence around us, power, protection." The image would hardly connote power and protection unless a house were the central part of the cluster. Number nine has the subject "Two hills, mountains or rocks, opposite to each other" paired with "Greatness, simplicity. Sequestered life, serenity, innocence of manners, repose, friendship."[9]

"Liberty" is mentioned several times, underlining that this didactic approach becomes moralizing in intent. This was clearly significant to Cozens's thought, since in 1772 he set out his imposing and ambitious plan for a *Morality*; it was to be a series of epic poems on each of the human virtues and vices thought important enough for the purpose, illustrated by a series of pictures of subjects representing the same themes.

Charles Davy, both painter and musician, is pivotal in linking these particular theories of response to music and visual art. He wrote a preface to his own translation of a French travel account, *Description des glacières, glaciers et amas de glace du Duché de Savoie*, written by the Swiss Marc Théodore Bourrit in 1773. Bourrit's illustration of the *Mur de glace at Bossons* shows the tiny, vulnerable human in the immensity of the glacier, an image of the sublime, while the text itself is informed by a Goethe-like scientific approach. Davy is vague in his connecting of the arts; he does not engage with the Platonic and Aristotelian classification of the modes in music with which he surely was familiar, nor with *Beauty* (that Aristotle had posited as being without an opposite) as placed by Burke in contradiction to *Sublime*. Here is part of the preface:

> The *general* effect of a survey of Nature is Delight; whilst every species of Landscape, like every different species of Melody excites its own peculiar genuine emotions, nor are they limited to the imagination only, they make their passage through it to the heart, and lead to acts of Gratitude and Adoration ... [as a footnote he adds:] The several species of *Melody*, have never yet been accurately determined; whereas those of *Landscape* are found to be no more than sixteen, from whose different combinations, with the addition of accessory circumstances, all the varieties of Landscape are derived; but it is not meant to be affirmed of Landscape, as of Melody, that [it] is capable of exciting only an Emotion.[10]

He continues by publicizing the Cozens treatise that performs this analysis.

Looking back to treatises on music prior to those of Geminiani, the German critic Johann Mattheson was very influential in his examination of the effect of music on the senses. Following Locke, he wrote that sentiment (*die Empfindung*) is the source of all ideas. Mattheson was to translate *Pamela*, the key eighteenth-century novel of sentiment, in 1742. In his *Kapellmeister* text of 1739 he wrote:

> For it is the true purpose of music to be, above all else, a moral lesson. Those who are learned in the natural sciences know physically, as it were, how our emotions function. It would be advantageous to the composer to have a little knowledge of this subject. Since, for example, joy is an expansion of our vital spirits best expressed by large and expanded intervals. Sadness, on

the other hand, is a contraction of those same subtle parts of our bodies. It is, therefore, easy to see that the narrowest intervals are the most suitable. Love is a diffusion of the spirits. Thus, to express this passion in composing, it is best to use intervals of that nature. Hope is an elevation of the spirit; despair, on the other hand, a casting down of the same.[11]

There is a tendency here to follow Descartes's paired opposites of emotions, originating with Aristotle; yet in contrast to the terms either stemming from the classics or in reaction against them, *sentiment*, which came to be used with increasing frequency by eighteenth-century British and French authors, seems modern.

Two of the most influential theoretical manuals for the performer were C. P. E. Bach's *Versuch über die wahre Art das Clavier zu spielen* of 1753 and, three years later, Leopold Mozart's *Violinschule*. In his work, Bach numbers and lists all the embellishments: seven types and twenty-four subtypes. The idea of sorting and classifying is again paramount, but Bach does not attribute a power of creating emotion to any of them in particular. Rather, he advises that various of them be employed in the appropriate emotional context. He wrote: "No one disputes the need for embellishments ... They connect and enliven tones and impart stress and accent: they make music pleasing and awaken our close attention. Expression is heightened by them; let a piece be sad, joyful or otherwise and they will lend fitting assistance."[12] For Bach, therefore, ornaments assist the feeling rather than create it. There is a parallel with the structure of English novels of the period, such as *Pamela*, in this statement: "Music must languish, it must startle, it must be gay, it must move boldly from one sentiment to another."[13]

Geminiani published the first of his treatises, the *Rules*, in 1748. It contains little on expression in performance achieved through ornamentation; the preface describes only a few of his symbols in a text without music examples (the four *Compositions* follow). The introduction to the *Treatise of Good Taste* (1749) describes all the ornaments and shows their various resolutions and combinations in musical examples, after which come four songs, three sonatas, and four airs. *The Art of Playing on the Violin* (1751) reproduces the introduction to the *Treatise*, with some minor variants in examples XVIII and XIX.

In *The Treatise of Good Taste*, however, there are points at which Geminiani expands his teaching to include the emotions:

> Of the Turned shake ... [it] is fit to express gaiety, but if you make it short and continue the length of the note plain and short, it may then express some of the more tender passions.

> Of the superior appoggiatura ... [it] is supposed to express love, affection, pleasure etc.

> Of the beat. This is proper to express several passions; as for example if it be performed with strength and continued long, it expresses Fury Anger Resolution or if less strong—mirth, satisfaction.

> Of the Close Shake ... ending it very strong may express majesty dignity etc. but shorter lower and softer, affliction, fear etc.[14]

He ends with a plea for expression, an apologia for the emotional power of pure instrumental music. It had previously been seen as defective in this regard in comparison to vocal music, much as landscape was judged weak in comparison to the communicative power of gesture and expression in paintings or sculptures of the human figure:

> Men of purblind understandings, and half Ideas may perhaps ask, is it possible to give meaning and Expression to Wood and Wire; or to bestow upon the Power of raising and soothing the Passions of rational Beings? ... with regard to musical Performances, Experience has shewn that the Imagination of the Hearer is in general so much at the disposal of the Master, that by the Help of Variations, Movements, Intervals and Modulation he may almost stamp what Impression on the Mind he pleases.[15]

The German music critic Friedrich Wilhelm Marpurg expressed a similar idea, also writing in 1749:

> The rapidity with which the emotions change is common knowledge, for they are nothing but motion and restlessness. All musical expression has as its basis an affect or feeling ... He who is fortunate, in any respect, to capture the enthusiasm of that great people of poets, orators, artists will know how precipitately and variously our soul reacts when it is abandoned to the emotions.[16]

It would appear that the distinction noted by Aristotle, the *real* effect of music as compared to the *signs and marks* of affect in visual art, is still influential at this point, though the distinctions are becoming dissolved between the various artistic media.

The response to landscape developed in a different direction in the early nineteenth century, with Constable as prime mover. Cozens's other major treatise, concerning the idea of facial beauty and expression, was retrospective in aesthetic terms. He published the *Principles of Beauty Relative to the Human Head* in 1778, with engravings by Francesco Bartolozzi. The aesthetic tradition behind this was the classically influenced theorizing world of the French academies, exemplified by Charles Le Brun's *Conférence sur l'expression générale et particulière* of 1668, in which the types portrayed represent the sort of person that most perfectly expresses each sentiment—for example, a bearded old man with wild hair is used for "scorn and hatred," while a mature, classical-looking female with elaborately arranged hair represents "wonder," and a younger, softer-looking female with disheveled hair portrays "rapture." Cozens produced images of *Melancholy*, suggesting dejection or grief, and *Steady*, suggesting a resolute, firm character; others he included were *Majestic*, *Sensible*, *Tender*, *Languid*, and *Penetrating*. The distinction between the differing functions of feeling as depicted here is analyzed by Amy Schmitter: "[E]ighteenth-century spectator- and judgment-centered moral theories gave the emotions a double role for our moral judgments: insofar as they represent the enduring dispositions of character expressed in actions, they are the objects of moral evaluations; but they also generate the judgments themselves."[17] There is a continuing discussion in aesthetics arguing that either the sentiment exists within the art object or it subsists in the mind or body of the spectator or audience. As John Dewey wrote in the 1930s,

"There is … no such thing in perception as seeing or hearing plus emotion. The perceived object or scene is emotionally pervaded throughout."[18] By the mid-eighteenth century, after the long run enjoyed by the theories of Plato and Aristotle on the purposes of music, poetry, and painting, it appears that the idea of virtue being instilled by art was waning.

We shall conclude with the artist so profoundly influenced by Cozens's method, John Constable. His *Various Subjects of Landscape* of 1833—a collection of twenty-two engraved plates of views, many of his beloved Stour Valley—combines a concern with the poetry of painting, with the specifics of time and place to move the aesthetic into the realm of "landscape as portrait" rather than generator of a "background feeling." They are expansive landscape views, with all the objects mentioned in Cozens's *Various Species* included—differing cloud formations, groups of trees and rural buildings—all deliberately composed to show how the natural world can foster the development of a unity of feeling. He consciously follows Cozens in his theory, but the emotions are subsumed into the image, marking the beginnings of what may be termed the pathetic fallacy. The rational approach of seventeenth-century French theory has been displaced by the cult of sentiment and the intensely personal visual world of the Romantic era. The Cozens and Geminiani treatises on composition and ornamentation seem to propose the evocation of emotion for the sake of itself; yet the engendering of these emotions is a result of deliberation, despite the connection with Reynolds and the prevailing aesthetic of adherence to idealized nature. They stand precisely on the cusp of this change in sensibility.

Notes

1 In preparing this research I was particularly indebted to the work of the Cozens scholar Kim Sloan and to Ryan Mark for help with the Geminiani material. The essay was originally given as a RMA lecture at Birkbeck College, University of London, June 4, 2011.

2 Aristotle, *The Basic Works*, ed. Richard McKeon (New York: The Modern Library, 2001), 1309–1312.

3 Joshua Reynolds, *Discourses* (London: Seeley and Co., 1905), 209.

4 Henry Angelo, *The Reminiscences of Henry Angelo* (London: H. Colburn and R. Bentley, 1830), 1: 212–215.

5 Adolf Paul Oppé, *Alexander and John Robert Cozens. With a reprint of Alexander Cozens' A new method of assisting the invention in drawing original compositions of landscape* (London: A. and C. Black, 1952).

6 Beckford diary entry of August 15, 1781; quoted in Oppé, *Alexander and John Robert Cozens*, 44.

7 William Beckford, *The Vision, Liber Veritatis*, ed. Guy Chapman (London: Constable and Company; New York: Richard K. Smith, 1930), 4–5.

8 "Non fumum ex fulgore, sed ex fumo dare lucem cogitat, ut speciosa dehinc miracula promat." *Ars Poetica*, V. 143–144, http://www.thelatinlibrary.com/horace/arspoet.shtml.

9 These three quotations from Kim Sloan, *Alexander and John Robert Cozens: The Poetry of Landscape* (New Haven and London: Yale University Press, 1986), 49–56.

10 Charles and Frederick Davy, *A relation of a journey to the glaciers in the Dutchy [sic] of Savoy* (Norwich: Richard Beatniffe, 1775), unpaginated.

11 *Concerning Sound and the Natural Science of Music* part I, chapter III, paragraphs 54–59 of Johann Mattheson, *Der vollkommene Kapellmeister* (Hamburg, 1739), in Hans Lenneberg, "Johann Mattheson on Affect and Rhetoric in Music (I)," *Journal of Music Theory* 2, no. 1 (April 1958): 51–52.

12 C. P. E. Bach, *Essay on the True Art of Playing Keyboard Instruments*, trans. W. J. Mitchell (New York: Norton, 1949), 76.

13 Bach, *Essay*, 16.

14 Francesco Geminiani, *A Treatise of Good Taste in the Art of Musick* (London, 1749), modern edition ed. Robert Donington (New York: Da Capo Press, 1969), 2.

15 Ibid., 3.

16 Friedrich Wilhelm Marpurg, *Der Critischer Musicus an der Spree*, September 2, 1749, in Bach, *Essay*, 81.

17 Amy M. Schmitter, "17th and 18th Century Theories of Emotions," *Stanford Encyclopaedia of Philosophy*, http://plato.stanford.edu/entries/emotions-17th18th/.

18 *Art as Experience* (1934), in John Dewey, *The Later Works, 1925–1953*, ed. Jo Anne Boydston et al. (Carbondale: Southern Illinois University Press, 1986), vol. 10, ch. 3.

Further Reading

Burke, Edmund. (1757) 2008. *Philosophical Enquiry into the Origin of our Ideas of the Sublime and the Beautiful.* Edited by James T. Boulton. London: Routledge.

Descartes, René. (1649) 1989. *The Passions of the Soul.* Translated by Stephen Voss. Indianapolis: Hackett.

Hume, David. (1757) 2009. *Dissertation on the Passions.* Edited by Tom Beauchamp. Oxford: Clarendon Press.

Montagu, Jennifer. *The Expression of the Passions: The Origin and Influence of Charles Le Brun's "Conférence sur l'expression générale et particulière."* New Haven and London: Yale University Press, 1998.

IV.2 Convergence in Conception

26

LEONARDO AND THE PARAGONE

Tim Shephard

The Italian term *paragone*, meaning literally "comparison," has taken on a range of significances within art history that make it somewhat difficult to define. Although the term is sometimes taken to refer to the specific rivalry of painting and sculpture, Leonardo's posthumously assembled *Trattato della pittura*—the central text of the paragone tradition—spreads its net considerably wider to include both poetry and music. We can perhaps best think of the paragone as a kind of speculative investigation proceeding through a comparison of various arts, which loomed large in the Renaissance reception of the ancient discourse on the arts. The end point of the investigation, from the point of view of Renaissance artists, was always and inevitably to elevate the status of their own medium above the others; the paragone must therefore be seen in the context of visual artists' quest for parity of status with the other arts across the fifteenth and sixteenth centuries. Music played an important part in the tradition of the comparison of the arts, in both its ancient and Renaissance incarnations, and also in the question of the status of the visual arts, but its role has been largely overlooked in modern scholarship.

Modern discussions of the comparison of the arts in the Renaissance soon reach for the phrase *ut pictura poesis* (as is painting, so is poetry), from Horace's *Ars poetica*. These three words, carrying the authority of antiquity, suggest an equivalence between painting and poetry, an idea that artists certainly found very attractive, for the study of letters enjoyed high status in Renaissance Italy. However, as several scholars have pointed out, when understood in context this brief quotation cannot really bear the weight of interpretation traditionally placed upon it. Horace's practice in the *Ars poetica*, familiar from many other ancient texts, is to treat his subject partly through analogy, and while analogies to music and painting are used repeatedly throughout the treatise, no extended comparison of the arts is attempted.

A more useful ancient source in establishing principles for a comparison of the arts is Aristotle's *Poetics*. Although this text entered into circulation in Renaissance Italy only toward the end of the fifteenth century, the *Poetics* codifies some important concepts that could also be found elsewhere in ancient texts, and which were certainly familiar to Italians earlier in the fifteenth century. Like Horace, Aristotle makes frequent use of analogies between the arts to explain poetry. However, unlike Horace, he also elaborates an overarching rationale for the similarity of the arts: the concept of "imitation." Initially, he outlines this concept in relation to what we would now identify as poetry, drama, song, instrumental music, and dance, although for him all five come under the general heading "poetry": "We are to discuss both poetry in general and the capacity of each of its genres ... Now, epic and tragic poetry, as well as comedy, dithyramb, and most music for aulos and lyre, are all, taken as a whole, kinds of mimesis [i.e. imitation]. ... [A]ll the poetic arts mentioned produce mimesis in rhythm, language, and melody, whether separately or in combination."[1] Aristotle is quite specific here about the different means through which the arts imitate. Elsewhere he is also specific about what they imitate—namely, character and emotion seen through action—and in the process of elaborating this idea he locates painting within the same system: "Since mimetic arts represent people in action, and the latter should be either elevated or base ... they can represent people better than our normal level, worse than it, or much the same. As too with painters: Polygnotus depicted superior people, Pauson inferior, and Dionysus those like ourselves."[2] The imitation of men's character seen through action is, for Aristotle, a pursuit with ethical implications: the subject of imitation should be either exemplary, counter-exemplary, or realistic.

Alongside Aristotle's account of imitation, we must place two other ancient systems for understanding the relationships between the arts: the Muses and the Liberal Arts. The Muses—usually, but by no means always, given as nine in number—were generally taken to represent different aspects of musico-poetic practice, including (as in Aristotle) varieties of song and choral dance. The precise nature and social significance of their hybrid area of artistic responsibility, generalized under the term *mousike*, is a topic of discussion among classicists and ancient historians. The Muses configure the practices they patronize as enjoying a familial relationship one with another: conventionally, they were identified as sisters, daughters of Zeus and Mnemosyne. Some authorities, for example Diodorus Siculus, identified the Muses' characteristic activities as "liberal arts," meaning those arts that could appropriately be pursued by people of high status. In later antiquity, this connotation meant that the Muses were conflated with, and to some extent usurped by, Martianus Capella's system of personified Liberal Arts, which included Grammar, Dialectic, Rhetoric, Geometry, Arithmetic, Astronomy, and Music. This system came to shape and define the medieval system of education, and remained important throughout the fifteenth century. It introduces a problem of status: if these arts are identified as "liberal," or suited to the education of gentlemen, then all other arts, by implication, are consigned to a lower status as "mechanical" and below the notice of the elite.

In the system of the Liberal Arts, music and letters are joined by mathematics, and in fact it is through an association with mathematics that music finds its place there. According to a well-known story, Pythagoras was the first to discover that harmony is governed by proportion, after listening to the sounds made by a blacksmith's differently sized hammers as they struck the anvil, and he built upon that premise a mathematical theory of consonance. This proportional theory established music as governed by reason, as opposed to sentiment, and thereby underpinned its claim to high status among the arts. The liberal status of music was also supported by the practical realities of Renaissance Italy: it was regarded as a near-essential social skill within elite culture, and so really was a part of the education of a high-born youth—although what noble youths learned from their music tutors was generally quite different from what Martianus Capella had in mind. Indeed, strictly speaking, the prestige of music's Liberal Arts status did not attach to musicians by merit of practical skill, but through knowledge of its "speculative" philosophical and theoretical aspects. A distinction was made by some musical authorities in the Renaissance—drawing on earlier practice and inspired ultimately by Boethius—between the *musicus*, who possessed a philosophical understanding of music, and the *cantor*, who merely knew how to sing.

The system of the Liberal Arts as codified by Martianus Capella had no place for the visual arts, leaving them to be classified as "mechanical" and not suited to the education of gentlemen. Nor, at the beginning of the fifteenth century, was there a visual equivalent to the philosophically expert "musicus." This problem of status was certainly a reality in Renaissance Italy. Castiglione, listing facility in painting among the accomplishments of the ideal courtier, finds it necessary to pre-empt the question of status with an extended defense of the visual arts:

> I should like us to discuss something else again which, since I consider it highly important, I think our courtier should certainly not neglect: and this is the question of drawing and of the art of painting itself. And do not be surprised that I demand this ability, even if nowadays it may appear mechanical and hardly suited to a gentleman. For I recall having read that in the ancient world, and in Greece especially, children of gentle birth were required to learn painting at school, as a worthy and necessary accomplishment, and it was ranked the foremost of the liberal arts ...[3]

Castiglione's view enjoyed some ancient support. At the very opening of the *Imagines* by the third-century Greek sophist Philostratus, painting is identified as enjoying a rational basis similar to that claimed for music: "Whosoever scorns painting ... withholds his praise from symmetry of proportion, whereby art partakes of reason."[4]

This argument was reprised at great length in the first extended comparative discussion of the arts in the Renaissance, found in the *Della pittura* of Leon Battista Alberti. The author signals his claims for the status of painting at the very outset: in the first three sentences, visual artists are placed alongside musicians and other practitioners of the Liberal Arts as leading intellectuals. The first book of the treatise is devoted entirely to elaborating the idea that the fundamentals of painting are to be found in geometry (itself a Liberal Art), and not least in the mathematics of proportion. In Book 3, he returns to the theme, requiring the painter to be "as learned as possible in all the liberal arts," but first and foremost in geometry.[5] The central point implicit in this posturing is made explicit in Book 2: Alberti turns on its head the assumption that painting is illiberal, claiming that in the ancient world, "although almost all other artists were called craftsmen, the painter alone was not considered in that category."[6] To further demonstrate the point that "the art of painting has always been most worthy of liberal minds and noble souls," he turns to the classics, hunting out references to the place of painting in the education of the elite.[7]

It is in the context of his discourse on the mathematical foundations of painting that Alberti explains his well-known perspective technique. In a sense, systematically constructed perspective is the center-point around which his entire argument for painting as a mathematical art turns. It is designed to do for painting exactly what the proportional theory of harmony did for music. Leonardo, as we will see, certainly saw a connection between the two systems, and I suspect many other artists did too. Some of the most interesting and persuasive fifteenth-century adventures in perspective were produced by artists working in a wood-inlay technique called *intarsia*, which was characteristically used to decorate the wainscoting in private study-rooms, as well as church choirs and sacristies. Alongside cityscapes, musical instruments were among the most popular subjects for representation in intarsia; it appears that instruments were considered to present a particularly interesting perspectival challenge (as Albrecht Dürer's 1525 woodcut showing a man attempting to draw a lute in perspective confirms). Functional musical notation was also common in intarsia. Perhaps the interest was not only in the forms presented by instruments, but in the irony of harnessing musical harmony to the ends of demonstrating the mathematical basis of visual art. The cityscapes performed an identical function: architecture was self-evidently founded upon mathematics, and had therefore been allotted an intermediate status by Martianus Capella as a junior partner to the Liberal Arts.

A particularly potent example is presented by Johannes Ockeghem's song "Prenez sur moi," which appears in an intarsia panel made for the private apartment of Isabella d'Este in the ducal palace at Mantua. The song is a canon in which three voices are to be realized from the single notated one. No time signature is given, and the unconventional key signature leaves the singer at a loss as to the starting notes for the three parts; in other words, without serious expertise in both the proportional system of meter and the proportional system of harmony, the song will not work. In the Mantua intarsia, this song which foregrounds the proportional basis of music is presented beneath a perspective cityscape demonstrating the proportional basis of visual art.[8] To my mind, there is a clear intention here to measure the claims of one art to Liberal Art status against those of the other: if music qualifies, so does visual art.

The Pythagorean theory of music that underpinned its status as a liberal art was concerned not only with the resonance of hammers on an anvil, but also with the resonance generated by planets circling in the heavens. According to this notion, often referred to as the "harmony of the spheres," the motions of the planets produced tones in the proportions required for harmony, and their harmony represented the harmony of the universe. Further, according to the Pythagorean tradition, the harmony of the heavens is reflected in the harmony of the healthy human soul. This theory was transmitted by no less an authority than Plato, and was repeated by such popular authors as Quintilian, so it enjoyed a substantial mainstream circulation in Renaissance Italy.

The special relationship proposed by this theory between musical harmony and the soul extended well beyond analogy, and brings us back to the question of imitation. In a famous passage in the *Republic*, Plato considers the utility of the arts to the state in terms of the extent to which they do or do not imitate virtue, and are therefore useful or harmful in education. This section includes the well-known passage in which musical modes and rhythms are chosen and rejected according to the states of mind that they imitate: warlike and temperate types of music are sanctioned, everything else is excluded. The reason for Plato's caution is that for him, music has the power to reshape a man's soul into the character it imitates. This idea remained popular in Renaissance Italy—the Florentine philosopher Marsilio Ficino, for example, counseled his reader thus: "remember that song is a most powerful imitator of all things. It imitates the intentions and passions of the soul as well as words; it represents also people's physical gestures, motions, and actions as well as their characters and imitates all these and acts them out so forcibly that it immediately provokes both the singer and the audience to imitate and act out the same things."[9] The same point was made more frequently through any of a range of anecdotes from the ancient world demonstrating the power of music to influence men's behavior.

The power of music to shape the soul into its image gave a particular charge to its role in education. If music imitates character and influences the soul, it follows that music imitating virtuous character will train the soul to virtue—a notion common enough to find a place in Castiglione's non-specialist discussion of music in the *Courtier*. Implicit in this, however, as Plato clearly understood, is the acknowledgment that music's power could also have a corrupting effect. Quintilian, for example, in *Institutio oratoria*, laments the effeminate and lascivious character of the music played in the theaters of his day, blaming this phenomenon for destroying the manliness of his contemporaries.

As we have seen, Alberti was at pains to demonstrate that painting, too, had an important place in education, and it is interesting to observe that he subjects the imitative character of visual art to a very similar analysis. In *Della pittura*, Alberti configures painting as, like music, an imitation of the character of men through their actions, with the power to impose the character that it imitates upon the soul of the viewer:

> The *istoria* [i.e. the narrative or scenario] will move the soul of the beholder when each man painted there clearly shows the movement of his own soul. It happens in nature that nothing more than herself is found capable of things like herself; we weep with the weeping, laugh with the laughing, and grieve with the grieving. These movements of the soul are made known by movements of the body. ... Thus all the movements of the body should be closely observed by the painter. These he may well learn from nature, even though it is difficult to imitate the many movements of the soul.[10]

Alberti here formulates the theory of visual imitation as a direct analogue of the well-known theory of musical imitation. This conception of the ethical power of imitation in the visual arts became a commonplace in Renaissance Italy, and was used to theorize the didactic character of much fifteenth-century painting.

It seems likely that here, as with painting's claim to a mathematical basis, visual artists were aware that they were laying claim to features that also gave music its intellectual status. An interesting case in this respect is presented by the pastoral revival of the early sixteenth century. Three things serve to characterize the pastoral mode: a wandering herdsman, music (usually songs about unrequited love), and a landscape comprising dramatic uplands, flower-strewn valleys, shade-giving trees, and ever-flowing fountains. The shepherd wanders the landscape in a state of love-lorn introspection, singing of his woes. In the tenth of Virgil's *Eclogues*—the touchstone text for Renaissance pastoral—a real man, Gallus, finds the pastoral world assembling around him as he "pines" (which, in the context of pastoral, we can read as "sings") in his love-sickness. Many elite Italians of the early sixteenth century wanted to replicate exactly this scenario, and the musical culture of the time supplied them with plenty of "pining" material with which to do so.

Within this conception, the shepherd's song evidently imitates his state of mind—that is, hopeless, amorous longing. As we learn from the example of Gallus, this musical representation of love-sickness is in fact the point around which the entire conceit revolves: to enter the pastoral world, a "real" Italian need only make music that imitates what we might call a pastoral state of mind. This musical feature of pastoral gives pastoral painting a very particular character. In a work such as Giorgione's *Concert champêtre*, the musical imitation of love-sickness becomes in itself the action imitated by the artist to convey the protagonist's state of mind. So long as the viewer knows to think within the poetics of the pastoral mode, no other cue is necessary to understand the scene. In this example, the artist is certainly employing the mechanics of imitation described by Alberti—that is, imitating character through action: indeed, the shepherd's state of mind and resulting actions are in a sense the entire purpose and subject of pastoral. However, he achieves his visual imitation by appropriating the similar imitative capacity of music.

Leonardo engaged vigorously with many aspects of this rich tradition of competitive comparison. He approached the paragone from a distinctive, multidisciplinary perspective, as painter, sculptor, architect, musician, and poet; and he engaged with all these arts not only as practitioner, but as natural philosopher. The quality and kind of his musicianship is mentioned frequently among his early biographers: it appears that he was what is commonly referred to as an *improvvisatore*—a poet-musician who sang or recited improvised verse while accompanying himself on a stringed instrument, usually the violin-like *lira da braccio*.

Like Alberti, Leonardo was extremely concerned to establish the rational basis of painting as a way of elevating its status. To do so, he developed a visual conception of proportion, asserting pointedly and repeatedly the similarity of painting and music in this respect: "there arises from [painting] harmony of proportions (*proportione armonicha*), just as many different voices joined together in the same instant create a harmony of proportions which gives so much pleasure to the sense of hearing that the listeners remain struck with admiration as if half alive."[11] Here and elsewhere he borrows the musical concept of "harmony" to describe the felicitous effect of proportionality in painting, but he also sought to establish "beauty" as its visual equivalent: he claims, for instance, that musical harmony is "composed the same way as is that outline of the members which creates human beauty."[12] Leonardo extends the equivalence of visual and musical harmony to the point of appropriating music's claim to imitate the design of the human soul. To make this point, he recalls the alleged response of King Mathias (of Hungary) to a poet who has presumed to compete with a painter: "Do you not know that our soul is composed of harmony, and that harmony is generated only in those instants in which the proportionality of things can be seen or heard?"[13] The reflection of the soul in musical harmony, here extended to painting, was (as we have seen) the basis of its claim to special influence over men's behavior.

However, it was not enough for Leonardo to establish that painting enjoyed the same rational basis and the same powers as music; he wanted also to establish that painting was superior to music. Drawing on his studies in the medical tradition, he argued that the proportional beauty of painting is addressed to sight, the foremost sense, whereas musical harmony is apprehended by the lesser sense of hearing:

"Painting serves the eye—the noblest sense and nobler than the ear ... much greater [than the effect of musical harmony] is the effect of the beautiful proportions of an angelic face represented in Painting, for from these proportions rises a harmonic concert which hits the eye in one and the same instant just as it does with the ear in Music."[14] To encapsulate this idea of similarity in form but difference in status, Leonardo defined music as "the younger sister of painting."[15]

He continued these efforts to diminish the relative status of music in his deliberations on other aspects of the Pythagorean musical tradition. As part of his investigations into the senses, he conducted numerous experiments in acoustics—incidentally, using the results to inform innovative designs for musical instruments. In particular, he took Pythagoras's study of the sounds produced by hammer blows and extended it into a wide-ranging investigation of percussion and resonance, incorporating objects and surfaces with varying properties. Among the results of these experiments was the conclusion that "There can be no voice where there is no movement or no percussion of air," and with this insight he was able to unpick Pythagoras's extrapolations concerning universal harmony: "It would follow therefore that the heavens in their friction not having air between them would not produce sound. ... And if they made a sound it would not be able to spread."[16] The implications of this claim for the aesthetics of music were profound: if the planets could produce no sound, then it would be difficult to sustain the idea that the universe was organized on musical principles; and if there was no music in the heavens, then their harmony could not be reflected in the human soul—and music's privileged relation to the soul was broken.

Although, as we have seen, Leonardo was content to let music's traditional divine attributes stand when they helped him to make an argument against poetry, when it came to a competition between music and painting, he could draw arguments from his study of acoustics to throw them into serious doubt. Meanwhile, through his study of optics, he was able to transfer the same qualities directly to painting. Leonardo saw sight as the sense that presented the world to one's apprehension; the other senses, for him, served merely to convey to us qualities of the things we see. He also praised sight as permanent and immediate, whereas sounds are transitory and enter the ear in sequence: sound "dies instantly after its creation," an accusation that would continue to plague music in later aesthetics.[17] According to the ancient discourse on the senses, the sense-organs were but conduits, and it was the soul that actually operated the powers of sense. Leonardo was thus able to describe a special relationship between the eye, as the foremost sense, and the soul; and as the visual arts were the only arts that presented themselves to the eye, that special relationship extended to painting. He encapsulated this conception through a Ciceronian formulation, calling the eye "the window of the soul" (although in this he was somewhat disingenuous, for Cicero—in the *Tusculan Disputations*—had assigned this honor to eye, ear, and nose all three).[18]

Leonardo's view of sight also informed a reconfiguration of the mechanics of imitation that transferred the honor of imitating God's design for a universe of harmonious proportions from music to painting. Painting, Leonardo argued, represents nature in its permanent and unchanging forms, just as they are apprehended by the soul; he called it "the sole imitator of all the manifest works of nature."[19] Nature, meanwhile, brings forth all visible things according to the design of God. The painter, therefore, imitates the proportional beauty of the universe as it has been created by God. This conception of visual imitation is summarized very neatly by Castiglione, whose discussion of painting is thought to rely heavily on Leonardo's ideas: "when all is said and done, the very fabric of the universe, which we can contemplate in the vast spaces of heaven, so resplendent with their shining stars, in the earth at its center, girdled by the seas, varied with mountains, rivers and valleys, and adorned with so many different varieties of trees, lovely flowers and grasses, can be said to be a great and noble painting, composed by Nature and the hand of God. And, in my opinion, whoever can imitate it deserves the highest praise."[20] With this idea, Leonardo appropriates for painting more-or-less exactly the privilege that musicians had previously claimed as their exclusive province—that of imitating the construction of the universe.

Leonardo's *Paragone*, and his notebooks more generally, contain the most explicit and wide-ranging evaluation of the similarities of music and painting attempted up to his day. However, as we have seen, most of the themes and theories that informed his discussion had been present—if less explicit—in the Italian discourse on the arts throughout the fifteenth century, and have their roots in ancient combinatorial schemata for the understanding of the arts. In particular, the Pythagorean conception of harmonious proportion, which gave music its rational basis and thus its membership of the Liberal Arts, inspired attempts to elaborate a similar conception of visual proportion in support of visual art's claim to the same status. Along with this came efforts to appropriate the other aspects of Pythagorean music theory, including the configuration of harmony as a system capable of comprehending the universe. Also, the particular power over the soul that was encoded into the ancient theory of musical imitation prompted artists to claim a similarly charged imitative capacity for painting. These strands effectively sum up music's part in the paragone up to the death of Leonardo in 1519. In them we see music playing an important role in the process of elevating the status of the painter from craftsman to fully fledged participant in elite intellectual culture—a role that Katherine McIver has also documented by other means. With the help of music's "speculative" tradition, Renaissance artists pieced together a visual equivalent to the category "musicus," and assigned it to themselves.

Notes

1 Ch. 1. *Aristotle: Poetics*, 2nd ed., ed. and trans. Stephen Halliwell, Loeb Classical Library (Cambridge, MA: Harvard University Press, 1995), 29.

2 Ch. II. *Aristotle: Poetics*, trans. Halliwell, 33.

3 Baldassare Castiglione, *The Book of the Courtier*, trans. George Bull (London: Penguin, 1967), 96–97.

4 Bk. I. *Philostratus: Imagines*, ed. and trans. Arthur Fairbanks, Loeb Classical Library (Cambridge, MA: Harvard University Press, 1979), 3.

5 Leon Battista Alberti, *On Painting*, rev. ed., trans. John R. Spencer (New Haven: Yale University Press, 1966), 90.

6 Ibid., 64.

7 Ibid., 66.

8 For a reproduction, see Daniele Bini ed., *Isabella d'Este: La primadonna del Rinascimento* (Modena: Il Bulino, 2001), 64.

9 *Marsilio Ficino: Three Books on Life*, ed. and trans. Carol V. Kaske and John R. Clark (Binghamton, NY: Renaissance Society of America, 1989), 358–359.

10 Alberti, *On Painting*, 77.

11 *Trattato della pittura*, pt. 1, ch. 41, according to A. Philip McMahon's division of the text. Quoted,

as Italian text with the author's own translation, in Emanuel Winternitz, *Leonardo da Vinci as a Musician* (New Haven: Yale University Press, 1982), 205.

12 Pt. 1, ch. 39. Winternitz, *Leonardo*, 211.

13 Pt. 1, ch. 28. Winternitz, *Leonardo*, 209.

14 Pt. 1, ch. 41. Winternitz, *Leonardo*, 205–206.

15 Pt. 1, ch. 39. Winternitz, *Leonardo*, 210.

16 Quoted, from passages in Leonardo's notebooks not included in the *Trattato*, in Winternitz, *Leonardo*, 111 and 106.

17 Pt. 1, ch. 39. Winternitz, *Leonardo*, 211.

18 Pt. 1, ch. 30.

19 Pt. 1, ch. 6. Quoted in *Leonardo on Painting*, ed. and trans. Martin Kemp and Margaret Walker (New Haven: Yale University Press, 1989), 13.

20 Castiglione, *Courtier*, 97.

Further Reading

Azzolini, Monica. "In Praise of Art: Text and Context of Leonardo's 'Paragone' and its Critique of the Arts and Sciences." *Renaissance Studies* 19, no. 4 (2005): 487–510.

Blackburn, Bonnie J. "Leonardo and Gaffurio on Harmony and the Pulse of Music." In *Essays on Music and Culture in Honor of Herbert Kellman*, edited by Barabara Haggh, 128–149. Paris: Minerve, 2001.

Farago, Claire. *Leonardo da Vinci's Paragone: A Critical Interpretation with a New Edition of the Text in the Codex Urbinas*. Leiden: Brill, 1992.

Kemp, Martin. *Leonardo da Vinci: The Marvelous Works of Nature and Man*. London: Dent 1981.

Lee, Rensselaer W. "*Ut pictura poesis*: The Humanistic Theory of Painting." *The Art Bulletin* 22, no. 4 (1940): 197–269.

McIver, Katherine A. "Maniera, Music, and Vasari." *The Sixteenth Century Journal* 28, no. 1 (1997): 45–55.

Murray, Penelope and Peter Wilson, eds. *Music and the Muses: The Culture of Mousike in the Classical Athenian City*. New York: Oxford University Press, 2004.

Winternitz, Emanuel. *Leonardo da Vinci as a Musician*. New Haven: Yale University Press, 1982.

27

POUSSIN AND THE MODES

Sheila McTighe

On November 24, 1647, Nicolas Poussin wrote from Rome to his Parisian patron Paul Fréart de Chantelou, telling about his paintings' relation to the modes of ancient music. According to the artist, a mode established that "when all the things that entered into the composition were put together proportionally" the work had "a power to induce various passions in the souls of viewers."[1] This was indeed a crucial element of ancient modes of music: the proportionate arrangements of notes in a mode conveyed not only mood but *ethos*, a manner not only of feeling but of behaving. From the accounts given later by Poussin's admirers, it appears that the artist's ideas about the modes predated this letter, and had been passed on orally to his companions during conversations in Rome during the 1640s. The immediate textual source for Poussin's 1647 statement was part 4, chapter 5 of Gioseffo Zarlino's *Le Istitutioni harmoniche* (1558). However, Giovanni Battista Doni's *Compendio del Trattato de' generi e de' modi della musica* (Rome, 1635), and Doni's presence at the Barberini court in Rome during the 1620s and 1630s, also probably informed Poussin's understanding of the musical modes. The system of the modes was a long-standing element in treatises on music, as well as in rhetoric and poetics, and remained a current topic through the end of the seventeenth century. However, the function of the modes both in theory and in practice was changing throughout the seventeenth century.

Poussin's thoughts on the ancient modes came at a turning point in the concept of musical modality and in the definition of musical representation. Within the visual arts, the modes of music were also caught up in a revision of the doctrine of *ut pictura poesis*. This notion that painting and poetry were sister arts, both of which focused on the expression of human passions and the representation of high moral actions, extended to the analogy that painting was "silent music," while music itself, like painting, made images in the listener's mind. The centrality of Poussin's often-quoted letter for understanding relations between music and the visual arts in early modernity cannot be overemphasized. His letter juxtaposes painting with both music and poetry as the models for how the visual image should elicit a powerful response from its audience. Yet the nature of that response was being redefined. At the same time, the relationship of service and honor that bound artists, musicians, and poets to their patrons, or to the broader audience that received their works, was increasingly coming into question. The internal contradictions within Poussin's letter on the modes of music show us some of the fault lines that were, in future, to split apart musical, poetic, and painterly expression.

The letter was quoted, verbatim or in paraphrase, so many times by later artists and writers that it is worth citing here at length. The context of the letter is also crucial. Poussin was chiding his patron Chantelou for having complained about getting a less attractive painting than the one Poussin had recently sent to another French patron, Jean Pointel. The artist protested that the difference between the two paintings in question had nothing to do with his devotion to his respective patrons, but arose instead from the difference in the two subjects that he depicted. The nature of the subject determined the manner of the painting, and "It is in this that all the artifice of painting lies." He continued:

> Those fine ancient Greeks, inventors of all beautiful things, found several Modes by means of which they produced marvelous effects. This word Mode signifies properly reason or the measure or form which we use to make something, which constrains us from going too far, making us operate in all things with a certain mediocrity and moderation, and this mediocrity and moderation is nothing other than a certain manner or determined order, which has within it the procedure by which the thing conserves its being.

> As the Modes of the ancients were a composition of several things put together, from their variety was born a certain difference of Mode by which one could understand that each retained in itself a certain "je ne sais quoi" of variety, principally when all the things that entered into the composition were put together proportionally, from which came a power to induce various passions in the souls of viewers. From this the ancient sages attributed to each their separate properties that they saw arise from them; for this reason they called the Doric mode stable, grave and severe, and used it for material that was grave, severe and full of wisdom.

> Passing to things pleasant and joyous, they used the Phrygian mode because its modulations were finer than any other mode and its aspect more acute. These two manners and no other were praised and approved by Plato and Aristotle, who esteemed that the others were useless. They found this mode [the Phrygian] to be vehement, furious and very severe and said that it left people astonished. I hope before a year is out to paint a subject in this Phrygian mode. The subjects of frightful war are best done in this manner.

> They also claimed that the Lydian mode was best for lamentable things because it has neither the modesty of the Dorian nor the severity of the Phrygian.

> The Hipolydian contains a certain suavity in itself and sweetness that fills the soul of viewers with joy. It is best for divine matters, glories and Paradise.

239

The ancients invented the Ionian with which they represented bacchanals, dances and festivities, for its joyous nature.

Good poets have very diligently and with marvelous artifice joined words to verses and used the meter according to the manner of speech. As Virgil observed throughout his poem, since he used all three manners of speaking, he accommodated the actual sound of the verse with such artifice that it properly seems that he puts before our eyes with the sound of his words the things of which he writes, such that when he speaks of love, one sees that he chose with artifice some words that sound sweet, pleasant and gracious to hear, or when he sang of a feat of arms or a naval battle or a storm at sea he chose hard, bitter and unpleasant words so that when hearing or pronouncing them they give us horror. So when I gave you a painting where such a process is observed, you imagined that I did not love you.[2]

Poussin's description of the Greek modes of music is problematic, in that he gave two contradictory views of the Phrygian mode, joyous or belligerent, without telling us, as Zarlino's text did, that there were differences of opinion about this mode among ancient authors. Poussin reduced the modes to just a handful, rather than the seven or thirteen that were discussed in music treatises. He didn't even state that the theory of the modes pertained to music, and indeed with his reference to the language of Virgil he made his point seem rather to lie in the analogy of painting with poetry. Worst of all for later readers of his letter, he gave no real explanation of how he used this theory of modality in creating his own paintings.

On several occasions in the 1660s through the 1680s, the painter Charles Le Brun and the royal historiographer André Félibien gave their own explanations of Poussin's practice of the modes, perhaps from their recollection of his conversations on the subject in Rome. Poussin's letter to Chantelou on the modes was probably not available to them. They interpreted his comments as describing the general expression or overall passion that prevailed in an image. To a certain degree, they hardened Poussin's observations into a rule for painterly decorum and a recipe for establishing the unity of a painting. Le Brun brought up Poussin's modes during two of the lectures he gave at the Académie Royale de Peinture et de Sculpture. In March 1670 he explained Poussin's procedure as "conforming to the harmonic proportion that musicians observed in their compositions; he wanted that, in his paintings, all things might keep their reciprocal accord and conspire toward the same end." The specific elements in this accord were color harmonies, light, and the movements of figures. In depicting a mournful subject, Poussin "established the lugubrious character through a feeble light, by somber hues, and by a languor that is seen in the movements of each figure."[3] Félibien later echoed Le Brun's account, saying "what made the Modes of Music capable of elevating or lowering courage, affliction or joy, was the manner by which voices and sounds were ordered ... thus M. Poussin represented his figures with more or less strong actions and colors that were more or less vivid, according to the subjects he depicted."[4]

Modern scholars have been less certain of how to relate Poussin's letter on the modes to his individual works. Some, such as Denis Mahon, dismissed the letter as derivative, confused, and irrelevant to the two paintings that Poussin was discussing with Chantelou, the *Ordination* given to Chantelou himself (private collection, on loan to the National Gallery of Scotland, Edinburgh) and *The Finding of Moses* made for Pointel (Musée du Louvre, Paris). More often, studies of Poussin's work describe the letter on the modes of music as general evidence of the artist's reverence for antiquity and his effort to subordinate every element of painting to the aim of expression. Charles Sterling, however, proposed that the clearest example of Poussin's practice of modal painting can be seen in his two self-portraits of 1649 and 1650 (Figures 27.1 and 27.2). These paintings were made just after the letter on the modes of music, and they were painted for Pointel and Chantelou, the two patrons whose rivalry set off Poussin's discussion. Sterling saw the earlier work for Pointel as an example of the Phrygian mode—apparently in that mode's joyous rather than warlike aspect—while the later portrait for Chantelou embodied the grave Dorian mode. Louis Marin took up this suggestion, reading the portraits as a form of modal counterpoint. It is worth keeping in mind that the portraits were never meant to be seen side by side, nor were they ever hung together during the seventeenth century, thus never explicitly displayed as a juxtaposition of modes. Only for Poussin himself, and perhaps for his two rival patrons, would the play of contrasts in the two canvases have been evident.

As with Le Brun's and Félibien's discussion, in these modern accounts of the self-portraits, Poussin's modes are read as manipulations of color, light, and movement. The contrast between the two self-portraits emerges from variation in the handling of chiaroscuro, in the contrast of warmer or cooler hues, and in stability versus implied motion in the figures. Above all, Poussin's own expressive demeanor establishes the tone, as he looks out at the viewer from one canvas smiling and from the other in severe reverie.

The self-portraits remain promising examples of the modes of music made manifest in painted images. But to focus only on variations in depicted light, color, and movement may be to overlook the essential nature of the modes as Poussin described them: they consist of a proportionate relationship of parts. In music, the parts that are thus related are musical intervals, conceived as divisions in the length of a sounding string. Although the proportionate intervals between notes are abstract, and exist only temporally, they can be expressed as a numerical proportion: the interval we call the octave establishes a proportion of 2:1, the fifth takes the proportion of 3:2, the fourth a proportion of 4:3. And these proportions may be expressed spatially as the relationship of areas or forms. Thus, famously, Pythagoras equated the proportions that governed musical harmony and those that could be discerned in the cosmos as a whole.

Naomi Barker, a musician and musicologist, has taken up this aspect of modality in analyzing a broad range of Poussin's paintings that mainly predate the 1647 letter on the modes. She explains that interval ratios can be expressed visually, by treating the width and the height of the painting as "string lengths on a monochord."[5] The measurements of height and width may be divided proportionately, working either from top to bottom or vice versa, and from side to side. Laying these divisions in a grid over the painted composition may reveal that significant forms lie at the crossing points, locating the focal points within the composition via proportional ratios. Such a method of analysis demonstrates that, just as Poussin described in his letter, the Ionian mode with its intervals of the octave, fourth, and fifth, was the mode of bacchanals and dances, such as the *Bacchanalian Revel before a Term of Pan* and *The Triumph of Pan* (both in the National Gallery, London). Along with compositions based on these proportions, the paintings share a blond color palette and surface patterns of triangles, together with a dynamic play of diagonal lines across the painted canvas. Similarly, the proportionate relations within the Dorian mode, based on ratios of the octave, minor third, and minor sixth, appear to underlie such depictions as Poussin's *Judgment of Solomon* (Musée du Louvre, Paris) and the two series of *Seven Sacraments* (private collections, on loan in part to Dulwich Picture Gallery, London, and the National Gallery of Scotland, Edinburgh). The heavy vertical and horizontal emphases in the compositions, falling along lines determined by these proportions, go together with a darker, autumnal palette and the figures' stable, fixed poses to yield a tone of somber religious gravity.

These suggestions point toward the real impact of the concept of modality on Poussin's works. However, many questions remain to be asked about the nature and extent of the artist's ideas on this matter. We know that during the 1640s Poussin, together with his friend the Franco-Flemish sculptor François Duquesnoy, measured antique sculptures in Rome, investigating ancient systems of proportion. How did this activity feed into his interest in and awareness of modal proportionality? Behind Poussin's self-portrayal in the portrait made for Pointel (Figure 27.1) is a low-relief tomb sculpture based on a work by Duquesnoy, which was itself derived from study of the antique. In what way did this sculpted form, which Poussin chose to depict as his backdrop, interact with the supposedly Phrygian modal proportions at play in this image? Are there traces of any method of composing a scene modally within Poussin's working drawings, or within the mark-making on the canvases themselves? In other words, how did the concept of the modes affect Poussin's understanding of antique art as a source for modern images, and how did it affect his practice as a painter, which goes beyond the abstract composition of an image, into its construction in pigment on canvas?

An important part of Poussin's letter on the modes has often been left out of the discussion, namely the issue of reception. While the mode of a work might determine its form, the aim of the ancient musician in using any given mode went beyond formal concerns, seeking to bring about changes in the *ethos* of its audience. The mode of the work would supposedly alter the emotions and state of mind of its auditor. This metaphysical aspect of ancient modality was steadily falling out of favor through the seventeenth century, as theorists turned toward the formal properties intrinsic to music—melody, harmony, rhythm—to define its nature. The ancient link between the proportions governing intervals in music and those underlying the heavenly spheres gave way not only to a new cosmology, but to pragmatic issues in performance, as musicians learned to "temper" the tuning of their instruments rather than tune them by the strict ratios of proportionality.

A sense of these changes informs the polite incredulity with which André Félibien recounted the ancient function of the musical modes. In his life of Poussin, first published in 1672, Félibien has his fictional interlocutor Pymandre interject a warning about the dangers of too literal a use of the musical modes: "It would be dangerous, said Pymandre, if Painting had as much power as Music to move the passions; excellent Painters would be in a position to create much disorder." He then told the tale of a Danish king who wished to see the effects of Dorian, warlike music on his court. On hearing a musician perform in a bellicose mode, the audience erupted into battle, during which the king himself, enraged by the music, killed four of his own subjects. Félibien commented: "Those who believed that Music was necessary to great Politicians ... did not intend that such use be made of it; and I believe also that it was not the intention of Poussin to put those who looked at his paintings in such great danger." Yet he immediately stressed that Poussin "exactly observed these Maxims about which I have just told you, and one will see in his works the marks of his application to make them conform in all things to the subjects he was treating." The power of the modes to alter the behavior of an audience (a phenomenon external to the work of art) recedes, in Félibien's understanding of Poussin's modality, in favor of their power to impart expressive unity (a property intrinsic to the work). As one author has suggested, the later seventeenth-century understanding of the modes of music is caught up with an emerging sense of the work of art as an internally coherent mechanism, in keeping with a turn toward the model of mechanism in a range of intellectual disciplines during the later seventeenth century.

Poussin's own contradictory understanding of the modes of music can best be appreciated if we look at the context of his 1647 discussion. His discussion of the modes is embedded in the midst of statements about patronage and viewers for his works. In fact, the overall theme of his letter on the modes is his servitude towards Chantelou. He began the letter by promising that he would work exclusively for his patron, in order to finish his series of the seven Sacraments paintings. He went on to say that, in deference to Chantelou's wishes, he would also serve M. de Lisle, Chantelou's friend, as part of his service to Chantelou himself. But before painting for anyone else, Poussin somewhat wistfully expressed the hope that he could paint a work "as if for myself, without subjecting myself further to the whims of others." The demands of the type of patronage called *servitù particolare*, wherein an artist took on a contractual obligation to work primarily for one patron and his network of relations, chafed at Poussin. He wanted the independence to choose his own subjects, to find his own inventions.

Buried in this understandable desire for autonomy is a curious contradiction with the very point of his discussion of the modes. He was instructing Chantelou that the effect of his paintings did not depend on the esteem he felt for his patron, that the painting's subject alone determined the tone of the work, and, implicitly, that its mode would affect any viewer and all viewers in precisely the same way. In proposing to make a work as if solely for himself, liberating himself from meeting the needs of a patron, Poussin appears to accept that the character of the audience—himself alone—would indeed change the nature of the image. In a letter written just before the letter on the modes, Poussin had revolted at the thought of painting for the poet Paul Scarron, another acquaintance of Chantelou. The artist loathed Scarron's burlesque travesty of Virgil and did not want to work for him. Again, the nature of the patron at least in part determined Poussin's response to the task of representation. He thus remained trapped by the very complaint that Chantelou had raised. Was the image a form of privileged communication between the artist and a specific individual patron? Chantelou suspected that this was why Pointel got the sweeter, lighter painting. Or was the work an internally coherent system that would mechanically elicit the same modal result in any viewer—in effect, a more modern, quasi-autonomous work of art? Poussin's theory of the modes was an attempt to cope with contradictions in the system of the arts that went much further than his own tiff with Chantelou. In a way characteristic of many seventeenth-century negotiations between antiquity and modernity, Poussin looked for a classical precedent to paper over the cracks between theory and practice, between contemporary art and its audiences.

If we turn back to the 1649 and 1650 self-portraits, their modalities would seem to repeat the difference that set off Chantelou's complaint to Poussin. The portrait given to him is undoubtedly more severe, more Dorian, than the smiling, Phrygian likeness sent to Jean Pointel, just as the Ordination painting had been darker and more solemn than the sunnier Moses scene. There are indications that Poussin used modality here in a more complex way, however, in order to address himself to the desires of both of his friends and patrons. Behind Poussin in the portrait delivered to Chantelou we see framed canvases, facing away from us and toward us. On the uppermost canvas, in a fragment of a painting within the painting, we see a woman whose crown holds a single eye: this is a symbol of *Pittura* or *Disegno*, a figure of the reasoned art of painting itself. Holding out her arms to embrace an unseen figure, she is within the work yet reaches beyond it. Poussin explained that she recalls the bonds of friendship. Presumably she reaches out to the absent viewer, the distant friend. But that friendship is expressed in and through the art of painting, an art which the portrait presents as the very identity of Poussin himself. In his portrait for Pointel, behind the artist we see a tomb with its classical relief as designed by Duquesnoy. Although depicted as if turning, moving, and very much alive, the artist stands before the tomb, as if by analogy the painting itself were an entombment of his effigy. More joyous though Poussin's depicted expression may be, his effigy stands, just as in the portrait for Chantelou, at the crossroads between the two termini of living presence and its absence, death. Crossing his wrists, the artist holds in one hand a book whose title declares its subject to be light and color, and in the other hand a double-ended brush, black pigment at one end, white at the other—the two termini of all light and all color. In the one hand, he holds theory expressed in words, in the other hand he holds the means to practice painting. Different modes may govern color, light, and expressive movement in these two works, but both portraits dwell on the same question of painting's address to its viewers, and it is an address that must explicitly move from presence to absence and back again.

It may be that Poussin used the mode of each work not to harmonize with the *ethos* of his absent patron, but to supplement or alter that person's prevailing state of mind. He had chided Chantelou in the letter on the modes for, in effect, his lack of seriousness. So it is the Dorian mode, grave and philosophical, in which his painted likeness is couched, with its lesson on friendship rather than servitude in painting. We know less about Pointel, so we may only surmise that his need was for joy, not philosophy. Within the constraints of its modality, each painting represents a similar image of the artist and his artistry. The aim of both paintings was to communicate across the gap between distant friends, to form a bond between individuals, and to express their mutual admiration for the highest forms of art. Finally, in these works that embody a difference of mode, Poussin brings together the powers of word and image, of musical harmony and painterly communication.

This synthesis of the arts under the guise of modality was not to last long. Already in the Académie discussions from 1667 onward, the discussion of musical modes was slipping away from the problems of communication and reception, moving instead toward defining painting as a unified and autonomous mechanism. The debates about color and the instantaneity of painting would lead toward new definitions of what was intrinsic and unique to the visual arts, destroying the sisterhood of poetry, music, and painting. Music could serve as an analogy to painting, but not as a literal model for it. In the early eighteenth century, the artist Antoine Coypel put it thus: "Each painting must have a mode that characterizes it. The harmony will be sometimes bitter and sometimes sweet, sometimes sad and sometimes gay, in keeping with what one represents. One can follow the example of the enchanting art of music."[6] With this, despite its superficial similarity to Poussin's letter on the modes, we have come far from Poussin's utopian desire to harness music's "power to induce various passions in the souls of viewers."

Notes

1 Nicolas Poussin, Letter to Paul Fréart de Chantelou, 24 November 1647, in Ch. Jouanny, ed., *La Correspondance de Nicolas Poussin* in *Archives de l'Art Francais*, nouvelle période V (Paris, 1911), 370.

2 *La Correspondance de Nicolas Poussin*, 370–375. The translation here is mine; I have punctuated the letter for greater clarity where Poussin ran several phrases or sentences together. Another, slightly more literal translation can be found in Anthony Blunt, *Nicolas Poussin* (London: Pallas Athene, 1967; revised edition 1995), 367–370.

3 Charles Le Brun's comments on Poussin's *Plague of Ashdod* (Musée du Louvre, Paris), as transcribed by Guillet de Saint-George, published in André Fontaine, *Conférences inédits* (Paris, 1903), 116–117. Cited (in French) by Jennifer Montagu in "The Theory of the Musical Modes in the Académie Royale de Peinture et de Sculpture," *Journal of the Warburg and Courtauld Institutes* 55 (1992): 238.

4 André Félibien, *Entretiens sur les vies et sur les ouvrages des plus excellens peintres anciens et modernes* (Trevoux, 1725). In this edition the discussion of Poussin's modes can be found on pp. 322–28.

5 Naomi Joy Barker, "'Diverse Passions': Mode, Interval and Affect in Poussin's Paintings," *Music in Art* 25 (2000): 10.

6 Antoine Coypel, "Sur l'esthétique du peintre" (1721), published in Henri Jouin, *Conférences de l'Académie Royale de Peinture et de Sculpture* (Paris, 1883), 328.

Further Reading

Allard, Joseph C. "Mechanism, Music, and Painting in Seventeenth-Century France." *Journal of Aesthetics and Art Criticism* 40 (1982): 269–279.

Barker, Naomi J. "'Diverse Passions': Mode, Interval and Affect in Poussin's Paintings." *Music in Art* 25 (2000): 5–24.

Bialostocki, Jan. "Das Modusprobleme in der bildende Kunst: Zur Vorgeschichte und zum Nachleben des 'Modusbriefes' von Nicolas Poussin." *Zeitschrift für Kunstgeschichte* 24 (1961): 128–41.

Lee, Rensselaer W. *Ut Pictura Poesis: The Humanistic Theory of Painting.* New York: W. W. Norton, 1967.

McTighe, Sheila. *Nicolas Poussin's Landscape Allegories.* Cambridge and New York: Cambridge University Press, 1996.

Montagu, Jennifer. "The Theory of the Musical Modes in the Académie Royale de Peinture et de Sculpture." *Journal of the Warburg and Courtauld Institutes* 55 (1992): 233–248.

Moreno, Jairo. *Musical Representations, Subjects and Objects: The Construction of Musical Thought in Zarlino, Descartes, Rameau and Weber.* Bloomington: Indiana University Press, 2004.

28

WAGNER'S GESAMTKUNSTWERK

Diane V. Silverthorne

In his famous essay "Richard Wagner and Tannhäuser in Paris," Charles Baudelaire wrote of his desire to penetrate more deeply into an understanding of Wagner's singular works. Determined to exchange the sensuous pleasure of listening for knowledge, Baudelaire found in the master's writings the reasons for Wagner's "natural, even inevitable" turn to Greek theater for the establishment of the new conditions of lyrical drama. After all, as Wagner wrote to Franz Liszt, "if we wonder why thirty thousand Greeks could follow with sustained interest the performance of Aeschylus's tragedies, we must see that it was due to the alliance of all the arts concentrated on the same goal, the production of the most perfect and only true artwork."[1] This was the beginning of Wagner's project. It led to his study of the interrelationship between the plastic and mimetic forms of art, as Wagner described, and thence to an examination of the relationship between music and poetry. The light that dawned in the darkness of this search was Wagner's *Gesamtkunstwerk*, or "total work of art."

Wagner's writings on the *Gesamtkunstwerk*, the overpowering effect of his music dramas, his cult-like following, and the legendary Bayreuth Festspielhaus experience—in other words, the idea of Wagner—provided an irresistible impetus for the aspirations of artists in all fields of cultural production at the end of the nineteenth and in the early twentieth centuries. Artists consciously sought to evoke Wagner's name, casting themselves as followers and seekers of the utopian ideal of the *Gesamtkunstwerk* as paradigm for a modern art which was clearly still vested in late-nineteenth-century Romanticism. The insistent presence of Wagner's *Gesamtkunstwerk*, reinforced by the uniquely expressive powers of his music, was made manifest in painting and literature by figures as diverse as Baudelaire, artist Wassily Kandinsky, and theater director Max Reinhardt, who embraced Wagner's idea of the total theater as a festival experience. Wagner's legacy has been as important to historians and practitioners in the visual and literary arts as to those in music, whether they reacted against Wagner's ideas or embraced them as a paradigm. The *Gesamtkunstwerk* has been creatively re-interpreted, depending on the interests of its proponents; this was a particularly marked tendency in fin-de-siècle Vienna.

Although he rarely used the term *Gesamtkunstwerk*, Wagner's theories of the synthetic artwork are found in various manifestations: in his "Zurich writings" of 1849–57, principally *The Art-Work of the Future* (1849) and *Opera and Drama* (1851), the second of which provides a more fluent articulation of his earlier ideas. These two books were written in the shadow of the Dresden uprising, in which Wagner was an active participant, and are imbued with his revolutionary spirit. This larger political and social vision was inspired in part by his readings of Friedrich Engels and Ludwig Feuerbach, particularly the latter's *Principles of the Philosophy of the Future*. Wagner's significant body of writings, notoriously opaque at times, was a way of working out his ideas for what he knew was going to be a significant undertaking on a scale never before envisaged: the four operas of *The Ring of the Nibelungen*.

The Art-Work of the Future (*Das Kunstwerk der Zukunft*), a phrase that Wagner used together with "the collective artwork" ("das gemeinsame Kunstwerk") to signify the *Gesamtkunstwerk*, was founded on the principles of an idealized vision of Greek theater. As Wagner wrote, "in any serious investigation of the essence of our art today, we cannot make one step forward, without being brought face to face with its intimate connection to the art of ancient Greece."[2] Greek tragedy had made use of instrumental music, verse, song, dance, mime, and narration to bring the fullest expression to the drama. The Athenians' manifestation of Greek tragedy was an embodied experience in which all people were joined. Just as the enactment of the tragic drama brought the ancient Greeks into a direct relationship with their gods Apollo and Dionysus, so Wagner's *Gesamtkunstwerk* would be spiritually transformative, a unifying religious experience.

Wagner's writings on the *Gesamtkunstwerk* united three central ideas. The first of these was derived from Wagner's view that Greek drama was the apex of human creative achievement. As an antidote to degeneracy in all the arts, a return to Greek ideals would produce "the ideal expression of art concentrated into one focus to bring forth its highest conceivable form."[3] The *Gesamtkunstwerk* would draw on three classical art-forms of Greek drama, enumerated by Wagner as music, poetry, and dance (or gesture, as he later described it), to create a single dramatic unity. Wagner placed great stress on each individual art-form coming together in its own "native truth and beauty." Mystically, he declared that each would gain in strength "by giving itself away" in the cause of a unified art-work, transformed into a greater entity than the sum of its parts.[4] The essential idea of synthesis, as opposed to the autonomy or separateness of each art form, lies in this principle.

Secondly, Wagner's *Gesamtkunstwerk* would use myth, or *mythos* as he referred to it, as the material and texture of the drama. *Mythos* was true for all time. It would convey universal truths that transcended differences of religion, time, and place. Perhaps surprisingly, Wagner used *mythos* to denote spareness rather than monumentality. Only through *mythos* could the essence of drama be comprehended. Understandable to all, it would manifest itself in utmost concentration, through the human voice, poetry, and music. Wagner would use *mythos*, embodied through the protagonists of his works, to speak to the fullness of the human condition.

The third idea that Wagner passionately advocated was the spirit of community, which according to him had been lost since the time of Greek tragedy—just as the arts had lost their individual strengths since their separation. The *Art-Work of the Future* would be a collective endeavor: a community joining practitioners of the arts and their audience in a spirit of fellowship. Wagner used the word *Volk* to denote its particularity to the German people, who would lead this revitalization of art, replacing it at the center of human achievement as the Greeks had done. This modern form of drama would rest with a new kind of "tone poet" (as opposed to the "word-poet"), who would "rouse the whole inner emotional faculty."[5] Wagner's constant stress on the inwardly driven, expressive capacity of the arts in their unified state to "express the inexpressible" is one of his most significant legacies.

Inextricably linked to the *Gesamtkunstwerk* were its perceived utopian powers as an antidote to a divided and fractured world. The *Gesamtkunstwerk* held out the promise of aesthetic unity to replace chaos, uncertainty, and fragmentation. It was an aspirational ideal, never to be fulfilled in its totality. Perhaps this is what haunts virtually every modern production of Wagner's *Ring*. The search for *Gesamtkunstwerke* always carries with it the aspiration of a *becoming* future, never a point of arrival.

Actors and Singers (1873), which includes Wagner's 1870 essay on Beethoven written to celebrate that composer's centenary, is also essential for a full understanding of Wagner's *Gesamkunstwerk* theories. By then, Wagner had read Arthur Schopenhauer's *The World as Will and Representation* (1819). Wagner's engagement with Schopenhauer was an epiphany. He saw these writings as a brilliant and profound articulation of his own deeply felt views about art and music. Schopenhauer had attributed to music a unique position in the hierarchy of the arts, which Wagner glossed as follows: "in Music itself is an Idea of the world."[6] Wagner also embraced Schopenhauer's darker vision of the world, of redemption through the complete annihilation of the will, a powerful idea that would become the dominating force for *Tristan und Isolde*. In so doing, Wagner acknowledged that the *Gesamtkunstwerk* could not simply exist as the joyful unification of the arts that he had first proposed. However, certain constitutive elements of his Greek ideals remained as *sine qua non* in the union of the arts to create a greater single entity, the central importance of myth, together with community, transposed increasingly in his writings to the term "purely human" (*Rheinmenschlich*). Above all, his *Gesamtkunstwerk* called for the synthesis of modern, emancipated forms of the fine arts in which music dominated.

Wagner saw Beethoven as the first true exponent of Schopenhauer's transcendental idea of music, and used his essay to justify a privileged place for music in the *Gesamtkunstwerk* and, of course, his music dramas. Beethoven's symphonic music, even before the Ninth Symphony, was distinguished by a metaphysical and poetic state expressing the essence of the musical spirit. Wagner cast Beethoven as a great path-breaker (and by implication, Wagner as his even greater successor) in a world in which "the vision of paradise" promised by the arts had been debased. He argued that Beethoven had been ill-served by existing analysis, and his Ninth Symphony misunderstood. Beethoven's greatness in music was equal to that of Goethe, Schiller, and Shakespeare in poetry; with his greatest gift, the Ninth Symphony, he emulated the act of creation at the "vanishing point," a nexus between consciousness and unconsciousness.[7] The Ninth was no longer constrained by time and space, the distinguishing characteristics attributed respectively to music and art in aesthetic debates of the period. It was now possible to see how words and music could be fused into a single expressive unity.

Wagner's words on this subject are worth citing at length, since they relate to his ideas on the synthesis of the musical and visual worlds. He made particular use of the term *Schein*, meaning *semblance* or "the appearance of things," to denote this elision. Beethoven, he wrote, had taken the "illusive surface" (*Schein*) of the visual world, and by virtue of its ingenious play with semblance, "la[id] bare *the Idea* (of music) concealed beneath."[8] The synthesis of these two worlds, which Wagner described as the light-world and the sound-world, existed on the edge of dreams. Dreams were analogous to music, only entering the visible world through a form of consciousness drawn from the noumenal realm. As Wagner declared, "the character (of the dream world) speaks out to us most straightforwardly from the works of the plastic arts."[9] Through his writings on Beethoven, Wagner bridged the principles of the Attic model of the *Gesamtkunstwerk* and his practice as music dramatist.

Wagner's writings on the opening of Bayreuth are also essential for a complete understanding of his visionary *Gesamtkunstwerk* project, and another seeming paradox. Despite his emphasis on the collective endeavor, the notion of the "total artist" (*Gesamtkünstler*)—a single, artistic mastermind imposing an overarching vision on the total work—became influential at this time. The Festspielhaus (Festival Theater), as the new opera house was called, embodied Wagner's insistence that art (and his art in particular) was the new religion. It had innovative architectonic features, such as a series of proscenium arches; the auditorium was darkened to intensify the audience's experience of the drama. Both of these effects were intended dramatically to alter visual perceptions of distance from the characters on stage. Wagner denoted the physical and metaphysical space between drama, stage, and audience as the "mystic gulf."[10] In this space something magical happened: between the spectator and the stage picture, nothing was plainly visible other than "a floating atmosphere (*Stimmung*) of distance," the "deeds of music made visible."[11]

The term *Stimmung* is a persistent *leitmotif* in Wagner's writings on the *Gesamtkunstwerk*. He associated it with the desired effect of the musico-dramatic performance on its audience. It relied on "the exclusion of all useless detail … Color itself would be turned into action," a sentiment taken up later by the European theater-reform movement, which stripped theater sets of their historicist accretions and used lighting for expressive impact.[12] *Stimmung*, Wagner implied, was an immanent force. It would bridge the real and metaphysical gap between audience and stage, evoking an imaginative leap across the darkened reaches. Even audiences further afield sought *Stimmung* as the ultimate Wagnerian experience in the years after Wagner's death. It was "the real festival experience, a harmony, a continuity of atmosphere … in a word the almost untranslatable, *Stimmung*, the subtle force," as the *Musical Times* described in 1911.[13] Wagner's ideas therefore prefigured early theories of psychological aesthetics, empathy, and form that emerged in the writings of German art historians and philosophers in the last decade of the nineteenth century, notably Wilhelm Worringer's *Abstraction and Empathy* (1908). They continue to act as a point of reference for inquiry into issues of perception and visuality in contemporary scholarship.

In his writings on Bayreuth, Wagner (almost) acknowledged the work of an admired contemporary, the celebrated German architect Gottfried Semper—particularly his unfulfilled designs for the Munich Theater. The two met in flight from Dresden and continued a rather disputatious acquaintance. Like Wagner, Semper strove to "see beauty as a unity, not just as a sum or a series," and the expression of unity through multiplicity of form, bound together by a single, guiding idea.[14] Also like Wagner, Semper wrote of his fascination for the experience of the Greek *theatron* and the magic of Greek dramatic performance. Semper's spectacular building designs for theaters and museums, over which he exercised control in every aspect, united the arts of architecture, painting, and sculpture, producing a glittering synthesis of materials—as if the building itself was a performance, intended to astonish the spectator and make him aware of his presence within a larger communal ritual. By 1892, the German philosopher Wilhelm Dilthey, writing on aesthetics, regarded Semper as the progenitor of the *Gesamtkunstwerk* in architectural form. After Wagner and Semper, the *Gesamtkunstwerk* became, for many of its followers, the inspiration for architecture and its synthetic partnership with painting and the applied arts that aspired to transform life through art, particularly within Europe's Art-Nouveau and other early modernist movements.

Out of the Spirit of Music

It was, however, philosopher Friedrich Nietzsche's first published work, *The Birth of Tragedy: Out of the Spirit of Music* (1872)—containing in its original edition a paean to his mentor, Wagner—that created a nexus of ideas for the dissemination of Wagner's *Gesamtkunstwerk* in the arts more widely, particularly in the German-speaking world. This work took its stepping-off point from Wagner's essay on Beethoven, which had celebrated the greatness of the composer's Ninth Symphony in creating a sublime synthesis of poetry and music. Developing Wagner's idea that ancient Greece represented the highest form of culture, and fifth-century Attic tragedy its most perfect expression, Nietzsche argued that great art was characterized by the essential opposing forces of the rational (Apollonian) impulse and the irrational (Dionysian) impulse. In Attic Greece, epic poetry represented the purest distillation of the Apollonian impulse, its powers closest to the art of image-making. The Dionysian impulse was exemplified by the unbounded, quasi-orgiastic forms of music (despite the ancient convention that the god Apollo represented music).

Nietzsche described these two opposing forces, respectively, as the art of the image-maker or sculptor, and the imageless art of music. These opposing impulses would ideally meet in the embodiment of the artist "as imitator," an artist of "both dream and intoxication at once."[15] In so doing, music would be made visible as a symbolic, dream image. Laying down a specific challenge to the visual arts, Nietzsche enjoined the artist "to transform Beethoven's 'Hymn to Joy' into a painting, placing no constraints on the imagination."[16] Using the term *Schein*, Nietzsche argued for the essential characteristic of the theatrical in art, a term of approbation in his writings, in which the untrammeled confusion of the Dionysian was masked and made bearable by the golden radiance of the Apollonian. Nietzsche's expanded realm of *Schein* became a transcendent force in the visual arts, acquiring, by association, the signification of light.

Nietzsche died in 1900. Had he survived for a further two years (and been in his right mind), he might have witnessed one of the most convincing expositions of Wagner's *Gesamtkunstwerk* as an extra-musical event, and the transformation into painting of Beethoven's "Hymn to Joy." Fin-de-siècle Vienna's exponents of the modern fine and applied arts, as well as music, were imbued with Wagnerism and the search for the modern, synthetic artwork.

Wagner's Ideas in Other Spheres

Music formalist Heinrich Schenker (1868–1935) aptly described the impact of Wagner's ideas in Vienna, which were "beginning to fall apart into a thousand, productive elements, each with a life of its own."[17] This was exemplified by the artists of the Vienna Secession, who in 1902 staged a celebration of the idea of Beethoven and his Ninth Symphony in an extraordinary art exhibition in their purpose-built pavilion. References to mythic symbolism in the surface decorations, such as three stylized gorgon faces above the entrance to the exhibition pavilion (Figure 28.1), were intended to transcend religious and political tensions to provide a space which was universal in spirit.

Both building and event were devoted to a modern aesthetic through a synthesis of painting, architecture, and sculpture, and, ever since its inception, the "Beethoven Exhibition" has been acknowledged as a paradigm of Wagner's *Gesamtkunstwerk* in the visual arts. It was the first (and perhaps only) modernist art exhibition in Europe to devote every element, from its temple-like staging to its exhibited artworks, to a single, overriding idea: a celebration of the visionary powers of the composer and his "Art-Work of the Future," the Ninth Symphony. A series of murals, including Gustav Klimt's famous *Beethoven Frieze* inspired by the musical ideas of the last movement of the Ninth and Schiller's "Ode to Joy," appeared to rise to Nietzsche's challenge. They gleamed with the brilliance of gold leaf, jeweled surfaces, and colored glass, evoking Nietzsche's *Schein* and eliding reality with abstraction.

From here, visitors proceeded to the central setting of the Beethoven monument (sculpted by the celebrated Leipzig artist Max Klinger), which brought them to a devotional state (*Andacht*) that Wagner attributed only to the aesthetics of the *Gesamtkunstwerk*. The exhibition paid tribute to Klinger's Wagner-inspired conception of *Raumkunst* (literally, "an art of space"), uniting the plastic arts in a demarcated space to create a higher artistic experience. Devoted to a single, overriding theme, the exhibition captured the Wagnerian ideal: musical ideas aspiring to an expressive synthesis of all the arts. Yet here, the visual arts dominated. Absorbing the audience in the experience, the exhibition prefigured installation art of the later twentieth century.

On the stage of the Vienna Court Opera, music director Gustav Mahler formed a partnership with Alfred Roller (1864–1935), a founding member of the Vienna Secession and an instinctive synthetic artist, who had come to Mahler's attention as director of the 1902 Beethoven Exhibition. Together they wanted to attain visually what Mahler sought to do musically: to realize the *Gesamtkunstwerk* aspirations that Wagner never achieved in his lifetime. Roller was the first stage designer famously to orchestrate different light and color effects, for a groundbreaking new production of *Tristan und Isolde* (1903). The most inwardly driven of Wagner's music dramas, it was composed in the heat of Wagner's engagement with Schopenhauer's ideas and is closest to an exposition of music as the Will's unmediated expression. Roller drew on the theories of the visionary stage designer Adolphe Appia (1862–1928) at a turning point in the history of stage design. Appia's *Music and the Art of the Theater* (1899), recognizing the limitations of Wagnerian stage designs, had presciently identified the mysterious affinity between music and light. With its unifying function, lighting would dramatize the action involved and thus achieve the same significance as a musical motif. Roller's production of *Tristan und Isolde* offered a realistically star-filled night sky for the first time. The "gushing colors" of other lighting effects made it possible for the audience to appreciate the strange dissonances of Wagner's poetic text, notably Tristan's "How do I hear the light"—perhaps the effect of sensory correspondence that Wagner had wished for. Wagner wanted to convey the essence of underlying realities perceived by the senses as "an undreamed-of super-reality" (*Überwirklichkeit*).[18] Transforming lighting into an expressive force as Wagner had desired, Roller's 1903 production won the accolade of *Stimmung*, suggesting the super-reality of Wagner's mystic gulf.

In 1911, in a modernist re-interpretation of Wagner's *Gesamtkunstwerk*, Arnold Schoenberg published the text of his expressionist music drama, *Die Glückliche Hand* (The Lucky Hand), which was imbued with the spirit of stage-design ideas emanating from the Vienna Opera House. The mythic protagonists of Wagner's music dramas were reduced, in this work, to the essence of the "purely human": Woman, Man, and Gentleman. Schoenberg brought together an anonymous chorus, music, mime, the idiom of "sung-speech," his own set designs, and a lighting crescendo (similar to Roller's celebrated *Tristan* effects) that correlated with the music and drama in this condensed work. The use of *leitmotifs* and various symbolic objects was recognizably Wagner's. If the dramatic elements taken individually seem dissonant, or forced against the grain of unity, they nevertheless converge as *Gesamtkunstwerk* in their cumulative effect.

Wagner's notion of *Gesamtkunstwerk* exerted an incontestable impact on the visual, literary, and dramatic arts throughout Europe, as these few examples have shown. As stated at the outset, Baudelaire's passionate writings on his synaesthetic experience of Wagner's music fueled the spread of Wagnerian ideas as the touchstone for Symbolist writing, art, and drama. Stéphane Mallarmé challenged Wagner's *Gesamtkunstwerk* ideas but did not renounce them. Instead, he promoted the idea of synthesis in a single medium, putting the concept to the test in his poetic work *Un coup de dés jamais n'abolira le hasard* (1897). Later, seeing a world shattered by the Great War, architect Walter Gropius fermented his ambition to use the fine and applied arts to transform art and life. Gropius loosed the *Gesamtkunstwerk* from its specifically Wagnerian context to form the Bauhaus, whose manifesto espoused "an artwork of unity." It is largely due to Wagner that music was not only used as an analogy and model in the search for new expressive forms of art, but also acted as a powerful catalyst in the release of painting from its traditional task of mimesis.

In his essay "Wagner's Relevance Today" (1963), Theodor Adorno viewed the existence of the Wagnerian *Gesamtkunstwerk* and its derivatives "only as a dream of convergence, an abstract utopia between music and the painterly arts, before the media permitted it."[19] This was certainly true, yet it is not the whole truth. In the staging of Wagner's music drama as *Gesamtkunstwerk*, painting with light using new technical effects, and the "will to art," various protagonists made a transformative contribution to its visual as well as musical realization. Wagner's almost unresolvable yet essential search for unity between inner and outer worlds, between the arts and their audience, lives on, as does his notion of the modern artwork as both revolutionary and redemptive. Consciously or unconsciously, seekers of the *Gesamtkunstwerk* continue to find traces of its "one thousand productive parts," a splintering effect ascribed more recently to the resonant spaces of post-modernist art. As various commentators have also observed, the idea of the *Gesamtkunstwerk* almost always lies outside music. It may be found in the after-effects of John Cage's

252

aesthetic of "all-sound," or manifested in the desire for social transformation that is implicated in the fragmented detritus of Kurt Schwitters's *Merzbau* project (c. 1923). In London, at the opening ceremony of the 2012 Olympic Games, Wagner's *Gesamtkunstwerk* ideas were suggestively in evidence, uniting "the common people" in a dramatic, synthetic spectacle of dance, mime, music, and light, with no less a Wagnerian sign than the forging of the Rings amidst showers of Loge's fire.

Notes

1 Charles Baudelaire, "Richard Wagner and Tannhaüser in Paris" (1861), in *Baudelaire, Selected Writings on Art and Literature*, trans. P. E. Charvet (London: Penguin, 1992), 324–357 (333, 336).
2 Albert Goldman and Evert Sprinchorn, eds., *Wagner on Music and Drama: A Compendium of Richard Wagner's Prose Works* (hereafter WOMAD), trans. H. Ashton Ellis (New York: Dutton, 1964), 77.
3 Ibid., 77, 78.
4 *Richard Wagner's Prose Works* (hereafter RWPW): *Art-Work of the Future*, VI, trans. William Ashton Ellis (London: Kegan Paul, 1892, 1893), 149.
5 WOMAD, 207.
6 R. Wagner, "Beethoven," in *Actors and Singers*, trans. W. A. Ellis (Lincoln: University of Nebraska Press, 1995), 57–126 (65).
7 Wagner, "Beethoven," 63.
8 Ibid., 70.
9 Ibid.
10 WOMAD, 101.
11 WOMAD, 366.
12 RWPW, *The Theatre*, VIII, 330.
13 B. Smith, "The Bayreuth 'Stimmung': A Subtle Force," *Musical Times*, August 1, 1911: 519.
14 G. Semper, *Style in the Technical and Tectonic Arts; or Practical Aesthetics*, trans. Harry Francis Mallgrave and Michael Robinson (Los Angeles: Getty Research Institute, 2004), 72.
15 Friedrich Nietzsche, *The Birth of Tragedy and Other Writings*, ed. Raymond Geuss and Ronald Speirs (Cambridge: Cambridge University Press, 1999), 19.
16 Ibid., 18.
17 Cited in Nicholas Cook, *The Schenker Project: Culture, Race and Music Theory in Fin-de-Siecle Vienna* (Oxford: Oxford University Press, 2007), 85.
18 Heinrich Porges, *Wagner Rehearsing the "Ring": An Eye-Witness Account of the Stage Rehearsals of the First Bayreuth Festival*, trans. R. L. Jacobs (Cambridge: Cambridge University Press, 1983), 4.
19 Theodor W. Adorno, "Wagner's Relevance Today," in *Can One Live after Auschwitz? A Philosophical Reader*, ed. Rolf Tiedemann, trans. Rodney Livingstone (Stanford: Stanford University Press, 2003), 314–352 (321).

Further Reading

Baudelaire, Charles. "Richard Wagner and Tannhäuser in Paris." In *Charles Baudelaire: Selected Writings on Art and Literature*, translated by P. E. Charvet, 324–357. London: Penguin, 1992.
Follett, Danielle and Anke Finger, eds. *The Aesthetics of the Total Artwork: On Borders and Fragments*. Baltimore: Johns Hopkins University Press, 2011.
Goehr, Lydia. *The Quest for Voice: Music, Politics, and the Limits of Philosophy*. Oxford: Clarendon Press, 1998.
Goldman, Albert and Evert Sprinchorn, eds. *Wagner on Music and Drama: A Compendium of Richard Wagner's Prose Works*. Translated by H. Ashton Ellis. New York: E. P. Dutton, 1964.
Magee, Bryan. *Wagner and Philosophy*. London: Penguin Books, 2000.
Nietzsche, Friedrich. *The Birth of Tragedy and Other Writings*. Edited by Raymond Geuss and Ronald Speirs. Translated by Ronald Speirs. Cambridge: Cambridge University Press, 1999.
Schopenhauer, Arthur. *The World as Will and Representation*. Translated by E. F. J. Payne. Indian Hills, CO: The Falcon's Wing Press, 1958.

Shaw-Miller, Simon. *Visible Deeds of Music: Art and Music from Wagner to Cage*. New Haven and London: Yale University Press, 2002.

Silverthorne, Diane V. "Music, Modernism and the Vienna Secession: Musical Form in *Ver Sacrum*." In *Music and Modernism c. 1849–1950*, edited by Charlotte de Mille, 26–52. Newcastle-upon-Tyne: Cambridge Scholars, 2011.

Wagner, Richard. *Actors and Singers*. Translated by William Ashton Ellis. Lincoln: University of Nebraska Press, 1995.

29

RĀGAS, MOOD, AND REPRESENTATION

Jonathan B. Katz

In this chapter we examine a remarkable and much celebrated example of the confluence of musical and visual ideas in South Asia. The Indian *rāgamālā* ("series" or "garland" of rāgas) is most commonly understood as a pervasive and fruitful pictorial tradition which was particularly vibrant in northern, central, and Deccani Indian miniature painting schools between the early sixteenth and the nineteenth centuries. Its precise relation to the actual practice of music is unclear, and some scholars have even rejected any genuinely aesthetic connection, but the rāgamālā may in fact reflect a certain understanding of an idea which is unique to the Indian musical tradition.

Underlying much of the music of the Indian subcontinent is a melodic principle which, when understood and described theoretically, has for centuries been called *rāga*. It is by far the most important melodic concept in what are considered the "classical" and "semi-classical" genres of both North Indian (Hindustani) and South Indian (Carnatic) musical repertoires. It also dominates the melodic character of many more popular and devotional kinds of music throughout India, even when the technical name itself may not be applied.

A rāga is a melodic structure which, fascinatingly, constitutes a specific aesthetic and structural entity but at the same time has to be brought to life, even "reincarnated," in a performance in order to transform a theoretical notion into a reality. In other words, a specific idea, which a practicing musician or experienced listener would be able to call to mind, becomes "embodied," and is uniquely represented, or rather recreated, in a live performance. A parallel may perhaps be seen in the nature of a religious icon, for there too the idea, which may often include a set of necessary constituent ingredients if it is to be the true definition of a personage or deity, will be differently represented each time an artist paints or sculpts an actual image. What is recognized by the educated observer is the idea behind the concrete image, and the artist may have been more or less faithful to that background idea, and may have exercised more or less creative energy and talent in bringing it to life. In both the icon and the rāga are seen, or heard, specific characteristic features which combine to create that identity. Look at the icon, or hear a performance "in" a rāga, and you become quickly conscious of the underlying "meaning" of what you experience.

Music, of course, has the crucial additional element of time; here, then, the transformation of idea into reality is also a shift in "dimension." We might describe the pre-performance understanding of a rāga as "pre-discursive," and the performance itself as "discursive." A "correct" and powerful performance, whether an improvised *ālāp* (discursive exploration and unfolding of the rāga by a vocalist or melodic instrumentalist) or a composed song using a particular rāga, will be judged partly on the persuasiveness with which it presents the true characteristics of the rāga without violating its "grammar."

The word *rāga* itself is Sanskrit, and has passed directly into all of the Indian vernacular languages. At its root is a verb (*ranj*) meaning "to be colored" or "to glow," and a frequent metaphorical extension of this in Sanskrit was the sense of emotional "coloring" or "passion." Hence a common early meaning of the noun *rāga* was "feeling." As a musical term it was explained by early Indian theoretical writers as "that which gives delight," and our sources for the history of Indian music suggest that in the course of the second half of the first millennium of our era, perhaps by the later eighth or earlier ninth century, the word not only became well established as a category term but was also used for individual, nameable structures which could be described and differentiated one from another; and the "delight" an individual rāga gave was partly related to its very individuality.

What distinguishes one rāga from another is primarily its melodic formation and secondarily its associated emotional "meaning" or "reference." Right from these early times up till the present day, the pitch content has been prominent among the characteristics of a rāga. The constituent pitches can be set out as a scale, but this will never be enough to define the rāga. For a rāga is much more than a scale, as it essentially contains notes which are particularly prominent or emphasized and others which are less so, as well as characteristic melodic patterns (including zigzags) in rising and descending passages, and definitively characteristic ornamentation of particular notes. Furthermore, the precise intonation of some notes will often be determined by the rāga in which they are used. The notion, indeed, of "ornamentation" should be applied with caution here, for in Indian music the embellishment of a note is often a part of that note's essential identity within its rāga context, transmitted from teacher to pupil along with other features of the rāga. Two or more rāgas may well have the same basic pitch content—that is to say, the same constituent notes—but will treat these notes quite differently, stressing different characteristic combinations and sequences, or perhaps dwelling more prominently on the upper or the lower part of the octave, or again, the one rāga omitting different notes from the others in ascending or descending note sequences.

The emotional associations of rāgas seem to have been derived from various sources. Some of the names themselves of individual rāgas clearly originate in geographical toponyms and suggest regional associations, perhaps with local styles of performance or prominent song melodies known to have been popular, or even with particular musicians. The earliest context for the theoretical description of music was that of the Sanskrit drama and all of its ingredient arts including music, dance, and poetry. Early Sanskrit dramaturgical sources and written treatises clearly link individual rāgas with the content and mood, and with the structural positioning within the drama, of certain types of poetic texts set to music; alongside the pitch-definitions of the kind described above, these sources tell us, for instance, that this or that rāga is to be performed in the context of one of the standard rasas (sentiments) that were prescribed for certain moments and stages in the unfolding of the dramatic plot.

Many medieval Indian music-theoretical treatises aimed at comprehensive definitions of the musical "material" from which performances would be created, and offered classified lists of melodic, metrical, and compositional forms as well as the instruments, types of voices, qualities of musicians, etc. It seems that a large body of recognizable "regional" melodies were gradually subsumed within more "classical" rāga systems. Classificatory strategies were devised to make sense of the enormous range of existent forms, so that what were considered older and earlier-established rāgas were considered to have "engendered" other forms which shared certain characteristics with these "parents."

A particularly prominent and influential central Indian music treatise of the thirteenth century, the *Sangītaratnākara* ("Jewel-mine of Music") by Shārngadeva, devotes its formidably comprehensive second chapter to the listing, classifying, and defining of rāgas, and offers both instrumental melodic examples and illustrative song compositions for some of those rāgas treated as the most important. These songs are devotional pieces addressed to various deities, and here is another strong association of melodic form with an associated intentional "meaning." In some other cases a deity is mentioned even when no illustrative composition is offered. For example, the "secondary" or "derived" rāga (technically termed a *bhāshā* or "dialect") *Velāvalī* is defined as follows (the notes in Indian music are named in a solfeggio system, ascending from tonic to tonic—sa, ri, ga, ma, pa, dha, ni, sa): "*Velāvalī*, which is derived therefrom, has a high *dha* [sixth note of the scale], a low *ga* [third note] and equally balanced notes. Having *dha* as its initial and final and principal note, and an oscillation on its *sa* [tonic note], it is dear to the god Hari [Vishnu] and is employed in the portrayal of conjugal affection between separated lovers."

In addition to describing actual musical practice, the medieval Sanskrit treatises in this traditional discipline known as *Sangītashāstra* (musicology) included much material that was already "antiquarian" by the time they were written, in an effort to bring together a musical "lore" that could account for all known forms and place them in a theoretical system. It is quite likely that some of the ascriptions of specific sentiments to certain rāgas and bhāshās reflect this traditional lore, especially aimed at a supposedly complete classification, rather than the actually current preoccupations of musicians. Certainly in more recent times it has been quite possible for a single rāga to be used for singing song texts over a wide range of different moods and emotions, and certainly a performance in a particular rāga can move through many quite contrasting degrees of mood and intensity. But the "identifiability" of the rāga, and certain traditional associations, still characteristically remain in its understanding and memorizing by musicians and listeners.

Such associations retained a greater importance in the music of North India than in the South. It is true that in the southern (Carnatic) classical music tradition too there has always existed a recognition, or assumption, of the distinctive aesthetic and emotional significance of individual rāgas; in the instrumental music of the temple *nāgasvaram* (large shawm) tradition there is still a common observance of the appropriate ritual performance hours for particular rāgas. But South Indian music theory and teaching after the seventeenth century came to place greater emphasis on the scale-types of the rāgas, and on their characteristic melodic "direction," than on the extra-musical associations found in the earlier tradition of musical lore still current in the discourse of Hindustani musicians.

And those associations can be powerful psychological influences on musicians. From the period following the composition of the Saṅgītaratnākara we begin to find stories of the strong evocative power of rāgas and their performance. The earlier connection of music with Sanskrit drama had now been largely replaced by associations with vernacular (especially Hindi) devotional religious and secular poetry, and indeed with genres which combined the two. Hindustani music fostered strong shared notions of "appropriate" times and seasons for the performance of particular rāgas, and still today many musicians will resist breaking with tradition and singing or playing a "morning rāga" in the evening, or vice versa. One of the most famous legends from the sixteenth century tells of an event in the career of the Emperor Akbar's renowned court musician Naik Gopal. The emperor asked him to sing the rāga *Dīpak*, which was popularly associated with brilliance, light, and fire. If brilliantly performed, this rāga was believed to have the power to create heat and light in the form of fire. The singer was said to have pleaded with the emperor to withdraw the royal command, but when Akbar insisted, Naik Gopal entered the river Jumna and stood so that the water reached his neck. When he began to sing, the water became hot and flames burst forth from the singer's head.

The notion that a rāga can be encapsulated in thought led naturally to the practice of encapsulating its character or sentiment in words, and musical treatises began to include, among the technical descriptions of the listed rāgas, evocative poetic verses. For example, in some texts, especially of the Eastern Indian region from the sixteenth century, each rāga description is complemented by what is referred to as a *mūrti*, literally an "icon" (the same word is used for the statue or picture of a deity positioned for veneration in a temple or shrine). Sometimes this is referred to as an *udāharana* ("exemplification") and sometimes as a *dhyāna* verse, a word commonly applied to a mental representation of, or meditation on, the attributes of a deity in iconographic systems of other kinds.

An example may be taken from a compendious musical treatise called the *Saṅgītanārāyana*, a work composed at a seventeenth-century Orissan royal court as much to serve the needs of connoisseurship as for the practical guidance of musicians themselves. The rāga *Velāvalī*, or rather the female "*rāginī*" as she is now classed, is given the same basic technical description as we find in the earlier medieval texts (the model was no doubt the Saṅgītaratnākara verse given above), with a slight variation in the account of one its notes. Then is given its *mūrti*: "Velāvalī, who has the color of a blue lotus, having given her lover a sign of assignation adorns her body with fineries, constantly thinking of Smara [the god of love], her personal deity." The author of the treatise then tells us that another source gives a "slightly different" expression of the image of this *rāginī*. For other rāgas and rāginīs more strikingly variant versions are offered, and clearly we are dealing here with separate conceptions, originating perhaps from different regions or even devotional traditions.

Here, then, we see two ideas of classification, first the more strictly music-technical and second the imaginative; we may assume that both were considered at this time appropriate for connoisseurs to study and appreciate. The female depiction of many of the rāgas is itself closely connected with a classificatory idea not entirely separate from the music-technical, for the idea of "parent" and of derivative or "offspring" rāgas which we have already seen in earlier sources has apparently led to that of a "family" system in which some rāgas are understood to be primary and others secondary, literally "engendered" from those when united with "wives."

Painted representations of such rāga images begin to appear in the sixteenth century, and many of the Sanskrit and vernacular dhyāna verses are preserved as textual inscriptions alongside these miniature paintings, or sometimes on the back of them. If we except some regional variants, three prominent systems of classification, with which the artists work, have been commonly identified. First there is what has come to be named (after a magisterial study by Klaus Ebeling, mentioned below in "Further Reading") the "painters' system," which is used in about half of all the inscribed paintings throughout the field in different parts of India. Second, there is the so-called "Hanuman's system," used in some two dozen sets and given this name because when the list appears in the seventeenth-century Sanskrit text Sangītadarpana ("Mirror of Music") written by the scholar Dāmodara (its first appearance so far documented) it is attributed to "Hanuman," a supposedly ancient music theorist and commentator. The third is the more elaborate system of a scholar-priest named Meshakarna or Kshemakarna, which is not later than the sixteenth century and admits borrowing material from older sources. This is the system used, with some freedom and iconographic license, by the painters of the Punjab hills. In addition to these three systems, we should also take into account some regional types such as are found in Eastern (Bengali and Orissan) musical texts. A Sanskrit text called the Sangītadāmodara, for instance, composed in the early sixteenth century by the prolific Eastern music and dance theorist Shubhankara, was highly influential in the Orissan region, where illustrated palm-leaf manuscripts used his verses as the basis for pictures.

The Sangītaratnākara itself does not refer to a rāga/rāginī classification, but at least one such system did exist before this time in a Jain Sanskrit text of the twelfth century. One possibly even earlier source for the classificatory idea is a text composed in Bengal with the title Brhaddharmapurāna. This presents a story in which the god Nārāyana tells the sage Nārada about six rāgas, each of which has six wives, with each member of the scheme having one attendant. This text seems to be the earliest available source for the iconographic idea behind the dhyāna verses, namely the personification (or deification) of the rāgas, and perhaps even for the dhyānas themselves, as a couple of rāgas are there described in dhyāna-like iconographic terms. There are thus some reasons to think that the whole idea may have originated in Bengal and then spread to other parts of India with the diffusion of devotional teachings and practices.

The first extant painted source appears to be the set of forty-two illustrations included in a Western Indian Jaina manuscript of c. 1475, in which the depictions of the rāgas and rāginīs are clearly deities. Here the images are named but are not accompanied by dhyāna verses, though it is likely that they are indeed based on a textual source. In later sources, however, the figures depicted are no longer deities but humans, including character types known from literary and dramaturgical traditions such as the romantic heroes and heroines known as nāyakas and nāyikās.

The rāgamālā became a favourite subject for artists in many of the court and provincial schools of painting. The commonest structure for a series was a primary set of six male rāgas, each with a fixed number of wives or consorts, usually five, the rāginīs, but this was not the only available system. Sometimes (as in the

Kshemakarna scheme) the "family" was extended to take into account a larger number which could be classed as "sons" of the couples, and in one known set of verses (for which no images have yet been found) the primary set is of eight, each with three consorts. A common feature, however, is the principle of regularity itself, which seems to match the efforts found in some texts of music theory to order the large repertoire of known rāgas in a systematic scheme.

In his review article on three major published inventories of rāgamālā paintings and verses (see "Further Reading" below), H. S. Powers surveys much otherwise scattered information to show how both images and texts could migrate and combine, and different local traditions could sometimes use a different selection of a body of apparently available iconographic elements. Influences were apparently felt from other subjects of painting and associated literary themes, and it is more than likely that many, or most, of the painters worked primarily in pictorial artistic traditions, and at some distance from musical practice itself.

A few images are notably stable and consistent across poetic and iconographic systems, representing perhaps popular themes commonly recognized almost everywhere. For example, the common, though not universal, image of the rāginī *Bhairavī* is of a female devotee honoring the god Siva (or more rarely Vishnu). Other representations are much more fluid and flexible, and perhaps show very different regional prototypes, and even varying understandings of these essential themes within a region or school. The example shown here (Figure 29.1) from a Rāgamālā set painted in the late eighteenth century in Kotah, Rajasthan, is an image, with text inscription, of the rāginī variously called Kāmodanī (as here), Kāmodikā, Kāmodī, etc. The different schools of painting contain, in her case, a variety of images. If there is a theme central to all or most of them it is that of a young female figure, in some verses (including the Sanskrit lyric dhyāna inscribed here) described as having long loose tresses, and often sitting alone in a forest and yearning for her absent lover. In this version there is no mention of the lover, but the verse tells us that she sits upon a seat of flowers, has a soft and fair body, and her dress is as bright as the moon. In a verse found in the Eastern Indian texts, she is indeed said to be in company with her lover, collecting flowers and delighting in their fragrance. The rāga itself was frequently listed, with more stable technical musical features than these iconographic details, in the classificatory systems in music treatises, and seems to have been commonly performed.

The decline and demise of the rāgamālā tradition of painting may be explained partly by a general reduction in Indian court patronage of painting. The last real flowering may be seen in the Rajasthan school of nineteenth-century Jaipur. The systematic classification of musical structures also underwent considerable change, and pedagogical methods were devised in which the more technical description of rāgas came to take precedence over the more "affective" kind of definition. But the association of rāga and mood has never been entirely lost in Indian, and particularly in Hindustani, music. Efforts to find genuine musical significance in the rāgamālā have often foundered because a direct parallelism was sought between identifiable visual features in the paintings and identifiable audible features in the musical structures. This chapter has offered a different suggestion, namely that certain common conceptual and organizational principles may be shared between the paintings and the music, and that, even if many of these artists were not in fact very familiar with the practice and theory of music, the underlying idea of a rāga picture, and even more so that of a series of such pictures, reflects an aesthetic insight that does indeed relate to a specifically Indian understanding of melodic creativity.

Further Reading

Dahmen-Dallapiccola, Anna L. *Rāgamālā-Miniaturen von 1475 bis 1700.* Wiesbaden: Harrassowitz, 1975.

Ebeling, Klaus. *Rāgamālā Painting.* Basel: Ravi Kumar, 1973.

Glynn, Catherine, Robert Skelton, and Anna L. Dallapiccola. *Ragamala: Paintings from India: From the Claudio Moscatelli Collection.* Exhibition catalogue. London: Philip Wilson and Dulwich Picture Gallery, 2011.

Katz, Jonathan. "Music and Aesthetics: an Early Indian Perspective." *Early Music* 24, no. 3 (August 1996): 407–420.

Lath, Mukund. "Some Thoughts on the Early History of Rāga-paintings." In *Jain Art and Architecture,* edited by R. C. Dwivedi, 37–46. Jaipur: Centre for Jain Studies, University of Rajasthan, 1980.

Powers, Harold S. "Illustrated Inventories of Indian Rāgamālā Painting." *Journal of the American Oriental Society* 100, no. 2 (1980): 473–493.

Waldschmidt, Ernst, and Rose Leonore Waldschmidt. *Miniatures of Musical Inspiration in the Collection of the Berlin Museum of Indian Art.* Part 2. Berlin: Museum für indische Kunst, 1975.

Widdess, Richard. "Sugar, Treacle and Candy: History and the Concept of *Rāga* in Indian Music." In *Ethnomusicology and the Historical Dimension,* edited by Margot Lieth Philipp, 71–81. Ludwigsberg: Philipp, 1989.

———. *The Rāgas of Early Indian Music.* Oxford: Clarendon Press, 1995.

IV.3 Convergence in Practice

30

ARTISTS AS MUSICIANS AND MUSICAL CONNOISSEURS

Musicians, *Mélomanes*, and Ideas of Music among Nineteenth-Century Artists

Peter L. Schmunk

Describing the proliferation of concerts in Paris in 1832 as "epidemic," the anonymous writer in *L'Artiste* drew a vivid comparison with the contemporary outbreak of cholera: "This year concerts are extremely popular. We are not overwhelmed, but, rather, infected. … On every occasion, concerts proliferate … under all guises … instrumental, vocal … classical, romantic … Paris is invaded by concert and by cholera."[1] Sociological and institutional studies confirm this arresting argument. Not only in Paris, but in London and Vienna as well, there was an explosion in the number and significance of concerts during the second quarter of the nineteenth century. The establishment of concert halls, standing orchestras, and subscription concert series made music of the highest level of sophistication more accessible and affordable than ever before. As a result, shopkeepers, clerks, and notaries, as well as artists, were able to hear the symphonies of Beethoven, the chamber music of Schumann, and the operas of Wagner, i.e., to have the kinds of musical experiences that had largely been restricted before the nineteenth century to those who could pay for their creation and performance directly.

Similarly dramatic expansions occurred in the performance of music at other venues. Café-concerts, for example, where food and drink were served alongside musical entertainment of a light and popular type, and which proliferated in Paris after the installation of gas lighting in the second quarter of the nineteenth century, grew in number from a handful around 1850 to nearly 200 by the early 1880s. The opera house, the ballet, and the dance hall, famously portrayed by Degas, Seurat, and Toulouse-Lautrec, were other important sites for the consumption of musical culture.

In the domestic realm, the spread of concerts was paralleled by an enormous increase in the acquisition of instruments, especially the piano, which could be played either independently or as an accompaniment to singing or another instrument. Writing in 1851, presumably with some exaggeration, Edouard Fétis (son of the Belgian musical scholar F. J. Fétis) declared that "there is not a home, even of the smallest bourgeois, where one does not find a piano. The instrument forms, in all necessity, a part of the furniture of every family; you will find it as far as janitors' lodges."[2] The piano became both a center of leisure and social activity in the home and an emblem of bourgeois prosperity and cultural aspiration. Numerous paintings, by artists as diverse as Caillebotte, Renoir, Vallotton, and Denis, portray the piano almost invariably as played by women, a social dynamic that has been explored in several scholarly studies. Daumier and other caricaturists could portray the piano as a place of amorous interaction, or lampoon young women's display of modest pianistic skills to captive dinner guests, because these were common social practices. Such rituals offered the cartoonists visual metaphors that a general audience would readily understand, as when Daumier, in 1869, personified Liberty as a woman at an upright piano whose singing was, according to the caption, "decidedly full of voice."

The publication of sheet music for the piano was a particularly dynamic industry during the nineteenth century in the enormous output of its production and in the shrewd responsiveness of publishers to the needs and interests of an ever-expanding pool of consumers. A considerable portion of the sheet music published at this time was the result of transcription, i.e., the adapting of a composition written for another instrument or group of instruments to the capacities of the piano and a particular level of performance expertise. An enthusiast of music in the nineteenth century was more likely to get to know the symphonies of Beethoven, or the music of a new opera, through a piano transcription than through an orchestral performance. Authenticity was readily sacrificed by both publishers and consumers for a composition's availability in an accessible form. Publishers realized as well that they could enhance the sale of sheet music through the visual appeal of a cover image, and thus many artists—even major figures such as Manet, Toulouse-Lautrec, and Bonnard—found employment in providing images for the music market.

Music journals, which included articles, reviews, reports from correspondents in other cities, and advertisements, appeared in growing numbers as publishers sought to exploit the widespread interest in musical subjects. One historian asserts that 260 such publications emerged between the years 1798 and 1848, the number no doubt increasing in the second half of the nineteenth century. Through the medium of the written word, such journals contributed to the spread of musical culture, the reputations of composers and performers, the consumption of specific musical commodities, and the dissemination of critical and philosophical ideas. Much of this discourse gave to music a status of the highest prestige. Writers varying in their diffusion and influence pronounced music "the most romantic of the arts" (E. T. A. Hoffmann), "the art of the century" (H. R. Haweis), and "the most powerful of all the arts" (Arthur Schopenhauer). The Horacian dictum *ut pictura poesis* was reformulated by the critic Louis Viardot in 1859 as *ut pictura musica*, with music displacing poetry as painting's rival art. Indeed, to compare a painting to a symphony, or a painter to a musician, was to give the visual arts the highest praise.

In such a milieu—with much local variation—nineteenth-century artists were potentially engaged with music in myriad ways. They could experience different kinds of music as listeners in a variety of places, public and private. A great number of artists did this, some of whom may justifiably be considered *mélomanes*, individuals with a deep love, a mania, for music. But in exploring the interests of artists in music and its possible influence on them, one should not think simply in terms of music per se, but rather in the broader sense of musical culture, the rich fabric of institutions, performances, social rituals, economic exchanges, literary and visual commentary, and critical discourse that made music a pervasive aspect of nineteenth-century life.

The researcher who chooses to explore this influence confronts a number of challenging questions. What was the actual experience of music, if any; what were the preferences and interests held by a particular artist? Was that artist also a musician and, if so, at what level of technical skill? Was the artist interested in music as sound or spectacle, or both? In what ways did the artist understand music? What ideas about music did the artist hold that might have been applied to the practice of painting? Answers to these questions can be elusive. The listening habits and musical preferences of an artist are often difficult to establish with any certainty. One must draw on a variety of direct and indirect sources such as journal entries, correspondence, and the recollections of acquaintances to assemble, at best, an approximation of an artist's experience of music. And even in cases where this experience seems to have had a profound and influential effect, artists did not often articulate their understanding of music in specific terms. The influence of music on painting may lie purely in the realm of inspiration and intuition. To demonstrate something of the variety of ways in which music was experienced and came to have an influence on the practice of painting over the course of the nineteenth century, the following discussion focuses on a selection of major artists.

Eugène Delacroix (1798–1863) was among the very first and most important nineteenth-century artists to develop a passionate interest in music. As a youth, he played both the violin and the guitar, and, beginning in 1820, the harpsichord as well. George Sand, the intimate companion of Chopin, insisted that Delacroix had a genuine technical understanding of music and might have been "a great musician if he had not chosen to be a great painter."[3] He was certainly a deeply engaged listener, attending opera and orchestral concerts at public venues and hearing chamber and vocal music in the homes of the affluent social elite, thus participating in both new and old patterns of musical patronage. The artist's journal entries contain numerous observations on the performances and compositions he heard. He was especially fond of the music of Mozart and selected operas then in currency, such as Rossini's *Cenerentola* and Cimarosa's *Il Matrimonio Segreto*. The new music of his own time received a less enthusiastic response. Delacroix was ambivalent toward Beethoven, dismissive of Verdi (to whom he referred with malicious sarcasm as Merdi), and contemptuous of Berlioz both as a person and as a composer. Though we may perceive, or unthinkingly assume, a stylistic affinity between contemporaries such as Delacroix and Berlioz, working in different artistic media, such connections were as often as not unappreciated by the artists themselves. Delacroix's tastes in music being somewhat conservative, he found the greatest inspiration in the music of an earlier time.

One of the most important outcomes of Delacroix's interest in music was the reflection that it prompted on the similarities and differences, the strengths and weaknesses, and the precise nature of the different arts. He regarded music and painting as similar to one another and superior to literature because of their very vagueness and imprecision, qualities previously thought to be a deficiency, which left the mind free to wander and to respond in subjective ways. On the other hand, he found the temporal nature of both music and literature tiring, because the listener was forced to remember ideas over time and able only gradually to grasp an impression of the whole, whereas painting presented a coherent whole directly and immediately. Delacroix's close friendship with Chopin provided other opportunities for consideration of the comparative nature of the arts. He was particularly intrigued by Chopin's explanation of the systematic character of music, an insight that confirmed and encouraged his own search for visual principles that might define the relationships between colors and their appearance in visual experience.[4]

While still in his twenties, Delacroix became familiar with the writings of Germaine de Staël, who played a pivotal role in introducing to France ideas that were then current in German philosophy and cultural discourse. Published in 1810, her book *De l'Allemagne* (*On Germany*) contains a well-known passage that Delacroix was to endorse:

> The impressions one obtains from the fine arts bear not the slightest resemblance to the pleasure derived from any form of imitation. The human spirit harbors innate feelings that can never be satisfied by real objects, and the painter's or poet's imagination consists in giving shape and life to such feelings. Music, the foremost of the arts, what does it imitate?[5]

Delacroix may have begun thinking about this observation on the non-imitative nature of music as early as 1824, when he noted in a journal entry that "in music, for example, form predominates over matter. ... In Mme de Staël I find exactly the same method that I use to develop my own ideas about painting. This art, like music, is higher than thought; hence it has the advantage over literature, through its vagueness."[6] He certainly knew and agreed whole-heartedly with the thinking of de Staël when he repeated the passage given above in an essay entitled "Realism and Idealism." Out of these ideas of music—the validation of its vagueness and the recognition that its capacity to communicate powerfully did not depend on the portrayal of material objects—emerged the concept of "musicality." In the same essay, Delacroix wrote:

> There is an impression that results from a particular juxtaposition of colors, lights and shades: what one might call the music of painting. Even before knowing what a picture represents, imagine going into a cathedral and positioning yourself at so great a distance that you cannot determine the subject of the picture. Often, you will find yourself seized by this magical chord; sometimes, even the grandeur of the lines alone can produce the same effect.[7]

The affirmation of a painting's musicality led Delacroix to retain a quality of sketchiness even in his finished works, to seek a greater simplicity through the elimination of superfluous details, to appreciate indefiniteness, and to find pleasure in "those scenes whose subjects have no explanation," for "in them painting triumphs alone, as music does in a symphony."[8]

Delacroix's notion of the "music of painting" was promoted by a number of critics, especially Charles Blanc and Charles Baudelaire, and thereafter had a significant influence on many late-nineteenth-century painters. One of these was James Abbott McNeill Whistler (1834–1903), whose familiarity with music came more through his friendships, his domestic arrangements, and social activities, and whose tastes in music tended toward the light and popular. Beginning in 1867, however, Whistler adopted musical terms for the titles of his works, thereby discouraging a conventional narrative reading of his art and directing a viewer's attention to a painting's qualities of mood and formal harmony. The idea of a musical title for a work of visual art was not entirely Whistler's own. It seems to have originated with the critic Paul Mantz, who characterized Whistler's early portrait of *The Woman in White*, exhibited at the Salon des Refusés in 1863, as "nothing other than a symphony in white."[9] When Whistler exhibited in 1867 a large painting of two women lounging on a white sofa, he gave it the novel and provocative title *Symphony in White, No. 3*, boldly inscribing those words on the work itself. Likewise, at the suggestion of Frederic Leyland (a patron of the artist and a pianist especially devoted to the music of Chopin), Whistler adopted the title "nocturne" for his monochromatic scenes of boats on water. Though the word "nocturne" refers generally to things of the night, Whistler's subsequent remarks indicate that he intended the term in its musical sense.

> Why should not I call my works "symphonies," "arrangements," "harmonies," and "nocturnes"? As music is the poetry of sound, so is painting the poetry of sight, and the subject-matter has nothing to do with harmony of sound or color. ...

> The great musicians knew this. Beethoven and the rest wrote music— simply music: symphony in this key, concerto or sonata in that.

> On F or G they constructed celestial harmonies—as harmonies—as combinations, evolved from the chords of F or G and their minor correlatives.[10]

The anti-narrativity that Whistler cultivated from an early date in his art was thus refined in his painting practice and signaled to his viewers by titles that, in referencing music, direct a viewer's attention to a painting's formal components. As other artists sometimes repainted or touched up a painting years after its initial completion—and Whistler did this, too—he also altered the titles of his works, adopting the musical terms best suited to the character of particular paintings: *Harmony in Blue-Green—Moonlight* became *Nocturne: Blue and Silver—Chelsea*; the *Golden Screen* became *Caprice in Purple and Gold: The Golden Screen*. As much as any nineteenth-century painter, Whistler exemplifies the transformation of the theoretical formula *ut pictura poesis* to *ut pictura musica*.

Camille Corot's (1796–1875) life-long interest in music led to rather different outcomes. Numerous drawings record his attendance at opera productions throughout his adult life; when he was in Paris he regularly attended concerts of the Conservatoire and Pasdeloup orchestras. Biographical anecdotes relate that he played the violin and had prints of his favorite composers—Mozart, Gluck, Paër, and Beethoven—attached to the walls of his bedroom. Corot designated money in his will for a performance of the Adagio movement of Beethoven's Ninth Symphony at his own funeral. Moreau-Nélaton, the artist's early biographer, reports that when one of his favorite pieces was performed, Corot would make "singularly apt comments; indeed he could analyze a symphony like a picture."[11] Corot's response to music was thus analytical as well as emotional; his observations were aimed, at least in part, at identifying analogies between aural and visual modes of expression.

Unlike the other artists discussed here, Corot portrayed musicians and the performance of music in numerous paintings and in a variety of ways. In several landscape paintings from the 1840s and 1850s, small foreground figures hold musical instruments, while others dance or listen, implying the presence of a particular kind of music consonant with the character of the landscape. In *Landscape, Setting Sun* (also known as *The Little Shepherd*) from 1840, for example, the twilight stillness of a forest resonates in the relaxed pose of a solitary shepherd and the implied unaccompanied melody coming from his upheld flute. A contrasting sentiment pervades the *View near Naples* of 1841, where the sunny, open character of the landscape is echoed in lively dancing and music made by peasant figures holding cymbals and a mandolin. In these and other similar works, Corot has treated landscape and music as analogous signifiers of particular moods, the one amplifying and inflecting the other. And just as images based on literature assume a viewer's familiarity with their textual sources, these landscapes require for their full appreciation an awareness of the sounds and emotional connotations of the instruments they include. Corot's musical imagery introduces an aural dimension to the viewing experience.

During the final decade of his career, Corot painted a number of works that place musical instruments in the hands or proximity of solitary figures, either a cello-playing monk or a woman in peasant costume in the artist's own studio. In each of the six studio interiors, painted c. 1865–72, the female figure in peasant attire sits before an easel displaying a Corot landscape (Figure 30.1). The things around her vary from work to work—a book, an attentive dog, an open paintbox—but include, in four of the six paintings, a mandolin which the figure plays or holds in prominent view. In these small but complex paintings, the female figure may be seen as model, viewer, muse, and as the artist's alter ego. In the latter role, she, like the artist, forms a bridge between music and painting. In those versions where the mandolin is not played but is held alongside the seated figure, its alignment with the easel suggests the foundational role of music as inspiration and model for Corot's art.

While the other artists discussed here were frequent concert-goers and had easy access to musical culture of various kinds, the isolation and poverty of Vincent van Gogh (1859–90) through most of his career precluded such experiences. In spite of this seclusion, he became aware of music's potential as a model for painting through writings such as Charles Blanc's *Les artistes de mon temps* (1876) and *Grammaire des arts du dessin* (1874). Having absorbed these texts, Van Gogh began to include musical metaphors in letters discussing particular painters and their art, and he made a quixotic effort to learn music from a small-town church organist. Apparently these were not piano lessons in the usual sense but lessons in music theory that might yield, for Van Gogh, insights applicable to the organization of color in a painting. While this effort was fruitless at the time, it prepared the artist to be receptive to the abundant discourse on music and its value as a model for painting, as well as the frequent opportunities to hear concert music, that he would encounter in Paris a year or two later.

In the south of France in subsequent years, Van Gogh invoked the model of music on numerous occasions for the brilliantly colored paintings he was then producing. Excerpts from correspondence of this time indicate something of the range and focus of his ideas of music:

> Painting as it is now promises to become more subtle—more like music and less like sculpture—and above all it promises *color*.

> Why do I understand the musician better, why do I see the raison d'etre of his abstractions better?

> In a painting I want to say something comforting, as music is comforting. I want to paint men and women with that something of the eternal which the halo used to symbolize, and which we seek to convey by the actual radiance and vibration of our coloring.

> By intensifying all the colors one arrives once again at quietude and harmony. There occurs in nature something similar to what happens in Wagner's music, which, though played by a big orchestra, is nonetheless intimate.[12]

Neither a musician nor a *mélomane*, Van Gogh lacked a technical understanding of music and had only minimal experience of its performance in the concert hall. Nonetheless, the pervasive discourse on the "music" of painting among artists, theorists, and critics in the 1880s prompted him to become conversant with this idea of music and then commit to its application in his own practice of painting. For Van Gogh, music provided a model of abstraction that encouraged him to simplify, exaggerate, and intensify the elements of visual form "to express [him]self forcibly."[13] This method was manifest especially in his treatment of color, but may be seen in other elements of his art as well, including line, shape, and brushwork. He rationalized his efforts to arrange brilliant colors in calculated combinations that might yield effects of harmony and calm by invoking the example of Wagnerian orchestration. And the consolation that he sought in life and art, he also linked to music, associating it especially with Wagner and Berlioz—though admitting to never hearing the latter's music. Van Gogh's citation of these composers might be regarded as name-dropping that pretended to a degree of cultural sophistication; it was also to participate in a discourse then widely current and understood by the artists with whom he corresponded, regardless of their actual experience of music.

In striking contrast to Van Gogh's musical dilettantism, Odilon Redon (1840–1916) might have become a professional musician had he not pursued a career as an artist. Responding in 1894 to the questions of a friend preparing a lecture on his art, Redon wrote: "When I was born [my brother Ernest] already played; still in the cradle, I heard Beethoven and Bach. I was born on a sound wave. There is not a recollection of my early childhood which is not linked to melody, to music of quality. Later as an adolescent, I listened to then still little-known works by Berlioz, Schumann, Chopin. Our family home was filled with it. Music certainly left its mark on my soul."[14] Redon learned to play both piano and violin in his youth, performing on the latter instrument in amateur orchestras in the city of Bordeaux. Settling in Paris in the mid-1870s, he was, in his own words, a "faithful listener of concerts"; in early 1875 he began attending the weekly gatherings of writers, artists, and musicians at the home of Berthe de Rayssac.[15] There he established a lasting friendship with the young musician and future composer Ernest Chausson. The two formed a violin–piano duo, playing on Sunday evenings at the Chausson family house and on Wednesdays at the salon of Madame de Rayssac. Chausson's surviving letters to Redon indicate a shared devotion to the music of Beethoven and Schumann. And Arï Redon, the artist's son, quoted his father as saying in his later years that Schumann, Chopin, Gluck, Berlioz, and Beethoven "represent to me five luminous and vivifying points of a mystic star which has sustained me lightly throughout life, making me forget its rigors. Oh! that beautiful art. It is more powerful than the one I exercise."[16]

This sentiment of exalted praise for the art of music was conveyed visually in Redon's lithograph *The Celestial Art* from 1894, portraying an enraptured listener and an angel playing a violin. However, Redon's lifelong devotion to the performance and experience of music is reflected in surprisingly few images on musical subjects. It was rather in the "indeterminacy" of music, in its capacity to provoke imaginative contemplation, that Redon found a compelling alternative to realism in painting. Even Fantin-Latour's ethereal portrayals of scenes from the music dramas of Wagner were too grounded in naturalism, too "parasitic upon the object," for Redon. And he discounted the same artist's emphasis on color as an inadequate means of translating music into painting. Though his skills as a performer and his understanding of the structure of music likely surpassed almost all other artists of the time, Redon was uninterested in finding formal equivalents between music and painting. The quality of music that he sought to emulate was not its logical structure, but the open-endedness and ambiguity of its meaning that afforded the listener a rich subjective experience: "The art of suggestion exists whole in the exciting art of music, and more freely and radiantly; but it is also mine by a combination of several elements brought together, of forms transposed, or transformed, without any relationship to contingencies, but having, nonetheless, a certain logic."[17] In an image by Redon, a few objects or parts of objects—e.g., a severed head, a few flowers, a shell, the branch of a tree, a chalice—inhabit an ambiguous space. Their interaction is evocative, often charged, but unresolved.

Redon was one of many nineteenth-century artists drawn to the subject of Orpheus, the consummate musician of Greek myth who could charm wild beasts and move rocks and trees. Among the painters discussed here, both Delacroix and Corot devoted major works to the story of Orpheus. Unlike these earlier images, which portray recognizable narrative episodes, Redon's *Orpheus* pastel of c. 1898 (Figure 30.2) relates only loosely and ambiguously to the mythic tale. The musician's severed head and emblematic lyre float in the lower half of the image. A rising serrated contour above suggests a mountain, with a few flowers glowing against its darkened side. Almost nothing possesses weight or depth, in an image that conveys sensations of radiance, reflection, and levitation. The arrangement of pink, lavender, apricot, and oxblood colors certainly possesses "musicality," as Delacroix understood it a half-century earlier, a formal harmony that has an expressive impact apart from the subject depicted. But it is the haunting mystery of this story, and of music in general, to which Redon was especially drawn and which he powerfully expressed in the painting.

Notes

1 "Paganini," *L'Artiste* 3 (1832): 109, cited in Nina Athanassaglou-Kallmyer, "Delacroix, Paganini, and the Cholera Epidemic of 1832," *Art Bulletin* 83, no. 4 (2001): 700.

2 Arthur Loesser, *Men, Women, and Pianos: A Social History* (New York: Simon and Schuster, 1954), 386.

3 Letter from George Sand to Théophile Silvestre, January 5, 1853, in George Sand, *Correspondance*, ed. G. Lubin (Paris, 1976), 2: 534–535; cited in Barthélémy Jobert, *Delacroix* (Princeton, N.J.: Princeton University Press, 1997), 30.

4 See especially the entry for April 7, 1849, in *The Journal of Eugene Delacroix*, trans. Lucy Norton (London: Phaidon, 1951), 99–100.

5 Madame de Staël, *De L'Allemagne* (Paris, 1869), 407. This passage was repeated by Delacroix without acknowledgment of source in his essay "Réalisme et idéalisme," in Delacroix, *Oeuvres littéraires* (Paris: G. Crès, 1923), 1: 65–67.

6 Journal entry for January 26, 1824, in *The Journal of Eugene Delacroix*, 24.

7 Delacroix, *Oeuvres littéraires*, 1: 63, cited in Peter Vergo, *The Music of Painting* (London: Phaidon, 2010), 69.

8 Journal entry for January 13, 1857, in Delacroix, *Oeuvres littéraires*, 2: 138.

9 Paul Mantz, "Salon of 1863," *Gazette des Beaux-Arts* 15 (July 1863): 60–61.

10 "The Red Rag," in *The World*, May 22, 1878; cited in *Whistler on Art*, ed. Nigel Thorp (Washington, DC: Smithsonian Institution Press, 1994), 51–52.

11 Étienne Moreau-Nélaton, *Histoire de Corot et de ses oeuvres, d'après les documents recueillis par Alfred Robaut* (Paris: Floury, 1905), 201–2.

12 Vincent van Gogh, *The Complete Letters of Vincent van Gogh*, 3rd ed., 3 vols. (Boston: Bulfinch, 2000), L528, 3:21; L522, 3:10; L531, 3:25; W3, 3:431.

13 Ibid., L520, 3:6.

14 Letter of June 15, 1894 to Edmond Picard. This letter subsequently appeared in *L'Art moderne* (August 25, 1894), the periodical of the Belgian artists' association *Les Vingt*. The translation cited here is from John Rewald et al., *Odilon Redon, Gustave Moreau, and Rodolphe Bresdin* (New York: Museum of Modern Art, 1961), 9.

15 Odilon Redon, *To Myself: Notes on Life, Art and Artists*, trans. Mira Jacob and Jeanne L. Wasserman (New York: Braziller, 1986), 19.

16 Arï Redon, *Lettres de Gauguin, Gide, Huysmans, Jammes, Mallarmé, Verhaeren ... à Odilon Redon* (Paris: José Corti, 1960), 25.

17 Redon, *To Myself*, 22.

Further Reading

Blanc, Charles. *The Grammar of Painting and Engraving*. Translated by Kate Newell. New York: Hurd and Houghton, 1874.

Delacroix, Eugene. *The Journal of Eugene Delacroix*. Translated by Lucy Norton. London: Phaidon, 1995.

Morton, Marsha L. and Peter L. Schmunk, eds. *The Arts Entwined: Music and Painting in the Nineteenth Century*. New York: Garland, 2000.

Redon, Odilon. *To Myself: Notes on Life, Art, and Artists*. Translated by Mira Jacob and Jeanne L. Wasserman. New York: Braziller, 1986.

Schmunk, Peter L. "Music and the Art of Corot." *Southeast College Art Conference Review* 13, no. 4 (1999): 354–63.

Van Gogh, Vincent. *The Complete Letters of Vincent van Gogh*. 3rd ed., 3 vols. Boston: Bulfinch, 2000.

Vergo, Peter. *The Music of Painting: Music, Modernism, and the Visual Arts from the Romantics to John Cage*. London: Phaidon, 2010.

Whistler, James McNeill. *Whistler on Art*. Edited by Nigel Thorp. Washington, DC: Smithsonian Institution Press, 1994.

31

MUSICAL SPACES

The Politics of Space in Renaissance Italy

Tim Shephard

The concept of "space" has received close attention across several disciplines during the last few decades, perhaps because it offers an attractive way to describe the relationship between activities and the environments in which they take place. As a concept, it has been amply and usefully theorized. In his classic study of what he called *The Production of Space*, Henri Lefebvre argued that space is not a neutral setting for social activities, but is itself socially produced—both literally, in the sense of planning, and imaginatively, in the sense of the way we conceive of and act in our surroundings. As W. J. T. Mitchell points out in his preface to the second edition of the influential anthology *Landscape and Power*, within this discourse it is normal to distinguish between "space" and "place": for Mitchell, space should be understood as a flexible and various set of dimensions describing the ways in which we experience and value a location; while place indicates simply the location itself. This amounts to a distinction between a site or location that is taken to be physical and neutral in character (place), and an imaginative conception of that location that imbues it with varied meanings, directing our lived experience of it (space). While there is clearly more than one way to construct the distinction between place and space—indeed, within geography the words' meanings are almost exactly reversed—the view described by Mitchell works well as a tool of analysis.

The account of space offered by Lefebvre sets up a generative relationship between what people do and the environments in which they do it: the activities produce the space. This generative function has in turn been subjected to further theorization at the hands of Michel de Certeau, whose book *The Practice of Everyday Life* has informed much subsequent discussion of space. De Certeau describes the ways in which people "spatialize" (i.e. experience and make meaning out of) the places and objects available to them, calling this "practicing." In his own words, de Certeau's "practicing" means "ways of operating," or "schemata of action" in everyday life.[1] De Certeau's term rather neatly encapsulates the range of imaginative and physical activities that constitute the "producing" of space, and helps us to tease out the questions of agency and action involved. Thus, in Mitchell's formulation, "a space is a 'practiced place,' a site activated by movements, actions, narratives and signs."[2]

Seen in these terms, the concept of space becomes an extremely useful tool for thinking about the coordination of activities across different media. Both musicking (Christopher Small's very useful term) and image-making can be seen as spatializing practices, numbering among the "movements, actions, narratives and signs" mentioned by Mitchell. Musical and visual cultures can therefore be studied as mechanisms for giving meaning to places, or "producing spaces." Their effects in this regard are inevitably experienced in combination, and this is in itself justification for studying them together. However, the discourse on space has always acknowledged that its production frequently falls within the scope of hegemonic control and can be the subject of planning and design, so that the arts can sometimes be deployed purposefully in coordination to inscribe particular meanings upon a site. In such cases, the study of both music and image together is not only justifiable but essential.

The architectural theorists of Renaissance Italy dealt with space in a strikingly similar manner. For them, a location took on meaning through a combination of architectural design, use, and decoration. In the writings of Leon Battista Alberti and Filarete, for example, the role of decoration in the production of space is given a particular priority: in describing the decorations of an ideal city, Filarete prescribes good judges for the walls of the hall of the chief magistrate; wise counselors of Rome in the hall of the Palazzo del Commune; the inventors of the arts in the guildhall; and Venus and Priapus above the entrance to the brothel. These prescriptions were made with a view to controlling the decorum of space—that is, to directing the ways in which people assigned meanings to locations in their day-to-day activities. As a means of control, such decorations relied on a theory of emulation that underlay much didactic activity in Renaissance Italy: it was widely acknowledged that people would imitate the models of behavior placed before them. In the words of Paolo Cortesi, writing on the ideal palace around 1500, painted decoration should feature "the lessons of history brought to life. For [by the sight of these paintings] either the appetite of the soul is aroused or the capacity for motion ... may be prompted by the striking life-like imitation, in the painting, of the thing represented."[3]

These Renaissance sources propose that a site can be pre-emptively "spatialized" by designing it in a way that will influence and direct the spatializing activities that people subsequently pursue within it. In de Certeau's terms, the "tactical" (i.e., bottom-up) practicing of place can be shaped in advance by "strategic" (i.e., top-down) planning and administration. This technique ensures that a site will be spatialized in the most appropriate and useful way—or rather, in a manner that fits closely with relevant contemporary ideals. For instance, the example of the Roman senators will ensure that the city counselors meeting in the Palazzo del Commune conduct their business in a wise and dignified fashion, according to a set of civic ideals modeled on those of ancient Rome. In the case of a city that is subject to a single ruler, Renaissance theorists are perfectly open to the implication that the design and production of space lies, in the first instance, within the power of the prince alone, so that the ideal ducal city can be seen as a multimedia installation authored by the prince according to a more or less coherent program. This is precisely the conceit underlying Filarete's *Treatise on Architecture* of c. 1464, in which a duke directs every aspect of the building and decoration of a new city.

The clearest real-life examples of this kind of princely authorship of space can be found in the building, decoration, and use of the spaces of the palace. Here we encounter numerous examples of the coordinated deployment of music and art to create spaces that serve the ends of the ruler, shaping the lived experience of his associates and subjects. Among the most charged spaces of the palace, and one of the most obviously musical, was the court chapel, a space notionally designed for the ruler's private observance but in practice often built with a much wider range of users in view. Contemporary political philosophy required of a prince that he gain a reputation for elaborate piety, as one among a number of virtues that should provoke feelings of love and awe in his subjects. Most of the various petty despots of Renaissance Italy paid at least some attention to this injunction, and none more so than Ercole I d'Este, Duke of Ferrara 1471–1505.

At the very beginning of Ercole's reign, an image of the Virgin Mary posted on the wall in an alley near his stables began to work miracles. It quickly became the object of a popular cult. Ercole immediately adopted the image, clearing the area around it to erect a temporary open-air church where Mass was sung by his choir every Saturday in the presence of a large crowd. This move constitutes an interesting and potent institutionalization of what had previously been a marginal space. The cultic spatializing practices associated with the image would in themselves have encoded the alley with ecclesiastical, or at least devotional, significance; Ercole's actions served to hijack those practices by reframing them, through a combination of musical and visual means, as a formalized observance contingent upon his sponsorship.

Ercole's adoption of this image soon took a more elaborate turn. He built a new court chapel, larger and more publicly accessible than the existing ones in his palace, and moved the image into it, together with its sung Saturday Mass and its popular cult, by means of a splendid procession attended by the entire city. In this form, his court chapel acted as a kind of interface between his palace and his subjects, using their desire to venerate the image of the Virgin to draw them within the ambit of his sponsorship, and into a space redolent of his piety. These actions prompted one of Ercole's courtiers to write a detailed account of the whole affair, in which the chapel is described as a composite of visual and aural elements—including, of course, the cult image, the ancona into which it was incorporated, and the choir of twenty who sang Mass in its honor—all of which combine to produce a space evidencing the laudable magnificence of Ercole's piety.

Another palace location that was almost always the subject of fascinating spatializing practices involving music and image was a room referred to in modern scholarship as the *studiolo*. The studiolo was, notionally at least, a study-room in which the prince could engage in studious and literary recreation. According to contemporary political philosophy, in addition to being pious, the prince should be well-educated and cultured, with sufficient expertise in the arts to exhibit good taste and judgment. Music-making enjoyed an important place within this scheme: it was viewed by many as an admirable and relaxing pastime, and was considered to be allied to literary pursuits via lyric poetry. The studiolo was intended to facilitate, and of course to evidence, the prince's efforts in these veins. Studiolo decoration therefore usually made reference to the Muses, as symbols of poetry and music, and the Liberal Arts, as symbols of learning.

Princely studioli present a more literal coordination of the musical and the visual than we found in the court chapel, in the sense that their visual decorations almost always featured music prominently—in the guise of notation, instruments or music-making. In my research I have argued that in some cases these representations of music were meant to encode into the space particular ways of interpreting the ruler's real musical pastimes, which were very likely among the activities characteristically pursued in studioli. The privileged courtiers and guests who were granted access to this relatively private part of the palace would have watched the ruler displaying his accomplishments on the lute or viol, surrounded by images that suggested particular ways of understanding the significance of music-making. In this scenario, the prince has an unusual degree of control over the spatializing of the studiolo location, controlling both the design of the space and the activities taking place within it.

A famous example, and one in which the combination of music and image is particularly straightforward, is the two studioli made in the 1470s for Federico da Montefeltro, duke of the small state of Urbino. Federico's fame derived from his immense success as a mercenary commander, a popular career among Italian nobles at that time; however, he had received a humanist education and was also renowned for his scholarly and literary interests. His studioli featured wainscoting stretching from the floor to around head height decorated using a wood-inlay technique called *intarsia*, above which were paintings. The intarsia in both rooms simulated the appearance of cupboards hanging open, within which were visible various objects related to the study of the primary scholarly curricula of the age: the Liberal Arts (grammar, logic, rhetoric, arithmetic, geometry, music, and astronomy) and the *studia humanitatis* (i.e., in essence, the humanities). We find the armillary sphere and astrolabe of Astronomy or Urania; the dividers, set square, and plumb bob of Geometry; any number of books that might be associated with either Rhetoric or Grammar; and a large collection of musical instruments and even notated music.

The number and range of musical objects is in fact quite astonishing. In the intarsie of the studiolo in Federico's palace in the town of Gubbio, near Urbino, there are percussion instruments, including a tabor and a tambourine; stringed instruments, including two lutes, a cittern, a harp, a rebec, and a fiddle; wind instruments, including two cornettos, a horn, and a pipe; and a portative organ. In his studiolo in the palace in Urbino, meanwhile, several songs are also to be found, with legible text and musical notation. The equipment lies about as if caught up in an ongoing process of regular use. These musical elements may be connected with the Muses, who are also invoked by other aspects of the decoration; but they likewise pertain to the Liberal Art *Musica*, who appeared as part of a series of paintings of the seven Liberal Arts above the intarsia in the Gubbio studiolo. (Music owed its place among the Liberal Arts to the Pythagorean mathematics of consonance, which connected music with astronomy via the notion of the "harmony of the spheres.")

In this case, although we know that Federico did keep musical instruments in his palaces, it is not clear whether we should envision him pursuing musical pastimes in these rooms. The fictive cupboards and their contents create an illusion of studious recreation: if the duke actually made regular use of the objects depicted, such an illusion would be superfluous. Rather, the decoration was primarily intended to convey messages about Federico's character to the favorites and visitors who were afforded the honor of meeting with him in this room. One of those messages was that the duke was knowledgeable in the field of music. In fact, music was the chosen medium for a concise statement of the overall message to be found in the Urbino studiolo: a song depicted in intarsia sets the words "Bella gerit musasque colit Federicus omnium maximus Italicorum Dux foris atque domi" (Federico, the greatest leader of all Italians, outdoors and at home, he fights wars and cultivates the Muses). Federico here claims that the contemporary ideal according to which a prince should balance the active life (*vita activa*) and the contemplative life (*vita contemplativa*) is realized in his person.

A rather different case is presented by the studiolo of Alfonso I d'Este, son of the Ercole mentioned above and successor to his duchy of Ferrara. Alfonso was also a military man, a famous expert in artillery, and in his youth had been reputed dissolute; but he also pursued practical interests in the arts, throwing pots, turning wood at a lathe, and playing several different musical instruments. His studiolo formed part of a new apartment within his palace complex constructed and decorated during the 1510s and 1520s. Alfonso had his studiolo decorated with paintings depicting bucolic and pastoral scenes from classical literature featuring Bacchus and Venus, divinities with particularly sensual associations. Bacchus was also closely associated with music, and several of the paintings featured scenes of music, feasting, dancing, and general frivolity in the countryside. We know that traditionally the Este had taken a particular pleasure in their country estates, where they regularly enjoyed those same diversions; during his reign Alfonso built two new country villas, and he kept musical instruments in at least one of them. At the Italian courts in the early sixteenth century, it was extremely fashionable to think of the countryside and its recreational possibilities in terms of the bucolic and pastoral strains of classical literature (in particular Virgil and Ovid), which featured rustic gods, shepherds, satyrs, and nymphs in amorous entanglements and, importantly, in musical recreation. Perhaps, then, the paintings made for Alfonso's studiolo draw just such a classicizing veil over the entertainments he actually enjoyed at his country estates.

This circumstance suggests that the room may have been used for musical recreation; but it also gives us clues as to how Alfonso thought about and experienced his musical recreation when he pursued it at his villas, in particular the relationship between music and the rural landscape. Another, very similar clue takes the shape of a song written at Alfonso's court at exactly the time when the studiolo decoration was taking shape. Adrian Willaert's "Quid non ebrietas" sets a portion of Horace's fifth epistle, in which the themes of nature, feasting, and wine are reprised. The text locates us in the context of Roman senatorial leisure, a model to which Italian nobles and literati frequently looked when designing their own recreations. In high summer, Horace invites a friend to dinner at sunset, entices him with the promise of wine, and reminds him that the following day is a holiday. He continues, "I shall begin the drinking and the scattering of flowers, and shall suffer you, if you will, to think me reckless"; then follow the lines set by Willaert:

> What a miracle cannot the wine-cup work! It unlocks secrets, bids hopes be fulfilled, thrusts the coward into the field, takes the load from anxious hearts, teaches new arts. The flowing bowl—whom has it not made eloquent?[4]

This song resonates so fundamentally with the bucolic vision of leisured music-making depicted in the studiolo decoration that in a very real sense it belongs in the room. It provides a good example of the way in which a patron could propagate a reflection of meaning between visual and musical elements in order to design particular meanings into a space, thus shaping any subsequent spatializing practices pursued therein.

"Quid non ebrietas" resonates most obviously with one of Titian's paintings for the room, the *Bacchanal of the Andrians*, depicting the inhabitants of the island of Andros enjoying a Bacchic festival. In the foreground of this painting, almost falling into a stream of wine, is a scrap of paper on which appears a single line of music, preceded by the word "Canon," which indicates that a puzzle must be solved in order to sing the song successfully. The only text given to explain the canon is the text of the song, which reads "Qui boyt et ne reboyt, il ne scet que boyre soit" (Who drinks and does not drink again, he knows not what drinking is). Trial and error shows that the single line of music can be realized as an ever-repeating canon in four voices, with any number of the voices reading the song the right way up (as it appears to the Andrians in the painting), and any number reading it upside down (as it appears to the viewer)—but only if each voice moves up a single scale degree upon each repeat. The text taunts the baffled viewer who cannot divine this last instruction: he who does not drink again (i.e., repeat the song) is ignorant of drinking.

"Qui boyt" can be read as extending a degree of control over the day-to-day activities pursued in the room on Alfonso's behalf, somewhat in the manner of Federico's "Bella gerit" discussed above. Titian's *Andrians* realizes a passage from the *Imagines* of the late-antique Greek writer Philostratus, in which the festive scene is described through the conceit of a song sung by the Andrian men. It seems obvious that "Qui boyt" is intended to recall this framing device, and it is therefore only in singing it that the viewer completes the conceit of the painting, and understands its meaning. Any visitors invited to sing the song, however, would find themselves forced to ask Alfonso for the resolution of its puzzle canon. Once it is resolved, in singing the song the viewer finds himself interpolated into Alfonso's picture as one of the Andrian men. Through this mechanism, the *Andrians* makes explicit the capacity of visual decoration and music collaboratively to control the meanings encoded into a space by inflecting the activities pursued within it.

These various examples serve to indicate a range of questions and circumstances within the study of music and visual culture that the concept of space can help us to address. My own research has focused in particular on the roles played by musical and visual practices in producing the spaces of the Renaissance palace, to a large extent within the control of a single patron. The force and utility of "space" in this context derives, paradoxically, from the extent to which it deflects attention away from music and art, configuring them not as ends in themselves but as means deployed in coordination toward the end of producing space. The musical and the visual form important, complementary components of the vocabulary through which spaces are assembled as texts to be "read" and experienced. I have found this perspective to be a useful alternative to attempts to enfold music and art, as essentialized traditions, into a single aesthetic system comprehensible only on the level of philosophy and metaphor. Through space and its theoretical frameworks, the combined study of musical and visual cultures can engage meaningfully with the lived realities in which those cultures are implicated.

Notes

1 Michel de Certeau, *The Practice of Everyday Life*, trans. Steven Rendall (Berkeley: University of California Press, 1984), xi.

2 W. J. T. Mitchell, "Preface to the Second Edition of *Landscape and Power*: Space, Place and Land-scape," in *Landscape and Power*, 2nd rev. ed., ed. W. J. T. Mitchell (Chicago: University of Chicago Press, 2002), x.
3 This translation and the original Latin can be found in Kathleen Weil-Garris and John F. d'Amico, "The Renaissance Cardinal's Ideal Palace: A Chapter from Cortesi's *De cardinalatu*," in *Studies in Italian Art and Architecture, 15th through 18th centuries*, ed. Henry A. Millon (Rome: Edizioni dell'Elefante, 1980), 45–123, at 90–91.
4 I.v.16–19, quoted in the Loeb translation by H. Rushton Fairclough.

Further Reading

Certeau, Michel de. *The Practice of Everyday Life*. Translated by Steven Rendall. Berkeley: University of California Press, 1984.

Dennis, Flora. "Sound and Domestic Space in Fifteenth- and Sixteenth-Century Italy." *Studies in the Decorative Arts* 16, no. 1 (2008–9): 7–19.

Gerbino, Giuseppe. *Music and the Myth of Arcadia in Renaissance Italy*. Cambridge: Cambridge University Press, 2009.

Howard, Deborah and Laura Moretti, eds. *The Music Room in Early Modern France and Italy: Sound, Space and Object*. Oxford: Oxford University Press, 2012.

Krims, Adam. "Music, Space, and Place: The Geography of Music." In *The Cultural Study of Music: A Critical Introduction*, 2nd ed., edited by Martin Clayton, Trevor Herbert, and Richard Middleton, 140–148. New York: Routledge, 2012.

Lefebvre, Henri. *The Production of Space*. Translated by D. Nicholson-Smith. Oxford: Blackwell, 1991.

Mitchell, W. J. T. "Preface to the Second Edition of *Landscape and Power*: Space, Place and Landscape." In *Landscape and Power*. 2nd rev. ed. Edited by W. J. T. Mitchell. Chicago: Chicago University Press, 2002.

Shephard, Tim. *Echoing Helicon: Music, Art and Identity in the Este Studioli*. Oxford: Oxford University Press, forthcoming.

Welch, Evelyn. "Sight, Sound and Ceremony in the Chapel of Galeazzo Maria Sforza." *Early Music History* 12 (1993): 151–190.

32

BUILT ARCHITECTURE FOR MUSIC

Spaces for Chamber Music in Sixteenth-Century Italy

Laura Moretti

In the course of the sixteenth century, secular music flourished in Italy as never before. The musical forms which developed in this period included *canti carnascialeschi*, the *villanella*, and the *balletto*. In elite circles the dominant type of composition was the madrigal, which emerged from a particular Italian literary culture and became a vehicle for remarkable linguistic and expressive inventions. Alongside the classic madrigal, the *madrigale rappresentativo* developed as a series of narrative compositions with humorous or popular themes. Meanwhile, the performance of purely instrumental music developed in all the courts of Italy, encouraging the invention of new kinds of instruments and the refinement of the technical aspects of existing ones.

The introduction of music printing favored the development and diffusion of secular music. The first printing press to use movable type for music was that of Ottaviano Petrucci da Fossombrone (1466–1539) in Venice. From Petrucci's press numerous volumes of secular music were to appear. Music publishing developed rapidly during the Cinquecento: among the other celebrated exponents were Andrea Antico (1470/80–post 1539), active in Rome and Venice and Petrucci's main rival; and Antonio Gardano (1508/09–1569) and Girolamo Scotto (d. 1572), both of the latter belonging to famous families of printers in Venice.

The main centers of secular music in Renaissance Italy were, above all, Venice and Rome, but others of importance included Milan, Mantua, Modena, Ferrara, Bologna, Florence, Naples, and Palermo. In particular, the princely courts of the Medici, Farnese, Gonzaga, Este, and Sforza developed as major centers of musical performance commemorated in numerous sources, both literary and visual. Another important source of patronage evolved in the academies, such as the Accademia "Platonica" in Florence, the Accademia degli "Intronati" in Siena, the Accademia degli "Incatenati" in Verona, the Accademia degli "Invaghiti" in Mantova, the

Accademia dei "Concordi" in Ferrara, the Accademia di Santa Cecilia in Rome, and the "Camerata fiorentina."

The principal venues for the execution of the secular genres described above were the princely courts, but villas and palaces of other elite families also became important. All over Italy non-noble households also commissioned music to accompany family celebrations, as well as for personal enjoyment.

In his *L'Antica musica ridotta alla moderna prattica* (Rome, 1555), Nicola Vicentino makes a clear distinction between chamber, church, and folk music. This source has been recognized as one of the first in which the term "chamber music" (*musica da camera*) is explicitly mentioned. The performance of music in rooms of quite small size, mainly in private houses, before an audience of limited size, was a common practice in Italy in the mid-sixteenth century, and even before. The performers could be the hosts in the company of friends, or professional musicians recruited for the occasion. One of the most important elements in chamber music is in fact the social dimension: the pleasure of making music in a domestic or semi-public environment with friends and relatives. This practice maintained its salient characteristics also in the wealthy Italian Renaissance courts, where salaried musicians—often retained on a permanent basis—were more common. This musical practice is portrayed in visual sources, which can help to convey the idea of the setting. One of the most famous is Lodovico Pozzoserrato's *Concerto in Villa*, now in Treviso, Museo Civico, which shows a small group of instrumentalists and singers playing together in a domestic context (Figure 32.1).

Many of those who commissioned musical compositions were also major patrons of architecture. The rapid development of more complex social rituals among elite families brought a demand not only for sophisticated entertainments such as musical activities, but also for a more complex and refined arrangement of domestic space. Although specific precedents in antiquity were unknown, the general ambition to live *all'antica* encouraged responses to various passages in Vitruvius, as Sebastiano Serlio indicates, in order to articulate specific settings for cultural events. Architectural responses are to be found across a broad social spectrum, from the dwellings of princes and cardinals down to the houses of merchants, educated professionals, and artisans. The new patronage comprised a wide range of individuals of broad cultural ambitions, both literary and artistic (many were also collectors of antiquities), who were open to new ideas. Their involvement often extended to direct intervention in decisions concerning architectural design, iconography, and even decorative detail.

The great halls of palaces and villas were undoubtedly the main settings for ambitious musical performances, as Palladio himself affirmed in his *Quattro libri* (1570): "Halls are designed for parties, banquets, as the sets for acting out comedies, weddings, and similar entertainments, and so these spaces must be much larger than the others and must have a shape that will be as capacious as possible so that many people can gather in them comfortably and observe what is going on."[1]

In addition, we find references to music rooms—described as "studi di musica," "stanze de' suoni" or "della musica"—during the sixteenth century. From the room in Cipriano Moresini's villa described by Anton Francesco Doni, to the "stanza de' suoni" appearing in the inventory of Niccolò Gaddi's Florentine palace, these spaces, whose designated function was to house large numbers of instruments and books, are recorded in documentary sources, literary texts, and theoretical writings on architecture. Francesco Sansovino's inclusion in his *Venetia citta nobilissima et singolare* (Venice, 1581) of a chapter on "Studi di Musica" in his account of notable sights within private Venetian *palazzi* highlights how the accumulation of instruments might follow wider patterns of collecting by including supposedly "ancient" or exotic examples, or by suggesting an encyclopedic comprehensiveness. Sansovino mentions four examples of "Studi di Musica" in Venice, located in the houses of Cavalier Sanudo at San Giovanni Decollato; of Catarino Zeno at the Crociferi, where an organ with four rows of pipes built in 1494 by Lorenzo da Pavia was housed (still preserved at the Civico Museo Correr in Venice); of Luigi Balbi at Santa Maria del Giglio; and of Agostino Amadi, probably at Santa Croce. These rooms housed notable collections of musical instruments and books, and in Sansovino's opinion were the most noteworthy examples among many others. Ippolito Baccusi, in the dedicatory letter of his first book of motets entitled *Motectorum cum quinque, sex et octo vocibus* (Venice, 1579), mentions Balbi's collections of instruments and states that in this house there were frequent gatherings of people for musical performances.

Often the owners of renowned collections of instruments were musicians themselves. In their houses it was quite common to find dedicated rooms for the storage of musical instruments and/or for musical performances. Marco Mantova Benavides, who owned a huge collection of instruments, is the dedicatee of the *Intabulatura di lauto libro sesto* by Melchiorre Barberiis, who, in the dedicatory letter, praises Benavides as a talented performer. The room in which the collection was kept no longer exists, but in 1624 it is recorded to be in the courtyard of his Paduan residence, to be quite large ("gran camerone ornatissimo"), to house a huge collection of musical instruments—including an organ, harpsichords, and viols—and to host musical performances by Paduan musicians.

Rooms where performances of music took place were frequently also called "ridotti," and, although located in private dwellings, they presented a semi-public character. The ridotto of Mario Bevilacqua in Verona was very famous. It was located on the ground floor of his palace, designed by the architect Michele Sanmicheli around 1530. Here, every day it was possible to hear musical performances, as attested by contemporary sources. Don Pietro Ponzio da Parma dedicated his *Ragionamento di Musica* (1588) to Bevilacqua, setting it in his ridotto. As Ponzio writes in the dedication, in Bevilacqua's house "di continuo risuona l'armonia" (harmony resonates all the time). The palace also housed collections of paintings and sculpture and a huge collection of musical instruments, which—from an inventory dated 1593—we know comprised seventy-seven items. Musical performances took place every Thursday, and drew a vast audience. The performers included salaried musicians, but also talented amateurs. Many works published in the fourth quarter of the sixteenth century are dedicated to Bevilacqua, and from the dedicatory letters it is possible to delineate a clear picture of his musical interests and the cultural climate in which he lived and operated.

During the sixteenth century, an interest in the acoustical characteristics of spaces specifically designed for the performance of music in private contexts gradually developed. Paolo Cortesi, in his *De Cardinalatu* (1510), mentions music rooms ("cubiculum musicae" in the singular) when describing the ideal cardinal's palace, stressing the need for good acoustics: "The music rooms have been given a round vaulted ceiling lest the voice wander or be lost. And hence we read that bronze vases or earthenware jars are often put into niches [*cellae*] in the walls of the music room. This is done for the sake of music, so that sound coming from the middle of the room strikes against the empty vessels, making both singing and playing sound much sweeter."[2]

In the first half of the sixteenth century the well-known patron of art and literature Alvise Cornaro (c. 1482–1566) built in his house in Padua a vaulted octagonal room with niches, the so-called "Odeo Cornaro." This room was drawn by Sebastiano Serlio in book VII of his treatise, published in Frankfurt in 1575 and then in Venice in 1584 with the title *Delle habitationi di tutti li gradi di homini* (Figures 32.2 and 32.3), and we know that it was used for learned conversations and musical performances. According to Serlio, the particular design of this room offered special acoustic qualities. What is especially interesting is Serlio's description of the building's architectural design, which offers important evidence regarding its intended use: "I remembered having seen in Padua in Italy at the house of Messer Luigi [i.e. Alvise] Cornaro, an apartment at the entrance to the courtyard facing the beautiful loggia—an apartment which that noble gentleman had built as a place for music since he took pleasure in all the noble arts and all the exalted virtues, and especially in architecture [...] Here musicians are to play—this is very suitable since the form is one which tends towards the circular, and the *salotto* is completely vaulted with brick, a material which has no humidity in it whatsoever. And the four niches, through their concave rotundity, receive the notes and hold them."[3]

Serlio's testimony clearly establishes two crucial points: first, that the Odeo Cornaro was used for music, and second, that performances took place in the central *sala*. The excellent acoustic qualities of this room are described in several documents written not long after its construction. For example, in a letter dated 8 February 1562, Mario Savorgnan, the well-known military strategist, wrote to Alvise Cornaro: "What can I say of the marvels of your house and gardens? Through these, with your skill you teach others to live in equally healthy and pleasant surroundings, to escape the harmful extremes of the seasons and to create for themselves a temperate climate and perpetual springtime, and finally a Paradise filled with angels from the entire celestial hierarchy, with such consonance and harmony that one could not hope to hear a sweeter, more gentle voice except in heaven; even when music is not played well here it sounds excellent and the consonances better, the voices harmonizing together with marvelous intonation."[4] Considering its other noteworthy characteristics—the scholarly reference to antique precedents, the elaborate interior decoration, the place of the Odeo in the overall complex of the Paduan patron, and not least its selection by Serlio for inclusion in his treatise—we can easily grasp the crucial role of music in this context.

Notes

1 Book I, Chap. XXI. Translation from Andrea Palladio, *The Four Books on Architecture*, ed. Robert Tavernor and Richard Schofield (Cambridge, MA: MIT Press, 1997), 57. For the original Italian see Andrea Palladio, *I Quattro Libri dell'Architettura* (Venice: De' Franceschi, 1570), 52.

2 Quoted in Flora Dennis, "When is a Room a Music Room? Sounds, Spaces, and Objects in Non-courtly Italian Interiors," in *The Music Room in Early Modern France and Italy*, ed. Deborah Howard and Laura Moretti (Oxford: Oxford University Press, 2012), 39.

3 Sebastiano Serlio, *Sebastiano Serlio on Architecture*, 2 vols., ed. Vaughan Hart and Peter Hicks (New Haven: Yale University Press, 1996–2001), 2: 364. For the original Italian, see Sebastiano Serlio, *Il settimo libro d'Architettura* […] (Frankfurt, 1575), 218.

4 Quoted in Laura Moretti, "The Function and Use of Musical Sources at the Paduan 'Court' of Alvise Cornaro in the First Half of the Cinquecento," *Journal of the Alamire Foundation* 1 (2010); 44. For the original Italian, see Emilio Lippi, *Cornariana: studi su Alvise Cornaro* (Padua: Editrice Antenore, 1983), 170–171.

Further Reading

Baron, John H. *Intimate Music: A History of the Idea of Chamber Music*. Stuyvesant, NY: Pendragon Press, 1998.

Dennis, Flora. "Music." In *At Home in Renaissance Italy*, edited by Marta Ajmar-Wollheim and Flora Dennis, 228–243. Exhibition catalogue. London: Victoria & Albert Museum, 2006.

——. "When is a Room a Music Room? Sounds, Spaces, and Objects in Non-courtly Italian Interiors." In *The Music Room in Early Modern France and Italy*, edited by Deborah Howard and Laura Moretti, 37–49. Oxford: Oxford University Press, 2012.

Feldman, Martha. *City Culture and the Madrigal at Venice*. Berkeley: University of California Press, 1995.

Howard, Deborah, and Laura Moretti, eds. *The Music Room in Early Modern France and Italy: Sound, Space and Object*. Oxford: Oxford University Press, 2012.

Moretti, Laura. "The Function and Use of Musical Sources at the Paduan 'Court' of Alvise Cornaro in the First Half of the Cinquecento." *Journal of the Alamire Foundation* 1 (2010): 47–61.

Schiltz, Katelijne. "Church and Chamber: The Influence of Acoustics on Musical Composition and Performance." *Early Music* 31, no. 1 (2003): 64–78.

33

URBAN SOUNDSCAPES

Hearing and Seeing Jerusalem

Abigail Wood

How might attention to the urban soundscape inflect our visual understanding of city space?[1] In recent years, a sub-discipline of "sound studies" or "sonic anthropology" has generated lively scholarly activity among both ethnomusicologists and anthropologists. Pioneering the field, Murray Schafer's 1977 volume *The Soundscape: our sonic environment and the tuning of the world* both introduced the term "soundscape" into popular use and staked out some of the contributions that close attention to sound might make to our understanding of the natural and urban environment. Schafer calls for heightened attention to the sounds around us, proposing exercises of "ear cleaning" to help students to pay attention to, and to document, the sonic environment. Since Schafer's book, and especially during the decade since 2003, academic work focusing on sound has flourished, addressing the relative absence of the acoustic environment both from the visually dominated field of anthropology and also from an ethnomusicology which has traditionally been concerned only with that subset of sounds labeled "music."

Scholarly approaches to the urban sound environment have been particularly inflected by anxieties about increasing noisiness as a consequence of modernity. In his introduction, Schafer cautions his reader about "the dangers of an indiscriminate and imperialistic spread of more and larger sounds into every corner of man's life"; his negative view of industrial and electronic noise, and romantic nostalgia for a quieter time, are widely echoed by later scholars.[2] Noise is frequently perceived to be a negative effect of urban life, the sonic detritus of a dehumanized industrial, high-capitalist society, to which individuals are subjected as they go about their everyday lives. Rowland Atkinson considers the role of sound in urban place-making, suggesting that "urban sound, even its complexity, has a tendency for repetition and spatial order which, while not fixed, also displays a patterning and persistence, even as these constellations and overlapping ambient fields collide and fade in occasionally unpredictable, multiple or purposeful ways."[3] He frames urban noise as largely hostile or unwanted, able to penetrate private living spaces or act as a medium of control over public and interstitial spaces. This perspective is also reflected in Philip Glass's soundtrack to Godfrey Reggio's iconic film *Koyaanisqatsi* (1982), in which images of natural landscapes accompanied by open, diatonic intervals are counterposed with shots of urban industrialization, decay, and demolition accompanied by frenetic, jagged, dissonant sounds.

The role of recorded sound in shaping the urban acoustic experience has also been addressed by several scholars. Tong Soon Lee documents the shift of the Islamic call to prayer in Singapore from loudspeaker to radio, reflecting changes in urban living and the atomization of previously geographically coherent communities. The loudspeakers of the visually iconic minaret—first turned outwards, then inwards, owing to city noise laws—are counterposed with the disembodied "invisible" voice conveyed by radio waves, marking a rupture in habits of communal living. Jonathan Sterne turns to urban commercial spaces; focusing on the Mall of America in Bloomington, Minnesota, he discusses the ubiquitous presence of programmed recorded music, most famously sold as a commodity by the Muzak Corporation. Sterne suggests that such music is experienced in a way that passes "in and out of the foreground of a listener's consciousness" as it colors spaces, shapes flows of movement through the mall, and seeks to engender affective responses from consumers.[4] By contrast, Charles Hirshkind and Michael Bull consider more intimate listening experiences, focusing on, respectively, the "ethical soundscape" of Islamic sermon tapes and the use of personal MP3 players. Others, including Ruth Finnegan and Tia DeNora, have documented urban musical practices as social phenomena. Both authors describe music as a technology of the self; Finnegan via participation in amateur musical activities, and DeNora through individual listening practices.

The use of the term "soundscape"—derived from "landscape," itself originally a term from the visual arts—and the focus on space, place, topography, and concern for visible and invisible sound sources hinted at in the studies mentioned above all point to a close relationship between sonic and visual approaches to the study of city life. Yet, given this convergence, it is remarkable that the specific relationship between urban sound and visual culture remains less explored. Two reasons go some way toward explaining this omission. First, sound studies has been explicitly conceived by many of its protagonists as a counter to the historical domination of the visual in anthropology; conversely, ethnomusicologists come to the study of the senses with a de facto focus on auditory material. Second, and perhaps more influentially, auditory and visual experiences have often been presented as polar opposites, embodying fundamentally different modes of perceiving the world with the ability to afford radically different insights.

A prominent protagonist of the latter view is Jacques Attali. "For twenty-five centuries," he writes, "Western knowledge has tried to look upon the world. It has failed to understand that the world is not for the beholding. It is for hearing. It is not legible, but audible. Our science has always desired to monitor, measure, abstract, and castrate meaning, forgetting that life is full of noise and that death alone is silent: work noise, noise of man, and noise of beast. Nothing essential happens in the absence of noise."[5] Attali's polarized juxtaposition of vision and hearing, suggesting that the ear can offer different and perhaps "truer" insights into ideological and political processes, is echoed in London-based sound artist and researcher Peter Cusack's recordings of Chernobyl, which deliberately counterpose the well-known photographs of industrial disaster and bare, ravaged land with the sounds of the choruses of nightingales and frogs who have proliferated in the exclusion zone in the absence of human inhabitants.

In recent years, however, these supposed inherent differences between vision and hearing have been analyzed and critiqued. Cautioning against the essentialization of sonic and visual experiences, Jonathan Sterne reproduces a "litany" of oft-supposed differences between hearing and seeing: "hearing is concerned with interiors, vision is concerned with surfaces, ... hearing tends towards subjectivity, vision tends towards objectivity; ... hearing is about affect, vision is about intellect; hearing is a primarily temporal sense, vision is a primarily spatial sense; hearing is a sense that immerses us in the world, vision is a sense that removes us from it."[6] Sterne asserts that this litany is steeped in ideological baggage, assuming that sound offers a less rational mode of apprehending the world than vision, and reproducing religious Christian dogma concerning the distinction between the letter and the spirit. Likewise, in an essay entitled "Edison's Teeth," Steven Connor suggests that the senses are not as easily separable as is frequently assumed.

In the remainder of this chapter, I probe the relationship between sound and vision in the urban environment via ethnographic material drawn from my own research on sounds in public spaces in Jerusalem. I consider the intervention of the urban soundscape in the experience of time, then space, two areas in which scholars in sound studies have frequently suggested that hearing might particularly enhance or challenge the understanding of the city that is afforded by visual stimuli. Finally, I consider places where the hearing and sight are more closely entangled, pointing to the need for a closer examination of the interrelationship between sound and visual stimuli in the urban environment.

Jerusalem provides a thought-provoking case study: it is difficult to imagine a city more visually iconic. From the golden cupola of the Dome of the Rock to the weather-beaten stones of the Western Wall, from the broad rotunda of the Church of the Holy Sepulcher to the city walls and alleyways, images of Jerusalem have captured the Western imagination for hundreds of years. The spaces of the walled Old City are very often mediated through pictures (photographs, postcards, maps, drawings) and through textual narratives, from psalms to poetry to newspaper clippings. Elevated in both Jewish and Christian thought as an icon of coherent urban space (the city built "at unity with itself" of Psalm 122 in the translation of the Book of Common Prayer; the "New Jerusalem" descending complete from Heaven in the New Testament book of Revelation), Jerusalem appears often in nineteenth-century Orientalist art, on the covers of academic books describing "the city," in news stories about Middle East unrest, and in colorful advertisements for travel to Israel and Palestine.

Echoing the trends discussed above, academic discussions of space and placehood in contemporary Jerusalem are likewise often dominated by visual imagery. Discourse frequently centers on narratives or maps, which tend to emphasize physical and other divisions between communities and privilege exclusive ownership. Each area is identified with one particular community or group: the Muslim quarter, the Christian quarter, the Jewish quarter, the Armenian quarter. However, despite the harsh and ever-present realities of conflict, this description is not sufficient to convey the ways that people actually use the spaces of the Old City, which frustrate such straightforward mapping. Sitting in one spot, one might observe, in succession, groups of Armenian priests, Western tourists, Palestinian shopkeepers, and ultraorthodox Jews occupying the same space, each bringing different sound worlds into play, which in turn change the character of the space and influence the interactions of others. Despite the line on the map dividing the Temple Mount and Western Wall plaza, one still hears the muezzin at the Western Wall, just as one hears church bells in shops, pilgrims on market streets, and so on. These sounds also remind us that the noises of the "archetypical" secular, post-industrial city spaces described by Schafer, Atkinson, and others are not the only kind of modern urban soundscape.

Sound and Urban Time

Perhaps the most commonly remarked property of sound, often contrasted to visual stimuli, is its temporal nature. The ecology of sound structures and textures time, as vividly illustrated by Steven Feld's 1991 audio CD *Voices in the Rainforest: A day in the life of the Kaluli people.* Feld's hour-long compilation of ambient field recordings condenses an archetypical daily flow of sound in the Bosavi region of Papua New Guinea, illustrating Kaluli designations of time, from "Real Morning" to "Inside Night." In Jerusalem's Old City, the temporal flow of the soundscape is dominated by the sounds of religious institutions, which articulate parallel, repeating cycles of time. The five daily Muslim calls to prayer, the siren announcing the Jewish Sabbath, and the cycles of Muslim and Jewish festivals—the Eid *takbīr* (festival prayer) echoing through the streets on Muslim holidays, the cannon announcing the end of the Ramadan fast, the *shofar* (ram's horn) marking the approach to the Jewish high holidays—follow the rising and setting of the sun and the lunar calendar, contrasting with the secular 24-hour clock. Even the church bells, based on clock time, expose competing structures of time, articulating the different patterns of prayer observed by the dozens of Christian denominations based at the shrines in Jerusalem.

Ears are attuned to specific frameworks of sound: as I wait to record a group of mainly South American Catholic pilgrims about to follow the Franciscans on their weekly procession along the Via Dolorosa, I am astounded that they ignore the loud sound of the call to prayer from the al Aqsa mosque, coming from a minaret just meters from where they sit. Sometimes the times marked by differences in sound are perhaps noted only by insiders: the quiet tread of bare feet and rubber shoes on a Jewish fast day, when leather shoes are proscribed by religious law; the stream of celebratory fireworks on the day that the results of the tawjīhi—the general secondary school examination in Jordan, the West Bank and Gaza—come out.

Yet the mixing of sounds emanating from visually and topographically distinct sources textures the experience of time. Sometimes, sounds cohabit in frayed proximity. At other times, the temporality conveyed in sounds is shared. I am invited for the traditional afternoon meal of the Jewish Sabbath with Esti, a religious Swiss-Israeli woman living in the Jewish Quarter. As family and guests chat before the meal, the *adhān* begins, the voice of the muezzin easily audible through the open windows. "Shkia!" (sunset) Esti announces, urging those present to prepare to eat: it is traditional to begin the meal by sunset. We sit down to a traditional European meal: chopped liver, meat and rice, apple cake with stewed plums; Esti and her son discuss the correspondence of the Muslim and Jewish prayer times: the muezzin, says Esti, also marks the time of full sunrise, the time preferred by Jewish sages for the morning prayer. As we speak, the cuckoo clock on Esti's door plays "Edelweiss" on the hour; outside her house a group of young Jews gather on the wide Cardo to sing together as the Sabbath draws to a close.

The temporality of sound is also reflected in the way it is experienced: while certain sound constellations are typical of particular places, the soundstream itself is ever changing. The story told by sounds as we hear them is incomplete and often ambiguous. Waiting for members of my research team to rejoin me during a late-night field trip, I write:

> It's 11.30pm and we are in the church of the Holy Sepulcher. I am dis-located, lost. I heard chanting and left the others to make a recording: I walked around and the sound of chanting continued—but I could never figure out where it was coming from. It's a confusing acoustic space. Lack of direction. New spaces open up. The chanting fades in and out. I hear one of my team members and jump up, but it's not her ... I walk around the church twice. Everywhere, Russian pilgrims with covered heads. Priests in black. Copts swinging incense by the shrine. Downstairs, people alone, draped over stones. The sound of footsteps squeaking on the stone. I walk everywhere twice, or at least I think I do ... but I don't find my team or the chanting monks.[7]

While I could replay the recording I made that evening, it is more difficult to recapture the indeterminacy of the moment: the impact of the sounds. The lack of information is also striking—in contrast to the framing of a photograph, which makes a clear distinction between the present and the absent, here there is no complete picture, and the visual and auditory images fail to match up.

Sound and Urban Space

Just as sounds convey information about time, they also reflect the physical spaces in which they are made. Beyond the reverberations of street architecture, sound can also reveal information about the physical environment beyond what is imme-diately visible.

In visual terms, inside and outside spaces are usually clearly defined. One is public and visible; the other is often hidden from view, and entrance may be restricted, marked by a threshold or doorway. Sound, however, does not respect such thresh-olds. Walking along a market in the Old City, I chance upon the doorway to a mosque nestled among shops that I have passed tens of times. I had never seen the inside space, but this time I hear it: sound spilling out of the doorway reveals the activities of an inside space. Likewise, sitting in the stone plaza outside the Holy Sepulcher church on a Sunday morning, I wait for an Armenian procession to leave the church. The monks are visually striking: they march two by two, wearing black pointed hoods, preceded by two *kawass* (ceremonial guards) in Ottoman garb and followed by seminary students wearing blue school blazers. As I wait, I watch Israeli policemen preparing for the procession, moving dawdling pilgrims and tourists out of the path. Yet I hear the procession before I see it—the regular beat of the steel-capped staffs of the kawass on the church's floor resounds in the reverberant stone space and echoes among the flagstones of the walled plaza, challenging the sharp architectural and visual delineation of interior and exterior spaces.

Interior sound spaces that are revealed on the streets do not have to be heard. Public noticeboards play an important part in street life in most urban spaces, advertising concerts, festivals, special offers, political events, and more. Via posters, musical events are performed to many more people than their immediate audience, announcing their presence in the city soundscape. In downtown West Jerusalem, I happen upon a bright orange poster advertising women-only dance and exercise classes. While, following Jewish religious codes of modesty, the dancing intentionally takes place behind closed doors, out of the sight of men, the poster brings this dancing into the narrative of the public sphere.

Sounds are also actively manipulated by street users to shape the immediate urban environment, from a group of teenage boys washing a car on the Via Dolorosa, from which pours loud Arabic pop music, to the ubiquitous practice of playing recordings of the Koran among Muslim shopkeepers, or a group of youths forming a spontaneous drumming circle in the Jewish Quarter's Hurva square. Particularly early in the morning, the sound of the Koran seeps through the street, at once creating a calm, slowed-down environment, and also marking personal space—the same sound that joins street users together into a shared acoustic environment also discourages extended conversation, maintaining personal space while each shopkeeper prepares for the day ahead. Here, we encounter a more material manifestation of visual and auditory difference: while changing the visual street environment is out of the reach of most, the ability to re-paint the street in sound is available to just about everyone, demonstrating an embodied awareness of the acoustic characteristics of urban spaces.

Hearing and Seeing: Urban Sonic and Visual Culture

The examples discussed above largely counterpose aural and visual cues: what can the urban soundscape tell us that we can't see? As discussed at the beginning of this chapter, one of the achievements of the recent burgeoning of "sound studies" has been the reinsertion of sound into the visually dominated anthropological gaze, at the same time dislodging the traditional disciplinary divide whereby music—the aural—is reserved as the specialist terrain of musicologists and ethnomusicologists. Yet auditory and visual experiences also inhabit a messier sphere of sensory experience. Even silent objects can be noisy: sound also creeps into the visual, symbolic and commercial ecology of the city. Musical instruments are artifacts as well as noise-makers: in a tourist storefront, a rabab and a stack of tambourines rub shoulders with a row of small hand drums in the style of the west African djembe, with the rather incongruous label "Jerusalem" colorfully painted on their bodies (Figure 33.1); nearby, glazed onto a ceramic plate, a colorful angel plays something that looks like a Middle Eastern oud; a tourist handles a long, curly ram's horn. Such objects, embodying the potential of both sight and sound, satisfy Western visitors' expectations of the East as well as revealing the global trading networks that sustain the city.

Photographs, too, cue auditory memory: visual and aural images intermingle, and sounds are reinserted into silent scenes. I look at a black-and-white photograph of a shepherd and his sheep on the Mount of Olives with Hagop, a Jerusalem Armenian whose father was a renowned photographer. "Look how quiet it is," he observes. "No cars, no horns, nothing." When I point out the animals in a photograph of the Old City streets, he says "No tractors"—the loud sound of the tractors that collect rubbish is a reference point in this part of the city.[8]

Sometimes it is difficult to separate auditory and visual experiences. I take a visiting American tourist to a rooftop in the Old City on a late May morning, knowing that the bells of the Lutheran Church of the Redeemer and Holy Sepulcher will soon begin ringing—the slow, deep European bells of the Lutheran church contrasting with the fast, higher ringing of the Eastern Orthodox bells at the Holy Sepulcher—followed by the Islamic call to prayer, which frequently overlaps with the bells at this time of day. As the sounds begin to intermingle, my companion, delighted by their counterpoint, pulls out his camera and begins photographing the nearest church tower. This audiovisual confusion perhaps reflects an unthinking push to the visual modality, reflected in the domestication of pocket-sized technologies: almost every tourist or pilgrim wields a still camera, yet it is rare to see a traveler record sound in isolation from visual photography. Yet resonance between modalities of perception is also an intrinsic part of the urban experience: the suffusion of electronic noise from toys on sale during Ramadan echoes the suffusion of candies, the smells of freshly ground coffee and herbs, and the physical density of the crowds on the way to the al Aqsa mosque, all contributing to the collective experience of the festival. Urban architecture frames urban music: a visiting choir from St. Petersburg sings in an underground Russian Orthodox chapel and an oud player busks in the arched space of the Ottoman-era Jaffa Gate, the visual city providing both acoustic and visual resonance for their musical performances.

Envisioning the Urban Soundscape

As affirmed by the fertile and growing field of sound studies, studying the soundscape offers a useful corrective to hegemonic visual and narrative representations of urban space. Sound offers an inroad to consider the city as a physical, sensory environment—yet urban noise has perhaps too frequently been dismissed as an unwanted consequence of industry and modernity. The case study I offered here makes a case for a textured understanding of urban sound, which in turn helps to uncover how both sound and visual cues interact to frame human encounters and experiences. The line between the visual and the auditory city is far from clear-cut. Both visual and auditory cues participate in a broader sensory, aesthetic, and political realm that extends beyond their own immediate spatial boundaries, reiterating the importance and presence of the full sensorium in the urban experience.

Notes

1 This chapter is based on research conducted in 2009–12 in Jerusalem's Old City, supported by small grants from the British Academy and SOAS, University of London. All names of individuals appearing in this paper have been changed. All responsibility for the material I cite above, however, and all errors of citation or interpretation, are my own.

2 R. Murray Schafer, *The Soundscape: Our Sonic Environment and the Tuning of the World* (Rochester, VT: Destiny Books, 1977), 3.

3 Rowland Atkinson, "Ecology of Sound: The sonic order of urban space," *Urban Studies* 44, no. 10 (2007): 1907.

4 Jonathan Sterne, "Sounds like the Mall of America: Programmed Music and the Architectonics of Public Space," *Ethnomusicology* 41, no. 1 (1997): 25.

5 Jacques Attali, *Noise: The Political Economy of Music*, trans. Brian Massumi (Minneapolis, MN: University of Minnesota Press, 1985), 3.

6 Jonathan Sterne, *The Audible Past: Cultural Origins of Sound Reproduction* (Durham, NC: Duke University Press, 2003), 15.
7 Fieldnotes, 14 November 2009.
8 Fieldnotes, 23 September 2009.

Further Reading

Atkinson, Rowland. "Ecology of Sound: The Sonic Order of Urban Space." *Urban Studies* 44, no. 10 (2007): 1905–1917.

Attali, Jacques. *Noise: The Political Economy of Music*. Translated by Brian Massumi. Minneapolis, MN: University of Minnesota Press, 1985.

Connor, Steven. "Edison's Teeth: Touching Hearing." In *Hearing Cultures: Essays on Sound, Listening and Modernity*, edited by Veit Erlmann, 153–172. Oxford and New York: Berg, 2004.

Corbin, Alain. *Village Bells: Sound and Meaning in the Nineteenth-Century French Countryside*. New York, NY: Columbia University Press, 1998.

Lee, Tong Soon. "Technology and the Production of Islamic Space: The Call to Prayer in Singapore." *Ethnomusicology* 43, no. 1 (1999): 86–100.

Samuels, David, Louise Meintjes, Ana Maria Ochoa, and Thomas Porcello. "Soundscapes: Toward a Sounded Anthropology." *Annual Review of Anthropology* 39 (2010): 329–345.

Schafer, R. Murray. *The Soundscape: Our Sonic Environment and the Tuning of the World*. Rochester, VT: Destiny Books, 1977.

Sterne, Jonathan. "Sounds like the Mall of America: Programmed Music and the Architectonics of Public Space." *Ethnomusicology* 41, no. 1 (1997): 22–50.

——. *The Audible Past: Cultural Origins of Sound Reproduction*. Durham, NC: Duke University Press, 2003.

34

MUSIC IN SOCIAL AND ARTISTIC CONTEXT

Women Qin Players

Mingmei Yip

Among the cultured elite of China, the qin 琴 was considered the most refined form of music, which should be played only by classically educated scholars. It was one of the four literati arts, the others being the board game of *qi* 棋, or *weiqi* 围棋 (Go in Japanese); *shu* 书, meaning calligraphy or books; and *hua* 画, meaning painting. Although the four arts were supposedly reserved for men, there are many instances in which gentlewomen excelled at them. The freedom of women to pursue these arts, as well as other forms of learning and artistic activity, depended on social factors such as class, wealth, family background, tradition, and historical period, as well as the obvious individual factors including talent and personality. However, while some gentlewomen were free to develop their artistic talents, the qin was also played by women of lower social status—especially prostitutes and actresses—despite the disapproval of the literati because of the supposed lofty nature of the qin. In this article, I will discuss women's relationship with the qin and also their position in the male-dominated qin culture. I will consider women qin players according to five categories: gentlewomen, court ladies, prostitutes, nuns, and legendary figures.

Attitudes toward Women and Qin

Attitudes toward women playing the qin were not consistent, but instead diverse and often ambivalent. In traditional textual sources, however, the negative comments predominate. The Song-dynasty *Dongtian Qinglu Ji* 洞天清錄集 (*Purity and Blessing of the Cavernous Heaven*) states the following: "When Daoists play the qin, even if the qin is not pure it will turn pure. When vulgar people play the qin, or women and girls, especially prostitutes and actresses, even though the qin itself is not vulgar, it will turn vulgar."[1] According to the Ming-dynasty qin manual *Qinpu Zhengzhuan* 琴譜正傳 (*The Authentic Transmission of Qin Tablatures*), certain kinds of people are not worthy to play nor even listen to the qin: "Those who fail to understand the virtue of sound (of the qin) include wanderers, failed scholars, elderly bachelors, and bitter women, who can only feel comfortable with trivialities."[2] It was assumed that women could not perform as well as men. The Song-dynasty *Gujin Yaqin Lu* 古今雅琴录 (*Lists of Elegant Qins from Past to Present*) says: "From Emperor Yao until the Song, through nine dynasties spanning two-thousand-seven-hundred and twenty-five years, eighty-five people excelled in the qin, [and] among them only three were women."[3]

However, early texts, particularly the *Shi Jing* 詩經 (*Classic of Poetry*), suggest that women's lives were not as constrained before Ruism 儒家 (Confucianism) became the dominant ideology. The *Shi Jing* is a collection of songs, many of folk origin, which is thought to have been compiled during the Western Zhou (1046–771 BCE) and early Spring and Autumn periods (approximately 770–221 BCE). These songs often depict men and women together, contrary to later ideas that they should be separated. In several poems of the *Shi Jing*, the qin even functions as a metaphor for harmony between men and women. For example, the poem entitled *Guan Sui* 关雎 (Guang! Cries the Osprey) reads: "The refined young lady, we greet her with the qin and the se." (The se is a larger zither that resembles the modern zheng.) Another poem, *Chang Di* 常棣, reads: "Wife and children should harmonize like the qin and the se played together."

The qin as a symbol of harmony between men and women persisted beyond the Zhou, though it seems to have been less common than the moralistic disapproval found in manuals of female deportment. Yet, in the midst of repressive attitudes, we find some texts that are quite supportive of women's playing the instrument. Li Yu 李漁 (1611–80) of the Ming, famous for his diverse artistic talents, encouraged women to take up qin playing in his *Xianqing Ouji* 闲情偶寄 (*Casual Memories of Leisurely Sentiment*): "Among the tunes of silk and bamboo [string and wind instruments], the qin is considered the best … If women learn [the qin], their personality can be transformed. [Men] who want to live in the gentle village [among women], cannot be without this instrument for self-cultivation."[4] Li Yu continues:

> Many hire famous teachers to teach their beautiful concubines [to play the qin] … The qin and the se serve to glue man and woman so they become one, and to join emotions so they will never separate.

> Beside the flowers and under the moon, in a beautiful scene and pleasant occasion, [with] cool water beside the pavilion … perhaps then the husband will play the qin and the wives follow, or the women play [the qin] and the man listens; or two voices sing simultaneously, their lingering tones in unison.[5]

This passage expresses a quite different view of qin playing by women than many of those quoted earlier, and assumes a much more congenial interaction between men and women than do Ruist guides to feminine deportment. Echoing the *Shi Jing*, Li Yu suggests that qin playing in the household could serve the purpose of improving harmony between husband and wife. The emphasis is less on virtue and more on pleasure.

The Five Categories of Women Qin Players

Gentlewomen, Guixiu 閨秀: Ladies of the Inner Chamber

Gui 閨, or *guifang* 閨房, refers to the chambers where women lived. X*iu* 秀 means elegance. *Guixiu* thus refers to cultivated, elegant ladies from wealthy or high-ranking families. Located at the backs of residential compounds, the inner quarters could be visited only by women or male relatives such as husbands and sons.

Although *shu yuan* 書院, academies, were in existence from the eighth century onward, many men still received their education within their family household. Women, being restricted to the home, were educated mainly by family members or by private tutors. Although most private tutors were men, some women became famous as teachers and traveled to teach in different households.

According to *Qinshi Xu* 琴史续 (*Continuation of the History of Qin*), which discusses forty-seven women qin players from the Song dynasty onward, qin playing by women in this social group is often referred to as *guixiu qin* 閨秀琴, qin from the elegant inner chamber, or *guige qinpai* 閨阁琴派—qin style of the elegant inner chamber. These women often addressed each other as *guixiu qinyou* 閨秀琴友—qin friends from the elegant inner chamber (Figure 34.1).[6]

Huanghou and Nushi: Empresses, Queens, and Court Ladies

Qin playing was not confined to private households, but played a part in court life at both amateur and professional levels. Categories of court ladies who might play the qin include: *huanghou* 皇后, the empress; *huangfei* 皇妃, the emperor's consorts; and *nushi* 女史, court ladies conversant with the classics. These women, especially empresses and the imperial concubines, came from prestigious families where they had received excellent private tutoring. Some became renowned as poets or qin players.

Court ladies playing the qin are frequently depicted in paintings. The best-known is a scroll attributed to Zhou Fang 周仿 (active 780–810) of the Tang. This painting shows three court ladies and two maids. One court lady is tuning the qin while other two look on. Later paintings that depict the lives of imperial ladies, commonly entitled *Hangong Chunxiao,* 汉宫春晓 (*Spring Morning in the Han Palace*), usually include a scene with women playing and listening to the qin.

One of the best-known examples is a long scroll by the Ming dynasty painter Qiu Ying 仇英 (c. 1494–1552). This intriguing work gives us a peek into the normally hidden lives of imperial women as well as male officials. In the imperial garden, we see women admiring peacocks, lotus flowers, and scholars' rocks, while others chat with one another. Inside the palace, women engage themselves in a multitude of artistic activities including embroidery, chess, creating and viewing paintings, as well as dancing and playing music. Instruments depicted include the *pipa* 琵琶, *yuan* 阮, *zheng* 筝, *konghou* 箜篌, clappers—and, of course, the qin. In one scene a woman holds a qin while another removes its brocade cover. In another, two women recline side by side under a tree, reading a book together, while a qin lies in the grass beside them.

In contrast to the happy mood depicted in these paintings, qin music about court women universally expresses melancholy. The titles of these pieces, like the paintings, commonly begin with the two words *hangong* 汉宫, the Han Palace. Some examples are: *Hangong Qiuyue* 漢宮秋月 (*Autumn Moon over the Han Palace*); *Hangong Chunxiao* 汉宫春晓 (*Spring Morning of the Han Palace*); *Hangong Chunyuan* 汉宫春怨 (*Spring Lament of the Han Palace*); *Hangong Qiuyuan* 汉宫秋怨 (*Autumn Lament of the Han Palace*). For example, the *jieti*, or explanation of the title, for *Autumn Moon over the Han Palace* states:

> The music evokes court ladies during an autumn evening, with a manner of suppressed melancholy, disappointment in their hearts … perpetually sad. The tone of this piece is of bitter lament like sobbing, but while bitter, it is not angry. While sad, it causes no pain.[7]

It is notable that the visual and aural representations of the lives of court ladies have opposite moods. Paintings show opulently adorned women enjoying themselves, while qin pieces present their lives as lonely and sad. In general, unpleasant events were not considered suitable for inclusion in painting, while they were customary in music.

Women Entertainers and Courtesans

When they hear the Chinese word *ji* 妓, or the phrase *changji* 娼妓, contemporary Mandarin speakers think of prostitutes. However, in ancient China, *ji* was also used to refer to women entertainers who performed in the emperor's court or at rich people's mansions. The *ji* who played the qin are referred to as *qin ji*. 琴妓. The word *ji* has two variations, one with the *ren* "person" radical 伎, meaning entertainer; and the other with the *nu* 女 "woman" radical, implying a prostitute 妓. In the phrase *qin ji* the former term meant a professional woman qin musician, while the latter referred to prostitute qin players.

The Song qin manual *Taigu Yiyin* 太古遺音 (*Ancient Tunes from Antiquity*), states: "Whenever playing the qin, it must not be in front of prostitutes or actors and actresses for this is disrespectful to the sage's instrument, and certainly they must not be allowed to hold the sacred instrument."[8] Similarly, a Yuan-dynasty article states: "The presence of a vulgar man, a courtesan, an actor or actress, a drunken and noisy atmosphere, these all are bad conditions for playing the [qin]."[9] These prostitutes were not those "who lean by the door and sell their smiles," but prostitutes of the highest rank, the *mingji*, 名妓, celebrated prostitutes, or courtesans. Like the many-talented gentlewomen, *mingji* were erudite, talented, and artistic. While *guixiu* were educated, respectable women in society, *mingji* were the *guixiu*'s fallen counterpart. While *guixiu* were women for whom activities outside the household were usually discouraged, courtesans, on the other hand, because of their dealings with rich merchants and famous literati, were professional women who led public lives.

Unlike lower-class prostitutes, *mingji* had the opportunities for literary pursuits such as poetry, dance, music, painting, calligraphy, opera singing, and performing. Although most courtesans were trained to play the *pipa* 琵琶 and the *zheng* 箏, some were accomplished on the qin, and so referred to as *qinji*—琴妓 qin prostitutes.

The Ming dynasty is considered the era in which *mingji* flourished. In the city of Jinling 金陵, along the Qinhuai 秦淮 river, dwelled the renowned *Qinhuai Bayan* 秦淮八艳, the Eight Beauties of the Qinhuai area. Among these eight beauties, five played the qin.

Nuns

Though qin music is usually associated with Confucian virtue and restrained emotion, it was also influenced by Daoism and, to a lesser degree, by Buddhism. Many
poems were composed with titles like "Listening to the Daoist ... play the qin" and
"Listening to the Monk ... play the qin," indicating that many *fang wai* 方外 "outside the dusty world" of Daoist and Buddhist priests were attracted to the qin and
became influential as performers. The instrument, with its soft, meditative tone,
emphasis on breathing, and rich philosophical lore, is ideal for monks and nuns to
practice as a means of self-cultivation and meditation.

However, in comparison to the many poems which describe a Daoist priest or
Buddhist monk playing the qin, similar poems describing a Daoist or Buddhist nun
playing the qin are rare. While Buddhist monk players attained fame and respect,
only a few Buddhist nuns were known as qin players. Either women in the religious
order were discouraged from playing the qin, or their status as a nun qin player was
considered too insignificant to be recorded. While there is a lineage of Buddhist
monk qin players, none is known for nuns.

Legendary Figures: Nu Wo 女蜗娲, Bodhisattvas, and Zhong Kui's Sister

The invention of the qin is attributed mostly to mythical male figures such as Fu
Xi 伏曦羲, Shen Nong 神农, and Huang Di 黄帝 (Yellow Emperor). However,
a female mythological figure in ancient Chinese history, Nu Wo 女蜗娲, the
serpent goddess, has also been credited with inventing the qin.

Nu Wo was believed to be the legendary emperor Fu Xi's wife (some say sister).
Both figures possessed a human head and a snake's body. Nu Wo was credited with
many things: creating the universe, mending the sky, inventing marriage, codify-
ing ritual music, and inventing instruments, including the mouth organ, flute, and
qin.

Although Avalokitesvara, the Bodhisattva of Compassion, was originally represented as a male, in China by the beginning of the Ming dynasty, feminine forms
had come to predominate. Guan Yin 观音, meaning literally "observer of sound," is
the goddess's name in Chinese. The word "sound" here refers to the cries of suffering
sentient beings.

Guan Yin can appear in different forms, such as ten-thousand-armed Guan Yin;
son-sending Guan Yin; fish-basket Guan Yin; sutra-holding Guan Yin; and many
more. Sometimes this bodhisattva is also depicted playing the qin, often as playing
in a celestial orchestra in the Pure Land (Figure 34.2).

The qin-playing Guan Yin motif appears in texts, paintings, reliefs, and frescoes
for the following purposes: (1) as an offering to the Buddha; (2) as praise to the Buddha's virtue; (3) as an *upaya*, a skillful means to lead sentient beings to the Dharma;
(4) *Yiqin shuofa* 以琴说法, to use the qin to preach the Dharma; (5) as a welcoming
gesture to devotees.

In Chinese paintings and woodblock prints, Zhong Kui 钟馗, the legendary ghost
catcher, is always depicted with bulging eyes and a full beard, and wearing a scholar's hat and a robe. A common genre of painting shows Zhong Kui marrying off his
sister, with the demons he has subdued as guests.

In contrast to Zhong Kui himself, who was mostly depicted as uncouth, his sister was depicted as beautiful. In the marriage procession, an object which looks like a qin in a silk case is always seen carried by a small ghost; however, neither Zhong Kui nor his sister is ever shown playing the instrument. Since the qin is also seen in other paintings of the ghost-queller, its presence symbolizes Zhong Kui's literati background as a *Jinshi* 进士, or eminent scholar.

Conclusion

A well-known qin reference, the *Jinyu Qinkan*, published in 1926 in Shanghai, recorded two hundred and twenty-five qin players, among whom only twenty-five were women. In recent decades, China, Taiwan, and Hong Kong have seen a revival in qin playing. While in ancient China women qin players were few, today there are more and more women who learn to play this ancient instrument. It seems a fact that among young beginners, more girls than boys are learning the instrument. Today playing the qin, by both women and men, is no longer just for intellectuals, but is popular at all levels of society. Qin players include film stars, factory workers, university professors, jewelry store sales associates, and many others. With the prominence of women, a new era of qin music has begun.

Notes

1 Zhao Xiju: 赵希鹄 *Dongtian Qinglu Ji*, 洞天清禄集 quoted in Chien-Yuan Tang 唐健垣, *Ch'in Fu* (*Collection of Materials on the Chinese Seven-stringed Zither*), 2 vols. (Taipei, Lian Guian Publishing Company, 1971), 2: 1–69.
2 *Qinpu Zhengzhuan* 1547, in *Qinqu Jicheng* 琴曲集成 (*Collection of Qin Compositions*) (Beijing: Zhonghua Shuju, 1981), 2: 392.
3 *Gujin Yaqin Lu* is quoted in the Ming dynasty *Qinshu Dachuan* 琴譜大傳 (*Big Collection of Qin Tablatures*), 1590, under the section *qinqu chuanshou* 琴曲傳授 (transmission of qin compositions), in *Qinqu Jicheng*, 5: 208.
4 Yi, Cunguo 易存国, *Zhonggguo Guqin Yishu* 中国古琴艺术 (*The Art of Chinese Guqin*) (Beijing: Renmin Chubanshe, 2003), 287.
5 Ibid. English translation by the present author.
6 Zhou Qingyun 周庆云, *Qinshi Shu* 琴史续 (*Continuation of the History of the Qin*) (Shanghai, 1919), juan 6, 11–12.
7 Yanglun 扬伦, before 1609. *Boya Xinfa* 伯牙心法 (*Boya's Method from the Heart of Yanglun*), quoted in Za Fuxi 查阜西, *Cunjian Guqin Qupu Jilan* 存见古琴谱辑缆 (*Compilation of Extant Ancient Qin Compositions*), 2nd printing (Beijing: Renmin Yinyue Chuban She, 2001), 227.
8 *Qinyou suoji* 琴有所忌, "prohibitions of the qin," in *Taigu Yiyin* 太古遗音 1511 in *Qinqu Jicheng*, 1: 30.
9 This is the ninth rule of qin playing according to Wu Cheng吴澄, *Qinyan Shize*,琴言十則 (*Ten Rules of Qin Playing*). Reprinted in R. H. Van Gulik, *The Lore of the Chinese Lute* (Tokyo, Japan and Rutland, Vermont: Sophia University, in cooperation with The Charles E. Tuttle Company, 1969), 75.

Further Reading

Cahill, Suzanne. "Material Culture and the Dao: Textiles, Boats, and Zithers in the Poetry of Yu Xuanji (844–868)." In *Daoist Identity: History, Lineage, and Ritual*, edited by Livia Kohn and Harold D. Roth, 102–126. Honolulu: University of Hawai'i Press, 2002.
DeWoskin, Kenneth J. *A Song for One or Two: Music and the Concept of Art in Early China*. Ann Arbor: Center for Chinese Studies, University of Michigan, 1982.

Ko, Dorothy. *Teachers of the Inner Chambers: Women and Culture in Seventeeth-Century China*. Stanford: Stanford University Press, 1994.

Van Gulik, R. H. *The Lore of the Chinese Lute*. Tokyo and Rutland, VT: Sophia University, in cooperation with C. E. Tuttle Co., 1969.

Yung, Bell. *The Last of China's Literati: The Music, Poetry, and Life of Tsar Teh-yun*. Hong Kong: Hong Kong University Press, 2008.

35

MUSIC IN NEW MEDIA

Fabian Holt

This chapter provides an analytical survey of developments in audiovisual media in music since the 1980s. The chapter is based on research and examples in Europe and North America, but the emphasis is thematic and conceptual rather than geographic. Musically, the period has frequently been characterized as eclectic, especially in urban and cyber culture narratives, and as retrospective with reference to retro styles, band reunion tours, tribute albums, CD box sets, and classic rock radio stations.

Changes in musical practices and genres in this period, however, need to be examined within new media dynamics and broader processes of social change. For instance, the increasing individualization of music consumption and the diversification of the media landscape in new digital worlds stimulate a wide range of dispersed micro-level creativity rather than a few long-term genre evolutions. Moreover, genres such as indie rock and electronic dance music have evolved in complex processes of not only digitization but also festivalization and consumerism. New communication technologies have become entrenched in everyday music-making and experience, creating more communication channels and layers of mediation, representation, and communication than ever before. This creates expectations for visual accompaniment to online communication about music in the form of photo and video. While new opportunities emerge, artists are also challenged to constantly provide new online content, especially for the many without support from a recording company. Artist and audience identities are complexly visually mediated through online music stores, social networking sites, magazines, and video blogs with search engines, interactive features, and multimedia content that to some extent are outperforming conventional communication channels such as physical stores, print publications, and street posters. At a more fundamental level, new digital literacies have made a transition from text to interactive audiovisual communication, exemplified by live televisual encounters, cross-media storytelling, and videos for sharing and documenting experiences.

While the materiality and space of the visual have changed in the digital age, contributing to broad erosions of communication contexts, conventional functions of the visual remain the same. Above all, the music industry continues to approach images for promotional purposes. This has not changed since the days of broadsides, posters, and album covers. Industry mogul Walter Yetnikoff primarily perceived MTV as a tool for increasingly global music marketing and said simply, "the more images the better."[1] Today, DIY indie rock musicians are using short online videos of performances to build a fanbase and create audiences for their tours. This does not mean that the genres of visual mediation are not perceived artistically. A prominent music video director such as Martin de Thurah, who has worked with James Blake, Röyksopp, Kanye West, and others, has a nuanced poetics of music video as a distinct art form.[2] There are also constants in the catalogue of subject matters and representational practices. Images are commonly used to situate music in social settings and geographical locations that enhance narratives of art and authenticity within genre discourses. Images of sexually suggestive bodies and social stereotypes are also widely used for immediate appeal to unconscious desires. Cultural research provides more and more evidence and critique of these forms of commercial exploitation and their implications for social and psychological health. A significant contribution is Barry Sherman's and Joseph Dominick's 2006 article "Violence and Sex in Music Videos: TV and Rock 'n' Roll."

Digital networked media have also created platforms for expanding the avenues of musical culture. A landslide occurred with the rise of media cultures focused on the theatrical–visual staging of amateur bodies in performance competitions. Narratives of musical performance and experience now routinely include TV talent shows and video games, in addition to the conventional avenues of music scenes, concert halls, and recording studios. These avenues are further altered by the extension of communication platforms with blogs, chat rooms, and social networking sites. A new level of mediation is felt particularly among amateurs and semi-professional artists now that a broad population communicates via everyday computing devices. Teenagers now commonly upload an ad hoc video recording of a performance to YouTube and get a couple of hundred views.

With this extension and transformation of the field of musical culture, new conceptions of performance, experience, and canonicity emerge. This raises questions about what should be included in a historical account. The present chapter considers changing forms of audiovisual mediation of musical experience and communication, adopting the perspective that music cultures respond differently to the technology-driven changes and the complex dynamics of the large-scale process of mediatization. The chapter focuses on the dominant media cultures to illustrate broad dynamics that also help to explain smaller cultures.

The chapter is organized into three sections. Following the introduction above, the second section considers social networking as a key context of everyday communication about music. This involves friendship dynamics and mediations of musical experience, illustrated by Facebook, the most popular site of its kind since 2008. According to its public information pages, Facebook has about half a billion daily users, and almost every private and public organization has a page there. To complement this perspective, the third section accounts for evolutions in networked video-sharing sites as a new arena for music video and video recordings of musical performances. Conceiving of YouTube as a complex architecture of mass and niche cultures, the section highlights the transition from television to more diversified broadcasting, from the corporate brand space of industry giant Vevo to micro platforms in niche genres such as classical music and jazz. Throughout the chapter, examples illustrate connections between media spheres and serve the general point that contemporary music cultures unfold along multiple platforms and cannot therefore be adequately framed in narratives of individual platforms and devices.

Music in Everyday Social Media Culture

Often dismissed by intellectuals as the epitome of triviality, in the 2000s the cul-ture of social networking has evolved into a key site of everyday interpersonal and professional communication. The first platform of mainstream participation was MySpace, which opened up new possibilities for musicians and audiences. MySpace profile pages were designed as home pages with multimedia content. The now-dominant Facebook platform instead privileges friend communications and inter-action through a conversational design. A social networking site is a space not just for experiencing media content or getting information but primarily for "hanging out" among friends in mediated everyday-life worlds. The primary communication space for the majority of personal users is one's immediate social network of friends, acquaintances, family, colleagues, etc. Within this context of narrating selves, users experience and communicate about popular photo and video genres for collective amusement, social distinction, memory sharing, and social bonding. Communica-tion itself sustains the kind of affect that might be associated with Baudrillard's notion of media ecstasy. Friendship-driven communication within a digital-atten-tion economy creates an economy of popularity in which user acts of clicking and viewing translate into public opinion and consumer interest. This has implications for how musical life is represented in contemporary life.

Key aspects of these dynamics are illustrated in the circulation of so-called "after videos" or "trailers" for electronic dance music festivals. One of the key interna-tional industry players is ID&T, which started in the Netherlands in the early 2000s with the event Sensation White, in which all participants are dressed in white. The audience emerges as one visually homogeneous and themed crowd in a fantasy world. The individual visual identity of each ID&T event is used in the entire dig-ital universe of the event, including the website, app, and Facebook page. In style and in the conception of space and design techniques, ID&T builds on the legacy of Disney World consumer culture examined in Sharon Zukin's 1995 book *The Cultures of Cities*. The events generally appeal to discotheque-goers as a spectacular dance party featuring world-famous DJs in a large, open-air setting, separated from everyday life and society as a gated area with its own currency. The first after video of the festival Tomorrowland (Figure 35.1) strategically frames the festival experi-ence as an event with a unique magic that comes to life only once a year. This story is told through a cinematic narrator and moving images of pretty young girls expressing happiness and erotic pleasure within large dance crowds, and through the accompanying soundtrack that builds up energy like a DJ set. The floating sounds in the introductory sequence build up a tension that culminates with the sight of a huge crowd dancing in front of the main stage. In addition to the visual identity, the media layers of the festival experience are integrated through the emphasis on the naming of a "land," a mythical space, and through the *carpe diem* motif: "yesterday is history, today is a gift, tomorrow is mystery" (which was also used in the 2008 movie *Kung Fu Panda*).

The first Tomorrowland after video had 50 million views on YouTube within a year and helped to sell out the festival in one day to audiences from over 75 countries. A research assistant of mine in the festival's core age group (she is 23) reported from Tomorrowland 2012 that everyone she talked to had watched the after video, although no one remembered where and how they discovered the video. My assistant let her Facebook friends know that she was leaving for the festival with a couple of friends, and some of her friends commented "Oh, you techno girls, what's going on with you?!" The comments gently made fun that their friends would attend what was perceived to be a superficial event with disco music familiar from commercial radio. The popularity of the video led ID&T to expand the after video from 2012 and conduct film premiere screenings in cinemas before the online release later the same day. Within 24 hours of the release, the 2012 after video had almost 2 million views, 40,000 Facebook likes, and 20,000 shares. One should not underestimate the communication power of 20,000 people sharing the video with all their Facebook friends within 24 hours. In this case, that power translates into a larger audience interest for the international events of ID&T, which is currently expanding. More importantly, when this integrated cinematic event and video gains so much attention in the most powerful mass media of our time, there can be little doubt that it impacts on public perceptions and horizons for festival and concert culture. This is boosted by a communication strategy that creates a digital universe and employs cinematic storytelling to emphasize the consumer experience and the party sociality associated with a cultural event. In a word, the international trajectory of the ID&T events represents a Disneyfication of popular music into special events in the era of social media. This has implications not just for festival culture but also for the existing ecosystems of the art worlds and public spheres of musical culture that constitute the conventional arena of music studies.

Video serves similar functions in other electronic dance music festivals, including the Sonar festival in Barcelona, which also caters to a broad international audience. During the 2000s, it has moved from conventional TV ads to brand and audience building through short videos uploaded to YouTube. The videos have been art oriented to signify sophistication, presented in the context of daytime events at Barcelona's Museum of Contemporary Art. In 2011, the video was a fictional sales presentation delivered by the festival organizers. In 2012 it was an atmosphere piece featuring an old man who was then pictured on festival posters around Barcelona holding a beer produced by the main sponsor of the event. Narratives and signs thus permeate layers of online and material culture. Another similarity is the construction of festival personae via visual media, so far mainly in the form of photos on the festival's website.

However, there are also contrasting visual cultures among festivals with electronic dance music. Festivals appealing to images of subcultural notions of authenticity with performances in the streets (as opposed to gated areas), such as the Distortion festival in Copenhagen, Denmark, or in the desert during the Burning Man festival in Nevada, tend to have a more DIY-based visual culture, with participants producing images as part of the festival experience. The media editor of the Distortion festival has focused on a long-term strategy of getting user videos uploaded to the festival's website rather than having them more dispersed in remote blogs and personal websites. The editor adopted a Creative Commons license policy whereby the festival does not have to pay for the videos, while certain forms of commercial use in other contexts require permissions from the producers.[3] In Facebook mediations of the Distortion experience, conventional narratives of simply showing presence in a special event give way to more ambitious narratives of authentic lived and mediated cultural experience with a subtle performance of habitus. The mediations are saturated with photos and videos whereby participants engage in the kind of self-presentation that is stimulated by social networking. In affective group interactions, the dance vibe from clubs is recontextualized into the broad daylight of streets in which anyone can watch and film.

Diversified and Corporatized Broadcasting

The mediation of musical culture in everyday social networking practices discussed above provides a context for understanding the fundamental change in broadcasting culture. As with social networking, the changes in broadcasting occur within communication infrastructures and power relations in mainstream society, not just in musical life, and the changes have implications for perceptions of what it means to make music and participate in musical culture.

The erosion of the relative monopoly of broadcast media described in Bill Ryan's *Making Capital from Culture* can be illustrated from the perspectives of amateur, DIY, and corporate music cultures. The distinctions between these cultures are fluid and contextual, but they constitute powerful domains that impact on each other, argues Patricia Lange. With mass participation, amateur culture has accelerated, challenging domains of corporate professional culture. Amateur culture proliferates across media, also in mass, popular reality television shows that have become the subject of a critical literature on self-realization in neoliberalism, from Zygmunt Bauman's *Consuming Life* to Laurie Ouellette and James Hay's *Better Living Through Reality TV*. Corporate professionals also play a role in the dominant video-sharing site YouTube, which was purchased by Google for $1.65 billion in 2006 with the prime purpose of making advertising revenues from free video sharing among users. While serious newspapers such as the *New York Times* offer useful reports on the ongoing developments, the deeper implications for communication dynamics have been studied by scholars such as Henry Jenkins, Manuel Castells, and José van Dijck. In both YouTube and video-game culture, many amateurs do not have the musical skills to play an instrument and are performing *to* music, to a playback device in a setting with many visual effects.

The career trajectories of talents being discovered on YouTube or in talent shows illustrate how these televisual cultures produce new aesthetics and recontextualize existing practices. The careers of stars such as Adele, Lily Allen, Justin Bieber, and Lana Del Rey were jumpstarted by MySpace or YouTube, and talent shows did the same for Kelly Clarkson and Paul Potts. The case of Potts is illustrative. He has generally been perceived as a reality TV construct by the classical music establishment, but his many performances in public spaces normally used for popular music and his YouTube flashmob performances have recontextualized opera and contributed to a cultural transition in the field that has only just begun. In Denmark, for instance, symphony orchestras have started doing flashmob performances of popular repertoire in train stations and broadcasting the performance to YouTube so as to reach everyday social media culture. So far this can be isolated to an activity outside the concert hall, but the images create expectations for a more participatory and informal concert culture, as these are dominant effects of social media. Participatory media culture creates expectations for a sense of mediated interaction, ownership, and transparency in relation to production processes and audience community-building. The Berlin Philharmonic now routinely offers short videos that mediate the experience in Facebook, along with interviews with the world-famous Sir Simon Rattle in informal settings, and a separate website for full-length concerts, as we shall see.

YouTube has taken over MySpace's former role as the dominant resource for exploring new music as well as a wide range of other performances and cinematic genres. The service has gained its position by social media functions such as embedding, by the sheer volume (the number of videos is unparalleled), and by Google's leading database search engine. YouTube is a mass culture phenomenon, with a growing share of daily global internet users going up from 25 percent in 2011 to 30 percent in 2012, according to Alexa.com. The mass-culture notion of an "MTV hit" in the 1980s now extends to the notion of a "YouTube hit," but it is now determined by view counts and is applicable to amateur videos. More importantly, YouTube is a mainstream public sphere for a variety of genres: not just music, but also political speeches, advertisements, and instructional videos. At the same time, YouTube is a land of myriad niche publics. Like other media with a wide penetration, YouTube becomes folklore, shaping new performance genres such as the flashmob and in contemporary urban cultures, as in the case of the DIY videos of the band Das Racist of Queens, New York. The videos of Das Racist portray a world in which hanging out in streets, playing video games, and riding the subway with iPods all play into musical performance, with media references in rap lyrics (for example, in "Ek Shaneesh" and "Chicken and Meat"). YouTube thus represents complex media architecture with a mass public culture of video consumption and production, but a platform that shapes particular ethics, attitudes, and styles of expression. An obvious impact of YouTube is the increasing visibility of activities that were previously more hidden or simply beyond the radar of old mass media, whether in private spaces or subterranean clubs. There are many examples of YouTube videos of dance moves creating trends in local scenes, from Brooklyn vogue dancing to Korean Gangnam-style dancing. There is a growing sense that every form of musical performance can be searched, watched, and mediated by the internet user.

The launch of Vevo in 2009 signaled how the conventional music industry was moving into the corporate infrastructure of the global digital communications system. Vevo is a brand platform within YouTube that offers videos by artists under contract with the corporate recording industry. Vevo is designed to sell music via links to the iTunes music store and sites selling concert tickets and merchandising, but also to generate advertising revenues, which are significant, given the mass interest in these star performers. The advertising revenues are shared with Google and form part of the company's larger strategy for making YouTube a gateway to consumers for the business world. The videos themselves are produced within the MTV tradition, although absorbing new genre elements such as anime and sometimes adding extended feature film elements such as Lady Gaga's "Telephone" or Kanye West's video suite "Runaway," both of which expand the universe of the individual song and the artist. The biggest change, however, is not in video style but in the consumption via media sharing and social networking sites in browsers and mobile devices.

Finally, new and established professional musicians are creating an ever-expanding field of small-scale production. The field of indie rock, for instance, has expanded in the process of what Chris Anderson called the long tail of distribution, resulting in fewer superstars and many more niche artists with greater control and revenue share at small recording companies. Across popular music genres, many artists have gone from major to indie recording companies in the 2000s, including not only rock bands such as Sonic Youth, Wilco, and Bad Religion but also pop stars such as Prince and Robyn, and the rappers Fat Joe and Cormega.

Today, many niche genre artists in jazz and classical music have adapted to the new media culture by creating their own YouTube channel and using it for relatively conventional forms of broadcasting. Broadcasting is part of their musical tradition and a way of maintaining the deeply rooted performance and listening practices among artists and audiences. The YouTube channel of a jazz artist such as Pat Metheny, for instance, features a number of short performances, among them performances that are recorded specifically for the audience of this YouTube channel. A performance of "A Girl From Ipanema" is shot with close-up in a small room to heighten the chamber music intimacy, with the detailed expression of his fingers and face, but the video simply shows the performance and does not create a non-musical drama or dance for the music. Here, YouTube video enables a virtual jazz club concert experience in a world where such venues have declined and the genre of jazz mainly has public presence at summer festivals.

In the sphere of classical music, world-famous orchestras started streaming performances live, in some cases migrating existing broadcasting arrangements from radio to an internet website, and now always also with spin-offs to their YouTube and Facebook pages. Examples include the Metropolitan Opera in New York, the Mozart festival in Salzburg, and the Berlin Philharmonic. The latter has created, with funding from a major German bank, a website designed as a virtual concert hall, with a high-quality photo of the real concert hall as a point of entry and with the main content being a video archive of live performances that can be watched in their entirety in high audio and visual quality. Each season, a number of performances are broadcast live. The website service is called "the digital concert hall" and stands out from popular music artists and festival broadcasts for a number of reasons. First of all, the digital concert hall has been a long-term investment because its dynamics are radically different from the communication ecstasy promoted in social media. The number of views does not match the criteria of standard advertising and it is ads-free and not linked to a commercial vendor. The financing is therefore a sponsorship arrangement as part of long-term brand management, building on the reputation of the high-culture traditions of the orchestra, Berlin, and Germany. Again, the video recordings stay close to the ideal of an intimate live music performance, with close-ups of musicians and no other theatrical staging or storytelling during extended performances.

Like the Metheny channel, the YouTube channel of the Berlin Philharmonic gives a taste of a traditional performance culture, but the digital concert hall goes one step further to the model of complete live transmissions that previously existed only on television. Digital audiovisual media and the internet allow a cultural niche institution such as the Berlin Philharmonic to be independent of broadcasting corporations, but not without corporate sponsorship. Thus, new media have also led to a growing emancipation or erosion of long-standing alliances among cultural and media institutions, with the new allies being mainly corporate sponsors.

Conclusion

The history of music and visual culture since the 1980s is characterized by a broadening of communication platforms, by the growing media presence of amateur and

DIY culture, and by the transition to a pervasive digital environment in which music is not just distributed but complexly mediated within a broader mediation of social life. The role of media technologies in this time period thus involves a further level of pervasiveness in social life, as illustrated by a shift from narratives of how music is circulated by and presented in the media to narratives of how musical culture is transformed and constructed through media; this shift has become an axiom of contemporary mediatization theory with scholars such as Sonia Livingstone and Stig Hjarvard. The dominant popular media cultures of Facebook and YouTube illustrate the growth of computer-based communication spaces. The interfaces and forms of communication in these spaces are visually dominated, and they allow media users to see much more of musical life past and present around the globe. The evolution cannot simply be accounted for in terms of expanded vision for the media user, however. It is crucial that the relations between image and music are cast not in abstract terms but in particular communication dynamics to highlight the important evolution from the virtual images in micro publics of the early internet age, to contemporary culture where the majority of the population participates in the production and circulation of images so that many performance spaces, music scenes, festivals, and dance cultures can be watched, increasingly with moving images, by any media user. This change in the online visuality of musical culture resembles the transition from graphic maps to photosynthetic maps such as Google Street View.

The large-scale mediatization process, in which media become more powerful agents of change, has a series of important analytical consequences for music studies and for studies of audiovisuality in music in particular. Studies of the audiovisual have tended to focus on "texts" such as recordings, videos, and television commercials, but an account of Facebook in musical life cannot meaningfully be limited to musical practices, artifacts, or even discourse; it also needs to analyze how music is mediated through the forms of everyday sociality, communications, and the popular culture contexts of social networking culture. The intensified process of mediatization is an evolving context for analysis of musical performances, recordings, and the boundaries of music culture in the coming years. Relatively little research has appeared on how new media practices change the boundaries of the musical landscape, and without a broader conception of media in long-term social processes important accounts of practices such as interactive video games tend to tell the story of the practice and its internal dynamics, while failing to explain some of the larger implications for power dynamics in musical culture and the perception of music in social life. A general challenge to the fields of visual studies and sound studies is to integrate new media perspectives more, as both fields are still dominated by their origin in the study of the "old" media of the broadcasting era.

It follows that mediation needs to be recognized as a complex form of power in contemporary musical life. The expanded media spaces and communication tools are instruments of power for artists, audiences, and organizations. The examples above have suggested how pop star and reality celebrities of our time shape the horizons of musical culture, including within historical institutions such as opera and the symphony orchestra. The power of media can finally be traced to the industry level. The Silicon Valley technology industry of the 1970s has become one of the most profitable industries in the world and dominates innovation in the communications infrastructure of contemporary society. To understand current social change, then, one might look further into the agendas and the place of music in the discourses of this relatively new industry. This would strengthen the ground for critical interventions and cultural critiques of the dominant discourses of communication and information services. A key to understanding the significance of music in contemporary society is precisely that it is not primarily communication and information; otherwise it would have little experiential value. Music is generally more expressive than communicative; its powers lie in embodied experience and in subtle meanings that transcend other modalities of social experience. Music cannot represent information or illustrate knowledge in a quick and precise way, like visual diagrams, road maps, or photos, but it has other capacities that are often left out of conversations about new media.

Notes

1 Walter Yetnikoff with David Ritz, *Howling at the Moon: The True Story of the Mad Genius of the Music World* (London: Abacus, 2004), 128.
2 Interview with author, 7 May 2011.
3 Festival media manager, anonymous, conversation with author, 7 March 2012.

Further Reading

Baym, Nancy, and danah boyd. "Socially Mediated Publicness: An Introduction." *Journal of Broadcasting & Electronic Media* 56, no. 3 (2012): 320–329.

Bull, Michael. *Sound Moves: iPod Culture and Urban Experience.* London: Routledge, 2007.

Holt, Fabian. "Is Music Becoming More Visual? Online Video Content in the Music Industry." *Visual Studies* 26, no. 1 (2011): 50–61.

Ito, Mizuko et al., ed. *Hanging Out, Messing Around, and Geeking Out: Kids Living and Learning with New Media.* Cambridge, MA: MIT Press, 2010.

McQuinn, Julie, ed. *Popular Music and Multimedia.* Farnham: Ashgate, 2011.

Miller, Kiri. *Playing Along: Digital Games, YouTube, and Virtual Performance.* Oxford: Oxford University Press, 2012.

Mjøs, Ole J. *Music, Social Media and Global Mobility: MySpace, Facebook, YouTube.* New York: Routledge, 2012.

Sexton, Jamie, ed. *Music, Sound and Multimedia: From the Live to the Virtual.* Edinburgh: University of Edinburgh Press, 2007.

Part V

HYBRID ARTS

36

PAGEANTRY

Kelley Harness

What pageantry, what feats, what showes,
What minstrelsie, and prettie din,
The Regent made in Metalin
To greet the King

(Shakespeare, *Pericles, Prince of Tyre*)[1]

Thus the personification of the fourteenth-century poet John Gower encourages audiences to imagine the festivities with which Lysimachus, governor of Mytilene, welcomes Pericles, his king and future father-in-law. Audience members need only recollect the play's earlier scenes to find ample models of the sorts of festivities to which Gower alludes. Examples of pageantry fill this play of c. 1607, from the stage directions calling for music to accompany the arrival of Antiochus's daughter in scene 1, to the elaborate procession of knights in scene 6 in anticipation of an off-stage tournament.

Pericles heads the list of references under the first definition of the term "pageantry" in the *Oxford English Dictionary*: "Pageants or tableaux collectively; the public performance or display of these."[2] Binding the governor's "feats," "showes," "minstrelsie," and "prettie din" together in a single entity results in a fairly apt illustration of the term's third definition in the *OED*: "Splendid display; gorgeous, colourful, or spectacular show; pomp." Although this usage first appeared in print in 1651, the activity certainly preceded it, and the modern-day reader can attest to its continued and ubiquitous presence in the areas of sport (e.g., the opening ceremonies of any recent Olympic Games) and politics (from royal marriages and commemorations of a long-sitting monarch in the UK to political conventions in the US). Always lurking in the background, of course, is the *OED*'s second definition: "Show without substance; mere acting or show; empty or specious display."

Yet the creators and audiences of pageantry invest it with meaning, capable not only of entertainment but also of communication, and both musical and visual media play crucial roles in creating and conveying these messages. When US presidential candidate Mitt Romney announced his choice of running mate in August 2012, he did so in front of a decommissioned naval battleship (the USS *Wisconsin*; an allusion, in part, to Rep. Paul Ryan's home-state) and accompanied by music from *Air Force One*, an action film in which a fictional president (played by Harrison Ford) thwarts terrorists from Kazakhstan aboard the hijacked presidential plane. The use of music to create an aural and symbolic link to a real or imagined past is a common feature of political pageantry: George Frideric Handel's anthem "Zadok the Priest," composed for the coronation of King George II in 1727, has been performed at the coronation of every British monarch since, and it returned as the first tune in a musical medley that accompanied the concluding fireworks at the queen's diamond jubilee celebrations outside Buckingham Palace in 2012.

Although civic pageantry of this sort occurred much less frequently in the sixteenth and seventeenth centuries, it included at least some of the same events and many of the same aims. According to Bonner Mitchell, "The chief purpose of civic pageantry has always been to represent the majesty of the state to its citizens and to foreigners."[3] Sponsored by courts and cities to honor state visitors or celebrate important events in the lives of the ruling family (e.g., births, weddings, funerals), and witnessed by representatives of the principal European courts, pageantry was at once a highly visible form of conspicuous expenditure, a means of cementing alliances, and a vehicle for celebrating the past and projecting a glorious future. Its events were often commemorated in published descriptions. Establishing bibliographic control has occupied much modern scholarship, although several scholars have also addressed issues of pageantry's meaning, both generally and with respect to specific rulers and locations. The published accounts tend to focus on visual images, which might include inscriptions on temporary triumphal arches or detailed descriptions of participants' costumes, but they also often attempt to recreate pageantry's visual representation of social hierarchy by recording precisely the arrangement, according to precedence, of the individuals whose physical presence constituted part of a specific event. While musicians' involvement might be noted, such as the trumpeters who marched in a procession, references to music are often quite general, rendering its exact nature difficult to ascertain. Exceptions do exist, however, two of which will be discussed below. In these instances the participation of musicians went beyond just adding another visual component to the spectacle. Music contributed both structure and, possibly, meaning to an event.

Florence, 1539

One of the most detailed records of sixteenth-century pageantry can be found in Pier Francesco Giambullari's description of the festivities celebrating the 1539 marriage of Duke Cosimo I de' Medici of Florence and Eleonora of Toledo. Giambullari's account is particularly valuable for the author's precise record of visual images: minute details of the triumphal arch under which the bridal party passed on its way to the city center; head-to-toe descriptions of the costumes worn by every mythological and allegorical personage involved in the entertainment for the bridal banquet; and an explanation of the subjects and meanings of the large, temporary paintings that adorned the second *cortile* of the Medici palazzo on Via Larga. Giambullari also includes complete texts for all the music performed as part of the festivities, as his title page proudly proclaims, and, although he neglects to name the composer (Francesco Corteccia), he does conclude his account with the notice that the music had recently been published in Venice.

As might be expected, one theme that runs throughout the festivities is that of future offspring, the tangible result of a successful political alliance between two families. This message was particularly prominent in the bride's procession through the city, beginning with the triumphal arch at the Porta al Prato, whose facade depicted allegorical representations of, among other attributes, Fecundity, Security, and Eternity, along with scenes celebrating the military exploits of Cosimo's father, Giovanni delle Bande Nere. From boxes on either side of the arch, singers and instrumentalists performed Corteccia's eight-voice motet *Ingredere, ingredere* at Eleonora's arrival. The event planners clearly invested the motet's text with some significance, for it was reproduced in its entirety on the arch itself:

INGREDERE INGREDERE FOELICISS. AVSPICIIS VRBEM TVAM HELIONORA AC OPTIMAE PROLIS FOECVNDA ITA DOMI SIMILEM PATRI FORIS AVO SOBOLEM PRODVCAS VT MEDI- CEO NOMINI EIVSQVE DEVOTISS. CIVIBVS SECVRITATEM PRAESTES AETERNAM.

(Come in, come in, under the most favorable auspices, Eleonora, to your city. And, fruitful in excellent offspring, may you produce descendants similar in quality to your father and forebears abroad, so that you may guarantee eternal security for the Medici name and its most devoted citizenry.)[4]

The other principal theme of the 1539 Florentine festivities was Cosimo himself. Because he was descended from a minor branch of the family, Cosimo and his advisors sought to (1) highlight the military exploits of his father; (2) align the young duke with the older, illustrious branch of the family; and (3) assert that the representative of this newly pre-eminent offshoot on the family tree promised to surpass his predecessors. This latter theme dominated the visual imagery of the twelve large paintings hung on the east and west sides of the second courtyard of the Medici palace, the space that hosted both the wedding banquet on July 8 and the play with musical *intermedi* performed the following evening. The paintings on the east wall featured Cosimo's ancestors, often in less-than-flattering situations: one depicted Lorenzo the Magnificent attempting to negotiate peace with Naples in the aftermath of the Pazzi Conspiracy, while another, by Agnolo Bronzino, showed "the many difficulties of Duke Alessandro [Cosimo's immediate predecessor] in Naples, with the firm opposition of his powerful adversaries," according to Giambullari.[5]

Directly opposite the east wall, six paintings represented Duke Cosimo in analogous situations—scenes in which he is shown as having fared far better than his relatives. For example, the painting paired with that of Lorenzo the Magnificent depicted Cosimo's election by a unified council of forty-eight. Reading the paintings from south to north, that is, moving toward the temporary stage, Bronzino's painting of Duke Alessandro was paired with one by the same artist celebrating the Neapolitan proxy marriage between Duke Cosimo and Eleonora, daughter of the viceroy of Naples.

Music served to reiterate and sharpen the messages that the paintings provided. For the post-banquet entertainment, the court presented a multi-part pageant. First, Apollo and the Muses offered musical tributes to the bride and groom, the latter being compared to his illustrious forebears in a sort of musical counterpart to the surrounding paintings. Then, the goddess Flora and personifications of Tuscan rivers and towns paid musical homage to the couple in a topographical pageant.

In combination with stagecraft, music delivered an even more pointed message the following night in the *intermedi* performed before, after, and between the five acts of Antonio Landi's comedy *Il commodo*. Giovanni Battista Strozzi composed the *intermedi* texts, while Francesco Corteccia again supplied the music. Several scholars have noted the significance of these intermedi to the history of theatrical solo singing in Florence. They also made important contributions to what Nino Pirrotta termed "temporal perspective," that is, the compression created by temporary shifts from real to musical time. In the madrigals of the first and sixth intermedi, sung before and after the comedy by Dawn and Night, respectively, Strozzi created a poetic bond analogous to the paired paintings on either side of the stage by means of similar opening and closing lines: for example, Dawn's "Vattene Almo riposo, ecco ch'io torno; Et ne rimeno il giorno" (Depart, blessed Repose, for here I am again, bringing back the day) can be compared to Night's "Vienten' almo riposo: ecco ch'io torno; Et ne discaccio il giorno" (Come, blessed repose, for here I am again, banishing the day"),[6] a textual parallelism not mirrored, however, in Corteccia's music. By means of stage machinery designed to reinforce this sense of temporal progress, the architect Bastiano [Aristotile] da San Gallo ensured the proper movement of the audience's eyes from the past to the glorious present. Vasari described in detail the device that accomplished this feat, consisting of a crystal ball filled with distilled water, which was backlit and then pulled by means of a winch from east to west, so that it replicated the movement of the sun. Thus in the final *intermedio*, as the personage of Night arrives and the sun is in the west, all eyes would have been drawn to the magnificent painting of the bridal couple, the illumination of a new era in Florentine politics.

In the Florence pageantry of 1539, music not only confirmed the festivities' magnificence, that is, as a visual display of the court's access to talented composers and musicians, but also served as a vehicle for communicating and heightening politically charged messages. Giambullari's inclusion of the full text of each madrigal and motet, coupled with his detailed descriptions of the musicians' costumes and instruments, suggests a privileging of the music's visual and semantic properties. Although he notes that four trumpeters headed the procession of the bridal party through the city, he does not spend time on the other likely occasions for instrumental music, just as he passes briefly over the actual food served at the wedding banquet. But instrumental music was an essential part of pageantry, especially outdoor genres such as triumphal processions and tournaments.

Florence, 1608

Nearly three-quarters of a century after the Medici court celebrated the marriage of Duke Cosimo I, Florence welcomed another new bride to Florence for the marriage of his grandson and namesake, Cosimo II, the eighteen-year-old crown prince who would assume the role of grand duke just a few months after his wedding. The year was 1608, and, as with Cosimo I's marriage to Eleonora of Toledo, the union celebrated and reinvigorated the Medici family's ties to the Habsburgs. Befitting the family's elevation in status over the intervening years, this time the Medici were able to marry their son to an archduchess, Maria Magdalena, cousin of the reigning Holy Roman Emperor Rudolf II. The court celebrated Maria Magdalena's arrival with an unprecedented series of events, including a play with lavish musical intermedi, a mock naval battle on the Arno River, and a horse ballet (*balletto a cavallo*) in the Piazza Santa Croce.

This horse ballet, performed October 27, 1608, and entitled *Ballo e giostra de' venti*, marked the first instance of a genre that would prove popular in Florentine pageantry for much of the century. Horse ballets and other equestrian genres allowed the Medici rulers to display publicly the military prowess of the Tuscan knights and Medici princes. An extant letter by Lorenzo Franceschi, the author of the 1608 work, confirms that the court was especially concerned to exhibit Cosimo's agility and skill to his future subjects. The work certainly provided an opportunity for the prince to demonstrate both physical strength and mental discipline. But it also acknowledged the long-standing relationship between the Medici and Habsburg families, a theme that recurred throughout the month-long series of events, from the archduchess's initial entrance into and triumphal procession through the city to the mock naval battle, which dramatized Jason (again played by the crown prince) capturing the Golden Fleece. The very notion of a horse ballet paid homage to Habsburg contributions to equitation: not only had Maria Magdalena's uncle Archduke Maximilian II introduced the Spanish horses that would lend their name to the imperial riding school in Vienna in 1562, but in 1580 her father had founded the stud farm that still produces the famed Lipizzaners. Even the specific subject of Franceschi's work linked the 1608 horse ballet to imperial spectacles, for among the festivities in Vienna celebrating the 1571 marriage of Maria Magdalena's parents was a tournament in which mounted riders were costumed according to a theme devised by the painter Giuseppe Arcimboldo—the first such unified tournament given in the Empire. The theme of that tournament centered on the conflict between Juno and Europa, each surrounded by her subject nations and attributes, including the personified winds, the main roles in Franceschi's *Ballo* of 1608.

The *Ballo e giostra de' venti* exemplifies the multiplicity of readings inherent in pageantry, readings dependent on a viewer's fluency with visual and, to a lesser extent, musical symbols. In 1608, Franceschi helped audience members to understand what they were seeing by means of a poem published and distributed to the spectators. Those who read all forty-seven octaves would have learned that the work was about the theme of princely virility in service to the Church, disciplined through wisdom and temperance. They would have been encouraged to think about the winds' traditional role as navigational aids, having guided three famous sailors—Jason, Ulysses, and Aeneas—to their long-sought goals (that is, the Golden Fleece, Ithaca, and the Latin shore, respectively). Franceschi predicts that favorable winds will secure future naval victories, especially now that the Habsburg and Medici houses are united. Readers would have been encouraged to view the entire work in terms of navigation: in addition to the presence of mariners and marine deities as participants, a 32-point compass rose—also known as a wind rose, which indicated the cardinal directions on both compasses and maps at this time—occupies a prominent location in both contemporary published sources, surrounded by a quotation from the *Aeneid* (6:130): *Ardens evexit ad æthera virtvs* (ardent manliness lifted up to heaven) (Figure 36.1). The *balletto a cavallo* illustrated this motto corporeally, using both equestrian and human bodies to mirror the concentric circles of the wind rose. Through words and bodies, the *Ballo de' venti* thus celebrated and promoted Tuscan naval superiority.

Audience members who, through lack of access or interest, did not read Franceschi's circulating octaves still would have been able to comprehend at least something of what was going on, based on participants' costumes and the banners that some of them carried. Instrumental music, now lost, punctuated the sectional construction of the event, and its performers participated in its underlying narrative. At the start of the work twenty-four musicians, costumed as creatures associated with water, accompanied the entrance of Aeolus, king of the winds, who rode into the arena surrounded by twelve footmen dressed as mariners, "who represented his first students, to whom he had taught the observation of the winds and the use of the sails."[7] Twelve trumpeters appeared disguised as tritons, four drummers (on nakers) were costumed as tempests, and eight players of *pifferi* (wind instruments) and *sordine* (probably double reed instruments) appeared to be sirens. The same musicians also accompanied the entrance of the *carro dell'Oceano*, a triumphal float replicating a rock decorated with coral, sponges, and moss, pulled by what appeared to be two whales and on which sat Deiopeia, Aeolus's beloved, surrounded by her own retinue of nymphs of the sea, rivers, and lakes. A surviving request for costumes reveals that twenty-six nymphs joined Deiopeia on her float. These nymphs added their own musical sonorities to the mix, performing on viols and violins.

The arrival of Deiopeia's float signaled the conclusion of the first section of the spectacle: King Aeolus and his court made a circuit of the performance space, after which the king made reverence to the bride. Franceschi based the next section of the entertainment loosely on the first book of the *Aeneid* (1.81–156): with his staff Aeolus struck an artificial mountain that dominated the west end of the piazza, effecting the release of thirty-two riders—including Prince Cosimo—depicting the winds, as well as 128 *venticelli* (breezes) on foot, just as Aeolus's minions buffeted Aeneas's ships. After this initial display of speed and power, the king restored order and harnessed his subjects, a discipline demonstrated visually in the orderly movements of the riders and their mounts. Prince Cosimo, as Zephyr, led eight rows of three riders each—a principal wind flanked by two companion winds—in a counterclockwise tour of the piazza to the sound of trumpets, their rows alternating with one of the eight transverse winds riding the horses trained as jumpers (*saltatori*). The riders formed the spokes of a wheel, which turned until each group arrived at its proper location, then realigned into three concentric circles, the eight principal riders in the center, the jumping horses one level out, and the remaining sixteen horses forming the perimeter (Figure 36.2). According to Franceschi, "the trumpets ceasing, Deiopeia and the other nymphs began to play violas and violins, and the eight principal winds began to dance"[8] to this new, sweeter sound that could be heard throughout the piazza, he affirms.

Cosimo and the seven other riders in the inner circle began nine choreographed *mutanze* (variations) in which the prince's skill on horseback would either shine or falter. The principal means by which these riders moved from place to place was by the *courbette*. In dressage, this term refers to an air above the ground that consists of a hop executed on the horse's rear legs. In visual art, such as equestrian monuments, courbette signifies a rearing pose "allegorically interpreted (by analogy with the art of equitation) as a prince properly governing his people."[9] Alfonso di Ruggieri Sanseverino, the ballet's choreographer, built excitement by gradually increasing the number of riders who participated simultaneously in each figure, culminating in a variation in which all eight riders executed a series of half turns and courbettes at the same time. Alternating with these nine mutanze, the remaining twenty-four riders performed what the description terms intermedi, which consisted of interwoven patterns and jumps. These movements added variety to the event but also, as Rinuccini attests, allowed the eight principal horses to catch their breath.

Music of a different sort accompanied at least some of the intermedi. Whereas the first intermedio is headed by the direction "Intermedio, e mutano s[u]ono i Violini," for the second intermedio the description reads "Intermedio, suona per li Saltatori," meaning it was "played" by the jumping horses. The emphasis on horses as sounding bodies recalls the actual noises that would have been a crucial part of the event, a clamor that would have served as a constant reminder of the military exercises to which equestrian pageantry was intended to allude.

According to contemporary reports, the audience greeted the *Ballo de' venti* enthusiastically. The eighteen-year-old crown prince apparently acquitted himself well, and the balletto a cavallo became a regular feature of court-sponsored festivities honoring, or in some cases anticipating, the marriages of Medici princes and princesses through much of the seventeenth century. Subsequent horse ballets included spoken and sung texts as well as instrumental music, giving audience members a clearer sense of their underlying narratives than the audience probably enjoyed in 1608. As already noted, many of Franceschi's complex, interrelated messages were likely lost on most of the audience in 1608, since the *Ballo de' venti* included no means of conveying them with any precision, aside from the banners carried by some of the participants and the circulating poetry. Even court insiders couldn't always figure it out: although diarist Cesare Tinghi knew that the work was about King Aeolus and the winds, he mistakenly reported that the noblemen on horseback were costumed as Indian girls. But perhaps that didn't matter, for the more important message, the one Franceschi had articulated ten months earlier, was indeed apprehended: a frail teenager had blossomed into a worthy knight, able to discipline his horse and claim his bride, all to the harmonious sound of violins.

These two Florentine examples illustrate an element of pageantry that has remained consistent to the present day, namely, the ability for an individual event to be "read" along a continuum of ever more precise interpretations depending on the degree to which an audience member is an initiate into its symbols. Visual images and music are not only implicated in these readings but are crucial to them.

Notes

1 William Shakespeare, *Pericles, Prince of Tyre* (London: Henry Gosson, 1609), sig. 12r.
2 *Oxford English Dictionary*, 3rd edition (online), www.oed.com.
3 Bonner Mitchell, *The Majesty of the State: Triumphal Progresses of Foreign Sovereigns in Renaissance Italy (1494–1600)* (Florence: Leo S. Olschki, 1986), 1.
4 Pier Francesco Giambullari, *Apparato et feste nelle noze [sic] dello Illustrissimo Signor Duca di Firenze, et della Duchessa sua consorte, con le sue stanze, madriali, comedia, & intermedij, in quelle recitati* (Florence: Benedetto Giunta, 1539), 10; translated in Andrew C. Minor and Bonner Mitchell, *A Renaissance Entertainment: Festivities for the Marriage of Cosimo I, Duke of Florence, in 1539* (Columbia, MO: University of Missouri Press, 1968), 103 n13. Minor and Mitchell also include an edition of the entire motet (104–117).
5 Minor and Mitchell, *A Renaissance Entertainment*, 132.
6 Ibid., 224, 342, 349.
7 [Camillo Rinuccini], *Descrizione delle feste fatte nelle reali nozze de' Serenissimi Principi di Toscana D. Cosimo de' Medici, e Maria Maddalena Arciduchessa d'Austria* (Florence: Giunti, 1608 [1609]), 51: "che tali furono i primi suoi allievi, a' quali avea insegnato l'osservazion de' venti, e l'uso delle vele." Translation mine.
8 "E cessando le Trombe incominciarono Deiopea, e l'altre Ninfe, a sonar di Viole, e Violini, e gli otto venti principali à ballare." Lorenzo Franceschi, *Ballo e giostra de' venti* (Florence: Giunti, 1608), sig. Av; translation mine.
9 Charles Avery, "Equestrian Monument," *Oxford Art Online* (www.oxfordartonline.com).

Further Reading

Béhar, Pierre and Helen Watanabe-O'Kelly. *Spectaculum Europaeum: Theatre and Spectacle in Europe (1580–1750)*. Wiesbaden: Harrassowitz, 1999.

Bowles, Edmund A. *Musical Ensembles in Festival Books, 1500–1800: An Iconographical and Documentary Survey*. Ann Arbor: UMI Research Press, 1989.

Cummings, Anthony M. *The Politicized Muse: Music for Medici Festivals, 1512–1537*. Princeton: Princeton University Press, 1992.

Minor, Andrew C. and Bonner Mitchell. *A Renaissance Entertainment: Festivities for the Marriage of Cosimo I, Duke of Florence, in 1539*. Columbia, MO: University of Missouri Press, 1968.

Mitchell, Bonner. *Italian Civic Pageantry in the High Renaissance: A Descriptive Bibliography of Triumphal Entries and Selected Other Festivals for State Occasions*. Florence: Leo S. Olschki, 1979.

Nagler, A. M. *Theatre Festivals of the Medici, 1539–1637*. New Haven: Yale University Press, 1964.

Pirrotta, Nino and Elena Povoledo. *Music and Theatre from Poliziano to Monteverdi*. Translated by Karen Eales. Cambridge: Cambridge University Press, 1982.

Strong, Roy. *Art and Power: Renaissance Festivals 1450–1650*. Woodbridge, UK: Boydell Press, 1984.

Treadwell, Nina. *Music and Wonder at the Medici Court: The 1589 Interludes for "La pellegrina."* Bloomington: Indiana University Press, 2008.

Watanabe-O'Kelly, Helen. *Triumphall Shews: Tournaments at German-Speaking Courts in their European Context 1560–1730*. Berlin: Gebr. Mann Verlag, 1992.

37
OPERA
Sarah Hibberd

Opera's origins lie in the various festivals, pageants, masques, ballets, *intermedi*, and other theatrical entertainments that took place across Europe in the sixteenth century, which combined drama with music and often lavish visual spectacle. The multimedia character of these performances was retained as opera established itself across seventeenth-century Europe, and has remained a part of its conception ever since: all opera necessarily includes the arrangement and movement on stage of individual characters and choruses, together with scenery, costumes, and special effects and lighting. The element of visual spectacle proved to be particularly fascinating to the French court at the turn of the seventeenth century: alongside the *comédie-ballet* and *tragédie en musique* (as exemplified by the works of Jean-Baptiste Lully) it cultivated the *opéra-ballet*, which was more closely related to trends in poetry and the visual arts. The form consisted of a prologue and three or four *entrées*, in which the sung element served as a pretext for a splendid *divertissement*, as typified by André Campra's *L'Europe galante* (1697), in which each entrée offered a contrasting stereotype of love (in France, Spain, Italy, Turkey); Louis de Cahusac described them as "pretty Watteaus, piquant miniatures that demand precision of design, grace of brush stroke and brilliance of color."[1] Indeed the integration into the drama of ballet, pantomime, and visual spectacle inspired by painting continued to characterize the French approach to opera: Jean-Philippe Rameau's tragédies (including his first, *Hippolyte et Aricie*, 1733) included a spectacular fête or divertissement in each of their five acts, which enhanced the dramatic action. In *Hippolyte*, this included a sea monster carrying off the hero in Act IV. French traditions were incorporated in Gluck's reforms to Italian *opera seria* in the second half of the eighteenth century as well: in his final work, *Iphigénie en Tauride*, created for Paris in 1779, he integrated aria, chorus, and ballet into dramatic tableaux of great flexibility and effect, and in so doing achieved new levels of expressive power.

With the emergence in the second half of the eighteenth century of a civic society and public space (as conceptualized by Habermas), the central concern of the new bourgeois art (including drama and emergent traditions of opera, such as *opera buffa*, *opéra comique*, and *Singspiel*) was the replacement of courtly formalism with an approach to individual and social existence that related to real experience. A crucial element of this new aesthetic, as specified by Denis Diderot, Gotthold Ephraim Lessing, and others, was a pictorially composed stage, evoking mood and local color and offering a truthfulness of representation. With the eruption of the French Revolution (the impact of which was to make itself felt across Europe for at least the next half century) and a developing aesthetic of heightened emotion, increasing attention was paid to creating scenes of shock that drew the audience into the unfolding drama and overwhelmed all their senses. With the widespread emergence of national (political) consciousness during the nineteenth century, further attention was paid to local color—whether recognizable moments from European history or the exotic East of colonial exploits—with (apparently) accurately rendered scenery and costumes often inspired by museum artifacts, paintings, and historical and travel writing. Multiple choruses represented clearly differentiated peoples (representing distinct nations, races, religions), and the increasingly ambitious use of machinery and lighting contributed to the overwhelming effect. Opera became ever more enmeshed in political culture, as illustrated most clearly by the grand operas of July Monarchy Paris, which depicted moments from history that resonated with recent political events (often—though not always—the Revolution), brought to life vividly with musical and visual symbols and magnificence. In Italy, owing to tighter censorship, the plots were more often based on literary models rather than specific historical events, but the genre was no less politically charged as a component of Italian identity during the Risorgimento. With Verdi's *Aida* (1871), an Italian opera commissioned for the new opera house in Cairo that drew on Verdi's experiences in composing for Paris, opera arguably reached its most visually magnificent zenith: individual human tragedy plays out against a massively realized setting, flavored (visually and musically) with the exoticism of Pharaonic Egypt, and incorporating ballets, processions, ceremonies, and a split stage in the final act representing the temple of Vulcan and its vaults in which the lovers expire. Productions in the 1930s reputedly incorporated real elephants and horses, and it is still common for modern directors to magnify the visual grandeur inherent in the work.

In more recent times, such ambitions have been reignited, and extended to the use of film projection and ever more sophisticated technological advancements. On the one hand, we might look to landmark productions of repertory works such as Patrice Chéreau's 1976 centenary *Ring* at Bayreuth, which combined a spectacularly realized nineteenth-century mythical dreamscape with industrial references (including the model of a vast steel dam for the opening scene of *Rheingold*), reflecting modern social and technological anxieties and offering an allegorical reading of the nineteenth century. On the other hand, we might look to newly conceived works that expand our definition of opera, such as Chen Shi-zheng's *Monkey King*, created in partnership with Damon Albarn and Jamie Hewlett for the Manchester International Festival in 2007, and incorporating circus acts and animations.

In spite of this spectacular history, it has taken some time for scholarship to acknowledge opera as an integral part of wider visual as well as musical culture. In part—as far as historical works are concerned, at least—this is because of the nature of extant source materials, from which it is often difficult to establish what a staging might actually have looked like. There has been a concomitant reluctance to consider how the visual dimension related to the music, and thus to understand a staging as not merely a straightforward visual embodiment or reflection of the drama, but as an intrinsic element of the conception. Nevertheless, in the twenty years since the early 1990s the situation has begun to change. Scholars are acknowledging opera's multimedia character and asking challenging questions of its relation to visual culture.

Visual Components of Opera

From the nineteenth century, we find increasing quantities of visual materials that help us to understand how a staging was conceived. Sketches for sets and costumes give us glimpses of the physical appearance of individual characters (often in a variety of costumes), and the scenery for specific scenes and acts. Moreover, technical manuals such as Gilbert Austin's *Chironomia, or a Treatise on Rhetorical Delivery* (London, 1806), Carlo Blasis's *The Code of Terpsichore* (London, 1828), or Aristippe Félix Bernier de Maligny's *Théorie de l'art du comédien* (Paris, 1828), though rooted in eighteenth-century practice, offer some insight into the lexicon of gestures, facial expressions, and stances that were available to singers in the first half of the century. Aspects of set design and the use of technology are also detailed in such works as Jean-Pierre Moynet's *L'Envers du théâtre: Machines et décorations* (Paris, 1874), which provides information on how stock effects such as appearances and disappearances, collapsing buildings, storms, and shipwrecks were achieved. The drawings and detailed descriptions in such publications help us to understand the craft of staging, and offer snapshots of the intended visual effects that situate opera within a wider theatrical culture. But these necessarily capture isolated moments, and offer little information on the transitions between sets, between different types of action (acting, singing, dancing), the movement of people on stage, and the interaction of music, visual display, and drama.

Artists' drawings, etchings, and paintings created after attending a performance can often provide a more telling impression of the overall emotional effect. Céline Frigau has demonstrated how prints in the collection at the Bibliothèque-musée de l'Opéra in Paris tend to offer idealized versions of works that magnify, for example, the imposing quality of the scenery (in contrast to small human figures), or that bring together consecutive moments from the drama in a single image, and thereby evoke the cumulative effect on the spectator. Art of the period was more broadly influenced by new techniques of melodramatic gesture and tableau in the theater, and such responses to individual works were appreciated as independent artworks as much as souvenirs of a performance. Descriptions of operas in press reviews tended to be similarly allusive, and emphasized the emotional effect on the audience of particular moments of the drama. In his introduction to the volume *Les Beautés de l'Opéra* (Paris, 1845), Théophile Gautier noted how "so much splendid scenery, so many charming costumes, so many magnificent processions disappear without trace."[2] This collection of literary essays (by Gautier, Jules Janin, and Philarète Chasles) evokes the atmosphere created in operas and ballets performed at the Paris Opéra in the 1830s and 1840s by describing the lighting effects and the costumes, the emotions generated in crowd scenes, the expressions on the performers' faces, and the reactions of the audience.

Together, then, such visual and literary source materials help us to appreciate the means by which visual effects were achieved, and the impact they had on the spectator, offering insight into conventions, stock effects, and taste, and something of their place in wider visual culture. As stagings became ever more spectacular and complicated, however, and as the practice of reviving existing works became more prevalent, the need to record staging details more precisely and comprehensively became pressing. In Paris, *livrets de mise en scène* began to appear when a *Comité de mise en scène* (under stage director Jean-Baptiste Solomé) was established at the

Opéra in 1827. This body of staging manuals includes transcriptions of both original stagings and much later productions, from the Opéra and from other houses, including the Opéra Comique. Together, they reveal important information about conventions and the evolving approach to realism during the middle decades of the nineteenth century—and the move toward ever greater magnificence and pomp. Aimed at those intending to revive the work in Paris, or to create it in the provinces or abroad, they contain information concerning the movement and placing of characters and choruses (including processions and dancing), the use of *practicables* (moveable platforms, such as staircases or large rocks), the use of drop-curtains with scenery painted on them, as well as some commentary on the use of machinery and lighting, details of costumes and props, and occasional cues with the score or libretto to synchronize movement. But they also include evocative descriptions, presumably to help the singers and/or director understand the emotion behind their actions or the intended effect on the audience. Witness the instructions for the final scene of the first grand opera, Daniel Auber's *La Muette de Portici* (1828):

> During this final scene, the curtain of clouds has disappeared and revealed an angry Vesuvius; it throws out swirls of flame and smoke; the lava comes as far as the foot of the stairway. The music must be managed so that the chorus begins as soon as Fenella has disappeared into the lava.
>
> After the final chorus, everyone moves about with the greatest terror. A man arrives at the top of the stairway; the top of the terrace, at the sound of an explosion, collapses and swallows him and three children, two held by the hand, one on his back. All see this tableau of horror and group themselves as follows.
>
> Alphonse in the center of the stage; Elvire, head buried in his chest; pages and women surround her in diverse groups.
>
> The people fill the stage; mothers carry their children; men support their wives; some fall to the ground, others support themselves against the colonnades.
>
> Those who come via the terrace expire on the steps; one cannot go too far in painting the terror in every movement of these characters.
>
> Underground noises continue; tam-tam strokes, thunder, tremors, roaring, everything happens at once. Just as the curtain is lowered, the arch should fall, from Vesuvius to the steps, stones of all sizes that could come from the crater: there must be many.[3]

Such excerpts offer insights into the industry behind the scenes dedicated to creating such effects. This comprised painters (often with specialties—landscapes, architecture, or even simply trees, water, or people); machinists (adept with pulleys and ropes); technicians responsible for producing flames or smoke; hordes of less skilled people to operate machinery and to throw *papier mâché* rocks onto the stage; and someone to orchestrate the activity and ensure the realization of every detail of the tableau. The singers must also have been acutely aware of the need to contribute to the overall stage picture, placing themselves correctly in relation to each other and to various objects—and to avoid the carefully orchestrated collapse of buildings around them.

In the mid-1850s, the Milanese firm Ricordi started publishing *disposizioni sceniche* at Verdi's suggestion, on the French model, though it was not until later in the century that staging was recognized as an intrinsic part of an opera in Italy. It has been demonstrated how such manuals can help clarify not only the intended action, but also the musical execution. Thus, David Rosen has explained how Riccardo's reluctance to leave the stage at the end of *Un ballo in maschera* (1858), which gives his rival the opportunity to stab him fatally, is documented (and thus explained) only in the *disposizione scenica* (there is nothing in the score or libretto); and Andrew Porter has explained how the blocking (i.e. positioning of characters) prescribed in the manual helps one to get the right balance between off-stage chorus and on-stage chorus, semi-chorus and soloists in the notoriously tricky passage in Act II scene 4 of *La forza del destino*. Moreover, certain staging effects (from changing lighting to the movement of characters) seem to have been composed into Verdi's scores, suggesting a closely conceived relationship between music and visual effect in the composition process. Wagner's detailed instructions are further evidence of this increasing composer-driven interest in controlling all aspects of a production. Gundula Kreuzer has demonstrated the complex ways in which such neglected visual elements of an opera as the raising of the main curtain or the use of drop-curtains and veils mid-scene have been effectively written into Wagner's scores, to the extent not simply that they become fixed, but also that the boundaries between music and image become permeable. For example, the orchestra seems almost to push the curtain up at the beginning of *Rheingold*, with its crescendo of rising Eb major arpeggios. By taking account of staging instructions one becomes aware of the "visual" qualities offered by the music, which contribute to the overall effect.

Yet, if music, text, and visuals are each considered and sanctioned by the composer, and are intricately related to each other, why should the detailed information contained in staging manuals so rarely feature in modern critical editions? Currently, it is unusual to include more than the odd direction, transferred from the score. Part of the problem is the conflicting information often found in staging manuals, score, and libretto, and the practicalities attendant upon incorporating such quantities of information into a single volume. Moreover, reproducing (supposing one can) the "original" staging does not necessarily bring us closer to the opera, and in fact can draw attention to its divergence from modern visual norms—the visual representation seems to date more than the poetry or music of an opera. As James Hepokoski has pointed out, spontaneous theatrical (not to mention socio-political) contexts are lost, and so when we see a historical staging we are in fact experiencing a modern historicized commentary. Nevertheless, awareness of what a period staging might involve can still be valuable to a modern director and conductor for practical and aesthetic reasons.

Opera in its Visual Context

An alternative and arguably more productive approach to understanding the visual dimension of opera is to move away from the archives and approach the problem from the other end: what was the visual literacy of opera audiences? At one level, we should acknowledge that stage and costume designers and set painters often worked not only at other theaters and opera houses, but also as independent paint- ers, interior designers, and illustrators, and so their designs and techniques in the opera house should be understood as an integral part of wider visual as well as musi- cal culture—and thus as historically situated. At another level, we should recognize opera—along with other forms of theater—as being at the forefront of technologi- cal advancements and experimentation, and thus participating in an exciting, more broadly conceived multimedia environment.

As noted above, French opera in particular tended to prize the visually spec- tacular. Art—in a variety of media—was an important reference point for both the creators and the spectators of opera during the long nineteenth century. Paintings often provided inspiration, whether for scenery, or for the arrangement of figures on stage. Thus, as Kirsten Gram Holmström tells us, *tableaux vivants*, based on familiar artworks, were often found embedded in plays and operas (and even in concerts) at the turn of the eighteenth century. By the 1830s, there was more interest in animat- ing such recognizable images, and Géricault's *Raft of the Medusa* (*Scène de naufrage*) provided a model for the third act of Louis Niedermeyer's opera *Le Naufrage de la Méduse* (1837) at the Théâtre de la Renaissance, which intensified the gruesome depiction of death and desperation, and embedded it in an unfolding narrative that sought to bring the event back to life in an arresting and emotionally charged scene. The final tableau of Giacomo Meyerbeer's *Le Prophète* (1849) was inspired by another popular—and spectacular—painting, John Martin's *Belshazzar's Feast*, which it brought to life in a more imaginative way, the exaggerated perspective and grandeur of the palace serving to underline the hopelessness of the small figures caught in the extravagantly depicted conflagration.

Special effects, too, were often inspired by developments in other forms of vis- ual entertainment. The Degotti brothers Ignazio and Ilario, who arrived in Paris from Turin (via Rome and Naples) and in David Charlton's assessment helped to establish the Théâtre Feydeau as the cradle of Romantic stagecraft in the 1790s, produced the overwhelming effect of a blazing castle in Luigi Cherubini's opera *Lodoïska* (1791), and a sublime Alpine landscape with an avalanche engulfing the entire stage in the same composer's *Eliza* (1794). Such works were created at a time when Parisian audiences were gripped by other spectacular illusionary effects, including that of the Panorama (the depiction of a vast landscape on the interior wall of a rotunda, patented by Robert Barker in London, and quickly established in Paris in the late 1780s), and the phantasmagorical performances of the magician and physicist Etienne-Gaspard Robert, known as Robertson, who summoned up dead heroes and destroyed enemies using a magic lantern technique to project an image on a wall or gauze screen. Audiences entered a dark cavern and saw these images accompanied by music, sound effects, and the voices of ventriloquists.

Some thirty years later, in 1822, the stage designer Louis Daguerre and the archi- tectural painter Charles Marie Bouton opened their Diorama, which displayed enor- mous paintings, mostly landscapes and cathedrals, under changing lighting effects of the type Daguerre had developed for the stage at the Théâtre de l'Ambigu-Comique and the Opéra, that suggested the passing of time. These included stunning sunrises and sunsets, moonlight, and storms, as well as the simulated movement of flames, smoke, water, and clouds. The most popular subject in the 1820s was the "Ruines de la chapelle de Holyrood," exhibited from 1823. It depicted a ruined Gothic chapel lit by moonlight, into which was introduced the figure of a woman in white, praying. Such displays clearly combined an interest in the realistic recreation of nature and historical ruins—inspired in part by Salon history paintings, and by such evocative writing as the novels of Walter Scott—with a desire for the visceral immediacy of spectacular visual display. Similarly, the effects created at such popular theaters as the Théâtre de la Porte Saint-Martin were widely celebrated. At the premiere of Charles Nodier's *mélodrame Le Monstre et le magicien* (1826), an extremely simplified adaptation of Mary Shelley's *Frankenstein*, audiences were delighted to see the monster pass through walls and floor without any opening being visible—this was the first use in Paris of the *trappes anglaises*. Such entertainments drew audiences from all social and political backgrounds, apparently keenly complicit in this trickery of the eye.

These effects were, of course, absorbed into opera of the late 1820s and early 1830s. The diorama technique of double-painting a canvas so that its image changed when illuminated from different sides was employed in Auber's *La Muette de Portici*, for example. As we have seen, an erupting Vesuvius, the subject of a diorama and a number of popular plays, provided the climax of the same opera. And Meyerbeer's *Robert le diable* (1831) revealed in two celebrated scenes the influence of two more dioramas: the moonlit cloister in Act III, the setting for a ballet of nuns, was reminiscent of "Ruines de la chapelle de Holyrood"; and the interior of Palermo Cathedral at the end of Act V recalled cathedral dioramas such as Bouton's "Trinity Chapel, Canterbury Cathedral" (1822). Several reviewers commented on the derivation of such moments, and audiences appeared to delight in the same sorts of illusions that they had experienced outside the opera house.

Although we tend to associate such spectacular visual effects with French opera during the nineteenth century, Wagner (in spite of his disdain for the diorama) employed lantern projections for the first performances of *The Ring* in 1876, which, as Jonathan Crary and others have noted, came out of this tradition of popular entertainment. The Ride of the Valkyries, for example, was created with images painted on glass slides that were projected by a magic lantern onto the stage. Crary notes that the way in which the diorama disoriented the viewer through "the disjunction between its illuminated imagery and the darkened space of the spectator" was a technique explored by Wagner in order to control emotional responses to his dramas.[4] The art theorist Paul Souriau was one of the first to describe Wagner's work as "phantasmagoric" in 1893, situating it in a line of illusion and suggestion that reaches back to late-eighteenth-century phantasmagoric displays and spectacles of the sort Wagner may well have encountered in Paris.

David Levin has challenged the prevailing idea that opera is primarily a musical genre in provocative ways, arguing for a more sophisticated analysis of the other components of this multimedia genre. In 1994, he pointed to the need to rethink the value of the libretto, and acknowledge it as containing not just a single "meaning" to read in the context of the music, but as being unstable, heterogeneous, with multiple meanings; he encouraged musicologists to borrow the methodologies and vocabularies of scholars from other disciplines and open themselves up to opera's complexities. In 2010, he took a slightly different approach, demonstrating how critical analyses of modern stagings can help us to further develop our understanding of individual operas and the meanings they contain—and the genre of opera more broadly. The next step might be to historicize the visual dimension, and think more carefully about staging conventions and the visual context in which opera was created and received. It is only by becoming more comfortable with such visual materials and practices, by learning to interrogate them more rigorously, and by acknowledging the often complex ways in which music, staging, and drama interact in a given work, that we can begin to appreciate opera as an "unsettled," multimedia form, as embedded in visual as it is in musical and literary cultures.

Notes

1 Louis de Cahusac, *La danse ancienne et moderne: ou Traité historique de la danse*, 3 vols. (Paris: J. Neaulme, 1754); cited in James R. Anthony, "L'Europe galante," *The New Grove Dictionary of Opera*, ed. Stanley Sadie (London: Macmillan, 1994).
2 Théophile Gautier, "Prospectus de l'ouvrage," accompanying the reprint of a selection of *notices* from *Les Beautés de l'Opéra* in Théophile Gautier, *Souvenirs de théâtre, d'art et de critique* (Paris: G. Charpentier, 1883), n.p.
3 Louis Jacques Solomé, *Indications generals et observations pour la mise-en-scène de* La Muette de Portici, repr. in Robert H. Cohen, *The Original Staging Manuals for Twelve Parisian Operatic Premières, 1824–1843* (Stuyvesant, NY: Pendragon Press, 1991), 47.
4 Jonathan Crary, *Suspensions of Perception: Attention, Spectacle, and Modern Culture* (Cambridge, MA: MIT Press, 1999), 252.

Further Reading

Crary, Jonathan. *Suspensions of Perception: Attention, Spectacle, and Modern Culture*. Cambridge, MA: MIT Press, 1999.
Gernsheim, Helmut and Alison Gernsheim, *L. J. M. Daguerre: the History of the Diorama and the Daguerreotype*. London: Dover Publications, 1968.
Hibberd, Sarah. "*Le Naufrage de la Méduse* and Operatic Spectacle in 1830s Paris." *19th-Century Music* 36, no. 3 (Spring 2013): 248–63.
Hibberd, Sarah and Richard Wrigley, eds. *Exchanges and Tensions between Art, Theatre and Opera in France, c. 1750–1850* (Aldershot: Ashgate, forthcoming in 2013).
Holmström, Kirsten Gram. *Monodrama, Attitudes, and Tableaux – Vivants*. Stockholm: Almqvist & Wiksell, 1967.
Latham, Alison and Roger Parker, eds. *Verdi in Performance*. Oxford: Oxford University Press, 2001.
Levin, David. *Unsettling Opera: Staging Mozart, Verdi, Wagner, and Zemlinsky*. Chicago: University of Chicago Press, 2007.
Sadie, Stanley, ed. *The New Grove Dictionary of Opera*. London: Macmillan, 1994.
Smart, Mary Ann. *Mimomania: Music and Gesture in Nineteenth-Century Opera*. Berkeley: University of California Press, 2005.

38

BALLET
Interactions of Musical and Visual Style

Philip Weller

Musical and Visual Perspectives

Visual style is an integral part of all theatrical dance, and is intimately bound up with the very idea of ballet. Whether we are consciously aware of it or not, the visual environment is always to the fore when we experience, or even just think about, the possibilities of balletic form and narrative. The disciplined physicality of ballet is in itself an essentially visual language, even with minimal scenic apparatus and "functional" modern costuming. Human movement and gesture, and the way the body is made obedient to choreographic intention, are radically visual in nature and effect.

This fact offers a whole new way of appreciating, cognitively and expressively, the flow and force of music. Choreographic form and movement are always spatialized and, furthermore, act as reference points for the audience in its response to the musical continuity. Musical form possesses its own rhythmic–textural patterning and character. These are nevertheless transformed through the addition of a whole new rhythmic layer in the shape of the dance, working as a kind of spatial and gestural counterpoint. Moreover, in actual performance the rhythmic life of the musical score will be subtly inflected by its concurrence with the detailed rhythmic articulations and "line" of the dance. This intimate structural and expressive concurrence is then further intensified through more conventional "surface" visual elements such as scenery, costumes, color, lighting, and so on.

This distinctive type of visuality can be easily seen in different ways at different periods of ballet's history: in the grand formalities of court ballet and the English masque in the seventeenth century; in the brilliant and colorful *entrées* of the French *opéra-ballet* of the early eighteenth century; in the "expressionistic" subjects of the *ballet d'action* in the later eighteenth century; in the new atmospheric settings and patterns of movement of the Romantic ballet, after 1830; and in the amazing vividness and variety of the ballets of the Diaghilev era (1909–29) and beyond.

The visual dimension of ballet, then, is as strong as that of opera. This is hardly surprising, given their shared status as theatrical genres, underpinned with (more or less) continuous music running in parallel with the visual spectacle. In each case, the way the two strands are not simply juxtaposed or interwoven but made to inter-act governs the broader cognitive and communicative dimension of the piece as a whole. This type of interaction informs its larger rhythmic and expressive life, and the way it "inhabits" or "works on" our perception.

The fact that ballet is a staged performance art unfolding in time necessitates the same kinds of presentational strategies, broadly speaking, as in opera. These then serve as a larger frame for the specifically musical and human elements within each genre. Such modes of presentation include, principally: a carefully evolved approach to scenic layout and set design; a spatialized visual form; a cogent sense of direction and production; and a lighting environment existing in relation to stage space, costume, figure, gesture, movement, mood, and so on. These elements are variously emphasized, according to circumstance, in different eras and within dif-ferent traditions of ballet.

Some General Questions

One pressing general question is to interrogate the exact nature of the collaborative work that may have gone into the original making of a ballet, in any given instance. For his iconic *Rite of Spring* (1913), for example, Stravinsky himself selected Nicho-las Roerich (1874–1947) as scene painter and designer, working with him inten-sively in 1912 *before* there was any question of specific choreographic style:

> (Robert Craft:) Did you choose Nicholas Roerich to do the *Sacre du Printemps* décors?

> (Igor Stravinsky:) Yes. I had admired his work for [Borodin's Polovtsian Dances from] *Prince Igor* and imagined he might do something similar for the *Sacre*; above all, I knew he would not overload. Diaghilev agreed with me and accordingly, in the summer of 1912, I met Roerich in Smolensk and worked with him there in the country house of the Princess Tenischev, a patroness and liberal who had helped Diaghilev. I still have a good opinion of Roerich's *Le Sacre*. He had designed a backdrop of steppes and sky, the *Hic sunt leones* country of old mapmakers' imaginations. The row of twelve blonde, square-shouldered girls against this landscape made a very striking tableau. And Roerich's costumes were said to have been historically exact as well as scenically satisfying.[1]

The creative imagination of the musician can be observed here working not in the abstract but very much *ad rem*: materially, visually, spatially, as well as sonically. And it can be seen that the process of making is a socialized, dialogic one, although in the case of Stravinsky the question of visualization was something on which he held very definite views. Nevertheless, whatever his own conviction, he always accepted the pragmatic need for collaboration and teamwork, and was in any case subjected to the company "rules of engagement" when working for Diaghilev.

A further general point, which applies in principle to any ballet (though in prac-tice much more to some than to others), is the question of alternative or multiple choreographies. Certain ballets have survived, at least in everyday consciousness, through their title and concept, even though they may bear scant resemblance to their earlier incarnation(s): often they have not only new choreography, but also new scene settings and design, and even new music.

The case of the elegant rustic comedy *La Fille mal gardée* is instructive. It is one of the few more or less familiar "repertoire" pieces to have survived, after a fashion, from the earlier history of ballet. It was created by the eminent pupil of Jean-Georges Noverre, Jean Dauberval (1742–1806), for performance at the Grand Théâtre de Bordeaux on 1 July 1789. In 1791 Dauberval himself restaged the work for the King's Pantheon Theatre in London; and the *premier danseur* Eugène Hus, creator of the principal male role of Colas in Bordeaux, then staged it himself at the Paris Opéra in 1803 (having already used the ballet's libretto in 1796 for a comic opera *Lise et Colin*, set to the music of Pierre Gaveaux). In the modern era, *La Fille mal gardée* has normally been presented in one of two different versions: (1) Alexander Gorsky's version to the music of Peter Ludwig Hertel, originally staged for the Bolshoi Theater in Moscow in 1903, though based in turn on important earlier productions (St. Petersburg, Berlin); or (2) the production staged by Frederick Ashton for the Royal Ballet in 1960 to music adapted by John Lanchbery from Ferdinand Hérold (Paris, 1828) with other pragmatic period additions. So, although the performance of *La Fille mal gardée* has a continuous tradition of sorts, it is refracted through a range of visual and choreographic, and also musical, prisms—this being the normal state of affairs for the eighteenth and nineteenth centuries—prompting questions about the integrity and "identity" of the balletic work in which all of its component elements are implicated.

This point about an evolving identity relates directly to the visual character and environment of a ballet as it makes its mark upon the world. In this sense a ballet always exists not just abstractly, *in potentia*, but in a bodily and spatial sense, *in actu*, as inscribed within a particular performance tradition. A ballet may conceivably have survived only through its libretto or scenario, hence with its basic story and choreographic premise intact, but with such features as its musical score, its specific dance components, and its visual design mostly or entirely absent, lost in the flux of time.

The active, embodied nature of dance makes its historical repertoire a fruitful object of study not only for scholars, critics, and historians, but also for dance practitioners and choreographic specialists of one kind or another. And it remains true, perhaps, that the most efficient and effective way of preserving a ballet is precisely by maintaining it in the performed repertoire—though there have been many serious and committed recreations of particular historical choreographies at various points in the twentieth century, typically combining the sympathetic yet also sharply interrogative reading of visual traces and notational records with an eminent dancer's physical and visual memory of the experience of the production itself.

Romantic Ballet: Evolution, Survival, Revival

The revolution of the Romantic ballet was as much visual as it was musical and choreographic. There were new types of stories, of course, and new types of step and gesture. But the changes in setting and atmosphere were based as much on questions of visual style as on a straightforward taste for white, floaty ballerinas able to perform difficult arm- and footwork lyrically, or for virtuosic national and exotic dance types, with costumes to match. The revolution in subject matter was indissoluble from changes in several areas concurrently: in step vocabulary and dance technique, in scenery and lighting, and in the kind of music that matched the Romantic ethos and aesthetic.

From the later eighteenth and through the course of the nineteenth century, the established companies in Paris, Milan, and Copenhagen, as well as Vienna and St. Petersburg, consolidated and significantly extended their dancing style and repertoire. Because they were organized performing institutions and maintained a working repertoire, they also generally kept hold of their design material, to a greater or lesser extent. These paper records in effect began to form a kind of archived collection, though not yet in any systematic sense, with the result that some ballets of the period have a quantity of useful documentary and visual materials surviving.

Moreover, in addition to high-quality engravings (which had been used as a medium of visual illustration since the beginnings of ballet), the nineteenth century was very much the age of the popular lithograph, so that prints of solo artists (especially the great virtuoso ballerinas), as well as of group scenes, figure compositions, and general views of ballet productions within theater interiors, are relatively plentiful. As a result, our knowledge of costume is often extensive—with photography, beginning in the 1850s and 1860s, aiding the quest considerably—while that of set design is very reasonable. Moreover, whether or not the actual theater spaces still exist, the typical nineteenth-century stage set-up is well known.

Despite all this, few ballet productions or choreographies of the Romantic era survive in a fully realizable state. The various elements generally have to be pieced together through a process of creative reconstruction, and in this area of investigative research lies one of the key roles played—for dance historians, scholars of theatrical production, and enthusiasts alike—by the surviving visual materials of ballet.

Yet, despite the availability of dance notation (developed in the French dance academy during the late seventeenth century), its use was in practice somewhat rare and haphazard. At any rate, it seems to have been more usual for dancer-choreographers to recreate their own version of a ballet visually, from having watched it, as August Bournonville did with *La Sylphide*, which he "took" from Paris (1832) to Copenhagen (1836).

In fact, the number of ballet works which have come down to us in anything like their original state from the mid-nineteenth century is absolutely tiny. *Giselle* (Paris, 1841) has survived in a reworked yet broadly authentic form emanating from St. Petersburg (1884); a handful of Bournonville choreographies have been brilliantly and lovingly preserved by the Royal Danish Ballet in Copenhagen (*La Sylphide*, 1836; *Napoli*, 1842; *Le Conservatoire*, 1849; *The Kermesse in Bruges*, 1851; *A Folk Tale*, 1854); and that is about it, for the first period of the Romantic ballet.

A little later, emerging out of the turbulent context of Paris in the 1870s (the very period when Degas was painting his famous ballet pictures), there are two French works which survive in a recognizable, though again somewhat adapted, form: *Coppélia* (1870) and *Sylvia* (1876). The former is an elegant tale of passion and sentiment based on E. T. A. Hoffmann, the latter a Romanticized mythological plot of essentially picturesque and decorative character. Both were choreographed to first-rate musical scores by Léo Delibes (1836–91).

All these pieces are internationally known, and enjoy classic status across the globe: the Parisian ballets continuously so, since their creation, through the familiarity of innumerable revivals and restagings throughout the Western world; the Copenhagen ballets only since World War II, once the Royal Danish Ballet began to tour. During the 1950s the Bournonville pieces began to gain a worldwide audience, and the totality of the spectacle they present—mainly in costume and choreography, but also in their scenery—served to establish for critics, historians, and audiences alike a compelling link back to the mid-nineteenth century. Their vividness and immediacy exist simultaneously in depth and at the surface, built into the very structures and patterns of the dance movement and acting, yet also present in the larger visual picture. These pieces are unique in that they have been maintained in an unbroken line of production and performance within a single company, whereas the Parisian works all survive in authentic but "exported"—and hence adapted—versions.

The lasting value of all these works lies precisely in the perpetual artistic challenge that they pose. As with the written musical repertory, their classic status cannot be taken for granted, but must be continuously reasserted through performance. They need to exist in a state of continuous revival, and thus of "perpetual becoming." And the visual and physical nature of these ballets, standing in a relationship of productive tension to the permanent "givenness" of the musical score, ensures that the received version of the piece as a whole will be appropriately rethought and kept alive by this means.

Relations between musical style and choreographic language were not, and are not, fixed and immutable. The multimedia nature of theatrical dance means that it is not just desirable but necessary—for historians, critics and practitioners alike—to constantly (re)interrogate all aspects of the spectacle and their potential for interaction. Historical choreographies, where they have survived, are fascinating in their own right, but dance readings of musical scores are never, and never can be, definitive. Over the last hundred and fifty years or so, ballet has acquired a substantial and important repertory, many parts of which are (rightly) affectionately and at times jealously guarded. But this is a modern development which was never part of the original ethos: in many instances it was only the visual material—designers' drawings, costume drawings, engraved set designs—which survived at all.

Baroque and Rococo: Visual Artists at the Ballet

There are a number of peripheral connections between dance and art which throw an interesting sidelight on the relationship between the aesthetic commitment of "pure" visual artists and the "applied," essentially pragmatic world of the theater. Such connections are, of course, long established: they go back to the expensive and prestigious Renaissance spectacles created at princely courts in northern Italy. One universally famous case was the staged *Festa del Paradiso*, performed to a poetic scenario by Bernardo Bellincioni in the Castello Sforzesco in Milan in 1490, for which Leonardo da Vinci acted as designer, engineer, and "aesthetic impresario." Such courtly festivities, and the court ballets and *intermedi* which followed during the sixteenth and seventeenth centuries, were the direct antecedents of opera and ballet in the narrower, generic sense. Indeed, the French *ballet de cour* was in essence a flourishing Italian tradition, grafted onto a more disciplined and closely defined

French rootstock. Acclimatized within France and its world of courtly entertainment and decorum, this tradition produced—from the *Balet Comique de la Royne* of 1581 onward—a stream of ballet productions on diverse subject matter which would continue, in a succession of evolving types, through to the end of the Ancien Régime.

All these kinds of staging broadly shared a common set of visual characteristics, so far as their stage aspect and design were concerned. They also shared a general physical language of movement and gesture—naturally subject to evolution and reform over time (with changes in costume and step vocabulary, abandonment of the mask, new models for scenic construction, and so on), yet with an overall cogency that expressed a classical visual system endowed with real integration and resilience. These varied characteristics, like the choreographic language itself, were matched in a variety of ways with the structural and stylistic features of the music composed or adapted for the ballet-master's purposes.

In the heyday of Baroque and Rococo stage spectacle, even so eminent a public artist as François Boucher (1703–70) would still design costumes and scenery for both opera and dance, including in particular the Paris production of Noverre's smash-hit ballet *Les Fêtes chinoises*, presented by the impresario Jean Monnet at the Opéra Comique to great public acclaim (1 July 1754), with music possibly by Jean-Philippe Rameau. More generally, there is a clear element of the scenic *tableau* within Boucher's painterly idiom, and both his pastoral and his mythological subjects carry more than a hint of theatricality, of "staged" visual presentation.

Bernardo Bellotto (1722–80)—nephew and student of Canaletto, who in turn had learned his trade as a set painter working with his father—did not himself work in the theater, but he did produce a very famous etching that shows, in rich circumstantial detail (including the full pit orchestra), a 1758 performance at the Vienna Burgtheater of *Le Turc généreux*, one of the entrées of Rameau's hugely successful opéra-ballet of 1735, *Les Indes galantes*: this performance was choreographed in a more modern and dramatic dancing style (of which Bellotto's print shows clear traces) by the Viennese ballet-master Franz Anton Hilverding (1710–68). Bellotto's is one of the most developed of all eighteenth-century ballet prints (Figure 38.1). And it is in part through the survival of pictorial scenes such as this, which record theatrical dance "in action" (however stylized the record may be), that we can begin to observe the visual environment for ballet at its most copious and expressive, away from the schematic formulations of treatises and technical designs.

Eighteenth-century ballet prints exist in a sheer variety of types that the seventeenth-century examples, for all their richness of execution, cannot quite match. A quantity of prints emanating from London included one or two very striking, part-satirical scenes engraved by the Italian specialist Francesco Bartolozzi (1727–1815), probably after original designs by Nathaniel Dance (1735–1811). A view of a scene from *Jason et Médée*—a Noverre choreography of 1763, newly staged at the King's Pantheon Theatre in 1781—shows three star performers of the era: Giovanna Baccelli (Creusa), Gaétan Vestris (Jason), and Mme Adelaide Simonet (Medea). The dancing style—deriving from Noverre in 1763, but here very much the (re)creation of Vestris himself—embodied the taut, highly projected expressivity of the *ballet d'action*. Yet the print also contains an element of humorous exaggeration: the rich English satirical tradition in the decades either side of 1800 found ample material in the theater of the time, not least in the movement and gesture of ballet.

(A quick comparison with Gainsborough's Tate Britain *Portrait of Giovanna Baccelli* (1782), one of the most evocative and exhilarating of all dancer portraits, will serve to confirm this satirical edge in the print.) The Bartolozzi print is also notable in including a view of some of the orchestral musicians in the pit, and even a short musical excerpt in accurate music notation. The very fact of having devised what is in effect a "multimedia print"—close to the radical aesthetic suggestions, say, of Denis Diderot—serves to underscore the way in which the larger rhythmic and expressive continuity of the ballet is by necessity articulated within a combined, fully integrated musical–visual environment.

All this visual and scenic information allows us to envisage a frame and context for the living physical language of choreography and gesture, and for the audience's reception of the musical score—in expressing the larger rhythm of the spectacle as a whole, the music thereby also lays down the ballet's general continuity and proportions, and its aptness for particular dance styles. The changes that occurred in musical composition over the more than three centuries spanning the Italian and French court ballets, the English masque, the dance elements within seventeenth-century opera and opera-ballet, and the enormously productive developments of the eighteenth and nineteenth centuries, were far-reaching indeed. The varied possibilities for interaction offered a spectrum of possible "visualizations" of ballet scores (as Stravinsky would later call them) which, if it obviously cannot rival the stylistic plurality of the twentieth century, nevertheless makes of Enlightenment dance a rich source of cultural study, and of material apt for practical revival.

Early Twentieth-Century Perspectives: Energy, Variety, Audacity

The notion of visuality as a powerful agent in the nature and making of dance—as both aesthetic quality and communicative medium—took on tremendous new vitality in the first half of the twentieth century. Visual immediacy and vividness acted as a primary factor in the reinvention of ballet as a total spectacle. This was a mode of reinvention that maintained a strong awareness of tradition (above all technically, as a professional discipline for dancers and *maîtres de ballet*), yet was also essentially modernist and to a degree eclectic in outlook, answerable only to itself. The process of reinvention occurred through the Diaghilev period and beyond, with astonishing effects on virtually every aspect of dance and staging, as well as on musical concept and idiom. It resulted in a renewed vitality for ballet, both in its New Music audacity and in the immersive visual character of its spectacle, across the Western arts world in the early and middle decades of the twentieth century.

So far as critics and audiences were concerned, it became a source of strength—and of endless discussion—that theatrical dance was now presented in the form of individual, fully integrated artistic projects, the character and visual style of which were new and modern and typically unpredictable, over and above whatever special musical and choreographic virtues any particular ballet might possess. One consequence of this intensified process of planning and dance-making was that the engagement of composers and artist-designers became the object of careful thought and choice. Leaving aside the practical question of commissioning either absolutely new music, or else brightened-up new versions of pieces recovered from the past, the creation of a specific musical and rhythmic style needed to occur in tandem

335

with the planning of the visual and choreographic aspects, with all that this implied of risk, daring, trial, and (possible) error.

If the art form has subsequently traveled far beyond what Diaghilev could have envisaged—musically, visually, choreographically—both in stylistic terms and simply in subject matter (or the apparent lack of it, in the case of abstract, plotless ballets), then the vitality and energy of this modern journey of theatrical dance emerged out of the wider Ballets Russes phenomenon, including their rivals, emulators, and later spin-offs. Specifically, the impetus came from what Diaghilev's company, driven by his determination and taste, had created in the twenty years of their existence. This example showed, too, how an awareness of the intrinsically balletic character and a creative (rather than simply antiquarian) understanding of the historical dimension of the dance could be successfully combined within a form of theatrical presentation that was unabashed in its energy and élan, characterized by a varied modernity that was both stylish and forceful.

From the design point of view, what other company could or would have envisaged hiring such artist-designers as Picasso, Braque, Gris, Matisse, Derain, Sert, Utrillo, Laurencin, de Chirico, Rouault, as well as the clutch of brilliantly chosen Russians (Bakst, Benois, Roerich, Tchelichev, Larionov, Goncharova, and so on)? Of the non-Russians, the list of Picasso's contributions is especially striking, beginning with *Parade*, the iconoclastic cubist project (devised in collaboration with Jean Cocteau and Erik Satie) of 1917, but becoming more amenable and even "tasteful" after World War I. The very fact of using such artists as part of a scheme of carefully assembled multimedia projects serves to demonstrate the cultural ambition of Diaghilev's envisaged form of balletic modernity—modernism that was incisive, yet also colorful and even sometimes expansive. This was underlined not only by the company's astonishing critical and popular success, but also by the rival activity of the Ballets Suédois, based in Paris, in the years 1920–25.

Rolf de Maré's Swedish company went so far as to take the idea of modern design as the governing idea for their type of ballet. They arrived at a new balance of elements which tended to privilege visual style and stage layout, thereby giving prominence to new types of "plastic figure composition" and visual effect, to some extent at the expense of dance itself (as critics have claimed). Taking the long view, this was without doubt true: their particular type of scenic-choreographic form did not catch on, and is preserved now mainly through a large body of visual material, including many evocative black-and-white photographs. Yet the work done by de Maré's artist-designers—above all by Fernand Léger (1881–1955) in *Skating Rink*, to music by Arthur Honegger, then in the quasi-African ritual of *La Création du Monde*, to the famous Darius Milhaud score; and by Francis Picabia (1879–1953), who made the concept and designs for *Relâche* of 1924, to Satie's music—made possible a new ballet-hybrid that could have seen the light of day by no other route.

No theater historian would now claim this hybrid as an important new evolutionary stage for ballet. It was a brilliant development in its own terms, but, viewed in the clear light of day, something of a balletic dead end. Not merely its eclectic avant-gardism (something it after all shared with the later Diaghilev) but also its continuous, seemingly fearless experimentalism served to carry it along the road to self-dissolution. The final stage of the Ballets Suédois was symbolically reached precisely through the brilliantly satirical *Relâche*: this extraordinary Dadaist event was, in the last resort, a fundamentally anti-balletic show that took their radical aesthetic to an extreme. Both the design-led production style and the company itself disappeared after a brief series of performances in 1925, leaving the way open for Diaghilev to colonize the territory of the balletic avant-garde unopposed for the remainder of the 1920s.

Yet with its combination of extreme chic and extreme modernity, the Parisian–Swedish ballet has its place in the avant-garde culture of its time and offers fascinating insights into the wealth of experimental ideas that were in ferment during the interwar period. Their achievement serves to demonstrate, once more, the truly intimate connection between ballet and the visual world, in every dimension: design, choreographic pattern, musical contour, mime, gesture, scenic rhythm, physical movement; a connection which forces any committed observer to constantly reassess the nature of the rhythmic and expressive relations between music, dance, and the visual–spatial environment within which the art of ballet operates.

Epilogue

Ballet has enjoyed a long and fruitful, if at times precarious, existence. Between the courts of Renaissance and Baroque Italy, the long history of French and Russian dance institutions, the brilliant technical innovations of the Italian ballet-masters of the eighteenth and nineteenth centuries, the emergence of ballet in such centers as Stuttgart, Vienna, London, and Copenhagen, as far as the explosive and transformative diversity of the twentieth century, is a vast journey. And it is one in which the totality of the spectacle, in abstract as well as narrative form, stands at the heart of the scenic and expressive language. If, over time, it is evident that this relationship changes almost beyond recognition in its outward manifestations, then there remains a guiding principle at work: that of a combined visual language of movement, rhythm, musical contour and continuity, spatial layout, stage lighting, color, costume, and set design, all running in parallel and interacting in manifold ways.

This is the creative and communicative medium of ballet, the generative potential of which enables and sustains choreographic invention. The musical element which supports this invention is expressive of carefully elaborated movement, as well as of atmosphere and character. The musician thereby supports dance in *its* expressive language, bringing gesture and physical–spatial rhythm closer to music than in other related genres such as opera or film, or even certain types of theatrical melodrama, to which it is, arguably, closest.

In terms of dance language and its representational potential, the abstract and the narrative are in fact remarkably close; and in ballet generally, the musical and the visual are perhaps more intimately connected than almost anywhere else. As Stravinsky observed, if the greatness of Balanchine was compounded of many talents and a very particular visual and spatial awareness, the most significant factor of all was his deep and resourceful musicianship.

Note

1 Igor Stravinsky and Robert Craft, *Conversations with Igor Stravinsky* (London; Faber and Faber, 1959), 94.

Further Reading

Beaumont, Cyril W. *Ballet Design Past and Present*. London: The Studio, 1946.

Buckle, Richard. "The Royal Danish Ballet at the Royal Theatre, Copenhagen." *Ballet* 11, no. 2 (July 1951). Extracts reprinted in: Richard Buckle, *Buckle at the Ballet*, 312–317. London: Dance Books, 1980.

Denby, Edwin. *Looking at the Dance*. New edition with an introduction by B. H. Haggin. New York: Curtis Books, 1968.

Joseph, Charles M. *Stravinsky and Balanchine: A Journey of Invention*. New Haven: Yale University Press, 2002.

———. *Stravinsky's Ballets*. New Haven: Yale University Press, 2011.

Kendall, Richard and Jill DeVonyar, eds. *Degas and the Ballet: Picturing Movement*. Exhibition catalogue. London: Royal Academy, 2011.

Kirstein, Lincoln. *Nijinsky Dancing*. London: Thames and Hudson, 1975.

Näslund, Erik, ed. *Les Ballets Suédois, 1920–1925*. Paris: BNF-Louis Vuitton, 1994.

Noverre, Jean-Georges. *Letters on Dancing and Ballets*. Translated by Cyril W. Beaumont. London: C. W. Beaumont, 1930.

Pritchard, Jane, ed. *Diaghilev and the Golden Age of the Ballets Russes, 1909–1929*. Exhibition catalogue. London: V&A Publishing, 2010.

39

DANCE

Visual/Musical Effects in Two
Dance Performances

Flaviana Sampaio

Over the course of the twentieth century, the art world saw several shifts in artists' approach to their practice. In part, these upheavals were motivated by a rejection of the established forms of the past, including the traditional understanding of the relationship between the arts and the appropriate use of their media. Dance performances partook of these changes, and their effects can be seen clearly in dance practice today. Among the artists whose activities found a central position in this rethinking of art are two whose work will provide the case studies for this chapter: my discussion is based around *Lamentation* (1930) by Martha Graham, and *Nearly Ninety* (2009) by Merce Cunningham.

Graham and Cunningham were approximate contemporaries, and their careers overlapped to an extent: from 1939 to 1945 Cunningham was a soloist in the Martha Graham Dance Company. Besides this period of practical collaboration, their work is similar in the extent to which it departs in interesting ways from the fantastical narratives characteristic of conventional ballet. However, Cunningham radically revised some traditional features of dance that Graham retained. These two dancers developed very particular views and intuitions about the making of dance and its capacity for representation, and in response my analysis of their performances will focus on visual aspects—lighting design, costume, and effects combining music and movement. Their distinctive approaches to these features will help us to understand some of the ways in which the relationships between performance components within dance have been refigured over the last hundred years.

The making of dance can be thought of as a process of coordinating movement, visual and spatial effects, and music, with a view to manipulating the effects produced by these elements upon the audience. According to the dance theorist Ivar Hagendoorn, "Choreography is not just about inventing movements, it is about evaluating the perceptual and emotional effects of a particular movement or spatial configuration. Choreographers continue adjusting a certain movement or position until it matches the effect they had in mind (or until the day of the premiere)."[1] One of the elements at the choreographer's disposal in pursuit of an intended effect is the visual design of the scene. The presence of the bench in *Lamentation*, and the large platform in *Nearly Ninety*, highlight the extent to which the placement of objects in relation to the dance—or, indeed, the visual design of an "empty" space through lighting effects—contributes to the performance.

The process of making dance, therefore, does not belong entirely to any single artistic field or mode, and rejects conventional disciplinary conceptions of arts expertise. As the unconventional activities of artists such as Graham and Cunningham make clear, there is neither a specific nor a general way to learn choreography, especially in the forms it has taken since 1900. In tandem with artists challenging disciplinary boundaries in other media, Graham turns to the concept of "practice" to convey the business of the choreographer: "I believe that we learn by practice. Whether it means to learn to dance by practicing dancing or to learn to live by practicing living, the principles are the same."[2]

Usually, dance has been configured as an art concerned with the relationship between space and time; but this is not the only possibility. In my view, more promising is the idea of dance as a visual art: this conception seems to offer a richer and broader understanding of dance. According to one formula, advocated for instance by Robert Scott, the "visual arts" can be defined as those that can be seen. A conception of dance as a visual art, therefore, might proceed from a new analysis of the extent to which its visible elements shape the experience of choreographic design in performance. For example, the relationship between space and time in dance is frequently articulated through lighting: each performance uses a specific time-space, and the lighting acts between these axes in a defined and planned manner, proposing structural, aesthetic, and conceptual relations between them. Once we recognize the role of lighting in dance, we can begin to think also about what it illuminates: the dancer himself, followed by set design, make-up, costume, and props.

The conventional view of the relationship between dance and music assigns to music a generative relationship. The choreographer responds to the music, creating dance movements that are synchronized with events in the music. This conception relies on a sense that music is in itself spatialized, and capable of exhibiting properties of movement; that music can be thought of in terms of trajectories, reliefs, and gestures that might be "translated" or "embodied" as dance. Music is, of course, widely understood and described in terms of this analogy, and so it is generally found to be persuasive. Drawing on a neuroscientific study of dance, Hagendoorn even argues that we see music and dance as the same thing. In particular, he suggests: "A buildup of expectation on an auditory level can find its realization on a visual level. The final moments in many ballets are either a concurrence of exaltation in both sound and movement or the opposite, a slow fading away."[3] This binary of waxing and waning, tied to changes in speed and intensity, effectively encapsulates the usual relation between visual and musical elements in dance.

The relationship between music, movement, and visual effects, meanwhile, has been theorized by the influential scenographer Adolphe Appia. Appia saw dramatic action, emotional content, music, and visual environment as working together inseparably to create a total "living" performance—a view that is obviously similar to Wagner's *Gesamtkunstwerk*. For Appia, lighting functioned as the primary unifying element, and should enjoy a reciprocity of representation with music and movement. In Christopher Baugh's summary, "The music achieved a physical embodiment through the eurhythmic movement of the performers, whilst the light could represent the music within the entire space."[4] All three he saw as visually expressive at a profound level, addressed to "the inner essence of all vision."[5] Appia's emphasis on reciprocal representation, which in practice means synchronization, has strongly colored audiences' expectations regarding the relationship between music, movement, and visual effects in subsequent stage performance. The two performances discussed here, to differing extents, challenge these expectations as well as those built upon the simpler premise of the choreographer responding to "movement" in music.

Graham's short solo *Lamentation*, viewed in the 1976 performance by Peggy Lyman, is characterized by a very clear treatment of space. In the center of the stage, a single dancer sits on a simple bench, facing the audience. The viewer's attention is drawn immediately to the costume, designed to prompt an enhanced exploration, indeed a problematization, of movement: it is a long, purple tube used as a skin enveloping the dancer's entire body, stretching and morphing with her movements, generating a kaleidoscope of images of the dancer while she remains seated on the bench. In this case, the lighting, although reaching the entire stage, is static. The make-up does not effect any distortion to the dancer's appearance, or function as a mask. This performance does not invite analysis through a range of visual features; rather, the visual effect is focused upon the carefully thought-through costume, and the other visual features of the performance—including the dancer's movements—are subsumed within it, so that its own visual properties, including texture and color, are foregrounded.

This solo is constructed out of Martha Graham's very characteristic exploration of movement. Her interest here focuses on gravity and severity in bodily action, drawing on her doctrine of contraction and release. Graham described the central theme of the dance as "the tragedy that obsesses the body, the ability to stretch inside your own skin, to witness and test the perimeters and boundaries of grief, which is honorable and universal."[6] Within Graham's conception, the costume was carefully designed to articulate, even sculpt, the grief-laden body and its perimeter of skin: "It must reveal the body, reveal the beautiful line of the waist, the hips, the shoulders, the turn of the head. The costume must speak to all of these things."[7]

Lamentation makes use of a short work for piano, No. 2 from Zoltan Kodaly's *Zongoramuzsika* (Music for Piano) op. 3, of 1909. The music—halting and undulating, exhibiting Kodaly's characteristic meditative melancholy—lends a mood of tension and uncertainty, and in combination with the visual effects it imposes a sense of restlessness upon the audience. Although the short piece is used in its entirety, and thus effectively determines the length of the dance, there is no attempt at the kind of "representational" relationship envisaged by Appia. The dancer's movements are coordinated with the music, but one could hardly call them "synchronized"; and to the extent that the dancer's movements are transmitted through the medium of the purple costume, the primary visual effect is also coordinated with the music. The lighting, however, remains unmoved.

Martha Graham explained the rationale underlying her approach to music thus: "I never believed in the necessity of interpreting either music or story in dance. I believe in writing a script of movement or a musician writing a script of music. Two can join and they do join."[8] Graham here envisages a "joining" of movement and music, but not in the sense that the dancer embodies or represents the "movements" found in the music. Rather, Graham appropriates the music as a component of her own conception—interestingly, in all of the very extensive discussion of *Lamentation* to be found on the internet, the music is almost never identified beyond Kodaly's name. Graham had worked with the choreographer and composer Louis

Horst, and admitted his influence on this aspect of her practice: "Louis felt that music for the dance should not overshadow the dance movement. He did not want me to use strings in any of the compositions for my dances. He preferred piano, percussion, and wind instruments."[9]

The Merce Cunningham Company's performance *Nearly Ninety* also departs from convention in this respect, but presents a more radically ambiguous relationship between music, dance, and visual effects. The aim, as Merce Cunningham explains, was to create a very particular dynamic among the elements of the performance: "What we have done in our work is to bring together three separate elements in time and space, the music, the dance and the décor, allowing each one to remain independent. The three arts don't come from a single idea which the dance demonstrates, the music supports and the décor illustrates, but rather they are three separate elements each central to itself."[10] Within this conception, the movements implied by the music and the movements of the dancer are conceived separately and are therefore asynchronous—Cunningham's approach in this respect was indebted to his long collaboration with John Cage. There was no intention to "fit" the music to the dance movements; instead, music and dance stand as independent entities which nonetheless generate complex interferences and interactions, giving rise to unusual and unexpected effects in performance.

This unconventional approach to the relationship between music and dance shaped Cunningham's practice in interesting ways. He explains, "I think perhaps one of the obvious things that conditions our work would be: we don't dance to music, it does not push us; we really have to do it ourselves."[11] The question of what "pushes" what is a moot point here: even when a dance is not created in direct response to music, the music, once introduced, will still inflect the dancing in performance. Rather, the important point concerns the type of relationship constructed through Cunningham's creative practice: the moment of intersection is delayed until the performance.

The scene of *Nearly Ninety* is dominated by a huge object that works as a set design and also as a place where the musicians play live. In front of this object is a projection showing images of fluid spaces, for example streams of water. The dancers are fourteen in total. One type of costume used is a unitard in two contrasting colors, one light and one dark. These colors appear in straight and geometric lines, distinguishing the parts of the body. Each leg has a color, and the torso has a different design for each dancer. The make-up does not invite any particular focus on the face. Nor does the lighting, as Cunningham explains: "We never like lighting to focus, to dramatize something."[12] The choreography reflects his interest in how movement operates—there is no story to be told in his works. The body and its possibilities of movement through space are the "subject" of the dance. Thus, music does not have a role in the process of making the dance, but its presence in the performance inevitably allots it a role in audience interpretations of the dance.

Cunningham's approach to the relationships between the arts in his performances is to dissolve any sense of the traditional structures binding them together, and at the same time to establish each on an equal footing. This is directly analogous to his approach to space, in which his aim is to break down the traditional relationships between spatialized components both across and behind the proscenium, establishing each space and "view" of the performance as equally important: "The space could be constantly fluid, instead of being a fixed space in which movements relate. We've grown up with ideas about a fixed space in theater to which spectator and dancer refer. But if you abandon that idea you discover another way of looking. You can see a person not just from the front but from any side with equal interest."[13]

Cunningham's ideas about the relations between performance spaces and between performance components are, I think, not only similar but interconnected. His aim was to construct a performance that did not impose or privilege a particular "way of looking," whether that refers to an angle of view, a focus of attention, or a particular relationship between music and movement. Audience members are left to assemble both their own "view" and their own combinatorial perspective from the elements presented. This is quite different from earlier practice, including that of Martha Graham, in which the audience expects to—and is expected to—encounter the performer head on, center-stage, dancing "to" music.

For Cunningham, his "other ways of looking" and their departure from tradition are the inevitable result of changes in the broader visual (and, one might add, musical) culture. "The time we live in forces us to rearrangements of all sorts. It's probably like the sixteenth century, when America was discovered, and also printing. At present, electronics has almost changed our mode of thinking. Our daily lives will change even if we're not aware of it, and I'm convinced that that will have many consequences. How can people do all that they do every day in a perfectly natural way and still go to the theater as in the nineteenth century?"[14] The modern-day dance audience has acquired audiovisual habits outside the performance space that include the capacity to scan vast amounts of information within a multimedia environment in a matter of moments. They are also accustomed to orienting themselves in relation to that environment through highly flexible modes of interaction that offer a considerable degree of choice and self-direction. In Cunningham's view, it is unreasonable to ask an audience to set these habits aside as they enter a venue for a performance. Within this conception at least, the relationship between music, movement, and visual effects in contemporary dance is no longer one of coordination, but one of conjunction, the nature and meaning of which depend very literally on one's point of view.

Notes

1 Ivar Hagendoorn, "The Dancing Brain," *Cerebrum* 5 (Spring 2003): n.p.
2 Martha Graham, *Blood Memory* (New York: Doubleday, 1991), 3.
3 Hagendoorn, "The Dancing Brain," n.p.
4 Christopher Baugh, *Theatre, Performance and Technology: The Development of Scenography in the Twentieth Century* (Basingstoke: Palgrave Macmillan, 2005), 110.
5 Ibid., 105.
6 Graham, *Blood Memory*, 117.
7 Ibid., 269.
8 Ibid., 212–213.
9 Ibid., 75.
10 Merce Cunningham, and Jacqueline Lesschaeve, *The Dancer and the Dance* (New York: Marion Boyars, 1985), 137.
11 Ibid., 130.
12 Ibid., 173.
13 Ibid., 18.
14 Ibid., 131.

Further Reading

Baugh, Christopher. *Theatre, Performance and Technology: The Development of Scenography in the Twentieth Century*. Basingstoke: Palgrave Macmillan, 2005.

Clifford, James. *The Predicament of Culture: Twentieth-Century Ethnography, Literature and Art*. Cambridge, MA: Harvard University Press, 1988.

Cunningham, Merce and Jacqueline Lesschaeve. *The Dancer and the Dance*. New York: Marion Boyars, 1985.

Graham, Martha. *Blood Memory*. New York: Doubleday, 1991.

Hagendoorn, Ivar. "The Dancing Brain." *Cerebrum* 5 (Spring 2003). http://www.dana.org/news/cerebrum/detail.aspx?id=2930.

Scott, Robert. *Design Fundamentals*. New York: R. E. Krieger, 1980.

40

MUSICALS

Dominic McHugh

Whether on stage or on screen, the musical forges an intense but often problematic relationship between its aural and visual aspects. Like opera, the genre's disparate strands have long been a site of creative friction, as directors and designers battle with composers and musical directors over the relative priority given to a show's physical and musical elements. A popular dictum reminds us that "Nobody leaves the theater humming the scenery," thereby positing music as the supreme element, while another—"The orchestrations should sound like the sets"—suggests that integration is the key to a successful musical. However, prolific orchestrator Don Walker (*Carousel, Fiddler on the Roof*) advised: "A theatrical composer, in addition to being aware of and respectful towards the story, must be sensitive to all physical movement on the stage and, where appropriate, underline it. Since the final result onstage is everything, it matters not how it was achieved."[1] In other words, the music should serve the action on the stage. These three different positions represent the tensions between music and the visual that musicals have to negotiate.

That the musical's basic paraphernalia broadly resembles that of opera has caused numerous debates over the origins of the genre, largely without fruitful conclusions. Some have even seen its roots in ancient Greece, on the basis of the presence of drama, dance, and music in Athenian theater, while other theories involve Offenbach, Gilbert and Sullivan, or Charles M. Barras's *The Black Crook* (1866). Yet the Broadway musical's identity is so closely tied to the place in which it has mostly thrived—indeed, the genre is often referred to simply as "Broadway," the avenue on which many of Manhattan's theaters can be found—that it is perhaps more effective to approach the musical's early years through notions of geography and architecture (the latter being a particularly rich aspect of the genre's visual culture). The heart of New York's modern theater district lies in the Times Square area, stretching roughly from Forty-Second Street to Fifty-Third Street, and it was here that the genre came of age in the middle decades of the twentieth century.

The venues that housed these works—impressive, monolithic buildings such as the New Amsterdam Theater, which dominated the skyline in those days—started to emerge in the early years of the century, as impresarios began to buy up cheap plots of land in an area that had once been famous only for attracting thieves and lowlifes, and to build theaters on them. The arrival of the New York subway in 1904 brought about a cultural change, facilitating social interaction between audience members from different districts. As Jeffrey Magee has observed, it is no coincidence that the titles of the first two musicals by the early Broadway pioneer, Irving Berlin, reflected two of the most common messages to be heard on the early subway trains: *Watch Your Step* (1914) and *Stop! Look! Listen!* (1915). The latter's use of the imperative to "look" and "listen" also hints at how the visual and the musical were already emerging as two distinct aspects of the genre, since the title also referred to the audience's engagement with the piece.

In itself, of course, the word "musical" suggests a certain generic bias in favor of music rather than dramatic or visual elements. But this term seems to have evolved only after the growing multivalence of shows' diction meant that more specific terms such as "musical comedy" or "musical play" became unrepresentative of the objects they were trying to describe. On Broadway, the plots of early musicals were loose at best, and the shows' scripts (or "books") were normally structured as showcases for popular performers to deliver their star turns. The revue style of show, which consisted of a string of musical numbers and sketches rather than a through-narrative, reached the height of its popularity in the 1910s and 1920s with the famous *Ziegfeld Follies*, presided over for more than twenty years by the entrepreneurial Florenz Ziegfeld. Here, star singers and comedians performed their acts alongside the *Follies'* main feature, which was its large chorus of show girls, who were usually cascaded down an elaborate staircase set.

Ziegfeld's approach was unquestionably visual rather than musical, operating on the philosophy that audiences were more likely to be satisfied if they could see how their money had been spent. The *Follies* were ephemeral in nature, and a new edition was brought out annually; the patchwork aesthetic of the construction of the show meant that it was rarely a forum for a composer to thrive in, since star acts such as Fanny Brice, Bob Hope, and W. C. Fields would often bring in their own material, with no concept of an overarching "score." However, a major exception to this rule was the 1919 edition (hailed by many, including Ziegfeld himself, as the best of the series), for which Irving Berlin served as principal songwriter. The hit number of the evening, "A Pretty Girl is Like a Melody," not only played on the "Ziegfeld Girls" trademark but also started to forge a closer relationship between the visual and the musical by using music as a metaphor to intensify the elegance associated with one of the series' main physical components (i.e. the spectacle of the girls on the staircase).

Two years later, a new branch of Berlin's work on Broadway continued to exploit this argument of equivalence between music and visual production. In 1920, he joined forces with veteran producer Sam H. Harris to buy a plot on West Forty-Fifth Street, on which they built an intimate new venue called the Music Box Theater. The title emphasized the importance of the music in the theater's plans and, unusually, the venue's main purpose was to showcase the work of a composer—Berlin himself, of course. Between 1921 and 1924 he was responsible for writing an annual variety-type show, made up of songs and sketches, called the *Music Box Revue*. The 1921 edition's unique feature was that Berlin himself appeared onstage as the penultimate act, making visible the creative force behind the music. Throughout the show, Berlin wove the score together with fragments of a song called "Say it With Music," and the metaphor of the visual embodiment of music was extended into a featured chorus of girls called the "Eight Little Notes," each representing a pitch in the diatonic scale. In the second-to-last scene, the Notes then arrived onstage to "interview" Berlin (in song) about his career and his compositional method. This association of pitches with people, and of a show's diegesis with a composer, was a new landmark in the genre's ongoing negotiation between the musical and the visual.

Later in the same decade, technological developments brought about the birth of the "talking picture," and it is surely no coincidence that the first widely distributed "sound film" was a musical, *The Jazz Singer* (1927). With the exception of one scene of dialogue, only the movie's musical numbers involved a synchronization of the soundtrack with the onscreen events. At once, this meant the songs—most of which were performed by Broadway veteran Al Jolson and again included an Irving Berlin song, "Blue Skies"—were the highlights, and these brief moments of synchronization helped to draw attention to the connection between music and the visual; audiences would specifically attend the film to witness this novelty. On the other hand, the movie also set the tone for almost all future Hollywood musicals in its relegation of the composer to much lower down the pecking order than the star and director: it is almost always the case that Broadway shows are referred to in connection with the composer (Bernstein's *West Side Story*) or writing teams (the Rodgers and Hammerstein shows), whereas film musicals are the property of the director (Vincente Minnelli's *An American in Paris*) or star(s) (the Astaire–Rogers movies). Paradoxically, music itself seemed less important than the staging of the musical numbers, which were in turn more important than the rest of the film.

Nevertheless, the success of *The Jazz Singer* helped to give birth to the movie musical as one of the main Hollywood genres, and it was soon followed by a raft of other films that similarly employed Broadway stars in stories set in the theater, thereby allowing directors to use the performativity of songs as "lyric moments" to exploit the sound technology. In particular, the 1930s musicals of director-choreographer Busby Berkeley (made for Warner Bros.) were famous for their lavish production numbers involving large groups of chorus girls in geometric or kaleidoscopic patterns. Just as the possibility of using sound now allowed music to play a more active role in film, Berkeley expanded the visual possibilities of the medium by creating numbers that referenced the surrealist works of Salvador Dalí and Man Ray. This notable early connection between the movie musical genre and contemporary visual art was made possible through an intensification of the musical numbers into dream sequences that had little diegetic significance but were nevertheless the cornerstones of the films. Of particular note is the "Shadow Waltz" from *Gold Diggers of 1933*, in which a chorus of girls play neon-tubed violins that glow in the dark; in one section of the sequence, all the artificial lights are turned off and only the neon violins are visible, with the violinists lined up in the shape of one large violin, shot (in Berkeley's trademark fashion) from above. This was perhaps the analogue of Irving Berlin's chorus of "Eight Little Notes," where the visual image underlines a reference to music.

Yet a different strategy in one of the 1930s' most sophisticated movie musicals proved much more innovative in the genre's ongoing negotiation between music and the visual. For Rouben Mamoulian's *Love Me Tonight* (1932), Rodgers and Hart devised a six-minute musico-dramatic sequence woven together with the song "Isn't It Romantic?" The number begins in a tailor's shop, in which Maurice Chevalier's character begins the song spontaneously, without a musical introduction; as the chorus continues, the camera pans into his reflected image in a three-paneled mirror, thereby trebling his visual impact and drawing attention to the extraversion of

347

his performance. Chevalier's customer takes over the song, and refers to it in the lyric as "a very catchy strain." He then leaves the shop and walks down the road away from the camera, crossing paths with another man who walks toward a taxi waiting outside the shop. The driver whistles a few notes of the melody and sings "At last I've got a fare!" The cab takes off and the driver continues to whistle the melody; his customer turns out to be a composer and he starts to join in, declaring he will write it down.

As the dictation goes on, the composer starts naming the notes as they are being sung, and the shot suddenly cuts to a scene on a train, where the composer is still writing down the song. A group of soldiers on the train overhear him, and they stand around and join in. Another cut takes us to a country road, down which the soldiers are marching and still singing the song. They are overheard by a gypsy violinist, who is then observed playing the melody to a group of other gypsies around a camp fire. They all start to sing along, and the music carries to the window of the solitary heroine, played by soprano Jeanette MacDonald, who then sings the final refrain alone, looking wistfully from her balcony into the distance. Thus Mamoulian, Rodgers and Hart satisfy two objectives: by starting the sequence with Chevalier and ending it with MacDonald, the number foreshadows the outcome of the story (the pair will end up together, even though they have not yet met); and by making the number semi-diegetic, the characters are singing a song in the story but more in the manner of a folk song, so they are no longer bound by a theater setting (as in many previous movie musicals). A large-scale, loose musical form thereby allows much more potential for the story to develop in a range of settings and liberates the visual potential of the movie.

While many of the other popular musical films of the 1930s maintained some sort of link to a theatrical context—Fred Astaire typically played a dancer or performer in most of his movies with Ginger Rogers, for instance—the treatment of song and film in *Love Me Tonight* paved the way for the next major landmark of the movie musical, *The Wizard of Oz* (1939). As with *The Jazz Singer*, the film was partly a milestone for its exploitation of a relatively recent technological development, this time the use of color. Though *Oz* was by no means the first film to use Technicolor, it was one of the earliest successful color movies, and part of this success was specifically because of the crucial narrative metaphor of this visual aspect of the film: when Dorothy (Judy Garland) is in Kansas in the opening scenes, the film is in sepia tones, but when she arrives in Oz, the color is introduced. Oz represents her dreams and aspirations, and it is a place of color and music: one song exhorts the characters to "Follow the Yellow Brick Road," drawing attention to the color, while one of the film's highlights is the extensive "Munchkinland Sequence" involving a chain of over ten movements or mini-songs. Again, the performativity of the musical numbers is specifically employed as part of the film's expressive discourse: the world that Dorothy dreams of "over the rainbow" is a place of musical and visual wonder.

The Wizard of Oz was the first of a group of musicals produced by MGM over the following decade and a half that expanded the potential of the dual musical–visual focus. In Minnelli's *Meet Me in St. Louis* (1944), for instance, the film is split into four segments representing the seasons of a single year (1904); each is signaled by the appearance of a postcard of the family home with the exaggerated trappings of the time of year (snow, autumn leaves, etc.). This type of device has been referred to by film scholar James Naremore (borrowing a term from Roland Barthes) as "season-ness," i.e. an intense feeling of the presence of the seasons in the film, but in the context of the present discussion it is important to note how this is underlined in the musical numbers. Popular turn-of-the-century folk songs are juxtaposed with new songs written by the team of Hugh Martin and Ralph Blane, and almost all of them are bound up with this visual cue of "season-ness": the climax of the winter scene, for instance, is Judy Garland's poignant rendition of "Have Yourself a Merry Little Christmas," framed by a snow-filled garden.

Similarly, Gene Kelly's two mid-career masterpieces, *An American in Paris* (1951) and *Singin' in the Rain* (1952), are especially vital in this discussion because of their self-conscious visual references to music and performativity. *An American in Paris* was an overt attempt to make a film that was as artistic as it was commercial: the score contains a mixture of Gershwin's popular Broadway songs with his 1928 tone poem that provided the film's title. Not only does this suggest a broad mixture of genres, but one might say more specifically that the visual aesthetic of the film as a whole takes its cue from the generic flexibility of the jazz-infused tone poem alone. Kelly plays a painter, and the decision to film on location in Paris carried a connotation of European art that reached its climax in the closing ballet sequence set against backdrops inspired by famous Parisian works of art. For instance, in one section Kelly portrays the dancer in Toulouse-Lautrec's *Chocolat dansant dans un bar* (1896), while other parts refer to the works of Renoir, Van Gogh, Rousseau, Dufy, and Utrillo. Thus ballet, art music, and visual art interact in one of the movie musical's most ambitious projects.

Singin' in the Rain takes a slightly different tack, however: the movie is set in the late 1920s and the plot deals with the creation of an imaginary follow-up to *The Jazz Singer* called *The Dancing Cavalier*. Frequent reference to the technique of shooting a movie musical makes film itself the work's topic, and this scheme of metafilm helps Kelly and his co-director Stanley Donen to deconstruct the genre. The plot's key love triangle between Don Lockwood (Gene Kelly), his female co-star (Lina Lamont, played by Jean Hagen) and the chorus girl hired to dub her unpleasantly squeaky voice (Kathy Selden, played by Debbie Reynolds) is only resolved when Don publicly reveals Kathy's identity, and the process of dubbing is constantly depicted in the film. There was a double irony, however, in that this also drew attention to the fact that even the actors in the film were lip-synching to their own recording, rather than singing live on set, and even more amusingly, Debbie Reynolds herself had to be dubbed in two of the movie's more challenging songs (by an uncredited voice artist, Betty Noyes).

These and the movie's many other explorations of the film-making process reveal the way in which the visual aspects of movie musicals help to bridge the gap between the disembodied voice on the soundtrack and the onscreen performer. On Broadway, though, the middle of the century brought different challenges. Liveness could be taken for granted, of course, but the increasing artistic ambitions of the 1940s and 1950s also made stage musicals much more expensive. The new aesthetic brought in by Rodgers and Hammerstein's first show, *Oklahoma!* (1943), followed by their *Carousel* (1945), *South Pacific* (1949) and *The King and I* (1951), as well as Lerner and Loewe's *My Fair Lady* (1956), Cole Porter's *Kiss Me, Kate* (1948), Irving Berlin's *Annie Get Your Gun* (1946) and Frank Loesser's *Guys and Dolls* (1950), among many others, revolved around the adaptation (albeit often loose) of pre-existing literary material such as plays, poems, short stories, and memoirs.

In turn, the musical aspects became more ambitious, which explains the attraction of composers from the world of art music, such as Kurt Weill, Leonard Bernstein, Morton Gould, Meredith Willson, and Jerome Moross, to the Broadway stage: all of these figures produced musicals during this period. Likewise, the expansion of the dance aspects attracted leading names from ballet such as Jerome Robbins, George Balanchine, and Agnes de Mille as choreographers of musicals. The staging, too, became much bolder and also cinematic, as can be seen from Oliver Smith's double turntables employed to change the scenes smoothly in *My Fair Lady* and his iconic fire-escape sets for *West Side Story* (1957).

Together, the designs for these two shows alone hint at the extent to which Hollywood had started to push Broadway in a much more visual direction, making the overall experience more fluent and imposing rather than simply a loosely connected series of musical numbers. However, the critical literature on Broadway of this period has somewhat myopically read this as a move toward the integration of all the musical's disparate aspects; Rodgers and Hammerstein were especially fond of the term "the integrated musical." In fact, if the songs had become completely integrated into the scripts of musicals, the key ingredient of the genre would have been undermined: the songs of *Oklahoma!*, *My Fair Lady*, *West Side Story*, and so on needed to be highlights of these musicals, otherwise they would simply have been momentary events in the diegesis, turning the pieces into so-called "plays with songs." Yet the blocking of the numbers on the stage in itself points toward the importance of the performativity of songs in musicals: the songs are almost always "staged" as emotional, entertaining peaks in the show, and this is a convention of the genre that audiences are conditioned to buy into (or, by the same token, is often the aspect of musicals that some people cannot accept, causing them to dislike the genre). Music alone is unable to bear this weight: the staging, costumes, choreography, and design are the conduits through which the music in musicals can be made acceptable, and are legislated for in the diegesis.

But technology was again to cause a change in aesthetic, this time with an impact on the stage musical. Expense reduced the Hollywood musical to a trickle in the 1960s, with the exception of a few big-budget stage-to-screen adaptations of successful shows like *The Sound of Music* and *My Fair Lady*, and in turn the emergence of rock-and-roll and youth culture fought against the "artiness" of Broadway shows. It is no accident that *West Side Story* became much more successful in the decade following its premiere: the plot's defiant teenagers, violence, and sexual promiscuity were matched by an edginess in the music that made the package resonate in the new culture. By the middle of the 1970s, musicals had started to undergo a complete change of flavor that in some ways represented a move back to the sex and sparkle of the *Ziegfeld Follies*—and, in consequence, away from art music. Though the challenging musicals of Stephen Sondheim had a cult following and were often critically appreciated, the dominant forces in the theater became composer Andrew Lloyd Webber, director Harold Prince, and producer Cameron Mackintosh. In particular, their collaboration on *The Phantom of the Opera* (1986) became a worldwide phenomenon, but in spite of its strong story and the enduring popularity of many of its songs, it also summed up the change of attitude and approach toward the music in musicals. Though the lead character of Christine is a soprano in the story, many of her highest notes are pre-recorded, as are other sections of the show when the actors are moving from one part of the set to another and are unable to sing

350

live. The pit band includes synthesizers to replace some of the live instruments; the sounds produced by the music box that plays a prominent part in the story are pre-recorded; and the score as a whole requires the entire cast and band to be connected to a state-of-the-art sound system that allows the sound engineer to manipulate what the audience hears, including the speakers through which they hear it.

Thus the dominant aspect of the show was Maria Bjørnson's lavish set. Whereas the highlight of a show like Bernstein's *Candide* (1956) was the experience of Barbara Cook singing "Glitter and Be Gay" backed by a large orchestra, all performing live—an equivalent case, in that the song calls for a bravura display of coloratura fireworks, like the numbers sung by *Phantom*'s Christine—the "all-singing, all-dancing" set provides the experience of "liveness" in *Phantom*, almost as if it has displaced the actors and become the star. The success of *Phantom* and other shows of the same period validated the shift of dynamic from music to the visual experience, and most musicals now involve click tracks, or at least a partly virtual orchestra. Because audiences can see the dancers performing onstage, the dance aspect cannot involve equivalent compromises (e.g. a reduction in numbers), and the set is now usually the most expensive component of a musical. In turn, the music has to be carefully synchronized to the movement of the set and is beholden to it, acting more as a soundtrack than as the focus of liveness that it had represented in the mid-twentieth century.

The tension between music and the visual currently rests in the latter's favor, therefore. But the cycle is by no means at an end. When New York's Lincoln Center revived Rodgers and Hammerstein's *South Pacific* in 2008, it became the biggest hit of the season, largely on the basis of the use of the full original orchestrations. Then in 2011, the University of North Carolina's School of the Arts went a step further by reproducing the original sets, costumes, choreography, and orchestrations of Rodgers and Hammerstein's *Oklahoma!*, using only light amplification to help the young singers. Both of these productions were so successful that they were televised and became nationwide phenomena, with critics consistently drawing attention to the impact of the orchestra. Perhaps in recognition of this, some recent musicals have started to expand the size of the pit, including, ironically, Lloyd Webber's most recent show, *Love Never Dies* (2010). Whether these recent examples bring about another cultural change back in the direction of music remains to be seen, but it is clear that this negotiation between music and the visual lies at the heart of the musical's concerns.

Note

1 Steven Suskin, *The Sound of Broadway Music* (New York: Oxford University Press, 2010), 251.

Further Reading

Feuer, Jane. *The Hollywood Musical*. Indiana: Indiana University Press, 1993.

Knapp, Raymond. *The American Musical and the Performance of Personal Identity*. Princeton: Princeton University Press, 2006.

Magee, Jeffrey. *Irving Berlin's Musical Theater*. New York: Oxford University Press, 2012.

Naremore, James. *The Films of Vincente Minnelli*. Cambridge: Cambridge University Press, 1993.

Suskin, Steven. *The Sound of Broadway Music*. New York: Oxford University Press, 2010.

41
FILM I
Bollywood—Music and Multimedia
Anna Morcom

Music is always in some way a combination of hearing and seeing, not to mention other senses. Whether live, recorded, or in memory or imagination, it is experienced in a given place and time. As Philip Bohlman states, music is characterized by "embeddedness" in other human activities.[1] Or, to cite the more traditional ethnomusicological phrase, music exists in a "cultural context." However, configurations and interactions of hearing and seeing (and of course other forms of experience) vary greatly with different kinds of music. Some musical forms consciously or explicitly embody imagery and scenes, for example Indian *raga*, program music, or music that is a part of drama or music video. More implicitly, music is grounded in place and is always associated with cultural phenomena, identities, and environments, for example the clear, high-pitched *a capella* nomadic songs of the vast nomadic Tibetan grasslands of Tibet, or the overlapping rainforest textures of the music of the Papua New Guinean Kaluli people described in Steven Feld's well-known work. However, in the context of nationalism, multiculturalism, identity politics, marketing, and tourism, music's associations with given peoples and places is in many cases honed, essentialized, and reified, and images and meanings become foregrounded in newly politicized and/or commercialized ways.

With electronic media and multimedia, the configurations of seeing and hearing involve more complexly layered possibilities. Recorded music is easily transported from place to place and can become appropriated with extraordinary rapidity. Hence, for example, as rap has gone global, it no longer just exudes images of black, ghetto America, or not to everyone. With multimedia or screened music, visuals are attached to the music, and these audiovisual products can similarly travel and become appropriated in new places, contexts, and cultures of living and listening. Thus, recorded and screened musics involve levels and speeds of de-, re-, and trans-contextualization that live musics do not.

Hindi film music is, in its primary form, a visual, multimedia music; cinematic, and narrative: the songs exist as visual sequences within a given parent film. However, they are also detachable from the film, and circulate independently in the real world. Since the advent of gramophone, radio, and, later, cassettes, they have been played without their visual sequences. With the expansion of television and video recorders in the 1980s, Hindi films gained a new, domestic context for viewing, and song sequences were watched separate from their parent films on television programs devoted to film songs or song compilations on video. The exponential growth of television in the 1990s following the entry of cable television in India, the spread of other audiovisual recorded media like the VCD and DVD, and, most recently, the rise of the internet have all caused film songs increasingly to circulate in audiovisual form.

Since the earliest days, film songs have also been accompanied by the images not only of the parent film, but of Indian cinema in general, and the paraphernalia of film hoardings, posters, and fan magazines. This visual paraphernalia too has increased with the growth of television, the internet, and easily interactive audio-visual media. In addition to circulating in recorded audio or audiovisual forms, film songs are re-performed in a vast range of genres, including traditional "folk" music. Thus, film songs in recorded, re-recorded, and re-performed forms have permeated musical cultures to an extraordinary level, changing some of them beyond recognition. The circulation of the films and the detached song and dance sequences has also been transnational, with countless musical and visual cultures across the world having appropriated aspects of film music or visual imagery. As new playback technologies and media platforms emerge, possibilities continue to proliferate.

The study of musical/visual cultures of Hindi film songs is thus limitless, with "Bollywood" (as Hindi cinema has become known since the late 1990s, amid global changes in its visibility and status) engendering cultures that vary vastly from place to place. Bollywood in Europe, America, and Australia is now a high-profile musical, visual, and consumer culture that foregrounds Hindi film songs, dance, and fashions to give a colorful, exuberant, cool, glamorous, sumptuous, successful, and fit image of South Asians. In Tibet, on the other hand, it involves more of a mix of Nepali touristic paraphernalia with Indian film songs, and an imagined link to India as the place where exiled friends and family, as well as the Dalai Lama, can be found. In India itself, brass bands play Hindi film songs in wedding processions across North India, permeating public space with these re-performed film tunes during the wedding seasons. In some areas, not only the groom's friends dance but also professional dancers, often cross-dressed boys. Since Hindi film songs became "cool" in India around the 1990s and 2000s, and social norms began to relax in India's upper middle-class circles, highly designed Bollywood nightclubs have sprung up, attracting well-presented girls in sexy yet classy clothes, sometimes in "ethnic chic" styles, and gymed-up boys in trendy shirts, with gelled hair, all singing and dancing along to the film tunes while drinking expensive alcoholic or soft drinks. At another level of society were the beer bars of Mumbai (closed down in 2005), where seductive girls swirled to film songs while wearing bejeweled Indian *gagra choli* dresses, and the lower middle-class "common man" enjoyed a dream of living like a *nawab* or prince, with wine, women, and song. There is also a range of other South Asian cinemas. These include Tamil, Telegu, Malayalam, Sinhala, Bhojpuri, Gujarati, Marathi, Punjabi, and Nepali cinema, and also B cinemas of South Asia. B movies, with their far lower budgets, offer legally censored (limited) erotic content, often in song sequences; and in many exhibition spaces, illegal pornographic sequences with musical accompaniment are added in. Tamil and Telegu cinemas are big-budget and glossy, operating in global circuits comparable to those of Bollywood. However, Bhojpuri and Punjabi cinemas (let alone B movies) have rather different networks and visual cultures.

Indian film music is a local, national, and global leviathan, permeating and engendering cultural activity across social hierarchies, geographies, and media platforms in complex configurations of music, imagery, dance, material objects, commodities, and meaning. In this short chapter, I focus on two aspects that are key to the way film music exists and proliferates as visual culture. While I concentrate primarily on Hindi film music, most of the points I make will have relevance to other Indian film musics. First, I examine how Hindi film music, in its very sounds and structures, embodies visual, narrative, and cinematic dimensions. Second, I look at ways in which the visual and narrative dimensions of film songs shape their reception and appropriation beyond the film, focusing on parallels and synergies of musical cultures in real life and the situational use of music in Hindi films. I use ethnographic methods to examine industrial processes, the production of Hindi film music, and aspects of its wider life. I also use analysis of songs and texts. I focus on narrative, media, multimedia, and the interaction of people with film music. I refer more briefly to historical, sociological, and political perspectives on film music, which are also essential aspects of understanding Hindi film songs and visual culture. I do not refer to lyrics in this chapter. Many parallels exist between lyrics and music in Hindi film songs. However, lyrics have also created particular nuances of imagery and meaning in film songs, particularly in the use of Urdu poetry, and their role in visual culture is a topic in itself.

Film Songs as Narrative and Multimedia Music

Since the earliest days, commercial South Asian films in Hindi and other languages have contained songs and song sequences. Indeed, early Indian cinema drew strongly from theatrical traditions that also incorporated songs and music. While popular music in the Western world has developed largely independently of cinema, in India, film music continues to dominate.

To state an obvious if sometimes overlooked fact: Hindi film songs are made first and foremost for Hindi films. They exist only because there is a film and are popular songs written for it rather than pre-existing pop songs used in it, as in the Western compiled-score model. Film songs thus differ fundamentally from non-film pop songs. With private album music (which is on a very limited scale in India), singers will write their own songs or have songs written for them, and will sing them in a way that foregrounds their own persona. A given album will have its own logic and coherence, and will relate to the singer, his or her image, vision, and voice. If there is a video, it is secondary to the song. With film songs, on the other hand, it is the screenplay writers and director that decide what kind of songs should be written, where they should go in the film, which characters sing them, and what those characters' emotions are. They will also decide the settings, the scenes, and—in conversation with art directors and choreographers (the latter particularly important in Indian cinema since the 1990s)—will create the visuals for the given songs. These cinematic aspects strongly influence what kind of song is sung, its timbre, the singers, the expression, the orchestration, and so on.

The music director (as a film song composer is called) plans the music in sittings with the director, who describes the song situations, the story, the settings, the characters, the scenes, their emotions, and even shot-to-shot details of the song picturization. Thus, film songs are fundamentally situational songs. As one music director stated, "film music is the director's conception of the situation";[2] and film directors are very much authors of film songs, as well as the music directors. Certain examples illustrate the situational nature of film songs particularly clearly. For instance, in *Yaraana* (1995), the heroine (who is a dancer) murders her sadistic husband at the end of a long dance sequence. The music as a whole is an edgy, percussive, harsh version of disco, which falls into heavy dissonance and sound effects at the end when she stabs her husband. This is an extreme example, but it illustrates the structural logic of film music and its fundamental difference from non-film pop music. Similarly, because film songs embody cinematic scenes, they must often transcend boundaries of space and time. For example, in the 1980 film *The Burning Train*, a group of singers and passengers enjoy singing along to a *Qawwali* (Sufi devotional song) with some Qawwali singers who happen to be on the train. They do not realize that there is a bomb on board the train. In a parallel scene, one of the heroes chases the train by car in a daredevil ride. The song constructed for this scene consists of a Qawwali interspersed with lengthy clips of spaghetti-Western-style chase music, featuring violin runs, vibraphone, brass, and bass. Such extraordinary fusion is an expression of this idiosyncratic situation and the vision of the music director, arrangers, and film director. Although Hindi cinema is famous for love and romance, it is also interlaced with action, melodrama, grittiness, or violence in a way that American film musicals have not been. Many film songs therefore require their visual or cinematic contexts in order to make sense—or, if not those, at least a knowledge of Hindi cinema, its conventions, images, and tropes.

A great many film songs are not overtly situational. Still, on analysis, decisions of style and idiom will relate to the situation and setting, as well as the wishes of the director. For example, the same film composer may write songs for a historical epic, a contemporary thriller, and a family melodrama, producing very different music for each to suit these greatly contrasting genres. Film composers follow their own artistic development and experiment with new sounds, as do those working independently of films. However, the necessities of expressing particular times, places, peoples, and situations also shape the parameters of musical styles and flavors that they use.

The cinema is also embodied in film music at deeper levels of style. Film songs by the late 1940s came to be performed by markedly larger orchestras, often adopting a Hollywood-style, symphonic sound. This violin-dominated and often intensely melodramatic sound is characteristic of the classic period of Hindi film music, from the late 1940s till the 1990s, and marks the inextricable link of this genre of popular music with the cinema. However, the large, Western-style orchestras found in Hindi films also need to be seen from a historical, sociological, and (post)colonial perspective. The performers of Western instruments, and the arrangers of Hindi film songs and background music, are overwhelmingly Goan Christian or Parsee. Because Goa was a Portuguese colony, large numbers of Goans learned Western instruments and also staff notation and arrangement, whereas in mainstream Hindu and Muslim India, Western (classical) music has had almost zero institutionalization.

The small Parsee community in Bombay was also involved in elite European culture. A widespread colonial music scene of dance music, jazz, cabaret, and orchestral music relied on such performers as well as European performers, and, in the case of jazz, black performers too. In the lead-up to independence and at independence itself, when the market for this kind of musical culture drastically shrank, unemployed Goan musicians in particular converged on the film industry. From this time, as well as the big Hollywood sound, jazz, cabaret, and other global dance styles entered film songs and song scenes, with increasingly extravagant nightclub and cabaret scenes woven into films to showcase these kinds of music. Thus, the visual culture of Hindi cinema felt the influence of these musical cultures strongly.

Also around this time, technological changes enabled far larger orchestras to be recorded. Earlier Hindi film orchestras had involved both European and Indian instruments, and orchestras grew over the first two decades of Hindi film songs. However, grand orchestras like those in prestigious cinema halls in the silent era had not been possible in sound film. Another ingredient in these changes was the influx of black money into the film industry in the postwar period. Thus, political, social, and technological history merged in the Indian film industries in particularly striking ways from the late 1940s, and extraordinary and large-scale fusions of melodramatic orchestra music, popular music styles such as swing or jazz, and Indian classical or folk styles emerged.

While cinematic and situational forces have from the earliest times shaped individual film songs, and Hindi film music as a genre, a number of devices aim at turning film songs into semi-independent popular songs. Films must enable songs to exist in their plots, for example with protagonists who are performers, or a story that intersects fortuitously with musical performances (such as an anti-hero who frequents a cabaret or dance bar). A strong identity as a song is also achieved through the use of catchy tunes and a clear refrain-verse structure, and the burden of situational music is fitted into instrumental sections which are less prominent to listeners and intrude less on the song. With film songs, it is sometimes difficult to distinguish musical interludes, introductions, and instrumental endings from backing music, since they use many typical Hollywood film-scoring idioms as well as musical codes that have developed from and for the Indian filmic context. Thus, Hindi film songs can be understood as lying on a continuum between backing music on the one hand and (non-film) popular song on the other. Backing scores rarely have any purpose independent from their films. Pop songs, by contrast, are intended to work without any particular visual reference, though they are of course connected with images: album covers, images of the performer, images associated with the genre, and so on. As *situational songs*, film songs bridge the two, existing in the dual contexts of the fictional filmic world and the real world. Directors and music directors aim to balance the situational needs of the song scene within the film against the song's "audio value" and, increasingly, its "video value." The situational needs often conflict with the song's autonomy, pulling it more in the direction of a background score. Yet, because Hindi cinema permeates Indian society and people are familiar with the conventions and images of the cinema, songs do not exist entirely outside the filmic context that gives them so much of their flesh and meaning. Thus, the filmic and real worlds interact and permeate each other, as I explore in more detail below.

Narrative, Situation, and the Permeability of Real and Cinematic Worlds

Hindi film songs are entwined with cinematic narratives, scenes, and visuals in their very music: from Hollywood scoring styles and codes, to Indian musical codes that evoke certain places, seasons, and emotions, to long instrumental interludes that cover onscreen action or spectacle, to sometimes idiosyncratic juxtapositions

356

of style or sudden changes of idiom. Beyond this, direct association through co-occurrence links film songs with films, stars, scenes, and images. This has been compounded since the 1980s and the 1990s in particular with the explosion of television and other visual media.

However, the visual culture of Hindi film music can be explored beyond the inherent multimedia, narrative, visual, and cinematic nature of these popular songs, or their indexical associations with the cinema and its visual, dramatic idioms. The situational nature of film songs can be seen to drive patterns of appropriation and consumption in real life that are very different from those of popular music in other parts of the world. This phenomenon helps to explain the extraordinary saturation of film songs in Indian musical culture.

Hindi films are an imitation or representation of Indian society in various guises. They draw from the musical culture of the real world in terms of the placement of songs within narratives and the kinds of musical styles used. Thus, an entire corpus of devotional Hindu songs or *bhajans* exists in Hindi films, paralleling their use in the real world. The same goes for Qawwalis, wedding songs, or songs for the spring festival of *Holi*. Similarly, songs exist in nightclub scenes in Hindi films, in courtesan salons, and in discos (since the 1970s), as they do in the real world. Such songs as these imitate real-life genres but also adapt them according to particular narrative demands and "*filmi*" aesthetics of excess. They in turn are appropriated back into these genres, fitting the context, yet with an added layer of modernity, trendiness, and glamor. Songs are also appropriated across categories in wider genres of regional "folk" musics. In India, the practice of parody or tune-borrowing is well established, and the film industry has provided a vast storehouse of pre-existing melodies for many "folk" traditions. Thus, devotional songs based on film disco numbers have been created or produced in a typically *filmi* style. As audio playback equipment has become more readily available, recorded songs are also used. Thus the interchangeability of filmic and real-life musical contexts has in many cases blurred the boundary between "popular music" and "folk" or "traditional" music in India.

In addition to songs performed live, as it were, in the film narrative, there are also vast numbers of film songs that involve no formal performance context; rather, the protagonists (typically the hero and/or heroine) simply break into song, most commonly singing about love. These songs are suitable to be performed, of course, in bars, restaurants, and nightclubs, and also in a range of now more illicit genres of seductive, erotic performance. While courtesans used to be at the center of Indian performing arts culture, colonial and nationalist reforms led them to be driven out of classical performing arts and heavily stigmatized. They continued to sing and dance, but lower in the cultural hierarchy, outside of high-profile national genres. Cross-dressed males also perform widely as females in theatrical and dance traditions across India. Many of them are transgender, seeing themselves as feminine. In these zones of seductive, erotic performing arts, the extensive repertoire of love songs and sexy dance songs from Hindi films is ideal for providing the kind of affective and erotic entertainment that customers seek, and they have therefore been heavily appropriated.

The synergy of film and real-life musical culture has led to a particularly explosive transformation of music-making at weddings in North India and Indian diaspora in the US, Europe, and Australia. Traditionally, a musical soirée known as a *sangeet* was held for the bride and her female family members and friends. Songs specific to the occasion were sung by all. Since the late 1990s in particular, sangeets have begun to expand in imitation of filmi song-and-dance wedding scenes, themselves huge extravaganzas of spectacle and color that had incorporated and vastly elaborated on the musical practices of real-life weddings. The result is that many wedding *sangeets* now involve the bride, groom, and many friends and family members performing a choreographed medley of film songs, chosen for appropriateness (sometimes ironic) to the bridal couple. This performance in front of all the guests sometimes costs enormous sums of money to put on. Changes in the representation of dance in Hindi films, global fashions, visual media, and changing socio-cultural ideas of the respectability of dance for women have also helped to drive a larger revolution in popular dance that has taken place in India.

Conclusions

Songs are at the heart of the emotional expression of Hindi film, and offer some of its most stylized and characteristic aspects. They also feature its most visual and sensual excesses in the form of scenery, clothes, expressions, dance, gesture, and of course poetry. Film songs are carefully constructed both to fit into film narratives and to be detachable from them. In their ability to transcend the boundaries of the real and fictional worlds, they contribute immensely to making the film a porous and interactive text, able to give and take much to and from the real world and to be something larger than itself. The vast culture of film music that exists outside of the parent film is shaped by the characteristics of these songs—inherently situational, multimedia, narrative, and cinematic in ways relating to the experience of listeners in given contexts—but also shaped by dynamism and change in real-life musical culture. From this point of view, it is difficult to cite film songs as a genre, since they permeate so many genres in so many places. Rather, they constitute a behemoth of multimedia popular culture.

Notes

1 Philip Bohlman, "Ontologies of music," in *Rethinking music*, ed. Nicholas Cook and Mark Everist (Oxford: Oxford University Press, 1999), 19.
2 Utpal Biswas, quoted in Anna Morcom, *Hindi Film Songs and the Cinema* (Aldershot: Ashgate, 2007), 48.

Further Reading

Booth, Gregory. *Behind the Curtain: Making Music in Mumbai's Film Studios.* New Delhi: Oxford University Press, 2008.
Gopal, Sangita and Sujata Moorti, eds. *Global Bollywood: Travels of Hindi Song and Dance.* Minneapolis and London: University of Minnesota Press, 2008.
Manuel, Peter. *Cassette Culture: Popular Music and Technology in North India.* Chicago: University of Chicago Press, 1994.
Morcom, Anna. *Hindi Film Songs and the Cinema.* Aldershot: Ashgate, 2007.
——. "Film Songs and the Cultural Synergies of Bollywood in and beyond South Asia." In *Beyond the Boundaries of Bollywood: The Many Forms of Hindi Cinema*, edited by Rachel Dwyer and Jerry Pinto, 156–187. New Delhi: Oxford University Press, 2011.
Ranade, Ashok Da. *Hindi Film Song: Music beyond Boundaries.* New Delhi and Chicago: Promilla and Co. Publishers in association with Bibliophile South Asia, 2006.

42
FILM II
David Neumeyer

This chapter offers three case studies as exemplars of the analysis and interpretation of music in film, the topic explored more generally in Chapter 8 of the present book. In the first instance, the attention is on music's relation to filmic space, or, the role of symphonic background music as narrator in the classical Hollywood sound film (*Laura*, 1944; underscore by David Raksin). The second analysis explores the same issues in a contemporary film, albeit one built on classical principles (*La Vita è bella* [*Life is Beautiful*], 1997; underscore by Nicola Piovani). The final reading focuses on a single unusual moment: the juxtaposition of music and painting in the final minutes of *Girl With a Pearl Earring* (2003; underscore by Alexandre Desplat).

Case Study 1: Music and Narrative Levels in *Laura*

One of the best-known Hollywood films of the 1940s, *Laura* was an immediate success with audiences, as was the eponymous song, which was performed and recorded by many prominent popular vocalists and quickly became a jazz standard as well, in both respects joining another famous song that originated in a film: Victor Young's "Stella by Starlight," from *The Uninvited*, also released in 1944. Although it has a secure place in the canon of film noir, *Laura* is not a gritty mystery with an ambiguous moral grounding, in the manner of *The Glass Key* (1942) or *The Blue Dahlia* (1946), but, like the nearly contemporaneous *The Big Sleep* (1946), combines aspects of the detective film with a couple-forming romance. There certainly are dark moments—the basic plot, after all, devolves from the murder of a young woman—and some classic night scenes. The latter, however, are exactly those one would expect in the police investigation of a murder. In fact, in sum, the film's *mise-en-scène* is to a large extent bright and open: the elegant apartments of Laura (Gene Tierney), her mentor Waldo Lydecker (Clifton Webb), and rival Anne Treadwell (Judith Anderson); the modern advertising agency where Laura works; even a busy restaurant, with its large spaces and tall ceilings. Perhaps the best characterization of *Laura* is that it thoroughly mingles traits of film noir, a police procedural, and a romance that happens to involve a detective (Dana Andrews's character Mark McPherson). The first of these dominates the film's opening half, the last dominates the film's second half (that is, after Laura, who had been thought dead, reappears), and the police procedural ties the two together.

Kathryn Kalinak points out a number of ambiguities and internal contradictions that also work to remove *Laura* from the category of the spare and relentless style of film noir. Chief among these are the characters themselves. McPherson loses his tough-man persona fairly quickly as he falls in love with Laura (the first strong evidence of this being when he returns to the apartment at night). Laura herself is a young woman of sexual experience, but certainly no *femme fatale*—she maintains her persona of a contemporary professional woman throughout and sometimes seems more bewildered than engaged by the twists and turns of the investigation. And Waldo, the eminent but sharp-tongued critic who eventually turns out to be the murderer, is clearly represented at the beginning as homosexual, according to Kalinak, even though the story demands that he be in love with Laura and, as the plot unfolds, he increasingly shows the traits of an intensely jealous heterosexual lover. Anything but a gangster, Waldo has mistakenly shot another woman after deciding to kill Laura because she defied him with her intention to marry a shallow, unworthy playboy (acted with surprising plausibility by none other than Vincent Price).

Kalinak also recounts the chain of production shifts and disagreements that engendered these results, as author, screenwriter, producer, director, and—ultimately—even composer jousted over priorities in the film's narrative and characterization. For our purposes here, and arguably for the film's overall character and tone, the most important of these concern narration and, along with that, the music. Vera Caspary's novel is divided into three parts, each of which is narrated by one of the principal characters: Waldo, McPherson, and finally Laura herself. In the film, these would be most efficiently reproduced through voiceover narration (as if each character is recalling events that the screen then represents for us): the voiceover is the level of the narrator, or the storyteller, while the screen representation itself, with its sounds and speech, is the level of the narration, or the story. Early in the writing process, however, Laura's voiceover was dropped; later McPherson's was also. In the end, only Waldo's voiceover was retained, and then mainly in short fragments. All this, of course, opened up a considerable space for music.

At the most basic level of analysis, the question is one of presence or absence: is music there or not? And what difference does that make? We might, of course, complicate a simple off/on, yes/no response by noting that music-like qualities of rhythm and pitch modulation can be observed in speech and effects. Even in classical Hollywood sound films, we can speak of the counterpoint of conversation or of sound editing that interweaves speech and carefully chosen sound effects. The deliberate and widespread exploitation of these qualities, however, belongs to a much later time—the contemporary era of sound design that launched with the introduction of Dolby noise-reduction technology in the early 1970s. In the classical sound film, on the other hand, the absence of music can support a "real-world" or realistic everyday emphasis in the image track; when music is introduced, then, it can have a greater effect of dramatic emphasis, heightened emotion, psychological depth, or even elevation to the mythic. Where the scene should go, what it should bring out, in such cases comes under the control of an almost continuous underflow of musical commentary, as the composer, "speaking" through the orchestra, takes on a role almost indistinguishable from that of a voiceover narrator.

The first half of *Laura* is mostly taken up by Waldo's account, the greater part of which is rendered as a flashback while Waldo sits with McPherson in a restaurant and offers a history of his relationship with Laura. From the beginning of the film until McPherson re-enters Laura's apartment (at minute 40 of the film's total of 87), virtually the only music we hear is the song, which is first played by the orchestra over the main titles and continues under (that is, at a lower volume than) Waldo's initial voiceover. Two prominent diegetic statements follow several minutes later: on a record in her apartment (at minute 13; Vincent Price's character, Shelby Carpenter, even draws attention to it), and, at 21:30, by a violinist and his trio in the restaurant. Rumba and foxtrot arrangements of the theme are heard behind the first party scene (at 24:00): we presume these are also diegetic, played on an unseen record player. Dramatic underscoring is relatively little and mostly unobtrusive: as a suspicious Waldo walks through the street toward Laura's apartment, and during their subsequent confrontation (after 28:30). In both cases, the figures introduced here, and juxtaposed with occasional snippets of the theme, are restated and developed in the later dramatic cues.

Throughout the film, music participates substantively in forwarding the narrative and in explaining it to us as it unfolds. Although the diegetic cues are important in underlining the theme's significance in viewers' memory, the primary device is the symphonic underscore, which, as Claudia Gorbman describes it in her well-known "seven rules" for music in the classical Hollywood sound film, acts temporally (for pacing or to smooth over transitions), referentially (to characterize things, people, or places), and psychologically (as revealing hidden or not physically evident emotion or as reinforcing or highlighting expressed emotion).

An example of the first category is in the fact that music crosses the temporal barrier between the detective's falling asleep and Laura's entry into the apartment. The image track employs a subtle jump cut (essentially the same view of McPherson asleep, but shot at a slightly different angle) while the music downplays even that indication of passed time. Music thus keeps the focus on the continuity of his changed feelings, an important dramatic consideration that helps to increase the effect of his consternation a few seconds later when Laura opens the door and walks in.

A simple example of the opposite effect—accentuating rather than smoothing over scene change—occurs a few minutes earlier, at the end of Waldo's narration. Laura speaks to him over the phone to cancel their dinner engagement, saying she is going to her country cottage to think over her situation; music goes out under the noise of her setting down the receiver, and the scene then returns to the restaurant, now in after-hours silence at the end of Waldo's long story. This contrast of music with "real-world" absence of music emphasizes the importance of this final shift from flashback to present time.

Referentiality is served both formally—in a film whose title is a woman's name, the classical model dictates that the musical theme during the opening title sequence be the music associated with her—and compositionally, through the many re-orchestrations, tempo, and style changes to which the theme is subjected. At the very beginning, the rich but also upbeat rendition drops off quickly behind the first narration, becoming much more subdued and nostalgic as Waldo speaks about "the day that Laura died." The violinist in the restaurant offers up a frankly romantic version, almost in the manner of a vocalist singing a ballad (as a point of interest, we never hear the theme sung; Johnny Mercer added lyrics after the film was released and "Laura" was then published in sheet-music form). Since this performance occurs just before the flashback starts, we can take it as emblematic of the older Waldo's conception of Laura, while the rumba and two different foxtrot arrangements position her quite differently, as a contemporary social and

361

professional person. Finally, when Shelby describes the recording as "not exactly classical but sweet," it's evident that he is really offering his characterization of Laura herself. She will appear on screen for the first time about three minutes later, at the start of the flashback.

Finally, with respect to music-as-emotion, the dramatic cues—which contrast sharply through their non-thematic character—emphasize Waldo's anger as he spies on Laura, then the tension in their confrontation, and finally McPherson's inner turmoil as he catches repeated glimpses of Laura's portrait (hanging prominently over the fireplace) while he goes over the apartment again. Music gradually transforms itself from a slow parade of ominous woodwind and brass figures, replete with stingers (sudden, sharp chords), into a more flowing line carrying increasingly longer segments of the "Laura" theme—though still timbrally distorted. All this traces the shifting emotions of McPherson, who had returned to the apartment at night in order to search for additional clues but, once there, is forced to admit to himself that he has fallen in love with this missing woman whom he presumes to be dead.

In Chapter 8 of the present book, I referred to Robynn Stilwell's notion of the "fantastical gap," or an ambiguous middle space between the diegetic and nondiegetic. The violin in the restaurant and the record on the record player are clear instances of the diegetic, and the orchestral underscore certainly fulfills the role of the nondiegetic. In only one instance can we point to ambiguities that fit the "fantastical gap": the music played during the two parties. The character of the music and the volume level are compatible with recorded music being played in the spaces shown on the image track, as I noted earlier, but we never see the physical source of the sound, nor do we ever observe someone changing a record when the arrangements change. The hint of spatial ambiguity introduced in this way allows an otherwise neutral, Muzak-like background music to take on some of the qualities of nondiegetic music. Here, as I noted above, the dance arrangements of the theme deepen the portrayal of Laura as a woman of her generation and thereby sharpen the contrast with the older—and old-fashioned—Waldo.

Case Study 2: Diegetic/Nondiegetic Separation in *La Vita è bella*

As the final seconds of *Laura* unfold, the viewer realizes that the entire film is to be understood as a voiceover narration by Waldo, as if he were speaking from the dead. A much more recent film, Roberto Benigni's tragi-comedy *La Vita è bella* (hereafter *Life is Beautiful*), similarly, is cast as a retrospective in which we hear the voice of the narrator only briefly at beginning and end. In later life, a man named Giosuè tells the story of his childhood, and particularly of his father's unusual but ultimately effective actions meant to save his wife and son during the trauma of imprisonment in a concentration camp.

Life is Beautiful is neither a Hollywood product nor classical, but it does belong to a very broad group of contemporary films that are firmly built on classical principles. In many respects, in fact, its treatment of music is considerably simpler than was the case with *Laura*. *Life is Beautiful* has a large amount of music, most of it underscore: it is present for slightly over half the film's one-hour-and-fifty-six-minute duration, though only occasionally for more than a minute or two at a time (in this latter respect, it differs substantially from *Laura*, which has a similar percentage of music, but concentrated in fewer and longer cues). In *Life is Beautiful* music is even more obviously involved in guiding and underlining the narrative—its frequent entrances and exits interrupt the flow of action and speech to underline or emphasize something in what we see. The surface and mood of the story change dramatically from the first half of the film to the second, but the persistence and consistency of the background music reminds us that all this is a reminiscence of Giosuè's, told at some later date. Thus, the voiceover narrator may disappear from the sound track after the film's first few seconds, but the music maintains a constant link to him. The most telling evidence of this, apart from the frequent, short interruptions, is that the score's three musical motifs (main theme, a love theme, and a Nazi theme) never appear as diegetic music: they belong to the narrator—they are his musical voice, so to speak—not to the world of the story itself. Furthermore, the three melodies are closely related: although not immediately obvious, the love and Nazi themes are both derived from the main theme.

In its first half, *Life is Beautiful* largely fits the genre of the romantic comedy (although, early on, a few ominous notes do point toward the film's darker second half). Generally speaking, dialogue-heavy comedies tend to minimize both music and effects in order to allow dialogue the opportunity to achieve maximum clarity. On the other hand, romantic comedies will sometimes highlight music, and, initially at least, *Life is Beautiful* is designed as a couple-forming romance, despite the many absurdities introduced by Benigni's hijinks. The film does open with a classic farce: brakes fail and the car carrying Guido [Benigni's character] and his friend speeds down the hillside and through the street of a town lined with a crowd awaiting a dignitary, for whom Guido is mistaken. The farcical coincidences continue, but with a strangely certain trajectory toward the marriage of Dora and Guido and the establishment of their family through the birth of their son. We hear the principal musical theme (from the opening credits) repeatedly but only in short fragments, juxtaposed with a love theme that is a hidden (slowed-down) variant of the main theme, as noted above. What music accomplishes in the first part of *Life is Beautiful*, then, is to keep the viewer's attention on the romance, rather than be diverted by the farce.

If the romance of the first hour justifies its thirty minutes of music, the same amount of music in the second half is more of a mystery. Guido and his son, Giosuè, are taken to a concentration camp, and Dora insists on joining them. From this point on, the music does not change in its method—the second hour also has about thirty minutes of music, with a preponderance of underscore but some prominently placed diegetic cues—nor in its goals: if music participated fully in the elaborate fantasy that brought the couple together and Giosuè into the world, music now participates fully in the fantasy that Guido constructs for his son in order to protect him, to divert the child's attention from the disturbing and dangerous aspects of their confinement in the camp.

Everything the music does is correct but predictable, according to the conventions of symphonic underscoring and the employment of diegetic music. There is, in other words, no critique of the image, no sense that something might be wrong with the narrative we are offered. The one unconventional treatment of music is simply the fact that it does continue into and through the second half—we would normally require that music be a part of the happy everyday life of the first half, then be banished for the most part during the grim, "too real" second half.

All this points very effectively to Guido's determined efforts to keep up the fantasy of everyday life. We are being told through the music that the two halves are of a piece, that they are in fact the same story with the same character behaviors, motivations, and goals. The underscore points to the "wholeness" of Guido's life and his fantasies: his irresponsible behavior nevertheless leads to love and to Giosuè's birth, and the same strategy of fantasy ultimately, even if implausibly, keeps his family safe. And this after all is the crux of the story that our narrator—Giosuè in later life—is telling us.

Case Study 3: Music and Image in Girl With a Pearl Earring

Girl With a Pearl Earring is a historical film in which Griet (played by Scarlett Johansson), the daughter of a painter who has gone blind, has come to work as a servant in the house of Johannes Vermeer (played by Colin Firth). Over the course of time, he comes to recognize that she has aesthetic instincts that belie her status as the girl who cleans his studio, and it doesn't take long before she becomes his informal assistant. Griet eventually poses for the film's title painting, which has been commissioned by Vermeer's wealthy—but also lecherous—patron. In the course of their work together, both painter and subject begin to realize that sexual tension is steadily growing between them. Also sensing this, Vermeer's wife demands that Griet leave. She does so, returning to her parents' home. The film ends with a trio of brief scenes:

(1) at 1:31:08, the patron sits alone amidst his treasures, contemplating the finished painting. Music is slow and dark, in a very low register, played by double basses. The music stops just before the end of the scene, as he sighs audibly.

(2) at 1:31:40, Griet is at home. A servant of Vermeer's enters and gives her a packet, which she opens slowly to reveal a pair of pearl earrings, one of which she wore while sitting for the painting. Ambient sounds are noticeable (chickens, birds); the servant speaks; Griet does not. There is no music until we see the pearls, at which point a bright, short figure is heard several times; unthematic, it is the introduction to a piece, not its melody.

(3) at 1:33:10 a fade to black and then we see the painting itself, at first as an extreme close-up of the pearl, after which the camera moves very slowly out until the entire painting is visible, at which point the camera stops (1:34:25); the painting, artist, and present venue are named; and then the end-credit sequence begins.

The first two of these scenes are conventional, although at the same time important because they provide concise closure for the film's narrative. Scene 3, on the other hand, attempts something "impossible": replacing the inexorable motion of the film (the "moving picture") and reinstating the image. It takes seventy-five seconds for the entire painting gradually to come into view, and the static image (without zoom) lasts fourteen additional seconds. Indeed, even more is attempted: restoring not only the image but also the aesthetic mode of painting. The image is still framed, but the shot—the kinetic traveling of the film itself (as a series of individual images)—is replaced by the traveling of the eye around and across the details of the image, in the common mode of contemplating a work of visual art.

Music is fully involved in this. Near the end of scene 2, just as Griet turns her head and the viewer sees a tear running down her face, we hear the first passage in the piano, then a quiet "chime" sound in celesta or glockenspiel that mimics the tear falling down her face (as if recalling the sound of raindrops falling on a wet surface). When the scene changes to the painting and we begin to see the pearl come into focus, strings and a woodwind melody are added. Every now and then we hear one beat of a muffled percussion instrument. This is a music of repetition rather than of movement, of contemplation rather than direction, and it ends just as the name of the painting appears, to be replaced—in a clear contrast—by the more energetic melody that opened the film.

Through experimentation and years of commercial practice, the code of the narrative feature film became very efficient at the three things it must accomplish: create the illusion of reality, address the viewer, and represent space. The sound track generally, and music within it, is central to those effects. Sound can not only affirm the depicted physical space but also expand it through offscreen sound as well as define it narratively through the opposition of diegetic and nondiegetic. The illusion of reality, paradoxically, highlights a film's constructedness, that is, a film *creates* a reality for us to observe. Finally, a narrative film addresses the viewer directly through voiceover narration and musical commentary, but in addition through the emphases that can be achieved by the mutual influence of sound and image. In the closing minutes of *Girl With a Pearl Earring*, three spaces are defined: the opulent home of the patron, Griet's family home, and the "unattached" space of the painting. In the first is a large, gloomy nighttime room crammed with paintings and animal trophies, and music both mimics and expresses the dark sexual desire we see in the patron's face. In the second is daylight, and the absence of music now takes on significance as confirming the safety of a real, if domestic, world. Music enters again as a sonic emblem of the bittersweet magic of the pearls. Finally, the painting, which was visible in the patron's home, moves outside the diegetic realm, into what we might call the mythic space of pure art—and music is there to contemplate it, along with the stationary camera and its slow-moving zoom-out. From the diegetic to the mythic we pass outside the frame of the narrative and into the end credits.

Further Reading

N.B. This list of case study exemplars is, in the main, a selection from a much longer list compiled by Robynn Stilwell and appended to her "Case Studies: Introduction," in *The Oxford Handbook of Film Music Studies* (New York: Oxford University Press, 2013).

Brown-Montesano, Kristi A. "*Pathètique* Noir: Beethoven and *The Man Who Wasn't There*." *Beethoven Forum* 10, no. 2 (2003): 139–161.

Buhler, James. "Star Wars, Music, and Myth." In *Music and Cinema*, edited by James Buhler, Caryl Flinn, and David Neumeyer, 33–57. Middletown: Wesleyan University Press, 2000.

Franklin, Peter. "*Deception*'s Great Music: A Cultural Analysis." In *Film Music II*, edited by Claudia Gorbman and Warren Sherk, 169–198. Sherman Oaks, CA: The Film Music Society, 2004.

Gabbard, Krin. "Borrowing Black Masculinity: The Role of Johnny Hartman in *The Bridges of Madison County*." In *Soundtrack Available: Essays on Film and Popular Music*, edited by Pamela Robertson Wojcik and Arthur Knight, 295–318. Durham, NC and London: Duke University Press, 2001.

Kalinak, Kathryn. "'Not Exactly Classical, but Sweet'—*Laura*: New Directions." Chapter 7 in her *Settling the Score: Music and the Classical Hollywood Film*. Madison: University of Wisconsin Press, 1992.

Magee, Gayle Sherwood. "Song, Genre, and Transatlantic Dialogue in *Gosford Park*." *Journal of the Society for American Music* 2, no. 4 (2008): 477–505.

Martin, Ruth Lee. "Framing Ambiguity and Desire through Musical Means in Sally Potter's Film 'Orlando'." *Music, Sound, and the Moving Image* 5, no. 1 (2011): 25–37.

Morris, Mitchell. "In Marginal Fashion: Sex, Drugs, Russian Modernism, and New Wave Music in *Liquid Sky*." In *Composing for the Screen in the USSR and Germany*, edited by Robynn J. Stilwell and Phil Powrie, 161–177. Bloomington: Indiana University Press, 2007.

Neumeyer, David and Laura Neumeyer. "On Motion and Stasis: Photography, 'Moving Pictures,' Music." In *Music, Meaning and Media*, edited by Richard Littlefield, Erkki Pekkilä, and David Neumeyer, 11–33. Imatra/Helsinki: International Semiotics Institute, 2007.

Pekkilä, Erkki. "Stardom, Genre, and Myth: Music in Aki Kaurismäki's Film *The Man Without a Past*." In *Essays on Sound and Vision*, edited by John Richardson and Stan Hawkins, 155–174. Helsinki: Helsinki University Press, 2007.

Stilwell, Robynn J. "'I just put a drone under him …': Collage and Subversion in the score of *Die Hard*." *Music & Letters* 78, no. 4 (1997): 551–574.

Stilwell, Robynn J. "Symbol, Narrative, and the Musics of *Truly, Madly, Deeply*." *Screen* 38, no. 1 (1997): 60–75.

43

MULTIMEDIA ART
Video Art-Music

Holly Rogers

Video art is often considered a visual genre. But the electromagnetic basis of the video format enabled sound and image to be recorded and projected simultaneously in an easy, portable way. As a result, the medium could produce a live form of audiovisual synergy rarely possible before. As earlier chapters in this volume point out, attempts to capture temporal elements in the static arts proliferated as the twentieth century progressed, with movement and transient fluidity becoming prominent themes for many Impressionists, Cubists, and those involved with Orphism, Vorticism, and Synchronism. And yet Karin von Maur has argued that in many cases, the governing force was not simply time but, rather, musicalized time: "Never before in the numerous programs and manifestos of the avant-garde did there appear so many temporal concepts, such as rhythm, dynamics, speed, and simultaneity, or musical terms such as cadence, dissonance, polyphony, etc., proving the existence of a close link between the temporalization tendencies in art and the reception of musical phenomena."[1] Film technology provided a significant boost to the possibility of "musicalized time" as it enabled the static image to burst into life, a leap into temporalization that manifested itself most clearly in the early visual-music films of Oskar Fischinger and Hans Richter and the mid-century experimentation of Californian visual-music artists Jordan Belson, James Whitney, Hy Hirsh, and Harry Smith. Although film equipment allowed images to become temporally and aurally active, the arrival of the video medium onto the commercial market in 1965 encouraged a form of live, interactive audiovisuality able to significantly expand audiovisual, cinematic space. Video was cheap and easy to use: it could be managed by one person; it could manipulate sound and image in real time; it could use the space around it as a creative material; and it could engender a new mode of activated spectatorship.

While it is true that video became a useful tool for visual artists seeking to move their images through time, many early video protagonists actually began their careers as musicians; Nam June Paik (experimental composer), Steina Vasulka (classical violinist), and Robert Cahen (electro-acoustic composer), for instance, all trained and worked as performers or composers before turning their attention to moving image work. Others came to the format without formal training, but with an established working relationship with music: Tony Conrad, for instance, was a member of the Theatre of Eternal Music (also known as The Dream Syndicate) alongside La Monte Young and John Cale; Bruce Nauman explains that his ideas about time were fertilized by the music of Steve Reich and Philip Glass; and Bill Viola developed his audiovisual and spatial tropes during his time performing as part of David Tudor's experimental group, Composers Inside Electronics (where he became involved with Tudor's "Rainforest" project). With the new audiovisual equipment in hand, these early protagonists produced highly musical pieces that paved the way for an intermedial aesthetic that would characterize video work for the next fifty years.

As music and art came together, the spaces that had previously held them apart became an integral part of the new aesthetic. Using the Duomo in Florence to illustrate the dynamic spatial forces at play between sound, image, and visitor in his work, for instance, Viola explained how the ability of sound to travel "around corners, through walls, or totally immerse, even penetrate the observer" could produce an "aural architecture" able to physically activate the hinterland between painting and music.[2] Such interest in the spatial aspects of audiovisual work relocated creative and receptive emphasis from object to process—from artifact to audiovisual space—a relocation that lies at the heart of the popular tri-partite designation "video installation art." Audiovisual at a material level, and frequently used by musicians, video technology gave rise to a genre able to command several levels of audio engagement at once: first, its technological make-up meant that sound and image could be produced concurrently, and this demanded an audiovisual commitment from its user; second, video's audiovisuality could be projected live to create a transient and site-specific intermedial space; and third, when displayed, video could immerse artist, performer, and audience within a single, interactive environment.

During the decades immediately preceding video's commercial availability, the spaces in which art and music were received, and the strategies of listening and viewing encouraged within them, became an increasingly important component of the creative process. This spatial curiosity not only called into question conventional concert- and art-venue decorum; it also pressed at the time-honored boundaries that separated the arts. Traditionally, visual art, unlike music, does not require a spatio-temporal realization. But the emergence of installation art during the last century questioned the silent, static nature of painting and sculpture by highlighting the spaces in which artwork was situated, a move that repositioned attention from the piece presented to its contextual relationships. Visitors were encouraged to move around the installed work at will in order to reconfigure its spatial attributes and their own bodily relation to it in a personal and unique way.

Performance art and Happenings took the ideas of spatial expansion and audience activation even further. Speaking of his Events, the architect of the Happening, Allan Kaprow, explained that people did not "come to look *at* things" but rather became a fundamental part of the work, a change that replaced the artist-as-creator with a fragile, impermanent, and collectively articulated art event. According to Kaprow, art no longer had to be a finite and collectable artifact: instead, it could arise from the interaction between visual and audio components, audience members, and the space in which they all collided: "There is, therefore, a never-ending play of changing conditions between the relatively fixed or 'scored' parts of my work and the 'unexpected' or undetermined parts," explained Kaprow: as a result, it is "possible to experience the whole exhibit differently at different times. These have been composed in such a way as to offset any desire to see them in the light of the traditional, closed, clear forms of art as we have known them."[3] Kaprow's desire to blur the boundaries between art and life was closely connected to the ideas advocated by members of the Fluxus alliance, artists and musicians who emphasized humorous anti-art gestures and impermanent situations. In 1964, George Maciunas explained that "Fluxus is definitely against art-object as non-functional commodity—to be sold and to make a livelihood for an artist. It could temporarily have the pedagogical function of teaching people the needlessness of art including the eventual needlessness of itself. It should not therefore be permanent."[4] The promotion of art that encouraged a free dialogue between its "scored" sections and the "undetermined" elements performed by its visitors initiated a shift between art-as-object and art-as-process: according to Maciunas, a work not only reflected its context but could also mediate it. Such mediation lay at the heart of early video work.

As artists began to move their work into temporal and spatial realms, composers started to demonstrate a new awareness of the ways in which sound could spread through a performance arena and into the audience. Of course, an interest in the spatialization of music performance can be found throughout the centuries, from the *cori spezzati* (separated choirs) favored by Venetian polychoral composers Adrian Willaert and Andrea and Giovanni Gabrieli during the sixteenth century, through to the physical movements of musicians in works such as the final Adagio of Haydn's Symphony No. 45 (the *Farewell*, 1772), which requires musicians to leave the stage one by one. Spatial effects can also be found in many orchestral works, such as the feuding timpanists that flank the orchestra in the Allegro finale of Nielsen's Fourth Symphony (*The Inextinguishable*, 1916), or the chilling offstage trumpet and horn cries that haunt the fifth and final movement of Mahler's Symphony No. 2 (*Resurrection*, 1888–94). As the twentieth century unraveled, the spatialization of performers and audience members became more pronounced. One of the first steps toward a refreshed relationship between music and its spaces of articulation came in the form of works that discarded permanent and determined sequences of sounds in favor of performer-driven processes similar to the fluid events orchestrated by Kaprow: Morton Feldman's four *Intersections* (1951–53), for example, and Terry Riley's *In C* (1964) give creative command to the performer, ensuring a different interpretation in every recital. John Cage took this idea further by proposing that music is not something a musician produces but, rather, something a listener perceives: any sounds can be music, in other words, provided that they are heard as such. In performances of *4'33"* (1952), incidental, "environmental sounds" from the performance space become part of the experience, an inclusion that dissolved the physical and creative boundaries between composer, performer, and audience.[5] Although working to a very different aesthetic, Luciano Berio often provided very specific stage directions for his performers: in *Circles* (1960), he asked the percussionists to execute "frantic gyrations," while the singer was requested to trace a "half circle" rotation until she became "absorbed into the ensemble."[6] Asked to meander at will between six small ensembles positioned all around her, the solo clarinetist in Pierre Boulez's *Domaines* (1968) was afforded control over the structure of the piece: as she reached each musical domain, a different segment of music was performed. Other composers sought to collapse not only the familiar seating formations of instrumental performers, but also the traditional bifurcation of concert venues, in which audience members remain physically separated from the musicians. In performances of *Terretektorh* (1966), Iannis Xenakis dotted his orchestra through the audience, who were seated in a circle around the conductor. As a result, each listener received a differently spatialized version of the music.

Even within this most cursory foray into the expanding spaces of early-twentieth-century music and art, it is easy to identify for video work a dual lineage. Set against a historical backdrop of intense experimentation that ranged from the conceptual work of Marcel Duchamp and the performance-based practices of Kaprow on the art side, to the heightened spatialization of Cage, Boulez, and Xenakis in the arena of music, the video format provided a new means by which to expand traditional methods of art and music consumption. As we have seen, the arrival of early video technology provided artists with the opportunity to easily sound their visual work, and composers the means by which to visualize their music. In so doing, those using the portable video equipment could become artist-composers, able to draw together the expanding spaces of music performance and art exhibition into a single, inter-medial unit. Perhaps because it rested at the intersection between disciplines, video was at first considered to be a facilitator for convergence, rather than as a genre in its own right. During the 1960s and early 1970s, for instance, the medium was pri-marily included in multimedia events, where it acted like an adhesive able to draw together audiences, performers, and technologies. This makes it difficult to identify a single orthodoxy at play within early video art-music, although shared influences did provide loose stylistic alliances—the Fluxus "dematerialization" of the object, for instance, or the desire for audiovisual synergy. Yvonne Spielmann refers to these early years as video's "integrating birth," arguing that any new medium, before it can coalesce into a genre, must first define itself in relation to existing media.[7] But we can take Spielmann's idea one step further by speaking not only of integration, but also of amalgamation. While it is true that a new genre was in the process of becoming, two ancient disciplines were also beginning to merge physically and aesthetically.

Video's place in the multimedia milieu of the 1960s can be seen in one of its first public appearances as a creative medium. *Nine Evenings: Theater and Engineering* was a series of multimedia events staged at the 69th Regiment Armory, New York, during October 1966. Organized by Billy Klüver, an electrical engineer, *Nine Eve-nings* presented work created by New York artists and musicians, including Cage, Tudor, Robert Rauschenberg, Robert Whitman, and Merce Cunningham, in col-laboration with engineers from the Bell Telephone Laboratories. By bringing music and art together with new technologies such as video, wireless sound transmission, closed-circuit television, Doppler sonar devices that could translate movement into sound, and infrared television cameras, Klüver hoped to develop integrated audio-visual performativity, an anticipation that was realized in Whitman's *Two Holes of Water—3*. To produce his highly theatrical piece, Whitman used seven cars, film, live performers, closed-circuit television, and a typewriter (Figure 43.1). A mini-ature fiber-optic video camera placed inside the pocket of fellow artist Les Levine captured real-time images of the performance, which were instantly relayed through a closed-circuit system to Whitman. The artist inter-spliced these images with foot-age from broadcast television to produce a live montage that was projected, via equipment attached to the cars, onto large screens placed around the Armory. In a similar way, sounds from the cars, typewriter, and audience were picked up by micro-phones and combined with pre-recorded noises, including the sound of crickets and the soulful enunciations of Bertrand Russell. By videoing and projecting live images and sounds, Whitman not only made use of video's ability to synergistically unite many disparate elements, he also drew the audience into the heart of the piece. Site-specific and interactive, then, the audiovisual space created by *Two Holes of Water—3* rejected traditional methods of art display and music performance.

The first American exhibition given entirely to video and television work was held a few years later, in 1969 at the Howard Wise Gallery, New York. "TV as a Creative Medium" included work by many early proponents of video, including Paik, Ira Schneider, Frank Gillette, and Aldo Tambellini, and represents an attempt to identify, or even to forge, an emerging video community. As Davidson Gigliotti explains, "TV as a Creative Medium was a catalytic event around which a video art community began to coalesce. New names and faces had appeared on the scene every year since 1965, but until the Spring of '69 there had been no center, no real cohesion, no sense of a community of purpose. After the show at the Howard Wise Gallery, it was possible to identify oneself as a video artist, and to recognize other video artists."[8] Significantly, this early attempt at identifying for video a cohesive community included several audiovisual pieces, an incorporation that not only brought sound into the normally silent gallery world of art exhibition, but also indicated the musical direction in which video was heading. Included were several pieces by Paik, among them a rewired television linked to two microphones. The monitor showed a moving cluster of colored lines which morphed and warped in response to the sounds being received by the microphones. Here, sound and image were created *simultaneously* by a single medium. Joe Weintraub's AC/TV (Audio-Controlled Television), a device able to "[t]ranslate music into a complex kinetic image on the screen of any color TV" sought a similar fusion: "The brightness is controlled by the volume of the music. The colors are controlled by the pitch. The patterns are dependent on both … As soon as I became aware of the Color Cathode Ray Tube, I realized that the red, blue and green guns in the CRT were ideally suited for audio control by the low, middle and high frequencies of music."[9] As part of the show, Paik premiered one of his collaborative cello works: *TV Bra for Living Sculpture* was one of several intensely musical pieces that the artist-composer produced with avant-garde cellist and mixed-media performance artist Charlotte Moorman. Hailing from New York, Moorman was a key protagonist in the city's experimental arts scene and established the Avant-Garde Festival, a series of radical and influential events situated beyond the threshold (and remit) of traditional venues. Described by one reviewer as "the show-stopper of this quite dazzling exhibition," *TV Bra* was intended to "humanize" and demystify the new electronic technology.[10] But it was also one of the earliest examples of audiovisual video composition. For this piece, Moorman sported an undergarment made from two small television screens which showed live TV footage and a closed-circuit feed of the performance. When she improvised on her cello, the sounds passed through a processor, distorting and modulating both the live broadcast TV and her own, looped image. The unique ability of video simultaneously to record and play back music and image was used to condense the performer and the broadcast world beyond into a transient, interactive, and intermedial space.

These early uses of video, then, produced a unique moment in history. Those using the technology could become (or invite their audiences to become) artist-composers, producing work able to collapse the space–time divide that previously had held apart the visual and musical arts. As a result, creative practice could move

371

fluidly between the space that traditionally separated and distinguished disciplines. By the 1980s, however, this moment was no longer unique, as video had become a well-respected and "aesthetically independent genre."[11] Although we must be wary of oversimplification and reduction, it is possible to distinguish between video's first wave of experimentation and its subsequent developments in terms of what Catherine Elwes calls "contrasting spatial dynamics."[12] During its first decade, video work was sculptural. Artist-composers placed emphasis on video's physical apparatus in order to produce an activated mode of consumption. This could either be in the form of multimedia presentation, as we saw in Whitman's *Two Holes of Water—3*, or sculptural, as demonstrated by the striking sartorial presentation of Paik's *TV Bra* or his later *TV Chair* (1968) and *TV Bed* (1972). Other artists placed all their focus on the TV monitor: for *Untitled* (1968), Otto Piene covered a television set displaying a diagonal line with silverpainted plastic pearls; Frank Gillette and Ira Schneider created a bank of nine TV monitors that displayed different views of the audience for *Wipe Cycle* (1969); and Nauman asked visitors to walk down a narrow wooden passage toward their own videoed image for his *Live-Taped Video Corridor* (1970).

Although audiovisuality and interactivity still resonate strongly in contemporary video work, later trends have leaned toward what Liz Kotz describes as a "seductive immateriality."[13] While exceptions to this binary are not difficult to find—Gabriel Barcia-Colombo's recent interactive audiovisual items and Camille Utterback's *Potent Objects* (2003) are just two examples—many artist-composers have embraced flat-screen technology to create more immersive, cinematic environments in which the apparatus blends with its surroundings. Using as a starting point Norman Bryson's belief that the Western oil paint tradition has been "treated primarily as an erasive medium" able to take attention away from "the surface of the picture-plane," Jay Bolter and Richard Grusin cite point-of-view television, webcams, and period dramas as examples of genres that make us think we are "'really' there."[14] In such instances, they argue, "the logic of immediacy dictates that the medium itself should disappear and leave us in the presence of the thing represented."[15] Viola's work embodies the notions of immersivity and intermediality particularly well. Although he also produces single-screen works, his most powerful pieces exist in multidimensional forms that reside in dark spaces cut off from the outside world. *The Stopping Mind* (1991), for instance, consisted of four projection screens hanging several feet from the blackened walls of a dark room. Speakers nestled in each of the four corners and another hung from the center of the ceiling. At first the room was still and silent: then, in "a burst of frantic motion and cascading sound," images taken from natural scenes began to jostle against urban landscapes.[16] Spreading across the four screens, the randomly generated images were delivered in short bursts, gaining in nervous haste each time. These visual bursts were presented with sounds taken from the original location. Like the image track, the electro-acoustic noises became increasingly warped and insistent with each appearance, until a level of amplified distortion resulted in what Viola referred to as "frightening" sounds.[17] Visitors were asked to step into the heart of this alternation between stasis and "frantic motion"; to be thoroughly immersed in the evolving nightmare. With the edges of each screen disappearing into a "seductive immateriality," visitors were thoroughly sutured into Viola's audiovisual diegesis. During performances of the *TV Bra*, it was possible for visitors to be included in the work's closed-circuit feed, thus appearing on Moorman's televisual clothing and assuming a degree of interactive engagement. However, the performance remained sculptural, rather than immersive. The "aural architecture" of *The Stopping Mind*, on the other hand, was immersive but not interactive; the visitors were physically absorbed into the audiovisual creation but could not alter its course.

Other forms of recent audiovisual video place the interactive element at the aesthetic heart of the work. David Stout's investigation into video noise—"a random grouping of black and white pixels changing position every 25–30 times a second"—makes use of computer technology to create responsive forms of audiovisuality, for instance, and can be traced back to the early intermedial experiments of Weintraub and Paik.[18] In works such as *SignalFire* (2003–04), the artist produces feedback loops and digital image processes through hybrid laptop instruments in order to create a direct audiovisual response from video noise, a transformation that suggests "the potential power of artificially intelligent sound-image engines" (Figure 43.2).[19] Like the pieces by Whitman and Paik above, these processes could include an interactive element, as Stout explains: "This sound and any sound emitted from the 'viewer' in the immediate environment can be directed back into the system to effect various mutations of visual form, color, scale and movement. Consequently, the individual works are unpredictable and capable of affecting the visual and sonic behavior of each other, producing an ambient or environmental effect which transforms the viewer into a participant and the singular composition into a net-worked system. As these works grow in size they will more importantly grow in behavioral complexity."[20] Two of Christa Erickson's installations that deal with the fragility of memory play on the conceptual links between sound and image through more gentle forms of interactivity. *Replay: Rewind* (2002–04) uses an ultrasonic sensor to activate projected images and an audio counterpoint whenever a visitor sits on a piano stool in front of the screen; in *Whirl* (2007), the grainy moving images of children at play and the shaky, distant sounds of nursery rhymes whispered through a record player become animated only when the visitor blows temporary life into a pinwheel. Adi Marom's interactive digital animation, *Machinema*, relied on a similar form of physical interactivity. Spread over 120 flat screens at the IAC Building, New York (2009), the piece lay dormant until a visitor assumed control over a large crank: as soon as the gears began to shift to the sound of loudly protesting ratchets and cogs, the installation ground into motion, sending birds, waves, clouds, and the sun across the screen to give the illusion of mechanical interaction.

The musical strategies at play in contemporary video art are particularly clear in work that encourages interactivity through the use of touch-screen interfaces and sensors. Once visitors cross the normally forbidden threshold that separates art and life in order to interact with a work, they become the material of the piece, able to assume varying levels of compositional control. *Cantique 3* (2004), a participatory video piece created by Marie Chouinard, for instance, allowed visitors to play the installation. The profiles of a man and a woman rested dormant on two large screens, each connected to separate touch-screen panels. On the screens—one each for the man and the woman—were five lines that resembled a musical stave: but instead of musical notes, small snapshots of the characters rested on the lines. Visitors were invited to move the snapshots up and down and along the staves in order to create a corresponding reaction in the faces on the big screens, which burst into aggravated movement and harsh, extended vocalizations. When played together, the man and woman created an audiovisual counterpoint composed entirely by the visitors.

At a time when even the youngest child can engage in audiovisual play on her mobile phone, it is difficult to imagine a time when moving images and sounds could not easily be produced together. But before 1965, live forms of audiovisuality were difficult to produce. Emerging at a time of cultural shift between art-as-object and art-as-process, video technology provided a simple means with which to create visual music, or sonic images: as a result, it enabled several strands of creative experimentation to pull together to form a new audiovisual space that radically redefined the traditions of music performance and art exhibition. Video's "acoustic architecture," then, represented a critical intervention, or coming together, of two spatially expanding disciplines. With this in mind, it makes sense to speak not of video installation *art*, but rather of video *art-music*. Not only does this recognize the importance of sound in video's material make-up, the ways in which it has been used, and the expanded spaces of its reception; it also acknowledges the historical importance of a technology able to draw together two separate artforms. Once established, this new form of art-music and the "activated spectatorship" it encouraged has proliferated into sculptural, immersive, interactive, and virtual forms that can now be found in most major galleries and large-scale music events.

Notes

1 Karin von Maur, *The Sound of Painting: Music in Modern Art* (Munich: Prestel, 1999), 44.
2 Quoted in Jörg Zutter, "Interview with Bill Viola," in *Bill Viola: Unseen Images*, ed. Marie Louise Syring (Düsseldorf: Städtische Kunsthalle, 1992), 100.
3 Allan Kaprow, "Notes on the Creation of a Total Art," in *Essays on the Blurring of Art and Life*, ed. Jeff Kelley (California: University of California Press, 1993), 11–12. Kaprow's essay was first published in 1958.
4 George Maciunas, "240.XXII George Maciunas (Fluxus objectives and Ideology) 1964," in *Fluxus etc. Addemda II: The Gilbert and Lila Silverman Collection*, ed. Jon Hendricks, exh. cat. (Pasadena: Baxter Art Gallery at the California Institute of Technology, 1983), 166.
5 Wim Mertens, *American Minimal Music*, trans. Jan Hautekiet (New York: Alexander Broude, 1983), 22.
6 Stage direction quoted in Robert Adlington, *The Music of Harrison Birtwistle* (Cambridge: Cambridge University Press, 2000), 48.
7 Yvonne Spielmann, *Video: The Reflexive Medium* (Cambridge, MA: The MIT Press, 2008), 117.
8 Davidson Gigliotti, "Video Art in the Sixties," in *Abstract Painting 1960–69* (Long Island City, NY: Institute for Art and Urban Resources Inc., 1983), 43.
9 Joe Weintraub quoted in exhibition flyer.
10 Reviewer quoted in John Gruen, "Art in New York," *New York* 2, no. 23 (June 9, 1969): 57.
11 Spielmann, *Video*, 87.
12 Catherine Elwes, *Video Art: A Guided Tour* (London: University of the Arts), 153.
13 Liz Kotz, "Video Projection: The Space Between Screens," in *Art and the Moving Image: A Critical Reader*, ed. Tanya Leighton (London: Tate Publishing, 2008), 379.
14 Norman Bryson, *Vision and Painting: The Logic of the Gaze* (New Haven: Yale University Press, 1983), 92; Jay Bolter and Richard Grusin, *Remediation: Understanding New Media* (Cambridge, MA: The MIT Press, 1999), 6.
15 Bolter and Grusin, *Remediation*, 6.
16 Bill Viola, "The Stopping Mind," in *Reasons for Knocking at an Empty House: Writings 1973–1994*, ed. Robert Violette (London: Thames and Hudson, 1995), 213.
17 Quoted in *Bill Viola: European Insights*, ed. Rolf Lauter (Munich: Prestel, 1999), 310.
18 David Stout quoted in Spielmann, *Video*, 225.
19 Ibid.
20 Ibid., 226.

Further Reading

Elwes, Catherine. *Video Art: A Guided Tour*. London: I. B. Tauris, 2005.

Gaudreault, André, and Philippe Marion. "The Cinema as a Model for the Genealogy of Media." *Convergence* 8, no. 4 (2002): 12–18.

Hall, Doug and Sally Jo Fifer, eds. *Illuminating Video: An Essential Guide to Video Art*. New York: Aperture Press, 1991.

Knight, Julia, ed. *Diverse Practices: A Critical Reader on British Video Art*. Luton: University of Luton/ Arts Council England, 1996.

Meigh-Andrews, Chris. *A History of Video Art*. Oxford: Berg, 2006.

Rogers, Holly. *Sounding the Gallery: Video and the Rise of Art-Music*. Oxford: Oxford University Press, 2013.

Schneider, Ira and Beryl Korot, eds. *Video Art: An Anthology*. New York: Harcourt Brace Jovanovich, 1976.

Spielmann, Yvonne. *Video: The Reflexive Medium*. Cambridge, MA: MIT Press, 2008.

Youngblood, Gene. *Expanded Cinema*. New York: E. P. Dutton & Co., 1970.

44

MUSIC, VISUAL CULTURE, AND DIGITAL GAMES

Roger Moseley

There is growing recognition that the twenty-first-century media landscape has been profoundly shaped by the rise of digital games to an unprecedented level of cultural prominence. Most commonly registered through its seismic impact on the economic terrain of the entertainment sector, the digital game has also transformed the stock of symbolic and social capital in which global popular culture has traded since the late 1970s. In recent years, moreover, digital games have opened up new modes of representation, expanded the critical lexicon, and stimulated distinctive contributions to debates surrounding music, the visual arts, film, literature, and new media.

While all media reflect the material and ideological conditions that make them imaginable, the case of the digital game is particularly telling. It channels a dizzying array of pre-existing art forms, media, and genres that includes calligraphy, painting, comics/*manga*, cartoons/*anime*, graphic novels, science fiction, board games, theater, opera, film, television, sports, radio, advertising, recorded sound, electronic music, dance, and performance art. Significantly, however, digital games combine and remediate these elements under the technological aegis of the computer, which both establishes and enforces the protocols that govern their interaction. In this sense, the digital game unites two of the furthest-reaching innovations of the twentieth century, both closely associated with the Hungarian-American mathematician John von Neumann: the discipline of economic game theory, which he developed with Oskar Morgenstern prior to World War II, and the hugely influential computer architecture developed in the postwar years that bears von Neumann's name and is ubiquitous today. It should be no surprise, then, that the digital game has served as a lightning rod for debates concerning the representation of violence, the rationalistic quest for domination in zero-sum conflicts, and the relationship between reality and simulation: it stands in synecdochically for the economic, technological, and militaristic operations of late capitalism writ large.

For the purposes of architects, fighter pilots, and surgeons as well as game players, computers can calculate or approximate the relevant optical or acoustic data required to simulate environments via complex sets of rules. While doing so, the computer's central processing unit (CPU) is effectively blind and deaf to distinctions between different types of data, since all information must be transcoded into bits. The computer can thus both visualize auditory data and "sonify" visual data as commanded, and this media-agnosticism has been identified as a hallmark of the digital age. Yet the mechanisms by which computers store and process binary information evoke Lessing's distinction between what Daniel Albright terms the "spatially juxtapositive arts ... of painting, sculpture, and architecture, and the temporally progressive arts of ... poetry and music."[1] Bits are either stored as spatially divergent but temporally fixed structures of memory, or executed serially in temporal sequence as code. The static configurations of bits as memory can be correlated to the spatial properties of the image (and in some early computers they were visible as such); the execution of bits as code, conversely, is more closely analogous to the transduction of a score into a musical performance.

These distinctions help to reveal the culturally embedded presumptions as well as the physical and mathematical principles that underpin the von Neumann architecture. They remind us that binary code is not ideologically neutral: for human purposes it is modulated into audible, visible, and haptic stimuli that, in pointing beyond themselves, are perceived as mimetic rather than (or as well as) simulational. The sonic and graphical output of digital games is often iconic in that it is understood to refer to sources, objects, or concepts, even though they might have no counterparts in the physical world. In practice, most digital games deploy both simulation and mimesis as representational strategies, and the boundaries between the two can be difficult to distinguish.

The tropes of simulation and mimesis have also informed the two leading critical approaches to digital games that have emerged in recent years. While one emphasizes the technical and material factors that determine the forms and patterns of games according to their prevailing rules, the other understands digital games primarily to remediate audiovisual elements from other contexts and concentrates on the phenomenological and social experiences that games afford, drawing on approaches informed by film theory, art history, visual culture, literary criticism, anthropology, and (ethno)musicology. By privileging algorithmic, procedural, and code-based factors, the first approach could be characterized as an attempt to foreground how digital games operate; by focusing instead on visual representations and audible phenomena, the second approach addresses the questions of what, and how, digital games mean.

Considered dialectically, these two perspectives offer complementary insights into the visible, audible, haptic, psychological, social, cultural, and ideological aspects of digital gameplay. While the computer serves as "an arbiter, an umpire, a scorekeeper, and a dungeon master," in the words of Atari pioneer Nolan Bushnell, the contingent and adaptive ways in which audiovisual relationships unfold in the course of play are dependent to a large degree on players and developers as well as on technological possibilities and constraints.[2] Differing levels of familiarity, skill, and motivation will result in divergent experiences; moreover, players can choose whether to submit to a game's ludic logic and its developers' intentions or to subvert them by relying on exploits within the game, by altering its code, or by interpreting its outcomes. In what follows, I will sketch a brief overview of the development of the digital game that takes account of the technological and material factors peculiar to its operation while also attending to the powerful cultural forces that have shaped its audiovisual modulations.

Beyond its immediate history, media-archaeological antecedents of the digital game are scattered among the mathematical and technological innovations of philosophers, inventors, and polymaths such as Filippo Brunelleschi, Gottfried Wilhelm Leibniz, and Athanasius Kircher. In the early fifteenth century, Brunelleschi established geometrical optical linear perspective as a painterly technique, which was codified and demonstrated by his acquaintances Leon Battista Alberti and Masaccio. In the seventeenth century, Leibniz not only had a hand in the invention of binary but also developed differential calculus, which offered a means of digitizing the analog trajectories of bodies in motion and thus rendered them computable. For his part, Kircher developed the *lanterna magica,* a forerunner to the slide projector, which, to the horrified amazement of onlookers, could throw ghostly images of demons and skeletons onto walls. (He also developed combinatorial systems of music composition and worked on technologies related to mechanical musical reproduction.)

As media theorist Friedrich Kittler pointed out, there is a thread that connects these innovations: all are related to the waging of war. Perspective, particularly as deployed by Leonardo da Vinci and Albrecht Dürer, became a technological means of aiming firearms accurately. Similarly, Leibniz's calculus was developed to calculate the ballistic behavior of cannonballs, while Kircher's *lanterna magica* was conceived as a means of sending encrypted military intelligence over long distances. Through and beyond these examples, Kittler argued that the relationship between war and technologies of diversion is undeniable: "The entertainment industry is, in any conceivable sense of the word, an abuse of army equipment."[3] To return to our immediate historical frame, it is clear that digital games were spin-offs made possible by technologies designed for the purposes of the US military-industrial complex. Correspondingly, the operations that govern them issued from the development of the earliest computers by von Neumann and his collaborators and competitors in the aftermath of the Manhattan Project, in which von Neumann played a critical role. This helps to explain why the development of the digital game was closely tied to the relationship between the US and Japan, nations whose military, political, and technological fortunes were bound together by the means, motives, and consequences of the atomic bombs dropped on Hiroshima and Nagasaki in 1945.

William Higinbotham's *Tennis for Two* (1958), one of the earliest electronic games made accessible to the public, illustrates these relationships and co-dependencies. Higinbotham had worked on the Manhattan Project before becoming head of the Brookhaven National Laboratory's Instrumentation Division, and his game was played not on a television but on a triggered-sweep cathode-ray oscilloscope. This analog display technology had been developed as a means of visually representing the invisible as reflected through sound (sonar) or radio waves (radar); it was concerned with providing data that tracked aircraft and seacraft for military purposes. From its formative moments, then, the video game dealt (as had Leibniz) with representations of bodies in motion, whether they took the form of airplanes or of tennis balls. It challenged players to process images in order to provide timely and accurate input that coincided with (or brought about) spatial collisions, forcing together what Lessing wanted to keep apart. The agonistic and violent qualities of such games, not to mention the imbrication of sonic and optical media technologies, were thus integral to their development rather than overlaid onto it. The repurposing of hardware for ludic purposes enacted a shift from mimetic representation of external phenomena (such as airplanes) to the simulation of physical laws governing the motion of an imaginary object (the "tennis ball") via analog computation, in the case of the Donner Model 30 that powered *Tennis for Two*.

Although audio-related technologies from sonar to vacuum tubes made major contributions to the development of the computer, early digital games such as *Spacewar!*, developed at the Massachusetts Institute of Technology in 1962 by a team including Steve Russell, Martin Graetz, and Wayne Wiitanen, produced no intentionally musical sounds. The very title of Atari's tennis simulator *Pong* in 1972, however, signaled the supplanting of the audible relay clicks of *Tennis for Two* by onomatopoeic sine-wave bloops and bleeps. Hardware designed for video display was repurposed to create auditory feedback that represented the binary logic of hitting, bouncing, and missing through distinctions of frequency. In human terms, these different pitches articulated the zero-sum representation of victory, deferral, and defeat.

When ballistic data were processed by the digital computational power of von Neumann's serial architecture rather than by televisual relays and gates, relatively complex artificially intelligent responses could be calculated and performed by the machine itself. This facilitated the solitary apocalyptic drama of *Space Invaders*, developed by Tomohiro Nishikado in 1978, in which a lone human is pitted against endless waves of computer-controlled alien adversaries. In *Space Invaders*, it is immediately apparent that the computer has transformed from neutral arbiter into sworn enemy: the phalanx of aliens unremittingly sweeps the screen in a pattern that emulates in slow motion the sweep of the electron beam that plots their bitmapped images pixel by pixel. As the player reduces the aliens' number via laser cannon, the decreased load on the CPU accelerates their movement. As Neil Lerner has observed, this effect is matched by an increase in the tempo of the soundtrack's reiterated descending tetrachord that, in a positive feedback loop, both registers and stimulates the player's quickening pulse as the stakes rise. The increased motion that accompanies the redistribution of the burden of execution from CPU to human is thus represented both visually and aurally.

While arcade games such as *Space Invaders* had dedicated sound chips, such luxuries were prohibitively expensive when it came to developing hardware for the domestic marketplace. In order to generate sound, Atari's enormously successful 2600 home console (released in 1977) followed *Pong*'s lead by commandeering its video hardware—the Television Interface Adaptor chip—for sonic purposes. Musical tones were produced by dividing the clock speed of the CPU until its frequencies entered audible range, resulting in characteristically ill-tempered intervals. More broadly, the lack of dedicated processing power, memory, and hardware resources for sonic processing placed severe timbral, dynamic, and polyphonic restrictions on composers. As the parameters most congenial to efficient digital encoding, pitch and rhythm were granted primacy, as they had been by the transmission of European music via alphanumerical tablature between the fourteenth and eighteenth centuries. Like the rules of a game, technological constraints afford opportunities for their ingenious circumvention, as composers as diverse as Rob Hubbard, Koji Kondo, and Nobuo Uematsu demonstrated throughout the 1980s: their soundtracks from the early home console and microcomputer era remain among the most celebrated of all time.

Perhaps the most popular and influential game of the 1980s was *Super Mario Bros.*, released for Nintendo's Famicom console (known in the US as the Nintendo Entertainment System) in 1985. Alongside Nishikado's vaguely aquatic *Space Invaders*, Shigeru Miyamoto and Takashi Tezuka's sprite-based designs for Mario, his allies and adversaries, and his vaguely psychedelic mushrooms have become iconic representations not merely of their symbolic referents but of digital gaming as a whole. Kondo's music exhibits an analogous degree of formal economy and semiotic clarity as it choreographs gameplay. As Peter Shultz has pointed out, musical topoi depict the game's four archetypal locales in ways that filter the four-movement symphonic archetype through idioms ranging from calypso to heavy metal.

As mandated by the von Neumann architecture, the images and music of *Super Mario Bros.* are structured by a digital latticework: the sprites are constituted by the spatial configuration of pixels on the screen, while the music is produced via the sequential execution of encoded pitches and rhythms. For artists such as Miyamoto and Tezuka and composers such as Kondo, restrictions on the amount of data storage available necessitated a reliance on looping, which had the consequence of driving sprites, themes, and sound effects deep into players' memories and intermedial networks. The power of these neurological and affective connections, now compounded by nostalgia, can be witnessed in the Pavlovian responses provoked by the images, music, and sound effects of games from the 1970s and 1980s in many who originally played them decades ago. Indeed, the lasting influence of *Super Mario Bros.* could be gauged as much from the retro-themed revival movements it has helped to inspire across both visual and musical cultures (the "pixel art" and "chiptune" scenes, respectively) as from the game's own attributes. Although trained on the 1980s, this orientation can bring a longer history into focus: the programming of music for mechanical reproduction is rooted in the pinning of cylinders for music boxes and organs, illustrated by Kircher in the seventeenth century, whereas the history of pixel art includes the pointillism of Seurat, Signac, and Pissarro as well as the manifold forms of tapestry and mosaic (media through which pixel art has itself often been remediated and marketed).

Japanese games have evinced a particularly strong attachment to two-dimensional game-worlds and character design, reflecting cultural attachments to *manga* and *anime* as well as the traditions of calligraphy, painting, and *ukiyo-e* (the mass-produced woodblock prints of the "floating world"). In part, these relationships were consciously constructed. With *Dragon Quest* (1986), Yuji Horii and Akira Toriyama adopted the procedural logic of Western role-playing games based on the dice-rolling *Dungeons and Dragons* template, but transformed their Tolkienesque iconographical and literary tropes into colorful *manga*-inspired artwork and even a haiku-based password system, resulting in what is widely acknowledged as the first Japanese role-playing game (JRPG). More recently, the distinctive aesthetic of pixel art has informed Takashi Murakami's Superflat movement, which both exploits and critiques the "flattened forms" of Japanese fine art, graphic design, and popular culture.

Along analogous lines, one might argue that the Western predilection for three-dimensional games, and especially the first-person shooter (FPS) genre, reflects not only the influence and military applications of Brunelleschi's invention of perspective but also the very concept of Cartesian subjectivity. *Doom* (1993), id Software's breakout FPS hit, even draws on Jesuit iconography: Kircher's demons and skeletons now take the forms of pixelated denizens of hell. (Rather than being projected onto a wall, in *Doom* they populate labyrinthine quasi-3D environments ostensibly located on Mars's moon Phobos.) In both Japanese and US contexts, however, one must be careful not to essentialize. Games of all types have been developed in both nations (and far beyond), while influence has flowed freely and multilaterally since the earliest days of the medium. Although *Space Invaders* bore the impression of Western media from H. G. Wells's novel *The War of the Worlds* (1898) to George Lucas's *Star Wars* (1977), for instance, the programmers of *Spacewar!* at MIT had earlier acknowledged the impact of Japanese *tokusatsu* movies such as *Godzilla* (1954) and *Rodan* (1956) on their game.

As hardware increased in sophistication over the ensuing generations of handheld and home-based game consoles, so did the graphical and sonic capacities available to artists and composers. The CD-based optical storage medium of Sony's PlayStation console, released in 1994, drastically increased the resources available for audiovisual storage and retrieval, making the manipulation of recorded sound and cinematic visuals possible on a previously inconceivable scale. The implications for digital games were encapsulated by the epochal *Final Fantasy VII* (1997), a standout entry in Square's venerable JRPG series that allowed for unprecedented sweep and scope through its full-motion video sequences and use of sophisticated digital sound synthesis and sampling.

At the turn of the millennium, consoles such as Sony's PlayStation 2 and Microsoft's Xbox featured digital surround sound, a technology that interlaced the fields of sound design and music composition. The celebrated soundscape of Bungie's futuristic FPS *Halo: Combat Evolved* (2001), created and programmed under the direction of Martin O'Donnell, demonstrated how the ability to locate sound precisely in virtual space sharpens its function as a feedback mechanism that provides gameplay information. Driven by an interactive engine, a distant descendant of Kircher's combinatorial compositional algorithms, the Dorian mode of *Halo*'s monkish main theme segues seamlessly into and out of pounding battle music, affording players the illusion that it has been composed expressly to amplify their exploits. *Halo* blends the cybernetic function of sound as provider and reflector of information in the game space with the traditional cinematic function of music as affective soundtrack. Correspondingly, the first-person perspective of the game's cyborg protagonist, Master Chief, overlaps with that of the player/viewer who simultaneously controls and observes him as he carries out his objectives.

The relationship of sound to the visual components of digital gameplay has itself been construed in ways that recapitulate the dynamics of older media. As one might expect, high-budget cinematic games such as *Halo* and Naughty Dog's *Uncharted* (2007) are amenable to theoretical approaches derived from film studies: concepts such as audiovisual counterpoint, diegesis, and acousmaticism are readily applicable. The digital game's fundamental elements of computation and interactivity, however, suggest that other models might better account for the situations and issues thrown up by gameplay. In particular, adaptive music, often based on looping modules, aims to create closer connections between player actions and sonic outcomes; as mentioned above, this is one factor behind *Halo*'s success. In other cases, such as Nintendo's *Super Mario Galaxy* (2007), sound effects and "stings" triggered by player actions are cued to rhythmic figures whose melodic contours are programmed to match the harmonic context at any given moment, somewhat after the manner of a figured bass realization. In this way, the benefits of a scripted sound-track are combined with those of spontaneity, insofar as a soundtrack that conforms to player actions emerges according to Hollywood-based criteria of convergence and positive feedback.

In the commercial context of Hollywood itself, digital games have been compre-hensively remediated. Not only have successful franchises from *Super Mario Bros.* and *Tomb Raider* to *Resident Evil* and *Silent Hill* been adapted for the cinema screen; game tropes have also offered thematic material for films such as *Existenz* (1999), *Gamer* (2009), and *The Hunger Games* (2012). The high-octane visual rhetoric of games has also informed action sequences, chases, and explosions in film, partly owing to technical resources such as computer-generated imagery and motion capture that both media share.

Perhaps less predictably, digital game soundtracks from the 1980s and 1990s have recently enjoyed an unexpected afterlife as concert music. In particular, game composer and impresario Tommy Tallarico's *Video Games Live* concert series has featured performances by orchestras as renowned as the Los Angeles Philharmonic of music from popular game franchises. Concerts have met with wild acclaim from fans, who themselves supplement the gameplay videos displayed on stage by dress-ing up as (or "cosplaying") their favorite characters. In a strangely recursive twist, these events recreate the technological conditions of silent cinema in the 1920s, and yet their participatory ethos clearly exceeds that historical frame, as well as the social conventions that regulate most contemporary performances of orchestral music.

The striking contrast between the monochromatic blocks of *Pong* (1972) and the stunningly detailed tropical vistas of Crytek's *Crysis* (2007) poses historiographi-cal challenges to art historians and media archaeologists who would account for it. There is no doubt that exponential increases in graphical and sonic processing power have contributed to radical expansions of both the technological possibili-ties and the stylistic protocols of visual and aural representation, and that these resources are often configured to pursue ever-greater resolution, fidelity, or photo-realism. The problems that most exercise graphic artists (such as the interplay of light sources and the depiction of complex phenomena such as fur, smoke, water, and grass) are those that have preoccupied painters for millennia, while the bench-mark for sound designers and composers is still "naturalness," whether in the form of an environmental soundscape or as the verisimilitude of a sampled symphony orchestra.

That notwithstanding, enterprises such as *Video Games Live* and phenomena such as the chiptune and pixel-art scenes belie the notion that the development of computer graphics and sound should be understood in teleological terms directed toward eliminating a perceived gap separating the "virtual" from the "real." Far from being archaic, the "primitivism" of *Pong* was thoroughly modern insofar as it evoked iconic works by painters such as Piet Mondrian, Kasimir Malevich, Mark Rothko, and Barnett Newman, not to mention the technological innovations of video artists such as Nam June Paik and Steina and Woody Vasulka. Likewise, while the mono-phonic sonic profile of early digital games might evoke comparisons with the dawn of notated Western music, it was more closely entwined with the contemporaneous development of synthesizers and the MIDI protocol. These games' musical charac-teristics are thus most fruitfully apprehended in the immediate contexts provided on the one hand by popular music culture (with a particular focus on electronic genres such as disco, synthpop, and techno) and on the other by avant-garde composers as divergent as La Monte Young, Iannis Xenakis, Karlheinz Stockhausen, Steve Reich, and Philip Glass. In the light of Terry Riley's minimalist landmark *In C*, for example, the soundtrack for Rockstar Games' *Red Dead Redemption* (2010) could be dubbed *In A Minor*: while its musical idioms draw heavily on the familiar soundscape of the Western, its modal uniformity allows for all manner of timbral, affective, and topical cues to be triggered and looped according to the arbitrary and emergent agenda of gameplay events.

In other contexts, disavowing naturalism can reflect more radical ideological and aesthetic commitments. The work of game developers and artists such as Jason Rohrer and JODI demonstrates how graphical techniques from the 1980s have accrued new layers of symbolism that can be pressed into the service of twenty-first-century preoccupations with history, memory, and meaning. In a similar vein, the potential for creating subversive meta-games based on the explicit and implicit codes that regulate normative gameplay, representation, and behavior has been tactically exploited by Cory Arcangel, Anne-Marie Schleiner, and Eddo Stern, among others. Drawing on the ludic traditions of Dada and Fluxus, their work has come closest to gaining avant-garde cachet for the medium of the digital game.

As several scholars have noted, the attributes of timing, rhythm, and digital dexterity that are crucial to digital gameplay are also fundamental to musical performance. The isomorphism between musical and digital play arises in part through their common transduction through code, whether it take the form of staff notation, tablature, or C++. In order to become music, the code must be "performed" by human, machine, or a combination of the two. This relationship has been explored by game developers such as Masaya Matsuura, who established the "rhythm-action" genre with *Parappa the Rapper* (1997). The genre's popularity peaked with Harmonix's *Guitar Hero* and *Rock Band* franchises (2005–10). In recent years, plastic guitar controllers have yielded the living room to devices such as Microsoft's Kinect, signaling a shift from instrumental instruction to the choreography of dance moves (or, rather, from the inputting of code via the digits to the surveillance of the human body by camera and microphone. The CPU might be blind and deaf, but Kinect equips it with prosthetic eyes and ears.) Such games flip the conventional hierarchy of visual elements over their sonic counterparts. Their visual representations of gameplay often foreground the material elements involved in the mechanical reproduction of music, such as Kircher's pinned organ barrel or the piano roll, while iconographic depictions of the performance are relegated to the background.

When it comes to digital games, "literacy" does not issue solely from knowledge of programming languages, important though that may be. For many players, it derives from mastering a vast array of visual, sonic, tactile, and affective codes. The syntax, grammar, and tropic logic of these codes can be processed semiotically through representations native to the digital game and those from other media. The blending of simulation and mimesis that is so characteristic of digital games thus requires a bifocal approach. Mimesis, which indexes the distance between an object and its representation, interacts and interferes with the logic of simulation, creating a parallax that can be interpreted from various cultural perspectives. On the one hand, critics might recognize the elements that define and distinguish the medium, and acknowledge their historical and epistemological lineages. On the other, they can reflect on the ecology in which games participate today, an ever-shifting environment that shapes the meanings derived from the processing and audiovisual modulation of binary code. While digital games can simulate—and even enact—the nefarious dynamics of globalized corporate empires, they can also enable marginalized voices to contribute to a vibrant discourse that sustains creative resistance and self-expression. For musicologists, art historians, and other scholars of audio-visual culture, the strategic challenge of coordinating interdisciplinary approaches to digital games thus poses both daunting risks and exciting opportunities.

Notes

1 Daniel Albright, *Untwisting the Serpent: Modernism in Music, Literature, and Other Arts* (Chicago and London: University of Chicago Press, 2000), 9.
2 Quoted in Chris Melissinos and Patrick O'Rourke, *The Art of Video Games from Pac-Man to Mass Effect* (New York: Welcome Books, 2012), 25.
3 Friedrich Kittler, trans. Geoffrey Winthrop-Young and Michael Wutz, *Gramophone, Film, Typewriter* (Stanford: Stanford University Press, 1999), 97.

Further Reading

Bogost, Ian. *Unit Operations: An Approach to Videogame Criticism.* Cambridge, MA: MIT Press, 2006.
Clarke, Andy, and Grethe Mitchell, eds. *Videogames and Art.* Bristol: Intellect Books, 2007.
Collins, Karen. *Game Sound: An Introduction to the History, Theory, and Practice of Video Game Music and Sound Design.* Cambridge, MA: MIT Press, 2008.
Dyer-Witherford, Nick, and Greig de Peuter. *Games of Empire: Global Capitalism and Video Games.* Minneapolis: University of Minnesota Press, 2009.
Galloway, Alexander R. *Gaming: Essays on Algorithmic Culture.* Minneapolis: University of Minnesota Press, 2006.
Huhtamo, Erkki, and Jussi Parikka, eds. *Media Archaeology: Approaches, Applications, and Implications.* Berkeley: University of California Press, 2011.
Kittler, Friedrich. *Optical Media: Berlin Lectures 1999.* Translated by Anthony Enns. Cambridge: Polity Press, 2010.
Wolf, Mark J. P., ed. *Before the Crash: Early Video Game History.* Detroit: Wayne State University Press, 2012.

IMAGE CREDITS

Figure 12.1 photo © Victoria and Albert Museum, London / V&A Images, reproduced by permission. Figure 13.1 photo courtesy of Peter Willi/The Bridgeman Art Library, both reproduced by permission. Figure 14.1 photo © Trustees of the British Museum, reproduced by permission. Figure 15.2 photo © Réunion des Musées Nationaux/Art Resource, NY, reproduced by permission. Figure 15.3 photo courtesy of The Phillips Collection, Washington, DC. Figure 16.1 photo © Finnish National Gallery/Central Art Archives/Jouko Könönen, reproduced by permission. Examples 18.1–3 scores reproduced by permission of the publisher. Examples 20.1–3 reproduced by permission of the Jean Gray Hargrove Music Library, University of California, Berkeley. Figure 27.1 photo © BPK, Berlin, Dist. RMN-Grand Palais/ Jörg P. Anders, reproduced by permission. Figure 27.2 photo © RMN-Grand Palais (Musée du Louvre)/Jean-Gilles Berizzi, reproduced by permission. Figure 29.1 photo © Ashmolean Museum, University of Oxford, reproduced by permission. Figure 30.1 photo © National Gallery of Art, Washington, reproduced by permission. Figure 30.2 photo © The Cleveland Museum of Art, reproduced by permission. Figure 32.1 photo © Museo Civico, Treviso, reproduced by permission. Figures 34.1 and 34.2 photos courtesy of the author. Figure 35.1 photo reproduced by permission of the festival organizer. Figures 36.1 and 36.2 photos courtesy of the Getty Research Institute, Los Angeles, reproduced by permission. Figure 38.1 photo courtesy of Private Collection/The Bridgeman Art Library. Figure 43.1 photo courtesy of Experiments in Art and Technology, reproduced by permission. Figure 43.2 photo by Julie West, courtesy of the artist, reproduced by permission.

INDEX

ROUTLEDGE RESEARCH

MUSIC

Routledge Research is our home for cutting-edge, upper-level scholarly studies and edited collections. Titles are characterized by dynamic interventions into established subjects and innovative studies on emerging topics covering many disciplines.

FEATURING SERIES IN:

Routledge Research in Music • Routledge Studies in Ethnomusicology
Routledge Studies in Popular Music • Routledge Studies in Music Theory